Marx and Engels

SUNY series in
Political Theory: Contemporary Issues

Philip Green, editor

Marx and Engels

Their Contribution to the Democratic Breakthrough

August H. Nimtz, Jr.

State University of New York Press

Published by
State University of New York Press, Albany

For information, address State University of New York Press,
State University Plaza, Albany, NY 12246

Production, Laurie Searl
Marketing, Fran Keneston

Library of Congress Cataloging-in-Publication Data

Nimtz, August H.
    Marx and Engels: their contribution to the democratic breakthrough / August H. Nimtz, Jr.
        p. cm.—(SUNY series in political theory. Contemporary issues)
    Includes bibliographical references and index.
    ISBN 0-7914-4489-9 (alk. paper)—ISBN 0-7914-4490-2 (pbk. : alk. paper)
    1. Democracy. 2. Marx, Karl, 1818–1883—Contributions in political science. 3. Engels, Friedrich, 1820–1895—Contributions in political science. I. Title. II. Series.

JC423.N535 2000
320.53'2'0922—dc21   99-053178

10 9 8 7 6 5 4 3 2 1

Contents

Preface

This book unabashedly challenges what has become an article of faith for much of the world at the end of the twentieth century—the supposed incompatibility between the projects of Marx and Engels and political democracy. In the process I challenge another orthodoxy—the proclivity of intellectuals to redo Marx and, to a lesser extent, Engels in their own image, to be primarily intellectuals or just "great thinkers." Coming on the heels of the one hundred and fiftieth anniversary of the *Communist Manifesto* such a retrospective look at its two authors is not only opportune but necessary.

I make three related arguments. First—my most sweeping claim—Karl Marx and Frederick Engels were the leading protagonists in the democratic movement in the nineteenth century, the decisive breakthrough period in humanity's age-old struggle for democracy. Second, they played such a role because they were first and foremost political activists, and not simply "thinkers," who constituted a revolutionary partnership. This much too ignored dimension of them is crucial in understanding why history knows no other example of two who were more successful in promoting their own political perspective. Third, their active involvement in the revolutionary upheavals in 1848–1849 as communists allowed them to draw lessons and conclusions that enhanced their effectiveness in the fight for democracy. Implicit in the latter is the claim that it was exactly their success in advancing the fight for socialism that advanced the democratic struggle.

The conclusion reached by Dietrich Rueschemeyer, Evelyne Stephens, and John Stephens in their well-received work, the most important contribution to date on the long-debated issue about the relationship between the development of capitalism and democracy, is the point of departure for this book. Their central argument is that the "self-organization of the working class"[1] in the second half of the nineteenth century was responsible for the democratic breakthrough, that is, the institution of "universal suffrage," the "responsibility of the state apparatus to the elected parliament," and the acquisition of civil liberties—a finding about which Marx and Engels could have justifiably said, "We told you so!" While convincing at one level of analysis, that is, structure, there is, however, a crucially important gap in their argument—the role of agency. The working class was certainly the product of the capitalist mode of production but was its politicization and self-organization, as their analysis seems to imply, inevitable? As the historian Eric Hobsbawm notes in his instructive overview of the workers' movement in the last quarter of the nineteenth century, "There was no necessary connection between the willingness to strike and organize, and the identification of the class of employers (the 'capitalists') as the major political adversary."[2] The basic argument here is that Marx and Engels are unequivocally that missing agential link. Their contribution was indispensable in the proletariat's political self-organization. If capitalism was the necessary condition for the democratic breakthrough because it brought into existence the working class, then conscious political leadership such as Marx and Engels provided was, in other words, the sufficient condition.

It is not possible in the space of one book to "prove" all of these claims. My aim is to provide enough evidence to make a more than credible case. Neither is the book organized around these claims. Because, as I argue, Marx and Engels's programmatic conclusions rested on practice and what they liked to call "the real movement of history" or the "lessons" of the class struggle, their politics can only be fully comprehended in time. Thus, the chronological structure of the book.

The first argument about Marx and Engels's indispensable role in the democratic breakthrough is the most difficult of the three to actually "prove." A proof would require a volume that focuses specifically on the agential side of the nineteenth-century democratic movement in its entirety. What I do here is to lay the foundation for this claim. Chapter one shows how Marx's and Engels's path to communism originated in their radical democratic posture, a product of both the French and Industrial Revolutions. Strange as it might sound to twentieth-century ears, in Marx and Engels's time, certainly on the eve of the 1848 revolutions, communists saw themselves as simply the most extreme wing of the democratic movement. Chapters two to four describes how they implemented their new or "scientific" communist perspective by becoming the most uncompromising component of that movement before and during the 1848–1849 revolutions. A thorough look at their involvement in these upheavals unmistakably discloses that they gave detailed attention to and worked out the strategy and tactics for an issue that they are often accused of neglecting—the national question and its relation to the democratic revolution. Chapter five is most pertinent since it constitutes a necessary step in a proof—a comparison of Marx and Engels with other leading nineteenth-century figures usually associated, at least today, with the democratic movement. Like Marx and Engels, Alexis de Tocqueville not only wrote about the 1848–1849 revolution in France but was one of its key actors. The comparison reveals that Marx and Engels's democratic credentials were far more deserved than those of the author of *Democracy in America*.

Of the three arguments, the second, which is in fact the heart of this book, is the easiest for which to make a case. I present evidence throughout that leaves little doubt that Marx and Engels were indeed revolutionary activists who functioned as a political team. Chapter ten shows how that partnership was maintained by Engels even after Marx's death. In the process I demonstrate that any treatment of them that fails to portray them in this light is not only inadequate but misleading. Marx's theses, that the "educator must himself be educated . . . [through] *revolutionary practice*" and that "philosophers have only *interpreted* the world . . . the point, however, is to *change* it," written in 1845 at the commencement of the partnership, were instantiated by everything they did thereafter. Therefore, this book rescues Marx and Engels from the clutches of those who have too long depoliticized them by treating the two as only theorists or intellectuals, rather than how they saw themselves and wanted to be regarded and what they, in fact, were.[3]

The "great thinker" myth has its base, of course, in the fact that Marx spent innumerable hours in the British Museum, especially between the 1848–1849 upheavals and the resurgence of political activity in 1864, doing research for *Capital*. But it is absurd to conclude, as the renowned historian A. J. P. Taylor does, that: "[Marx] is indeed the only man who has changed the whole destiny of the human race simply by sitting in the British Museum."[4] "Simply by" ignoring Marx the revolutionary activist is it possible to utter such nonsense. A more recent example is provided by the Marxologist Terrell Carver who would have us believe, in his introduction to *The Cambridge Companion to Marx*, that he "left political organization almost entirely to others . . . nor was he . . . ever involved directly in the politics of his land of exile," and "was not himself a direct actor in German politics"[5]—claims that fly in the face of reality, as this book demonstrates. "Yet," for Carver, "Marx's words have changed the world . . . markedly since his time. How?" His answer: Marx's writings.

The self-importance of intellectuals that Carver betrays is exactly what Marx denounced in his first collaboration with Engels. "Ideas *cannot carry out anything* at all. In order to carry out ideas men are needed who can exert practical force." He and his partner were, above all else, revolutionary activists who profoundly understood that they had to actively put into practice what they wrote, as well as learn from practice what to write—tasks that are in general alien to the intellectual world, especially that of the Marxologist.[6] Chapters six and seven, unlike any other treatment of the period of the lull in political activity in Marx's life, rectify this standard portrayal by putting Marx and Engels's literary and scientific endeavors, especially the research for and writing of *Capital*, in the context of "party building" activities—preparation for taking the political helm as soon as opportunities permitted. Without the necessary party activities during this period, the Marxist current, a tiny socialist tendency at the time, could not have succeeded in outdistancing other and more popular radical currents and have had such an impact on "the whole destiny of the human race."

Evidence for the third argument is found in those chapters that detail their practice in the aftermath of the turbulent events of 1848 to 1851, specifically chapters seven through ten. I demonstrate how the core idea they distilled from that experience, the necessity of independent working-class political action—the subject of the second half of chapter four—was the fundamental criterion they employed in their practice to the very end. The real movement of history had unmistakably revealed in the defeats of those revolutions that neither the liberal bourgeoisie nor middle-class reformists had respectively the desire or fortitude to fight for democracy. Only the proletariat in alliance with the peasantry and urban petit bourgeoisie could, they argued, so ensure its victory. Thus, the oft-repeated accusation about Marx's supposed disparagement and ignorance of the peasantry is another myth disposed of here. The related myth, that their perspective was not meant for underdeveloped countries, is also disputed. As chapters nine and ten make clear, not only did they intend their project for such societies but also, for one in particular, they accurately foresaw *and* actively promoted its revolutionary potential—czarist Russia in the last decades of the nineteenth century.

A critical assumption of this book is that Marx and Engels constituted a political team with the same perspective. Hence, I reject the claim (to be discussed in chapter ten) that they were philosophically dichotomous. I do so on the grounds that this claim cannot be located in what they took most serious—their practice. Whatever nuances, or even differences, in emphasis on theoretical questions that may have existed between them were not meaningful because they were not manifested in their politics. For Marx and Engels, as I show throughout the book, political practice was their alpha and omega and there is nothing to suggest that they failed to *act* in unison. This includes as well, as I argue, Engels's practice after Marx's death.

One of the advantages in undertaking this study is the availability today, unlike any other time, of the most complete record in existence of every known writing and utterance of the two revolutionaries. The forty-seven volume (at the time of this writing) English edition of the *Marx-Engels Collected Works (MECW)* constitutes the most thorough record in print of the known extant materials. Combined with the new edition of the projected one hundred and fourteen volume *Marx-Engels Gesamtausgabe*—about half completed—which includes materials not in the *MECW*, specifically their notebooks and the correspondence they received, their written and spoken record is the most accessible to date. The English words and expressions used by Marx and Engels in texts written in German, French and other languages, appear in small caps in *Marx-Engels Collected Works*. Quotations which include this material retain this typographical differentiation.

Exactly because of the long history of bowdlerization and misrepresentation of what Marx and Engels actually said, a practice that began even before Marx died in 1883—leading him to say on more than one occasion that if this is Marxism then "I am no Marxist"—I make my case by extensive quotation of what they said rather than, as is so often done, relying on snippets and paraphrasing. For this reason and the fact that I draw on their published record in its entirety, not just the usually cited canonical "texts"—which make up at most about one-tenth of their total output— I beg the reader's indulgence. While I realize that I too can be accused of biasing the written record, it seems to me that this is minimized by copious quotations accompanied by adequate contextualization. A more economical approach increases the risk of distortion. The reader, I am convinced, will find this approach rewarding as she or he reads what Marx and Engels had to say on a variety of issues rather than what is so often misleadingly reported and, hopefully, will want to read more of the two—in their own words. What they "meant" by their pronouncements is obviously important but not a priority of this project. My concern is what they actually said *and* did to the best of our ability to discern.[7] Enough ink has been spilt on discussions and debates on the meanings of their texts. Let the hermeneutical exercise proceed at least on the basis of their practice in its entirety.

Clearly not everything Marx and Engels wrote or said, or so reported, is of equal reliability. For that reason I employ to some extent what Hal Draper calls his list of their writings "in descending order of reliability" with regard to both published and unpublished writings including their correspondence. Draper prioritizes, in order: "books and major essays," "articles published under their control," "articles composed as political statements," "articles in which remarks on issues occur only in passing," "journalistic articles, written as hack work," "articles published not under the control of the writer," "unpublished manuscripts" and "letters" about which he makes further qualifications, and lastly, "private notes, notebooks and workbooks."[8] One slight modification I make is to give more weight to their correspondence while taking into account the precautions he offers. Engels's letters in his last decade are especially valuable; owing to time constraints, he employed them to make political points that he did not have time to make in more formal writing—with the understanding oftentimes that they would be published in his lifetime. Another key source not on Draper's list but one I draw on extensively in the chapters on the First International are the minutes of the organization's General Council. Because Marx and Engels, along with other GC members, voted on the minutes of the previous meetings, which often quoted them, and were very vigilant about their accuracy, I would place the GC minutes high on his list. Lastly, I give more weight to points that are repeated regardless of where they appear. This is consistent with my focus on their political practice in time, the threads of continuity, as well as modifications and ruptures.

This book in some ways was inspired by Draper's insufficiently heralded work on Marx and Engels. Among his many contributions certainly none is more valuable than his *Marx-Engels Chronicle: A Day-by-Day Chronology of Marx and Engels' Life and Activity*, without which today no serious treatment of them can be done.[9]

Another advantage in doing this study now has to do with the blows that the Stalinist regimes in Eastern Europe and the former Soviet Union have sustained. One very salutary result is that the near monopoly that Moscow and its political allies exercised over the legacy of Marx and Engels has been broken. The most significant opening in almost five decades now exists for the broadest discussion about what Marx and Engels really said *and* did. Related to this outcome is another development, the increasingly recognized global crisis of capitalism. Economic insecurity and depression-like conditions, with all of the attendant social and political consequences—not the least of which is the recrudescence of fascism—are a growing reality for much of world humanity. Precisely because Marx and Engels claimed to offer an alternative to such a scenario it behooves those who make judgments about the relevancy of their prescriptions to know what they actually advocated. A fresh look at them allows us in a post-Stalinist dominated world to determine the extent to which the policies—programmatic and organizational—that have been posed, historically, in their name, be they of a Stalinist, Social Democratic, or any other variety, are consistent with what they understood their project to be. Hence, this book constitutes a necessary step in answering the question—the subject of a future volume—what happened to Marxism after Marx and Engels. A clear and thorough exposition of their perspective, as is done here, is crucial in determining what is and isn't Marxist continuity.

One final comment. In the spirit of Marx and Engels, I harbor no illusions that what is presented here will convince opponents or skeptics of the correctness of their practice. My purpose is to challenge the claims, or more specifically, the many misrepresentations and myths about their project. As they fully understood, one's class position and perspective are in the final analysis determinant as for being attracted or repulsed by what they had to offer. As for those who may find themselves in the former camp, my hope, on the eve of the twenty-first century, is that this book conveys the importance that they lent to the democratic struggle, the necessary prerequisite for "the social revolution"—a lesson that was all too often lost, tragically, on many a would-be twentieth-century revolutionary. Lastly, it can't be stressed enough—again, in their spirit—that only through the real movement, that is, practice that links up with the fights of the proletariat, the laboratory of the class struggle, can a real assessment of their politics be made.

Acknowledgments

Various drafts of this book, in whole or in part, benefitted significantly from the comments and suggestions of a number of persons. As well as his encouragement, the thoughtful questions and careful eye of Colin Leys are most appreciated. Philip Green, editor for the series, made it possible for the manuscript to become a book. The comparative assessment of the Marx-Engels team and Tocqueville in chapter five in the 1848 revolutions owes much to the feedback I received from Ron Aminzade, Roger Boesche, Mary Dietz, Lisa Disch, and Lansiné Kaba. Jim Farr's insights were especially useful in the very early and last stages of the project. The comments of graduate students in my comparative socio-political change seminar at the University of Minnesota who read earlier versions of the manuscript helped me to refine and clarify my arguments. Sharilyn Geistfeld, as well as those with whom I have political relations such as Chris Nisan, served as willing sounding boards and sources of faith in the project for many years. Lastly, the staff at SUNY Press, Zina Lawrence, Laurie Searl, and most importantly, copy editor Alan Hewat, are all to be thanked for their assistance. Of course, as always with such a project, I alone am responsible for what finally found its way into print.

CHAPTER ONE

The Democratic Urge and Commencement of a Revolutionary Partnership

Ideas cannot carry out anything at all. In order to carry out ideas men are needed who can exert practical force.

—Marx, *The Holy Family*

Philosophy and the study of the actual world have the same relation to one another as onanism and sexual love.

—Marx, *The German Ideology*

[S]tanding up in front of real, live people and holding forth to them directly and straightforwardly, so that they see and hear you is something quite different from engaging in this devilishly abstract quill pushing with an abstract audience in one's "mind's eye."

—Engels to Marx

[I]n this country [Germany] Democracy and Communism are, as far as the working classes are concerned, quite synonymous.

—Engels

About two years before Karl Marx's death a journalist spent a few days with him and his family at a beach side resort. One conversation was especially memorable: "[D]uring an interspace of silence, I interrogated the revolutionist and philosopher in these fateful words, *'What is?'* And it seemed as though his mind were inverted for a moment while he looked upon the roaring sea in front and the restless multitude upon the beach. *'What is?'* I had inquired, to which, in deep and solemn tone, he replied: *'Struggle!'*¹

Of all his qualities, nothing characterized Marx more than his willingness and joy in carrying out a struggle, the fight. In the popular family parlor game, Confessions, a semi-jocular questionnaire, Marx gave the following answers to his daughter Jenny: "Your chief characteristic. *Singleness of purpose*; Your idea of happiness. *To fight*; Your idea of misery. *To submit*."[2] Frederick Engels, Marx's lifelong political companion, recalled this side of his partner at his funeral. "Marx was before all else a revolutionist. . . . Fighting was his element. And he fought with a passion, a tenacity and a success such as few could rival."[3]

The same can be said of Engels. Amongst the earliest of his extant writings is the poem *Florida*, written when he was eighteen. A juvenile verse, it praises American Indian resistance to White European encroachment. At one point Engels assumes the voice of a Seminole:

> Peace to my brethren I shall not proclaim;
> War be my first word, battle be my last.

And concludes:

> Come then, White Man, if your desire it be,
> And you shall get the homage that's your due.
> From every bed of reeds, from every tree,
> Seminole arrows await to ambush you![4]

The poem reveals what would be another lifelong trait of Engels—one that he shared with his partner—confidence in the ability of the oppressed to overcome their oppressors. At Engels's funeral in 1895, the German Social Democratic leader Wilhelm Liebknecht remembered him in words similar to those that Engels had used to describe Marx twelve years earlier. "To all of us Engels showed the way and had been a *leader* en route; he was a *leader* and *fighter*; theory and practice blended with him into one."[5]

While fighters, both Marx and Engels recognized quite early in their lives that it wasn't enough to be a fighter; a fighter had to have a perspective—a program. The steps they took to form a partnership to formulate and carry out a program to transform the world in which they were born is the subject of this chapter. A necessary step in that process was their political break with the world in which they, especially Marx, had been intellectually reared, German philosophy. Their passage from the world of ideas to that of the practice of the proletariat enabled them to become thinking fighters.

THE QUEST FOR DEMOCRATIC RULE

Two historical events profoundly shaped the political trajectories of the "young" Marx and Engels—the Industrial Revolution and the French Revolution. The Rhineland, the province in Germany most affected by these two developments, was where Marx and Engels spent their formative years. Their radicalization, though by somewhat different routes, can be traced to the unfulfilled political hopes engendered by both seismic events.

Shortly before Marx and Engels were born, respectively, in 1818 and 1820, the Rhineland came under the autocratic Prussian administration after having enjoyed the relatively more politically open climate of French rule—the legacy of the Revolution. Though less repressive than others in the Prussian Empire, the Rhineland government denied political freedom to its citizens in most areas of public life. For the province's growing bourgeoisie the absence of civil liberties and political rights was especially galling given the freedoms its counterparts enjoyed in neighboring countries such as France, Belgium, the Netherlands, and, for sure, Britain. The setting in which Marx and Engels matured was one where liberal ideas flourished, owing to the social weight of the bourgeoisie in the province, but one where such ideas could not be implemented because of the dead weight of semi-feudal Prussian rule. Like others of their generation, they sought an answer to the most pressing political question of the day: how could Prussian authoritarianism be replaced by democratic rule and who or what segment of society would lead such a transformation?

The Young Marx

Prussia's repressive political climate confronted the young Marx in a most direct way. Hoping, after he received his doctorate in 1841, to get a teaching position at one of the state-run universities, where the "political correctness" of Prussian authoritarianism was the order of the day, Marx was warned by his friend, Bruno Bauer, a left-liberal university professor, to temper his increasingly radical ideas.[6] Shortly afterward Bauer himself was denied tenure at the University of Bonn because of his views. Since he was not willing to conceal his own democratic sympathies, Marx concluded that the academic route was not an option.[7] Bruno's dismissal no doubt raised questions for him about the efficacy of the liberal strategy of trying to win reforms within the framework of the authoritarian Prussian state.

Marx eventually got a job as editor of the recently founded liberal publication the *Rheinische Zeitung(RZ)* in Cologne, an industrial center in the Rhineland. The fact that its owners, composed mainly of the industrial and other wings of the bourgeoisie, were willing to hire Marx, a known member of the relatively radical Young Hegelian circle, testifies to the increasing frustration of the liberal bourgeoisie with the Prussian state.

Even before Marx assumed his duties in late 1842 he had fallen victim to the state censor's scissors. In an article he published outside the province, he argued that the "essence" of Prussian censorship is the false assumption that the bureaucrats who enforce it know what's best for the people. "There is no confidence in the intelligence and goodwill of the general public even in the simplest matter. . . . This fundamental defect is inherent in all our institutions."[8] Thus, almost from the beginning of his political career, opposition to the state's stifling of human potential, fuelled Marx's radical trajectory. Unlike many others before and after him, Marx's gut instinct, as his comment reveals, was to trust "the people" and not the state, however well intentioned it might be—a core trait that informed him to the end. Yet, at this stage he didn't have a programmatic answer to the age-old riddle: how could "the people" be expected to govern themselves if they had never been prepared?

Shortly afterward, he wrote to an acquaintance that he intended to do a critique of the political views of the then most influential philosopher in Germany, George Hegel (1770–1831): "The central point" of the critique would be a "struggle against [Hegel's advocacy of] *constitutional monarchy*. . . ."[9] This comment reveals the growing critique that Marx was beginning to make of the liberal opposition who saw a constitutional monarchy as the answer to the problem of censorship and lack of other political freedoms. Hegel's solution, he charged, was an obstacle to the "sovereignty of the people," or "true democracy." That liberal opponents to the regime embraced Hegel's position was evidence that they were "by no means equal to the task" to defend not only freedom of the press but any other political liberties.[10] Within a year, Marx would argue, without being specific, that the only answer to Prussian despotism was the "impending revolution."

The *RZ*, under Marx's editorship, came into increasing conflict with the government. On April 1, 1843, in spite of Marx's resignation two weeks earlier—which reflected the breach between him and the newspaper's liberal owners on how to respond to censorship—the organ was banned by the authorities. Although his tenure was brief, his political development deepened considerably. The government's ban made clear to Marx that "the mantle of liberalism has been discarded and the most disgusting despotism in all its nakedness is disclosed to the eyes of the whole world."[11]

In addition to getting a direct lesson in state oppression and liberal vacillation, Marx's editorship enabled him to begin clarifying his views on what was then considered to be the "left." "The Free," a Young Hegelian group, many of whom Marx had been associated with, called for sharp criticism not only of the government but the liberal opposition as well. Marx increasingly felt that their critique was too theoretical. He expressed a view that would forever inform his political practice. "The correct theory must be made clear and developed within the concrete conditions and on the basis of the existing state of things."[12] Also, in their enthusiasm to denounce the government these "theoretically correct" critics risked bringing down the state's wrath and the banning of the *RZ*. Thus, "[W]e arouse the resentment of many, indeed the majority, of the free-thinking practical people who have undertaken the laborious task of winning freedom step by step, within the constitutional framework, while we, from our comfortable arm-chair of abstractions, show them their contradictions."[13] Whatever, therefore, the theoretical shortcomings of those who were fighting for political freedoms they were at least engaged in struggle and, thus, care had to be taken not to do anything that threatened the limited political space that did exist. In other words, to be an armchair revolutionary theorist and not engaged in "practical work" was irresponsible.

After assuming the *RZ* editorship Marx's differences with "the Free" widened and eventually led to a break. They accused him of being a "conservative" because of his critique of their writings and their "communist" politics. "Communism," which at this stage of history was vaguely defined—the point of Marx's criticism—went beyond the egalitarianism of socialism by calling for the elimination of private property and an orientation toward the proletariat. In his defense Marx wrote, "I demanded of them less vague reasoning, magniloquent phrases and self-satisfied self-adoration, and more definiteness, more attention to the actual state of affairs, more expert knowledge. I stated that I regard it as inappropriate, indeed even immoral, to smuggle [in] communist and socialist doctrines, hence a new world outlook. . . . I demand a quite different and more thorough discussion of communism."

Marx then addressed one of Young Hegelianism's favorite topics—religion. "I requested further that religion should be criticised in the framework of criticism of political conditions rather than that political conditions should be criticised in the framework of religion . . . for religion in itself is without content, it owes its being not to heaven but to the earth, and with the abolition of distorted reality, of which it is the *theory*, it will collapse of itself. Finally, I desired that if there is to be talk about philosophy, there should be less trifling with the *label* 'atheism' (which reminds one of children, assuring everyone who is ready to listen to them that they are not afraid of the bogy man), and that instead the content of philosophy should be brought to the people."[14]

Precisely because communism was "a new world outlook," Marx demanded more of it than what was then being presented. Radical phrase mongering, including the flaunting of one's "atheism," was insufficient. It had to descend from the philosophical heavens, be made explicit, and relate to the "actual state of affairs." Marx's critique anticipated by a couple of years his "materialist conception of history."

After his departure from the *RZ* and very soon from Germany as well—it was clear to him by now that the political space was narrowing quickly for him—Marx sought to do exactly what he had demanded of the Free, that is, provide in writing an explicit "new world outlook." While it would take another year and a half before he could present his views, a comment he wrote about a recently published article by the philosopher Ludwig Feuerbach (1804–1872), whom he still held in high regard, hinted at what would be characteristic of this new approach. To Marx, Feuerbach's theses about the need to transform German philosophy seemed "to be incorrect only in one respect, that he refers too much to nature and too little to politics. That, however, is the only alliance by which present-day philosophy can become truth."[15] Consistent, thus, with his critique of the Young Hegelians, a philosophical perspective was valid only to the extent it addressed the "actual state of things," "practical work," or more specifically, "politics."

In spite of the suppression of the *RZ*, Marx was not deterred from journalistic pursuits. Newspapers and journals, he felt, were the best means to get one's ideas to the "people." Thus, he began almost immediately to get underway a journal that would be published in Paris, the *Deutsche-Franzsische Jahrbucher*, with one of the few Young Hegelians with whom he still maintained a political relationship, Arnold Ruge. That the journal aimed to reach out to French as well as German readers indicates the direction that Marx was headed—an internationalist perspective. Marx also hoped that the relatively more liberal environment in France had political lessons for the more oppressed Germans which could serve to "teach us to recognise the emptiness of our patriotism. . . ."[16] Although the venture was never really successful—only one issue, a double one, was ever published—it proved useful for Marx's self-clarification.

In the much too neglected exchange of letters with Ruge about the purpose of the journal, Marx put forward views that would forever be at the very core of his political being. Firstly, unlike Ruge, Marx was confident that the oppressed could liberate themselves. In reply to Ruge's pessimism about the current political reality in Germany—increasing state repression without, apparently, any resistance from the German people—Marx chided Ruge's analysis: "[T]here is absolutely nothing political about it. No people wholly despairs, and even if for a long time it goes on hoping merely out of stupidity, yet one day, after many years, it will suddenly become wise and fulfill all its pious wishes."[17]

Marx did not deny the reality of despotic rule in Germany and its impact on the German people. Despotism depended on "people who did not feel they are human beings." To be a human being "would imply thinking beings, free men, republicans. . . . Despotism's sole idea is contempt for man, the dehumanised man. . . . The despot always sees degraded people." It was the French Revolution in its overthrow of monarchy that "aroused again in the hearts of these people" the possibility of freedom with the creation of a "republic and an organisation of free human beings instead of the system of dead objects." If, as Marx said, unlike Ruge, he did "not despair of" the present state of affairs "that is only because it is precisely the desperate situation which fills me with hope." He wasn't referring to the shortcomings of the rulers or the passivity of the ruled:

> I simply draw your attention to the fact that . . . all people who think and who suffer, have reached an understanding, for which previously the means were altogether lacking, and that even the passive system of reproduction of the subjects of the old type daily enlists recruits to serve the new type of humanity. The system of industry and trade, of ownership and exploitation of people, however, leads even far more rapidly than the increase in population to a rupture within present-day society, a rupture which the old system is not able to heal, because it does not heal and create at all, but only exists and consumes. But the existence of suffering human beings, who think, and thinking human beings who are oppressed, must inevitably become unpalatable and indigestible to the animal world of philistinism which passively and thoughtlessly consumes.[18]

Marx's optimism, therefore, stemmed from the increased consciousness, the "thinking" of the oppressed, which is what the French Revolution represented, along with the economic changes taking place in Germany and the exploitation that these engendered. The latter developments accelerated an inherently unstable situation—the exploitation of increasingly conscious human beings.

As for the specific purpose of the *Deutsche-Franz_sische Jahrbucher* Marx then wrote:

> [W]e must expose the old world to the full light of day and shape the new one in a positive way. The longer the time that events allow to thinking humanity for taking stock of its position, and to suffering mankind for mobilising its forces, the more perfect on entering the world will be the product that the present time bears in its womb.

    Marx and Engels

The journal's role, thus, was to promote "thinking"—consciousness on the part of the oppressed. What Marx was also arguing for, perhaps for the first time, was the desirability of adequate preparatory time for a revolution. This is a view that would inform his approach to the strategy and tactics of revolution, beginning with the 1848–49 revolutions in Germany and France. Implicit here also is the idea that revolutions may occur before adequate preparation.

As to what the future society ought to look like, Marx made clear that "we do not dogmatically anticipate the world, but only to find the new world through criticism of the old one . . . constructing the future and settling everything for all times are not our affair. . . . I am not in favour of raising any dogmatic banner. On the contrary, we must try to help the dogmatists to clarify their propositions for themselves." Opposition to blueprints for the future was a stance Marx maintained throughout his entire life.

As for criticism, "I am referring to *ruthless criticism of all that exists*, ruthless both in the sense of not being afraid of the results it arrives at and in the sense of being just as little afraid of conflict with the powers that be."[19] To be effective, Marx called for criticism that addressed the "reality" that most Germans faced, above all religious and political issues. The only way to "influence our contemporaries" with regard to such issues is to take political reality as it exists. "We must take these, in whatever form they exist, as our point of departure, and not confront them with some ready-made system" à la utopian socialism. In essence, the perspective that Marx put forward for the new journal called for "making criticism of politics, participation in politics, and therefore *real* struggles, the starting point of our criticism, and from identifying our criticism with them."[20] Philosophy for Marx, therefore, could only be justified to the extent that it related to and participated in the "real struggles" that confront humanity.

He described his perspective at this stage in his political development as that of "critical philosophy." While Marx did not yet identify as a communist he singled out "communism," as then practiced, as a particular dogma—"a special, one-sided realisation of the socialist principle"—in need of clarification. (Like many other radicals at the time Marx often used "communism" and "socialism" interchangeably. When precision was required, "communism" was a particular expression of "socialism" that emphasized the proletarian dimension.) Its importance for Marx was that "communism is itself only a special expression of the humanistic principle." Motivated on the basis of assisting the oppressed to find their humanity, to become conscious, thinking beings, Marx now turned his attention to the criticism and, thus, clarification of the existing doctrines of communism.

If the liberal bourgeoisie had already failed to overthrow Prussian despotism and institute a "new world," then what segment or class in society could be counted on to do this? Within a year Marx proposed an answer. In critiquing Hegel, a necessary step on the road to an answer, Marx made his oft-quoted point that the "weapon of criticism cannot, of course, replace criticism by weapons, material force must be overthrown by material force; but theory also becomes a material force as soon as it has gripped the masses." But who are the "masses" at this stage in Germany's development?

After a comparative survey of German and French political history, and the dynamics of class conflict in both countries, he concluded that the hope of Germany's liberation lay in that segment of German society "which cannot emancipate itself without emancipating itself from all other spheres of society and thereby emancipating all other spheres of society. . . . This dissolution of society as a particular estate is the *proletariat*." Therefore, "philosophy finds its *material* weapons in the proletariat . . . [and] the proletariat finds its *spiritual* weapons in philosophy. And once the lightning of thought has squarely struck this ingenuous soil of the people the emancipation of the *Germans* into *human beings* will take place."[21] This comment, a major advance, reveals that Marx still had lingering illusions about philosophy.

Thus, by the end of 1843, less than a year after Marx began to look for an alternative to the liberal bourgeoisie to overthrow Prussian despotism his eyes were now focused on the proletariat. He was not specific about its composition or its contours, other than the fact that it was to the industrial proletariat that he looked. Neither did he harbor any illusion about what the German proletariat could achieve at that time. "The proletariat is coming into being in Germany only as a result of the rising *industrial* development." Yet he was clearly aware that the latter process was moving literally full-steam ahead.

Within six months of Marx's declaration of his new orientation, one of the most important milestones in German labor history occurred in early June 1844 in Eastern Prussia—the Silesian weavers' revolt. This uprising, which began as a protest by cottage industry weavers—thus, not quite yet a modern, that is, industrial proletariat—against manufacturers for higher wages, escalated into a two-day violent battle with the state militia. For Marx, the revolt confirmed the correctness of his new orientation. This was not the case for Ruge. His earlier pessimism about struggle against despotism resurfaced in an article he wrote about the revolt, which he saw as futile and ill-advised. Marx felt compelled to respond to Ruge in *Vorwärts*, a publication popular within the German exile community in Paris where Marx now lived. In his article Ruge learned how serious Marx was about "ruthless criticism."

First, Marx argued, Ruge failed to appreciate the significance of the strike. Referring to the song composed by the strikers, he said "recall *the song of the weavers*, that bold *call* to struggle . . . in which the proletariat at once, in a striking, sharp, unrestrained and powerful manner, proclaims its opposition to the society of private property."[22] Such consciousness, in Marx's opinion, was much more advanced than that even of workers in France and England. More importantly, "not a single English workers' uprising was carried out with such courage, thought and endurance."

Second, Marx severely criticized Ruge for not identifying with or relating to the strike.

> Confronted with the first outbreak of the . . . uprising, the sole task of one who thinks and loves the truth consisted not in playing the role of *schoolmaster* in relation to this event, but instead in studying its *specific* character. This, of course, requires some scientific insight and some love of mankind, whereas for the other operation a glib phraseology, impregnated with empty love of oneself, is quite enough.

Marx, in other words, was condemning Ruge for reneging on the perspective concerning the purpose of the *Deutsche-Französische Jahrbucher* that he thought they had agreed to in their exchange of letters. Referring to that earlier exchange, specifically where Marx said that the starting point of their criticism should be "participation in politics, and therefore *real* struggles," he elaborated:

> [W]e do not confront the world in a doctrinaire way with a new principle: Here is the truth, kneel down before it! We develop new principles for the world out of the world's own principles. We do not say to the world: Cease your struggles, they are foolish; we will give you the true slogan of struggle. We merely show the world what it is really fighting for, and consciousness is something that it *has* to acquire, even if it does not want to.

The manner in which Ruge looked at the strike, in Marx's opinion, was exactly what he thought they had agreed not to do.

Lastly, the strike revealed something even more important. Marx, who by this time, was espousing communism,[23] argued that the revolt indicated that Germany was destined for a social revolution as well as a political revolution. What Ruge apparently didn't understand was that while the two are interrelated they are separate processes. "*Revolution* in general—the *overthrow* of the existing power and *dissolution* of the old relationships—is a political act. But *socialism* cannot be realised without *revolution*. It needs this *political* act insofar as it needs *destruction and dissolution*. But where its *organising activity* begins, where its *proper object* . . . comes to fore—there socialism throws off the *political* cloak."[24]

This was Marx's first statement on the essentials of a socialist revolution. It reflected in part the intense reading he was doing on earlier revolutions, particularly the French Revolution. While he would elaborate these views in subsequent years on the basis of concrete experience, the essence remained—especially the notion that the political step was a necessary, but not a sufficient condition to the creation of a socialist society, a society where "the worker" would no longer be isolated through "*his own labour*" from "physical and mental life, human morality, human activity, human enjoyment, *human* nature"—that is, from "*life* itself." To realize such a society meant going beyond a political revolution—not merely a change in the state but an overthrow of property relations.

Marx's idea that a political revolution was insufficient for the end of despotic rule in Germany was also shared by his recently wed wife, Jenny, with whom he collaborated politically. Interestingly, he publicized her views by printing an excerpt from one of her letters in the same journal issue in which his article against Ruge appeared, perhaps as another way to hammer home his point. Commenting on the recent attempted assassination of the Prussian Emperor, Frederick William IV, she noted that the perpetrator, a very impoverished man, did not act out of political motives. This, for Jenny Marx, was "precisely a new proof that a political revolution is impossible in Germany, whereas all the seeds of a social revolution are possible."[25]

What is especially remarkable about the political conclusions that Marx had begun to reach is that he arrived at them in spite of his near abstention from active political involvement. His world, until then, had been one of middle-class intellectuals with few or no organic links to the world of the political activist. This is not to slight the battles he fought as a radical journalist against state censorship. But those who engaged in the kinds of "real struggles" that Marx increasingly looked to, such as the Silesian weavers, experienced the political actions of the state in a far more brutal way than middle-class fighters demanding liberal reforms. Thus, a worker who fought back against oppression was more likely to draw revolutionary conclusions from his or her experience than a rebel journalist.

One of the consequences of Marx's writings was that it led to a permanent political break with Ruge, and consequently severed almost all of his ties with the Young Hegelians.[26] Another result was that in April 1844, the Prussian government charged Marx with "high treason" and issued a warrant for his arrest if he reentered Prussia. From this point on his exile from Prussia was involuntary and his participation in politics took on a new challenge. In this context he began establishing ties with various exile groups and secret workers' organizations in Paris, although without joining any. Certainly, the most important political relationship that he established, at the end of August 1844, was with another Rhinelander, Friedrich Engels. As a result of this relationship, he would be able to round out the political perspective that he was forging, and, more importantly, begin to carry it out.

The Young Engels

The road that Engels travelled toward communism was in many ways similar to the one taken by Marx. As a Rhinelander, he too had been exposed to liberal influences. His father, a textile manufacturer, embraced many of the political aspirations of the region's bourgeoisie. In his first explicit political writing, an article for the RZ, Engels addressed the issue of liberalism. Like Marx at one time, he too looked to liberals for political leadership. He contrasted "North German" liberals to their counterparts in the southern provinces; the former were "distinguished by a high degree of consistency, a definiteness in his demands" which the latter had never achieved. Unlike the latter, North-German liberals were able to "launch a resolute vigorous and successful battle against each and every form of reaction. . . ." While the southerners had once contributed significantly to parliamentary government, they failed in the end to obtain it because, as Engels argued, they "proceeded from practice to theory . . . ; so let us begin the other way round and to penetrate from theory into practice. I wager anything that in the end we shall get farther this way."[27]

While still confident that at least some liberal opponents of the regime were willing to carry out the fight, Engels was already aware of the vacillation within their ranks. In addition, he recognized the necessity of a "theory" to inform the requisite political activity for the institution of political democracy. He was clearly not a revolutionary at this stage because he, like many liberal opponents of the regime, felt that liberties such as freedom of press and a representative government could be won without overthrowing the monarchy in the person of Frederick IV.

Like Marx, Engels also had to work his way through Hegelianism. Although a high school dropout, he affiliated himself with the intellectual Young Hegelian circle. Consistent with his belief in the need to move from "theory to practice," he took the initiative, through publications, to defend the views of the circle. It was in this connection that he came to write for the *RZ*, and, thus, attracted Marx's attention. One of the differences between Engels and Marx at this stage in their political development, is that the former, like most of the Young Hegelians, attached greater importance to the religious question. Raised in a highly devout family, unlike Marx, he had to spend more time grappling with this issue. Thus, whereas Marx's critique of Hegel tended to focus on political matters, Engels, like many of the Young Hegelians, gave greater attention to religion, and argued that the logical outcome of Hegel's system, in spite of itself, was atheism.

Toward the end of 1842 Engels embarked on an experience that was decisive in his political transformation. It was unlike anything that the Young Marx had experienced, and yet Engels's experiences were to be crucial in Marx's development, as well as in his own. This was his move to Manchester, England, the industrial heart of the most industrialized country at that time. Urged by his father to go and get commercial apprenticeship training in one of the family's factories, Engels used the opportunity to study bookkeeping, and, more importantly, the inner workings of industrial capitalism and all of its social and political consequences. One result was the publication in 1845 of one of Engels's best known works, *The Condition of the Working-Class in England.*

Engels's stay in England allowed him to provide Marx and other readers of the *RZ* and *Deutsche-Französische Jahrbucher* with a firsthand account of the reality of vanguard capitalism—the road Germany had yet to travel—from someone within their milieu. Indeed, because Engels had an intimate view of a much more developed capitalism, which his comrades in Germany lacked, he was able after only about a year in England to write his first economic work, "Outlines of a Critique of Political Economy," published in the *DFJ*. This made him "the best-read Young Hegelian on the subject of political economy."[28] The article exercised an enormous influence on Marx. Shortly after reading it, Marx began his own economic studies, which resulted in the so-called "Economic and Philosophic Manuscripts of 1844." Engels's article may even be said to have been the seed from which *Capital* sprang.

Just as influential as Engels's economic writings were his reports on the political situation in England, especially the activities of the proletariat. When Marx, for example, in defense of the Silesian weavers' revolt, made judgments about the relative resoluteness of the German proletariat vis-à-vis their counterparts in England, it was Engels's articles to the *RZ* on the workers' movement in England that he drew upon. As Marx was developing his orientation toward the German proletariat, Engels supplied *RZ* readers with data and assessments on what was then the most class-conscious proletariat in the world. It was the living struggle, the real experiences of the proletariat, the material that Marx had demanded to be the starting point of his analysis, that Engels was able to supply.

In England at that time the proletariat's political movement was Chartism, whose goal was the realization of basic democratic rights for working people, particularly suffrage. From the very beginning of his stay Engels sought to understand the revolutionary potential of the working class in England. While certainly hopeful, Engels entertained no illusions about the English workers, unlike many of their sympathizers on the continent. His observations on the late summer strike wave in 1842 are instructive.

The strikes failed, he argued, because the "whole affair was unprepared, unorganised and without leadership." When the Chartist leaders intervened and attempted to overcome these deficiencies they were ineffective. Primarily because "the only guiding idea . . . was that of revolution by legal means—in itself a contradiction, a practical impossibility. . . ." Yet Engels, a revolutionary by now, said all was not lost—the proletariat did learn something in the process: "the realisation that a revolution by peaceful means is impossible and that only a forcible abolition of the existing unnatural conditions, a radical overthrow of the nobility and industrial aristocracy, can improve the material position of the proletarians." And to make clear what he meant by "revolution"—"the revolution will be social, not political,"[29] that is, it would go beyond simply the overthrow of the state but involve a radical transformation of property relations. Aside from what Engels saw as its fetish with legality, the main problem with the proletarian movement in England was that it lacked a "theory" to guide "practice." Engels, in partnership with Marx, would soon take steps to ensure that the workers' movement from hereon would not have to reproduce this defect of the English movement.

Engels was not simply an observer and commentator on the English proletariat. Consistent with his notion of "practice," he established political relations with the various proletarian tendencies in England at the time, the Chartists, the followers of the utopian socialist Robert Owen, as well as the German exiles in the communist League of the Just. A particular interest of his was linking up with the Irish nationalist movement. This was inspired in part by Mary Burns, an ardent working-class Irish nationalist, with whom he established a personal union until her death in 1863. These ties laid the basis for the practical work that he and Marx later undertook.

Engels saw his role as one of helping to overcome the information barriers between English and continental socialists. Just as he had been writing in the *RZ* and other German publications to inform German revolutionaries and activists about the political situation in England, he began writing in English movement papers about doings on the continent. Although socialist consciousness had developed in different ways in England, France, and Germany, and there were consequently differences between them—albeit minor—"the thing wanted, is that they should know each other."[30] Thus, through his reports, Engels was an early pioneer in what would later be called proletarian internationalism.

His reports on the various socialist movements at that time—between 1842 and 1844—sought to draw a balance sheet on their strengths and weaknesses. Of particular interest, in terms of his later views on organizational and strategic matters, was his very briefly stated critique of the French communists' fetish for "secret associations." While sympathetic with the use of force in their struggle—a key difference between the French and English political realities—he nevertheless felt that "secret associations are always contrary to common prudence, inasmuch as they make the parties liable to unnecessary legal persecutions."[31]

In his effort to make English readers understand the reality of German communism, Engels made it clear that it was indeed the "party" to which he adhered. His identification with communism came about a half-year before Marx would do so. ("Party" in this sense referred to a political tendency and not an organized current. Again, it must be remembered that "communism" as both Engels and Marx then used the term would take on a quite different meaning for them while they formulated their joint program.) German communism's growing success, as he described it, was due to an active strategy on the part of the Young Hegelians to be the most resolute defenders of republicanism. The result was that "very soon the whole of the German liberal press was entirely in our hands. We had friends in almost every considerable town in Germany; we provided all the liberal papers with the necessary matter, and by this means made them our organs." Those who agitated for republicanism "developed farther and farther the consequences of their philosophy [and] became Communists." Engels counted "Dr. Marx" among the members of the communist "party." Finally, while the Germans have a much more developed philosophical basis than their counterparts in England and France, "in everything bearing upon practice, upon the *facts* of the present state of society, we find that the English Socialists are a long way before us. . . . I may say, besides, that I have met with English Socialists with whom I agree upon almost every question."

The tone of Engels's remarks reflected the degree of conscious political activity that emerged quite early in his political career—even before he became a "Marxist." Keeping in mind that his remarks were current—thus avoiding any temptation to ascribe purpose to actions that may not be warranted—it means that Engels certainly, if not the other Young Hegelians, deliberately and consciously sought to influence and win others to their ideas. Also, it was a conscious effort to push the fight for democracy further leftward than what liberals had intended. Finally, his comments also indicate that he still held German philosophy and English socialism in high regard.

In another article that Engels wrote for the English press he alerted readers once again to "Dr. Marx." The context was a discussion of the "favourable" political climate in Germany at the beginning of 1844 "for the commencement of a more extensive social agitation . . . and [for] the effect of a new periodical advocating a thorough social reform."[32] He was referring to the soon expected publication of the *DFJ*, whose co-editors "Dr. Ruge and Dr. Marx . . . belong to the 'learned Communists' of Germany." The periodical "could not . . . commence at a more favourable moment, and its success may be considered as certain." Though Engels's optimism about the journal was misplaced, it revealed the high regard in which he held Marx, and, in anticipation of the future, his readiness to promote Marx's ideas.[33] And just as Engels was singing Marx's praises, Marx was doing the same for Engels as he was reading and readying for publication in the *DFJ*, his seminal article "Outlines of a Critique of Political Economy." Thus, by the beginning of 1844 both men held one another's writings in high esteem and, more significantly, they each, independently of the other, had reached the same conclusion, which each began acting on—Engels perhaps more so than Marx at the time—the view that practice should be the outcome of revolutionary theory.

Engels completed his commercial apprenticeship and left Manchester for home in August 1844. He decided to stop over for a few days in Paris, where Marx was living. Unlike the first time they met, when Engels was on his way to England, this meeting lasted longer. The realization that they agreed on the basic issues of revolutionary politics resulted in the now-fateful decision to form a political alliance. With due apologies to John Reed—but with due justification—those ten days in Paris, from August 23 to September 2, 1844, could easily be called, "ten days that would shake the world."

The Partnership Begins

One Marxologist has described the Marx-Engels alliance as one in which "Marx was commander-in-chief of the revolution; Engels, executive officer."[34] While there is an element of truth in this, it could be taken, mistakenly, to suggest a sharp division of labor between the two, or that Marx only gave orders for Engels to carry out. The reality, as the entire record of their relationship will show, was quite different.

In the immediate aftermath of their decision to work together Engels appeared to be more of a task master, making sure that what they had agreed to in Paris would actually be executed.[35] The priority was the formulation of a joint perspective—a new communist world view. The first step in this direction was the clearing away of the Hegelian cobwebs. This took the form of a published polemic against former Young Hegelian associates, particularly Bruno Bauer, who had by now declared ideological warfare on Marx. "Ruthless criticism," without any fear of its consequences, was from now on a joint Marx-Engels endeavor.

Toward the Break with German Philosophy

The polemic against the Young Hegelians, the first literary product of the new alliance, *The Holy Family, or Critique of Critical Criticism*, was a rambling and tedious tract written largely by Marx. Engels contributed about a tenth of the final work. As much as he enjoyed reading it after Marx was finally able to have it published at the beginning of 1845, Engels frankly and correctly wrote to Marx that "the thing's too long. . . . In addition most of the criticism of speculation and of abstract being in general will be incomprehensible to the public at large, nor will it be of general interest." Engels's forthrightness not only set a tone that characterized their relationship until the end—based on honesty and equality—but more apropos, it was advice that revolutionary communists whose primary audience would be the proletariat had to heed.

Within the framework of this book, the most important part of *The Holy Family* is probably chapter VI, written by Marx, particularly the subsection that is translated in the *MECW*, as "'Spirit' and 'mass.'" As Hal Draper persuasively argues, given its contents, the more appropriate translation should be "'Intellectuals versus the Masses.'"[36] This section addressed what Marx had now come to recognize as a major failing of the Young Hegelians, their elitist attitude toward the oppressed. Simply put, they believed, like Marx and Engels at one time, that as philosophers they were the masses' "spiritual weapon"—its brain.

In their attempt to overcome Hegel, Bruno Bauer and the Young Hegelians equated "criticism" with Hegel's "Absolute Spirit." The problem with this equation, as Marx argued, was that "*criticism* sees itself incarnate not in a *mass*, but exclusively in a *handful* of chosen men, in Herr *Bauer* and his disciples. . . . On the one side is the Mass as the passive, spiritless, unhistorical, *material* element of history. On the other is *the* Spirit, *Criticism*, Herr Bruno and Co. as the active element from which all *historical* action proceeds. The act of transforming society is reduced to the *cerebral activity* of Critical Criticism," that is, what Bruno and his cohorts called their philosophy.[37]

To Bruno's "critical criticism" Marx counterposed "communist criticism." Substituting the former for Hegel's "Absolute Spirit" didn't really get beyond Hegel because it didn't address the fundamental problem that "*all progress of the Spirit* has so far been *progress against the mass of mankind*, driving it into an ever more *dehumanised* situation." Whereas, "communist criticism had practically at once as its counterpart the movement of the *great mass*, in opposition to which history had been developing so far." Marx then revealed who he meant by the "great mass." "One must know the studiousness, the craving for knowledge, the moral energy and the unceasing urge for development of the French and English workers to be able to form an idea of the *human* nobility of this movement."[38]

Thus, intellectuals like Bauer and his kind could never be the source for real transformation. After examining the dynamics of a real struggle, the French Revolution, Marx hammered home this point. "*Ideas* can never lead beyond an old world order but only beyond the ideas of the old world order. Ideas *cannot carry out anything* at all. In order to carry out ideas men are needed who can exert practical force."[39] As he had already made clear in his earlier critique of Hegel, the proletariat are the "men . . . needed." What Marx anticipated here was the radical reevaluation of philosophy and philosophers as agents of social change that he and Engels would make and then elaborate on within a year in their next joint work, *The German Ideology*.

The other issue that Marx anticipates in his critique is the old bugbear that critics of "Marxism" and then later, "Marxism-Leninism" would raise, namely, that Marx and Engels merely established a new model of elitist politics. This is not the place to discuss this criticism; it can only be addressed by examining the actual practice of Marx and Engels, and then later Lenin, in the context of real struggles—in other words, in the subsequent chapters of this book (Lenin must await another volume). Suffice it here to note that at the very earliest stage of his joint venture with Engels, Marx was skeptical of any liberatory endeavor that rested on the goodwill of a "handful of chosen men."

"We must strike while the iron is hot"

Engels's candidness about the style of *The Holy Family* indicates the mode of collaboration that he established at the outset with Marx—one that was crucial for the future literary productivity of the partnership. Upon returning to the Rhineland, Engels, inspired by the alliance just agreed to in Paris, immediately threw himself into political activity in order, as he wrote to Marx, to propagate "our principle." While the province "promises to be first rate soil," what was lacking was "a few publications in which the principles are logically and historically developed out of past ways of thinking and past history."[40] To overcome this deficit, it was imperative, as Engels saw from the beginning of the partnership, that he and Marx get their ideas into print as quickly as possible. Thus, his admonishment in the conclusion of his first extant letter to Marx: "[S]ee to it that the material you've collected is soon launched into the world. It's high time, heaven knows! . . . Down to work, then, quickly into print!"

In subsequent letters Engels was even more insistent. Getting in print, was, as he stated many times, the way "we . . . might exert influence . . . but we shall have to put our backs into it if we're to achieve anything, and that's all to the good when you're itching to do something." To encourage Marx, he wrote about his own writing schedule, and his effort to get *The Condition of the Working-Class in England* finished. He went so far as to provide advice on the discipline of writing—no doubt based on his own regimen. "You over there [in Paris] will also have to bestir yourselves. You should write an article every 4 or 6 weeks for [*Vorwärts*, a German weekly published in Paris] and not allow yourself to be 'governed' by your moods."[41] Regarding *The Holy Family*, "try and finish *before* April [1845], do as I do, set yourself a date by which you will *definitely have finished*, and make sure it gets into print quickly . . . it must come out soon."

While articles were useful, "what we need above all just now are a few larger works to provide an adequate handhold for the many who would like to improve their imperfect knowledge, but are unable to do so unassisted." Referring to "the material" that Marx had been collecting, Engels made clear what kind of larger work he had in mind. "Do try and finish your political economy book, even if there's much in it that you yourself are still dissatisfied with, it doesn't really matter; minds are ripe and we must strike while the iron is hot."[42] Even after he completed volume one of *Capital* in 1867, this urging from Engels would be a constant refrain that Marx would hear for the rest of his life.[43] Hence, evidence for the claim about Engels's role in the partnership as that of the executive officer.

This exchange also reveals that from the beginning of the partnership Engels tended to complete writing projects more quickly than Marx. Always cognizant of the inadequacy of language in describing the contradictions of social reality, Marx tended to struggle longer for precision in his formulations. Finally, and most importantly, the correspondence makes clear that, once formed, the Marx-Engels team wrote and published for political purposes—"to exert influence." Thus, from this point on, their writings can only be fully understood if looked at politically—what Marxologists almost invariably fail to do.

Given the absence of "larger works" and the reality that Marx's work on political economy was a long way from completion, in spite of Engels's tactful cajoling, Marx and Engels seriously tried for about the first half of 1845 to establish a "library of the best foreign socialist writers." Its purpose was to provide essential readings for aspiring German communists, who while enthusiastic, were still "hazy . . . and groping in the dark" for want of adequate literature.[44] The idea was to begin translating the classics of Fourier and other socialist utopians, the writings of and about participants in the French Revolution such as Babeuf and Buonarroti, even the English philosopher Jeremy Bentham ("although the fellow's so tedious and theoretical"), along with others. An indication of the seriousness that Marx and Engels accorded the educational needs of their "party" are the works that they considered for the library. Engels's comments to Marx are instructive. "I believe that it would be better here to sacrifice *theoretical* interest to practical effectiveness, and to start off with the things which have most to offer the Germans and are closest to our principles."[45] Consistent with their new orientation, the emphasis was now on practice; thus, the desirability of studying real struggles or ideas that came out of real struggles. What this foreshadowed was the irreparable break they were about to make with philosophy in general and German philosophy in particular. Owing to publication obstacles, the library was never realized. This failure, however, simply spurred the Marx-Engels team to move quickly beyond criticism of existing ideas and to write and publish what they stood for—their new communist world view.

Engels's comment to Marx that "We must strike while the iron is hot" makes clear that the outcome of those fateful ten days in Paris was indeed the establishment of a political team. It was the core of what would increasingly be called the "Marx party," or a political tendency. In his first extant letter to Marx, not only did he refer to "our principle" but also, "our people," that is, the growing number of partisans of communism as then understood. Engels's political activity when he returned to the Rhineland after Paris consisted of political organizing and propaganda as well as literary work. In this manner, he sought to give direction to "our people's activities" in the province, while Marx, he suggested, should form a "council" with partisans in Paris. Thinking in terms of a political team with a division of labor, Engels wrote that with such a "council" in Paris, "you will have all the less need of me and there is all the more need for me here. . . . And after all, one of us ought to be here because all our people need prodding if they are to maintain a sufficient degree of activity and not fall into all manner of shuffling and shifting."[46] Again, the image of Engels as task master and executive officer is not altogether undeserved.

It appears that Marx was also active along the lines that Engels urged. The record, however, is not as clear as that for Engels since, unfortunately, virtually none of his letters to Engels from this period survives.[47] What does exist is a police agent's report about Marx's activities at the beginning of February 1845. The "agent reported having seen Marx and his friends, including the publisher Börnstein and the poet Herwegh, at meetings of 'sometimes thirty, often one hundred to two hundred Germans.' The meetings took place in a wine shop in the workingclass quarter near the Porte de Vincennes . . . where many of the artisans lived. As the agent saw it, Marx and his friends were 'intriguers [who] take advantage of the poor German artisans, and also young business-people and clerks, to seduce them into communism.' The speakers . . . 'made speeches in which they openly advocated regicide, the abolition of all private property, the elimination of the wealthy classes and religion.'"[48] Notwithstanding the agent's own interpretation of what he witnessed, the account suggests that Marx's political activities in Paris were organizational as well as literary.

Engels's activism also took different forms. One involved covert intervention in the Associations for the Benefit of the Working Classes, which were organizations established by the liberal bourgeoisie in the wake of the Silesian weavers' revolt—a liberal effort to preempt future uprisings by giving the appearance of concern for the needs of workers. As such, their meetings provided a cover, in the framework of the repressive Prussian state, for political discussions about the "social" question. Thus, as Engels wrote to Marx, "our people" took the initiative to establish the organizations in the Rhine province and made sure that "we" would exercise decisive influence in how they operated.[49] Because these associations began attracting a mass following in the urban areas and communist organizing began to be effective, the Prussian authorities, who had initially been somewhat supportive in their establishment, banned them in the spring of 1845.

An activity that was new for Engels was public speaking. Its advantages for an activist became immediately apparent. "Standing up in front of real, live people and holding forth to them directly and straightforwardly, so that they see and hear you is something quite different from engaging in this devilishly abstract quill pushing with an abstract audience in one's 'mind's eye.'"[50] In February 1845, he addressed three meetings in Elberfeld, the industrial center of the Rhine province; the last meeting, the largest of these, had about two hundred in attendance, comprised almost exclusively of the local bourgeoisie and small shopkeepers. Significantly, "only the proletariat [was] excluded," apparently due to government interference. That "only" the proletariat was absent suggests that Engels still had yet to become a communist in the sense that he and Marx would later understand. This is not to imply that he thought that communism was irrelevant to the German proletariat. Commenting a few months earlier in a letter to Marx on the increasing crime rate in working-class neighborhoods in the Elberfeld area, he dispels any such interpretation. Working-class crime was in fact a measure of the advances in the proletarianization of the Rhine province because it represented a form of social protest. "If the proletarians here develop according to the same laws as in England, they will soon realise that this way of protesting as *individuals* and with violence against the social order is useless, and they will protest, through communism, in their general capacity as *human beings*."[51]

Engels's Elberfeld speeches reveal the extent of his political development at that time. They were probably the most concrete ideas in existence then—Marx certainly had yet to be so concrete—on the relationship between the reality of capitalism, the coming of socialist revolution, and the organization of a socialist society. He linked capitalist competition, monopolization, trade wars and protectionism, recessions, social pathology with increasing discontent on the part of the proletariat to the potential for violent revolution. Yet, his bottom line message to his mainly petit-bourgeois audiences, was that "a social revolution . . . *the open war of the poor against the rich*" could be avoided by "the peaceful introduction or at least preparation of communism." Making himself clear, Engels said, "If we do not want the *bloody* solution of the social problem . . . then gentlemen . . . we must make it our business to contribute our share towards humanising the condition of the modern helots."[52] Thus, while Engels may have then been more concrete than Marx about the reality of capitalism and socialist revolution, he had not yet fully grasped what Marx had increasingly come to see, namely, that only the proletariat could liberate itself—including the German proletariat, in spite of its relative underdevelopment. Engels still harbored illusions about the liberal wing of German capital, or at least liberal capital in the Rhine, both large and small; this would change within just a few months.[53]

Reunited in Brussels

In the beginning of 1845 Marx fell victim once again to the repressive arm of the Prussian state—this time via the French government of Louis Philippe. Because his regime—a constitutional monarchy—had been established by the revolution of 1830, it was obligated to maintain a certain liberal facade including tolerance and at times support of political refugees from neighboring countries. Indicative of the changing political climate within France, however, the government ordered the expulsion of Marx and other German exiles who had collaborated with the German exile newspaper *Vorwärts*; a month earlier the French authorities had banned the paper. Both the expulsion and banning orders were due to pressure from the Berlin government, which was feeling increasingly vulnerable to the criticisms and political activities of it opponents in exile in Paris. On February 3, Marx moved to Brussels. Though the government was also liberal, Marx was required to sign a statement promising not to publish any political writings in Belgium. He was then "immediately placed under secret surveillance as a 'dangerous democrat and Communist.'"[54]

Marx's move to Brussels was difficult, particularly for his wife and his ten-month-old daughter. Owing to onerous expenses, Engels proposed that a collection be taken among their communist contacts "so that the extra expense you have incurred thereby should be shared out communist-fashion between us all."[55] Not certain that this would be enough, Engels then wrote, "I shall, needless to say, have the greatest pleasure in placing at your disposal my fee for my first English piece [*The Condition of the Working-Class in England*]." This appears to be the first time that Engels offered Marx financial assistance; it wouldn't be the last. Engels's intent was to ensure that Marx could carry on his work with a degree of economic security.

Once settled in Brussels Marx continued his research on political economy. He had just signed a contract to write and have published a two-volume work to be entitled, *Critique of Politics and Political Economy*, which would take another two decades to complete. Related to this project was a plan to do a study of the French Revolution in the context of an analysis of the "modern state." Some of the proposed topics were "the constitutions of the state. Individual freedom and public authority," "state and civil society," "division of powers," "legislative power," "executive power," "judicial power and law," "nationality and the people," "political parties," and lastly, "suffrage, the fight for the *abolition* of the state and of bourgeois society."[56] Unlike the main project on political economy this plan was never realized.

A frequent criticism of Marx and Engels is that they ignored political structures and processes (an issue to be addressed in the Conclusions). Marx's plan makes clear that such issues were not unimportant to him.[57] That Marx never wrote this book says more about his priorities. More important was a thorough understanding of how the system of the private ownership of the means of production became an obstacle to "true democracy." Thus, the need to grasp the inner logic of the capitalist mode of production and prioritize the research for what would later be *Capital*. That having been accomplished—which it never was in Marx's lifetime—a work on the "modern state" could then be undertaken.

Throughout 1845 the Prussian authorities continued to close off the limited political space that still existed within its borders. By April, Engels realized that it was only a matter of time before the government would clamp down on him. He decided to leave Prussia and move to Brussels to collaborate more closely with Marx. The actions of the Prussian regime, unbeknownst to it, were therefore in part responsible for cementing the partnership that had been founded in Paris some eight months earlier. Its actions, along with those of the French and Belgian authorities, also provided very concrete lessons for both Marx and Engels on the class character of the state—a crucial component of their soon to be formulated new communist world view.

The partnership that began in Paris was able to be consummated in Brussels. With residences near one another Marx and Engels were able to have daily discussions that facilitated a homogenization of political and theoretical views. Brussels provided other benefits—its own binational character and proximity to the Rhine Province and Britain. Along with its multinational political exile community—albeit smaller than that of Paris—Brussels made it possible for the two to acquire a truly international perspective. In addition, the city was the capital of the second most industrialized nation in Europe—a fact, as the next chapter will show, of no small significance for the revolutionary team.

Although Marx intended to complete the political economy project in Brussels, other projects took priority. It had become clear to him, probably as a result of discussions with Engels, that he needed to do a more general methodological piece before writing a major work on political economy. To do so meant clearing away a few remaining philosophical cobwebs. The most important of these was the philosopher Feuerbach, with whom both Marx and Engels had until now agreed. In spite of his agreement with Feuerbach's critique of Hegel, Marx had once noted that he tended to ignore politics which, in Marx's opinion, was "the only alliance by which present-day philosophy can become truth."[58] In the spring of 1845 Marx began a reevaluation of Feuerbach.

Shortly before doing so, Engels, who was still in the Rhineland, wrote Marx that he had just received a letter from the philosopher in reply to their request which, apparently, asked him to join with them in their communist literary efforts. Feuerbach politely declined saying that he was too involved in his philosophical studies. "However, he says he's a communist and that his only problem is how to practise communism. There's a possibility of his visiting the Rhineland this summer, in which case he must come to Brussels and *we'll show him how* [italics added]."[59] Engels's editorial comment reflects not only the confidence that he and Marx possessed quite early in their partnership but, more to the point, their commitment to political activism.

By the end of the spring, perhaps after Engels had joined him in Brussels, Marx drafted his *Theses on Feuerbach*, which consisted of, as Engels later described, "notes hurriedly scribbled down for later elaboration." Less than three pages in length, the eleven theses would, in fact, constitute many of the core ideas in *The German Ideology*, written about half a year later. Although it cannot be proven, it's very possible that Engels's editorial comment about the noted materialist philosopher weighed heavily on Marx's mind when he drafted them.

The problem with Feuerbach and materialists like him, as the first thesis argues, is that "he does not grasp the significance of 'revolutionary,' of practical-critical activity."[60] Materialists as social determinists, according to the third thesis, "forget that it is men who change circumstances and the educator must himself be educated." Thus, their view is inherently elitist because it "is bound to divide society into two parts, one of which is superior to society. . . . The coincidence of the changing of circumstances and of human activity can be conceived and rationally understood only as revolutionising practice." In other words, the "educator," those who claim to know how to change society must themselves engage in revolutionary practice. Herein also is the kernel of Marx's answer to the age-old riddle about the unprepared masses' ability to rule themselves. And as the last, and most well-known thesis, aptly stated, "The philosophers have only *interpreted* the world in various ways; the point, however, is to *change* it." What these very concise, but not necessarily new, ideas foreshadowed was the removal of the pedestal upon which Marx and Engels had once placed not only philosophers such as Feuerbach but philosophy itself. If, indeed, the point was to "change" the world or the "circumstances" in which humans find themselves, then it was necessary to turn to those forces who were engaged in "revolutionary practice" and not to the Feuerbachs who were too busy with their philosophical studies.

A Momentous Trip

After about three months together in Brussels, Marx and Engels traveled to Britain in order to meet leaders of the Chartist movement, as well as various socialists, and to do research in Manchester libraries on British political economy. While it is not clear what motivated the trip for Marx—Engels had a number of personal matters he had to attend to—one must guess that Engels's book, *The Condition of the Working-Class in England*, which was published at the end of May and which Marx began reading immediately, was influential. For Marx, a trip to England was not only an opportunity to see advanced industrial capitalism with his own eyes and to get the most current data and thinking on political economy but, even more importantly, to meet the proletarian fighters that Engels had been talking and writing about—an opportunity to put flesh on the theoretical bones of his own writings.

The six weeks in England were quite fruitful, especially for Marx. The first four were spent in Manchester where Marx was able to utilize the libraries and take extensive notes on political economy. Through Engels, he also met workers and leaders active in the Chartist movement. The last two weeks were spent in London where, again, through Engels he met national Chartist leaders, such as Julian Harney (1817–1897). He also met for the first time German political exiles who belonged to the League of the Just, about which more will be said later.

A couple of days before they left London Marx and Engels participated in a meeting with leaders of the Chartist movement, the League of the Just, and other political exile groups in which they motivated the convening of an international conference of revolutionary democratic forces as a counterweight to the so-called Holy Alliance of monarchs. Engels seconded a motion to that effect: "That a public meeting of the democrats of all nations, residing in London, be called to consider the propriety of forming an Association for the purpose of meeting each other at certain times, and getting by this means a better knowledge of the movements for the common cause going on in their respective countries."[61] The language of the resolution, particularly the second clause, could easily have been taken from an article that Engels wrote for the English press at the end of 1843.[62] A very successful meeting did take place on September 22, 1845, in London out of which was born the Society of Fraternal Democrats. And although Marx and Engels were unable to attend the meeting, their role in making it happen no doubt encouraged them to take even bolder steps in what was, in hindsight, their first joint effort at proletarian internationalism.[63]

The German Ideology

The trip to England proved to be decisive in the further political development of the Marx-Engels team. More than anything it provided evidence that the proletariat, as Marx had already begun to argue, was indeed capable of taking its own destiny in its hands through its own practice *and* without the guidance of philosophy in general or German philosophy in particular. While there were already hints in his writings before Engels's second visit to England, the realization that German philosophy had little to offer the proletariat became most apparent for him in the aftermath of the trip. At this time, the most current and influential incarnation of Hegelianism was the self-styled current known as "True Socialism." With roots also in Feuerbach's materialist humanism, it envisioned a socialist world coming into existence on the basis of love and human understanding. It was just then that Marx-Engels decided to begin their long-planned theoretical work stating their new communist world view, *The German Ideology*, one of whose central arguments would be that only through "revolutionary practice" could communism be realized. Thus, True Socialism represented another philosophical diversion—a dissolution of the concrete fight for socialism into abstract calls for human understanding—from what had to be done.

With Engels leading the way the team began a concerted polemic against this latest pearl of wisdom of German philosophy. His first jab, "A Fragment of Fourier's on Trade," is especially instructive.[64] The problem with German theoreticians—and in a self-reflective moment, "I make no exception here of my own writings"—is that they have an inflated opinion of their own achievements, "comical arrogance." Also, to the extent that they draw on other socialist theorists they interpret them in a "bad, abstract, unintelligible and clumsy form," and invariably are attracted to "only what is worst and most theoretical: the schematic plans of future society, the *social systems*." That which is best in socialist writers in France or elsewhere, including the utopians, "the *criticism of existing society*, the real basis, the main task of any investigation of social questions, they have calmly pushed aside."[65] Engels's demand for concrete analysis based on the world as it exists is, of course, exactly what Marx had called for in his exchange of letters with Ruge in 1843.

As an example of what Germans should be doing, Engels then presented his readers with a translation of extensive excerpts of some of the writings of the utopian socialist Charles Fourier (1772–1837). Because Fourier was not a Hegelian, he therefore, with telling sarcasm, "unfortunately could not attain knowledge of absolute truth, not even of absolute socialism . . ." since he had no "absolute method." Thus, Engels ridiculed not only a preconceived "absolute socialist" society but also an "absolute method" for getting there.[66] Anticipating the perspective of *The German Ideology*, Engels concluded by noting that while Fourier could be criticized for his speculations about the future, he did so "after correctly understanding the past and the present; German theory [on the other hand] first of all arranges past history according to its liking and then prescribes to the future, what direction it should take." While True Socialism puts forward a "little 'humanitarianism' . . . a little moaning about the proletariat," like previous German theories it was characterized by a "boundless ignorance of political economy and the real character of society. . . . And with this tedious stuff they want to revolutionise Germany, set the proletariat in motion, and make the masses think and act!" Making the "masses think and act." That, for Engels, was now the real test for any theory.

Engels's conclusion makes clear that the recent visit to England was on his mind. "Let the Germans first acquaint themselves with the social movement abroad, both practical and literary—the practical movement included the whole of English and French history during the last eighty years, English industry and the French Revolution. . . . Only after they have seen what was done *before* them will they have an opportunity to show what *they themselves* can do."

In settling accounts with German philosophy—*The German Ideology* would do so more thoroughly—Engels was also closing a chapter on his own political development. As his self-reflection on his earlier writings and pronouncements indicated, he too had harbored illusions about the accomplishments of German philosophy. Recalling forty years later his political disposition when he first met the German political exiles of the League of the Just in his first visit to London, Engels wrote that "they were the first revolutionary proletarians whom I had seen" but he didn't agree with them, "for I still bore, as against their narrow-minded egalitarian communism ["communism which bases itself exclusively or predominantly on the demand for equality"], a goodly dose of just as narrow-minded philosophical arrogance."[67] Unlike the first meeting in 1843, the second one two years later was far more productive;

Engels came to the second meeting as an "educator" willing to learn from the revolutionary practice of proletarian fighters.

There was one other question on which Engels had displayed some ambivalence—an issue that needed to be resolved before the team could formulate their new world view. If Engels as well as Marx left London convinced that the proletariat could liberate itself, did this apply equally to German workers?—a working class that was not as advanced objectively and subjectively as its English counterpart. Engels's earlier pronouncements, especially his Elberfeld speech, suggested otherwise.

A few weeks after the Fourier article Engels wrote a piece for the Chartist newspaper, *Northern Star*, on recent developments in German politics. He discussed the significance of a recent protest in Leipzig, located in the province of Saxony, that the government had bloodily suppressed. The Saxons, he argued, must know now that in spite of "their constitution, liberal laws, liberal censorship, and liberal king's speeches [Frederick Augustus II]" they too were subject to the same brutal regime as other Germans. However, as a result of the repression the Saxon masses were beginning to stir for the first time and "the spirit of rebellion" was spreading, "notwithstanding all the talking of the Saxon Liberals."[68] Elaborating on this last point, he then looked at the larger German picture. While youth will be in the forefront of this mass stirring and eventual rebellion, "this youth is not to be looked for among the middle classes." If not from the "middle classes," then from whom?

> It is from the very heart of our working people that revolutionary action in Germany will commence. It is true, there are among our middle classes a considerable number of Republicans and even Communists, and young men too, who, if a general outbreak occurred now, would be very useful in the movement, but these men are "bourgeois," profit-mongers, manufacturers by profession; and who will guarantee us that they will not be demoralised by their trade, by their social position, which forces them to live upon the toil of other people, to grow fat by being the leeches, the "exploiteurs" of the working classes?

Engels's caustic comments reflected a reality he knew all too well. A few months earlier he had written to Marx about his "declared intention of giving up the huckstering business for good and all," that is, to sever his ties to his family's textile business. He may have had himself in mind when he qualified his indictment of "middle-class" communists.

> And if they remain proletarians in mind, though bourgeois in profession, their number will be infinitely small in comparison with the real number of the middle-class men, who stick to the existing order of things through interest, and care for nothing but the filling of their purses. Fortunately, we do not count on the middle classes at all. The movement of the proletarians has developed itself with such astonishing rapidity, that in another year or two we shall be able to muster a glorious array of working Democrats and Communists—for in this country Democracy and Communism are, as far as the working classes are concerned, quite synonymous. . . . The movement . . . goes on quietly, but steadily, whilst the middle classes spend their time with agitating for "Constitutions," "Liberty of the Press," "Pro-

tective Duties." . . . All these middle-class movements, although not without some merit, do not touch the working classes at all, who have a *movement of their own*— a knife-and-fork movement. [italics added][69]

Thus, by the fall of 1845, Engels was unequivocal in his belief that German workers, like their cohorts in England, were not only capable of taking their destiny into their own hands but in fact had begun to do so. Well-intentioned liberals could not be counted on to do what only the proletariat could do for itself. At best only a few of them would be able to break with their class interests and wholeheartedly embrace the proletarian cause. Within a little more than two years Engels's forecast about rebellion in Germany would prove correct. In addition, the positions he now held about the relationship between the petit-bourgeoisie and workers in the fight for democracy would be utilized by the Marx-Engels team in its participation in that revolt. As to what explained Engels's apparent shift in views it is difficult to know with certainty. Perhaps it was the more amicable meeting with the German exiles in his second trip to London—an encounter that was no doubt facilitated by Engels having left behind his "philosophical arrogance." Whatever the reason, in the aftermath of the visit the Marx-Engels team was now united in its views on the proletariat and thus able to tackle the last major task before engaging in revolutionary practice—a detailed statement of their new outlook.

Marx and Engels wrote *The German Ideology* between the end of 1845 and the about the first half of 1846. Unlike their first publication, *The Holy Family*, this was indeed a joint effort—a true collaboration. It's unwieldy subtitle, *Critique of Modern German Philosophy according to its representatives Feuerbach, B. Bauer and Stirner, and of German socialism according to its various prophets*, makes clear that it was intended to cut a wide critical swath through contemporary German philosophy. Any doubts that they had broken with philosophy are easily dispelled by this work.

> One has to "leave philosophy aside" . . . one has to leap out of it and devote one-self like an ordinary man to the study of the actuality, for which there exists also an enormous amount of literary material, unknown, of course, to the philosophers. . . . Philosophy and the study of the actual world have the same relation to one another as onanism and sexual love.[70]

More than a critique and a final settling of accounts with German intellectual traditions, the work set out for the first time the alternative perspective of the Marx-Engels team.

Given one of the arguments of this book, that Marx and Engels were first and foremost political people who should be approached as such, a case can be made that not much time need be spent in discussing the contents of *The German Ideology*. First, except for one small chapter, the book was never published in their lifetimes. When they realized they couldn't get a publisher, by the second half of 1846, they, in Marx's own words some thirteen years later, "abandoned the manuscript to the gnawing criticism of the mice all the more willingly since we had achieved our main purpose—self clarification."[71] Second, Marx did publish within a year another work that did present, very adequately in their view, their historical materialist outlook,

The Poverty of Philosophy, about which more will be said in the next chapter. Looking at *The German Ideology* manuscript four decades later, Engels noted that "the finished portion consists of an exposition of the materialist conception of history which proves only how incomplete our knowledge of economic history was at that time."[72] This admission might explain, lastly, why Engels, after the manuscript was found following Marx's death in 1883, always refused to lend it out or have it published.[73] In sum, then, *The German Ideology* for Marx and Engels was important in their own political development but for them was not a work of lasting political value such as *The Poverty of Philosophy* or *The Communist Manifesto*, of which they always welcomed new translations and printings.

Suffice it to say, nevertheless, that *The German Ideology* laid out for the first time the "materialist conception of history"—historical materialism—which was indeed a new communist world view. Its core was the explication of the origin and evolution of classes and, hence, the class basis of the state. The *Manifesto*, which would be written in two years, incorporated this perspective. While, as Engels's admission suggests, this core had to be elaborated on and concretized with new data both in time and place, it constituted from the outset that which distinguished what eventually came to be called "Marxist" or, as they called it, "scientific communism" from preexisting communisms. More would be added to the core with the appearance of *Capital* two decades later.

Finally, with regard to the proletariat and revolutionary practice, there was nothing in *The German Ideology* that had not already appeared or been anticipated in previous writings of Marx and Engels. For example, "Communism is for us not a *state of affairs* which it to be established, an *ideal* to which reality [will] have to adjust itself. We call communism the *real* movement which abolishes the present state of things." Or, the oft-quoted passage on revolution:

> Both for the production on a mass scale of . . . communist consciousness, and for the success of the cause itself, the alteration of men on a mass scale is necessary, an alteration which can only take place in a practical movement, a *revolution*; the revolution is necessary, therefore, not only because the *ruling* class cannot be overthrown in any other way, but also because the class *overthrowing* it can only in revolution succeed in ridding itself of all the muck of ages and become fitted to found society anew.[71]

What's expressed here is basically an elaboration of the third of the *Theses on Feuerbach*. Through revolutionary practice not only is the "educator" educated but the masses as well, thus, obviating the need for "a handful of chosen men" who know what's best for the masses in a postrevolutionary society. Also, what occurs in the latter is very much dependent on what takes place in the revolution itself. Herein, therefore, was Marx and Engels's answer to the historic query about the capacity of the masses for self-rule. Through their participation in the revolution itself the masses cleanse themselves "of all the muck" to make self-rule possible. The more thoroughgoing that process the greater their capacity.

Though made before he had fully grasped the proletariat's revolutionary potential, its ability to both think and act, Marx's above-cited point to Ruge about the desirability of adequate preparatory time for a revolution should be read alongside this conclusion because it would forever inform both him and Engels. "The longer the time that events allow to thinking humanity for taking stock of its position, and to suffering mankind for mobilising its forces, the more perfect on entering the world will be the product that the present time bears in its womb." Again, implicit here is the recognition that circumstances might not allow the revolutionary process adequate preparation.

This somewhat cursory treatment of *The German Ideology* does not suggest that it had nothing really new to offer in the sphere of revolutionary practice. To the contrary, the new class theory of the state was of supreme importance. If, indeed, as the new view argued, it is through the state that exploiting classes have historically exercised their rule, then it was incumbent upon the proletariat to overthrow the bourgeoisie and take state power. The end of class oppression would not be ended, as Feuerbach or the True Socialists claimed, through "love" or "human understanding" but rather through "revolutionary passion." Only with the proletariat in power would it be possible to institute "true democracy" and end the oppression of all, which would be signalled by the destruction of the state itself.

However confident Marx and Engels were about their new world view they knew that theory in and of itself was insufficient, but it "becomes a material force as soon as it has gripped the masses." This is exactly what the Marx-Engels team now set out to accomplish.

CHAPTER TWO

From Theory to Practice: Toward a Communist Party

[N]othing democratic must be allowed to take place in Brussels without our participating.

—Engels to Marx

You can regard Mr Marx as the head of our party (i.e. of the most advanced section of German democracy . . .

—Engels to L. Blanc

As long as democracy has not been achieved, thus long do Communists and democrats fight side by side . . .

—Engels

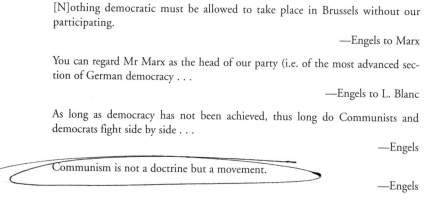

Communism is not a doctrine but a movement.

—Engels

In 1885, almost forty years after having written *The German Ideology,* Engels recalled how he and Marx intended to make use of their new theoretical weapon.

[W]e were by no means of the opinion that the new scientific results should be confided in large tomes exclusively to the "learned" world. Quite the contrary. We were both of us already deeply involved in the political movement and possessed a certain following in the educated world, especially of Western Germany, and abundant contact with the organized proletariat. It was our duty to provide a scientific substantiation for our view, but it was equally important for us to win over the European, and in the first place the German, proletariat to our conviction. As soon as we had become clear in our own minds, we set to work.[1]

The historical record bears out Engels's recollections. Even before the "scientific results" were on paper in the middle of 1846 the Marx-Engels team was active in establishing an organizational network to disseminate their new communist world view. Within a couple of years this effort would lead to the formation of what can justly be called the first Marxist communist party. Within three years the team would test its program in the heat of battle. This chapter begins by looking at the first organizations that Marx and Engels actually led, the Correspondence Committees, and then, the Communist League, the organization for which they wrote the *Communist Manifesto*.

PREPARING FOR REVOLUTION

The Marx-Engels team that "set to work" in 1846 was motivated not only by conviction but also a sense of urgency. While both had seen the need for revolution in Germany—Marx as early as 1843—there were increasing signs by 1846 that revolution was imminent. They were convinced that only with the creation of a new revolutionary party armed with a "scientific" perspective could a successful outcome to such an upheaval be assured. Marx recognized—again as early as 1843—the advantages of adequate preparatory time for a revolution. Beginning in 1846 he and Engels began to act on this conviction.

Communist Correspondence Committees

By February 1846 the Marx-Engels team, along with a Belgian communist, Philippe Gigot, had begun establishing "a new system of propaganda"—the Communist Correspondence Committees (hereafter, CCC).[2] Taking their name from the Jacobinic Corresponding Societies, the Committees, with their center in Brussels, sought to institute the exchange of letters among various socialists and communists on the continent and in England. The letters were to be "devoted to discussing scientific questions, and to keeping an eye on popular writings, and the socialist propaganda that can be carried on in Germany by this means." There was, however, a more basic political motive underlying this effort—the same one that initially led Engels to begin writing in the English radical press.

> The chief aim . . . will be to put the German socialists in touch with the French and English socialists; to keep foreigners constantly informed of the socialist movements that occur in Germany and to inform the Germans in Germany of the progress of socialism in France and England. In this way . . . ideas and impartial criticism can take place. It will be a step made by the social movement in its *literary* manifestation to rid itself of the barriers of *nationality*. And when the moment for action comes, it will clearly be much to everyone's advantage to be acquainted with the state of affairs abroad as well as at home.[3]

The CCC were intended, therefore, to be a network through which self-styled socialists and communists in different countries would begin to talk with one another in a systematic way. The discussions would allow individuals and groups to put forward their particular views in order to subject them to comradely criticism. Consistent with the perspective of the Marx-Engels team, discussions were not an end in themselves, but rather the basis for coordinated activity "when the moment for action comes."

The decision to form the CCC reveals a distinguishing feature of the Marx-Engels team at the very outset—a recognition of the need to organize to make ideas influential. While Marx and Engels were certainly not the first radicals who, in the aftermath of the French Revolution, tried to propagate their ideas, they were amongst the few who put in the necessary time and organizational effort. Picture, in contrast to them, the utopian socialist Fourier, who after receiving his theoretical revelations, announced that he would return home every day at noon to wait for whoever was willing to be anointed by his wisdom. It's reported that he did this for ten years without anyone taking up his offer. He was, if anything, persistent.

The CCCs, through "impartial criticism," constituted the first stage of Marx and Engels's organized effort to "win over the European proletariat to our conviction." Not everyone, however, was willing to debate and defend their views vis-à-vis the new communist perspective of the Marx party in such a venue. One such socialist, the influential French radical writer Pierre-Joseph Proudhon (1809–1865), declined to participate partly on the grounds that "he himself had outgrown a belief in revolution."[4] If Marx could not engage Proudhon within the framework of the CCCs, then he would have to find another format in which to take him on. He did exactly that in the following year with the publication of his well-known anti-Proudhon polemic, *The Poverty of Philosophy*, about which more will be said later.

One of the first actions of the Brussels CCC was to defend and make overtures to the Chartists. The positive reply of one of its leaders, Julian Harney, to Engels's entreaty on behalf of Brussels as well as his frank views about some of Engels's observations about the Chartists testifies to the kind of comradely relations that Marx and Engels, through the CCC, were able to establish with the English movement. A few months later, the Brussels CCC, on behalf of the "German Democratic Communists," congratulated the Chartist leader, Feargus O'Connor, on his recent election to the House of Commons and solidarized with him against detractors. Also, it volunteered to "circulate" Chartist publications, such as *The Northern Star*, on the continent.

This initiative suggests that Marx and Engels viewed the CCCs, or at least the one in Brussels, as a nascent political party that took collective stances. It means also that five months after visiting with the Chartists in England, the Marx-Engels team began acting in earnest on the political perspective it had recently arrived at by attempting to establish "party to party" relations with the Chartists, the most class conscious proletarian movement in existence. In other words, they were acting as a communist team, in the sense they argued for, by relating to the "real" movements and struggles of the proletariat. It should be noted that they opted to formalize their relations with the Chartists on an organizational basis. Seen by the Chartist leadership at this time as perhaps no more than sympathetic revolutionary writers with some following on the continent, Marx and Engels could very easily have maintained the earlier ties they had established with the Chartists at the level of the Marx-Engels team itself or perhaps, individually. That they chose the more formal route is indicative of the seriousness that they took organizational matters even at this very early stage in their partnership.

As expected, "impartial criticism" quickly revealed important political differences within the CCCs. The first significant political conflict pitted the Marx party against the German radical writer Wilhelm Weitling (1808–1871). A tailor, Weitling was distinguished as being one of the few non-middle-class socialists who was an accomplished writer as well as activist. Marx and Engels, in fact, had only a few years earlier sung his praises as an example of the working class producing its own theoreticians. Whatever his past achievements, it was clear by the end of March 1846, when the clash occurred, that he had become a "has-been." Much of what was written about this confrontation need not concern us.[5] What is relevant are the party-building implications of the dispute for the Marx-Engels team.

When Julian Harney agreed to collaborate with the Brussels CCC, he did so with the proviso that the League of the Just, the mainly German political exile group in London which he had just joined, would also be invited to participate. The reason for his hesitation, as he explained in his reply to Engels, was that he had "heard that *you* (the literary characters in Brussels) *had formed a society, confined to yourselves into which you admitted no working men.*"[6] The source of this clearly false allegation was none other than Weitling who had begun to resent the young middle-class upstarts in Brussels who were impertinently seeking support for a communist perspective that was very much at odds with his own increasingly metaphysical nostrums. What the Marx-Engels team had been victim to, perhaps for the first time as a team, was class baiting. There were lessons to be learned from this episode because it would not be the last time that they had to deal with such an accusation.

Weitling's slanders could have been a serious setback to Marx and Engels had not it been for the fact that they came in the wake of his own political demise within the German exile political community. His new schema in which the lumpenproletariat constituted the vanguard of the revolution—which was always around the corner, and thus it was a waste of time to attempt to understand the conditions that gave rise to revolutions—held little sway amongst proletarian fighters; his credibility began to wane. In the well-known debate with him in Brussels in March 1846, Marx, in front of a number of CCC members, demolished his argument—word of which apparently got back to the London exiles. The Brussels CCC then proposed to the League of the Just that they establish a London branch. In June, Karl Schapper (1812–1870), the head of the League, replied favorably to the proposal and indicated agreement with the split with Weitling that soon came. In the end, this success, the links made between Brussels and the League, proved to be the most important gain for the CCC during its brief existence.

There was still unfinished business with Weitling. One of his protégés who also happened to be a True Socialist, Hermann Kriege, began publishing a journal in New York, where he was living, that claimed to speak for German communism. On May 11, 1846, the Brussels CCC adopted a resolution severely criticizing his views and issued a widely publicized circular to that effect. The essence of the critique was that Kriege, in his advice to American workers, substituted "love" for class struggle, and subsumed communism within the framework of religion. "Kriege is . . . preaching *in the name of communism* the old fantasy of religion and German philosophy which is the *direct antithesis of communism. Faith*, more specifically, faith in the 'holy spirit of community' is the last thing required for the achievement of communism."[7] The circular sarcastically noted that in spite of his "religion of love" for "humanity," Kriege declared: "Any man who does not support such a party can with justice be treated as an enemy of mankind." It then went on to make a most compelling observation about this apparent contradiction.

> It is however a perfectly consistent conclusion of this new religion, which like every other [religion] mortally detests and persecutes all its enemies. The enemy of the party is quite consistently turned into a heretic, by transforming him from an enemy of the actually existing *party* who is *combated*, into a sinner against *humanity*—which only exists in the imagination—who must be *punished*.[8]

If ever there were a more telling and prophetic statement from Marx and Engels about what happens when communism is converted into a religion then this it must surely be. While they could never have anticipated the twentieth-century phenomenon of Stalinism in all its complexities, they certainly could have understood one of its essential qualities—"communism" as state religion.

The resolution against Kriege had been voted on with seven in favor and one, Weitling, against. The vote, the resolution and its contents all suggest that, by this time if not before, the CCC was functioning as an ersatz party. That Weitling participated in the vote means that, contrary to the often-made claim of Marxologists, the Marx party did not purge him after his ignominious defeat in the debate with Marx six weeks earlier. One could, therefore, participate in the CCC with a different line from that of Marx and Engels. It's true Weitling eventually left the CCC, but there is no evidence that he was ousted.[9] In all probability his departure signalled his failure to convince the rest of the branch that he had a better program than the Marx-Engels team.

In addition to establishing a CCC branch in Britain, the Brussels center, with Marx and Engels at the helm, made efforts to do the same elsewhere, particularly in Germany. Of invaluable assistance in their party-building work was the Silesian revolutionist, Wilhelm Wolff, who, after having read their writings, moved to Brussels in 1846 to work with them. Remaining until his death in 1864 one of the most loyal members of the Marx party, Wolff was the person to whom Marx dedicated *Capital* when published in 1867.

As new CCC branches were established, their organizational norms, which had been evolving, had by the middle of 1846 become a clear set of standard operating procedures. This is most evident in the Brussels CCC letter of June 15 to Gustav Köttgen, a communist in the Elberfeld area with whom Engels had only recently collaborated. Köttgen had written to Engels requesting assistance in setting up a CCC as a means for getting varied socialists and communists in and around Elberfeld (present-day Wuppertal) to begin working together. Marx and Engels wrote the reply to Köttgen on behalf of the Brussels CCC.[10] In it they made a number of recommendations and proposals that would forever be part of their political and organizational arsenal.

Their first advice was that the best way to overcome the "isolation" that characterized German communists was for them to come together "for the purpose of reading and discussion" in "regular meetings to discuss questions concerning communism." This was the only way in which they could "clear things up among themselves." They agreed with Köttgen that "cheap, easily understandable books and pamphlets with a communist content must be widely circulated." Such publications could be made available through "regular money contributions" from the membership. However, they had to "reject" his "suggestion to support the authors by means of these contributions, to provide a comfortable life for them. . . ." They then recommended that "a minimum sum for the monthly contributions" be fixed, "so that the amount of money that can be used for common purposes can be accurately determined at any moment." As for relations between the branch and the center in Brussels, "you should communicate to us the names of the members . . . since we have to know, as you know of us, who it is we are dealing with. Finally, we await your statement of the size of the monthly contributions earmarked for common purposes, since the printing of several popular pamphlets ought to be proceeded with as soon as possible."

Firstly, the call for "regular meetings" once again reflects the seriousness with which Marx and Engels took political work. More importantly, regular meetings allowed for the kind of "discussion" through which communists could achieve self-clarification. Second, that there should be "monthly contributions" from members also testifies to their seriousness. It also reflected their general view that communist organizations should be self-financing, particularly when it came to the publication of communist literature.[11] This, no doubt, was one of the lessons for Marx and Engels from the difficulties they had in getting commercial publishers to print *The German Ideology* or the "library of socialist writers." Lastly, their objection to "authors" being subsidized by the CCC is also telling. Although they did not explain why, it is safe to assume that it had to do with their principled opposition to an elite strata of "educators" within a communist organization. One might suspect, also, that Marx and Engels were especially sensitive to any appearance of privileges for "literary characters"—the language Harney employed to describe them—given the recent class baiting they had been subjected to. In a world in which educational opportunities were quite limited—the vast majority of workers were not in a position to become "authors"—it was necessary to take steps to avoid any possible charge of class privilege.

Along with the organizational recommendations, Marx and Engels addressed political questions that Köttgen had raised. One concerned the tactic of petitioning the Prussian authorities for reforms. They were doubtful, given the weakness of the communist forces at that time in Germany. "A petition is only useful when at the same time it appears as a threat, behind which there stands a compact and organised mass. The only thing you could do . . . would be to produce a petition furnished with *numerous* and impressive workers' signatures." A related question concerned the desirability of holding a congress to bring together disparate communist forces in Germany. Again, Marx and Engels were skeptical, given the reality of communist forces in Germany at that time. "Only when communist associations have been formed in the whole of Germany and means for action have been collected will delegates from the individual associations be able to gather for a congress with any prospect of success. . . . Until then the sole means of cooperation is the clarification of questions by letter and regular correspondence." Congresses, therefore, should only occur when there are real political forces who have adequate experiences under their belt to be represented at them.

In the letter's postscript, Marx and Engels took up the petition question anew. Realizing perhaps that their above response may have been a bit too negative, they recommended that if the CCC could not obtain at least five hundred workers' signatures they should consider a cooperative petitioning effort for liberal reforms with the "bourgeoisie of the area." If they were not cooperative,

> join them for the time being in public demonstrations, proceed jesuitically, put aside teutonic probity, true-heartedness and decency, and sign and push forward the bourgeois petitions for freedom of the press, a constitution, and so on. When this has been achieved a new era will dawn for c[ommunist] propaganda. Our means will be increased, the antithesis between bourgeoisie and proletariat will be sharpened. In a party one must support everything which helps towards progress, and have no truck with any tedious moral scruples.

This is a most remarkable addendum. Encapsulated in a highly distilled form, it is Marx and Engels's first joint statement of their strategy and tactics for communists in the fight for democracy.[12] It recommended that if the working class did not have the strength to move on its own, then for tactical and long-term strategic reasons it was incumbent on communists to embrace those bourgeoisie who were willing to fight for democracy, "pushing" them, if necessary, to ensure victory. Communists had an inherent interest in expanding the political space through the institution of civil liberties. The achievement of political democracy would make it possible to put the social question on the agenda—the struggle between the bourgeoisie and the proletariat. Communists, therefore, should put aside political self-righteousness, hold their noses if need be, and coalesce with the bourgeoisie in this fight—even if the bourgeoisie itself was reluctant to do so. Thus, the postscript afterthought recognized that the initial advice to get only workers' signatures on the petitions was sectarian. What one detects here is a note of caution against nascent ultra leftism. This would be their line in the upcoming 1848 revolution as well as in settings where bourgeois democracy had yet to be realized.

There was a final piece of advice for the new CCC from the relatively new but clearly seasoned Marx-Engels team. "For drafting the letters you must elect the person you consider most capable. Personal considerations must be utterly disregarded, they ruin everything." Party interests, therefore, should take precedence over personal ones—advice which many a would-be revolutionary has failed to heed and much to their regret. One can only speculate about who or what incident Marx and Engels may have had in mind from their own experiences—the break with Ruge?—in making this recommendation.

In sum, then, Marx and Engels's letter to Köttgen on behalf of the Brussels CCC was their first truly political writing that combines both organizational and programmatic themes. Only two and a half pages, it also constitutes, as their subsequent political activities make clear, a major document in the Marx party's arsenal of political writings.

In addition to the Wuppertal area, the Brussels CCC attempted with varying success to establish branches in North Germany, Cologne, and Silesia. At the end of August 1846, Engels moved to Paris to do the same. His strategy was to urge the Paris branch of the League of the Just to set up a CCC, as their London comrades had just done. Engels, however, encountered two obstacles within the Paris League, only one of which he was able to overcome.

The first was the ideological influences of Karl Grün, a True Socialist, and Pierre-Joseph Proudhon, who had just a few months earlier declined Marx and Engels's invitation to participate in the CCC. Although his own perspective at that time might be labelled "socialist libertarianism," Proudhon had recently begun to collaborate with Grün. The latter as a True Socialist had been the target of special criticism in Marx and Engels's then still unpublished *The German Ideology*. The other reason Proudhon rejected Marx and Engels's invitation was due to their stated opposition to the views of his new collaborator Grün.

Engels decided to attend League meetings and related events where the German exile proletariat congregated and begin through discussions and lectures to take on, first, True Socialism and, then, Proudhon's ideas. In spite of some initial gains, Engels knew it would not be easy. "But one must be patient, and I shall not let the fellows go until I have driven Grün from the field. . . ."[13] Toward the end of October, Engels was able to report to the Brussels CCC that he had made some headway with a group of about twenty cabinet makers by besting Grün's followers in a series of debates.

Recognizing that Grün's self-styled communism had little in common with his and Marx's views, Engels's tactic was to focus the debate on the definition of communism; he knew it would lead to the differentiation with True Socialism that he wanted. He proposed a definition of communism for debate and then a vote to determine "whether or not we were meeting here as communists." The "aims of communism" were:

> 1. to ensure that the interests of the proletariat prevail, as opposed to those of the bourgeoisie; 2. to do so by abolishing private property and replacing same with community of goods; 3. to recognise no means of attaining these aims other than democratic revolution by force.[14]

Engels also knew that his definition would not sit well with the Proudhonists. But at this stage the fight was with Grün's sympathizers. After two evenings of discussion the vote was taken. Thirteen agreed and two opposed Engels's definition. This had been a major turnaround since at the outset of the meetings Engels reported that "I had nearly the whole clique against me. . . ."

Engels's victory was limited, however. Grün's countertactic was to attack Engels's brand of communism at larger public meetings where it was known that police informers were present. This had a chilling effect on real discussion since German exiles in Paris were fearful of being labelled "revolutionary" by the police and therefore liable to persecution of some kind. This had been Marx's fate about a year and a half earlier.

In the fight with Grün's ideas, Engels said that the "main thing was to prove the necessity for revolution by force and in general to reject as anti-proletarian, petty-bourgeois, and Straubingerian Grün's True Socialism, which had drawn new strength from the Proudhonian panacea." What Engels is referring to here is the second obstacle he had to overcome in winning the German exiles to his and Marx's views—which in the end he was not able to surmount. A *straubinger* was "in general, a traveling journeyman; by extension, an artisanal worker still filled with the narrow guild outlook and its petty-bourgeois prejudices."[15] Artisans, in fact, constituted the overwhelming majority of the Prussian working class at that time, outnumbering the industrial proletariat about five to one.[16] The mainly artisanal makeup of the League of the Just also placed an objective limitation on the appeal of Marx-Engels's perspective. A "straubingerian" outlook was anticapitalist but from the vantage of the past—a tendency to orient toward a mythic past when, prior to the dissolving impact of capitalism on the social threads of society, humans lived in "harmony" and "love" in an idyllic "community." This was exactly what True Socialism appealed to.

Proudhon's "panacea" was also appealing. It would consist of associations in which artisans would market their own labor in order that they reap the profits. These were not unlike the so-called "labor-bazaars" of the Owenite utopian socialists which, by this time, as Engels sardonically noted, were bankrupt. A few years later Proudhon would come up with another panacea, mutual credit associations, which the Marx-Engels team would again have to critique. Owing to Proudhon's influence, Engels, who had once expressed some admiration for the French radical, began in 1846 reading him closely, particularly his then just published book, *The Philosophy of Poverty*. To counter his influence amongst French and German workers Engels realized that he and Marx would have to write a major polemic. He urged Marx to begin doing so. His partner didn't need much prodding, especially when Proudhon, shortly before his book's appearance, wrote to Marx: "'*J'attends votre férule critique*' [I await your severe criticism]. This criticism . . . soon dropped on him . . . in a way which ended our friendship for ever."[17]

By the beginning of 1847, Marx began writing what would be *The Poverty of Philosophy*—a deliberate twist of Proudhon's title—the Marx-Engels team's opening shot in what would be a life long struggle with Proudhon's influence. The importance that they gave to this project is shown by their decision to give up the effort to have *The German Ideology* published and instead concentrate their attention on the anti-Proudhon polemic.[18] In it Marx was able to explicate more concisely the historical materialist perspective of *The German Ideology* and sketch their view of political economy. He wrote it in French in order to reach the same audience that had likely read Proudhon's book. Also, in spite of his own dire economic straits, Marx financed the publication of the book out of his own pocket.

For purposes here, the most significant part of Marx's polemic is the last section, "Strikes and Combinations of Workers." There, in contrast to Proudhon, he applauded the rise of trade unions and pointed to their trajectory—the constitution of workers "as a class for itself" in order to wage "a veritable civil war" with capital. "But the struggle of class against class is a political struggle." His polemic, in fact, qualified him to become "the first leading figure in the history of socialism to adopt a position of support to trade unions and trade unionism, on principle."[19]

Finally, the struggle of workers with capital had a broader historical significance.

> An oppressed class is the vital condition for every society founded on the antag-
> onism of classes. The emancipation of the oppressed class thus implies necessarily
> the creation of a new society. For the oppressed class to be able to emancipate itself
> it is necessary that the productive powers already acquired and the existing social
> relations should no longer be capable of existing side by side. Of all the instruments
> of production, the greatest productive power is the revolutionary class itself. The
> organisation of revolutionary elements as a class supposes the existence of all the pro-
> ductive forces which could be engendered in the bosom of the old society.[20]

A very concise exposition of the perspective elaborated on in *The German Ideology*, the "materialist conception of history," Marx left no doubt that at this stage in history the proletariat was "the revolutionary class." Its struggle with capital, a political struggle, "is a struggle which carried to its highest expression is a total revolution"[21]—what Proudhon, he argued, either denied or disdained. Much of this perspective would be distilled a year later into the *Communist Manifesto*.

In the meantime it became clear to Engels that Paris was not the fertile terrain that they had hoped. The straubinger character of the League was the main problem. Though the League's London branch had a similar composition there was a major difference. "[T]hose members of the League who went westward [to England] . . . came under the influence of Chartism, at the time the most advanced workers' movement in the world. . . . The longer they lived in England the more they shook themselves free from their primitive egalitarian communism."[22] The Londoners still carried with them influences from the past, but in far less quantity than their comrades in Paris.

To summarize, then, the Marx-Engels team, following the formulation of their new perspective, began the quest for Europe's proletariat. To do so, they had to, first, both differentiate themselves from and critique other tendencies that spoke in the name of communism and/or sought the allegiance of the proletariat. The CCCs were the vehicle that Marx and Engels employed for this dual task. Just as Engels had done at the artisans' meetings in Paris, the strategy essentially involved putting up their ideas against competing ones and then letting the workers decide. After having bested to one degree or another their competitors, they had to then turn to the proletariat itself—the task of building a communist, in the Marxist sense of the term, workers' party.

THE COMMUNIST LEAGUE

While the League in London was willing to become part of the larger CCC network, they harbored, as their letter of acceptance in June 1846 suggested, reservations about working with the Marx-Engels team. Schapper, writing on behalf of his comrades, added that they thought Marx's "Circular on Kriege" was a bit too harsh on their former comrade. Like Weitling, Kriege too had spent some time in London as a member of the League. Their soft spot for Kriege reflected, in part, their suspicions about the "philosophical arrogance" of the two Rhinelanders, suspicions that could be traced in part to Weitling's earlier class baiting. They also reflected the lingering support for True Socialism within the League. Schapper's letter of July 17 to Marx is unequivocal on both counts. Not only does he defend the "spirit of brotherly love" à la True Socialism but then he says, "you proletarians of Brussels still have the professors' arrogance in a high degree."[23] The Marx-Engels team still had its work cut out for it.

One of the issues that Marx had apparently raised in his initial letter to the League concerned its conspiratorial style of organizing. Such was the modus operandi of virtually every revolutionary party after the end of the Napoleonic Wars in 1815. Ruling elites in Europe, in order to prevent another mass democratic revolution, curtailed whatever political space that was available. Thus, "all revolutionaries regarded themselves, with some justification, as small elites of the emancipated and progressive operating among, and for the eventual benefit of, a vast and inert mass of the ignorant and misled common people, which would no doubt welcome liberation when it came, but could not be expected to take much part in preparing it. . . . All of them tended to adopt the same type of revolutionary organization, or even the same organization: the secret insurrectionary brotherhood."[24]

The conspiratorial tradition had its origins in Babeuf's Conspiracy of Equals in 1796, an ill-fated attempt to resurrect the radical orientation of the French Revolution. It was left to one of his followers, Buonarroti, to codify his views in a book some three decades later that became a virtual manual for conspiratorial organizing. By the 1830s, in the aftermath of the Revolution of 1830 that brought Louis Philippe to power, the individual whose name became virtually synonymous with conspiracies, or revolutions led by a "handful of chosen men," was Auguste Blanqui (1805–1881). In 1839, Blanqui's Society of Seasons carried out an unsuccessful putsch in Paris against Louis Philippe's regime. Given the internationalism of political organizing at the time, a number of German political exiles had been involved or accused by the government to have been.[25]

Amongst the German exiles in Blanqui's failed putsch were members of the recently formed (1836) League of the Just, a split-off from the more middle-class and intellectual League of Exiles or, Outcasts. The splitters, mainly artisans, had grown suspicious of the intellectuals and the highly centralized top-down organizational structure of the old League—typical of Babouvist organizations. The two grievances the splitters had about the League of the Exiles, the intellectual composition of its leadership and its centralized character, was not coincidental. These two tendencies usually went hand in hand, as Marx and Engels had pointed out in their earlier polemics against the True Socialists (and Proudhon as well). Intellectuals were more likely to see themselves as "a handful of chosen men" and as such felt that they had the license to make decisions for the unwashed. Both issues would influence the relations between the Marx-Engels team and the League of the Just.

Schapper, one of the League's founders, went to London after a brief incarceration for his involvement in the 1839 events, where he established a branch. The Paris branches went underground and functioned that way for some time. Underground functioning explains in part why Engels could report as late as October 1846 that under the League's rules, in Paris at least, the penalty for divulging internal business to outsiders was "death by dagger, rope or poison"—clearly a legacy of the older League of the Exiles. It also explains, as Marx and Engels began to realize, why the Paris branches of the League were not as politically healthy as those in London.

The actual practice and track record of conspiratorial parties—a long trail of nonsuccesses—explained in part Engels's aforementioned critique of "secret associations."[26] Opposition to principled conspiratorial functioning became a hallmark of the Marx-Engels partnership. Their debate with Weitling a few months earlier was related in part to this matter since he too had been influenced by Babeuf's model of political organizing.[27] This also explains why he and Marx were concerned about the modus operandi of the League in London. Schapper addressed their concerns. "As far as conspiratorial ideas are concerned, we have long since gotten over such silliness . . . and we have seen with joy that you hold the same view. Naturally, we are convinced that one will not and cannot dispense with a thorough revolution, but to want to bring it about by conspiracies and stupid proclamations à la Weitling is ridiculous."[28]

The organizational statutes of the League also revealed a significant difference between it and its predecessor. Under rules adopted in 1838, the central committee, for example, was now elected annually, "not by the entire membership, to be sure, but by the leaders of the district in which its seat was located . . . leaders who themselves would have been elected by the membership of each local unit. . . ." The central committee's "basic function was confined to the execution of 'laws' that now had to be passed by a majority of the full membership. . . . Members now owed more limited obedience . . . and their expulsion could be pronounced only by the local units."[29] While a number of the old conspiratorial practices of the League of Exiles were retained, relatively speaking, the League of the Just was more open and democratic.

Schapper, offering further evidence that the old small-knit clandestine way of functioning was a thing of the past, described the League's activities, the most relevant being its participation in the German Workers' Education Association. Founded in 1840 by the League, the GWEA, with its membership of 250, served as its legal and, thus, public face. "The statutes of the London [GWEA], printed as a special pamphlet, became the pattern for all organizations of the same kind founded by members of the League everywhere German workers lived and legal organizations of this, or a similar kind were possible."[30] Not only did the GWEA provide self-help for its members and meet their social needs but most importantly, as Schapper knew that Marx and Engels would appreciate, it was the major means by which revolutionary ideas were disseminated to the German exiles community. The League did not, as Schapper had correctly assured Marx, operate as a secret body within the GWEA. While it no doubt placed greater demands on its members it seems that GWEA membership also entailed a certain degree of disciplined functioning, at least in the realm of education. The account points out elsewhere that both the League and the GWEA counted amongst its ranks not only Germans but English, such as Harney and other Chartists, and other nationalities. In conclusion, then, the League in conjunction with the GWEA offered the Marx-Engels team an ideal venue in which "to win over the European, and in the first place the German, proletariat to our conviction."

Fusion with the League of the Just

After accepting the Brussels CCC offer to establish a London branch and assuring it that its conspiratorial days were over, Schapper, on behalf of the League, then made a demand of his own to Marx. "'And finally we ask you to tell us more about your plans. It is true that you have told us what you want, but you haven't said how you think you will go about achieving it.'" Marx responded on behalf of Brussels on June 22, with his "plans." He proposed that the League's new CCC branch carry out a fight against "philosophical and sentimental communism" and, to this end, convene a congress in England that would bring together various communist groups and individuals to discuss these and other issues.[31] While Schapper indicated in his above-mentioned reply of July 17 that he was not necessarily in accord with Marx's assessment of True Socialism, he did agree with the need for a congress and proposed London as the site. Shortly afterward the Brussels CCC heard from Harney who accepted its invitation to join the CCC network now that the League had just agreed to do the same.

For reasons that are not clear, Brussels did not communicate with the new London CCC until October, when they sent them an update on the state of the movement in Germany. What is clear is that Marx and Engels became increasingly dubious about the revolutionary potential of the League in Paris, and thus, also possibly, the London branch, owing to the straubinger factor. While they viewed the London League more favorably, given its ties to the more industrially proletarian Chartists, they nonetheless had no illusions about what it represented—opposition to capitalism largely from an artisanal perspective. It would be useful to address this issue since it is sometimes alleged that the reason why Marx and Engels supposedly got it all wrong, that is, the revolutionary potential of the working class, is that they confused very early in their political partnership artisanal radicalization for that of the modern industrial proletariat.[32]

It should be remembered, firstly, that when Marx came to the realization at the end of 1843 that Germany's proletariat and not its liberal bourgeoisie would lead the overthrow of Prussian autocracy and institute democratic rule, he fully recognized that the "proletariat is coming into being in Germany only as a result of the rising *industrial* development." That is, a modern German industrial proletariat was still in the process of formation. This was still his position as well as his partner's two years later. Engels addressed this in an article written with Marx's input at the beginning of 1847.

> [The] division [of the German "working classes"] into farm labourers, day labourers, handicraft journeymen, factory workers and lumpen proletariat, together with their dispersal over a great, thinly populated expanse of country with few and central weak

points, already renders it impossible for them to realise that their interests are common, to reach understanding, to constitute themselves into *one* class. This division . . . restricts the workers to seeing their interest in that of their employers. . . . The journeyman stands under the intellectual and political sway of his master. The factory worker lets himself be used by the factory owner in the agitation for protective tariffs. . . . So little is the mass of the workers in Germany prepared to assume the leadership in public matters.[33]

This passage, which Engels had intended to elaborate on in a later article but unfortunately never did, makes clear that Engels and Marx had no illusions about the political consciousness of the German proletariat on the eve of the 1848 Revolution. This assessment stands in sharp contrast to their opinion of the English proletariat whose Chartist movement, in their view, represented the highest expression of proletarian class consciousness then in existence. This may also explain why Engels, until the fall of 1845, doubted the self-liberatory potential of German workers in comparison to those in England.

If Marx and Engels regarded the leaders of the League as "revolutionary proletarians," as Engels recounted some forty years later, they still saw them as straubingers with the consciousness of a "journeyman" and, thus, susceptible to sentimental communism à la Weitling or True Socialism. It was probably no accident that Marx and Engels's first choice in London for affiliation with the CCC were the Chartists and not the League. Only after Harney had made his membership conditional on the League's participation did the Brussels CCC reach out to it. It seems clear, then, that the priority for the Marx-Engels team was the establishment of ties with Europe's most advanced proletariat, the Chartists. To the extent that the League could facilitate this link, then, ties to it were necessary.

Engels drew attention to the limitations of the League only a few months after it had established a CCC branch. The issue concerned self-determination for the German-speaking province of Schleswig-Holstein, which was then under Danish control. London issued a position paper, an *Address*, which counterposed a variant of "proletarian internationalism" to bourgeois nationalism. It reflected the straubinger disdain for the growing bourgeoisie. This was aided by True Socialism's deprecation of the bourgeois democratic revolution as well as the theoretical shortcomings of the Chartists who were also by then influential in the League. In the absence of a historical materialist perspective, as Engels argued, the *Address* failed to understand that a modern proletariat had yet to develop in the province; peasants and artisans were the main inhabitants. Thus, in place of some yet nonexistent proletarian internationalism, the League should have, in Engels's opinion, come out in support of self-determination rather than leaving the field wide open to the bourgeoisie to so do. The position Engels argued for was one that became a key plank in the Marx-Engels program on the relation between national self-determination and the bourgeois democratic revolution.

By November 1846, Marx and Engels had become more pessimistic about the League. It was unfortunate, Engels wrote Marx, "because they, of all the Straubingers, were the only ones with whom one could attempt to make contact frankly and without *arrière-pensée*." Along with muddled political positions was "their perpetual envy of us as 'scholars.'"[34] Class baiting, in other words, was still a problem. The dilemma for the Marx party, as Engels saw it, was whether to end their relationship with the League and if so, how to do it with the least political cost. On the one hand, in spite of their shortcomings and "misgivings [about the "scholars"], they wish to learn from us." Also, the Leaguers did command a following amongst the artisanal class of the proletariat. On the other, "we have learnt from this business that, in the absence of a proper movement in Germany, nothing can be done with the Straubingers, even the best of them." Whatever the case, Engels concluded that a public confrontation with them would not be in order. "Vis-à-vis *ourselves*, these lads declare themselves to be 'the people,' 'the proletarians,' and we can only appeal to a communist proletariat which has yet to take shape in Germany." Without a doubt, then, Marx and Engels were quite sober about the reality of the working class in Germany at that time. The claim that they confused radical artisan politics with modern proletarian politics flies in the face of what they actually had to say on this score.

Unbeknownst, apparently, to Marx and Engels, relations between them and the League were beginning to take in November a decided turn for the better.[35] This was in spite of the just-made decision by London to issue a call to its branches, without consulting Brussels, for a congress to be held in May the next year. The *Address* in which the call was made also suggested that the "intellectuals" in Brussels, that is, Marx and Engels, were not to be trusted.[36] Again, the continuing problem of class baiting. However, this unilateral move for a congress reflected, oddly enough, a more propitious atmosphere within the League as a result of two developments. One was the decision of the League to move its central committee, the Central Authority, from Paris to London. In Paris the League had become moribund, owing, as the Authority explained a half year later, to factional strife due in part to the influence of Weitling and the "literary knight of industry and exploiter of workers," Karl Grün. Related to this move, as Engels explained forty years later, was the integration into the London leadership of "two men who were considerably superior in their capacity for theoretical perception to [Schapper et al.] . . . the miniature painter Karl Pfänder . . . and the tailor Georg Eccarius," both Germans.[37]

The second had to do with the situation in Germany. Drawing on the internal documents of the League, Oscar Hammen, certainly no sympathizer of the Marx-Engels team, was forced to admit the truth.

> This invigorated Central Authority, sensing that Germany was on the eve of a momentous revolution, recognized the need of an appropriate philosophy and program of action. Almost immediately it sent out an *Address* to all the League branches, calling for a clarification of views and policies. A "simple communist confession of faith to serve as a guide for all" was needed, as well as a policy in relationship to other radical movements. The various branches were instructed to discuss these matters and to prepare their recommendations. The *Address* then announced that a congress . . . would meet in London on May 1, 1847 . . . to formulate a final statement of principles and a program of action.

In their search for a philosophy and program of action, the London group eliminated one possibility after another. They were disillusioned with Weitling, their earlier hero. Cabet [the utopian communist] was found unacceptable when he appeared in London in January, 1847. Then they turned to Marx, perhaps because the Marxian stress on economics and class warfare meant more to them, exposed as they were to the Chartist movement in the advanced industrial society in England.[38]

Hammen's account is completely consistent with Engels's, again written some forty years later, about the "quiet revolution that was taking place in the League, and especially among the leaders in London. . . . The inadequacy of the conception of communism held hitherto, both the simplistic French egalitarian communism [of Cabet] and that of Weitling, became more and more clear to them. . . . In contrast to the untenability of the previous theoretical views, and in contrast to the practical aberrations resulting therefrom, it was realised more and more in London that Marx and I were right in our new theory."

The League's *Address* made clear that its search for a new theory was for the purpose of action. On January 20, 1847, the Central Authority in London authorized Joseph Moll, a watchmaker and one of its leaders, to travel to Brussels and Paris to meet respectively with Marx and Engels to convince them to join the League. As he explained to them, the League's leadership had now come to accept their views and was willing to abandon its conspiratorial style of functioning. To remove any doubts, London issued another *Address* in February that "spoke of the advent of a 'terrible revolution' and the need for strong men to seize the sword. But it warned against premature riots and conspiracies. . . . [It] called on [its branches] to combat any 'insipid love giddiness' and to clarify the difference between communism and socialism as methods for achieving a socialist society."[39] Thus, the Weitling and True Socialist influences were now declared to have been expunged from the League.

Moll made an offer that the Marx-Engels team could not refuse. About a decade later Marx explained their acceptance. They had, he said, been polemicizing for some time against utopian and sentimental socialist views. "We argued in popular form that it was not a matter of putting some utopian system into effect, but of conscious participation in the historical process revolutionising society before our very eyes." As for the doubts that he and Engels had about how far the League had evolved, Moll "argued . . . that if backward and refractory elements were to be overcome, our participation in person was indispensable, but that this could only be arranged if we became members of the 'League.' Accordingly, we joined it."[40] They began working immediately as League members. Marx transformed the Brussels CCC into a League branch or commune while Engels became active in the Paris communes. Brussels also established a commune in Liège "among Walloon factory workers." This, no doubt, was Marx's effort to transform the League from a mainly artisanal body into one based on the modern industrial proletariat. Marx also took steps to convince other CCC branches, such as the one in Cologne, to affiliate with the League.[41]

Moll's offer could not be refused because it represented the fruit of the victory that the Marx-Engels team had won in its line of march since Fall 1845, when it decided that its number one task was to "win over the European . . . proletariat to our conviction." Because the team had waged a successful war of "ruthless criticism" against other would-be communists who also sought the hearts and minds of the proletariat it was thus incumbent on it to now provide the leadership for which it had vigorously fought. It was as if Moll, on behalf of the Londoners—who constituted the real German proletarian movement at that time with all of its straubingerian tendencies—was saying to the Brussels "intellectuals," now that you've convincingly shown us the error of our ways show us the way forward (this was also the tone of Schapper's above-cited June letter). But, to do so, you will not be effective if you appear to be "schoolmasters" giving advice from "comfortable armchairs of abstractions"—in other words, doing what Marx had once castigated other would-be revolutionaries for doing. Moll was demanding that the Marx team embrace and be part of the real movement as it existed, to become members of the League. Marx and Engels had already shown by the time of Moll's visits that they were willing and able to thoroughly immerse themselves into that movement for the rest of their lives.

There is another and most crucial aspect to Moll's offer. It came on behalf of a working-class organization that consciously, after initial reservations and hesitations, chose the leadership of the Marx-Engels team. This must be fully grasped because not only in its own lifetime but even until today the Marx party has been accused of establishing or seeking to establish a new elite to lord over the working class. What Moll's overtures make clear is that the initial and effective link between the Marx party and the proletariat was made at the initiative of the latter.

The Central Authority of the League explained a few months later to its ranks what it had done. Recognizing the organizational and political "crisis" within the League, the Authority "took the necessary measures: sent out emissaries, removed individual members who were jeopardising the existence of the whole, re-established contacts, called the general congress. . . . At the same time it took steps to draw into the League other elements of the communist movement who until then had stood aside from it, steps which here highly successful."[42] The "other elements" were of course the Marx-Engels team. What is revealed here is not only a decision arrived at very consciously but also very confidently. These were not workers who came grovelling to Marx and Engels. The invitation came from the most international proletarian party in existence to serve what it decided was in its best interests. It recognized that it had a convergence of interests with the Marx-Engels team. However much the latter had striven to make links with the proletarian movement, in the final analysis such ties depended on the wishes of the working class itself.

Later in 1847, after the Marx party had consolidated its leadership in what became the Communist League, Engels addressed the charge of an erstwhile Young Hegelian that "communist writers are only using the communist workers . . . [they act as] prophets, priests or teachers who possess a secret wisdom of their own but deny it to the uneducated in order to keep them on leading-strings." Precisely because of the way in which the Marx-Engels team came to be part of the workers' movement, earlier that year, Engels could confidently dismiss this charge. Regarding such "insinuations, we do not take issue with them. We leave it to the communist workers to pass judgement on them themselves."[43] That is, only the working class had the right to decide if it was being used by the Marx party. This was good advice not only in 1847 but ever since whenever this charge is raised.

Preparations for the First Communist Party

The congress that the League had called for in May actually took place a month later, from June 2 to 9, in London. Owing, apparently, to financial difficulties, Marx was unable to attend.[44] However, Wilhelm Wolff, who had been briefed by Marx, represented the Brussels commune. Engels, after some parliamentary maneuvering with the typesetter Stephen Born, was elected to represent the three Paris communes—a decision that was later sanctioned by the congress.

The congress transformed the League profoundly. Engels, in collaboration with Wolff, played a major role in that process. It changed the League's name to the Communist League. As the "Circular of the First Congress of the Communist League to the League Members" explained, the old name reflected a particular historical situation that "does not in the least express what we want. How many there are who want justice, that is, what they call justice, without necessarily being Communists! We are not distinguished by wanting justice in general—anyone can claim that for himself—but by our attack on the existing social order and on private property, by wanting community of property. . . ."[45] Consistent with this new-found class perspective, the League's old motto, "All Men are Brothers," was changed to "Working Men of All Countries, Unite!" Obscure German organizational terms were abandoned because they belied the "anti-nationalist" character of the League "which is open to all peoples." In addition, "simple, clear names serves also to remove from our propagandist League the conspiratorial character which our enemies are so keen to attach to us."

The abandonment of the conspiratorial past was most reflected in the "Rules" for the new League that were drafted by the congress. Some years later Marx noted, "When Engels and I first joined the secret communist society, we did so only on condition that anything conducive to a superstitious belief in authority be eliminated from the Rules."[46] Indeed, the draft rules were a radical departure from the old norms. The most important of these was the provision for a delegated congress— one delegate from each "circle"—to be held once a year; circles were composed of communities, the League's most basic units. The congress was the League's "legislative authority" while the Central Authority was its "executive organ" and "responsible to the Congress." The Authority was to be composed of five members elected by the circle in the city where it was located. To cleanse the League of all remaining conspiratorial influences, the congress "resolved unanimously to remove the Paris Weitlingians from the League."

In compliance with the call for the congress, a draft statement of principles, or "credo," was adopted. Written by Engels, the "Confession of Faith" incorporated a number of the fundamental ideas of *The German Ideology*. It consisted of twenty-two questions and answers, a catechistic style that was popular in the German workers movement, that explained what communism is, the development and role of the proletariat, how communism would be realized—"enlightening and unifying the proletariat"—the issue of the family and the national question. The two questions that addressed the transition to communism testify to the Marxian influence. As to whether communism could be instituted "at one stroke," the answer was, "we have no such intention. The development of the masses cannot be ordered by decree. It is determined by the development of the conditions in which these masses live, and therefore proceeds gradually." Then how would this be done? "The first, fundamental condition for the introduction of the community of property [the basis of a communist society] is the political liberation of the proletariat through a democratic constitution." Thus, the political revolution, the democratic revolution, was the prerequisite for the socialist revolution—probably the most fundamental idea in the political strategy of the Marx party.

The congress resolved that the credo along with the draft rules would be sent to every circle for discussion "so that the proposals could be formulated for amendments and additions" and that another congress—apparently Engels's suggestion—would reconvene in six months for final adoption. As for both proposals, "we have tried on the one hand to refrain from all [utopian] system-making and all [conspiratorial] barrack-room communism, and on the other to avoid the fatuous and vapid sentimentality of the tearful, emotional Communists; we have, on the contrary, tried always to keep firm ground under our feet by the constant consideration of the social relations which alone have given rise to communism. . . . [W]e call on you again, to discuss the subject with particular zest." The congress also resolved to begin publishing a bimonthly paper to be financed through subscriptions and sales by the communities and circles. Finally, the "Circular" urged the ranks to "strenuously" implement the congress's decisions because the "revolution is drawing near in all its might . . . everywhere, in France as in Germany, in England as in America, the angry masses of the proletariat are in motion. . . ." Within a year, this prediction would prove to be true in at least two of the four countries mentioned.

Three months after the congress the Central Authority issued another circular to Communist League members. Unlike the first, which was written by Schapper and Wolff, the September circular was the work of Schapper, Moll, and the shoemaker, Heinrich Bauer, all of whom had been the leaders of the former League of the Just. Thus, this later and much neglected document measures in no uncertain terms the gains the Marx party had made within the League by dint of argument and not, as the erstwhile Young Hegelian referred to above would soon claim, some legerdemain or possession of "secret wisdom."

The document spoke the "plain truth" about the work that had been done since the June conference. While "emissaries," as mandated by the congress, had been dispatched as far as Lapland in Sweden and Wisconsin in the United States to set up new communities, very few of the previously existent branches had actually complied with the earlier circular's request for amendments and recommendations regarding the draft rules and the credo. Another directive that required local units to make financial contributions to the center in London had also been ignored. "So far we have only received a definite reply from the Brussels circle. . . ."[47] Brussels was also applauded for being the only circle to pledge and actually send into London regular financial contributions. Of course, Brussels was the headquarters of the Marx party, with Engels joining Marx there after the congress for about three months before returning to Paris. Their work testifies once again to the seriousness of their political commitment which put them in even better stead with Schapper and the others in London. It may have even chagrined the latter a bit that the "scholars" in Brussels were not just "thinkers" but activists who could outdo many of the old-timers of the League of the Just.

What is especially instructive in the document is the extent to which the old League of the Just leadership defended the decisions of the congress. The Hamburg circle, which evidently had not been represented at the congress, wrote to London upon receipt of the June circular that it objected to the name change of the organization, the expulsion of the Weitlingians, and the harsh characterization of Grün. Schapper and the others replied that unless the "Hamburg Brothers" had a counterproposal that they were prepared to defend, then the congress's decision would stand. The new "name says clearly what we are and what we want, which the previous one did not. . . . [W]e have no right to take mere emotions into consideration." As for the supporters of Weitling and Grün, "it is time we came to our senses and therefore we can no longer waste time on dreamers and system-mongers who have no energy for action—we will drag no corpse along behind us. . . . We are no elegant bourgeois and therefore do not beat about the bush but say what we think, i.e., call things by their names."

It then advised its members not be demoralized by the split. "For over ten years moderation, forbearance and unity have been preached in the League and with all this preaching, with all this brotherly love we have accomplished nothing. . . . Our opinion is that 100 active members are better than 1,000 of whom half are indecisive and luke warm. Instead of looking back and helping the lame to catch up, we march boldly forward, which will probably get others to their feet somewhat more nimbly as well."

And finally, to make clear what they meant by having "energy for action," the three authors asked the "Brothers in Hamburg" why they hadn't yet made a financial contribution to the League's propaganda efforts and begun in earnest to sell the one and only issue of its newspaper, *Kommunistische Zeitschrift* (Communist Journal). "Once more, Brothers," what is needed is will, and if that is lacking then at least "courage! courage! and once again courage! If people are unable or unwilling to go as far as we do—all well and good; if their intentions are honest, we shall not cease to respect them, but when we are called upon to step backwards in order to join up with such people, then we reply: Never!"

This rebuke of the supporters of Weitling and Grün and admonishment of the Hamburgerians are revealing for a number of reasons. One concerns its language and tone. Detractors of the Marx party oftentimes fault it with almost single-handedly having introduced into the workers movement the language of "ruthless criticism." The rebuke makes clear that the Schapper leadership needed no assistance in the employment of blunt and direct language. As working-class fighters, they were conscious of and took pride in their ability to communicate in such a fashion—to "call things by their names." In addition to their tone, these excerpts underline the importance of practice for Schapper et al.; action was the criterion for deciding who was and was not serious about politics. It was exactly for this reason that the fusion with the Marx team took place.

The September circular provides far too many other important insights about the genesis of the communist movement than can be explored here. Suffice it to note the amendments and additions of the Brussels circle to the congress documents. First, although Engels wrote the credo, Brussels, where Engels was at the time, had "a good number of important alterations . . . which we shall put before the [next] Congress for discussion." What this suggests is that the Marx-Engels team reworked, collectively in Brussels, the credo. It might suggest that Engels in his drafting of the credo had to bend more to the views of the League of the Just leaders than he had intended. On the other hand, it may simply have been the case that Engels in his haste to draft the document—the evidence suggests that it was written hurriedly— was not able to be as precise in his formulations as he might have wanted. In this regard, it is interesting to note that the Leipzig community, where the Marx party was not known to have had sympathizers, "believes that it was necessary to phrase the Credo in terms more scientific and more suitable for all social classes."

Brussels also had two proposals concerning the draft rules. One of the requirements for membership was "not to belong to any political or national association." The Brussels circle argued that it was "unpolitic" to require this "since by so doing we deprive ourselves of all opportunities for influencing such organisations." The Marx-Engels team was urging a more outward and less cloistered orientation than had been characteristic of the conspiratorial style of the old League. At the November congress it was agreed—possibly a compromise—that membership in "any anti- communist political or national association" was incompatible with membership in the CL. The other amendment from Brussels concerned the congress. The draft pro- posed that all congress decisions would have to be submitted to the communities for approval. Brussels objected, saying that "if the present period were a more revolu- tionary one, the whole activity of the Congress would be hindered by this restric- tion." Drawing on the studies Marx and Engels had done of the French Revolution, they added: "We recall that in 1794 the aristocrats put the same demand before the Convention, in order to paralyse all action." Thus, the congress should be the high- est decision-making body and it should be a body for action and not be stymied from so doing. To do otherwise would render the CL impotent—it would deny it the capability of acting as a revolutionary organization. These suggestions from Brussels reveal how seriously from the beginning the Marx-Engels team took orga- nizational as well as theoretical questions—a trait that would resurface on many an occasion in their future political work.

One other section of the September circular is worth noting. It mentioned that pro-Grün forces were still causing problems within the CL by their espousal of Proudhon's panaceas. Schapper and the others recommended that they read Marx's recently published, *The Poverty of Philosophy*, so that they stop "chasing [the] false ideas" of Proudhon. If they persisted in their pursuit, and "if they wish to remain men of honour, they should leave the League and start working on their own. . . . [S]eparation is better than an internal split." As Marx and Engels had hoped, the book, which was the first printed presentation of their new communist world view, began to influence the very people to whom it was directed—the most conscious layers of the European proletariat. The other piece of advice that the Central Authority leaders offered to Paris is also significant. It may well have been the first expression within the communist movement of what eventually became a norm of functioning—principled politics, the notion that programmatic agreement should be the only basis for political unity. Without it there is no *raison d'être* for joint political work.

As the September circular noted, the Brussels circle was most active following the congress. This was in fact a measure of the activism of the Marx party. In early August the old League of the Just units in Brussels were replaced by a new CL commune and circle with Marx as the president of the former and a member of the Central Authority of the latter. The CL then established a GWEA, which was "led by League members . . . [to] serve as a preparatory school for the League." Wolff was one of its leaders. Within a few months it claimed one hundred members. At the end of September various middle-class forces took steps to form the Brussels Democratic Association, which as its name implies, promoted the cause of liberal democracy. It eventually affiliated with the Fraternity of Democrats that Marx and Engels played some part in helping to organize in London in 1845. With Marx out of the country, Engels, along with GWEA leaders, intervened in its creation. As Engels explained in a letter to Marx, "it was essential to attend because . . . nothing democratic must be allowed to take place in little Brussels without our participating." The outcome was that Marx became its vice-president in November. In spite of the numerous hats that he was wearing Marx relished his many commitments. "I believe that . . . public activity is infinitely refreshing for everyone." Engels did the same when he returned to Paris in October to be active in CL politics by forging ties with the democratic left there.

In Defense of the Communist Party

Near the end of October Engels, in response to an inquiry from Louis Blanc, the French socialist, gave a brief description of the CL: "You can regard Mr Marx as the head of our party (i.e., of the most advanced section of German democracy . . .) and his recent book against Mr Proudhon as our programme."[48] It was precisely this view of the relationship between communism and democracy that explains why the Marx party was active in the three Brussels organizations. Their memberships constituted the essential forces in the Marx party's strategy for the coming revolution in Germany, as well as in Belgium—workers, liberal democrats, and communists.[49] Their strategy for the liberal democratic sector was to build within it a proletarian wing, as Marx did in his travels to Belgian industrial centers such as Ghent to establish chapters of the Democratic Association in working-class neighborhoods. Shortly after the June congress, this overall strategy along with various accompanying tactics was attacked by Karl Heinzen, the erstwhile Young Hegelian referred to above, whom the Central Authority of the CL called the "bitterest enemy of the Communists."

In their polemics against Heinzen, Marx and Engels elaborated for the first time their strategy and tactics for making a revolution. This was necessary since Heinzen fancied himself as the noncommunist revolutionary alternative. Engels led the charge in what effectively became by the late fall of 1847 the newspaper of the Marx party, the *Deutsche-Brüsseler Zeitung*, owing to a shortage of funds the CL was never able to publish more than one issue of its paper. Engels took on Heinzen's call for "immediate insurrection." It was "ridiculous" to do so without "knowledge or consideration of circumstances."[50] Rather, a "party press" was needed to "debate . . . to explain . . . to defend the party's demands" and to "rebut . . . the claims . . . of the opposing party." Through such discussions the "people," that is, "the proletarians, small peasants and urban petty bourgeoisie," will learn who their real oppressors are—"the bureaucracy, the nobility and the bourgeoisie." They will also learn that "the conquest of political power" by the forces who constituted "the people" is the precondition for the end of their "social oppression." This was therefore, as Engels concisely presented, the expected alignment of class forces in the coming revolution.[51] Note that this coalition did not include the bourgeoisie or even the liberal bourgeoisie. Marx and Engels had already concluded that it was problematic at best that the liberal bourgeoisie could be counted on to wage a fight to institute democracy.

Also, note Engels's inclusion of the small peasantry as part of the alliance of the "people." Thus, contrary to the standard charge, which has been repeated ad nauseam, that he and Marx ignored the peasantry, they clearly, even before the *Manifesto*, saw them as part of the revolutionary coalition. What Engels did argue, in opposition to Heinzen's position, was that the peasants were not capable of "seizing a revolutionary initiative" at that stage in Europe's history. The proletariat constituted the "vanguard" of the democratic revolution and both the peasantry and urban petit bourgeoisie would "depend on its initiative completely." What did the "conquest of political power" by the alliance of the "people" have to do with communists? As Engels explained, elaborating on a point he had made in late 1845 and echoing the postscript in the letter to Köttgen a year earlier: "[I]n the present circumstances, the Communists for the time being take the field as democrats themselves in all practical party matters. . . . [T]he political rule of the proletariat is the first condition for all communist measures. As long as democracy has not been achieved, thus long do Communists and democrats fight side by side, thus long are the interests of the democrats the same as those of the Communists." Marx said as much in a later issue of the *DBZ*: "The first manifestation of a truly active communist party is contained within the bourgeois revolution, at the moment when the constitutional monarchy is eliminated."[52] Again, the bourgeois democratic revolution as the strategic line of march toward the socialist revolution was not a new idea for the Marx party. In the context, however, of the impending revolutionary upsurge in Europe it took on a significance unlike anytime before in their politics. It explains the three organizational hats that Marx donned in Brussels.

In his polemic with Heinzen, Engels offered a concise description of communism. "Communism is not a doctrine but a *movement*; it proceeds not from principles but from *facts*. The Communists do not base themselves on this or that philosophy as their point of departure but on the whole course of previous history. . . . Communism, insofar as it is a theory, is the theoretical expression of the position of the proletariat in this struggle and the theoretical summation of the conditions for the liberation of the proletariat." Again, there is nothing here that had not already been stated by Marx or Engels. What Engels did was to popularize the most basic premises of their world view and reach, through this polemic, much wider audiences.

Lastly, Engels addressed the issue of issues in revolutionary tactics—the relation between reforms and revolution. Heinzen's problem, Engels argued, was that he, unlike communists who also advocated social reforms, confused the latter for the revolutionary outcome itself. For communists, reforms are "possible as preparatory steps, temporary transitional stages towards the abolition of private property, but not in any other way." This is perhaps the first discussion in print by either Marx or Engels—which would be elaborated in the *Manifesto* and immediately afterward for the 1848 Revolution—of what later in the Marxist arsenal became known as transitional demands.[53] Their effective application, as Engels emphasized, depended on a careful distinction between means and ends.

Many of the ideas that Marx and Engels hurled against Heinzen were repeated in one way or another by the various authors who contributed to the one and only issue of the *Kommunistische Zeitschrift*—"the first working-class organ that frankly called itself 'communist'"[54]—which appeared in September 1847. The trial issue was edited by Schapper, Moll, and Bauer. The editors revealed the extent to which they had broken with their artisanal political perspective. Machinery, for example, could be a progressive force if under "common ownership." Political work, also, should be done "openly where the laws permit, for our activities need not fear the light of day." A conspiratorial modus operandi was permissible only "where the arbitrary will of tyrants imposes secrecy upon us." As for the revolutionary process, the CL unlike other communists rejects instant revolution and recognizes the need for a "transitional period" to a "fully communised society." The "approaching storm" will be the fight for democracy: "We know that, on the continent of Europe, the discord between the aristocrat and democrat cannot be resolved without a clash of arms. . . ."[55] Thus, the basic revolutionary program of the Marx party had now been embraced by the Central Authority of the CL.

The Program for the Party

Along with their literary activities, Marx and Engels prepared for the upcoming CL congress. When Engels returned to Paris at the end of October, he found an intense discussion in progress on the "Credo" that he had drafted for the June congress. Through his intervention to limit a recrudescence of true socialist influences he was mandated by the circle to write a new version, *Principles of Communism*, which he submitted to the Central Authority in London. The *Zeitschrift's* editors announced that it is "our duty to submit the draft to our friends abroad in order to profit by their views in the matter. As soon as we receive replies we shall make the necessary emendations and additions, and shall print it in our next issue." Though a "next issue" never appeared, the *Principles* became the immediate basis from which the *Manifesto* was derived. It incorporated Marx and Engels's most recent thinking as stated in the polemics with Heinzen on the political alignment of class forces in the course of the revolution. It also addressed the issue of "peaceful" revolution. While desirous of such a transformation and rejecting the voluntarist perspective of con-spiracists, it said, however, that "should the oppressed proletariat . . . be goaded into a revolution, we Communists will defend the cause of the proletarians by deed just as well as we do now by word."[56] Another important addition concerned the inter-national character of the revolution. To the question, "will it be possible for this rev-olution to take place in one country alone?," the answer was an emphatic, "no. . . . The communist revolution will . . . be no merely national one. . . . It is a worldwide revolution. . . ." The revolutionary events of the following year would indeed give credence to this prediction.

Indicative of the political weight that the Marx-Engels team had in the CL on the eve of the congress is the letter of October 18 from the Central Authority to the Brussels circle. " 'London and Brussels are the pillars of the league at the present moment. . . . It is *absolutely necessary* that Brussels send delegates to the next con-gress, and in concert with London surgically cut away the 'rotten flesh' [i.e., the rem-nants of Weitling and Grün supporters] . . . we would be very happy if *Marx could come to the congress.*'"[57]

The second CL congress took place in London from November 30 to Decem-ber 8. Both Marx and Engels attended and played an active and decisive role in its deliberations; they also participated in and gave talks at CL-related public events. Unlike the June meeting, this congress had better and broader participation "at which members from Switzerland, France, Belgium, Germany and England were represented."[58] After ten days of what Marx and Engels later described as "heated" and "lengthy" debate, "all contradictions and doubt were finally over and done with, the new basic principles were adopted unanimously, and Marx and I were commis-sioned to draw up the Manifesto." That the Marx-Engels team was "commissioned" by the congress to write what would be the *Manifesto of the Communist Party*—based on Engels's *Principles of Communism*, which the congress had adopted—testifies to the victory it had achieved in its line of march to the European proletariat beginning two years earlier.[59]

The draft rules were amended only slightly. The proposal from Brussels that members be allowed to join other organizations was agreed to with the proviso that such organizations could not be antagonistic to the CL. The other proposal from the Marx party, that congress decisions be final and should not have to be approved by local bodies, was accepted in full. Also noteworthy, a new condition for membership was added; "subordination to the decisions of the League." Since League decisions were, under the newly adopted rules, arrived at in a most democratic way—in con-trast to what had been a relatively more authoritarian modus operandi—David

Riazanov, a Bolshevik historian and biographer of Marx and Engels, argued that the CL had now become a democratic centralist organization.[60] While there is some basis for Riazanov's claim, there was one important difference, as he himself noted, between the CL and the Bolshevik party under Lenin—the party in which the norm of democratic centralism was first explicated and developed. In the latter, the executive arm of the party, the political bureau, was elected by the central committee, which was in turn elected by the congress. Whereas, in the CL, the Central Authority, the executive organ, was elected by the circle in the place where it was located. Thus, under Leninist norms, the executive organ was more accountable to the party as a whole. Hence, there was more content to the "democratic" in Leninist democratic centralism than was the case for the CL.

That Brussels proposed a change in the draft rules to allow for multiple organizational affiliation for CL members is not surprising, since it was there that the Marx party was active in promoting the democratic sector of the "people's" alliance, specifically in the form of the Democratic Association. As mentioned above, its strategy was the building of a proletarian wing within the democratic movement, with Marx playing a key role in this effort in Belgium. He also began to take steps at the end of the year to create an international democratic movement by encouraging, with the assistance of the Chartists and the Society of Fraternal Democrats in London, the convening of an international congress. While promoting this movement Marx and Engels had the opportunity to speak out in defense of Polish self-determination. At one such event Marx gave a sketch of the relationship between the socialist revolution and the quest for national liberation. "The victory of the proletariat over the bourgeoisie is at the same time the signal of liberation for all oppressed nations."[61] This prescient idea would soon be elaborated on by Marx and Engels and become the basis for Lenin's very influential views on the national question.

The presence of the Marx party in the democratic movement was not welcomed by all liberals. In what may have been their first experience with red baiting, combined with a bit of German immigrant bashing, a Belgian publicist accused the CL "schoolmasters"—no doubt Marx and company—of wanting to take over the Democratic Association. Interestingly, Marx, possibly anticipating such an accusation, consciously declined to have the GWEA be the "*nucleus*" of the Association when it was originally proposed by the very same individual who subsequently redbaited him. The real issue, as Marx saw it, was a conflict over competing political perspectives. In spite of such opposition the Marx party stood its ground in the Brussels democratic movement until the government forced it to leave the country in March 1848.

The activism of Marx and Engels in the democratic movement may explain why, by mid-January 1848, they had not finished writing the *Manifesto*. In fact, Marx alone was charged by the congress to write the document, which was to be based on Engels's *Principles of Communism*. Engels worked briefly with Marx on the *Manifesto* after the congress and made some suggestions, the most important being that the catechistic style of the *Principles* be abandoned. The final product was certainly a joint effort. According to Hammen, Marx "once noted appreciatively that a German writer had used the *singular* verb when speaking of [Marx and Engels's] activities. In the same sense he apparently wished to have it known that Marx-Engels was the author of the *Manifesto*."[62]

On January 26, Schapper, Moll, and Bauer on behalf of the Central Authority sent a letter to the Brussels Circle Authority to direct Marx to complete and send the *Manifesto* to London by February 1. If it did not reach them by then "further measures would be taken against him."[63] This brief message makes clear that Marx was under organizational discipline to complete the document, giving further credence to Riazanov's claim that the CL was a democratic centralist body. It is also evidence for the point made earlier about the nature of the Marx party's fusion with the League of the Just, that is, a principled alliance in which both parties approached each other on an equal political footing. While Schapper and company certainly wanted the Marx-Engels team to be part of their party and its leadership they did so with the expectation that the Belgian duo, in spite of their middle-class intellectual origins, would function in the same way and with the same obligations of every other party member.

Marx completed the *Manifesto* before the end of the Central Authority's deadline and sent it to Schapper, who read over the proofs before its publication around the last week in February.[64] Hardly before the ink was dry on the document the long anticipated upheavals in Europe began. The document as well as the Marx-Engels team itself would now be tested by what the team regarded as the most important test of ideas—the real movement of history.

CHAPTER THREE

The Revolutions of 1848–1849: Participating in the "Real Movement"

As the Russian revolution of 1905 was ebbing after two years, revolutionaries engaged in a heated debate about what to do next. Lenin emphasized the "lessons" of the past and "revolutionary traditions," both their preservation and correct application to new circumstances. This, he argued, was the practice that distinguished Marxists from other revolutionary currents. Following the example of Marx and Engels, he wrote that the most important lessons were to be found in "revolutionary periods."

> In the activities of Marx and Engels themselves, the period of their participation in the mass revolutionary struggle of 1848–49 stands out as the central point. This was their point of departure when determining the future pattern of the workers' movement and democracy in different countries. It was to this point that they always returned in order to determine the essential nature of the different classes and their tendencies in the most striking and purest form. It was from the stand-point of the revolutionary period of that time that they always judged the later, lesser, political formations and organisations, political aims and political conflicts.[1]

Consistent with the second argument of this book, Lenin was absolutely right in this assessment of the practice of Marx and Engels. To prove this it is necessary to delineate as clearly as possible the Marx-Engels team's participation in the revolutionary events of 1848–49 and explicate the political lessons they drew from those upheavals—the focus of this and the following chapter. Subsequent chapters will allow us to determine the degree to which the Marx party actually employed, as Lenin argued, the lessons of 1848–1849.

Prelude to Revolution

A major reason why the Communist League (CL) was unable to have a regular newspaper by the fall of 1847 was the inability of its members to provide financial support. The Central Authority in London reported in September that "over half our members are out of work and in dire straits." The situation on the continent may have been even worse. What CL members were experiencing, like most toilers in Europe at that time, workers as well as peasants, was the deepest slump in the severe economic crisis of what had come to be called the "Hungry Forties." The crisis combined food shortages—the potato blight was a major factor—with the financial and banking crisis in England, which then spread to the continent. The latter had its origins in a modern phenomenon that was unique, as Marx later argued, to the capitalist mode of production, the tendency toward overproduction. The result was periodic business slumps. Deep slumps, or recessions, meant high levels of unemployment, as was the case in 1847. Because Britain was in the vanguard of industrial capitalism this phenomenon appeared there first, and then increasingly began to impact the course of economic activity on the continent.

As Germany became more industrialized and thus integrated into the growing international capitalist system, the pace of its economic life—slumps as well as booms—was increasingly synchronized with what occurred in Britain. Because the crisis of the late forties had its origins in both agriculture and commerce—hence combining both precapitalist and industrial capitalist processes—and because Germany at that stage in its development straddled both modes of production, the crisis manifested itself differently from one area to another. Thus, in the more industrialized Rhineland and the trading centers such as Hamburg and Bremen high rates of, respectively, unemployment and business failure was the norm. Whereas in the more agricultural regions to the east, the tendency was near famine-like conditions. The unevenness in the crisis, which reflected the unevenness in Germany's economic development, had enormous implications for its revolutionary process.

The economic crisis of 1847 combined with the political crisis. The French Revolution had launched the "age of revolution" and the attempt of the ancien régimes of Europe in 1815 to hold back the tide increasingly proved futile. The quest for democracy had sparked more than two hundred revolts between 1815 and 1848 from virtually every corner of Europe to the Americas. While the result in some countries, particularly after 1830, had been democratic openings, by the middle of the forties the political space on the continent was beginning to shrink. Marx and Engels's own odyssey from Germany via Paris and Brussels was very much related to the rightward direction of liberalism in Europe. In France, the combination of unfulfilled hopes for political democracy, growing disenchantment with public corruption, *and* the acute economic situation at the beginning of 1848 provided the tinderbox which only awaited the appropriate spark. Owing to the legacy of the earlier revolution, France was poised to set the political agenda for the rest of Europe.

The *Manifesto*

The "Marx party," as the closest associates of Marx and Engels increasingly began to be known, like many other political participants in the 1848–49 revolutions, anticipated the impending upheavals. What distinguished it, however, was the conscious effort it made to prepare for its intervention. The *Manifesto*, which appeared in February 1848, provided its supporters with an overall perspective to take into these events. It brought together for the first time in a relatively concise and popularly written statement—intended for the broadest possible distribution—their most essential ideas. Some parts of the document are especially important in light of Marx and Engels's activities over the course of the next two years.

Firstly, the original title of the document, *Manifesto of the Communist Party*, is instructive. Although it was commissioned by the CL, it was not called the *Manifesto of the Communist League*. As Marx explained some twelve years later, he used "party" to mean "the party in the broad historical sense."[2] Whereas the "'League,' like the *société des saisons* [of Blanqui] in Paris and a hundred of other societies was simply an episode in the history of a party that is everywhere springing up naturally out of the soil of modern society."[3] Or, as Engels many years later wrote, "the German 'Communist Party,' as we called it, consisted only of a small core, the Communist League. . . ." Thus, the "Communist Party," unlike the League, was not a particular organization, or to put it another way, the interests of the "party" could not be reduced to any specific organization. The organizational expression of the "party" could therefore take different forms in time and in place. This usage of "party" helps clarify the discussion at the beginning of the second part of the document, the "relation" of communists to the "proletarians." More specifically, "Communists do not form a separate party opposed to other working-class parties. They have no interests separate and apart from those of the proletariat as a whole."[4] Communists, however, were distinguished by their internationalism, their resolve and theoretical clarity in "understanding the line of march . . . of the proletarian movement." Given Marx's usage of "party," there was, then, no necessary contradiction between what he wrote here and his promotion of and participation in the CL.

Secondly, the *Manifesto* begins and ends on a similar theme—the necessity for communists to "openly" state and "publish their views, their aims." This was, again, an affirmation of the Marx party's rejection of the conspiratorial style of organizing that had long characterized revolutionary activities since the end of the French Revolution. That this point opens and ends the document indicates the seriousness with which it was treated.

Thirdly, not only does the document, especially in its first section, describe and explain the proletariat's role in the class struggle—"with its birth begins its struggle with the bourgeoisie"—but it stresses the *value* of struggle for the proletariat. In a particularly revealing passage, it states that "now and then the workers are victorious, but only for a time. The real fruit of their battles lies, not in the immediate result. But in the ever-expanding union of the workers." In the real world, then, the working class engages the bourgeoisie in battle regardless of whether it can actually win or sustain victories. Most importantly, this occurs whether or not there are a "handful of chosen men" who claim to know what's best for workers. Through such battles—defeats as well as victories—the proletariat learns for itself. This enormously important idea about the self-education of the proletariat harkens back to the third of the eleven *Theses on Feuerbach*, revolutionary practice and the education of the educator. Marx's polemic in 1844 with Ruge about the Silesian weavers' strike is also recalled: "We do not say to the world: Cease your struggles, they are foolish; we will give you the true slogan of struggle." For both the proletariat and its leadership education takes place through participation in the living class struggle. As the *Manifesto* explains: "The theoretical conclusions of the Communists are in no way based on ideas or principles that have been invented, or discovered by this or that would-be universal reformer. They merely express, in general terms, actual relations springing from an existing class struggle, from a historical movement going on under our very eyes." That communists, as Engels argued in his polemic with Heinzen, seek to generalize and disseminate the lessons of the workers' movement— the process by which the proletariat becomes "conscious" of its own movement— does not contradict the notion of self-education. The essential point is that the lessons derive from and are tested in the real movement.

Lastly, of the almost forty pages of the *Manifesto* less than three can truly be said to provide concrete strategies and tactics. This too was consistent with the earliest views of the Marx party, specifically its critique of and opposition to the schemata of the utopians. Again, only the living class struggle would reveal the appropriate strategic and tactical answers. This also applied to organizational questions as well. Although a list of ten "measures" to "raise the proletariat to the position of ruling class"—applicable to "most advanced countries"—can be found in part two of the document, the reality of the German revolution, as we'll see shortly, required the Marx party to supplement the *Manifesto* almost immediately after its appearance with a new list of demands.

The final page of the last part of the document is especially relevant since it provides a brief but important outline of the party's strategy for Germany "on the eve of a bourgeois revolution."

> In Germany [the Communists] fight with the bourgeoisie whenever it acts in a revolutionary way, against the absolute monarchy, the feudal squirearchy, and the petty bourgeoisie.
>
> But they never cease, for a single instant, to instil into the working class the clearest possible recognition of the hostile antagonism between bourgeoisie and proletariat in order that the German workers may straightway use, as so many weapons against the bourgeoisie, the social and political conditions that the bourgeoisie must necessarily introduce along with its supremacy, and in order that after the fall of the reactionary classes in Germany the fight against the bourgeoisie itself may immediately begin.

The general strategic perspective that the German proletariat would ally with its bourgeoisie "whenever" the latter waged a fight to overthrow absolutism and then immediately commence, in the wake of that victory, its fight to overthrow its erstwhile ally was also not new for the Marx party.[5] The very important qualifier, "whenever" (or, in the original, "as long as"),[6] meant that the alliance with the bourgeoisie was an open question since, as Marx and Engels had noted on many occasions, the commitment of the German bourgeoisie to a democratic revolution was problematic. What is new is the call for an alliance *against* the "petty bourgeoisie" as well. In the *Principles of Communism* and the polemic with Heinzen, Engels, however, had included the "urban petty bourgeoisie" as one of the allies of the proletariat in the fight for democracy. As the real history of the 1848–49 events in Germany makes clear, it would be Engels's strategic line that the Marx party would actually employ.[7]

A final comment concerns the strategic alliance for the communist party. As has so often been noted, there is virtually nothing in the *Manifesto* about the peasantry; what is stated is disparaging[8] and, hence, the basis for the frequently stated claim that the Marx party dismissed them. Again, Engels, as noted above, did include the "small peasantry" in the alliance with the proletariat.[9] The actual practice of Marx and Engels in the impending revolution revealed a concern with the peasantry that belied their near total silence on the subject in the *Manifesto*.

In conclusion, the *Manifesto* provided the communist party with an overall political perspective for its participation in the upcoming revolutions. While useful in preparing its cadre for the tasks ahead, it could only be a framework. Only the actual struggle would determine what needed to be done.

THE REVOLUTION BEGINS

While completing the *Manifesto*, Marx wrote elsewhere that the proletariat "alone will accomplish the coming French revolution."[10] Engels also wrote then that the "day of reckoning" was drawing near for the French bourgeoisie.[11] Unlike Germany, where the bourgeois democratic revolution was on the agenda, in France, the bourgeoisie, they argued, which had been in power since the revolution of 1830, would be challenged by the proletariat at the outset of the impending revolution. Within a month their predictions would be tested in the real movement.

Leading the Communist League in Brussels and Paris

As part of their preparatory activities Marx and Engels were actively involved in the democratic movement in Brussels and Paris. In general, "the democracy" included those who advocated political—republicanism—and social reforms; there was less consensus on what the latter entailed. Their strategy was to promote a proletarian wing within its midst. To this end Marx, immediately after the CL congress at the end of 1847, began a series of classes for the GWEA on political economy with particular focus on wages. This was followed by lectures to the Democratic Association on the topic of free trade. Plans were made to publish both series of talks in order to widely disseminate their contents. Marx's *Speech on Free Trade* appeared as a pamphlet about three weeks before the February revolution. The latter delayed the publication of the wage lectures until the following year, when they were serialized as *Wage-Labour and Capital*.

The lectures were intended to arm communist workers within the multiclass democratic movement with scientific arguments that explained the irreconcilable class differences between the proletariat and the bourgeoisie. Clarity on this most essential issue was mandatory for the proletariat as a whole. For German communists no illusions could be entertained about the temporary alliances they would have to enter into with nonproletarian forces in the fight for the bourgeois democratic revolution.

In spite of Engels's aforementioned frustration with the CL in Paris he was able to make links with much of the leadership of the democratic movement in France, some of whom would shortly be members of the revolutionary government. One of them, Ferdinand Flocon, became a minister in the provisional government and provided vital assistance to the Marx party. However, before this occurred the Louis Philippe government, feeling the heat of revolution on its neck, forced Engels to leave Paris, whereupon he immediately joined Marx in Brussels.

On February 22, street fighting and the erection of barricades began in Paris. Within two days Louis Philippe abdicated and a provisional government was installed. The February Revolution helped launch almost fifty similar outbreaks throughout Europe in the first four months of 1848. The democratic movement in Brussels was immediately galvanized by events in Paris. Having long anticipated what was unfolding in France, the Marx party threw itself into activity to raise Belgium's revolutionary pulse. The Central Authority of the CL in London, realizing that the revolutionary initiative had now shifted to the continent, decided to move to Brussels. Marx was elected chair of the Authority, Schapper as secretary, and Engels one of its seven members. Working through the Democratic Association, it proposed to the Brussels city government that in addition to the civil guard, composed mainly of "middle-class" elements, that the "working class" also be armed as a way of maintaining "public peace." The authorities, fearful of an echo of the Paris events, tried to head off such a confrontation by activating the civil guard—a legacy of Belgium's 1830 bourgeois democratic revolution. The proposal from the Association was a very conscious effort to limit the bourgeoisie's monopolization of access to arms. Although, not surprisingly, the authorities rejected the proposal, there is some evidence that Marx went ahead and donated money from his just-received inheritance to begin the arming of workers—an indication of the importance that he lent to such a step.[12] The combination of red baiting and German immigrant bashing made it easy for the government to force the Marx household, after a brief and somewhat brutal imprisonment, to leave the country. Almost at the same time that the Marxes had to leave Brussels, they received an invitation—"free France opens its doors to you"[13]—from Flocon to live in Paris, effectively overturning the order that had forced Marx to abandon Paris in 1845.

On the eve of Marx's departure from Brussels, the Central Authority convened for one last time. Since Belgium's political reality made it impossible for it to function and, "that at the present moment Paris is the centre of the entire revolutionary movement," it decided to move to the French capital. In addition, it "confers on League member Karl Marx full discretionary power for the temporary central direction of all League affairs with the responsibility to the Central Authority to be newly constituted and to the next Congress."[14] This momentous decision registered the enormous authority that the Marx party now held within the League, what it had achieved within the space of half a year.

Preparing for the German Revolution

Within a day of his arrival in Paris, March 5, Marx set about the reconstitution of the CL. This was critical since a rival group of German exiles in Paris was making preparations to export the French revolution to Germany via an armed expedition. Marx vehemently opposed their plans. To launch a well-publicized expedition from French soil with the clear backing of the French government would simply play into the hands of the German counterrevolution. The return, he argued, should be less public and prepared by the establishment of workers organizations in Germany.[15] Furthermore, the February Revolution was only the prelude to what would be the real struggle in France—that between the bourgeoisie and the proletariat. The outcome of that struggle would be decisive for the rest of Europe.

Marx tried unsuccessfully to dissuade the adventure from going forward.[16] Among its organizers was the Russian exile, Michael Bakunin. This would only be the first in a long line of political differences between the two. Just as Marx had predicted, the expedition was a fiasco when it was easily routed after crossing the Rhine by the more organized and better armed German army on April 1. This was the first time that the line of the Marx party, and that of an opponent group, was tested in a revolutionary situation. Subsequent events reveal that it passed its first revolutionary test with, if not flying colors, its banner at least intact.

The criticisms that Marx and Engels made of the armed legion offer another important lesson. Contrary to the oft-stated claim that they ignored ethnicity or the national question in their haste to get to the class struggle, their denunciation of the expedition shows that they understood all too well the reality of nationalist sentiment. As one of the legacies of the Napoleonic wars, the nationalist—often times nascent—opposition that was engendered in many locations on the continent taught Marx and Engels that any attempt to "export" revolution from France would have its opposite effect; it would be used by the right to undermine revolutionary struggles and in fact would allow the counterrevolution to counterpoise nationalism to proletarian internationalism. Nowhere was this so clear as in Cologne, where CL activists reported that in the aftermath of the failed expedition the hitherto very active pro-revolutionary forces in the town were placed on the defensive by the right.[17] For Marx and Engels the issue was never one of ignoring nationalism but rather a recognition of its reality in order to chart a revolutionary course that actually got to the class question. Within that framework they counterpoised an alternative plan for the return of the German exiles—the same one they would apply on countless occasions to the national question.

Along with a reorganization of the League's branches in Paris, a "German Workers' Club" was established as its public face. Marx, who was elected as Chairman of the newly unified CL district organization, drew up the draft rules for the Club. In anticipation of a return of CL members and supporters to Germany—protests and demonstrations were by now an almost daily occurrence inside the country following the February Revolution—the organization began to function in a more disciplined way.[18] Members, for example, who had been organizing the ill-fated armed expedition, were expelled. Marx, in this context, recommended to Engels that he "dismiss" Gigot, a founder of Brussels CCC, if he didn't "begin to show signs of activity" in the Brussels CL. "Just now the fellow ought to be more energetic."[19] Marx clearly believed that "activity" was a requirement of League membership, particularly in a near-revolutionary situation. In addition, presumably as a way to differentiate themselves from the expedition participants, who adopted the black, red, and gold colors of German nationalism, the CL agreed to Marx's proposal "that all League members shall wear a *red* ribbon." Again, at Marx's suggestion all members had to supply the organization with their names and addresses. Lastly, educational activities were also instituted. At their request, the London CL sent the Paris body one thousand copies of the *Manifesto* for study and propaganda work.

Developments in Germany justified the preparations in Paris. On March 3, for example, CL activists in Cologne organized a demonstration of five thousand workers and artisans to demand basic democratic rights.[20] There as in other towns the regime was beginning, albeit hesitantly, to respond with brute force. Commenting to Marx, Engels wrote, "If only Frederick William IV [the reigning Prussian monarch] digs his heels in! Then all will be won and in a few months' time we'll have the German Revolution." Neither Engels nor Marx realized that within weeks, on March 18, the long-predicted German upheavals would begin. The immediate stimulus was the uprising in Vienna a few days earlier, the capital of the Austrian Empire, which forced Emperor Ferdinand to bow to some of the protestors demands and Count Metternich, the architect of European reaction, into exile. In Berlin, after two days of barricade fighting, Frederick IV also conceded to the demands of the demonstrators and agreed to grant a constitution—without, significantly, saying when.

A Needed Addendum to the Manifesto

The League's activities took on a new urgency; the return to Germany was only a matter of time. After some delay Engels arrived in Paris to assist his partner. The key programmatic task was the concretization of the strategic line of the *Manifesto* for the new situation in Germany. Within a day of his arrival Engels and Marx began to draft what became, after the discussion and approval of the Central Authority, the *Demands of the Communist Party in Germany*. The seventeen demands were printed—apparently with Marx paying for it out of his own pocket[21]—as a one-page leaflet and distributed along with the *Manifesto*. By early April, the CL had been successful in having them published in a number of German democratic newspapers.[22] They were reprinted and disseminated throughout the duration of the German revolution. So effective was the campaign that the German populace, during the upheavals, was likely to have been more familiar with the *Demands* than the *Manifesto*.

The *Demands* reaffirmed the "people's" alliance that the *Manifesto* had placed in doubt. After listing the specific demands, it made clear to whom they were directed. "It is to the interests of the German proletariat, the petty bourgeoisie and the small peasants to support these demands with all possible energy."[23] Whereas the *Manifesto* had placed the petit bourgeoisie in the opposition camp, this new programmatic statement included them once again, as had the *Principles* and the anti-Heinzen polemic, in the alliance. The *Demands* were fundamentally the extreme left position of the bourgeois democratic revolution.[24] The first four called for a unified German republic based on universal suffrage, a paid legislative body—to ensure that "workers . . . be able to become members of the German parliament"—and the "universal arming of the people." The demand for a unified German republic was consistent with the view as expressed in the *Manifesto* that "the proletariat of each country must, of course first settle matters with its own bourgeoisie." A unified Germany, with a republican form of government, offered the most favorable terrain for the proletariat to "settle matters" with the German bourgeoisie.

The purpose of the sixth through ninth demands was "to reduce the communal and other burdens hitherto imposed upon the peasants and small tenant farmers without curtailing the means available for defraying state expenses and without imperilling production"—thus, the Marx party's first programmatic statement on the peasant question. Of the seventeen, numbers one through four and six through nine spoke to the distinct tasks of the German revolution as opposed to the ten "measures" listed in the *Manifesto*, whose purpose was "to raise the proletariat to the position of ruling class," that is, to advance the proletarian or socialist revolution. These demands and the *Manifesto* measures concretized the very important difference between the bourgeois and socialist revolution, which would soon be of crucial importance.

Along with programmatic preparations, the CL took a number of organizational steps for the return to Germany. The Central Authority began to send without fanfare—in contrast to the armed expedition—emissaries to various locations to reconnoiter the situation and test the political waters. The Marx team also made preparations for the publication of a party newspaper in Germany. Noteworthy is their decline of Flocon's offer of monetary assistance in this project. While assistance was indeed needed, the evidence suggests that by now, about two months after the February revolution, Marx and Engels had begun to have doubts about the resolve of the petit bourgeois radicals like Flocon in the provisional government and were reluctant to become beholden to them in any way.[25]

On April 1, the first of the three to four hundred CL supporters had begun to make their way back to Germany. Internal party documents suggest that Marx helped to finance this effort with monies from his recently received inheritance. Within a week, Marx and Engels and some of the other Central Authority members left Paris. After about two weeks all of them had found their way to the various localities in Germany as planned.

THE RETURN TO GERMANY

The strategic line that the Marx party pursued in Brussels and, perhaps to a lesser extent, Paris following the December congress of the League was the promotion of the democratic movement and the construction of a workers' component within its ranks. Within the workers' component the perspective was the construction of a communist tendency, namely the CL, to provide political direction. Once back in Germany, however, there would be significant shifts in emphasis in this two-prong strategy.

The emissaries that the CL had sent into Germany prior to the return of the bulk of its forces made an effort to lay the foundations for an all-German workers' association. An appeal was issued to that end from the town of Mainz by two CL leaders on April 5. Addressed to "Brothers and Workers," it warned that unless workers began to move expeditiously they would again be "deceived" by "a handful of men." Workers, therefore, had to organize themselves throughout the country. There needed to be "representatives from the working class to the German Parliament nominated and elected, and all other steps taken that are necessary for safeguarding our interests."[26] It proposed that Mainz serve as the organizing center for this effort. On their way back to Cologne Marx and Engels stopped in the town to discuss with the CL members the progress made so far with the appeal. Clearly, then, their initial strategy upon returning to Germany was to promote what the proletariat in Britain best exemplified, independent working-class political action, in order to put the German proletariat in the strongest position possible to defend its interests in the multiclass alliance needed to overthrow the Prussian autocracy and carry out the bourgeois revolution.

While other CL leaders and members returned to various towns in Germany, Marx and Engels decided not to make Berlin but rather Cologne, the largest city in the most industrialized province of Germany, their headquarters. Although the capitol of the Prussian empire, Berlin, in their opinion, "does not play the role of Paris as far as either Germany or the Rhineland in particular is concerned." Whereas Cologne was in the center of industrial Germany, Berlin was not even "a metropolis, it is a 'seat of the Court,'" that is, the capitol of feudal Germany. Also, the fact that some of the legal practices from the Napoleonic period still existed in the Rhineland, for example, trial by jury, allowed for a degree of protection from the arbitrariness of the Prussian authorities that prevailed in Berlin. Also, given Marx's editorship of the *RZ* four years earlier, it was more likely that a "party organ," a newspaper, could be established in the Rhineland capitol. Indeed, after some negotiations with the local bourgeoisie, the *Neue Rheinische Zeitung*—the New Rhenish Magazine (NRZ)—appeared for the first time on June 1, 1848, almost six weeks after the return of the Marx party.

The Rhineland bourgeoisie and authorities greeted the return of Marx and Engels, whose political reputations—known largely through their writings—preceded them, with both mixed emotions and trepidation. Engels made a most prophetic observation about the bourgeoisie in Barmen, his home town, from whom he had tried unsuccessfully to get financial support for the new paper: "[E]ven these radical bourgeoisie here see us as their future main enemies and have no intention of putting into our hands weapons which we would very shortly turn against themselves."[27] In Cologne, where the local bourgeoisie was a bit more confident, their approach to the Marx party appears to have been the embrace of death. Thus, a layer of them invested in the newspaper—whose editorial line would in theory be consistent with their avowed politics—to no doubt use the Marx-Engels team for their own political aims. The Barmen bourgeoisie foresaw correctly that the team, as it had already made clear in the *Manifesto* and elsewhere, had no intention of serving the interests of the bourgeoisie. Ludolf Camphausen, one of the Rhineland's most successful industrialists and once a major shareholder in the former *RZ*, took a somewhat different tack. Now, as a result of the March Revolution in Berlin, he was Prussia's first prime minister. In a not too subtle effort at co-optation, he offered Marx a position in his government.[28] Needless to say, the offer was politely but quickly turned down. Meanwhile, behind the scenes the city's police inspector reported on "the politically unreliable *Dr. Karl Marx*" in regard to his application to renew his Prussian citizenship. The government stalled on the request for more than a year and attempted unsuccessfully to use it to curtail Marx's political activities.

The Strategy for Workers: Marx v. Gottschalk

The Cologne that Marx and Engels returned to on April 11 was a highly politicized city owing in part to the massive March 3 demonstration mentioned earlier. Two days after their return, Andreas Gottschalk, a CL leader in the town since Fall 1847 and key organizer of the demonstration, called for a meeting to establish a workers' association. The call was so successful that within a few weeks more than five thousand workers had affiliated with the newly formed Cologne Workers' Society.

> By the end of June the membership had risen to nearly 8,000 [about a third of the eligible voters of the city]. Every one of its meetings at the Gürzenich Haus was packed to overflowing. The workers in their blouses sat before a platform adorned with the red flag, wearing red sashes across their breasts, some of them with red Jacobin caps on their heads. Many of the audience were women, and many were illiterate workers, porters and boatmen, who were particularly hard hit by the prevailing unemployment.[29]

On the surface, Gottschalk's effort would appear to be exactly what the CL leadership had been promoting through the Mainz appeal. Yet it quickly became clear that his approach to organizing workers was increasingly at odds with the line of the *Demands*. The strategy of the CL, as already emphasized, was to promote and help build the democratic movement and within it construct a proletarian wing, that is, build the "peoples alliance" in order to carry out the bourgeois democratic revolution. For Gottschalk, however, the construction of the Cologne Workers' Society was counterposed to the building of the democratic movement. "Though not guided by a definite programme, he was sufficiently critical of democracy to have declared at his first public appearance at the town hall, 'I come not in the name of the people, for all these representatives are of the people; no, I address myself to you only in the name of the labouring population.'"[30] Thus, for Gottschalk, only the workers—"the labouring population"—were important and not the other components of Marx and Engels's "peoples alliance."

Other differences between the CL leadership and Gottschalk became apparent. While the *Demands* had called unequivocally for a "republic"—in fact the very first demand—Gottschalk balked at this on the grounds that it would frighten, which was true, the bourgeoisie. Instead, he began to opt for a constitutional monarchy, just as the Camphausen government was doing, while the CL leadership, on the other hand, was actively fighting against such a political system. Another issue concerned upcoming elections for the All-German Frankfurt Parliament and the Prussian Constitutional Assembly—two of the concrete gains of the March revolution. Because workers would only have an indirect vote—they would only be able to vote for electors—Gottschalk advocated that the elections be boycotted. Again, Marx and Engels and the rest of the CL leadership opposed such a tactic.

At the heart of the growing dispute was Gottschalk's disagreement with the fundamental line of the League that the bourgeois democratic revolution was on the agenda in Germany to which every tactical move had to be subordinated. All energy, it felt, had to be focused on the fight for bourgeois democracy based on an alliance of the petit bourgeoisie, the small peasantry as well as the workers. As the Marx-Engels team had long argued, only with such a victory could the social question be placed on the agenda. Only the political revolution would provide the working class with the space to begin to forge the kind of class consciousness needed to prepare for and carry out a socialist revolution.

Gottschalk's approach recalls what Marx and Engels had advised against in their postscript of the letter to Köttgen two years earlier. Then the issue was whether workers should petition for freedom of the press by collecting only workers' signatures. Their counsel called for consideration of a cooperative petitioning effort, initiated by the communists, of the workers with the bourgeoisie. For the working class to try to do it alone would have been sectarian and, more importantly, would have made it more difficult for democracy to actually be instituted. Gottschalk's strategy, in other words, diverted the workers' movement from the fight for democracy and thus by default conceded the franchise for that fight to the bourgeoisie who, as Marx and Engels had already argued, would increasingly vacillate on the question of democracy. Neither was it surprising that Gottschalk supported a constitutional monarchy. In his opposition to an alliance between workers and the petit bourgeois democrats, and yet aware that the German proletariat was not sufficiently strong to take power, Gottschalk had no alternative but to turn to an enlightened monarch or what he called the "social monarchy."[31]

Gottschalk was not the only CL member who looked askance on a workers' alliance with the bourgeois democratic forces. Relocated in Berlin, Stephen Born, who had once collaborated with Engels in Paris to oppose the True Socialist tendency in the CL, also began to have doubts about such an alliance. This was facilitated by his growing distance from communism and emphasis on building a workers' movement that was increasingly sectarian toward non-working-class issues. The organization Born founded—usually considered to be the first general German workers association—"was organized along the popularly-preferred craft lines. . . . It was more interested in immediate action to improve the material well-being of the workers than in politics and revolution."[32] The body's newspaper ignored not only the peasantry but rural workers as well and "took little notice of foreign affairs . . . [a] general hostility to foreigners, foreign produce and foreign competition, and more than a hint of anti-semitism."[33] It was just this kind of a narrow workerist perspective—what would be called in the context of the early debates among Russian revolutionaries a half century later, "economism"—that Marx and Engels opposed in fighting for the people's alliance.

Many years later Engels explained the error of Born's and, by inference, Gottschalk's exclusive approach to the workers' movement in the 1848 upheavals. "In particular, strikes, trade unions and producers' co-operatives were set along going and it was forgotten that above all it was a question of conquering, by means of political victories, the field in which alone such things could be realised on a lasting basis."[34] They put, in other words, the workers' economic cart before the political horse—the political revolution.

Owing to its rule that "subordination to the decisions of the League" was one of the "conditions of membership," Gottschalk either decided or was asked to tender his resignation. At a May 11 meeting Marx asked him "what attitude towards the League he . . . now intends to adopt." He replied that he intended to resign because he didn't agree with the rules—"the present conditions" required new rules—under which "his personal freedom was in jeopardy." As he parted ways with the CL he said he would be willing to work with it if the need so arose. His departure was only apparently amicable, as subsequent events revealed. The rules and their enforcement give credence once again to the suggestion that the League operated in fact as a democratic centralist organization.

The CL leadership continued in its efforts to build a national workers' movement along the lines of the Mainz appeal and as part of the broader democratic movement. An important aspect of this was Marx and Engels's effort to maintain the proletarian internationalist dimension of the League—just as it was beginning to be rejected by Born in Berlin. Thus, in the midst of all his organizational tasks Engels began to translate the *Manifesto* into English. Such an undertaking, which Engels only got halfway through due to the exigencies of the movement in Germany, reflected the Marx party's view that the outcome of the revolution in Germany depended in the long run on developments in France and, especially, Britain. Throughout 1848 they were hopeful that the Chartists would lead a successful fight and take power. It was thus of utmost importance that Europe's most class conscious proletariat have access to the communist program that it had hitherto lacked in its previous struggles. The soon to be launched *NRZ*, in sharp contrast to Born's paper in Berlin, would continue and deepen this internationalist perspective by bringing German workers the latest news and analysis about the fights of their cohorts elsewhere in Europe.

Marx and other CL leaders in Cologne (Engels was in his hometown of Barmen for much of April and May) began to receive reports from League emissaries throughout Germany. Contrary to the optimism of the Mainz appeal, they indicated that the prospects for building branches of the League and workers' associations in order to affect the course of the growing mass democratic movement were not propitious. There was indeed much organizational activity among workers but it tended to be on the basis of defending and/or promoting guild privileges rather than advancing a class conscious proletarian perspective.[35] Engels seemed to have found a similar situation in Barmen (as well as a coterie of radical democrats "who fear for their fortunes and smell communism in the air and . . . who regard us as rivals"). The activities of the workers resembled, in other words, what Born increasingly promoted in the workers' movement in Berlin and then later elsewhere. The real movement showed that the artisanal or straubinger factor still weighed heavily on German workers.

On the basis of these reports the Marx-Engels team made an important shift in its practice. About the middle of May, in what was a conscious division of labor within the Central Authority of the League, Marx became very active in the Cologne Democratic Society, which he had earlier helped organize—later joined by Engels—while Schapper and Moll did the same in the Workers' Society that Gottschalk headed. This division allowed the CL leadership to begin implementing the strategy of the *Demands*, that is, seeking to win forces to the people's alliance from within both the democratic and workers' movements. Thus, very quickly, Schapper and Moll began promoting the *Demands* within the Workers' Society—apparently to Gottschalk's discomfort—in order to convince workers of the necessity of the alliance between workers, the petit bourgeoisie, and peasantry. Marx and Engels did the same—promoting the alliance—within the Democratic Society of Cologne.

The NRZ—the *Organ of Democracy*

On June 1, the first issue of the *NRZ* appeared. It's subtitle, *Organ of Democracy*, made it quite apparent that the paper intended to be the voice of the people's alliance—the vanguard coalition in the fight for the bourgeois democratic revolution. Reports from League activists in the field made clear that it would have been premature to declare the paper to be the voice of communist workers; such a constituency had yet to take form in Germany. What did exist, however, was a growing mass democratic movement in which the Marx party, through the newspaper, could lobby for a proletarian orientation. It should be remembered that "the democracy" was in general the proponents of political reform—republicanism—and less well-defined social goals. Three decades later Engels defended the strategy he and Marx adopted for the paper.

> If we did not want to do that, if we did not want to take up the movement, adhere to its already existing, most advanced, actually proletarian side and to advance it further, then there was nothing left for us to do but to preach communism in a little provincial sheet and to found a tiny sect instead of a great party of action. But we had already been spoilt for the role of preachers in the wilderness; we had studied the utopians too well for that, nor was it for that we had drafted our programme.[36]

The real movement in Germany, therefore, was the democratic movement. The obligation for communists was not to be sectarian about the movement but to intervene in it, help lead it in order that it be pushed as far to the left—i.e., within the framework of the democratic revolution—as possible. The *raison d'être* of the paper, as Marx explained two years later, was "its daily intervention in the movement and speaking directly from the heart of the movement, its reflecting day-to-day history in all its amplitude, the continuous and impassioned interaction between the people and its daily press. . . ."[37] The *NRZ* was to be, therefore, as Engels had argued for in his polemic a year earlier with Heinzen, a party paper—a political instrument in the promotion of the democratic revolution.

With the *NRZ* the Marx-Engels team made another major tactical shift. The aforementioned field reports from CL activists had indicated that the same obstacles for organizing a national proletarian movement made it difficult for the League to become an effective organization. For example, "as early as April 18 Wilhelm Wolff had written: 'In Cologne the League continues to vegetate in a great state of incoherence.'"[38] It was due in part to this reality that Marx and Engels proposed to the Central Authority that the League be dissolved. In its place they proposed, apparently, that the *NRZ*, whose editorial board was composed of League members—including Engels and Wolff—serve as the organizing center for the communist tendency in the German revolution. Following an unresolved debate, Marx, in his capacity as president with "discretionary authority," appeared to have dissolved or suspended the League early in June.

Marx's actions have been the subject of much debate by historians ever since, due in large part to the absence of documentation at the time of the decision. Political inclinations, especially in relation to stances for or against the Leninist perspective on the revolutionary party, have oftentimes fuelled the debate. For anti-Leninists, for example, Marx's actions go to prove that he, unlike Lenin, didn't make a "fetish" of the "vanguard party." The situation is complicated by the fact that in some locations, London certainly, the CL continued to function. A further complication is that Marx and Engels strongly suggested two years later—to be discussed in the next chapter—that it had been a mistake to shelve the organization. The only explanation Marx gave of what happened was written about a decade after the 1848–49 revolutions: "[D]uring the revolutionary period in Germany, [the League's] activities died down of themselves since more effective avenues existed now for the realisation of its ends."[39]

Engels, in his later history of the *NRZ* and the League, elaborated on Marx's explanation. Essentially, the mass democratic movement had engulfed League members who, in their oftentimes quite varied locales scattered throughout Germany, were increasingly separated from one another. "The few hundred separate League members vanished in the enormous mass that had been suddenly hurled into the movement." They stopped being League members and frequently became activists within this new movement. (This is probably what Stephen Born meant when he said in a letter to Marx before the latter shelved the CL, " 'The League is dissolved everywhere—and nowhere.'")[40] Moreover, "from the moment when the causes which had made the secret League necessary ceased to exist, the secret League lost all significance as such. But this could least of all surprise the persons who had just stripped this same secret League of the last vestige of its conspiratorial character."[41] For Marx and Engels, therefore, it made sense, given their well-known opposition to conspiratorial organizing, to dissolve the League since the political space existed in Germany after the March revolution to do open political work. In 1964 the testimony of Peter Röser, a leader of the Cologne Workers' Society at the time of the

League's dissolution and then later president of the "reconstituted" CL, was published in full for the first time and basically substantiated Marx and Engels's explanation.[42] His testimony also indicated that Schapper and Moll opposed Marx on the dissolution, a fact of some significance, as later events revealed. In light of Marx and Engels's later suggestion that the dissolution had been a mistake, again to be discussed in the next chapter, a more complete assessment of their actions in June 1848 must wait until then.

The NRZ as Organizing Center. The *NRZ* indeed became the organizing center for what had hitherto been the Central Authority of the League. It provided direction and coordination for the communist tendency's participation in both the democratic movement and the workers' movement—in Cologne, respectively the Democratic Association and the Workers' Society. The old Central Authority members such as Schapper and Moll and the newspaper's editors, all of whom had been CL members, constituted the effective decision-making body with Marx as the acknowledged leader. The paper itself was the propaganda and agitational arm of this center. As editor, Marx exercised decisive influence in what was written, as Engels explained in very blunt terms many years later. "The editorial constitution was simply the dictatorship of Marx. A major daily paper, which has to be ready at a definite hour, cannot observe a consistent policy with any other constitution. Moreover, Marx's dictatorship was a matter of course here, undisputed and willingly recognised by all of us."

To get the paper off the ground shares were sold, primarily to that wing of the bourgeoisie that identified with "the democracy" in opposition to Prussian absolutism. Although Marx went to great lengths to make clear that the paper was the voice of "the democratic party" and not that of communism—it never, for example, printed the *Demands* or referred directly to the *Manifesto*—he and Engels were successful in selling only about half the shares. This reflected the fears of the bourgeoisie that under Marx's editorship the *NRZ* would advocate a democracy far more radical than anything with which they could be comfortable. Their worst fears were confirmed. "Half of them deserted us immediately after the first number came out and by the end of the month we no longer had any at all." The departure of the bourgeoisie from the *Organ of Democracy* foreshadowed their course in the subsequent months of the revolution.

The original publication date for the first issue was to have been at the beginning of July. However, Marx and Engels decided to publish a month earlier even though everything was not in place. At the top of the first issue in bold print the editorial committee explained to its readers why it had moved sooner. "But since the renewed insolence of the reactionaries foreshadows the enactment of German September Laws [a reference to a series of laws introduced in France in 1835, which placed severe curbs on civil liberties such as freedom of the press] in the near future, we have decided to make use of every available day and to publish the paper as from June the first."[43] Thus, ten weeks after the March revolution, the *NRZ* editors were of the opinion that the political space that had opened with that revolution was being threatened by a counterrevolution. It was urgent now to take steps to head off such a turn and it was from that vantage point that the paper sought to affect the course of the revolution.

The article in the first issue that frightened half of the *NRZ*'s shareholders to withdraw their support from the paper was written by Engels on the aforementioned Frankfurt Assembly—the first all-German constituent assembly. The article set the tone for the paper's line on domestic matters, the essence of which was to advocate in the most uncompromising way for a "single, indivisible, democratic German republic." Engels's article ridiculed the recently elected delegates—mainly moderate liberals on the government payroll—who had been in session for two weeks, for not having taken any substantive steps toward this end. Underlying his and Marx's sharp rebukes of the Frankfurt Assembly was their fear that its irresolute behavior would embolden the reactionary forces that wanted to limit the political space that had been opened by the March Revolution. As they constantly emphasized, March had been "only a partial revolution" because it had not been "carried through to the end." Marx, in the paper's second issue, warned "the democratic party" that its illusions in the "moderate bourgeoisie" such as the Cologne bourgeoisie's own cohort and now Prussian Prime Minister Ludolf Camphausen, would only undermine its ability to resist the growing counterrevolution.

In agitating for a unified German republic, the most favorable terrain for the proletariat to take on the bourgeoisie, the *NRZ* editors were not expecting an instant outcome. "We do not make the utopian demand that at the outset a *united indivisible German republic* should be proclaimed, but we ask the so-called radical democratic party not to confuse the starting point of the struggle and of the revolutionary movement with the goal."[44] This, in fact, was almost the same language Engels had employed in his criticism of Heinzen almost a year earlier, namely, his failure to distinguish between reforms and revolution and the need to employ transitional demands. And in language that closely resembled what Marx had used with Ruge four years earlier, the editors explained how Germany's political transformation would occur. "The final act of constitution cannot be *decreed*, it coincides with the movement we have to go through. It is therefore not a question of putting into practice this or that view, this or that political idea, but of understanding the course of development. The [Frankfurt] National Assembly has to take only such steps as are practicable in the first instance."

It must be noted that the *NRZ*'s advocacy of a "single, indivisible, democratic German republic" was not unconditional. As the government in Berlin became increasingly reactionary Engels raised the possibility of the Rhine province separating from Prussia. German unity had to be on the basis of the dissolution of the old Prussian empire, and the Rhineland could not be forced to remain under Berlin's rule. After the revolution had been defeated, Engels, in 1850, referred to this position in answering the charge that the *NRZ* advocated the "ceding of the left back of the Rhine to France. . . . [T]here was only talk of a union of the Rhine Province with France in the sense that in the decisive battle between revolution and counter-revolution the Rhine Province would unfailingly fight on the revolutionary side, whether it was represented by Frenchmen or Chinamen."[4] While "only talk" at the time, Engels made clear that for his party national loyalty took a back seat to revolutionary internationalism.

As part of its efforts to counter the expected moves of the right, the paper warned workers in Cologne not to be provoked into premature actions against the military, which was spoiling for an excuse to limit civil liberties. On numerous occasions throughout the course of the revolution the Marx-Engels team would offer and carry out such counsel—what Draper calls "revolutionary restraint." Although his assessment, as Draper correctly notes, is somewhat one-sided and ignores Engels, the historian E. H. Carr was one of the first Marxologists to call attention to this characteristic of the Marx party's leadership: "Marx was the first revolutionary in history who consistently sought to restrain his followers. Again and again he preached the supreme folly of rash and premature adventures."[46] The rationale for this approach was the simple desire that the oppressed win their struggles by fighting on the most favorable terrain.

Given the increasing rightward direction of not only the various German governments but the liberal bourgeoisie as well, it might have been tempting for Marx and Engels to sit back and say we told you so. Indeed, the *Manifesto*, the *Principles of Communism*, and other writings had anticipated as much. But it was precisely because they were communists and not inevitablists that they actively participated in the class struggle in order to influence its outcome.

THE JUNE REVOLUTION

It was the events at the end of June and the response of the *NRZ* that drove away most of its remaining shareholders. Just as Paris had led the way for the March Revolution, the French capitol would once again be influential for the German revolution. Marx and Engels, as well as other astute observers, had been saying for months that France's February Revolution was only the prelude to the decisive battle—that between labor and capital. During the last week in June Parisian workers rose up massively and waged their long-awaited battle. The uprising reflected, more than anything else, the frustrations of Paris' working masses with the unfulfilled social expectations of the February Revolution, due in large part to the vacillations and betrayals by the liberal democratic government that took power after the deposition of the Louis Philippe regime. After four days the revolt was brutally suppressed. "Only four or five hundred of the rebels appear to have perished on the barricades, but more than three thousand were massacred by the soldiers of the *garde mobile* and the regular army after the fighting was over."[47] Another twelve thousand were arrested and charged, many of whom were deported to Algeria. In an initial assessment of the defeat Marx pointed to the "absence of leaders and means," reasons about which he would later provide a more detailed analysis. Engels, who in his youth did a one year stint in the Prussian military, wrote a series of articles for a "purely military description of the struggle to show our readers" how a nearly victorious insurrection of the Paris workers was carried out. He suggested that the techniques employed would be a model for future street and barricade fighting.

The *NRZ*, unlike any other paper in Germany, gave wholehearted support to the uprising. While almost every other paper, including even those of the left democrats, applauded the defeat of the Parisian "mob" and "anarchy" and the restoration of order, Marx wrote that the "momentary triumph of brute force [over the workers of Paris] has been purchased with the destruction of all the delusions and illusions of the February revolution, the dissolution of the entire moderate republican party and the division of the French nation into two nations, the nation of owners and the nation of workers."[48] The June Revolution had revealed the fundamental cleavage in French society, which from now on could not be hidden—the struggle between labor and capital. For Germany's liberal bourgeoisie, even its republican wing, such an assessment of the outcome in France struck too close to home. For those among their ranks who still owned shares in the *NRZ*, it confirmed their worst fears about how the Marx party viewed Germany's future. Not only did they withdraw their support for the paper but they increasingly agreed with government steps to place a cap on the revolutionary fervor released by the March Revolution in order to avoid, as they rationalized, a Paris outcome.

In Defense of National Self-Determination

The Paris events justified for Marx and Engels the attention they gave to international issues in the *NRZ*. Engels had written in the *Principles of Communism*—more explicitly than in the *Manifesto*—that the communist revolution would "not be a national revolution alone." The revolutionary process was intertwined, especially in Europe. This was why Engels, as noted earlier, tried unsuccessfully to translate the *Manifesto* into English upon his return to Germany. Marx, also, had argued only a few months earlier that the outcome of the struggle in Paris, of which February was only its "superficial beginning," would be decisive for the rest of Europe. Thus, in addition to a domestic line the *NRZ* had a definite foreign policy, as Engels explained many years later: "[T]o support every revolutionary people, and to call for a general war of revolutionary Europe against the mighty bulwark of European reaction—Russia." Under Czar Nicholas I, Russia not only epitomized the ancien régime but had the will and military capacity to roll back the democratic revolutionary process unleashed at the beginning of 1848. Thus, the furtherance of that process was inextricably linked to Russia's military defeat.

A related issue was the self-determination of oppressed nationalities, particularly those subjugated by the autocracies of Russia, Prussia, and Austria. The continuation and deepening of the revolutionary process was also linked to independence for such peoples. Hence, the *NRZ* roundly castigated the democrats of all stripes in the Prussian and Frankfurt Assemblies for supporting as well as escalating Prussian and Austrian imperial policies that oppressed the Poles, Northern Italians, and Czechs. The Polish situation was of particular importance, as Engels explained to his *NRZ* readers in late August: "So long . . . as we help to subjugate Poland, so long as we keep part of Poland fettered to Germany, we shall remain fettered to Russia and to the Russian policy, and shall be unable to eradicate patriarchal feudal absolutism in Germany. The creation of a democratic Poland is a primary condition for the creation of a democratic Germany."[49]

German participation in the suppression of the Czechs, as well as the Poles, was also an obstacle to the German democratic revolution. Referring to the use of German troops in putting down the popular uprising in Prague in mid-June, Engels vented his anger in words remarkably similar to ones that Lenin would use a half-century later to describe the Bolshevik policy on self-determination for nations oppressed by Russian imperialism. "A revolutionised Germany ought to have renounced her entire past, especially as far as the neighbouring nations are concerned. Together with her own freedom, she should have proclaimed the freedom of the nations hitherto suppressed by her."[50]

In another article and in more positive terms, Engels elaborated on this theme, which warrants reproduction in full. It is the first example in the Marxist arsenal of a political approach to the problem of patriotism and national chauvinism from the perspective of a proletarian foreign policy. Engels told his readers that in spite of Germany's infamous foreign policy record,

> Things are indeed beginning to look brighter. The lies and misrepresentations which the old government organs have been so busy spreading about Poland and Italy, the attempts at stirring up enmity artificially, the turgid phrases proclaiming that German honour or German power is at stake—all these formulas have lost their magic power. The official patriotism is effective only when these patriotic postures conceal material interests, only among a section of the big bourgeoisie whose business depends on this official patriotism. The reactionary party knows this and makes use of it. But the great mass of the German middle class and the working class understand or feel that the freedom of the neighbouring nations is the guarantee of their own freedom. Is Austria's war against Italy's independence or Prussia's war against the restoration of Poland popular, or on the contrary do they not destroy the last illusions about such "patriotic" crusades? However, neither this understanding nor this feeling is sufficient. If Germany's blood and money are no longer to be squandered, to her own detriment, in suppressing other nations, then we must achieve a really popular government, and the old edifice must be razed to the ground. Only then can an international policy of democracy take the place of the sanguinary, cowardly policy of the old, revived system. How can a democratic foreign policy be carried through while democracy at home is stifled? Mean while, everything possible must be done to prepare the way for the democratic system on this side and the other side of the Alps [i.e., Italy].[51]

Then, very consciously, Engels informed his readers about the attitude of the Italian democratic movement toward "the German people." He provided documentation to make his point, including a statement from the editors of a fraternal publication of the *NRZ* in Florence: "'[W]e whole-heartedly assure you that all Italians know who really violates and attacks their liberty; they know that their most deadly enemy is not the strong and magnanimous German people, but rather their unjust, despotic, and cruel government; we assure you that every true Italian longs for the moment when he will be free to shake hands with his German brother, who, once his inalienable rights are established, will be able to defend them, to respect them himself and to secure the respect of all his brothers for them.'"

Contrary, once again, to the oft-repeated claim that Marx and Engels ignored or underestimated the issue of nationality, Engels revealed a remarkable understanding of patriotism and, even more important, the political acumen about how it should be addressed. His was an appeal to those who in fact did not benefit from German imperialism. Whether or not "things [were] . . . beginning to look brighter," Engels, as a communist who was engaged in the real movement in order to influence its outcome, was encouraging his readers to make "things . . . brighter."[52]

Resistance to the Counteroffensive

The defeat of the June Revolution was exactly what the forces of reaction in Germany needed. Within weeks the Prussian authorities, as well as other German governments, took steps to roll back the gains of the "partial revolution," just as Marx and Engels had been predicting since the beginning of June when they rushed to launch the *NRZ*. Shortly before the June events the Camphausen government, caught between the rock and hard place of reaction and revolution, fell. Its replacement, the government of David Hansemann, another Rhinelander capitalist, proved quickly to be to the right of its predecessor. In early July it cracked down on the Cologne Workers' Society, arresting Gottschalk and another Society leader, Friedrich Anneke, and forced a number of other activists to flee the country. Because the *NRZ* wrote an article criticizing the arrests Marx and the paper were subjected to government harassment for a number a months. The authorities' charge that Marx defamed the police eventually became a pretext for the Prussian government to turn down his application for citizenship renewal. Later in July, the democratic associations in Stuttgart, Heidelberg, and the entire state of Baden were suppressed. The Hansemann government then introduced legislation to limit freedom of the press and the autonomy and effectiveness of the civic militias. The latter, a kind of citizens' army—composed only of property owners—had been formed by the government in the wake of the March revolution to maintain law and order. In some locales the militias resisted government control and began to be seen as a threat.[53]

In all of these antidemocratic moves by the authorities the *NRZ* distinguished itself by its loud opposition. A few excerpts from Marx and Engels's articles indicates the seriousness that these communists gave to the fight for basic democratic rights. Engels spewed forth his indignation at the suppression of the democratic associations in Stuttgart and Heidelberg in the opening paragraph of his protest. "You [Germans] believe you have made a revolution? Deception! You believe that you have overcome the police state? Deception! You believe that you possess freedom of association, freedom of the press, the arming of the people and other beautiful slogans which were bandied about on the March barricades? Deception, nothing but deception!" He ended by demanding that the authorities responsible for these actions "*be impeached* for violating the fundamental rights of the German people."[54]

Marx was just as indignant in denouncing the press law the Hansemann government introduced to the Prussian Assembly. As he explained to his readers: "From the day when this Bill becomes law, officials may with impunity carry out any arbitrary act, any tyrannical and any unlawful act . . . the press, the only effective control, has been rendered ineffective. On the day when this Bill becomes law, the bureaucracy may celebrate a festival. . . . Indeed, what remains of freedom of the press if that which *deserves* public contempt can no longer be held up to public contempt?"[55] Marx's words recall what he wrote six years earlier about the Prussian bureaucracy and its censorship laws, his first explicit political writing.[56] The *NRZ*'s denunciation of the proposed legislation to limit the civic militias is also instructive because Marx elaborated on the problem of the Prussian bureaucracy. Under the guise of protecting the constitution, the proposed legislation would create a series of regulations that in fact made the militias subservient to the bureaucracy and thus ineffective in protecting the constitution from the authorities. Constitutionalism and basic civil liberties, he argued, would now become subject to the bureaucracy; the censorship proposals were another example. "Prussian acumen has found out that every new constitutional institution offers the most interesting opportunity for new penal laws, new rules, new punishments, new supervision, new chicanery and new bureaucracy." The Prussian example revealed, therefore, that the existence of a constitution was no guarantee of democracy. Then, to make the links between foreign and domestic policy, he wrote: "The *Prussian reorganisation of Poland* [i.e., the perpetuation of Poland's partition] is followed by the *Prussian reorganisation of the civic militia!*"[57] Thus, to curtail the bureaucracy at home it had to be curtailed abroad—an insight that applies as much, if not more, to twentieth-century politics as it did to nineteenth-century Prussia.

As the foregoing examples suggest, Marx and Engels treated democratic rights and state processes from the perspective of the interests of the proletariat and its allies in the people's alliance—that is, what impact might the absence or presence of particular laws and procedures have on their ability to take state power. That this was their bias, which they did "disdain to conceal"—to employ the language of the *Manifesto*—does not in the least mean, as many a Marxologist has claimed, that they ignored democracy and its institutions. Any serious reading of the *NRZ* during its eleven months of existence would dispel such a notion. With a readership of six thousand, "one of the largest and most passionately read newspapers in Germany,"[58] the *NRZ* editors could rightly claim to be the foremost advocates of democracy in all of Germany.

TOWARD THE PEOPLE'S ALLIANCE

In spite, or perhaps because, of the regime's moves to cut off the democratic space, the Marx-Engels team stepped up its efforts to forge the people's alliance between the proletariat, the urban petit bourgeoisie and the small peasantry. The Prussian authorities unwittingly aided this process in two ways. First, by arresting Gottschalk they made it easier for the *NRZ* tendency to get a hearing for its perspective in the Workers' Society on the role of the proletariat in Germany's revolution. With Gottschalk and Anneke in jail, the former CL central authority leaders Moll and Schapper were elected, respectively, president and vice president of the Society. By September, the Society's newspaper began, as a result of their input, to reflect the views of the *NRZ*. They were able to deepen the political and educational work they had earlier promoted when Gottschalk was around, particularly the circulation and discussion of the *Demands*. Educational work was necessary, Schapper explained, "so that the coming revolution would represent 'an intellectual victory as well as a physical one.'"[59] Issues raised in the *Manifesto* and other writings of Marx and Engels also became topics for discussion such as the benefits of machinery in production and the organization of labor. Engels gave the final talk in the series on the latter topic at the beginning of September. Given that almost eight thousand members belonged to the Society, Moll and Schapper advocated its reorganization into smaller units—with less of a guild and craft orientation—in order to have more rank and file input into the educational activities.

A particularly significant topic of discussion that Schapper and Moll introduced was the "agrarian question" as part of the larger topic of the organization of labor. "The peasants were as much involved as the worker in the city, since there was also a 'proletariat' on the land. Fallow land should be turned over to this agricultural 'proletariat' and state domains should be administered for the benefit of society."[60] The *Demands*, particularly numbers six through nine, were the basis of Schapper and Moll's proposals. As further evidence that the *NRZ* was indeed the organizational center for the communist tendency, the paper began to take up in increasing detail the agrarian or peasant question.

The very first article, written by Engels on the eve of the June Revolution, focused on what would be the major issue in the *NRZ* approach to this topic. As spelled out by the sixth of the seventeen *Demands*: "All feudal dues, exactions, corvées, tithes, etc., which have hitherto pressed upon the rural population, shall be abolished without compensation." Within this framework Marx severely criticized a bill introduced by the Hansemann government that only pretended to obliterate the last remaining feudal dues in Prussia. The inadequacy of the bill went to the very heart of the character of the March Revolution. "It is the most striking proof that the German revolution of 1848 is merely a *parody of the French revolution of 1789*" in which the feudal obligation of the peasantry was eliminated within three weeks. "The French bourgeoisie of 1789 never left its allies, the peasants, in the lurch. It knew that the abolition of feudalism in the countryside and the creation of a free, landowning peasant class was the basis of its rule. The German bourgeoisie of 1848 unhesitatingly betrays the peasants, who are its *natural allies*, flesh of its own flesh, and without whom it cannot stand up to the aristocracy. . . . [S]uch is the result of the German revolution of 1848. That is much ado about nothing."[61] The acid test for the German bourgeoisie, therefore, was its willingness and capacity to end feudal property relations in the countryside. Four months after the March Revolution it had yet to measure up to its cohorts in France six decades earlier.

In posing the agrarian question within the Workers' Society and educating its readership about the continuing reality of feudal relations in the rural areas, the *NRZ* tendency was seeking to make the people's alliance a reality. What was required was the actual participation of the peasantry. To this end the Workers' Society sent a delegation at the end of August to Worringen, a few miles north of Cologne. After fruitful discussions with the peasants, a branch of the Society of about forty members was established.[62] This was the first concrete step of the Marx party in forging an alliance between workers and peasants. Within a few weeks it would be tested in battle.

The second unwitting assistance from the authorities to the Marx-Engels team resulted from their crackdown on the democratic associations. Precisely because the *NRZ* party had been the unique voice that warned about the impending antidemocratic direction of the government, its credibility was enhanced when the crackdown began. Also, just as Moll and Schapper stepped up their activity within the Workers' Society, Marx, Engels, and Wolff did the same within the Democratic Association. They spearheaded the convening of a congress of Rhineland democratic associations in mid-August—seventeen organizations were represented—out of which a provincial executive committee was formed that included Marx. They were also successful in getting agreement at the congress in organizing branches of the movement among the peasantry, although the regular Democratic Association proved to be less active than the Workers' Society in actually realizing this goal. Finally, the congress "specifically recommended the *Neue Rheinische Zeitung* by name as an *Organ of Democracy*."[63]

In addition to the proletariat and the peasantry, Marx and Engels made a conscious effort to reach out to the urban petit bourgeoisie, the third component of the people's alliance. To this end Marx participated in the Cologne Society of Workers and Employers, an association composed mainly of small shopkeepers and the self-employed. It was never as viable and active as the Workers' Society and the Democratic Association, however. That it had an overlapping membership with the other two bodies, particularly the latter, meant, nevertheless, that the urban petit bourgeoisie was well represented in the democratic movement and the alliance that the *NRZ* tendency sought to construct.

The influence of the Marx party in the democratic movement was reflected in the opportunity Marx was given to refute anew the nostrums of Wilhelm Weitling who, like a bad penny, had recently turned up in Cologne. Prior to his rebuttal Marx distributed copies of the *Manifesto* to Association members. Weitling had argued, as had Gottschalk, that a socialist revolution, rather than a bourgeois democratic revolution, was on Germany's agenda and that a proletarian "dictatorship" was necessary for this to be realized. According to the minutes from the meeting Marx replied as follows: "The dictatorship which Weitling proposed as the most desirable constitutional form is . . . regarded by Marx as impractical and quite unfeasible, since power cannot be attained by a single class; the intention to carry on a dictatorship in accordance with a system devised by a single brain, deserves to be called nonsensical. On the contrary, the governing power, just as the Provisional Government in Paris, must consist of the most heterogeneous elements, which by means of an exchange of views have to agree on the most appropriate mode of administration."[64] Schapper refuted Weitling's ideas along similar lines in the Workers' Society.

While Marx's remarks—as understood by whoever took minutes for the meeting—were consistent with his position on the people's alliance, and thus fundamentally not new, they provide the first glimpse of his vision of the new government in the aftermath of a revolutionary overthrow in settings such as Germany as well as France—where either the bourgeois or socialist revolution was respectively on the agenda. In either situation the first government was likely to be composed of forces from different classes who would have to find a modus operandi. Only experience, the Paris Commune in particular, would make it possible for this most prescient glimpse to be flushed out.

By the end of the summer the *NRZ* party was well placed, in Cologne at least, among the forces it considered essential to a successful revolutionary transformation of Germany. Just as he had done in Brussels on the eve of the 1848 upheavals, Marx, as head of the party, now wore the hats of the three organizations that represented these forces. While Germany's revolution could not be consummated in Cologne alone, it was possible that the Rhineland capitol would provide the spark for the rest of the country. By the middle of September 1848 it began to appear that indeed Cologne might play such a role. The Marx party would be subjected to its most severe test yet.

CHAPTER FOUR

The End of the Revolutionary Upsurge and the Lessons of Struggle

> History presents no more shameful and pitiful spectacle than that of the German bourgeoisie.
>
> —Marx, from the NRZ
>
> While the professors were evolving the theory of history, history ran its stormy course without bothering about the professorial history.
>
> —Marx, from the NRZ
>
> Our paper continues to stand by the principle of émeute [insurrection].
>
> —Marx to Engels
>
> Herr Marx (!) is becoming increasingly more audacious. . . . He takes the liberty . . . in his increasingly popular paper . . . to promote even greater feelings of discontent and indirectly calling upon the people to revolt.
>
> —Cologne Military Commander
>
> [The German workers must not be] misled for a single moment by the hypocritical phrases of the democratic party into refraining from the independent organisation of the party of the proletariat. Their battle cry must be: The Revolution in Permanence.
>
> —Marx and Engels, Address of 1850

The question that had politicized the young Marx and Engels, as well as millions of other Germans of their generation—how would democracy come to their land and who or what class would lead the way—was no longer an abstract query after March 18, 1848. By the end of the summer the question took its most concrete form yet. Marx and Engels had concluded three years earlier that real majority rule could only be realized if class society was eliminated, and that only the proletariat had an interest in and was capable of carrying out such a transformation. Yet they recognized that the best terrain on which to wage a fight against class society was one where a republic and basic democratic rights existed, that is, bourgeois democracy. Would, however, the German bourgeoisie, as its counterparts in Britain and France had done earlier, actually lead a bourgeois democratic revolution by overthrowing monarchial feudal rule? In the *Manifesto* and other writings they had suggested that this was an open question. Only the real movement would provide an answer to this historic query. While the behavior of the bourgeoisie in the first five months of the revolution hinted strongly at what that might be, only after September would it be known with certainty.

The counterrevolutionary forces in Germany had clearly been emboldened by the slaughter in Paris a few months earlier. The *NRZ* tendency, under Marx's leadership, however, was convinced that it was still possible to push the revolution forward. Hence, the decision to root its members in the leadership of the democratic movement of Cologne—the city that was expected to have a key role in consummating the bourgeois revolution. Indeed, by the end of the summer, Cologne flared up. From September to November the Rhineland capital was on the center stage of the German revolution with the Marx party at the helm. As the crisis deepened the party's workload increased. In addition to vital editorial responsibilities, Marx and the *NRZ* group were obligated to spend more time at mass meetings, demonstrations, and eventually on the barricades. By December the counterrevolution had triumphed in Prussia if not in its Rhineland province. By June of the following year it had triumphed in all of Germany. It was not until the summer of 1850 that Marx and Engels concluded that the revolutionary wave that began in Paris in February 1848 had come to a definitive end. What remained for them to do as communists— the subject of the second part of this chapter—was to draw a balance sheet of the momentous events, to distill and tease out the lessons of the real movement.

FROM REVOLUTION TO COUNTERREVOLUTION

A series of events at the beginning of September provoked a major crisis for the government in Berlin. Basically, the crown and its feudal and bureaucratic allies made moves in both domestic and foreign affairs that challenged the authority of the elected assemblies in Berlin and Frankfurt.[1] In anticipation of an impending showdown with the revolution, the counterrevolution took the initiative. In so doing it made it increasingly difficult for the liberal bourgeois Hansemann government to pretend, as had also been true with its predecessor, the Camphausen government, to be a mediator between both forces. As the fence upon which it was perched became increasingly razor thin it failed its balancing act and was eventually replaced in October by a more conservative government. In late June the *NRZ* had predicted that the policy of the Camphausen and Hansemann governments in providing a liberal bourgeois cover for the counterrevolution would only embolden the latter to "shake off this irksome mask" and establish a *Government of the Prince of Prussia,* that is, a government that made no pretense of its loyalty to the crown. The new government was a major step in this direction.

For a "Revolutionary Dictatorship"

As this crisis was unfolding Marx was in Berlin and Vienna in an effort to raise funds for the financially strapped *NRZ*—which Engels edited in his absence—and to strengthen ties with the democratic and workers' movements in both places. Immediately upon his return to Cologne Marx used the newspaper to agitate for defense of the revolution. At that moment defense meant support for the Assembly in Prussia against the crown and its allies. "Which of the two sides will win depends on the attitude of the people, especially that of the democratic party. It is up to the democrats to choose."[2] A day later Marx explained to his readers what had to be done to save the revolution.

> Every provisional political set-up following a revolution requires a dictatorship, and an energetic dictatorship at that. From the very beginning we blamed Camphausen for not having acted in a dictatorial manner, for not having immediately smashed up and removed the remains of the old institutions. While thus Herr Camphausen indulged in constitutional dreaming, the defeated party strengthened its positions within the bureaucracy and in the army, and occasionally even risked an open fight. The Assembly was convened for the purpose of agreeing on the terms of the Constitution. It existed as an equal party alongside the Crown. Two equal powers in a provisional situation! . . . [I]t was this very division of powers in a provisional situation that was bound to lead to conflicts. The Crown served as a cover for the counter-revolutionary aristocratic, military and bureaucratic camarilla. The bourgeoisie stood behind the majority of the Assembly. The Government tried to mediate. Too weak to act resolutely on behalf of the bourgeoisie and the peasants and overthrow the power of the nobility, the bureaucracy and the army chiefs at one blow, too unskilled to avoid always harming the bourgeoisie by its financial measures, the Government merely succeeded in compromising itself in the eyes of all the parties and bringing about the very clash it sought to avoid.[3]

Marx's assessment of the situation is most revealing. First, with regard to his advocacy of a "dictatorship" no more should be read into this than what is stated here. That is, in order to advance the democratic revolution "energetic" steps should have been taken to "smash" the ancien régime as quickly as possible. The longer this was put off the more would reaction be emboldened. To make clear whose interests he had in mind in urging the dictatorship, Marx immediately added that "in any unconstituted state of affairs it is solely the *salut public*, the public welfare, and not this or that principle that is the decisive factor." It was in this sense that Marx and Engels, as we'll see later, employed on occasion their often misrepresented "dictatorship of the proletariat."[4]

Second, the "principle" that Marx argued should have been subordinated to the interests of the "public welfare" was what he termed "the Montesquieu-[Jean Louis] Delolme worm-eaten theory of division of powers." To advocate the separation of powers between the crown and the Assembly in the aftermath of the March Revolution was to stifle the revolution, to place obstacles in the way of extending democracy.[5] The import of Marx's comments is that they provide more details—beyond the few nuggets he offered in his debate with Weitling in early August—on his thinking about the practical political issues in a revolutionary transition.

Marx summed up the situation in mid-September for his readers. "The inevitable conflict between two powers [the Assembly and the crown] having equal rights in a provisional situation has broken out." He then offered them advice. "The side that has the greater courage and consistency will win." A few days later Engels implored the German "Left" to find the courage to face up to the "unavoidable battles . . . which we hope will take us a little further and will at least free Germany from the traditional fetters of her past."

In Cologne the *NRZ* group took to heart the advice of Marx and Engels. Through their leadership in the democratic and workers' movements they helped organize protests against the machinations of the government and the vacillation of the assemblies in Berlin and Frankfurt. "Disdain[ing] to conceal their views and aims"—to employ again the language of the *Manifesto*—they began a mass distribution of the seventeen *Demands of the Communist Party in Germany*. "In the ensuing revolutionary agitation in Cologne, the Communists were evident everywhere. They appeared to be in command, almost like a party, or at least an overwhelming presence. Newspapers commented on the fact that the editorial staff of the [*NRZ*] occupied the public platform, gave many speeches, and initiated motions."[6]

Following a brutal provocation by Prussian troops stationed in the town, the *NRZ* group, which was active within the civic militia, initiated the formation of a special Committee of Public Safety—the inspiration of the French Revolution, no doubt—"a *committee* elected directly and publicly by the people . . . which undertakes the task of representing the interests of the part of the population not represented in the legally instituted authorities" and "watching over the preservation of the people's rights" against further Prussian actions.[7] Because Marx, Engels, and other *NRZ* people were active on the committee it was red baited by the liberal and right-wing press as "the first step towards revolution . . . the red republic [was] on the verge of being proclaimed . . ."

The political high point of Marx and Engels's activities in this period was their collaboration with the Workers' Society in mobilizing peasant opposition to the government and the counterrevolution. Throughout the crisis Engels in particular wrote constantly on the potential and need for peasant mobilizations in conjunction with the other democratic forces. "The peasant war begun this spring will not come to an end until its goal, the liberation of the peasants from feudalism, has been achieved."[8] As part of this effort, two close associates of Marx and Engels in the Workers' Society began publishing a new paper, *Neue Kölnische Zeitung für Bürger, Bauern und Soldaten* (New Cologne Newspaper for Townsmen, Peasants and Soldiers) to popularize the views of the *NRZ* among the peasantry. It "was to follow a 'social-democratic' slant, and would represent the interests of the 'working people, whether in the city or on the land, whether in civilian clothes or in a soldier's uniform.'"[9] The Marx party, in other words, was making its most concerted effort yet to realize the "people's alliance" it had begun to call for a year earlier.

Its greatest success, in the Rhineland at least, came on September 17 with the convening—in spite of police harassment—of a massive meeting of more than eight thousand near Worringen, ten miles north of Cologne. Schapper, who was elected to preside over the meeting—Engels was elected as secretary—proposed a unanimously adopted resolution that declared the meeting "in favor of a 'republic, and specifically the democratic-social, the *Red Republic*.'" Other adopted resolutions expressed support for the Committee of Public Safety and recognized the *NRZ* as the paper of the democratic party. Attended by peasants, workers, and the urban petit bourgeoisie from throughout the region, the Worringen meeting was the hitherto theoretical concept of the people's alliance in flesh and bones.

The *NRZ* party was under no illusion that Worringen and other successful mass meetings meant that a popular uprising was on the immediate agenda in Cologne. Marx, Engels, Moll, and other communists cautioned against such precipitate action. Applying the tactic of revolutionary restraint, Moll said before a Workers' Society meeting "that it was still necessary to 'restrict the battle to the mouth and the pen.' The Party was growing constantly. Many people, especially those on the land, were waiting for someone to bring them the 'humanist doctrines of democracy and socialism.' It was necessary to gain the support of the peasants . . . and to overcome the resistance of the army. Even the soldiers had a human heart and a sound mind. They were not robber gangs without a will of their own. . . .'"[10] As they also explained, success in Cologne depended on similar uprisings in Germany and elsewhere.

But the reality elsewhere was one of defeats—including a short-lived insurrection in Frankfurt—and not victories for the revolutionary forces. The bourgeoisie's fear of the proletariat, as Engels explained to *NRZ* readers, and the fact that "the people . . . are unorganised and poorly armed . . ." accounted for that reality. The very real possibility, as he saw it, of another and even more radical upsurge in France, this time "under the red flag," boded well for Germany's revolution.

The counterrevolution also understood that unless it seized the initiative Engels's hopes might very well be realized. Thus, in order to put an end to the growing radicalization within Cologne—Worringen was as instructive to the counterrevolution as it was to Marx and Engels—the Prussian government carried out a preemptive strike by issuing arrest orders the weekend of September 23 for most of the *NRZ* party, including Engels, and other democratic party leaders "on the charge of 'conspiracy aimed at revolution.'" Engels and a few others escaped the dragnet by fleeing the city and eventually the country.

Marx, whose own legal situation had been precarious since July, due in part to the government's defamation of character charge against him, provided leadership to the communist tendency in the September crisis from behind the scenes and therefore was able to avoid the "conspiracy" charges. When barricades began going up to protest the arrests of the democratic party leaders, Marx surfaced to lead the call for revolutionary restraint—persuading the rebellious forces, about two thousand in number, that an uprising in Cologne alone would be futile since "no large issue would drive the entire people into combat. . . ."[11] Marx had accurately assessed the larger reality of the revolution in Germany at that time. Encouraged by their success in stifling the revolutionary opposition in Frankfurt and Berlin, the Prussian authorities closed off further political space in Cologne by declaring martial law, "the suspension of all societies organized for political and social purposes, as well as the listed democratic and workers' newspapers."[12]

Marx "holds the *fort*"

Once martial law was lifted the *NRZ* was able to resume publishing on October 12. But with most of the editorial staff on the run, including Engels, Marx was left almost alone, as he wrote to Engels in November, "to hold the *fort* and to preserve the political position as all cost."[13] Even Hammen, certainly no partisan of Marx, writes that "the last three months of 1848 stand out as the heroic period for Marx."

While struggling to "hold the *"fort,"* that is, maintaining the *NRZ*, Marx was able to "preserve the political position" by taking on more organizational responsibilities. With Schapper in jail and Moll on the run, Marx was asked by the Workers' Society to become its president in mid-October—an acknowledgment of his leadership. In spite of a precarious legal situation and editorial obligations with the newspaper, "he was ready," as the minutes stated, "provisionally until Dr. Gottschalk was set free [in December], to accede to the desire of the workers."[14] Under his leadership the Society stepped up its work in the rural areas around Cologne by organizing new branches among the peasantry and holding another large rally at Worringen. It also regularized internal educational activity, which included discussions on the *Demands of the Communist Party*. Schapper, who was released from jail in mid-November, maintained this orientation when he resumed his activism in the Society, thus relieving Marx of many organizational obligations.

Although Marx continued to be active in the Democratic Association, it was clear at this time that he was beginning to prioritize the Workers' Society. An indication of what was to come was the decision of the Society, which he no doubt motivated, to send to the upcoming nationwide Democratic Congress in late October in Berlin its own representative "separately [from] the Democratic Association" of Cologne. The delegate was instructed to "attempt to persuade the . . . Congress to adopt some of the 'Demands of the Communist Party in Germany.'" While it is not clear why Marx supported a separate delegate it is possible that one of the lessons for him of the September crisis was that the Workers' Society was a more reliable ally in combat than the Democratic Association; the latter, unlike the former, had vacillated on support for the Committee for Public Safety. Precisely because of the educational work within the Workers' Society around the *Demands* and the fact that the organization actively distributed copies of them among the peasantry of the area, a representative from that body could be expected to make a more convincing case for their adoption at the Berlin Congress.

Marx and Engels's hope since the June days that another revolutionary uprising in France or elsewhere would be the needed shot in the arm for the German revolution appeared to materialize with the revolutionary outbreak in Vienna in early October. The political situation in Austria was not unlike that in Germany. A partial revolution in March resulted in an unstable division of power between the feudal reaction, which the Habsburg monarchy provided a cover for, and the constituent assembly or Imperial Diet, based on the revolution. And like its counterpart in Prussia the counterrevolution—headed by the government and thus in this aspect unlike Prussia—was emboldened by the outcome of the June days in Paris and perched to take the initiative. In this context Marx visited Vienna at the end of August and intervened in the debate within the democratic movement about how to proceed, specifically how to get rid of the counterrevolutionary government.

In its report on the debate at a meeting of the Vienna Democratic Association a newspaper hostile to the revolution wrote that "an *academic from abroad* really had the audacity to say" that rather than looking to either the Imperial Diet or Emperor to resolve the situation "*We must appeal to the people and must try to influence it employing every possible means. We must raise a storm against the Government, and must work towards this end in every possible way, even using Mephistophelian means, We must use the press, posters and discussions to achieve this.*"[15] In addition to having the "audacity" to make such proposals to the democratic movement in Vienna, Marx also sought to influence the workers' movement in the city with his program. Another paper reported that he "delivered a fairly long lecture on wage labour and capital" at a meeting of the Workers' Association at the beginning of September, in which he said that "the assertion that the interests of the capitalist and of the wage labourer are identical is false."[16] This talk was no doubt based on the lectures he had prepared in Brussels at the end of 1847 in his continuing effort to instill class consciousness in the working class.

About a month after Marx's visit to Vienna the revolution in Austria faced a final showdown. Marx's intervention a month earlier notwithstanding, the democratic forces in Vienna were not able to mobilize enough of "the people" throughout Austria to overcome the military might of the government. By the end of October the revolution in Austria had effectively come to an end. Just as Vienna had been a prelude to the March revolution that began in Berlin the October defeat would soon pave the way for the success of the counterrevolution in Prussia.

Thus, Marx's analysis of the defeat in Vienna anticipated by a month and a half his obituary for Prussia's revolution. He emphatically charged the German bourgeoisie—Vienna was the capital of the German part of the Austrian empire—with responsibility for the defeat. Before the final outcome was known, he wrote that ever since the June days in Paris *NRZ* readers should not have been surprised by the "baseness of the **bourgeoisie** [in original]." Paris struck fear of the proletariat in the hearts of Germany's bourgeoisie and thus predisposed it to "*hamper*" the course of Germany's bourgeois revolution. In exchange for the right to engage in commerce without interference from the monarchial feudal state, the German bourgeoisie, unlike its counterparts in France and England, was prepared to compromise the revolution, that is, not fight to create a unified German democratic republic. "History presents no more *shameful and pitiful spectacle* than that of the German bourgeoisie."[17] The lesson for the democratic forces was that "we . . . find ourselves called upon to break off any negotiation with the *bourgeoisie*. . . . It would . . . *convince* us that no peace with the *bourgeoisie* is possible, not even for the period of transition, and that the people must remain indifferent in the battles between the bourgeoisie and the Government and must wait for their victories or defeats in order to exploit them."[18] A few days later he wrote that the lesson of the counterrevolutionary bloodbaths of Paris in June and Vienna in October was "that there is only *one means* by which the murderous death agonies of the old society and the bloody birth throes of the new society can be *shortened,* simplified and concentrated—and that is by *revolutionary terror.*"[19]

Marx's assessment and policy recommendations represent the beginning of what was the most important strategic shift for the Marx party in the course of the 1848–49 revolutions. Until now, the question about the behavior of the German bourgeoisie in the fight for bourgeois democracy had been an open one that only the real movement could answer. The original version of the *Manifesto* stated that in Germany communists would "fight with the bourgeoisie *as long as* it acts in a revolutionary way, against the absolute monarchy, the feudal squirearchy, and the petty bourgeoisie [emphasis added]."[20] Vienna made clear, however, unlike any other event so far, that the German bourgeoisie was not prepared to act "in a revolutionary way." The lesson, therefore, was that communists and presumably "the people" also should be "indifferent" to the struggles of the bourgeoisie with the ancien régime. Such struggles, however real, were between allies who were on the same side of the barricades in opposition to the democratic forces. This conclusion was, thus, the initial formulation of an answer to the historic query, which would be elaborated on in coming months and years.

The Campaign for "Active Resistance"

The events in Vienna reverberated in Germany. The uprising provoked a debate within the democratic movement about how best to respond. Should aid be sent to the revolutionaries in the Austrian capital and if so what kind? Armed legions of volunteers? Marx and his old foe Arnold Ruge found themselves once again on different sides of the political divide. The latter, currently a member of the Prussian Assembly, espoused the view, which was adopted by the second All-German Democratic Congress meeting in Berlin at the height of the crisis in Vienna, that the German people should demand that their governments, including the one in Prussia, should "save . . . the cause of freedom in Vienna." Aside from lacking specificity, such a demand, Marx countered, also miseducated the people by encouraging them to look to their counterrevolutionary governments as their "saviors of freedom." The only realistic way to aid the Viennese revolution was "by defeating the counter-revolution at home."[21] Marx's position was, of course, consistent with his long-held view that only the proletariat could liberate itself and not, therefore, governments that represented alien class forces.

In the meantime mass protests erupted in the streets of Berlin to demand that the Prussian Assembly support the Vienna revolution. The left wing of the Democratic Congress—meeting in Berlin at a most opportune time—played a key role in organizing the protests; the same faction had been successful in the aforementioned effort of Marx to get the Congress to adopt some of the *Demands of the Communist Party.* The near-insurrectionary situation in Berlin led to a new governmental crisis. The Hohenzollern monarch, Frederick IV, inspired no doubt by the triumph of the Habsburgs in Vienna, unilaterally dismissed the government and replaced it with one totally subservient to the counterrevolutionary forces. The Assembly refused to recognize the King's government—what Marx derisively called "passive resistance"—which resulted in a month-long standoff between it and the crown, the final showdown between the reaction and the revolution in most of Prussia.

While appearing to be complicated, the situation was actually "very simple," as Marx explained to *NRZ* readers.

> When . . . two sovereign powers are no longer able to agree or do not want to agree, they become two hostile sovereign powers. The *King* has the *right* to throw down the gauntlet to the Assembly, the *Assembly* has the *right* to throw down the gauntlet to the King. The *greater right* is on the side of the *greater might*. Might is tested in *struggle*. The test of the struggle is *victory*. Each of the two powers can prove that it is right only by its *victory*, that it is wrong only by its *defeat*.[22]

The German revolution, as Marx correctly understood, had reached the stage that today would be called "throw down time." In such a situation "passive resistance" was inadequate.

Beginning on November 12, Marx, through the pages of the *NRZ*, launched a campaign of "active resistance." Picking up on a suggestion that had been floated in the Assembly, the *NRZ* declared in bold print that in view of the Assembly's just-reached decision to find the new government "guilty of high treason" for having decreed that the Assembly was adjourned and that the civic guards had to disarm, *"the obligation to pay taxes automatically ceases . . . to pay taxes is now tantamount to high treason and refusal to pay taxes is the primary duty of the citizen."*[23] (Bold in original.) Precisely because the crown and its government's actions had aroused the indignation of democrats of all stripes, the *NRZ*'s tax refusal campaign struck a responsive cord throughout the country.

The newspaper's tone was now agitational. Every day for a month the battle cry, "No More Taxes!!!," was the featured headline. Reports of growing support for the campaign from around the country were published daily. "Marx spared no expense to bring out the latest and greatest coverage of the news. Second editions were frequent, alternating with or augmented by supplementary editions, extra-supplements and extraordinary supplements [which could be used as posters], depending of the gravity of the hour. Marx made every effort to increase the circulation of the paper."[24] As an officer of the Rhineland Democratic Association Marx was able to mobilize its ranks on behalf of the campaign; all of its proclamations were published in the *NRZ*. Particular emphasis was placed on mobilizing support in the rural areas. "Berlin . . . and the provincial capitals, can only be safeguarded through the revolutionary energy of the countryside."[25] The effort received a big boost when the Prussian Assembly, three days after the *NRZ* openly advocated nonpayment of taxes, voted unanimously in favor of the appeal. According to Hammen, close associates of Marx in the Assembly led this effort.[26]

Given the stakes in the situation, Marx's strategy was to push the antitaxation sentiment as far to the left as possible. "*The people must put an end to the halfway measures of* [the] *March* [revolution], *or the Crown will put an end to them.*" When the governor of the Rhineland province issued a warning against the nonpayment of taxes, Marx took the offensive. Any official who challenged the authority of the Assembly and backed the government should be "1. *dismissed from office, 2. guilty of high treason* and provisional *committees of public safety* appointed in their place. . . . Where counter-revolutionary authorities seek forcibly to frustrate the formation and official activity of these committees of public safety, *force must be opposed by every kind of force. Passive* resistance must have *active resistance* as its basis. *Otherwise it will resemble the vain struggle of a calf against its slaughter.* "

To prevent a "slaughter" Marx and the other Democratic Association leaders, including Schapper, issued an "Appeal" to organize a "people's militia . . . everywhere. The cost of weapons and ammunition for impecunious citizens is to be defrayed by the community or by voluntary contributions." This last proviso was to ensure that wealth would not be an obstacle to participation in defense of the revolution. One of the weaknesses, in Marx's opinion, of the now-disbanded civic militia in the town was that uniforms and weapons had to be paid out of the individual participant's pocket, thus discriminating against those who could not afford to so do. The "Appeal" also stated that any local government bodies that did not support the Prussian Assembly "should be elected afresh by a universal vote."[27] On the basis of this call, Marx and the other Democratic Association leaders would be charged with "incitement to rebellion" and brought to trial in February.

The *NRZ* group also sought to build an armed contingent through the Workers' Society. Friedrich von Beust, a former military officer who worked closely with Marx in the Society, took steps to organize members of the National Guard (*Landwehr*) throughout Prussia into a "popular revolutionary army" to defend the revolution. In Cologne the Society motivated the formation of numerous armed "Free Corps" of which von Beust was elected overall commander. As increasing numbers of contingents emerged and apparently began to test their strength against the government forces, the latter moved decisively to halt this development. Von Beust was forced to flee the city and, thus, effectively ended the creation of a revolutionary army in Cologne.

With Marx playing such a public role in organizing the revolutionary forces in Cologne—whereas in the September crisis he operated from behind the scenes—it was inevitable that the government would attempt to prosecute him. The first attempt came shortly after the mass meeting in Worringen that Marx had helped organize to protest the actions of the government in Berlin. The meeting had launched a massive petition drive—more than seven thousand signatures were collected in two days—and elected a broadly represented "Peoples Committee" of twenty-five, which included Marx, to be the executive committee of a "body operating 'in permanence.'" Given his central role in the mass movement in Cologne and the readiness of large numbers of his supporters to mobilize in his defense, the government was forced to back down. In addition, Marx, who was well versed in the Napoleonic code, which still operated in the Rhineland, skillfully navigated the *NRZ* between legality and illegality in spite of the fact, as he wrote to Engels, that "our paper continues to stand by the principle of *émeute* [insurrection]."[28] Although the party of insurrection, the *NRZ* group, under Marx's leadership, defensively formulated its calls by portraying the government as the provoker of an uprising. But, if necessary, "the Rhine Province will sooner shed its last drop of blood than submit to the rule of the sword."

While there were indeed thousands if not tens of thousands of German workers and peasants who were willing to shed their blood in defense of the March revolution it was just as clear that this was not true for the vast majority of the bourgeoisie, the middle classes, and much of the self-proclaimed democratic party. The clearest sign of this was the vote of the Frankfurt Assembly on November 22 by almost two to one in opposition to the tax-refusal campaign. Rather than challenge the government it sought a compromise to solve the crisis. Marx was severe in his rebuke of the "assembly of professors"—in reference to the university professors who made up almost a quarter of the Assembly's members. He was even harsher when another group of academics a few days later declared to the king their opposition to the campaign. Since professors were state employees, their "indescribable fury at the *refusal to pay taxes*" was understandable. "No more taxes—and privileged erudition goes bankrupt." Their "prostitution before royalty" was motivated solely by their desire to protect the "monopoly" they exercised on the "scientific profession." But, "if" the revolution were to triumph, the "people . . . [will] put a speedy end to the whole evil of privileged erudition."[29]

The vote of the Frankfurt Assembly gave the counterrevolution the green light it had been looking for in the month-long standoff. Not able to reach an accommodation with the Prussian legislators, who were still engaged in "passive resistance," the government dismissed the Assembly. And on the same day, December 5, Frederick IV unilaterally imposed his own constitution. While it contained many of the liberal features that the Assembly had proposed, the document made clear in no uncertain terms that ultimate power rested with the monarch. Although the *NRZ* maintained the campaign for the nonpayment of taxes, it had become clear to Marx by December 17—when it discontinued the "No more taxes!!!" headline—that in the absence of any effective opposition to the King's move the counterrevolution had scored a major victory in Prussia if not in all of Germany.

Clarity on the Bourgeoisie

In an assessment made six months earlier of the "big bourgeoisie" as being "all along anti-revolutionary" Marx wrote that "we cannot here go into the question as to why. . . . For the present we merely report the fact."[30] In the aftermath of the victory of the crown and its allies Marx was now prepared to provide an answer in a series of articles published in December, "The Bourgeoisie and the Counter-Revolution." This was the Marx party's first major programmatic statement since the publication of the *Manifesto* and the *Demands*. As the title suggested much of the blame had to be placed at the doorstep of the bourgeoisie.

The essence of Marx's argument was that the antirevolutionary actions of the big bourgeoisie from the March days onward prepared the way for Frederick IV's coup in December. It had been a "fallacy" to think that the "gentlemen of this liberal opposition [i.e., the bourgeoisie in opposition to the absolutist state before

March] . . . betrayed their principles after the March revolution." To the contrary. They were well on the way to working out an accommodation with the crown and its feudal allies that would have allowed them the political and social space for the unimpeded accumulation of capital. Berlin's plebeian masses in March, however, inspired by their cohorts in Paris and Vienna, took matters into their own hands. Their revolution made it possible for the Prussian bourgeoisie to exercise political power—albeit together with the crown and its allies—for the first time. The only problem was that the hitherto powerless masses expected to at least share in the bourgeoisie's newly acquired power through the assemblies, especially the one at Berlin. More than anything it was the bourgeoisie's fear of those masses—particularly in light of the proletariat's assertiveness in France—that made them wary from the outset of their unsolicited deliverers. Germany's bourgeoisie, a late developer in comparison with its cohorts in France and Britain—it "developed so sluggishly, timidly and slowly"—had the misfortune of entering political life at the same time that its archenemy, the proletariat, was also knocking on the door to political freedom.[31] The same political liberties—freedom of association, the press, etc.—that the bourgeoisie needed to further its own material interests in relation to the ancien régime were also required by the proletariat in its daily struggles with its overlords, the bourgeoisie.

The German bourgeoisie looked askance upon the peasantry as well as the proletariat. As Marx and Engels had earlier noted, if the monied class was willing to betray the peasantry—a more natural class ally than the proletariat—then clearly was it incapable of acting in a revolutionary fashion. Thus, it was a mistake to equate Germany's revolution with the two prototypes—England in 1648 and France in 1789—revolutions in which the bourgeoisie led the overthrow of feudal property relations in the countryside. To the extent that the bourgeoisie disowned the March revolution it encouraged the counterrevolution, who wanted to maintain as much as possible its historic privileges. The June revolution in Paris, denounced by the German bourgeoisie and its middle-class allies, emboldened the counterrevolution, who began to sniff out any openings for an attack.

As 1848 began, with the expectation of an upsurge of bourgeois democratic revolutions in Europe, Engels wrote, "[F]ight bravely on, most gracious masters of capital! . . . but do not forget that 'The hangman stands at the door!'"[32] The wider the bourgeoisie opened the door to bourgeois democracy the better position the "hangman," the proletariat, was in to fit the noose around the neck of its erstwhile ally. Little wonder then that the German bourgeoisie vacillated on opening the door to the bourgeois revolution. Their hesitation, however, enabled the forces of feudal reaction, who had all along longed for the good old days of absolutism—particularly, access to the state purse without any obstacles from capital—to finally, on December 5, shut the door that had been partially opened by the March revolution.

There was a lesson in all of this—the long-sought answer to the historic question about how democracy would be instituted in Germany.

> The history of the Prussian bourgeois class, like that of the German bourgeois class in general between March and December, shows that a purely *bourgeois revo-*

lution and the establishment of *bourgeois rule* in the form of a *constitutional monarchy* is impossible in Germany, and that only a feudal absolutist counter-revolution or a *social republican revolution* is possible.[33]

Thus, the alternatives now before Germany were either a return to feudal absolutism or a republican revolution that addressed not only political reforms but as well major social reforms in the interests of the laboring masses—reforms that would go beyond and begin to infringe upon the interests of the bourgeoisie. If the bourgeoisie would not "fight bravely" for democracy then who or what forces would? Marx and Engels had already proposed an answer even before the March revolution—the people's alliance. It was to these forces that they now turned their attention.

Toward the Proletariat and Its Allies

In spite of Frederick IV's coup of December 5, Marx expected a revolutionary resurgence. Just as had been true in March, the larger Europe-wide context was still determinant. As he explained in a New Years Day article to *NRZ* readers, the "liberation of Europe, whether brought about by the struggle of the oppressed nationalities for their independence or by overthrowing feudal absolutism, depends . . . on the successful uprising of the French working class."[34] The latter in turn required a victory over the expected counterrevolutionary moves of England—"the country . . . that takes the whole world within its immense embrace"—and "only a *world war* can overthrow the old England." Thus, the fate of the German revolution was linked to the successful outcome of a world wide revolutionary process that combined national liberation, antifeudal and anticapitalist struggles "waged in Canada as in Italy, in East Indies as in Prussia, in Africa as on the Danube."[35]

While internationalism was not new in the Marx party's strategic arsenal it was given new emphasis in the wake of the December coup. The *NRZ*, the *Organ of Democracy*, began to call itself the "Organ of European Democracy." With the return of Engels in late January—the government dropped the charges against him and other *NRZ* editors stemming from the September crisis—the paper expanded its coverage of revolutionary events elsewhere, especially the Hungarian revolution against Austrian rule. As a "revolution in permanence"—a term that Marx and Engels were employing with more regularity—with a capable leader, Lajos Kossuth, and a "revolutionary organization," the Hungarian uprising offered the most immediate hope for a new upsurge in Europe.[36] With its long-term hopes pinned on France, the *NRZ* group took steps—eventually unsuccessful—to get out a French edition of the *Manifesto*.

Although Marx had written off the bourgeoisie in his seminal article "The Bourgeoisie and the Counter-revolution," a month later he advocated support to them—the last time he would do so. The occasion were the elections, authorized by the recently imposed constitution, at the end of January to the new Prussian Assembly. The question posed by the elections was whether to vote for liberal democrats who would oppose the constitution, or put forward candidates representing the "people's alliance" of workers, peasants, and the urban petit bourgeoisie, or abstain. Marx's view, which was adopted by the Workers' Society with some modifications, was that the "party of the people" was not strong enough to run its own candidates (a position that would undergo self-criticism the next year); it "exists in Germany as yet only in an elementary form."[37] The principled stance, as he argued at the Workers' Society January meeting, was opposition to feudal absolutism, that is, the imposed constitution. "We are certainly the last people to desire the rule of the bourgeoisie. . . . But we say to the workers and the petty bourgeoisie: it is better to suffer in modern bourgeois society, which by its industry creates the material means for the foundation of a new society that will liberate you all. . . ." Thus, it was necessary to "unite with another party [at least that wing of the bourgeoisie] also in opposition, so as not to allow our common enemy, the absolute monarchy, to win."[38]

In spite of the fact that opponents of the constitution won overwhelmingly in the Rhineland, throughout the rest of Prussia proponents, with the backing of the bourgeoisie, were successful. Big capital's support for a document that was objectively against its interests confirmed unequivocally for Marx that the German bourgeoisie was incapable of acting in a revolutionary way. The opposition Rhineland vote, however, which was mobilized by the joint efforts of the Democratic and Workers' Societies of the province, convinced the *NRZ* party that the potential for building the "people's party" was better than ever. In the elections "the petty bourgeoisie, peasants and proletarians ["the specifically *red* class"] emancipated themselves from the big bourgeoisie, the upper nobility and the higher bureaucracy."[39]

About three weeks after the January elections, an opponent newspaper accused the *NRZ* tendency of having been duped by the liberal democrats, whom it supported on the expectation that they would oppose the constitution—an expectation that was quickly unfulfilled. Marx's reply is instructive since it provides perhaps the first glimpse of Marx and Engels's approach to electoral politics. After explaining, just as he had at the aforementioned January meeting of the Workers' Society, why "we put *our* own views into the background" during the elections, he declared that "Now, *after* the elections, we are again asserting our old ruthless point of view in relation not only to the Government, but also to the official opposition."[40] As for the charge of having been duped by the liberal democrats, "It could be foreseen that these gentlemen, in order to be re-elected, would now recognise the imposed Constitution. It is characteristic of the standpoint of these gentlemen that *after* the elections they are disavowing in the democratic clubs what *before* the elections they assented to at meetings of the electors. This petty, crafty liberal slyness was never the diplomacy of revolutionaries."[41]

Thus, the "party of the people," while obligated, owing to the particular setting of mid-nineteenth-century Germany, to ally with the liberal democrats in the elections, should entertain no illusions about the latter and should take political distance from them as soon as the elections are concluded. A year later, to be seen shortly, Marx and Engels would extend this position by calling for complete working-class political independence from liberal democrats, specifically, by running workers' candidates in future elections.

To build the "party of the people," that is, the people's alliance, the *NRZ* team led an effort to reorganize the Workers' Society by eliminating the remaining guild and craft tendencies. There was also a decision to markedly increase educational activities. Like the old German Workers Education Associations that the Communist League directed, members, under the new rules adopted, were expected to take part in the educationals and to provide financial support. Marx and Engels agreed to give lectures every two weeks. The most important of these were an update of the lectures that Marx gave in Brussels at the end of 1847, "Wage-Labor and Capital," which were serialized in the *NRZ* during April. At the heart of these lectures was the thesis of the irreconcilable class interests of labor and capital, which was critical, in view of the growing counterrevolution, for workers to grasp. "We shall try to make our presentation as simple and popular as possible and shall not presuppose even the most elementary notions of political economy. We wish to be understood by the workers." The editorship of the Society's newspaper, which had been in the hands of a Gottschalk sympathizer, was also changed in order to reflect the new direction of the organization. Steps were taken to create, with the assistance of Stephen Born in Berlin, a national workers' organization; this was never realized owing to the demise of the revolution within a few months. As part of this campaign thousands of copies of the "Wage-Labor and Capital" talks from the *NRZ* were sent to associations throughout Germany.

Finally, on April 14 an announcement appeared in the *NRZ* stating that Marx, Schapper, Wolff, and Anneke were withdrawing from the Rhineland Democratic Association because it "includes too many heterogeneous elements for any possibility of successful activity in furtherance of the cause." It then went on to advocate a "closer union of the Workers' Associations . . . since they consist of homogeneous elements."[42] A few days later the Cologne Worker's Society held a general meeting and made a similar decision. Although not a declaration to end collaboration with the Democratic Associations, both decisions were a clear statement by the Marx party, in light of the reality of the previous year—specifically, the vacillation within the democratic ranks—that from now on its priority was building the worker's movement.[43]

Along with the revitalization of the Worker's Society the *NRZ* party stepped up its work among the peasantry. Again, educational work through the pages of the newspaper was a key component of this effort. At Marx's urging, Wilhelm Wolff, of peasant origin, wrote a series of articles in March and April titled, "The Silesian Billion." They provided a detailed account of the amount of money and property "the *Silesian* aristocracy alone had wrested from the peasants since the redemption of feudal dues began" more than thirty years earlier.[44] Their purpose, as Engels recounted some thirty years later, was "to influence" the peasants "by explaining to them the position they were facing" following the December counterrevolution and to go on the "attack" by demanding that they be repaid for what they had been forced to give to their former landlords.

> Few of the many inflammatory articles in the [*NRZ*] had such an effect as these, eight in number. . . . Orders for the newspaper from Silesia and the other Eastern Provinces increased at a furious rate; individual issues were requested and eventually [owing to press restrictions in Silesia] . . . someone came up with the idea of

secretly reprinting in Silesia the entire eight issues as near to the original in appearance as possible and disseminating them in thousands [10,000] of copies—a procedure to which the editorial board was naturally the last to object.[45]

The *NRZ's* propaganda campaign was certainly the most successful outreach of the Marx party to German peasants during the entire two years of the revolution.

While the Marx party had clearly taken steps to prioritize the building of the people's alliance, this did not mean that it favored the revival of the Communist League. This became apparent when Moll, who had eventually found his way back to London following his forced exile from Cologne in September, returned to the latter in February. He brought with him a proposal from the reconstituted Central Authority in London that the CL be reestablished in Cologne and other cities. In light of the growing counterrevolution throughout Europe the Authority had also adopted new statues that revived the old conspiratorial provisions. "Members were now forbidden to participate in 'any other political organization' (Art. 2), a reversal of Marx's 1847 advice and probably a deliberate repudiation of his united-front policy."[46] The political climate, it was argued, would only permit secret functioning. At a meeting of old CL members in the city to discuss the issue, Marx opposed the proposal on the ground that there was still sufficient political space that obviated the need for the League, especially if it meant having to operate as a secret organization. A vote was taken and Marx's view prevailed by a slim margin. Moll, in spite of the opposition in Cologne, went to other cities and tried, with mixed success, to revive the organization. About a year later Marx and Engels would reevaluate their opposition to reviving the League.

The Marx Party's Final Stand

A major consideration, no doubt, in Marx's objection to the resurrection of the League were the very significant legal victories that he, Engels, and other party members had just scored a few days prior to Moll's visit. In two separate jury trials Marx and Engels, first, and then Marx, Schapper, and the head of the Democratic Association were found not guilty of, respectively, the defamation of character charge stemming from the previous July and the charge of "incitement to rebellion" in connection with the tax refusal campaign in November. In both trials Marx and Engels defended themselves with the very same arguments they had been employing for the previous eight months in the *NRZ* in defense of freedom of the press and the right of rebellion. So persuasive were their speeches that it took both juries less than an hour to find them innocent. The jury foreman in the second case even "thanked Marx for his informative analysis."

Their success derived not just from cogent presentations to the juries but rather a very political approach to legal defense. As Marx argued in the second case, "[S]ociety is not founded upon the law. . . . On the contrary, the law must be founded upon society, it must express the common interests and needs of society— as distinct from the caprice of individuals—which arise from the material mode of production prevailing at the given time." This was the framework—their "materialist conception of history"—within which they defended themselves before, during, and after their trials. Their strategy always was to mobilize popular sentiment to protect themselves. This was one of the reasons they chose in 1848 to set up shop in Cologne rather than elsewhere in Germany; the legacy of the class struggle, the Napoleonic Code, provided more opportunities—press freedoms and jury trials for example—for such mobilizations. Thus, they always kept *NRZ* readers well informed about their legal situation including any provocations from the government; this also applied to other victims of government persecution such as Ferdinand Lassalle, as well as those with whom they may even have had political differences, such as Gottschalk. Building broad coalitions with democratic forces for political work was also part of their defensive strategy. Since their overall strategy was to milk the political space for every drop of advantage in order to get out their ideas and influence politics, the trial itself was treated as a political event. Thus, Marx and Engels's trial speeches, which were printed in full in the *NRZ*, were published as a pamphlet for even wider distribution. The day after the second trial Marx rubbed a bit of salt into the government's wounds. "[T]he case turned only on the political question: whether the accused [had the right] . . . to call . . . for resistance to the state power, to organise an armed force against that of the state. . . . After a very brief consultation, the jury answered this question in the *affirmative*."[47]

Four decades later, Engels, the "general," as he was sometimes called by close friends—in recognition of his military skills—recalled that his and Marx's success in warding off the government for so long was due not just to their political acumen. Many had wondered, he wrote, why in Cologne, where the Prussian authorities had garrisoned eight thousand troops, the government permitted the *NRZ* to act with impunity: "[O]n account of the eight rifles with bayonets and 250 live cartridges in the editorial room, and the red Jacobin caps of the compositors, our house was reckoned by the officers likewise as a fortress which was not to be taken by a mere *coup de main*." Engels's later assessment notwithstanding—Marx once chided him for focusing "too much on the military side of things"—the respite that the Marx party enjoyed had more to do with their accurate judgment of the relationship of class forces in Cologne.

Shortly after the trials, the military commander in Cologne wrote on February 17 to the provincial governor that "Herr Marx (!) is becoming increasingly more audacious now that he has been acquitted by the jury. . . . He takes the liberty . . . in his increasingly popular paper . . . to promote even greater feelings of discontent and indirectly calling upon the people to revolt. . . . The deportation of this man would strengthen the position of the police and restore to them greater respect, and I request Your Excellency's support in this matter. . . ."[48] Three weeks later other Cologne authorities wrote to the Minister of the Interior in Berlin that the impact of the *NRZ* is "all the more damaging since its impertinence and humour constantly attract new readers."[49] Although Berlin in mid-April gave local authorities in Cologne the leeway to find a pretext to exile Marx, it would not be until late May that they felt confident to actually do so.

In many ways the fate of Marx and Engels became a barometer of what was left of the revolution. The final crisis ensued when the Frankfurt Assembly at long last produced what it had been elected ten months earlier to do—an all-German constitution, which Hammen describes as "a monument of mid-19th century liberalism." It then asked the Prussian monarch to accept it and become head of state of the new German empire. The work of the Assembly was all for naught as Frederick IV eventually rejected its offer. As Marx and Engels had foreseen, the failure of the Assembly to come to the defense of the revolutionary process in previous crises discredited its work in the eyes of most Germans who desired a democratic republic. When the lower house of the recently elected Prussian Assembly voted to accept the Frankfurt Assembly's imperial constitution, the monarch, as Marx and Engels had also predicted, refused to abide by its decision and sent it packing. If Frederick IV's affront to the Frankfurt Assembly did not provoke much of a mass response, his dissolution of the Berlin Assembly certainly did, particularly since it was followed by similar dissolutions by monarchs in Germany's lesser states who had been emboldened by the Prussian monarch's move. Among the masses was a growing sense that the gains of the March Revolution were being threatened and had, thus, to be defended at all costs.

The *NRZ* party was optimistic about a resurgence of the revolution. Unlike the previous year, this time it did not look to the bourgeoisie and liberal democrats to lead the way. Engels, who was editing the paper while Marx was out of town on a fundraising campaign for the *NRZ*, wrote that "any one who supposes . . . [they] are capable of *that* [providing leadership] is greatly mistaken."[50] Its hopes this time were with the international situation, especially the Hungarian war of liberation. They should only act in concert with other parts of the country and take their lead from any victories in Hungary's revolution. When Engels's hometown of Elberfeld rose up in response to a military provocation he went there (Marx had now returned to Cologne) to assist in the military preparations to defend the town against Prussian reprisals.

By the middle of May, however, the broad-based sentiment to defend the gains of the March Revolution had begun to dissipate. The reason was best illustrated by what happened to Engels in his hometown. The local bourgeoisie, who initially, in the wake of the crisis in Berlin vis-à-vis the Frankfurt Assembly, were ready to oppose the Prussian monarch, became increasingly leery that Engels's presence in Elberfeld would radicalize the uprising beyond their bourgeois democratic desires—"afraid at any moment he would proclaim a red republic."[51] Much to the anger of the "armed workers" on the barricades, the bourgeois-controlled Committee of Public Safety asked him to leave after five days—"*since his presence could give rise to misunderstandings as to the character of the movement*"—which he did. Engels's experience was symptomatic of the increasing fear of the bourgeoisie and much of the middle class throughout the Rhineland and elsewhere in Germany that the situation was verging on a "revolution in permanence." Aware of this growing sentiment the Cologne authorities now felt confident to finally move against the *NRZ* team. On May 16 Marx was served with an exile order to be acted on in twenty-four hours. The following day an arrest order was issued for Engels for his Elberfeld activities. Similar orders were issued for other members of the team, which meant that the newspaper would effectively be put out of business. Failing to find a jury that would silence the *Organ of Democracy*, the Prussian authorities had to resort to force.

Taking advantage of the last remaining political space in Cologne, the editors put together one final issue of the paper—the famous "Red Number." Printed entirely in red ink, it bid farewell to its readers in a defiant, militant, and optimistic tone. The lead article, addressed "To the Workers of Cologne," warned them not be provoked into a revolt that would give the Prussian authorities an excuse to declare a state of siege. As for the editors of the *NRZ*, "their last word everywhere and always will be: *emancipation of the working class!*" (Bold in original.) More than twenty thousand copies of the paper were sold—the circulation at the time was almost six thousand—with many of them becoming collectors' items. As Engels recalled forty years later, "We had to surrender our fortress, but we withdrew with our arms and baggage, with band playing and flag flying . . ."

Still hopeful that the revolution was not expended, Marx and Engels went to Frankfurt to meet with the left Assembly members to urge them to assume the leadership of the insurrections in the southwest. Unsuccessful in that effort, they then went to Baden and the Palatinate in southern Germany where the most serious revolts were under way. There they tried in vain to convince the Baden provisional government "to gain the support of the peasant masses by abolishing all feudal burdens."[52] In order to broaden the struggle in Baden to other areas they urged, again vainly, the revolters to send their troops to Frankfurt to defend what was left of the Assembly so that it might be encouraged to become the center of an all-German revolt.

Given the obstacles they faced, Marx and Engels decided to split their forces. Marx went to Paris, as a representative of the democratic movement, to see what the prospects were for a French impulse to the European revolution while Engels participated in the military operations of the insurrectionary army of Baden. Although neither had much success, Engels, in a letter to Jenny Marx, said that aside from the military experience he gained there was at least "one member of the [*NRZ* who took part in the military actions since]. . . . It would have been said again that the gentlemen of the [*NRZ*] were too cowardly to fight."[53] One other *NRZ* member also took part in the fighting, Moll, and in the process was killed. Engels, who escaped to Switzerland, fought with one of the last contingents in Germany to be subdued by Prussian forces. For Marx it was important that Engels "write a history or a pamphlet" about the events. "Had you not taken part in the actual fighting, we couldn't have put forward our views about that frolic."[54]

Shortly after Marx's arrival in Paris in June the left republicans suffered a major defeat, because of an irresolute revolt, at the hands of the new French president, Louis Bonaparte. In the meantime the Hungarian revolution was being crushed by Russian troops, confirming Marx and Engels's prediction made a year earlier that Russia posed the greatest danger to the revolution. With the European revolution in retreat, Marx with his family and then, later, Engels decided to withdraw to London in order to assess the prospects for a resurgence of the upheavals that had begun seventeen months earlier. Writing to Engels of his plans to start a new publication, Marx said "In London we shall get down to business."[55]

Almost immediately after his arrival in London in late August 1849, Marx got down to the business of politics. He contacted the few remaining Communist League members who had not returned to Germany and began to help rebuild the organization. Although it is not clear how it was done, especially since he had opposed the reconstitution of the CL back in February, Marx became a member once again of the Central Authority and then later president. Engels and Schapper were coopted onto the Authority when they arrived in London later in the year. On Engels's recommendation, the military commander to whom he had served as an adjunct in the Baden campaign, August Willich, was also brought onto the body.

As a League leader Marx became active in the German Workers Education Association, which still functioned in London. Just as he had done in Cologne and earlier in Brussels he began giving lectures at GWEA meetings based on his "Wage-Labor and Capital" series as well as the *Manifesto*. For CL leaders and activists he gave more detailed lectures on these and related issues at his home.[56]

Through the League and the GWEA Marx devoted considerable time, energy, and increasingly limited money in assisting the political refugees coming into London from Germany and elsewhere. Refugee work quickly became embroiled with the politics of the German revolution. In response to an attempt by petit bourgeois democrats to undermine the influence of the League and the GWEA in the committee doing the work, Marx and other CL leaders decided to establish a new refugee body that gave "priority to members of the social-democratic party" while not excluding assistance, if available, to refugees from other tendencies.[57]

The most significant work that Marx and Engels engaged in during this period, in terms of lasting importance, was their literary activity—more specifically, the balance sheets that they drew on the 1848–49 revolutions. For this purpose Marx struggled heroically to begin a new publication, the *Neue Rheinische Zeitung. Politisch-Ökonomische Revue.* Unlike its predecessor, which was a "daily intervention in the movement and speaking directly from the heart of the movement," the "Political and Economic Review . . . provides the advantage of comprehending events is a broader perspective. . . . It permits a comprehensive and scientific investigation of the *economic* conditions which form the foundation of the whole political movement." Begun as a monthly and seen as a party publication—League affiliates and members were called upon to provide financial support—the *Revue*, it was hoped, would eventually become a daily.

The "Address" of March 1850

Just as the *Revue* was beginning to publish the first segments of Marx's assessment of what had occurred so far in France's revolution, Marx and Engels, on behalf of the Central Authority, drew a balance sheet on the League's participation in Germany's upheavals over the previous two years. As well as being a task and perspective report for the next stage in the revolution, the "Address of the Central Authority to the League, March 1850," stands out as one of Marx and Engels four most important party writings; the others, the *Manifesto*, the "Inaugural Address of the International Working Men's Association" of 1864, and *The Civil War in France*. Also, "More than any other writing by Marx and Engels . . . [the Address] has been the target of remarkable exercises in exegesis by ingenious Marxologists."[58] Its historic significance is testified to by Riazanov, the Bolshevik bibliographer. Referring to the March "Address" as well as a subsequent one in June of the same year, Riazanov writes that "Lenin, who knew them *by heart*, used to delight in quoting them" [italics added].[59]

The immediate background to the "Address" was the effort to revive the League in Germany. Marx, as CL president, wrote Peter Röser in Cologne at the beginning of 1850 to urge him to reestablish a branch in the town as well as in other Rhineland cities. He also indicated that the organization's new rules that had been adopted in his absence and those to which he objected would be changed at an upcoming congress. Until then, according to Röser, Marx said "I was to organise things on the basis of the *Manifesto*."[60] Since it had been Marx and Engels who were chiefly responsible for the fateful decision in June 1848 to suspend the activities of the League, it was incumbent on them in calling for its revival to evaluate that decision.

The "Address" began by assessing the decision. While League members had performed in an exemplary fashion during the two years of the revolution and were served well by their programmatic documents, especially the *Manifesto*. "At the same time the former firm organisation of the League was considerably slackened. A large part of the members who directly participated in the revolutionary movement believed the time for secret societies to have gone by and open activities alone to be sufficient." The result was that while the "democratic party, the party of the petty bourgeoisie, organised itself more and more in Germany, the workers' party lost its only firm foothold . . . and thus came completely under the domination and leadership of the petty-bourgeois democrats. An end must be put to this state of affairs, the independence of the workers must be restored." Because "at this moment when a new revolution is impending, when the workers' party . . . must act in the most organised, most unanimous and most independent fashion possible if it is not again to be exploited and taken in tow by the bourgeoisie as in 1848," the Central Authority decided to send a new emissary to Germany to do what Moll had not been able to at the beginning of 1849, to revive the League

Thus, in no uncertain terms the document made clear that it had been a mistake for Marx and Engels to shelve the League. Experience had taught that the decision disarmed the proletariat by depriving it of the leadership necessary to pursue its own class interests in the revolution. The document then spelled out the political basis for this conclusion.

The *Manifesto* had correctly warned that as soon as the liberal bourgeoisie took power it would turn on the working class. As Marx's articles, "The Bourgeoisie and the Counter-revolution," had pointed out, the liberal bourgeoisie did this by entering into a governing alliance with feudal reaction and thus betraying the democratic revolution. However, the bourgeoisie could not stabilize its bastardized rule owing to the external revolutionary situation that surrounded Germany. Internally, the "democratic petty bourgeoisie," now the leading opponent of the governing alliance, was at the same time "more dangerous to the workers than the previous liberal party. . . ." Many of them had been in the leadership of the democratic movement. Like the liberal bourgeoisie, they too would seek an alliance with the proletariat to overthrow the ruling coalition, which would then be immediately jettisoned once their aims were achieved. What the *Manifesto* had not been specific about, how the proletariat should position itself in order to successfully take on its erstwhile allies once the remnants of feudalism had been overthrown in the impending revolutionary resurgence, the "Address" could now do on the basis of the real movement, as seen in the experience of the two previous years.

The overall strategy was as follows: While "the revolutionary workers' party . . . marches together with [the petty bourgeois democrats] . . . against [the ruling coalition] it opposes them in everything by which they seek to consolidate their position in their own interests." As against the more limited demands of the petty-bourgeois democrats who "wish to bring the revolution to a conclusion as quickly as possible . . . it is our interest and our task to make the revolution permanent," that is, toward a socialist revolution.

To ensure that the revolution would be "permanent," preparations had to be made prior to its resumption. The proletariat, and "above all the League, must exert themselves to establish an independent secret and public organisation of the workers' party alongside the official democrats and make each community [League branch] the central point and nucleus of workers' associations in which the attitude and interests of the proletariat will be discussed independently of bourgeois influences." Thus, a revived CL would engage in both public and secret activities in order to maintain the political and organizational independence of the proletariat. While the *NRZ* team had served as the "nucleus" of the Workers' Society in Cologne, for example, from now on such public work would be done by CL branches operating in secret owing to the new political reality in Germany. Such preparation would be crucial in order to prevent, as would surely happen again—the insurrections in Spring 1849, including Elberfeld, were most instructive—the petty-bourgeois democrats from restraining "so-called excesses" of a revolutionary victory. Such independent organizing would enable the workers' movement to immediately establish alongside the new official governments that emerge after a victory "their own revolutionary workers' governments" in whatever form they take—"municipal councils," "workers' committees"—in order to undermine the "bourgeois-democratic governments."

The foregoing steps could only be successful if the workers are "armed and organised." Along with their independent political organizing there must be independent armed organization of the proletariat. Every effort should be made for workers to carve out their own armed space during and after the emergence of the new petit-bourgeois democratic governments. "Arms and ammunition must not be surrendered on any pretext; any attempt at disarming must be frustrated, if necessary, by force."

Once the revolutions have succeeded and the new petit-bourgeois-dominated governments have consolidated themselves, "their struggle against the workers will begin." Just as was true both before and during the revolutionary struggle, workers will need their own organizations. The Central Authority will transfer its seat to Germany and assist in this process. Especially important will be the creation "of at least a provincial association of the workers's clubs."

Finally, workers must pursue a completely independent course in the elections to the expected national assembly. In what was no doubt a criticism of the policy that Marx and Engels advocated in the two elections to the Prussian National Assembly, the "Address" stated "that everywhere workers' candidates are put up alongside the bourgeois-democratic candidates, that they are as far as possible members of the League. . . . Even where there is no prospect whatever of their being elected, the workers must put up their own candidates in order to preserve their independence, to count their forces and to lay before the public their revolutionary attitude and party standpoint." Workers were not to be taken in by petty-bourgeois claims that their candidates would split the vote and make it possible for reactionaries to be elected. "The advance which the proletarian party is bound to make by such independent action is infinitely more important than the disadvantage that might be incurred by the presence of a few reactionaries in the representative body."

As the opposition to the new petit-bourgeois government, the workers' party "cannot yet propose any directly communist measures." But "they must carry to the extreme the proposals of the democrats, who in any case will not act in a revolutionary but in a merely reformist manner, and transform them into attacks upon private property." In this context, the workers' party demands in the countryside must focus on strengthening the alliance with the rural proletariat. While the reformists will advocate turning over feudal lands to the peasantry, in order to "form a petty-bourgeois peasant class, which will go through the same cycle of impoverishment and indebtedness which the French peasant is now still caught in"—in spite of the land reform of the first French revolution—the workers "must demand that the confiscated feudal property remain state property and be converted into workers' colonies cultivated by the associated rural proletariat with all the advantages of large-scale agriculture. . . ." Marx and Engels would later modify their position on land reform and adapt it to concrete situations.

The document concludes by noting that the German proletariat was not in a position to take power and its fate was still dependent on what happened in France. "But they themselves must do the utmost for their final victory by making it clear to themselves what their class interests are, by taking up their position as an independent party as soon as possible and by not allowing themselves to be misled for a single moment by the hypocritical phrases of the democratic petty bourgeois into refraining from the independent organisation of the party of the proletariat. Their battle cry must be: The Revolution in Permanence."

Many of the conclusions that Marx and Engels drew in the "Address" were reached or anticipated by them in the previous eighteen months (certainly from the time of the Vienna revolution) as the preceding chapter and the first part of this one make clear.[61] What the "Address" does is to present these lessons in a fairly concise and distilled form. Clearly, the operative word throughout the document is political and organizational "independence" of the proletariat. It is from that stance that Marx and Engels criticized their decisions to shelve the League and not run workers' candidates in the elections to the Prussian Assembly. Independence of the working class was consistent with their long-held view that only the working class could liberate itself. And only an independent proletariat could assure a "revolution in permanence."

In one very important way the "Address" rounds out the *Manifesto*, more specifically its last and briefest section, "The Position of the Communists in Relation to the Various Existing Opposition Parties." The sketch on strategy and tactics for the German revolution could now be filled out on the basis, not of a blueprint or schema, but rather the living class struggle, the real movement of the previous two years. It cannot be overemphasized that the document is the product of that experience, particularly the betrayal and vacillation of, respectively, the liberal bourgeoisie and the petty bourgeoisie as well as the initiatives of the working class. This is important to understand in light of Marxologists who, for political reasons—oftentimes modern-day social democrats who hate the document for the same reasons that Lenin loved it—vainly attempt to have Marx and Engels disown the "Address."[62] It should be noted that those who engage in this chicanery almost never address the validity of the lessons that the document drew in light of what actually occurred in the German revolution.

One issue that the "Address" is surprisingly silent about is the alliance between the proletariat, the small peasantry, and the urban petit bourgeoisie that the Marx party sought to build during the revolution, especially in its final months. This does not necessarily mean, however, that they had abandoned this strategy. The conception of the alliance prior to the 1848 upheavals was one in which the proletariat would play the leading role. It can be argued that Marx and Engels's almost exclusive focus on the proletariat in the "Address" was due to their recognition, implicit perhaps, that unless the proletariat was clear on its class interests it would not be in a position to lead its allies. Thus, the alliance would be a moot strategy without the political and organizational independence of the proletariat.

As for the peasantry, while it is true that the March "Address" spoke only of the alliance between the proletariat and rural workers, the "Address" in June insisted that League members become involved in peasant associations to be able to exert political influence.[63] Just as the *NRZ* party did during the revolution, League members had to fight for the allegiance of the small peasantry, in other words, not concede them to the bourgeois democrats as the March "Address" seemed to imply. If anything, in their rush to have the small peasants protected from the ravages of the marketplace, as was the reality in capitalist France, Marx and Engels may have been guilty of focusing too much on the goal of permanent revolution without sufficient attention to the kinds of demands—most importantly land reform—that would assure the small peasantry's support for the alliance.[64] They would correct this error in further elaboration of their policies on the peasant question.

The March "Address" was taken to the continent by a special emissary and secretly distributed throughout Germany to League members. Functioning in a secret fashion, owing to the lack of political space inside Germany, did not signify that Marx and Engels had resorted to the conspiratorial style of politics that they had once denounced. This is clearly proven by a review they wrote in March for the *NRZ Revue* of two books by French police agents. The activities of one of them, a self-described "professional conspirator," revealed all that was wrong with conspiratorial politics. Rather than focusing on "the general organising of the revolutionary proletariat" the conspirator sees that "the only condition for revolution is the adequate preparation of their conspiracy."[65] They are the "alchemists of the revolution" because of their disdain for the "theoretical enlightenment of the proletariat about their class interests." For these and other reasons, especially the lifestyle that conspirators must of necessity pursue, this mode of functioning becomes a breeding ground for police informers. They noted that to "the extent the Paris proletariat came to the fore itself as a party, these conspirators lost some of their dominant influence, they . . . encountered dangerous competition in proletarian secret societies, whose purpose was not immediate insurrection but the organisation and development of the proletariat."[66] Thus, secret functioning as a way to prepare the proletariat as a class to take power was not to be confused with conspiratorial politics.

The Class Struggles in France

In addition to drawing a balance sheet on the German events, Marx and Engels did the same for the French upheavals upon which they had pinned their hope for a resurgence of the European revolution. In a series of articles written between January and October 1850 for the *NRZ Revue* that Engels later titled, *The Class Struggles in France, 1848–1850*, Marx, who wrote most of them, analyzed the reasons for the upsurge as well as its eventual defeat. The debacle that the French working class experienced in June 1848 could be explained by the underdevelopment of the industrial proletariat both materially—a reflection of the immature state of French industrial capital—and politically;"It makes no theoretical inquiries into its own task,"[67] that is, its own class interests (one of the reasons why Marx and Engels tried unsuccessfully to have the *Manifesto* translated into French). The Parisian proletariat, under the illusion that the republican bourgeoisie, who it had just helped to take power in the February revolution, would serve its interests, were betrayed by their erstwhile ally. Workers were forced to take on their new rulers, their class enemy, and eventually demand, "*Overthrow of the bourgeoisie! Dictatorship of the working class!*"

Disarmed politically, however, the workers of Paris became easy prey, in spite of their heroic resistance, to the counterrevolution in June. Thus, began "*bourgeois terrorism . . . [the] bourgeois dictatorship,*" a situation in which "the petty bourgeoisie and the peasant class . . . had to adhere more and more closely to the proletariat as their position became more unbearable and their antagonism to the bourgeoisie more acute."[68] Because the battle lines between the working class and the bourgeoisie were drawn unlike they had ever been—the outcome of the June defeat—the proletarian revolution was now on the immediate agenda in France, a revolution that would also be combined with the national liberation struggles on the continent. "And we exclaim: *The revolution is dead!—Long live the revolution.!*"

In the second and third articles in the series, written about the same time as the March "Address," Marx analyzed the class dynamics of the revolution in the aftermath of the June events. While Louis Bonaparte's victory over the left republicans in June 1849 represented a setback—the slaughter on the barricades the previous June had prepared the way—the Parisian by-elections of March 10, 1850, in which "socialist" candidates won, confirmed that the "constitutional republic" was to soon be replaced by the "social-democratic, the Red republic."

Although Marx and Engels had previously employed the term *dictatorship*, their first usage of the "dictatorship of the proletariat" or some variant was in *The Class Struggles*. In response to a criticism in 1850, which claimed that Marx was more interested in the *"rule and the dictatorship of the working class"* rather than in the *"abolition of class distinctions in general,"* he explained what he meant by the term. He referred the critic to the end of Part II of the *Manifesto*:

> If the proletariat during its contest with the bourgeoisie is compelled, by force of circumstances, to organise itself as a class, if by means of a revolution it makes itself the ruling class and, as such, sweeps away by force the old conditions of production, then it will, along with these conditions, have swept away the conditions for the existence of class antagonisms and of class generally, and will thereby have abolished its own supremacy as a class.

Thus, in defending himself, Marx provided in the antecedent clause a definition of his much-maligned "dictatorship of the proletariat"—the rule of the proletariat by means of force.[69]

In June, Marx began a detailed study at the British Museum of Europe's economy over the past decade. As he had explained to prospective readers of the *NRZ Revue*, it was necessary to understand "the *economic* conditions which form the foundation of the whole political movement." A "Review" article, May to October 1850, revealed the enormous breath of the reading he and Engels were doing on the world capitalist system. They concluded, basically, that the commercial crisis of 1847, which began in Great Britain, was indeed, as they had thought, the "foundation" for the revolutionary upsurge at the beginning of 1848. At the same time, for a host of reasons—such as the discovery of the gold fields in California—the crisis in Britain had come to an end by the Spring of 1848. "Renewed prosperity" in Britain began to spread to the continent in mid-1849 and became generalized in France and Germany by the end of the year.[70] Therein lay an important lesson.

> Just as the period of crisis occurs later on the Continent than in England, so does that of prosperity. The original process always takes place in England. . . . While, therefore, the crises first produce revolutions on the Continent, the foundation for these is, nevertheless, always laid in England. Violent outbreaks must naturally occur rather in the extremities of the bourgeois body than in its heart, since the possibility of adjustment is greater here than there.

There was a sobering lesson also in the fact that the Chartists had not been able to duplicate in the two previous years what their co-thinkers had done in France and Germany.

[T]he degree to which Continental revolutions react on England is at the same time the barometer which indicates how far these revolutions really call in question the bourgeois conditions of life, or how far they only hit their political formations.

With this general prosperity, in which the productive forces of bourgeois society develop as luxuriantly as is at all possible within bourgeois relationships, there can be no talk of real revolution. Such a revolution is only possible in the periods when *both these factors,* the *modern* productive *forces* and the *bourgeois forms of production,* come *in collision* with each other. . . . *A new revolution is possible only in consequence of a new crisis. It is, however, just as certain as this crisis.*[71]

Thus, by the summer of 1850, Marx and Engels had concluded that the economic conditions that gave rise to the 1848 upheavals had changed. Revolution in Europe was no longer imminent. Major political implications—to be discussed in Chapter Six—flowed from this historic assessment.

With the hindsight of four decades and shortly before he died, Engels explained, in a new introduction to the articles that he and Marx had written, why they—as well as many other revolutionaries—thought that revolution was still on the agenda in the first half of 1850. Their assumption had been that the French industrial proletariat, although a minority at the time, could, as other minority classes had done before in the history of social revolutions, lead the masses—in this case the peasantry and the petty bourgeoisie—in the overthrow of capitalism. "History had proved us, and all who thought like us, wrong. It has made clear that the state of economic development on the Continent at that time was not, by a long way, ripe for the elimination of capitalist production." It would take a number of decades before an industrial proletariat came into existence—along with other requisite developments, particularly national unity in the case of Germany—throughout France, beyond Paris and a few large cities, as well as in Germany, that was capable of leading the "complete transformation of the social organization."[72]

Three Notable Balance Sheets

A few comments are in order about three balance sheets that Marx and Engels drew in the aftermath of their new assessment of the revolutionary prospects for Europe. The first, written in the second half of 1850, was one of Engels's best-known works, *The Peasant War in Germany*—the first detailed application of the historical materialist outlook to a historical event, the peasant revolt of 1525. Engels's intent was to put the recent events in Germany in historical perspective, to deepen his and Marx's analysis of the defeats, while seeking at the same time to inspire present-day fighters by the example of their militant forbearers. The import of Engels's analysis was reflected in a comment Marx made to him in 1856 on the prospects for another German revolution: "The whole thing in Germany will depend on the possibility to back the Proletarian revolution by some second edition of the Peasants' war. Then the thing will be first-rate."[73] What 1525 and 1848 had failed to do would only be achieved, therefore, by a revolutionary alliance between workers and peasants—one of the most important lessons of Germany's second mass uprising.[74]

The next assessment was another work by Engels, *Revolution and Counter-Revolution in Germany*, written between 1851 and 1852. As Engels explained in its introduction, revolutionaries were obligated in the "interval of rest" between revolutionary upsurges "to study the causes" that lead to both the "outbreak [of 1848–49] . . . and its defeat; causes that are not to be sought for in the accidental efforts, talents, faults, errors or treacheries of some of the leaders, but in the general social state and conditions of existence of each of the convulsed nations." While it would be impossible to do "a complete history of the events," it was nevertheless necessary to do what was possible in order "to give us a clue as to the direction which the next and perhaps not very distant outbreak will impart to the German people."[75] The result was the most comprehensive statement by Marx and Engels on the German revolution.

Initially a series of articles, it summarized Marx and Engels's analysis from the pages of the *NRZ*. On occasion it elaborated on concepts and ideas they frequently employed. For example, "the incurable malady," of the Frankfurt Assembly members, "*parliamentary cretinism*, a disorder which penetrates its unfortunate victims with the solemn conviction that the whole world, its history and future, are governed and determined by a majority of votes in that particular representative body which has the honor to count them among its members, and that all and everything going on outside the walls of their house—wars, revolutions . . . is nothing compared to the incommensurable events hinging upon the important question, whatever it may be, just at that moment occupying the attention of their honorable House." It also gave Engels the first opportunity to write about the armed struggle and "the art of insurrection"—the first such pronouncements of the Marx party. His "axioms" make clear that the revolutionary restraint that he and Marx frequently counselled in Cologne did not stem from any fears of armed confrontation.

The last balance sheet on the 1848–49 revolutions is one of Marx's most famous writings, *The Eighteenth Brumaire of Louis Bonaparte*, written at the beginning of 1852. Although Engels often cited this work as a model for the application of historical materialist analysis to a concrete political event, Louis Bonaparte's coup d'état in December 1851, he was also correct when he wrote in 1895 that while it was written after the definitive end to the French revolution Marx "had very little to change" from what he and Engels had written in their final article in *The Class Struggle in France*.[76] Some formulations in the former, however, were given greater precision, such as the reasons for the failure of February to become a socialist revolution. There were, also, some issues that the book uniquely addressed—the worker-peasant alliance and the phenomenon of "bonapartism"—both of which will be taken up later.

Marx did make a noteworthy observation in the book that is most pertinent to this discussion on the lessons of 1848–49 and reflected profoundly that experience. It concerned the difference between socialist and bourgeois revolutions.

> Bourgeois revolutions, like those of the eighteenth century, storm swiftly from success to success, their dramatic effects outdo each other, men and things seem set in sparkling brilliants, ecstasy is the everyday spirit, but they are short-lived, soon

they have attained their zenith, and a long crapulent depression seizes society before it learns soberly to assimilate the results of its storm-and-stress period. On the other hand, proletarian revolutions, like those of the nineteenth century, criticise themselves constantly, interrupt themselves continually in their own course, come back to the apparently accomplished in order to begin it afresh, deride with unmerciful thoroughness the inadequacies, weaknesses and paltrinesses of their first attempts, seem to throw down their adversary only in order that he may draw new strength from the earth and rise again, more gigantic, before them, and recoil again and again from the indefinite prodigiousness of their own aims, until a situation has been created which makes all turning back impossible, and the conditions themselves cry out:

> Hic Rhodus, hic salta!
> Here is the rose, here dance![77]

The emotion as well as the elegance with which Marx delivered this most important lesson of 1848–49—an observation that many a twentieth-century revolutionary would learn only painfully—can be traced to an essential characteristic of all their conclusions. Even before they became communists Marx and Engels had concluded that only through participation in the real movement could the oppressed and its educators learn to liberate themselves. While many of the lessons that they drew about those two momentous years were anticipated in their writings, especially the *Manifesto*, which itself was based on their reading of the real movement in history, it was still necessary that they, along with the proletariat and its allies, go through that experience. Thus, the conclusions that they came to, chief among them that the liberal bourgeoisie in Germany was incapable of leading the charge for bourgeois democracy and that only an alliance of workers and peasants would ensure the institution of democratic rule, were the direct product of participation in the class struggle.

At the same time, as historical materialists Marx and Engels's framework for action was objective material reality. Hence their conclusions about the end of the revolutionary era as a result of their research in mid-1850. Yet their tendency throughout the two years was to prioritize political action, to test the limits of objective reality. While, for example, Germany's economic development placed limits on what could be expected from its proletariat, which they had written about before the March revolution, they recognized that only experience itself would provide the answer about the capabilities of the proletariat and its allies.

As already noted, a critical conclusion that Marx and Engels reached at the beginning of their partnership was that "*Ideas* can never lead beyond an old world order but only beyond the ideas of the old world order. Ideas *cannot carry out anything* at all. In order to carry out ideas men are needed who can exert practical force."[78] In the midst of the crisis in November 1848 they invoked this insight to castigate the Frankfurt Assembly, the "professors' assembly," for failing to support the Vienna revolution and the tax refusal campaign. "While the professors were evolving the theory of history, history ran its stormy course without bothering about the professorial history."[79] Exactly because they had broken with the world of ideas and become communists Marx and Engels threw themselves into the real movement by becoming participants in history's "stormy course" in order to "exert practical force."

Unlike any other event in their political lives the revolutions of 1848–49 were Marx and Engels's baptism of fire, the crucible in which they were politically forged. While their subsequent political experiences would allow them to add to and enrich the lessons of 1848–49, the latter, as Lenin correctly argued—to be substantiated in the following chapters—served as the anchor for all their future political analysis.

CHAPTER FIVE

Interpreting the 1848–1851 Events in France: Marx and Engels versus Tocqueville

> By so doing [resisting Bonaparte] it [the Party of Order] would give the nation its marching orders, and it fears nothing more than that the nation should move.
>
> —Marx, *The Eighteenth Brumaire*

> And yet it [Bonaparte's coup d'état] is inevitable, unless resisted by an appeal to revolutionary passions, which I do not wish to rouse in the nation.
>
> —Tocqueville, *Correspondence*

If it is true, as claimed here, that the 1848–1849 revolutions exercised an enormous influence on Marx and Engels's political strategy, how accurate, then, was their reading of that reality upon which their prescriptions were based? How did their assessments and conclusions stand up to those of their contemporaries and subsequent analysts? A definitive answer to such questions is obviously beyond the scope of this book. What would be feasible and instructive, however, is a comparison of their reading of political reality and the inferences they drew with a contemporary account from someone on the other side of the barricades. Such an account is to be found in the writings of Alexis de Tocqueville, who wrote about as well as participated in the 1848 revolution in France. A comparison of Marx and Engels with Tocqueville would not only constitute the beginnings of an evaluation of their political analysis but in the process provide further clarification of their politics.[1] But first, a brief introduction to accounts about the 1848 revolutions by contemporaries of Marx and Engels.

MARX AND ENGELS VERSUS THEIR CONTEMPORARIES

Given the unusual number of intellectuals who witnessed and participated in the 1848–49 events in Germany—for example, of the approximately five hundred members of the Frankfurt Assembly that Marx derisively termed the "professors' assembly," 104 were university teachers, of whom a good number were historians— one is struck by the relative absence of contemporary accounts about the German upheavals that are comparable in any way to those of Marx and Engels. What explains the writer's block that apparently gripped so many of these intellectuals? Sir Lewis Namier, in his classic work *1848: The Revolution of the Intellectuals*, is surprisingly silent on this matter. In France, however, the situation was different. "Nearly everyone who took part . . . either wrote a special book to defend his part, or described the revolution at length in his memoirs."[2]

One explanation for the absence of comparable accounts from Germany may have to do with the disillusionment that set in among intellectuals both during and after the revolution, individuals who in their majority were initially enthusiastic about the outbreaks in early 1848. This appears to be especially the case with the intellectuals in the Frankfurt Assembly. The role they saw for themselves in the revolution was that of the expert on the fine points of deliberating and writing a constitution. For them this was their revolutionary practice. While applauding their work, Hammen, who clearly is politically closer to them than to Marx and Engels, unwittingly exposes his heroes. "The resultant Constitution stands out as a monument of mid-nineteenth-century liberalism, but it never went into effect."[3] Indeed a monument! Hammen's sentence encapsulates the reality of nineteenth-century liberalism. Although capable of writing the perfect constitution replete with democratic guarantees, liberals were unwilling to take the political step that would have been necessary to guarantee the constitution itself—wage a revolutionary war against the counterrevolution. More fearful of the German masses than Prussian reaction, most Assembly members acquiesced in Frederick IV's rejection of their document. Demoralized by the realization that all their fine work went for naught, most Assembly members left Frankfurt and returned dejectedly to their homes. Such outcomes are not the stuff to inspire memoirs.

Marx and Engels, on the other hand, saw their role in a completely different light. As communists they began with the assumption, based on their reading of the real movement of history—specifically the French Revolution of 1789—that only through mass struggles could democracy be won and guaranteed. Their eyes were on, initially, the broad democratic movement and then later the forces that comprised the people's alliance—workers, peasants, and the urban petit bourgeoisie. They wrote in order to mobilize all of these forces. Except perhaps for Stephen Born's newspaper in Berlin, which had a much narrower focus, the artisanal proletariat, no paper other than the *NRZ* saw itself as a conscious organizer of Germany's popular forces. Although the counterrevolution had newspapers that it could count on, its possession of state power obviated the need for a publication to organize its activities. Thus, the absence of accounts during the revolution that are comparable to the writings of Marx and Engels may be explained by the unique way in which the latter functioned throughout the two years—as revolutionary communists.

In the aftermath of the revolution's end in Germany, the number of written accounts, comparable to what Marx and Engels produced, did not significantly increase. Those that were written seem to have been authored by those who, like Marx and Engels, went down to defeat fighting—the stuff that does inspire memoirs. The outstanding example is Carl Schurz's *Reminiscences* which was written, however, more than a half century after the fact.[4] Noteworthy, German revolutionaries such as Schurz, as well as many others who were political collaborators of Marx and Engels, migrated to the United States and continued their revolutionary activities by fighting against the slavocracy in the Civil War.

For France, again, the situation was different. In addition to Tocqueville, Marx and Engels's political opponent Proudhon—also a participant in the revolution—wrote two volumes on the events.[5] Aside from the limitations of space, a comparison of Marx and Engels with Proudhon would be difficult since each volume offers a different line on the course of the revolution, particularly Louis Bonaparte's role. Two other participants, Louis Blanc and the novelist Victor Hugo, also wrote accounts, which, again for practical reasons, cannot be addressed here.[6] There is also the interesting example of the German academic Lorenz von Stein whose influential *The History of the Social Movement in France, 1789–1850*, published in 1850, analyzed, inter alia, the February and June revolutions from a materialist and class perspective. In spite of the limited theoretical similarities with the method of Marx and Engels—but clearly from an antirevolutionary perspective—Stein's book, however, does not get beyond the June events. Finally, it might be mentioned that one of the greatest French novels, *Sentimental Education* by Gustave Flaubert, was based in part on the reality of the upheavals in 1848–49 which the author witnessed.

MARX AND ENGELS VERSUS TOCQUEVILLE

It is appropriate to focus on the accounts of Alexis de Tocqueville. His *Recollections: The French Revolution of 1848* was written almost at the same moment, between July 1850 and March 1851, when Marx completed *Class Struggles in France.*[7] The comparison here is primarily, but not exclusively, with the latter and those writings of Marx and Engels that appeared before the summer of 1850. This ensures, for comparative purposes, that Marx and Engels, who, unlike Tocqueville, wrote subsequent analyses about the outcome in France, do not have the unfair advantage of hindsight. For purposes of closure later writings of all three will be utilized in a more limited manner.

A major benefit in employing *Recollections,* is that of all other contemporary accounts about the 1848 revolution in France, it continues to be one of the most highly regarded by scholars. As Roger Price notes, both Marx's and Tocqueville's "views have exercised a substantial influence on writing about the revolution by both historians and sociologists ever since."[8] Another advantage in comparing the two is that both individuals, as political people and activists, are regarded even today as alternative poles of political attraction, which influences, not surprisingly, how their two accounts are received. Thus, for the Tocqueville partisan and anti-Marxist J. P. Mayer, "Tocqueville's understanding of the structure of the historic process was perhaps subtler than that of Marx . . . Tocqueville was a realistic sociologist; in comparison Marx was a Utopian."[9]

Mayer's opinion notwithstanding, a thorough reading of both accounts reveals that it was Marx who had a superior grasp of political reality and whose analysis more accurately anticipated the political outcome in France.

A number of preliminary considerations are in order. In one sense it may be unfair to compare *Recollections* to *Class Struggles*; the latter, although a little more than a third of the length of the former, was an explicit political analysis of the French Revolution of 1848 whereas Tocqueville's work was more of a private memoir. Unlike Marx's account it was never intended to be published but, as Tocqueville explained, only a "mental relaxation for myself and not a work of literature." Yet therein lies an important difference between the two men and their works that justifies a comparison. As a communist Marx was obligated to draw a balance sheet on the 1848 revolutions and to disseminate those lessons in order to influence subsequent events. Tocqueville, albeit a participant in the revolution—on the other side of the barricades as an officer in the national guard and Minister of Foreign Affairs in one of the governments—felt, on the other hand, no similar compulsion. Reflecting on the upheaval was for him a private affair.[10] Marx and Engels, who had to scrape for every penny to publish their accounts, had no such luxury. Thus, their approach to writing about 1848 was quite different from that of Tocqueville. Almost every paragraph in *Class Struggles* is pregnant with political analysis whereas *Recollections* requires the reader to wade through what is often interesting, sometimes fascinating, and never boring narrative to find proportionately fewer political insights.

On the Eve of Revolution

From the beginning of both accounts the degree of agreement is noteworthy. On the eve of the February Revolution both agreed that the monarch Louis Philippe represented not the aristocracy but rather the bourgeoisie. He was, for Tocqueville, "the head of the bourgeoisie," and for Marx the bourgeoisie's "crowned scapegoat," who ruled on their behalf. Like Marx and Engels, Tocqueville not only accurately predicted the Revolution but also its social content. In a draft of what was to have been "a programme in the form of a manifesto" for his parliamentary caucus in October 1847 Tocqueville wrote that revolution was once again on the agenda. "The French Revolution [of 1789], which abolished all privileges and destroyed all exclusive rights, did leave one, that of property. Property holders must not delude themselves about the strength of their position, or suppose that, because it has so far nowhere been surmounted, the right to property is an insurmountable barrier; for our age is not like any other. . . . Soon the political struggle will be between the Haves and the Have-nots; property will be the great battlefield. . . . Do you think it is by chance, or by some passing caprice of the human spirit, that on every side we see strange doctrines appearing . . . which all deny the right of property. . . . Who can fail to recognize in this the last symptom of the old democratic disease of the times, whose crisis is perhaps approaching?"[11]

And in a speech to the Chamber of Deputies on January 29, 1848, Tocqueville tauntingly asked his colleagues if they hadn't noticed that the "working classes . . . passions have changed from political to social? Do you not see that opinions and ideas are gradually spreading among them that tend not simply to be the overthrow of such-and-such laws, such-and-such a minister, or even such-and-such a government, but rather to the overthrow of society, breaking down the bases on which it now rests? . . . such opinions . . . must sooner or later . . . bring in their train the most terrifying of revolutions?" Tocqueville's insights were consistent at one level of analysis with Marx and Engels's *Manifesto*—the presumption that a new form of class struggle was now on humanity's agenda, that between the proletariat and the bourgeoisie.

As well as the similarities, it is instructive to note the differences in the forecasts of Tocqueville and Marx and Engels. In an article he wrote in November 1847 on the reform movement in France, that is, the campaign for the "extension of the suffrage," Engels drew attention to the differences between the "Liberals," "Democrats," and "Radicals" within the movement on how far to extend the suffrage. Only the "Radicals" supported universal suffrage and a republican form of government and only one paper, *Réforme,* "understands not merely Political Reforms, which will, after all, leave the working classes as miserable as before—but Social Reforms, and very definite ones." Tocqueville, it must be noted, "opposed *every* concrete proposal made to reform suffrage during the July Monarchy."[12] In the parlance of the period, he was a "latter-day republican," someone who became a republican advocate after the February Revolution.

Engels noted that the regime was more tolerant of middle-class rather than working-class participation in this movement owing in large part to its greater fear of the latter. Workers, however, were engaged in a far more important task—"the study of those questions of social economy. . . . Within a month or two, six thousand copies of M. Louis Blanc's work on "The Organisation of Labour" [which advocated state-financed worker cooperative production] have been sold in the workshops of Paris. . . . They read likewise a number of other works upon these questions; they meet in small numbers of from ten to twenty, and discuss the different plans propounded therein."[13] Engels clearly supported this effort, since he and Marx had concluded a few years earlier that only if the oppressed prepared for their liberation by becoming conscious of their tasks would they likely succeed. Thus, Engels confirms, but with greater specificity, Tocqueville's fears about "strange doctrines" and "ideas . . . spreading among" the workers.[14]

Engels assured his readers that the engagement in study by French workers did not in the least imply that "the revolutionary ardour of the people is decreasing. . . . On the contrary, the necessity of a revolution, and a revolution more thoroughgoing, more radical by far than the first one, is deeper than ever felt by the working people here." Rather than being provoked into a premature confrontation—"the government desires a riot, they provoke it by every means"—workers, Engels argued, sought the necessary knowledge to "guarantee the stability of their conquest; that will destroy not only the political, but the social power of capital that will guarantee their social welfare, along with their political strength." At the appropriate moment workers, he predicted, would take to the streets because "a collision between the people and the government will be inevitable." As for the middle-class reformers, it was his "fear" that "most . . . will hide themselves in the darkest corner of their houses, or be scattered like dead leaves before the popular thunderstorm. Then it will be all over with Messrs Odilon Barrot, de Beaumont and other Liberal thunderers, and then the people will judge them quite as severely as they now judge the Conservative Governments." Especially relevant is that the individuals Engels cited were the key members of the political faction to which Tocqueville belonged—called by the latter, the "moderate republicans."[15] The outcome for Tocqueville's party came remarkably close to Engels's forecast.

In sum, then, like Tocqueville, Engels also accurately predicted the revolution as well as its class content. However, unlike Tocqueville, Engels provided a more nuanced analysis that took into account the different shadings within Tocqueville's "Haves and Have-nots." It recognized from the outset that the most ardent republicans were a minority on France's political spectrum. This no doubt explains Engels's support for revolutionary restraint on the part of the working class—a sober recognition of what was likely to be achieved given the relationship of political forces. Armed with a sharper vision, Engels, in an important insight, noted that unlike the 1832 Reform Bill in England, the extension of the suffrage to the "small bourgeoisie" in France would have negative consequences for financial capital because the former, who were "so much oppressed and squeezed by the large capitalists . . . would be obliged to have recourse to direct aggressive measures against the moneylords, as soon as they get the suffrage." With a more nuanced view Marx and Engels were better equipped than Tocqueville for understanding, therefore, why big capital was quite content with Louis Bonaparte's overthrow of France's Second Republic at the end of 1851.

What most distinguishes Engels's analysis, on the eve of the revolution, from Tocqueville's is its employment of class resting on economic categories and dynamics. Tocqueville's classes, "Haves and Have-nots," were generic, whereas those of Marx and Engels were specific to the capitalist mode of production. Private ownership of the means of production and not property per se, as Tocqueville implies, was the basis, Marx and Engels argued, of the social as well as political "power of capital."[16] As stated in the *Manifesto*, "the distinguishing feature of Communism is not the abolition of property generally, but the abolition of bourgeois property." It was the varieties of capitals, for instance, financial versus industrial capital, that the more blunt "haves and have-nots" distinction failed to capture. Also, the dynamics of the capitalist mode of production were different from previous economic systems. Thus, the most glaring omission in Tocqueville's forecast was any discussion of the economic crisis that engulfed the working classes as well as the small bourgeoisie on the eve of the revolution—a factor that for Marx and Engels was of grave importance in trying to forecast a rise as well as an ebbing of the revolutionary tide in general and explaining the particulars of February. It was, as discussed in chapter four, their economic analysis in the summer of 1850 that allowed them to correct their mistaken assumption that the working class in France was in a position in 1848 to take power.

Explaining the February Revolution

Marx and Tocqueville differed sharply on the class character of the revolt. For Marx, what February did was to *"complete the rule of the bourgeoisie"* by instituting a bourgeois republic. It "finally brought the rule of the bourgeoisie clearly into view, since it struck off the crown [i.e., Louis Philippe's downfall] behind which capital kept itself concealed."[17] Because the proletariat had played a decisive role in its success the result was a *"republic surrounded by social institutions,"* that is, a bourgeois republic that instituted some social programs. For Tocqueville, however, "the real and only party defeated was the bourgeoisie."[18] The winners were the propagators of "those socialist theories . . . that later kindled real passions, embittered jealousies, and finally stirred up war between the classes. . . . Socialism will always remain the most essential feature of the February Revolution. . . ."[19] Subsequent events made clear that Marx had made a more accurate call at the outset of the revolution. That Tocqueville was still characterizing February two years later when he wrote his account as a socialist overturn reveals—in addition to his political biases—the limitations of his political analysis.

In this context it should be noted that earlier in *Recollections* Tocqueville upbraided "all those absolute systems that make all events of history depend on great first causes linked together by the chain of fate and thus succeed, so to speak, in banishing men from the history of the human race."[20] Tocqueville, instead, explained February on the basis of what in current social science parlance is called relative deprivation—a gap between rising expectations of the masses, due in part to the 1789 revolution and increased "prosperity," and their inferior social situation.

> Inevitably they were bound to discover sooner or later that what held them back in their place was not the constitution of the government, but the unalterable laws that constitute society itself; and it was natural for them to ask whether they did not have the power and the right to change these too, as they had changed the others. And to speak specifically about property, which is, so to speak, the foundation of our social order, when all the privileges that cover and conceal the privilege of property had been abolished and property remained as the main obstacle to equality among men and seemed to be the only sign thereof, was it not inevitable, I do not say that it should be abolished in its turn, but that at least the idea of abolishing it should strike minds that had no part in its enjoyment?[21]

Rising expectations were also due to "economic and political theories, which were beginning to attract notice and which tended to encourage the belief that human wretchedness was due to the laws and not to providence and that poverty could be abolished by changing the system of society." For Tocqueville, in fact, the real culprit in the outbreak was, as he wrote in a letter soon after February, socialist ideology: " 'The crisis from which the workmen in large manufactories were suffering . . . lasted a very short time, and though severe was not unexampled. It was not want, but ideas, that brought about that violent Subversion; chimerical ideas on the relations between labour and capital, extravagant theories as to the degree in which government might interfere between working men and employer. . . . I repeat, we have to contend with ideas rather than with wants.'"[22] Implicit in Tocqueville's insistence on an idealist over a materialist explanation of February was that opponents of any future outbreaks should take measures to limit the impact of ideas—foreshadowing the antidemocratic policies he would actually advocate after the June uprising.

In a broad historical sense Tocqueville is correct in pointing to the rising expectations of France's working classes as a result of 1789. However, to speak of "prosperity" or overall improvement in the standard of living of workers and peasants in France in the late 1840s is questionable. Marx and Engels are more persuasive in their explanation of the February upheavals in pointing to the particulars of the economic crisis that peaked in 1848 as the more immediate background factor. Their explanation, though not inconsistent with Tocqueville's, provides the specifics for understanding the actual timing of events—e.g., why 1848 and not 1846. The ups and downs of the business cycle, the uniquely boom and bust character of this new mode of production into which France's working population was being inexorably integrated, was the dynamic factor that fuelled their sense of relative deprivation.

Tocqueville's explanation for February revealed his politics in no uncertain terms. While opposed to "absolute systems" he looked to "providence" or divine ordinance to explain "human wretchedness," while embracing "the unalterable laws that constitute society itself . . . property, the foundation of our social order." The claim that poverty "was the work of laws and not of Providence," was as Irving Zeitlin shows, "a proposition whose validity Tocqueville continued to deny all his life."[23] Tocqueville the dispassionate social observer gave way to Tocqueville the latter-day republican. Yet what makes Tocqueville so interesting as a social commentator, particularly in this context, was his ability to grasp the principal dilemma of class society based on private ownership of the means of production and understand—but certainly not agree with—why the communist alternative would be appealing to the dispossessed.

In his introduction to *Democracy in America*, written almost fifteen years earlier, Tocqueville drew attention to a "universal" fact—the "gradual development of the principle of equality. . . . Would it, then, be wise to imagine that a social movement the causes of which lie so far back can be checked by the efforts of one generation? Can it be believed that the democracy which has overthrown the feudal system and vanquished kings will retreat before tradesmen and capitalist?"[24] His observation, therefore, that the end of feudal privileges as a result of 1789 exposed class privilege on the basis of bourgeois property as never before is completely consistent with Marx and Engels's position. In its opening pages the *Manifesto* states, "The modern bourgeois society that has sprouted from the ruins of feudal society has not done away with class antagonisms . . . it has simplified class antagonisms." Bourgeois democracy in the form of republican rule not only placed the proletariat on the best terrain to carry out its fight but revealed in the clearest light its true enemy, the bourgeoisie itself.

Thus, for Marx and Engels the value of February was that it removed the monarchist cover to bourgeois rule in France. While Marx and Engels could have agreed with Tocqueville's assessment that by the mid-nineteenth century or six decades after the 1789 revolution the property question was being posed in a way it had never been before—the *Manifesto* itself is testimony to their recognition of that reality—that is a long way from concluding that a particular revolt such as February represented the concrete expression of that question. Whereas Tocqueville, along with many revolutionary republicans, mistakenly believed that working-class rule was instituted with February, Marx and Engels, however, saw February as only the prelude to what took place in June—the struggle to put the working class in power.[25] To confuse the two events, or to assume that February was June, was politically costly. Since Tocqueville was on the other side of the barricades the costs were not as high to his side as they were to revolutionary republicans, as subsequent events revealed; the latter were unprepared to defend the June uprising, with many of them actually opposing it since they thought its goals had already been achieved in February. At the level of political and social analysis Tocqueville's statement about a general trend, while not incorrect, missed the complexity of the way that tendency actually unfolded. Marx and Engels, on the other hand, writing at both the time of the events and afterward in *Class Struggles*, provided a far more perspicacious reading of political reality.

Tocqueville concluded his analysis of the reasons for the February revolt with a discussion on the prospects for socialism and provided one of his most profound insights about the course of human history.

> Will socialism remain buried in the contempt that so justly covers the social-ists of 1848? I ask the question without answering it. I am sure that in the long run the constituent laws of our modern society will be drastically modified. But will they ever be abolished and replaced by others? That seems impracticable to me. I say no more, for the more I study the former state of the world, and indeed even when I see the modern world in greater detail, when I consider the prodigious diversity found there, not just in the laws but in the principles of the laws and different forms that the right of property has taken and, whatever anybody says, still takes on this earth, I am tempted to the belief that what are called necessary institutions are only institutions to which one is accustomed, and that in matters of social constitution the field of possibilities is much wider than people living within each society imagine.[26]

To entertain the possibility that nothing is written in stone when it comes to social organization echoes what was fundamental to Marx and Engels's approach. That Tocqueville could find himself in agreement with a basic premise of the founders of revolutionary communism says more about all three of them as keen social observers than as political allies.[27] As the subsequent course of the 1848 revolution revealed, Tocqueville was an active opponent of everything that Marx and Engels stood for. While he may have been "tempted" to consider a socialist alternative, his actions, especially from June onward, made clear that he was an active defendant of class rule. However, as astute social observers Tocqueville, Marx, and Engels had an advantage that many of their twentieth-century sympathizers did not, namely, the opportunity to witness the transition from the feudal to the capitalist mode of production with their attendant political forms. The period of history in which they all came of age politically may have impressed them with the fact that "in matters of social constitution" nothing is permanent, including the "right of property." Tocqueville's analysis betrayed his aristocratic contempt for the bourgeoisie and explains perhaps why he could have been objective in speculating about its circumscribed future, since the class he represented had already been passed by history. But again, lest we be taken in by Tocqueville the impartial observer, the operative word is speculation.

Towards the June Revolution

In the run-up to the June revolution Marx and Tocqueville were both very critical of the policies of the provisional government—but from different sides of the barricades. In Tocqueville's opinion, "there have been more mischievous revolutionaries than those of 1848, but I doubt if there have been any stupider."[28] Among their stupidities was the alienation of the peasantry. As an astute observer on the scene in his rural department of La Manche in Normandy, Tocqueville noted how in the aftermath of February trepidations in the countryside about the future course of the revolution, particularly with regard to the property question, tended to solidarize rural property owners regardless of the size of their holdings. "Ownership constituted a sort of fraternity linking all who had anything, the richest were the elder brothers and the less prosperous the younger; but all thought themselves brothers, having a common inheritance to defend. As the French Revolution [1789] had divided up ownership of the land *ad infinitum*, the whole population seemed part of one vast family."

Following February, the provisional government did not take steps to win over the peasantry as universal manhood suffrage was being instituted. "They forgot that their predecessors [in the 1789 revolution] at the same time that they gave every peasant a vote did away with tithes, abolished the *corvee* and other seignorial privileges, and divided the nobles' land among their former serfs, whereas there was nothing similar that they could do. By establishing universal suffrage they thought they were summoning the people to support the revolution, whereas they were only arming them against it." With insight that Marx would have appreciated, Tocqueville faulted the provisional government for not having the foresight to provide debt relief for small farmers. "In France every farmer owns some part of the soil, and most of their small holdings are encumbered with debt; therefore the creditor rather than the noble was their enemy, and it was he who should have been attacked."[29] The government's neglect of the small peasantry resulted in pro-republican forces losing big to conservatives in the May elections, possibly the first elections ever on the basis of universal manhood suffrage. The rural vote was decisive.

Marx would have agreed with much of what Tocqueville wrote about the provisional government's ineptness toward the peasantry. However, Marx had more to say on this question that was politically superior to Tocqueville's observations. It wasn't just a policy of benign neglect that undermined support for the revolution in the countryside. The imposition of a tax on the peasantry was the government's undoing. "Whereas the Revolution of 1789 began by shaking the feudal burdens off the peasants, the Revolution of 1848 announced itself to the rural population by the imposition of a new tax, in order not to endanger capital and to keep its state machine going."[30] The tax, as Marx argued persuasively, was due fundamentally to the regime's efforts to placate the bourgeoisie and, hence, finance capital, that is, the creditors of the small peasantry. Rather than tax the bourgeoisie to cover needed state expenditures, the provisional government decided to squeeze small peasants.

Furthermore, debt relief for small peasants, a proposal that Marx and Engels put forward in the *Demands* and discussed in the March 1850 Address, was for them not the panacea that Tocqueville took it to be. On numerous occasions Marx pointed out that the French Revolution of 1789 proved that land reform without the end of the market or capitalist property relations would simply result in a new subjugation for the peasantry, this time to capitalist creditors rather than landlords of old. Precisely because Tocqueville upheld, in practice certainly, the sanctity of private property and thus, by implication, capitalist property, he could only offer a palliative to small peasants and not a cure such as Marx and Engels offered. The subsequent history of capitalist property relations in the countryside have profoundly confirmed the latter's prognosis that under capitalism peasants would be converted into rural debt slaves. The policies of the provisional government ended up undermining an alliance between workers and peasants—the Parisian working class in particular, the most vigilant supporters of the government at this time, was seen increasingly by the peasantry as its opponent because of the tax—the only force that could have defended the gains of the February revolution.[31]

Explaining the June Days

Given the ineptness of the provisional government, Tocqueville confessed that his side, the opponents of revolution, should have taken advantage of the situation soon after February. "I had always thought that there was no hope of gradually and peacefully controlling the impetus of the February Revolution and that it could only be stopped suddenly by a great battle taking place in Paris. I had said that immediately after the 24th February, and what I now saw persuaded me that the battle was not only inevitable but imminent, and that it would be desirable to seize the first opportunity to start it." For Tocqueville, then, a pretext should have been sought to provoke the proletariat into a fight. He got his wish in June when the government ended the public works program, the most important of the social policies, in the eyes of Parisian workers, ushered in by February.

Marx saw this as a direct provocation. "The workers were left no choice; they had to starve or let fly. They answered on June 22 with the tremendous insurrection in which the first great battle was fought between the two classes that split modern society. . . . The Paris proletariat was *forced* into the June insurrection by the bourgeoisie. This sufficed to mark its doom." To understand the latter remark it is well to recall that on the eve of February Engels counselled revolutionary restraint on the part of French workers so that they allow themselves sufficient time to prepare for a fight—a luxury they were not afforded. Thus, for Marx it was no surprise that the workers who fought "with unexampled bravery and ingenuity" did so nevertheless "without leaders [and] without a common plan. . . ."[32] Their defeat, therefore, was inevitable.

Tocqueville's description of the June revolution is remarkably similar to that of Marx. For him it was the "greatest" insurrection in French history—owing to the number of participants—as well as the "strangest, because the insurgents were fighting without a battle cry, leaders, or flag, and yet they showed wonderful powers of co-ordination and a military expertise that astonished the most experienced officers." Whereas Marx attributed the lack of leadership to inadequate preparation, Tocqueville, reflecting his opposition to the insurrection, explained it by faulting the insurgents for being too radical. It was this fact that "prevented any man of standing from putting himself at its head."[33] While true that no leader was ever found—due in part as Tocqueville recognized to the imprisonment a month earlier of key republican figures—Marx and Engels had never placed their hope in any "man of standing" which is exactly why for them adequate preparatory time was crucial. As revolutionaries, and thus unlike Tocqueville, they praised those insurgents that did step forward to provide leadership, however inadequate, such as Joachim René Kersausie (1798–1874) whose name, Engels wrote, would go "down in history as the *first commander-in-chief of barricade fighting.*"[34]

Unlike Marx and Engels, who were in Cologne at the time, Tocqueville had the advantage of being on the scene of the insurrection. His *Recollections* provides the kind of detail that only someone present at the events could possibly describe. This is particularly true for understanding that reality from the perspective of the insurrection's opponents. Yet Tocqueville's picture is markedly inferior to that which Marx and Engels, on the basis of newspaper reports and other news from Paris, presented to their *NRZ* readers as the revolt was unfolding and in its immediate aftermath. Engels's details on what he termed the "purely military description of the struggle" still constitute primary source material.

Tocqueville also agreed with Marx on the class content of the uprising. "Another point that distinguished it from all other events of the same type during the last sixty years was that its object was not to change the form of the government, but to alter the organization of society. In truth it was not a political struggle (in the sense in which we have used the word "political" up to now), but a class struggle, a sort of 'Servile War.'"[35] On the basis of what he actually witnessed Tocqueville concluded "that the whole of the working class backed the revolt, either actively or in its heart. . . . In fact the spirit of insurrection circulated from end to end of that vast class and in all its parts, like blood in the body." Tocqueville is also most informative about the class composition of the insurgents' opponents. The "volunteers" who came to Paris from his own home district were "landowners, lawyers, doctors and farmers, my friends and neighbours. . . . The same was true almost everywhere in France. The most stick-in-the-mud little squire from the backwaters and the elegant, useless sons of the great houses all remembered that they had once formed part of a warlike ruling class, and all displayed dispatch and energy, such vigor there is in these old aristocratic bodies." It is precisely Tocqueville's frankness about the class character of the June days, which corroborates Marx's interpretation, that some modern-day analysts seek to deny.

Where Marx and Tocqueville sharply parted company was on the reasons for the insurrection. Like February, the June uprising for Tocqueville also had its roots in "the theory of socialism." The revolt was "a powerful effort of the workers to escape from the necessities of their condition, which had been depicted to them as an illegitimate depression, and by the sword to open up a road towards that imaginary well-being that had been shown to them in the distances as a right. It was this mixture of greedy desires and false theories that engendered the insurrection and made it so formidable." So once again Tocqueville resorted to his "socialist devil-made-them-do-it" thesis to explain June. Since it was naive for workers to think that they could change the conditions and institutions under which they lived they clearly must have been operating under some kind of "false consciousness," or, "false theories." Marx the materialist would have rejected the "socialist theory" culprit argument. The February revolution, in his view, had revealed the subjective as well as objective limitations of France's proletariat. "It makes no theoretical inquiries into its own task. The French working class had not attained this level; it was still incapable of accomplishing its own revolution."[36]

The situation in June had not changed significantly. While it was true, as he and Engels believed then, that February had opened the door to the socialist revolution it could not be deduced from that general proposition that the proletariat had come to such a realization by June. The causes for the uprising were quite basic—survival. The ending of the public works program meant that thousands of Parisian workers would have no means of subsistence. This is what Marx meant when he wrote that the workers were forced into the revolt—"they had to starve or let fly."

Exactly because Marx and Engels were on one side and Tocqueville was on the other side of the political divide their descriptions of the June events often read like mirror class images of each other. Their agreement, for example, on the lumpen-proletariat composition of the Gardes Mobiles, but from very different sides of the divide, is remarkable.[37] Or their assessments of the outcome of the defeat of the June revolution. Those "fateful days," Tocqueville concluded, "did not quench the fire of revolution in France, but they brought to an end, at least for a time, what one might call the proper work of the February Revolution. They delivered the nation from oppression by the Paris workmen and restored it to control of its own fate."[38] Marx's conclusion, again not inconsistent with Tocqueville's, was done from an opposite class vantage point as well as being richer and more precise.

> In the National Assembly all France sat in judgment upon the Paris prole-
> tariat. The Assembly broke immediately with the illusions of the February Revolu-
> tion; it roundly proclaimed the *bourgeois republic*, nothing but the bourgeois repub-
> lic. . . . The proletarians . . . had to be vanquished in the streets. . . . Just as the
> February republic, with its socialist concessions, required a battle of the proletariat,
> united with the bourgeoisie, against the monarchy, so a second battle was necessary
> in order to sever the republic from the socialist concessions, in order to officially
> work out the *bourgeois republic* as dominant. The bourgeoisie had to refute, arms
> in hand, the demands of the proletariat.[39]

Echoing, finally, Tocqueville's qualifier "at least for a time" Marx returned to the thesis that he and Engels had been arguing for since at least 1846: namely, that the bourgeois republic offered the proletariat the best terrain upon which to overthrow its adversary. Thus, the June defeat only hastened the day for the showdown between labor and capital. About June, then, "we exclaim: *The revolution is dead!—Long live the revolution!*"

In the midst of the June events and afterward another side of Tocqueville was revealed that is often overlooked by his latter-day liberal admirers. No longer content to be an astute observer of history, Tocqueville now sought to shape history—like Marx and Engels, but from the other side of the barricades. When it appeared at a crucial moment that the insurgents might prevail Tocqueville put aside personal angst and did what had to be done to defend the "country's safety" or, as Marx put it, "to perpetuate the rule of capital, the slavery of labour." Although initially hesitant, he went along with the decision of the National Assembly to institute what he termed "a military dictatorship under General Cavaignac." Regarding his initial hesitation, he later wrote, "In that I made a mistake, which luckily was not imitated by many."[40] Cavaignac, who had recently led France's conquest of Algeria, was given carte blanche powers, which Tocqueville enthusiastically endorsed, to employ the kinds of methods he had successfully used against Algeria's peasants. As for the claims of some that the Assembly was duped by Cavaignac partisans into voting for the dictatorship, he said: "If they did use this trick, I gladly forgive them, for the measures they thus caused to be taken were indispensable to the country's safety."[41]

But beyond simply voting for Cavaignac's dictatorship, he led the Assembly in going out into the battle zones to rally support among the government's troops for the general. When the faint-hearted in the Assembly began to vacillate on implementing their vote, it was Tocqueville who took the initiative. "'Gentleman,' I said, 'the Assembly may have been mistaken, but allow me to observe that, such a resolution having been publicly taken, it would be a disgrace for it to retreat, and a disgrace for us not to obey.'"[42] Because of his resolve Tocqueville was elected to be one of the sixty Assemblymen to "disperse through Paris, informing the national guards of the various decrees just passed . . . and thereby restoring their confidence. . . . [W]e put on our sashes and went out. . . ."[43] Thus, almost exactly at the same time that Marx and Engels were leading the fight for solidarity for the insurgents through the pages of the *NRZ*, Tocqueville was doing all he could to ensure that the revolt would be crushed.

In the Aftermath of the Revolution

The enthusiasm with which Tocqueville participated in the defeat of the insurgents—there is no mention in his account of the brutality of the government's actions[44]—foreshadowed not only his actions in the coming months but also the course of political developments in France. While it is true that Tocqueville's memoirs reflect a degree of angst about what had been done and fear for what it portended,[45] his actions following the June revolt, about which his *Recollections* are highly selective,[46] make clear that his fervent opposition to it was no momentary aberration. As André Jardin notes in his most informative biography, the "June Days disposed Tocqueville to adopt a conservative policy of order. . . . He now voted against the limitation of the workday to ten hours, against the abolition of the salt tax [which was especially onerous for peasants], in favor of continuing to allow men called for military service to hire substitutes instead of making military service obligatory for all—and, of course, against amnesty for those convicted during the June Days."[47]

As one of the eighteen Assembly members selected to draft the constitution—there were about nine hundred representatives in the Assembly—Tocqueville played a key role in what was eventually adopted. In the debate on the right to work Tocqueville's anti–working class stripes were most apparent. Prior to the June revolt an article in the draft preamble that obligated the state to provide workers with employment and assistance in time of need—one of the "social institutions," as Marx called it, of the February revolution—was met with silence from Tocqueville. However, after June, when it was proposed that the state "'recognizes the right of all citizens to education, work, and assistance'" as a substitute to the earlier draft article, Tocqueville objected vehemently. It was he who in fact led the charge that prevented its adoption in the final document.

> Tocqueville's speech on September 12 . . . broadened the discussion; recognition of the right to work led to the socialization of society, and it was therefore socialism itself that he was denouncing. The latter, in its different forms, had three constant principles: the worship of material goods, the abolition of private property, and the suppression of individual liberty. It was as remote as possible from the values exalted by the French revolution. The revolution of 1848 would deny the ides of 1789 if it established socialism.[48]

The speech made quite a stir and was later published as a pamphlet. In the opinion of one modern-day conservative Tocqueville partisan it was "an impassioned defense of democracy against socialism and an account of their fundamental incompatibility."[49] As Marx would have argued, more accurately, the speech was "an impassioned defense" of bourgeois property rights vis-à-vis the rights of workers and a recognition of the "fundamental incompatibility" of the two sets of class interests.

Tocqueville's success in having the right to work clause excluded from the constitution was not unexpected, in Marx's opinion. Aside from the fact that the pre-June draft article was "the first clumsy formula wherein the revolutionary demands of the proletariat are summarized" and that the "right to work is, in the bourgeois sense, an absurdity, a miserable pious wish," the constitution itself simply "put on record the *existing* facts." The final wording of the constitution registered what had occurred on the barricades in June. More specifically, Tocqueville's silence on the right to work issue before June as opposed to his vehement reaction afterward reflected fundamentally the fact of the defeat of the workers, the force that had been behind its initial inclusion in the earlier draft. What Tocqueville epitomized was the confidence that the enemies of the working class had gained as a result of their victory over them in the streets; his success in having the right to work clause left out simply registered that fact.[50]

There were two other constitutional issues in which Tocqueville played a leading role in the Assembly's deliberations: a unicameral versus a bicameral legislature and the popular election of the president. On the former issue he supported a bicameral body and his notes for the speech that he intended to give—he was unable owing to illness—presented his argument. Basically, he was fearful that a single body would concentrate too much power in the hands of the newly enfranchised masses: "It was necessary to 'fight the chronic disease of democracies—instability, capriciousness, and tyranny on the part of the legislative power,' and for that, to 'slow down popular movements. The ruling principle of democracy is that nothing is to be done despite the people and apart from the people, and not that the people can immediately realize every desire.'"[51] The legacy of the February revolution, however, still reverberated throughout France, in spite of June, and the Assembly gave in to popular sentiment and voted instead for a unicameral body—much to Tocqueville's distress.

On the issue of the election of the president, Tocqueville, again, was motivated by his fear of the masses. A popularly elected president, he felt, would be a check against a too-powerful Assembly. Even before the June Days he held this view; this was especially true after suffering the defeat on the bicameral question. "I was, I confess, much more concerned with putting a powerful leader quickly at the head of the Republic than with drafting a perfect republican constitution. At that time we were under the divided, vacillating rule of the Executive Committee [of the provisional government], socialism was at our doors, and we were drawing near to the days of June. . . ."[52] With his assistance the Assembly voted in favor of a popularly elected president, "and we know as well what followed from it—the election of Prince Louis-Napoleon as president of the French Republic [December 1848], his coup d'état [December 1851], and the authoritarian regime of the Second Empire [beginning December 1852]. Tocqueville was not the last to ironize over that institution he had taken such pains to ensure and define."[53] Thus, perhaps unwittingly, Tocqueville's contribution to constitutional government paved the way for its overthrow.

Since the two constitutional arrangements that Tocqueville proposed were inspired by Montesquieu's separation of powers doctrine, it is well to recall Marx's view of a similar proposal raised in the context of the German revolution. In that situation the issue was whether there should be a sharing of power between the crown and the Prussian Assembly. Marx and Engels bitterly opposed such an arrangement—"the Montesquieu-[Jean Louis] Delolme worm-eaten theory of division of powers"[54]—because in their view its intent was to stifle the revolution and limit the extension of popular rule, that is, democracy. The basis of Tocqueville's enthusiasm for separation of powers, to limit mass involvement in the decisions of the state, thus to limit the revolution, was exactly the reason why Marx and Engels opposed it. Again, the mirror class image of the two political perspectives. Unlike Tocqueville, Marx, of course, understood that in the final analysis constitutions do not protect freedoms or prevent coup d'états from occurring—only the mobilization of the masses offers any real likelihood of guarantees. Tocqueville, of course, found such an option too distasteful.

Tocqueville attributed the later constitutional crisis that preceded the coup d'état to a "big mistake" that he was in part responsible for—the enactment of a provision that made the incumbent president ineligible for reelection. "Our minds were not supple and quick enough to turn around and see that as soon as it was decided that the citizens themselves should choose the president, the ill was without remedy, and that any rash attempt to hinder the people in their choice would only increase it." Thus, the decision to institute the popular election of the president had let the genie, in the person of the masses, out of the bottle. The dilemma Tocqueville expressed was symptomatic of a larger contradiction surrounding the constitution, as Marx argued.

> The fundamental contradiction of this constitution, however, consists in the following: The classes whose social slavery the constitution is to perpetuate, proletariat, peasantry, petty bourgeoisie, it puts in possession of political power through universal suffrage. And from the class whose old social power it sanctions, the bourgeoisie, it withdraws the political guarantees of this power. It forces the political rule of the bourgeoisie into democratic conditions, which at every moment help the hostile classes to victory . . .[55]

The granting of universal manhood suffrage, created, therefore, an inherently unstable situation for the bourgeoisie. The fundamental incompatibility between labor and capital was aggravated by the newly obtained political rights of the working classes. As Marx would argue later, Bonaparte's coup was an attempt to resolve this contradiction.

Although Tocqueville was lukewarm in his support for the republic—"I . . . was indifferent to the Republic"[56]—he nevertheless felt it was worth protecting. Since he and his political cohorts, who were acting increasingly as an organized faction in the Assembly at this time, were not about to look to the masses for support, their solution was to work from within, to attempt to influence Louis Bonaparte, the newly elected president who took office in December 1848—and about whom Tocqueville had many qualms—to maintain the republic. Thus, their decision to accept posts within the new government of Odilon Barrot; Tocqueville became Minister of Foreign Affairs. Not unbeknownst to him he walked into a major foreign policy fracas that eventually led to his resignation. Although the issue, French intervention in the Roman revolution, occupied much of his time, he says little about it in *Recollections*.

Tocqueville's writer's block about the Roman situation may have to do with its outcome—an unequivocal failure in liberal foreign policy. Essentially what happened is that a French expeditionary force in late Spring 1849 intervened in the Roman revolution by overthrowing the republican government and reinstalling the Pope. Tocqueville, whose tenure as Foreign Minister began in June, was put in the seemingly uncomfortable position of defending the government's actions in the newly elected legislative Assembly; prior to taking office he had voted as an Assembly member for the appropriation to send the force. Nevertheless, his correspondence makes clear that however "great [a] misfortune" it might be to subject Rome "to all the horrors of war," especially since the dilemma had been created by his predecessor and he had misgivings about the policy, "to withdraw covered with shame . . . would be a frightful disaster."[57] In tones reminiscent of many a twentieth-century liberal foreign policy maker, liberal democracy abroad had to be sacrificed for the sake of imperial interests at home. In the choice between revolution from below versus order from above the latter had clear priority. Tocqueville attempted to assuage his liberal angst by getting assurances from the Pope that he would institute liberal reforms—which the latter eventually reneged on. Thus, in the end Tocqueville had nothing to show his liberal admirers for his Roman actions, which perhaps explains his silence in *Recollections*.[58]

The government's intervention in Rome was a clear violation of the new constitution. When Ledru-Rollin, leader of the left republican Montagne or Mountain faction in the Assembly, who lambasted France's actions, asked to see government documents related to the situation Tocqueville refused. A peaceful and poorly attended Mountain-led demonstration on June 13 against the government's policies gave the Interior Minister an excuse to declare a state of siege on the bogus claim that the protest was an attempt at another June uprising in Paris. (In Lyons, however, the proletariat did engage in a real revolt that was eventually overcome.)

Marx, who had just arrived in Paris from the barricades in Germany, wrote an article for a German democratic weekly about the June 13 events. The irresolute and inadequate response of the Mountain faction, he argued, undermined any confidence Paris' proletariat may have had in its leadership. The result was that the "chief actor in the drama of June 13 was not the *people*, but the 'Mountain.'"[59] Given the failure of the Mountain and other left republicans to support the uprising of the proletariat the previous June, "June 13, 1849 is only the retaliation for June 1848. On that occasion the proletariat was deserted by the 'Mountain,' this time the 'Mountain' was deserted by the proletariat." Tocqueville, too, had a similar assessment of June 13. "In June 1848, the army had no leaders; in June 1849, the leaders had no army."[60]

With Ledru-Rollin and his faction on the run and forced into exile, Marx—who was again forced to leave France—predicted that in spite of its victory, the counterrevolutionary alliance in the National Assembly, which Tocqueville was part of, "will not only disintegrate, [but] its extreme faction will soon reach a point when it will seek to discard even the irksome semblance of the Republic, and then you will see *how it will be blown away with a single breath and there will be a repetition of the February, but on a higher level.*" For Marx, therefore, the salutary aspect of June 13 was that it polarized the situation by removing from the scene the petit-bourgeois left republicans, whose role had been to blunt the class struggle, and encouraging the counterrevolution to end the republican experiment via an attempted coup or some similar move. Such a bid would propel the "people" back into the streets to make the revolution this time "permanent." It was only by the middle of 1850 that Marx and Engels had concluded—again, as discussed in the previous chapter—that "permanent revolution" was not on the agenda in France or anywhere else in Europe. On the other hand, Louis Bonaparte's coup d'état in December 1851 did indeed remove the counterrevolution's republican fig leaf.

As for the Roman intervention itself, the immediate situation that gave rise to the June 13 events, Marx explained in *Class Struggles* that Bonaparte's support for the papacy in opposition to the Roman Republic began almost immediately with his accession to office in December 1848 and was well known by the National Assembly and, hence, by Tocqueville. The basis for Bonaparte's position was no mystery. "The Roman revolution was . . . an attack on property, on the bourgeois order, dreadful as the June [1848] Revolution. Re-established bourgeois rule in France required the restoration of papal rule in Rome . . . to smite the Roman revolutionists was to smite the allies of the French revolutionists."[61] Thus, Tocqueville, a defender of Catholicism—at least for France—was not in all likelihood as uncomfortable as he implied in *Recollections* with Bonaparte's Roman policies when he decided to accept the Foreign Affairs portfolio.

Toward the End of the Republic

The June 13 events became the pretext for the government's crackdown on democratic rights throughout the country—policies that Tocqueville enthusiastically implemented and embraced and about which there is virtual silence among his latter-day admirers. With pride he recalled that "we introduced the following measures: a law to suspend the [political] clubs, another to suppress the vagaries of the press with even more energy than had been used under the Monarchy; and a third to regularize the state of siege." When an opponent of these measures in the Assembly charged that they established a "military dictatorship," Tocqueville quoted approvingly his chief minister's reply: "'Yes . . . it is a dictatorship, but a parliamentary one. No private rights can prevail over the inalienable right of society to save itself. There are certain imperious necessities that are the same for all governments, whether monarchies or republics.'" In Tocqueville's own words, "the only way to save freedom was to restrict it."[62] For Marx also, June 13 "makes the *legislative dictatorship* of the united royalists [the conservative coalition] a *fait accompli*. From this moment the National Assembly is only a *Committee of Public Safety of the party of Order.*"

Tocqueville justified his actions on the grounds that the way to "save freedom," that is, to "prevent the overthrow of the Republic and in particular to stand in the way of a bastard monarchy under Louis Napoleon [Bonaparte] . . . the most immediate danger," was to win over to his government's side the conservatives, the largest party, in the parliament. This was the party that Marx had referred to as the extreme faction of the counterrevolution that would, as he accurately predicted, eventually "seek to discard the irksome semblance of the Republic." Tocqueville was well aware that his antirepublican concessions to the conservatives were part of their strategy to end the republic. Unlike Marx, whose approach to defending the republic was to mobilize the masses—something that Tocqueville was incapable of doing—his tactic was to convince them that their interests would be furthered by his government. "They wanted order energetically re-established; in that respect we were their men, for we wanted the same as they, and we did it as well as they could desire and better than they could have done themselves. . . . [T]hey wanted to use our victory [over the Mountain faction in June] to impose repressive preventive laws. We ourselves felt the need to move in that direction although not wishing to go as far as they."[63]

Hence, the imposition of a "parliamentary dictatorship" was justified by Tocqueville as "concessions to the fears and legitimate resentments of the nation . . . after such a violent revolution." The "nation" of course meant Tocqueville's conservative allies; "such a violent revolution" is contradicted by Tocqueville himself who had written only a few pages earlier that June 13 was far less violent than the previous June revolt. In spite of these concessions Tocqueville recognized that "such measures, laws and language pleased the Conservatives but did not satisfy them. To tell the truth, nothing short of the destruction of the Republic would have contented them." This is exactly what Marx had foreseen a year earlier. Yet Tocqueville, caught in something like a Greek tragedy, continued to believe that the rightward direction of his government would save the republic—in spite of knowing the agenda of his conservative allies. "The leaders of the majority [in the Assembly] wanted to make use of us to get rigorous measures taken and repressive laws passed, so that government would be comfortable for our successors; and at that moment our Republican opinions made us more fit for the task than the Conservatives. They counted on being able to bow us out afterwards and bring their substitutes onto the stage."[64]

What explains Tocqueville's persistence in courting the antirepublican conservatives whose goal was the dismantling of the Republic? Since the party that he and his cabinet colleagues belonged to—those who wanted "to establish a moderate republic"—were a minority in the Assembly, it had to enter into an alliance, as he argued, with the conservative majority. "We have undertaken to save the Republic with the help of parties who do not love it. Therefore we can rule only by making concessions—only one must never give away anything of substance. In this matter everything depends on measure. At this moment the best, and perhaps the only guarantee for the Republic is our continuance in office. Therefore we must take all honourable means to keep ourselves there." Tocqueville's justification highlights what was the fundamental difference between his politics and those of Marx and Engels. Whereas the latter looked to the "people's alliance" with the proletariat at its head to ensure victory in the fight for democracy, Tocqueville, foreshadowing many a well-intentioned twentieth-century liberal, placed his hopes in enlightened latter-day republicans like himself. Thus, the necessity of "our continuance in office." Astute political maneuvering on their part was the "only guarantee" against the counterrevolution. It was beneath Tocqueville's aristocratic liberal dignity to look beyond the legislative arena for the only majority, as Marx argued, that had it in its interest to "save the Republic"—the masses. Marx and Engels's critique five years earlier of the Young Hegelians as "a handful of chosen men" who pretended to think and act on behalf of the masses was no less applicable to Tocqueville and his cohorts.

Since, as Tocqueville recognized, Louis Bonaparte represented "the greatest and most permanent of dangers" to the Republic, it was, thus, necessary to humor him—"to charm, or at least to content his ambition"—as well as the conservatives. To that end he promised Bonaparte that he and his party would seek to revise the article in the constitution—one that he had played a major role in having included in the document—"'which forbids the re-election of the President. . . . We would gladly help you to get that done.'" In a further suggestion to Bonaparte,

I went on to hint that perhaps in the future, if he governed France quietly, wisely and modestly, confining himself to being the first magistrate of the nation and not its suborner or its master, it was possible that, when his mandate expired, he might be re-elected despite Article 45 by almost unanimous agreement, for the Monarchic parties would not see the limited prolongation of his rule as the ruin of their hopes [of reinstalling a monarch], and even the Republican party might feel that a government such as his was the best way of getting the country used to a Republic and ready to acquire a taste for one.[65]

Having once feared a strong executive, Tocqueville was now willing to enhance its power—all in the name of saving the Republic. While Tocqueville was to later blame the coup on the excesses of the left, it didn't occur to him that he may very well have whetted Bonaparte's appetite for an unbridled executive with his hints and suggestions. More importantly, what Tocqueville's comments reveal once again, as was the case with his tact on the conservatives, is his aristocratically haughty assumption that he could personally and skillfully engineer democracy's institutionalization in France. With such talents who needed the masses to bring about democratic rule! Toward the end of *Recollections*, written about September 1851, Tocqueville had convinced himself that Bonaparte "seemed to like me better and better." Thus, the "Roman expedition in which . . . I firmly supported the President until his policy became exaggerated and unreasonable, finally put me in his good graces." Tocqueville was a shining example of the liberals who, as Marx noted, mistakenly thought they could use Bonaparte for their own purposes.

While the Roman events may have allowed Tocqueville to be in Bonaparte's "good graces" this didn't ensure his tenure as a cabinet minister. Looking for a pretext to assert his power vis-à-vis the Assembly, Bonaparte charged that the government provided insufficient support to his views on the Roman situation and called for its resignation. Thus, Tocqueville and his cohorts, shocked and depressed, were unceremoniously returned to the Assembly as ordinary members in November 1850. In the meantime Bonaparte began to look for a way to continue his presidency in spite of the constitutional prohibition. Tocqueville assisted him in this enterprise by leading an unsuccessful effort in July 1851 in the Assembly to revise the constitution.[66] Marx had correctly foreseen that the majority party of order would be "compelled to prolong the power of the President." While the majority of the Assembly had voted in favor of revision it lacked the requisite three-fourths majority. Frustrated with the Assembly's resistance, Bonaparte took matters into his own hands. On December 2, 1851, the anniversary of the coronation of his uncle Napoleon I, he carried out a coup d'état that dissolved the Assembly, which left him to rule unencumbered. Those Assembly members, such as Tocqueville, who put up symbolic resistance were arrested and spent a night in jail. A year later Bonaparte had himself crowned as Napoleon III. Thus, the official end to the Second Republic and the beginning of the Second Empire.

With remarkable insight Marx had painted in broad outlines more than a year earlier what in fact occurred. He was especially perceptive about the course that Tocqueville and the conservative coalition that his faction was allied with, the Party of

Order, would take. "In its struggle with the people, the party of Order is compelled constantly to increase the power of the executive. Every increase of the executive's power increases the power of its bearer, Bonaparte . . . it strengthens the fighting resources of Bonaparte's dynastic pretensions, it strengthens his chance of frustrating a constitutional solution by force on the day of the decision."[67] Seven months prior to Bonaparte's coup Marx thought, erroneously, that the Assembly would reach an accommodation with him. The reason he gave, however, accurately understood the sentiment of its members including Tocqueville; they "would prefer the lesser of two evils. They would prefer an Empire or a Dictatorship of Napoleon, to a Democratic and Social Republic. . . ."[68] Events would show that it was exactly this sentiment that facilitated Bonaparte's takeover.

Like Marx, Tocqueville anticipated a coup, if not its timing. A meeting with Bonaparte on May 15, 1851, left Tocqueville with the impression that "he is far from renouncing the possibility of a *coup d'état* on his own."[69] But however much Tocqueville saw himself as a key player in shaping France's democracy his liberalism prevented him from taking the necessary steps to prevent Bonaparte's actions. He allayed all doubts about his true loyalties in a letter written a few months before the coup:

> I believe that the Bonapartist current, if it can be turned aside at all, can be turned only by meeting a revolutionary current, which will be still more dangerous . . .
> The government which I should prefer, if I thought it possible, would be a republic; but, believing its continuance impossible, I should see without regret Louis Napoleon become our permanent ruler, if I could believe that he would be supported by the higher classes, and would be able and desirous to rule constitutionally. But . . . I [do] not believe either of these things to be possible . . .
> His reelection, therefore, especially if illegal, may have disastrous consequences. And yet it is inevitable, unless resisted by an appeal to revolutionary passions, which I do not wish to rouse in the nation.[70]

Thus, Tocqueville clearly recognized—what Marx had long argued—that only a "revolutionary current" could stop the "Bonapartist current," an option that for him was worse than the usurper. He was prepared to hold his nose and take a Bonapartist dictatorship over that of the "greedy"—as he referred to them in the June revolt—masses.

In the aftermath of the coup, with all its attendant horrors, Tocqueville had second thoughts about the Bonapartist option. Another letter two weeks after the coup revealed his doubts.

> What has just happened in Paris is abominable, in form and substance. . . . As for the event itself, it was contained as an embryo in the February, like a chick in an egg. For it to emerge, all that was needed was enough time for the incubation. As soon as socialism appeared, one should have predicted the reign of the sword. One engendered the other. I had been expecting it for a long time, and even though I am filled with shame and sorrow for our country and great indignation over acts of violence and certain contemptible actions that exceeded all bound, I feel little surprise and no inner confusion. . . . The nation, at this moment, is mad with fear of the socialists and a passionate desire to regain its well-being. It is incapable and, though I say it with much regret, unworthy of being free . . .[71]

Yet however much Tocqueville deplored the new situation he could not resist resorting to his "socialist" devil-made-him-do-it thesis to explain what happened. In what may be the first instance of blaming the victims of counterrevolution in the bourgeois era, the culprit was not Bonaparte but the perpetrators of February and certainly their successors in June. Tocqueville himself had played a key role in evoking the red scare in his diatribe against socialism during the right to work debate in the constituent assembly. It was precisely because he had assisted in instituting the "reign of the sword" during and after the June events that Tocqueville could "feel no inner confusion" about what Bonaparte had done.

What Tocqueville was incapable of grasping is the possibility that his as well as the actions of other well-intentioned "moderate republicans" may have paved the road to Bonapartism. This, in fact, was one of the central arguments in Marx's summary statement of the lessons of the revolution, *The Eighteenth Brumaire of Louis Bonaparte*, which was written about six months after Tocqueville had made his last entry in *Recollections* and about eighteen months after the last article in *Class Struggles*. (Unlike Marx, Tocqueville never completed a balance sheet on the entire revolution; he apparently found it easier to turn his attention to the 1789 revolution which resulted in his writing *The Old Regime and the French Revolution*, published in 1856.)[72]

Firstly, the state of siege of Paris that Tocqueville had enthusiastically supported in June 1848, Marx noted, was the "midwife" for the constituent assembly and its product, the republican constitution. "If the Constitution is subsequently put out of existence by bayonets [i.e., Bonaparte's coup], it must not be forgotten that it was likewise by bayonets, and these turned against the people . . . that it had to be brought into existence."[73] Thus, a precedent was established and it was only a matter of time that the "sabre and musket" would get the idea after subsequent state of sieges of "saving society once and for all by proclaiming their own regime as the highest and freeing civil society completely from the trouble of governing itself," that is, a permanent military state of siege led by Bonaparte.

Secondly, the actions of Tocqueville and the majority in the National Assembly in the course of the June 1849 events also played into Bonaparte's hands. By failing to uphold the constitution in the face of Bonaparte's violation of it with his Roman intervention, by defeating the motion of the Mountain faction that called for Bonaparte's impeachment because of the violation, and by violating the parliamentary immunity rights of the Mountain members with their arrests and banishment, the parliamentary Republic politically undermined itself vis-a-vis the presidency. "By branding an insurrection [the June 13 demonstration] for the protection of the constitutional charter an anarchic act aiming at the subversion of society, it precluded the possibility of its appealing to insurrection should the executive authority violate the Constitution in relation to it."[74]

Marx also pointed to the dismissal of Tocqueville and his fellow ministers as "a decisive turning-point" in Bonaparte's strengthening of his office vis-à-vis the legislature. "No one has ever sacked lackeys with less ceremony than Bonaparte his ministers. . . . With it the Party of Order lost, never to reconquer it, an indispensable post for the maintenance of the parliamentary regime, the lever of executive power." From then onward, the Party of Order, the conservative majority in the Assembly which Tocqueville's faction had blocked with, never really challenged Bonaparte's enlargement of the executive at the expense of the legislative power. It dared not do so, as Marx explained, because by "so doing it would give the nation its marching orders, and it fears nothing more than that the nation should move."[75] In other words, a real fight against Bonaparte would have required, as Tocqueville explained in his letter on the eve of the coup, "an appeal to revolutionary passions, which I do not wish to rouse in the nation." It was as if Marx had read Tocqueville's very own words.

Lastly, the failed attempt led by Tocqueville to revise the constitution in order to allow Bonaparte to run again for the presidency also played into the latter's hands. The problem, as Marx perceptibly diagnosed—he, in fact, had stated as much in *Class Struggles* eighteen months earlier—was that Tocqueville's party, "caught in inextricable contradictions," had boxed itself in a no-win situation due in large part to the parliament's prostration before Bonaparte for at least the two previous years. It couldn't afford a rejection of revision since this would provoke Bonaparte to use force to retain the presidency at the moment when his tenure ended in May 1852. Such a scenario would provoke "revolutionary anarchy" since Bonaparte would be lacking authority at that moment along with a parliament that "for a long time had not possessed it [namely, authority] and with a people that meant to reconquer it." But Tocqueville's party lacked the three-fourths majority needed to make a revision as required by the constitution. Interestingly, Marx presented Tocqueville in a relatively favorable light by noting that he qualified the motion for revision with another one which stated that the Assembly "had not the right to move the *abolition of the republic*."[76] Marx apparently didn't know that about five weeks later Tocqueville proposed "an overall revision of the Constitution not excluding even the republican form itself."[77]

While a majority voted on July 19 for revision, it lacked about one hundred votes for the required three-fourths. In spite of the defeat, as Marx underscored, "the majority of parliament declared against the Constitution, but this Constitution itself declared for the minority and that its vote was binding." Thus, Bonaparte was provided with a rationale for his coup because "had not the Party of Order subordinated the Constitution to the parliamentary majority on May 31, 1850, and on June 13, 1849? Up to now, was not its whole policy based on the subordination of the paragraphs of the Constitution to the decisions of the parliamentary majority? . . . At the present moment, however, revision of the Constitution meant nothing but continuation of the presidential authority, just as continuation of the Constitution meant nothing but Bonaparte's deposition [i.e., he had to step down since he could serve only one term]. Parliament had declared for him, but the Constitution declared against parliament. He therefore acted in the sense of parliament when he tore up the Constitution, and he acted in the sense of the Constitution when he dispersed parliament."

In other words, on two previous occasions, the vote of May 31, 1850, to rescind universal manhood suffrage—what Marx called the "coup d'état of the bourgeoisie"—and the vote of June 13, 1849, to reject the motion to impeach Bonaparte for violating the constitution with his Roman intervention, the parliamentary majority of the party of order had dismissed the constitution.[78] It had given Bonaparte an important precedent for doing the same. Also, that the constitution stood above the parliamentary majority allowed Bonaparte to rationalize his own standing above the parliament. Therefore, the failure to revise the constitution gave Bonaparte the handle he had been looking for ever since his election in December 1848. Perhaps for different reasons, Tocqueville could have agreed with Marx's observation that "if ever an event has, well in advance of its coming, cast its shadow before it, it was Bonaparte's coup d'état."[79]

Marx's critique of the actions of Tocqueville's party—how they prepared the way for Bonaparte's coup—is not just of historical interest. There is in fact a very modern ring to Tocqueville's anything-but-a-revolution strategy for defending liberal democracy. The twentieth century is replete with modern-day Tocquevilles who have pursued such a course. They have had about as much success as Tocqueville in preventing the rise of latter-day Bonapartes. That Bonaparte might correctly be termed a "premature totalitarian"—the lumpen hordes, described by Marx, that Bonaparte organized into partisan supporters clearly anticipated twentieth-century fascist gangs—is reason enough to take seriously the political strategy put forward by Marx as an alternative to that of Tocqueville.[80]

Alasdair MacIntyre characterizes Marx's and Tocqueville's perspectives on the events of 1848–1851 as rival theories for interpreting the behavior of major participants and "action-guiding interpretations of political transactions."[81] While true, more important than theory for interpretation is the matter of theory for political action. As he correctly notes, but unfortunately does not explore, "Tocqueville's diagnosis warrants in retrospect a very different response to one and the same situation warranted by Marx's diagnosis." It is indeed the response that Tocqueville made, as opposed to the one that Marx advocated, to the events that is of far more political significance—for some participants, in fact, a matter of life and death. It isn't enough to argue, as MacIntyre does convincingly, that both Marx and Tocqueville acted and interpreted the events of 1848–51 from different theoretical premises. There's more at stake here than simply interpretation. What must be addressed is the political consequences of their theories. The course that Tocqueville pursued, based on his deepest-held beliefs, assumed that republican democracy could be achieved and maintained without mobilizing the "revolutionary passions" of the masses. Marx and Engels, on the other hand, had concluded some years earlier that such mobilizations were a necessary prerequisite. Tocqueville, unlike Marx, was in a position to put his line to the test of the French reality. It failed miserably.[82] For Marx and Engels the real test of a theory was its effectiveness as a weapon for political action.

In this connection it is useful to recall Marx's preface to the second edition of *The Eighteenth Brumaire* in 1869 in which he took to task Proudhon's analysis of Bonaparte's coup d'état. "Proudhon, for his part, seeks to represent the coup d'état as the result of preceding historical development. Unnoticeably, however, his historical construction of the coup d'état becomes a historical apologia for its hero. Thus he falls into the error of our so-called *objective* historians. In contrast to this, I demonstrate how the *class struggle* in France created circumstances and relations that made it possible for a grotesque mediocrity to play a hero's part."[83] In other words, the class struggle made Bonaparte's accession possible but not inevitable. Had Tocqueville's *Recollections* and other writings on the French events been available to him, Marx could have subjected them to the same criticism.

In the immediate wake of the February revolution Tocqueville wrote a new preface to his *Democracy in America* in which he held up the American republican experience as a model for Europe. Referring to the upheavals of 1848, he wrote "almost all Europe was convulsed by revolutions; America has not had even a revolt." The lesson for revolutionary France was that "it was not force alone, but good laws, that give stability to a new government."[84] It was just this posture, what Marx and Engels called parliamentary cretinism, the mistaken belief that the legislative arena was the center of politics, that blinded Tocqueville to the possibility of the kind of upheaval that shook the American republic to its very foundations twelve years later. In fact, it was the revolutionary force unleashed by the Civil War and its aftermath—which Marx and Engels encouraged and applauded—that made the American ideals that Tocqueville so admired a reality for the first time. Yet for Tocqueville the very thought of the masses in revolutionary motion sent shudders up his spine; for Marx and Engels it was a spine-tingling thrill.[85] This difference in the essence of their political cores, not just rival political theories, was decisive in their different responses to the events of 1848–51.

Almost a decade earlier in 1841 Tocqueville, in a most self-reflective moment, admitted to his core:

> My mind is attracted by democratic institutions but I am instinctively aristocratic because I despise and fear mobs. At the most fundamental level, I passionately love freedom, legality, respect for rights, but not democracy. I hate demagoguery, the disordered action of the masses, their violent and unenlightened intervention in public affairs. . . . I belong neither to the revolutionary nor the conservative party. But, when all is said and done, I incline towards the latter rather than the former because I differ from the conservatives over means rather than ends, while I differ from the revolutionaries over both means and ends.[86]

Nothing better anticipates what his response would be to the French masses' "intervention in public affairs" in 1848–1849.

Three months prior to the February revolution Engels anticipated the "moment . . . at which a collision between the people and the government will be inevitable" and predicted that most of the prominent upper-class reformers, a number of whom formed the faction that Tocqueville later affiliated with, would "hide themselves in the darkest corner of their houses, or be scattered like dead leaves before the popular thunderstorm. Then it will be all over with Messrs Odilon Barrot [the chief minister of the cabinet that Tocqueville was a member of], de Beaumont [Tocqueville's lifelong friend and collaborator] and other Liberal thunderers, and then the people will judge them quite as severely as they now judge the Conservative Governments."[87] In one sense Engels's prediction was incorrect—aside from the fact that Tocqueville's pre-February reform credentials were highly questionable—because this party did not take flight after February or June. They, in fact, stood toe to toe *against* the people—behind of course the sabres and muskets of the military. They were enthusiastic participants, with Tocqueville in the lead, in implementing measures that limited the political space for the masses. One could argue that another error in Engels's prediction is that while Tocqueville and his cohorts were "scattered like dead leaves" it wasn't at the hands of the people but rather by Bonaparte.

Yet the spirit if not the letter of Engels's prediction was confirmed by events. For in the final analysis Tocqueville and his colleagues did take flight from the defense of the Republic. In Tocqueville's case the historical record makes clear that he consciously rejected the only course he knew would defend the Republic, mobilizing the revolutionary masses. In that sense he and his party took flight. The case can be made that he also hid himself—from politics. He retreated into his research not for the purposes of drawing a full balance sheet for public consumption on the events of 1848–51, including his own role, but for his own edification. Five days before Bonaparte's coup Tocqueville wrote "that he welcomed the inevitable disaster which would free him from the world of politics . . . 'I can only savor in imagination the time when, far from public affairs . . . away from political conversations . . . I will try to isolate myself from my time and my country to live by myself and for myself.'" [88] In the end, Tocqueville's class privileges allowed him the luxury of a withdrawal from political reality.

Tocqueville's retreat from politics stands in sharp contrast to what Marx and Engels did. They emerged from the 1848 events politically stronger and more confident. The chief result of these tumultuous years in their opinion was that the struggle for socialist revolution was placed on the political agenda for the first time. As a communist Marx responded to the 1851 coup by dropping everything else to write and publish a thorough political analysis of this event; most importantly, to explain to fellow fighters why the revolution did not advance. Tocqueville's response, on the other hand, resembled that of the German intellectuals who too had been disillusioned by their brief foray into the political arena. It is in this sense, again, that Engels's forecast about Tocqueville and his cohorts was indeed correct. In conclusion, Marx and Engels provided an account that was politically superior—as a basis for action—to what Tocqueville produced in explaining the course of the 1848 revolution. As well, it accurately foresaw Tocqueville's own political course.

CHAPTER SIX

Political Adjustments to the Long Lull in the Class Struggle

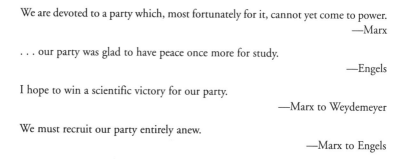

> We are devoted to a party which, most fortunately for it, cannot yet come to power.
>
> —Marx
>
> . . . our party was glad to have peace once more for study.
>
> —Engels
>
> I hope to win a scientific victory for our party.
>
> —Marx to Weydemeyer
>
> We must recruit our party entirely anew.
>
> —Marx to Engels

Toward the end of Summer 1850 Marx and Engels concluded, based on Marx's research on developments in the world capitalist economy, that the revolutionary wave that began in 1848 had come to an end and that the socialist revolution was not on the immediate agenda anywhere in Europe. A major upturn in western European economies was under way, which meant that the grievances of Europe's working masses that fed the 1848 upsurge were likely to diminish. Such a conclusion required organizational as well as political adjustments. Thus, beginning in the fall of the same year they began to reorient their party activities to this new reality. Their failure to win most Communist League members to this reassessment provoked a split in the organization that was in part responsible for its eventual demise. In the meantime Marx and Engels settled into what they dubbed the "scientific" work, the necessary step as they saw it to prepare for what would eventually be another upsurge in the class struggle. More than a decade would pass before they found themselves immersed in active political struggle. Along the way they consolidated around themselves a core of co-thinkers who together functioned as an informal party referred to by both partisans and opponents as the "Marx party." And whenever political reality demanded, they put aside the scientific work and mobilized their party to respond.

THE COMMUNIST LEAGUE: AN "EPISODE IN THE HISTORY OF A PARTY"

When Marx and Engels became active again in the Communist League upon their arrival in London in mid-1849 and helped in its revival through, for example, the writing and dissemination of the "Addresses" of March and June, they did so on the assumption that the 1848 revolutionary wave was still alive and well. Situated now in London, they also took steps to link up with other revolutionary exiles who also assumed that their stay in England was merely a brief respite from the upheavals of the previous year and a half. London would now be a launching pad for the next phase in the process.

While the March 1850 "Address" of the Central Authority of the League laid out the broad programmatic perspective for the organization's participation in the anticipated renewal of the revolutionary wave, with particular emphasis on the political and organizational independence of the proletariat, another "Address" that Marx and Engels issued in June took up more organizational issues.[1] Among various recommendations to League branches it warned against the efforts of opponents to "destroy the centralisation and strength of the party by fragmenting it. . . ." As for relations with opponent groups, the "workers' party can use other parties and party factions for its own purposes on occasion but must never subordinate itself to any other party." And as for "those people who were in the government during the last movement [the revolutionary upheaval in Germany in the previous Spring] and who used their position to betray the movement and to suppress the workers' party wherever it wanted to act independently [they] must be kept at a distance under all circumstances."[2]

There was specific advice for the German party on how to relate organizationally to peasant, labor, and sports associations—for example, the institution of two categories of membership, actual and supporters—although the "detailed organisation can be left to the leading districts. . . ." The document reported favorably on the increasing collaboration of the Central Authority in London with "delegates of the Blanquist secret societies"—all in "preparation for the next French revolution"— and the left wing of the Chartist movement led by Julian Harney. The final words of advice reflected Marx and Engels's optimism about the imminence of a new upheaval. "All members are urged to make the greatest possible efforts, especially at this moment when the situation is so critical that the outbreak of a new revolution can no longer be very far away."[3]

In expectation of a new revolutionary upsurge Marx and Engels became involved in a new organizational effort about which there has been much Marxological hue and cry ever since, the details of which need not concern us. Suffice it to say that the Universal or International Society of Revolutionary Communists, as they dubbed it, never got beyond the planning stage.[4] The basic reason is that by the middle of the summer, or after they issued the June "Address," they were no longer convinced that there was a need for such an organization. Revolution was no longer on the agenda.[5]

The Politics of the Split in the League

When Marx and Engels began to argue inside the League for their new view, based on Marx's recently done research, they encountered stiff opposition, especially from Willich. He took issue with Marx's claim that "communism could only be introduced after a number of years, that it would have to go through several phases and that generally its introduction could only be effected by a process of education and gradual development."[6] Willich argued, in turn, according to Marx's rendition—or at least as Marx's rendition was recalled—that communism "would be introduced in the next revolution, if only by the might of the guillotine [and that] . . . he and his brave men from the Palatinate [in Southern Germany where the stiffest resistance to the Prussian army in the Spring of 1849 occurred] would introduce communism on their own and against the will of everyone in Germany." Willich not only argued for instant communist revolution but also against the kind of measured analysis and research upon which Marx's scientific communism was based. Anticipating the future, Marx related that "the hostility between [him and Willich] was already great and he . . . feared it would lead to a split in the League. . . ."[7]

The expected split, which pitted Marx and Engels and a majority of the Authority on one side against Willich, to be joined soon by Karl Schapper, on the other, surfaced first in the refugee committee in which League members had been active. At the September 1 meeting of the Authority it erupted in full to such a degree that Willich actually challenged Marx to a duel, which the latter understandably declined. At the September 15th meeting of the Authority, Marx, in recognition of the irreconcilable differences with the Willich-Schapper faction and in an effort to preserve the League, proposed that the Authority be transferred to Cologne, that the Authority in Cologne draft new Rules for the League,[8] and that two independent districts of the League be formed in London. In advocating the last provision—"the way for us to separate without splitting the party"—Marx said that it was apparent that there were fundamental differences of principle at issue. In spelling out what he saw was wrong with the line of the Willich-Schapper faction Marx in turn provided his vision of the revolutionary process.

> In the last debate on "the position of the German proletariat in the next revolution" views were expressed by members of the minority on the Central Authority which directly clash with those in the last circular but one and even the *Manifesto*.[9] A German national standpoint was substituted for the universal outlook of the *Manifesto*, and the national feelings of the German artisans were pandered to. The materialist standpoint of the *Manifesto* has given way to idealism. The revolution is seen not as the product of realities of the situation but as the result of an effort of *will*. Whereas we say to the workers: You have 15, 20, 50 years of civil war to go through in order to alter the situation and to train yourselves for the exercise of power, it is said: We must take power *at once*, or else we may as well take to our beds. Just as

the democrats abused the word "people" so now the word "proletariat" has been used as a mere phrase. To make this phrase effective it would be necessary to describe all the petty bourgeois as proletarians and consequently in practice represent the petty bourgeois and not the proletarians. The actual revolutionary process would have to be replaced by revolutionary catchwords. This debate has finally laid bare the differences in principle which lay behind the clash of personalities, and the time for action has now arrived.[10]

Marx was apparently criticizing the Willich-Schapper faction's disagreement with his economic analysis that the upswing in England's business cycle was of fundamental importance for politics in continental Europe, including Germany. He, therefore, in addition, opposed their tactic of blocking with exile reformist forces who wanted instant revolution. While Marx and Engels viewed the revolutionary process from an international perspective, as made clear in the *Manifesto* and the "Addresses"— the March "Address," in addition to saying that "the [German] workers [would not be able to] propose any directly communist measures" when the democratic reformists took power in the next upsurge, explicitly stated that for "the German workers . . . the first act of this approaching revolutionary drama will coincide with the direct victory of their own class in France and will be very much accelerated by it"[11]—the Willich-Schapper faction viewed the German situation independently of that larger reality. It was exactly such national provincialism that Marx attacked.

Schapper continued to disagree with Marx's vision of a prolonged process through which German workers would come to power, saying that the "question at issue is whether we ourselves chop off a few heads right at the start or whether it is our heads that will fall." Giving a demagogic nod to Marx's internationalist perspective, he added that in "France the workers will come to power and thereby *we* in Germany too. Were this not the case I would indeed take to my bed . . . I would be able to enjoy a different material position." Along with this declaration of self-sacrifice for the revolutionary cause, he engaged in another bit of demagogy by suggesting that his opponents in the debate lacked his optimism about the prospects for German workers. "I am in general an enthusiast in this matter . . . I am a fanatical enthusiast." For his final jab, Schapper reverted to his old habit of class baiting Marx and Engels in rejecting Marx's proposal for establishing two independent League districts in London. "Marx is a personal friend of mine but you are in favour of separation—very well, we shall each go our separate ways. But in that case there should be two leagues, one for those who work with the pen and one for those who work in other ways."[12]

In reply Marx educated him on revolutionary self-sacrifice, revolutionary patience, and made a further elaboration of his vision of the politics of the transition to the dictatorship of the proletariat.

> As for personal sacrifice, I have given up as much as anyone; but for the class and not for individuals. And as for enthusiasm, not much enthusiasm is needed to belong to a party when you believe that it is on the point of seizing power. I have always defied the momentary opinions of the proletariat. We are devoted to a party which, most fortunately for it, cannot yet come to power. If the proletariat were to come to power the measures it would introduce would be petty-bourgeois and not

directly proletarian. Our party can come to power only when the conditions allow it to put *its own* views into practice. Louis Blanc is the best instance of what happens when you come to power prematurely.[13] In France, moreover, it isn't the proletariat alone that gains power but the peasants and the petty bourgeois as well, and it will have to carry out not its, but *their* measures. The Paris Commune [1792–94] shows that one need not be in the government to accomplish something. And incidently why do we hear nothing from the other members of the minority, especially Citizen Willich, who approved the circular [probably the March "Address] unanimously at the time? We cannot and will not split the League: we wish merely to divide the London district into two districts.[14]

Marx's rebuttal encapsulates in perhaps the most succinct form ever put by him or Engels—or, more correctly, the minutes keeper at the historic meeting (Marx and Engels signed the minutes, it should be noted)—the essence of their reading of what is involved in making a socialist revolution. Note again the people's alliance as the basis for a new revolutionary government, the same lineup that he argued for against Weitling's claim two years earlier that a socialist, rather than a bourgeois democratic revolution was on Germany's agenda. In that debate he also argued that the Provisional Government in France was not the dictatorship of the proletariat but rather a multiclass government.[15] Also noteworthy, contrary to some interpretations of what this reassessment of the potential for revolution after 1850 meant for Marx and Engels, they continued to defend the relevancy of the Central Authority "Addresses" and the *Manifesto*. That revolution was not on the immediate agenda did not, therefore, in any way invalidate the basic premises of both documents.

While the majority of the Authority voted for Marx's three proposals, Willich and Schapper rejected them and established a separate party. They were able to attract a majority of the members of the GWEA and the refugee committee to their new party, which prompted Marx, Engels, and the other Authority members who voted with them—Heinrich Bauer, Konrad Schramm, Carl Pfänder, and Johann Eccarius—to resign from the two organizations. Three weeks later they, along with Harney, curtly replied to a note from the Blanquists—collaborators of Willich—in the Universal Society of Revolutionary Communists, that "we have, long since, considered the association you speak of as dissolved by fact."[16]

The Cologne district, to which the Authority was now transferred, no doubt clearer about political reality inside Germany—unlike the exiles in London—sided with the Marx-Engels team and roundly denounced the splitters. "The Willich-Schapper attack, they told the members, was not directed against some kind of 'bourgeois socialism'; on the contrary—

> it damned the authors of the party Manifesto of 1848 and of the first 'Address of the Central Committee' of this year [i.e., the March Address], in which the policies of the party are expounded in detail; indeed, it also condemned the *Manifesto and the policies of the party itself.*"[17]

Thus, not only did Marx and Engels understand that the March "Address" was still applicable in the aftermath of their reevaluation of the potential for revolution in Europe but their comrades in Cologne as well.

With the Willich-Schapper faction functioning as a separate party the Marx-Engels League district in London proposed to the Authority in Cologne that they be expelled. The reasons they gave provide some insight into their expectations about internal party discipline. It should be remembered that new party Rules had yet to be promulgated.

1. They have communicated reports, and false reports at that, concerning the split in London to leaders of secret societies outside the League and to refugees of various nationalities.

2. They are in a state of open rebellion against the legally constituted Central Authority in Cologne; they act in defiance of the latter's decisions and have an emissary traveling around Germany to found a Sonderbund.

3. They have violated, and still violate, in their relations with the members of the London district, all obligations binding on members of secret societies.

4. They have, since the separation, broken all the laws of secret societies and to permit them to remain in the League any longer would only serve them to hasten its disintegration.[18]

The Cologne comrades agreed with the proposal and formally severed relations with the Willich-Schapper group at the end of November.[19]

As the Central Authority in Cologne was carrying out the expulsion, it drew up, in compliance with the decision of the September 15th League meeting in London, a set of new "Rules" which it sent to London in December for its approval. It's instructive to look at them, since Marx had a hand in editing them and voted for their adoption.

In general, the new "Rules" did not differ significantly from those of 1847.[20] The centralist character of the organization was reaffirmed. Whereas the "Rules" of 1847 stated that a condition of membership was "Subordination to the decisions of the League," those of 1850 required that "Members will swear to abide unconditionally by the decisions of the League." One condition of membership that was new stipulated that the individual "be emancipated from all religion, sever connections with any church organisation and not participate in any ceremony not required by civil law." It is not clear, unfortunately, what the basis was for this addition. Another condition elaborated a bit more on a provision in the earlier "Rules": "[S]how ability and zeal in propaganda, unswerving devotion to convictions and revolutionary energy." This stipulation is most interesting because it anticipated the issue that precipitated the historic split in the Russian Social Democratic Labor Party in 1903 that gave rise to the Bolshevik and Menshevik factions. It concerned the obligations of membership and more specifically the extent to which party members were expected to be organized in order to be as active as possible.

Significantly, one provision modified the December 1848 revision that forbade members to participate "in any other political organization."[21] Under the new "Rules" members were merely obligated to "stand aloof from all organisations and particular strivings that oppose or obstruct the progress of the League towards its goal." Another major change made expulsion more difficult or more in line with the 1847 "Rules." The use of the death penalty for "betrayal" in the 1848 revision was dropped.

At the beginning of January 1851, the London district of the League met, with Marx in attendance—Engels had now moved to Manchester—and approved with a couple of minor changes on Marx's part the "Rules" drafted by Cologne. The organization soon became moribund and at a meeting in November the following year Marx moved that it be dissolved (to be discussed shortly).

The Politics of "Mindlessness"

The critique that Marx directed at the Willich-Schapper faction regarding the revolutionary process had a basic resemblance to the one he reserved for another group of opponents—liberal and reformist democrats. The occasion was the unsuccessful attempt by exiled petty-bourgeois leaders from the failed revolutions on the continent, Ruge from Germany, Ledru Rollin from France, and Giuseppe Mazzini from Italy, to form in 1850 in London a new international democratic association, the Central Committee of European Democracy. The inaugural manifesto of the body was severely excoriated by Marx and Engels. It argued, in its own words, that the failure of the revolutions of the previous two years was due primarily to a lack of "'organisation. . . . We have sects but no Church, incomplete and contradictory philosophies, but no religion, no collective faith which rallies the faithful beneath a single banner. . . .'" The reference to "contradictory philosophies" meant "exclusivity in point of theory." Hence, any appeals to "intellect" should be set aside in order to "agitate the masses" who act out of "collective intuition."

> Life is the people in motion, it is the instinct of the masses [who accomplish "great things"] . . . by involuntary, sudden, electric association in the streets. . . . The hand-clasp of a worker in one of these historic moments which inaugurate an epoch will teach us more about the organisation of the future than could be taught today by the cold and unfeeling travail of the intellect . . .[22]

Marx and Engels termed the manifesto an "appeal to mindlessness." Aside from its denial of the class struggle and, thus, contradictory class interests—the real reason for "no collective faith"—it discounted the need for revolutionary theory and sought to reduce the revolutionary process to simply an organizational problem.

> Their ideas of social organisations are most strikingly expressed: a mass gathering in the streets, a riot, a hand-clasp, and it's all over. In their view indeed revolution consists merely in the overthrow of the existing government; once this aim has been achieved "*the* victory" had been won. Movement, development and struggle then cease, and under the aegis of the European Central Committee that would then be in control, there begins the golden age of the European republic and somnolence proclaimed for evermore.[23]

Thus, like the Willich-Schapper faction these liberal and reformist democrats patronizingly held that theory was either beyond the interest or competence of workers. For Marx and Engels, on the other hand, revolutionary theory in the hands of workers was the weapon for self-liberation. The conclusion they drew, based on their theoretical perspectives, was that any attempts to "make" a revolution in the new circumstances would simply set back the real movement. Both tendencies shared in their view a penchant for "playing at revolution."

Marx's characterization of the Willich-Schapper faction at the time of the split is instructive: "[T]hese people are still Communists in their convictions even though the opinions they are now expressing are anti-communist and could at best be described as *social democratic*" [italics added].[24] In his *Principles of Communism*, written three years earlier, Engels described "democratic socialists" as "either proletarians who are not yet sufficiently enlightened regarding the conditions of the emancipation of their class, or members of the petty bourgeoisie, a class which, until the winning of democracy and the realisation of the socialist measures following upon it, has in many respects the same interest as the proletariat."[25] It is in the first sense that Marx applied the label to Willich and Schapper, that is, workers who were not convinced that certain objective conditions had to exist before the proletariat could take power and carry out socialist measures. Reformists, such as those who formed the Central Committee of European Democracy, were best described by the second sense of the definition. Schapper, it should be noted, rejoined the Marx party and was one of its most active members until his death in 1870. On his deathbed, Schapper, after admitting to Marx some years earlier that he had the wrong position in the 1850, told him that while he had been faithful "to our principles, I am no theoretician."[26] No doubt he was alluding to his failure to see at the time Marx's long-term historical materialist view of Europe's development.

In Defense of the Party

The correspondence between Marx and Engels makes clear that they had grown weary with the internecine wars within the exile community. Also, while Marx continued to meet regularly throughout 1851 and 1852 with what remained of the League in London—again, Engels was now living in Manchester—and collaborated with the Authority in Cologne, he sought to reduce his own personal involvement in organized political activity including the League. Their priority at this moment was the continuance of the scientific work that had been interrupted by the events of 1848–51. However, political reality intervened once again to sidetrack their plans. In the spring of 1851 Prussian authorities began to crack down on political opponents and organizations. Thus, most of the leaders of the League in Germany were imprisoned and eventually brought to trial in the fall of 1852 on charges of conspiracy to overthrow the government. In what proved to be the last activity of the League, Marx organized an international defense campaign that involved legal, propaganda, and relief work on behalf of the defendants.

The primary target of the crackdown was clearly the party that Marx and Engels had successfully assembled in Germany since 1848. As the chief of police in Berlin explained, in a most accurate and prescient assessment, shortly before the arrests in 1851: "'It can now rightly be said of the Marx-Engels Party that it stands far above all the emigrants, agitators and central committees, because it is unquestionably the strongest in knowledge and ability. Marx himself is well known personally, and everyone realises that he has more intellectual power in the tip of his finger than the rest of the crowd have in their heads.'"[27] Marx was not unaware of the motives behind the actions of the authorities: "The trial . . . is directed *autant* against us as against the Cologne people; we too shall have some rough treatment . . ."[28]

The state's evidence against the accused consisted of the *Manifesto*, the March and June Addresses of 1850, the Rules of the Communist League, and a set of forged minutes of League meetings which tried to implicate Marx. In collaboration with the police and spies in other countries, the Prussian authorities, which included the king, constructed their case and after a year and a half put the detainees on trial in Cologne. While Marx had worked hard prior to the trial to publicize the detention of his comrades and to collect counterevidence in their defense, he and other League members doubled their efforts once the trial began in early October 1852. In collaboration, via an elaborate underground mail system, with the defense counsel at the trial, Marx directed the defense, which involved the collection and dispatch of relevant data on a daily basis. The extraordinary degree of mobilization of the party in London in carrying out this work was captured in part by Jenny Marx in a letter to Adolf Cluss, a party member in Washington, D.C.

> As you can imagine, the "Marx party" is busy day and night and is having to throw itself into the work body and soul. . . . [Regarding the prosecution's forged materials] We here had to supply all proofs of the forgery. Hence my husband had to work all day and late into the night. Affidavits had to be obtained . . . and the handwriting of the alleged minute-takers . . . officially authenticated to provide proof of forgery on the part of the police. Then every one of these things had to be copied out 6–8 times and dispatched by the most divers routes to Cologne, via Frankfurt, Paris, etc. . . . The whole thing has now become a struggle between the police on one side and my husband on the other—they blame him for every thing, the entire revolution and even the conduct of the trial. . . . A complete office has now been set up in our house. Two or three people are writing, others running errands, others scraping PENNIES together so that the writers may continue to exist and prove the old world of officialdom guilty of the most outrageous scandal. And in between while my 3 merry children sing and whistle, often to be harshly told off by their papa. What a bustle![29]

While the "Marx party" was able to impugn the prosecution's bogus evidence, such as the forged minutes, the Prussian state, through the selection of a jury sympathetic to the state, eventually achieved much of what it wanted. Seven of the eleven defendants received sentences from six to three years imprisonment while the remaining four were acquitted.

Immediately after the trial the Marx party took steps to publicize the trial proceedings in order to expose the Prussian government's frameup and rebut the charges. In addition, a broad-based committee was formed to raise funds for the families of the imprisoned. Along with news articles that Marx and Engels were able to get into the press in Europe and the United States, Marx wrote a pamphlet, *Revelations Concerning the Communist Trial in Cologne*, that unfortunately, owing to a police confiscation in Germany, only got limited distribution, mainly in the United States in the German exile community. Nevertheless, the pamphlet allowed Marx to go public for the first time with the politics of the Willich-Schapper split—which the prosecution raised in the trial—as well as a defense of the character and modus operandi of the League as a secret organization.

The effort that Marx poured into the Cologne trial, before and after as well, took a toll on his political economy research. It also came at great personal expense, as his letter to Cluss about the *Revelations* pamphlet makes clear:

> To appreciate to the full the humour of the thing, you must know that its author, for want of anything decent to wear on his backside and feet, is as good as interned and moreover, is and continues to be threatened with *truly ghastly misère* engulfing *his family* at any moment. The trial dragged me even deeper into the mire, since for 5 weeks, instead of working for my livelihood, I had to work for the party against the government's machinations. On top of that, it has completely alienated the German booksellers with whom I had hoped to conclude a contract for my Economy.[30]

The comment reveals once again the seriousness with which Marx and Engels took their political obligations. They expected no less from their comrades. In the same letter to Cluss, Marx urged him to form committees in the United States for the prisoners and their families. "Here [in England] it is a matter of party demonstration. . . . [Y]ou might specifically emphasise that this is not a case of begging for the revolution . . . but rather of a *definite* party aim whose fulfillment is demanded by the honour of the workers' party." A couple of months later, after Marx had learned that the German authorities had confiscated the bulk of the *Revelations* pamphlet, Jenny Marx wrote Cluss again, this time to impress upon him his political obligation in disseminating the publication in the United States.

> Since printing in Europe has become almost impossible but is now entirely a matter of honour for the party, you should at least have it printed *à tout prix* as a feuilleton. The publication of the pamphlet is now a necessity as against *all* our enemies, and will, more than anything else, further the interests of the Cologne people and sway public opinion in their favour. Interest in them must be awakened.[31]

As her entreaties to Cluss make clear, Jenny Marx, along with other activists who are often ignored in the standard Marxological tomes, functioned and saw herself as a serious party member.

Although *Revelations* was never distributed as widely as the Marx party had hoped in the immediate aftermath of the trial, in later decades it was republished in order to assist subsequent generations of revolutionaries in carrying out political defense work, a necessary activity of any revolutionary party. Much of what Marx and Engels had learned through the experience of the Cologne trial would serve them well two decades later in defense of the Communards of Paris.

By the end of the Cologne trial it was clear that it was no longer possible for the League to exist in Germany and its future elsewhere was also problematic. Thus, as Marx explained in a letter to Engels, "at my suggestion" on November 17, 1852, "the League here *disbanded*; similarly the continued existence of the League on the Continent was *declared* to be *no longer expedient*. In any case, since the arrests of Bürgers-Röser [leaders of the Authority], it had to all intents and purposes already ceased to exist there."[32] Some eight years later Marx briefly elaborated on this explanation for the dissolution to say that "moreover circumstances were no longer favourable for a propaganda society of this sort."[33] The first organization, therefore, to proclaim the program of scientific communism came to an end after five years of existence. In subsequent years, Marx and Engels would reflect back on the League's experience. "The 'League,' like the *société des saisons* in Paris [Blanqui's republican socialist organization from 1837–39] and a hundred other societies was simply an episode in the history of a party that is everywhere springing up naturally out of the soil of modern society."[34]

PREPARING FOR THE NEXT UPSURGE

In the framework of readjusting the Communist League to the fact that revolution was no longer on the immediate agenda, Marx and Engels had to reorganize themselves to carry out what they now saw as their key political task—a resumption of the scientific work. To that end Engels in mid-November 1850 moved to Manchester to work in his family's firm in order mainly to subsidize the Marx household so that his comrade would be able to devote undivided attention to his magnum opus.[35] As Marx later acknowledged, without the subsidies from Engels, which derived from the surplus value produced by the workers in the Engels family firm, *Capital* would never have been written. Until Engels moved back to London in 1870 it was primarily through frequent correspondence, which averaged a letter every other day, and periodic visits to each other that the core of the Marx party remained in tact.

The Party that "Swots" Together Stays Together

Even before the League's dissolution Marx and Engels had recognized, in the aftermath of the split in the League in the fall of 1850, the futility of continuing organized party work. The failure of most exiles to recognize that the era of revolution had come to an end put them at odds with Marx and Engels. Exile politics became increasingly sectarian, much of which was directed at the Marx party. The Willich-Schapper party, on the assumption that revolutions could be "made," behaved in a manner that had no basis in political reality, which explains in part why it became defunct two years after the split. In the absence of any real revolutionary opportunities Marx and Engels concluded that a withdrawal from organized activities was the best course to follow. Five months after the split Marx confidently wrote to Engels that "I am greatly pleased by public, authentic isolation in which we two, you and I, now find ourselves. It is wholly in accord with our attitude and our principles."[36] In reply Engels made an observation about exile politics that subsequent history has confirmed on more than one occasion. "One comes to realise more and more that emigration is an institution which inevitably turns a man into a fool, an ass and a base rascal unless he withdraws wholly therefrom, and unless he is content to be an independent writer who doesn't give a tinker's curse for the so-called revolutionary party. It is a real SCHOOL OF SCANDAL AND MEANNESS in which the hindmost donkey becomes the foremost saviour of his country."[37] A few days later Engels was more realistic about the extent to which he and Marx could avoid active political involvement. "By the mere fact of keeping oneself INDEPENDENT, being *in the nature of things* more revolutionary than the others, one is able at least for a time to maintain one's independence from this whirlpool, although one does, of course, end up by being dragged into it."[38]

For Marx and Engels, their self-imposed isolation gave them relief from exile politics in order to undertake the research—or, in current parlance at that time, to "swot," that is, to study—that would be necessary in preparing for the next revolutionary wave. Engels explained this to one of their party members in Switzerland in July 1851.

> We . . . have the satisfaction of being rid of the entire loud-mouthed, muddleheaded, impotent émigré rabble in London, and of being at long last able to work again undisturbed. . . . We have always been superior to the riff-raff and, in any serious movement, have dominated them; but we have, meanwhile, learnt an enormous amount from our experiences since 1848, and have made good use of the lull since 1850 to resume our swotting. If anything should blow up again, the advantage we shall have over them will this time be of quite a different order, and in fields, furthermore, of which they have small inkling.[39]

A couple of years later Engels made the same point to Joseph Weydemeyer who was doing political work for the party in New York. After a lengthy discussion on the likelihood of another revolutionary upsurge in Europe Engels expressed his optimism about the prospects for "*our party*" because it was "taking the stage under wholly different auspices." In the new situation, at the level of theory and program, many of the democratic and republican demands that the communists advanced in 1848 were now being touted by "our respected opponents." Thus, "this time we shall start off straight away with the *Manifesto*, thanks largely to the Cologne trial in which German communism . . . has passed its matriculation."

At the level of "practice," however, Engels explained that the reform democrats could be expected to vacillate on these demands in a revolutionary situation. Therefore, Engels feared—raising an issue of profound historical importance that will have to be explored in more detail later—"our party will find itself forced into power, whereupon it will have to enact things that are not immediately in our own, but rather in the general, revolutionary and specifically petty-bourgeois interest . . . we shall find ourselves compelled to make communist experiments and leaps which no one knows better than ourselves to be untimely." Yet as he lamented, "I don't very well see how it could happen otherwise." What Engels foresaw was exactly the reality that the Bolsheviks found themselves in sixty-four years later, to employ his language, an "advanced party" taking power in a "backward country"—and with many of the consequences that he had foreseen.

Whether the communist party would or would not have to come to power prematurely, to return to the issue at hand, "the main thing is that our party's rehabilitation in history will already have been substantiated in advance in its *literature.*" Engels was lauding the fact that the party, no longer saddled with the advocates of "mindlessness," had already made significant progress in its scientific work. "[W]e have all of us benefited substantially in exile. There are, of course, some amongst us who proceed on the principle: 'What need is there for us to swot? That's what *père* Marx is there for, it's his business to know everything.' But in general the Marx party does a good deal of swotting . . . our party's superiority has increased both absolutely and relatively. As indeed it must, for *la besogne sera rude* [it will be a tough business]."[40] What's significant here is Engels's stricture, made to another party member, that "swotting" was the responsibility of all members of the Marx party, not just its leader. In this regard, it is worth mentioning that although "père Marx" was the recognized leader of the party, he rejected—implicit in Engels's comment—any messianic interpretation of that role. In an angry letter to a one-time collaborator who was now slandering the party in 1850, charging that Marx sought to create a personal "dictatorship," Marx reminded him "that you did all you could to foist upon me the role of 'democratic Dalai Lama and incumbent of the future.' What proof have you that I ever accepted that absurd role?"[41]

One of the newer recruits to the party in the early 1850s in London was Wilhelm Liebknecht who spent much of his time with the Marx household. Like other neophytes in the party he too was impressed by the seriousness with which Marx took his research. As he recalled many years later,

> Marx went there [to the British Museum] daily and urged us to go too. Study! Study! That was the categoric injunction that we heard often enough from him and that he gave us by his example and the continual work of his mighty brain.
>
> While the other emigrants were daily planning a world revolution and day after day, night after night intoxicating themselves with the opium-like motto: "Tomorrow it will begin!," we the "brimstone band," the "bandits," the "dregs of mankind," [some of the epithets hurled at the Marx party by opponents] spent our time in the British Museum and tried to educate ourselves and prepare arms and ammunition for the future fight. . . .
>
> Marx was a stern teacher: he not only urged us to study, he made sure that we did so.[42]

The greatest fear of Marx and Engels during this period was that they would not be able to have the scientific "ammunition" in time "for the future fight." When it appeared that European economies were headed for a crisis in 1853, Engels, in the same letter to Weydemeyer, wrote, "I should like to have time before the next revolution to study and describe thoroughly at least the campaigns of 1848 and 1849 in Italy and Hungary." Engels's research, in addition to collaborating with Marx on political economy, focused primarily on military matters, which he was able to translate into major writings. Marx, too, was anxious about the economic climate in 1853. "I find that things have begun to move sooner than I should have liked (I think the COMMERCIAL DOWNFALL will begin in the spring as in 1847). I had always hoped that, before that happened, I might somehow contrive to withdraw into solitude for a few months and work at my Economy. It seems that this isn't to be."[43]

Marx and Engels, again, the inveterate politicians, were prepared to prioritize political activity over the scientific work if forced to do so by political reality. As it turned out, the next revolutionary era was a decade away, giving the Marx party sufficient time to "prepare arms."

In promoting the publication in 1859 of Marx's *A Contribution to the Critique of Political Economy*, the first installment of the long-awaited political economy project, Engels was on even more solid ground in reiterating the point about the Marx party as a swotting party that he had made six years earlier to Weydemeyer.

> Our party was propelled on to the political stage by the February Revolution and was thus prevented from pursuing purely scientific aims. The basic ["materialist"] outlook, nevertheless, runs like an unbroken thread through all literary productions of the party. . . .
>
> After the defeat of the Revolution of 1848–49, at a time when it became increasingly impossible to exert any influence on Germany from abroad, our party relinquished the field of emigrant squabble . . . to the vulgar democrats. . . . [Meanwhile] our party was glad to have peace once more for study. It had the great advantage that its theoretical foundation was a new scientific outlook the elaboration of which kept it busy enough; for this reason alone it could never become so demoralised as the "great men" of the exile.
>
> The book under consideration is the first result of these studies.[44]

That Marx, too, saw the book as a party publication is made clear by a comment to Lassalle explaining how his chronic liver ailment had forced him to delay its completion. "In it an important view of social relations is scientifically expounded for the first time. Hence, I owe it to the Party that the thing shouldn't be disfigured by the kind of heavy, wooden style proper to a disordered liver."[45] A few months before the book's publication, Marx left no doubt, in a letter to Weydemeyer, its purpose. "I hope to win a scientific victory for our party."[46] In a comment to Lassalle about the next book in the project—that is, *Capital*—Marx said it would "take a somewhat different form, more popular TO SOME DEGREE . . . because [it] has an expressly revolutionary function."[47]

With the appearance of *A Contribution* Marx felt vindicated by the decision he and Engels made a decade earlier about organized political activity, as he explained to Ferdinand Freiligrath who had until recently been a Marx party stalwart. "[I] was firmly convinced that my theoretical studies were of greater use to the working class than my meddling with associations which had now had their day on the Continent."[48] While it is true that Marx was disappointed with the initial attention that *A Contribution* attracted, especially in Germany, he gleefully reported to Lassalle in 1860 that "in Russia my book has caused a considerable stir, and a professor in Moscow has given a lecture on it."[49] The attention that the Russians gave to Marx's book was a harbinger of things to come.

What clearly distinguished the Marx party from any other revolutionary current of the nineteenth century was exactly the importance it attached to "swotting"—research and study based on what Engels termed at this stage, "the materialist conception." And an essential component of their study was the distillation of the lessons of the previous revolutionary wave, its causes, course, and outcome. One of the lessons of the 1848–49 upheavals was that it was indeed incumbent for revolutionaries to have done their homework beforehand—if, of course, political reality permits. Thus, the feverish effort with which the party worked, Marx in particular, to be prepared for the next round.

Functioning as an Informal Party

In rejecting organized party work after 1852 Marx and Engels did not, however, dismiss the need for coordinating in some fashion the political activities of themselves and their closest co-thinkers. In fact, from this time until the formation in 1864 of the International Working Men's Association they consciously operated as an informal party, a fact that is ignored by virtually every Marxological account.[50] A recognition of this reality clarifies their usage—especially in this period—of "party," which they employed in two senses. One was explained by Marx in a letter to Freiligrath in 1860. "By party, I mean the party in the broad historical sense."[51] The other was that of the informal Marx party, what Marx and Engels were clearly referring to in their above-quoted comments about *A Contribution*. The party in this second sense had, in fact, a precedent—the *NRZ* team that functioned after the League was suspended in Cologne in 1848.

That Marx and Engels still thought in party terms, that is, collaborative political work between themselves and others based on shared beliefs *and* expectations, after the end of the League is revealed by an exchange of letters about three months after the organization's formal dissolution. Ernst Dronke, a League member whose ties to the Marx-Engels team went back to the Correspondence Committee in Brussels, had irked Marx for failing to deliver on time needed funds from Engels. Dronke's negligence was symptomatic, in his opinion, of a larger problem that he raised in a letter to Engels in which he rebuked him and the other "milksops" in the party: "With their idleness, lack of stamina and inability to sustain any PRESSURE FROM WITHOUT, they are absolutely hopeless. We must recruit our party entirely anew."[52] Marx then listed with evaluative commentary some of the people he considered to be party members, which included, among the nine names, Lassalle ("despite his many 'buts,' is *dur* [hard] and energetic"), Liebknecht, and Wolff. Engels, in his reply, thought that "in the next affair . . . the 'best' of them will no doubt pull themselves together." He agreed with Marx about Lassalle, while noting his "foibles . . . and we are already aware that he will always make official business a pretext for indulging his lesser appetites and pursuing his own little private affairs." This assessment anticipated the party's break with Lassalle a decade later.

Engels then took up Marx's comment about the need "to recruit our party entirely anew."

> [O]nce we are back in Germany we shall, I think, find plenty of talented young fellows who have, in the meantime, and not without result, tasted the forbidden fruit. If we had the means to conduct propaganda scientifically and steadily for the space of 2 or 3 years, writing books about *n'importe quoi* [no matter what], as we did before 1848, we should have been appreciably better off. But that was impossible,

and now the storm is already brewing. You ought to finish your Economy; later on, as soon as we have a newspaper, we could bring it out in WEEKLY NUMBERS. . . . This would provide all our by then restored associations with a basis for debate.[53]

Clearly, Marx and Engels's respite from organized politics after 1852 was seen only as temporary; as soon as the scientific work had been completed organized political activity would be resumed. Also, Marx's rebuke of Dronke and other "milksops" shows that he expected their closest contacts to act—at least to some degree—as if they were in an organized party even if one did not exist. Just because the League had disbanded did not mean, in their view, that party obligations had ended. There is other evidence, as we'll see shortly, for this conclusion.

Engels's reply to Marx regarding party recruitment suggests that the forces that came to the party in the heat of the struggles of 1848–49 were not, in his opinion, garnered under ideal conditions, because the theoretical arms in place were not sufficient. It should be remembered that a longstanding position of Marx certainly, going back at least to 1844, before the partnership was formed, had been that adequate preparation was a prerequisite for proletarian self-liberation. Engels's assessment of the 1848–49 period might explain the remarks he made to Marx before the League's dissolution but after the split, that is, when both had concluded that the organization had outlived its usefulness in the exile conditions of London. The immediate issue was Harney, the Chartist leader with whom Marx and Engels had worked closely but who was now avoiding them while flirting with Willich and Schapper. Harney's behavior, Engels observed, should not be really surprising: "[H]aven't we been acting for years as though Cherethites and Plethites[54] were our party when, in fact we had no party, and when the people whom we considered as belonging to our party at least officially, *sous réserve de les appeler des bêtes incorrigibles entre nous* [with the reservation that between ourselves we called them incorrigible fools], didn't even understand the rudiments of our stuff?"[55]

Five months later, July 1851, again after the split but before the dissolution, finds Engels in a more optimistic mood about recruitment possibilities. In spite of the police crackdown underway in Germany reports indicated that the Central Authority in Cologne was making progress.

> I am delighted that, as I anticipated, small communist groups are being formed everywhere on the basis of the *Manifesto*. This is just what we lacked, the General Staff having hitherto been so weak. There'll never be any shortage of rank and file when it comes to the point, but it is agreeable indeed to have in prospect a General Staff not consisting of Straubinger elements, and admitting of a wider selection of men with a modicum of education than does the existing staff of 25.[56]

First, it should be recalled that the *Manifesto* did not figure prominently in the propaganda arsenal of the *NRZ* party during the 1848–49 events. By mid-1851, however, owing largely to the default of the reformists, communist ideas could get a serious hearing for the first time—the point made above and what the "Addresses" anticipated. Second, and more relevant, Engels's comment about the "Straubinger elements" recognized that the League was never able to surmount Germany's backwardness. The absence of a significantly large modern industrial proletariat—which presumed a level of education—placed limits on the League's effectiveness. Thus, Engels's hopes in more educated workers becoming members of the then-functioning League in Germany.

Basically, the problem Engels and Marx were grappling with was how to construct a new political party that would avoid the pitfalls of the League. When Marx said, "We must recruit our party entirely anew," he did not mean the reestablishment of another organized party at that moment. Rather, the goal was to lay the groundwork for such an effort once the scientific work had been accomplished, to create what Liebknecht later called a "party embryo."[57] It was with this objective in mind that both he and Engels approached the informal party work that occupied their attention until 1864.

The need to construct a modern communist party, one not based on "Straubinger elements," explains why Marx and Engels prioritized the Chartist movement over the League even before the latter's formal demise. England was the one country that had a modern proletariat which, also, had its own political movement. When Harney proved increasingly unreliable Marx and Engels began to work closely with Ernest Jones, the Chartist leader whose own views were more akin to theirs. As Marx explained, "we support him, *because* he *stirs up* 'UNFRIENDLY FEEL-INGS AMONGST THE DIFFERENT CLASSES.'[58] By early 1852 Engels was confident, as he wrote to Marx, that their collaboration with Jones was beginning to pay off, at the moment in which the Chartist movement was beginning to splinter into various tendencies. "

> Jones is moving in the right direction and we may well say that, without our doctrine, he would not have taken the right path and would never have discovered how, on the one hand, one can not only maintain the only possible basis for the reconstruction of the Chartist party—the instinctive class hatred of the workers for the industrial bourgeoisie—but also enlarge and develop it, so laying the foundations for enlightening propaganda, and how, on the other, one can still be progressive and resist the workers' reactionary appetites and their prejudices.[59]

Four years later, Marx, too, spoke confidently of the relationship of his party with Jones's wing of the Chartist movement: "[W]e are the Chartists' only intimate allies and that, though we may hold aloof from public demonstrations and leave it to . . . [our opponents] to flirt openly with Chartism, it is always in our power to resume the position already allotted to us by history."[60] With an eye toward the future, the Marx party consciously intervened in proletarian politics in England—before and after the dissolution of the League—in order to shape its direction.

Owing to his relationship with Jones, Marx was invited to participate as an honorary delegate in the initial meeting in March 1854 of the most important initiative in independent working-class politics in England during this period—the Labour Parliament movement. Although unable to attend, Marx sent greetings in which he advised that the movement's success depended on its going beyond trade unions to the representation of "the laboring classes" as a whole.[61] This message, whose kernel could be found in the *Manifesto*, that the working class needed an organization to represent it in its entirety, for which trade unions were inadequate, was one that the Marx party would have at the top of its agenda once the IWMA was formed. In one of his few acts of public political activity during this period, and at a time when his own personal situation was at a low point,[62] Marx attended two mass demonstrations in London—almost getting arrested at one—organized by the Chartists in the summer of 1855. Held to protest Sunday closing laws, which were particularly onerous on workers and their families, the actions proved to be the tonic that Marx needed.

Relations soured between the Marx party and Jones in the late fifties, due largely, as the former saw it, to his efforts in courting radical middle-class forces. This reflected not only the demise of the Chartist movement but also "the fact that the English proletariat is actually becoming more and more bourgeois."[63] As Marx opined in a letter to Engels, "the ass should begin by *forming* a party, for which purpose he must go to the manufacturing [i.e., working class] districts. Then the radical bourgeoisie will come to him in search of compromise."[64] As Jones's maneuvers proved futile, within a few years he found himself in agreement once again with the Marx party, in time for their collaboration in the IWMA. When Jones died in 1869, Engels wrote, "amongst the politicians, he was the only *educated* Englishman who was, *au fond*, completely on our side."[65]

The "Struggle in the Press"

To successfully "recruit our party entirely anew," Marx and Engels recognized that they needed "the means to conduct propaganda scientifically and steadily. . . ." As early as February 1851 Engels averred, "[T]he main thing at the moment is to find some way of getting our things published; either in a quarterly in which we make a frontal attack and consolidate our position . . . or in fat books. . . ."[66] With the demise of the *NRZ* and its successor, the *NRZ Revue*, the party was without its own organ. As a partial solution to this problem, they helped Jones in publishing his own paper, *The People's Paper*, which first appeared in May 1852, by contributing articles written by themselves—until 1856—and other party members. They assisted in other ways, as Marx mentioned to Engels: "In spite of my own money bothers I have spent days with him traipsing all over the place in connection with his paper's financial affairs." Marx's editorial and political support was also crucial in keeping the paper afloat until it went under in 1858, the time when relations between Jones and the party were estranged.

When two League-*NRZ* activists, Weydemeyer and Cluss, moved to the United States after the demise of the German revolution, Marx and Engels worked closely with them in establishing a party organ in their new country. Before Weydemeyer arrived in New York, Marx told him that his move was most opportune as a "source of livelihood . . . and being of service to our party. . . . [A]nd with the wholesale suppression of newspapers in Germany, it is only over there that we can conduct the struggle in the press."[67]

The "struggle in the press" was part of the larger goal of party-building work. Waiting for Weydemeyer when he arrived in New York in November 1851 were two letters from Marx with instructions to that end. One asked him to get the English translation of the *Manifesto* (Marx had just sent it, along with twenty copies of the German version, to a contact in the city) and see "if you can publish, distribute and sell it." Marx also requested that Weydemeyer send "20–50 copies for ourselves" to be distributed in England. Another instruction was that Weydemeyer look into the possibility of publishing a "kind of pocket library" of *NRZ* articles, since the paper "was not widely distributed in America." The specific articles he suggested for the collection were Wolff's "Silesian Billion" articles on the peasantry, a series of articles that Engels wrote on the Hungarian struggle for self-determination and his own "The Bourgeoisie and the Counter-Revolution." He also recommended, in addition to the *NRZ* articles, that Weydemeyer reproduce in pamphlet form his and Engels's anti-Heinzen pieces from 1847. Marx also suggested that in the future the *NRZ Revue* articles should be reprinted. These instructions are, thus, most revealing. They indicate what Marx regarded as the priority literature in the party arsenal as of October 1851.[68]

Marx and Engels, along with other party members whom they encouraged—"I am here at their backs, WHIP in hand, and shall have no difficulty in keeping their noses to the grindstone," wrote Marx[69]—sent contributions to the journal *Die Revolution*, the first Marxist periodical in the United States. Although only four issues ever appeared, because of financial constraints, the last one featured for the first time in print Marx's *Eighteenth Brumaire*.

After *Die Revolution*'s demise, Weydemeyer and Cluss and two other émigrés founded the first Marxist party in the United States, *Proletarierbund*, and in consultation with their London comrades, they got editorial control over *Die Reform* newspaper, which had began publication in 1853. This effort was linked to the new party's involvement in the formation of the American Labor Union, one of the first efforts to form a labor party in the United States *Die Reform*, which became the Union's paper, published numerous articles by Marx and Engels. Weydemeyer, through the newspaper and other political activities, played a crucial role—again, in consultation with Marx and Engels—in waging a largely successful and important fight inside the German émigré community to counter the pro-slavery influence of the Democratic Party, which had been promoted by True Socialists like Kriege and Weitling.

When Weydemeyer became editor of a proletarian newspaper in Chicago in 1860 he asked Marx for assistance who, in turn, sought correspondents for him. In making a request to Lassalle, Marx appealed to party obligations: "There is no question of payment. But as party work it is *very* important. . . . [Weydemeyer] is one of our *best* people."[70] Consistent with the line of the Marx party, Weydemeyer joined the Union army when the Civil War broke out and served with distinction. He remained, until his death in 1866, which was a severe setback for Marxist continuity in the United States—to be discussed later—a loyal party member.

In order to supplement the subsidies that Engels provided, Marx was for eleven years the London correspondent for one of the major bourgeois papers in the United States, the *New York Daily Tribune*. As an antislavery paper with a Fourierist editor,

Charles Dana, the *Tribune* allowed Marx—and Engels as well, since about a third of the articles were actually written by him in Marx's name—enough political space to get much of their politics into a paper that was read on both sides of the Atlantic. The arrangement began, in fact, with the publication in serial form of Engels's *Revolution and Counter-Revolution*. With the financial difficulties that faced party publications the *Tribune* proved to be at times the Marx party's only outlet during this period. As an example of its utility, it brought Marx to the attention—favorably—of the first major economist in the United States, Henry George Carey.

The other major bourgeois paper that Marx and Engels wrote for was the *Neue Oder-Zeitung* in Breslau, the only democratic paper that the German authorities permitted. In their view, "the *N. O.-Z.* expresses the most extreme views possible in the present condition of the Press."[71] Because it gave them their only direct access to democratic forces in Germany they attached greater political importance to getting their articles in it than in the *Tribune*. Also, because the *N. O.-Z* editors did not take editorial liberties with their articles, as did those of the *Tribune*, their writings were likely to be more reflective of their actual positions. It was the opportunity to navigate through the government's censorship obstacle course, as Marx expressed to its editor, "the UNDERHAND struggle AGAINST THE ESTABLISHED POWERS which incline me to work in the interest of this paper."[72] When it appeared that the paper might go under due to financial problems Marx, as an indication of the paper's importance to him, volunteered to forgo payment. In fact, the paper ceased publication in November 1855.

Since the focus here is on the party activities of Marx and Engels in this period, the content of their journalistic work, for practical reasons, has to be ignored. Nevertheless, it should be noted that their journalism allowed them to ground their theoretical premises to a degree they had not done before. They extended their empirical terrain to every corner of the world beyond Europe, which was later reflected in *Capital*. More than anything, the journalistic research impressed upon them the interconnectedness of the class struggle on a worldwide basis, particularly the links between the colonial and proletarian revolutions. In the process they were required to acquaint themselves with virtually every aspect of bourgeois politics, diplomacy, parliamentary politics, current political economy, etc.—all for the purpose of understanding how workers' interests were affected and, thus, how revolutionaries should respond.

In Anticipation of a New Revolutionary Era

That the Marx party is best seen is this period as a revolutionary party in waiting is testified to by its response to a request from industrial workers in the Rhineland in 1856 that it return there to lead them in a new uprising. Soliciting Engels's input, Marx outlined what he thought their response should be.

> I have, OF COURSE, declared that, *circumstances permitting*, we would range ourselves with the Rhenish workers; that any uprising, undertaken off their own bat, without prior initiatives in Paris or Vienna or Berlin, would be idiotic; that, should Paris give the signal, it would be advisable, whatever the circumstances, to

risk all, since then even the ill-effects of a momentary defeat could themselves be no more than momentary; that I and my friends would seriously consider what direct action might be taken by the working population of the Rhine Province, and that in due course they should again send someone to London, but do *nothing* without prior agreement.[73]

Clearly, the Marx party was prepared to mount the barricades again once conditions were ripe. Until then, revolutionary restraint was the order of the day.

If the party was still not convinced that circumstances required an organized formation, it nevertheless felt that the objective situation was improving, as instanced by the first worldwide capitalist economic crisis in 1857—the main reason why Marx, in spite of his even direr personal situation, was spurred to complete *A Contribution*. In terms of the party per se, the impending crisis meant that it was even more incumbent that party norms be maintained. It was the violation of those norms that was partly responsible for the break that the party made with Lassalle in 1862.

Foreshadowing the split, Marx told Engels in 1859 that "if Lassalle takes it upon himself to speak in the name of the party, he must in [the] future either resign himself to being publicly disavowed by us, since circumstances are too grave to take account of feelings, or else he must first ascertain the views held by others beside himself before following the joint inspiration of fire and logic. We must now absolutely insist on party discipline, otherwise everything will be in the soup."[74] A bit more tactful but just as firm, Marx wrote directly to Lassalle some months later:

> There is a possibility that things will come to a head again soon. In that case one of two things must prevail in our party: either no one speaks for the party without prior consultation with the others, or everyone has the right to put forward his views without any regard for the others. Now this last is certainly not to be recommended, since a public polemic would in no way benefit so small a party (which, I hope, makes up in vigour for what it lacks in numbers).[75]

The circumstances surrounding this dispute were the Italian War of 1859 and the position that communists should have taken. Lassalle's pamphlet, *The Italian War and Prussia's Tasks*, which Marx considered "an ENORMOUS BLUNDER," presented a counterline to that of Marx and Engels, which the latter explicated in his pamphlet, *Po and Rhine;* Lassalle had read Engels's pamphlet prior to writing his own. To provide further clarity on the question and to counter Lassalle's position Marx and Engels gave serious consideration to publishing "a party manifesto."[76]

Even the private behavior of party members had to be weighed carefully. Such was the case a year earlier when Marx consulted with Engels and Wolff about Lassalle's wish to defend his honor by engaging in a duel. Engels informed Marx that he and Wolff shared his view that for "members of the revolutionary party . . . duels, are on the whole untimely. . . ."[77] As Marx explained to Lassalle, "Our party must resolutely set its face against these class ceremonies and reject with the most cynical contempt the presumptuous demand that we submit to them. The present state of affairs is far too serious to permit of your consenting to such puerilities. . . ."[78] Five years later—two years after the party broke with him—Lassalle disregarded this comradely advice; he was mortally wounded by an opponent in a duel.[79]

It was especially important, with the prospect of a new revolutionary upsurge, that the party stand true to its principles. Thus, when Liebknecht in early 1859 attempted to mediate differences between the Marx party, without the agreement of Marx and Engels, and opponents in the newly revived German Worker's Educational Association, Marx reacted angrily. Liebknecht "talked a great deal of nonsense about having to defend me against the great odium felt for me by the workers (i.e., louts), etc. . . . I convened our people . . . and took the occasion to pitch into Liebknecht in a manner far from pleasing to him until he declared himself a contrite sinner."[80] Commenting some years later on the incident, Liebknecht said, "I found myself charged with the crime of violating our principles by my actions . . . of having made concessions to the Weitlingian and other sectarians that were inadmissible from a tactical and theoretical standpoint . . . of playing the role of 'mediator.' . . . Marx deprecated the 'mediator business;' if he had anything to say to the laborers he could say it himself."

Another example of Marx and Engels's expectations was their reaction to the historical drama that Lassalle wrote in 1859, *Franz von Sickingen,* a work whose political content they severely criticized—to be discussed shortly. Of relevance here is Engels's justification, as he explained to Lassalle, for his critique: "*Between ourselves* criticism has, of course, for years been necessarily as outspoken as possible in the interests of the party itself." And then, as a salve, he wrote: "[I]t is always a great pleasure to me and all of us when we are given fresh proof that our party, irrespective of the field in which it makes an appearance, invariably does so with distinction. And that is what you, too, have done on this occasion."[81] Regardless of how sincere Engels was in assuaging Lassalle, his comments make clear, once again, the seriousness he lent to the integrity of the party.

Defending the party's honor was also a necessity. When the noted German democrat Karl Vogt launched his slanderous book against the party at the end of 1859, Marx reacted forcefully. Just when he was on a roll with his political economy research and writing—*A Contribution* had just appeared—he decided to put it on hold, for a year in fact, in order to refute Vogt's charges. His response, which included the writing of *Herr Vogt,* was, as he argued, "crucial to the *historical vindication* of the party and its subsequent position in Germany."[82] Referring to one of the culprits in the slander campaign, a former League member, Marx wrote that "he had forgotten that he was confronting someone who would be *ruthless* the moment his own honour, or that of his party was at stake."[83]

A necessary weapon in the party's defense was its own organ or newspaper, the absence of which was a continual problem throughout the fifties. A temporary solution was found in May 1859, when the party in London, in collaboration with the German Workers Education Association (Marx had by now rejoined the organization after his resignation in 1850), gained editorial control over its paper *Das Volk.* To Engels, Marx wrote: "I consider *Das Volk* to be a dilettante rag like our Brussels and Paris papers [*Deutsche-Brüsseler-Zeitung* and *Vorwärts*]. But covertly and without intervening directly, we can use it to worry the life out of [our opponents]. Again, *the moment may come,* and that very soon, *when it will be of crucial importance that, not just our enemies, but we ourselves* should be able to publish our views in a London paper."[84] Given the poor financial shape it was in, the paper, as Marx explained to Engels, "can only exist by party sacrifices and hence we are asking *all* party members to make such sacrifices. . . ."[85] Although the paper folded after four months, it had the distinction in the late fifties of publishing articles that were truly party documents, the most important of which was the "Preface" to *A Contribution.*

Marx's reinvolvement in the GWEA, albeit on a limited basis, anticipated his return to organized political activity five years later. It, too, was done in the framework of an expected renewal of the European revolution. Karl Schapper, who had by now returned to the party after admitting his earlier political error, was the party member Marx counted on to lead its intervention in the organization. In the fall of 1859 Marx gave a series of lectures based on *A Contribution* to about twenty to thirty GWEA members. In spite of these new initiatives, Marx was still not convinced that he and Engels had been successful in their efforts "to recruit our party entirely anew." Commenting on the party forces they worked with in the GWEA, which included Liebknecht and Schapper, Marx wrote Engels in May 1859, "Never have we had a poorer STAFF."[86] The situation would only improve with the formation of the IWMA five years later.

One of the outcomes of the Vogt affair was the alienation from the Marx party of a long-time member, the poet Ferdinand Freiligrath, who preferred not to come to the party's defense. His poetry, he wrote Marx, was now his major concern; "he wishes to stand aside from the 'party' out of 'purity.'"[87] In his reply, Marx politely begged to differ with his friend. If the poet was looking for "purity," then it certainly was not to be found in the world of "bourgeois trade" where Freiligrath worked to subsidize his creative needs. The facts of political life are that indeed "dirt is thrown up by storms, that no revolutionary period smells of attar of roses, that even, at times, one becomes a target for all manner of garbage, goes without saying." But, in view of all the slanders and attacks against the party and the record of opponent parties both during and after the upheavals of 1848–49, "when one finally asks oneself what can actually be held . . . against the party as a whole, one can only conclude that what distinguishes it in this, the nineteenth century, is its *purity.*"[88] Thus, at the end of the decade and lull in the revolutionary process, Marx felt that his party could be proud of its record of principled behavior, and confidently looked forward to the soon-expected upturn in the class struggle.

Applying the Lessons of 1848

One of the key lessons of 1848–1852, that the revolutionary party must have in place its scientific work prior to the next upsurge, meant for Marx and Engels the prioritization of the long-awaited political economy project. Therefore, not surprisingly, the party issued no major programmatic statement between 1852 and 1864. Engels's pamphlet, *Po and Rhine,* written on the outbreak of the Italian (or Austro-Italo-French) War of 1859 was about as close as they came to such a statement; once the war commenced Marx and Engels, as already mentioned, seriously considered the publication of a "party manifesto."

The pamphlet was indeed a party document. In his appeal to Lassalle to get it published in Germany as soon as possible, Marx wrote, "[P]lease don't begrudge the considerable time and effort I cost you. I can only plead the GENERAL PARTY INTER-EST." In his letter to Engels that same day, February 25, 1859, Marx urged Engels to write quickly: "You must *set to* at once, time being *everything* in this case . . . it will be a triumph for our party." Referring to his *A Contribution*, which was about to appear in a few months, Marx noted that in "my 'Preface' I have done you a few *honneurs*; and thus it is all to the good if you yourself take the stage immediately afterwards. . . . Those dogs of democrats and liberal riff-raff will see that we're the only chaps who haven't been stultified by the ghastly period of peace."[89] Hence, *Po and Rhine*, as well as *A Contribution*, were seen by Marx as the weapons that would put the party back at the center of revolutionary politics and give it a head start vis-à-vis its opponents in the next round; also, it was further vindication for the priority that was given to "swotting" during the twelve years of political reaction.

Although Engels's pamphlet deals mainly with military matters, the politics of which are a bit tangential for our purposes here, there are programmatic aspects of it that relate to some of the lessons he and Marx drew about the 1848 revolutions. As the issue of German, as well as Italian, unification was being more sharply posed—issues related to the War—Engels opposed those German nationalists who wanted unity at the expense of the denial of self-determination for the Italians, the Slavs, and other peoples of central Europe. Unity on this basis, the "Central European great power theory," would lead to a German "Fatherland" in which "Germany would be the arbiter and master of Europe." It was exactly this brand of German nationalism—based on the supposed racial superiority of the "Teutons"—that the *NRZ* consistently opposed in 1848–49. At the heart of the matter was whether German unification would be achieved from above by either Austrian or Prussian imperialism—that Lassalle leaned toward the latter explains the basic political differences he had with Marx and Engels—or below through the revolutionary mobilization of workers, peasants, and the middle classes. "Instead of seeking our strength in the possession of foreign soil and the oppression of a foreign nationality, whose future only prejudice can deny, we should do better to see to it that we *are united and strong in our own house*."[90] Such advice—which was as sorely needed, if not more so, seven decades later as in 1859—was the concrete application of the line of the party throughout the 1848–49 revolution to the new reality of the impending war, that is, the demand for a unified German republic.

Contrary, again, to the oft-repeated claim that Marx and Engels either ignored or underestimated the pull of nationalism, they clearly understood that it was not enough to recognize the actuality of German nationalism. For communists, the challenge was how to present and fight for a proletarian perspective on the question. As the *Manifesto* had stated, the "proletariat of each country must, of course, first of all settle matters with its own bourgeoisie." A unified German republic, brought into existence from below, was the best terrain upon which the proletariat could "settle matters." It was for the same reasons that the Marx party promoted in its other writings both before and during the war a unified Italian republic based on revolution from below. Lastly, it should be noted that *Po and Rhine*, which was written anonymously in order that it not be ignored by the bourgeois press, had a major impact on the debate in Germany, fulfilling Marx's hope that it would return the party to center stage in the revolutionary movement.[91]

While *Po and Rhine* was the only explicitly programmatic document of the party during the lull that drew on the experiences of 1848–49, other writings, including the party correspondence, indicate that the lessons of the revolutionary period were also utilized in one fashion or another. The most important example concerned the German movement. In April 1856 Marx received a number of letters from activists in the Rhineland requesting his advice on what attitude workers should have toward the bourgeoisie in event of a new revolutionary outbreak. The letters, which expressed varying opinions on the matter, reflected the existent difference of opinions within the revolutionary party. The only letter, for which there is some evidence, that Marx responded to—his letter is not extant—was the one from a former League member, Johannes Miquel, who held that "the proletariat should ally itself not only with the petty-bourgeois democrats but also with the bourgeois liberals and refrain from such revolutionary measures as might frighten the bourgeoisie away from the revolution."[92] Marx was clearly not impressed, as he commented to Engels: "[T]he attempt to digest this 'wisdom' fairly 'turned my stomach.'"[93] In his evidently more tactful reply to Miquel, after having gotten Engels's "detailed 'OPINION,'" who in turn consulted with Wolff, Marx declared "that the sole ally of the proletariat in a future revolution is the peasantry, and insist[ed] on the need for a merciless struggle against the bourgeoisie."[94]

Marx's reply reveals, once again, that he and Engels continued to uphold the politics of the March 1850 Address, as well as *Revolution and Counter-Revolution in Germany*—the major balance sheets of the Marx party on the German revolution. His comment on the peasantry suggests that the worker-peasant alliance assumed even greater weight for the party since, as it was noted in chapter four, the March Address virtually ignored the rural toilers. Indeed, it was in the context of this discussion, in 1856, that Marx made his oft-quoted comment to Engels about the prospects for the next revolution in Germany: "THE WHOLE THING IN GERMANY will depend on whether it is possible TO BACK THE PROLETARIAN REVOLUTION BY SOME SECOND EDITION OF THE PEASANT'S WAR. In which case the affair should go swimmingly."[95]

The experiences of 1848–49 made the Marx party more conscious of the role of the peasantry in the democratic revolution. Marx's comments to Weydemeyer and Engels in 1851 about the prospects for Italy's national liberation struggle, headed by Giuseppe Mazzini, are instructive.

> I regard Mazzini's policy basically wrong . . . by failing to turn to the party of Italy that has been repressed for centuries, to the peasants, he is laying up fresh resources for the counter-revolution. . . . But admittedly it required some courage to tell the bourgeoisie and the nobility that the first step towards gaining Italy's

independence was the complete emancipation of the peasants and the transformation of their métayage [tenant sharecropping] system into bourgeois freeholdings.

. . . If Mazzini, or anyone puts himself at the head of the Italian agitators and fails this time to transform the peasants, *franchment* and *immédiatement*, from *métaires* [sharecroppers] into free landowners,—the condition of the Italian peasants is atrocious.[96]

Marx is clearly drawing on the German experience of the two preceding years in reaching these conclusions about the Italian revolution. In the absence, however, of a party organ or some other means for making these opinions public they remained as best as can be determined exactly that, internal party opinions.

One other example of how Marx and Engels applied the lessons of 1848–49 to the peasant question concerns Lassalle's above-mentioned historical drama, *Franz von Sickingen*. The work focused on the nobility and its opposition to the emperor during Germany's peasant revolt of 1525, and therein laid the problem in Marx and Engels's opinion. Whereas the hero in Engels's *Peasant War in Germany* is the peasant leader Thomas Münzer, in Lassalle's self-styled tragedy it is the knight von Sickingen. For Marx, the issue raised by the failure of the knightly class, in alliance with Luther, to overthrow the monarchial regime in 1525 was "the tragic conflict upon which the revolutionary party of 1848–49 justly floundered." Marx was referring, of course, to the absence in 1848–49 of a "proletarian revolution" "backed" by a "second edition of the peasants' war." Lassalle's error, in his view, was that he focused too much on the "*aristocratic* representatives of revolution" rather than the "representatives of the peasants . . . and of the revolutionary elements in the towns." And then is a most prescient comment, which anticipated Lassalle's own political direction, "Have not you yourself—like your Franz von Sickingen—succumbed, to some extent, to the diplomatic error of regarding the Lutheran-knightly opposition as superior to the plebian-Münzerian?"[97] Three years later Lassalle unsuccessfully tried to sell the nascent German working-class movement to Bismarck.[98]

Engels, who was intimate with the historical particulars of the events in the drama, provided more detailed commentary on the peasant question.

I should say . . . that neglect of the peasant movement is what has led you to give an incorrect idea, or so it seems to me, of one aspect of the national aristocratic movement . . . while at the same time allowing the *truly* tragic element in Sickingen's fate to escape you. In my view, it never occurred to the bulk of the nobility then subject directly to the emperor to form an alliance with the peasants; their dependence on the income deriving from oppression of the peasants did not admit of this. An alliance with the towns would have been rather more feasible. . . . The national aristocratic revolution could, however, only have been effected by means of an alliance with the towns and the peasants, particularly the latter; and to my mind the tragic element lies precisely in the fact that this essential condition, alliance with the peasants was impossible. . . . Here, in my view, lay the tragic clash between the historical necessary postulate and the impossibility of its execution in practice.[99]

If it was impossible for the nobility to enter into such an alliance with the peasantry in 1525, the townspeople, on the other hand, were not prevented from so doing in

1525, and certainly later, in 1848–49. This was the perspective of the *NRZ* party during those two tumultuous years and the one with which Marx and Engels sought through their commentary on his drama in 1859 to convince Lassalle. While the exchange with Lassalle was internal party business it nevertheless represented an effort on the part of Marx and Engels to win party members to the conclusions they had drawn about the worker-peasant alliance, conclusions that would be of dire importance—as will be seen later—in the future for the revolutionary party in Germany.

Marx and Engels commented, here and there, on the peasant question in other contexts during this period. The failure of the bourgeois democratic revolution in Spain, for example, could be explained by the fact that "the revolutionary party did not know how to link the interests of the peasantry to the town movement."[100] But it was in Russia that they began to see the most portentous developments. In the aftermath of the Crimean War (1854–1856) they anticipated rumblings in the Russian countryside. At the end of 1859 Marx wrote to Engels, "In Russia the movement is progressing better than anywhere else in Europe. On the one hand the constitutionalism of the aristocracy versus the Tsar, on the other of the peasants versus the aristocracy."[101] Engels's decision, a few years earlier, and Marx's, a few year later, to begin learning Russian testified to the importance they lent to the developments to the east.

To conclude, the test of any revolutionary party is not only how it responds to a revolutionary situation but also how it comports itself in its absence. As Marx had chided Schapper in his debate with him in 1850, "not much enthusiasm is needed to belong to a party when you believe that it is on the point of seizing power." In the face of political reaction and a deafening lull in the class struggle, as well as the most difficult personal circumstances, particularly for the Marx family, the Marx party, unlike any other revolutionary party of the 1848 upheavals, passed the test. Along with major achievements in the scientific work—the basic groundwork and draft of *Capital* was completed during this period—the party was able to mobilize itself whenever the party's survival was at stake. Thus, the priority that was given to the Cologne trial and to Vogt's slander campaign. It also mobilized in anticipation of the Italian War when it was necessary to present a working-class perspective on the ensuing conflict. Hence, the effort to get Engels's pamphlet *Po and Rhine* into print. All of these responses testified to the priority of politics for the Marx party even at the expense of the scientific work. As history later verified, it was no mere bravado or exaggeration on Marx's part when he said in 1859 that "we're the only chaps who haven't been stultified by the ghastly period of peace." The accomplishments of the party during the lull, both literary and political, were decisive in enabling it to assume leadership in the next revolutionary wave and, thus, to put the proletarian movement on footing far firmer than had been the case in any previous upheavals.

CHAPTER SEVEN

A New Revolutionary Era and the Birth of the First International

As in the 18th century, the American war of independence sounded the tocsin for the European middle classes, so in the 19th century, the American Civil War sounded it for the European working-class.

—Marx, *Capital*

To conquer political power has therefore become the duty of the working classes.

—Marx, Inaugural Address

The International was founded in order to replace the socialist or semi-socialist sects by a real organisation of the working class for struggle.

—Marx to Friedrich Bolte

Early in 1863 Marx wrote to Engels that "the ERA OF REVOLUTION has now FAIRLY OPENED IN EUROPE once more." The moment that the Marx party had been anticipating for at least four years had finally arrived. Within a year and a half Marx was deeply immersed once again in organized political activity, the central force in the International Working Men's Association—the first truly international proletarian organization. On the road to the IWMA, Marx, in particular, stepped up his activism in various campaigns. At the same time he struggled mightily to complete his magnum opus before the onset of revolution. Political reality, the need to direct the new organization through its infancy until its end, was largely responsible for only the first volume of *Capital* being published in Marx's lifetime. Contrary to the expectation of Marx and Engels that their party would begin straight away with the *Manifesto* when a new upsurge began, the composition of the IWMA required a protracted internal struggle to win its ranks to the basic plank of scientific communism—independent working-class political action. Many of the findings in *Capital* became the ammunition for Marx in that struggle. By the fourth year of the International's existence, the Marx party had become the hegemonic current in the first successful effort toward the realization of the call it raised two decades earlier, "Workers of the world unite!"

The basis for Marx's conclusion that a new revolutionary had begun in 1863 was the peasant uprising in Poland that year. However, even before the event other signs had already appeared on the political horizon that gave cause for optimism. At the beginning of 1860, Marx declared—and Engels concurred—"that the most momentous thing happening in the world today is the slave movement—on the one hand, in America, started by the death of Brown, and in Russia, on the other."[1] Marx was referring, of course, to the abortive rebellion of the abolitionist John Brown at Harper's Ferry, Virginia, a few months earlier, which in turn had stimulated at least one slave uprising in its aftermath. As for Russia, its "slaves," or serfs, had also been on the march for emancipation as he had noted the previous year. A year later, in a move to preempt a revolt from below, the czar abolished serfdom. Of enormous significance was that the Russian movement was coinciding with the one in the United States. Precisely because they viewed the class struggle from an international perspective they gave more weight to the conjuncture of struggles in various countries than to isolated ones. The fight against slavery and other precapitalist modes of exploitation was part and parcel of the democratic revolution, a necessary step in labor's struggle against capital.

The Civil War as a Revolutionary Struggle

Prior to the Civil War, it should be remembered, the Marx party, specifically, through Weydemeyer, had played an important role in winning the German émigré working class in America to the Republican cause. German-American support to Abraham Lincoln, with the expectation that he and his party would be "most hostile to slavery," was of some significance in his being elected president in 1860.[2] The "Forty-eighters," or "Red '48ers," as they were sometimes called, that is, political refugees of the 1848–49 German revolution, were the most ardent Republicans and opponents of slavery. The Civil War was for them an opportunity to continue the fight they had waged more than a decade earlier. Prussian feudal autocracy was not unlike the Southern slavocracy. Many served with distinction in the Northern army and included a number of current or former Marx party members, such as Weydemeyer, Willich, and Fritz Anneke.[3]

Once the War began, Marx and Engels, as pro-Union partisans, gave their undivided attention to its every detail. Their primary practice was winning through their journalism the English and German proletariat to the Northern cause. A key strategic issue in the war was whether British capital, led by the textile barons, would be able to get their government to intervene on behalf of the Confederacy, the most important source of cotton for its mills. At a certain stage of the crisis it was, therefore, necessary for supporters of the Union cause, particularly the proletariat, to organize an anti-interventionist movement in Europe. In Britain this effort was most successful.[4]

In addition to reporting on this campaign through his articles, Marx assisted in the organization in March 1863 of the largest of a number of English trade union–sponsored meetings in solidarity with the North.[5] The anti-interventionist sentiment and movement, Marx felt, was decisive in preventing the British government from coming to the Confederacy's defense. The fact that British workers, many of whom lost their jobs because of the Northern blockade against the export of Southern cotton to England and elsewhere, were in the forefront of this campaign was particularly gratifying for Marx.[6] For him it was one of the important signals that indeed a new "era of revolution" had arrived. His involvement in the mass rally of March 1863 in London in support of the Union was a harbinger of his return to organized political activity a year later.

Solidarity with the Polish Insurrection

When peasants in Polish Russia rose up in early 1863, signalling the onset of the new "era," Marx wrote Engels that though their party was minuscule it was more mature because of the lessons learned from the 1848–1849 experience.[7] But unlike the earlier upheavals, which began in France, the expectation now was that "the lava will flow from East to West," that is, the revolutionary process would begin in Russia's empire and move westward. As early as 1863, then, Marx and Engels began to fix their hopes on Russia as the spark for the European revolution—contrary then to the usual claims about their vision of the direction of the continent's revolutionary process.

The rebellion itself combined a movement for national independence with the struggle of the peasants to be free of feudal obligations. On the basis of previous uprisings, especially the Cracow uprising of 1846, the *Manifesto* had stated fifteen years earlier that in Poland communists "support the party that insists on an agrarian revolution as the prime condition for national emancipation. . . ." Marx and Engels maintained this position, along with their earlier views on the Polish national liberation movement,[8] in judging the latest revolt. Its success also depended on whether it "might yet become part of a general European movement. . . ."[9] Partly for this reason they expected that not only would the "lava . . . flow from East to West" but it would also be the spark for a Russian peasant revolt to fulfill the empty promises of the czar's 1861 "emancipation" of serfs. By the summer of 1863 their hopes were still unrealized, as Engels lamented to Marx: "What surprises me most is that a peasants' movement should not have risen in Greater Russia."[10] In the end, the 1863 revolt floundered, fundamentally for the reason the *Manifesto* suggested— no leadership emerged that was unswerving in its commitment to the "agrarian revolution as the prime condition for national emancipation." Another five decades would have to pass before that condition could be met.

In spite of the increasingly lost cause of the Polish revolt, Marx and Engels actively worked to support it. They made plans to write a pamphlet that analyzed the political, diplomatic, and military aspects of the uprising. Although the piece was never completed, owing largely to Marx's various illnesses, the research he conducted was extensive and took time away from his magnum opus—evidence, again, for the priority of politics for the Marx party even at the expense of the scientific work. Bismarck's backhanded support for the Czar's suppression of the rebellion required that the German proletariat be clear about the issues. Marx was successful in getting the GWEA in London to issue a "Proclamation on Poland" in the form of a leaflet, which he wrote—but did not sign for tactical considerations—that was unequivocal in its central message: "The Polish question is the German question. Without an independent Poland there can be no independent and unified Germany, no emancipation of Germany from the Russian domination that began with the first partition of Poland." After outlining how the German bourgeoisie had defaulted on the question of Polish independence, the leaflet turned to the tasks of the German proletariat:

> In this fateful moment, the German working class owes it to the Poles, to foreign countries and to its own honour to raise a loud protest against the German betrayal of Poland, which is at the same time treason to Germany and to Europe. It must inscribe the *Restoration of Poland* in letters of flame on its banner, since bourgeois liberalism has erased this glorious motto from its own flag. The English working class has won immortal historical honour for itself by thwarting the repeated attempts of the ruling classes to intervene on behalf of the American slaveholders by its enthusiastic mass meetings, even though the prolongation of the American Civil War subjects a million English workers to the most fearful suffering and privations.
>
> If police restrictions prevent the working class in Germany from conducting demonstrations on such a scale for Poland, they do not in any way force them to brand themselves in the eyes of the whole world as accomplices in the betrayal, through apathy and silence.[11]

Signed by eleven well-known GWEA members, including Wolff, the leaflet was reproduced and circulated in the émigré community in England and, on Marx's instruction, in Germany.[12] Wolff, who distributed the "Proclamation" in Manchester, wrote to Jenny Marx in December, 1863: "'As soon as I read the first few lines, I realised that this short vigorous proclamation could have come from no one but the Moor.'"[13] A model of communist propaganda and agitation it expressed in a very popular and concise form some of the basic theoretical premises of scientific communism; it was as well an appeal to action on the basis of proletarian internationalism. It held out as an example to German workers the successes of their counterparts in England. During the long hiatus between the two revolutionary eras it was the most concrete call to action by the Marx party. Along with Marx's efforts through the GWEA to help the Polish refugees collect money to finance the insurgency,[14] it too, like the anti-interventionist work that Marx participated in around the U.S. Civil War, anticipated by a year his return to organized political activity.

The Revival of the German Workers' Movement

Marx's effort to agitate the German working class on the Polish question was part of the larger campaign that he and Engels had recently begun to conduct in earnest— political intervention in the nascent German workers' movement. A couple of years before, the movement, centered in Leipzig and Berlin, began to stir anew after a decade of hibernation. Unlike, however, the earlier movement, this one, infected by the example of British trade unionism, was based on a modern proletarian rather than an artisanal/guild perspective. Owing to his activist past in the 1848 events as well as his connections with the Marx party, Lassalle was asked by the workers to lead the fledgling body, the General German Workers Association, which was founded in May 1863. Because of his energy and organizational experience Lassalle, as Marx and Engels always acknowledged, played a useful role in getting the new organization, the first truly German workers' association, off the ground. However, his help came with a price—the insertion of ideas and a mode of functioning that were antithetical to the interests of independent working-class political action. While Marx and Engels waged a relentless campaign against his influence in the German worker's movement after his death in 1864, they had to walk much more gingerly in taking him on during his brief tenure as the movement's leader, in order not to throw out the baby, the just-born GGWA, with the bath water of Lassalleanism.

A year earlier, after Lassalle visited him in London, during which he outlined his latest nostrums for Germany's workers, Marx had concluded that there was no basis any longer of a "political PARTNERSHIP" with him "since all we had in common politically were a few remote objectives."[15] Aside from the fact that Lassalle "gives himself all the airs of a future working men's dictator," Marx objected to his panaceas for the social emancipation of the German proletariat, among which were universal suffrage and Prussian state socialism. As for the former, Marx sarcastically noted in a letter to Engels, the "workers . . . are to agitate for *general suffrage*, after which they are to send people like himself into the Chamber of Deputies, armed 'with the naked sword of science.'"[16] Marx's opinion about the limitations of electoral politics for the proletariat, not the first time he or Engels made such a pronouncement, is most interesting here on the eve of the foundation of German Social Democracy—the significance of which will be discussed later. Marx also objected to his proposal that "they organise workers' factories, for which the *state* advances the capital and, BY AND BY, these institutions spread throughout the country."[17] The basis in political economy for the latter proposal, state socialism via the Prussian state—quintessential Lassalleanism—was his position that workers could not employ strikes to raise wages owing to the "iron law of wages."[18] These were precisely, as well as others, the political views with which Germany's modern labor movement came into the world, thanks largely to Lassalle, and against which the Marx party waged a ceaseless fight.

Liebknecht's return to Germany in 1862 was most opportune for the party. Although not without his own limitations, Liebknecht, with whom Marx and Engels had worked closely for almost a decade, was much more, unlike Lassalle or anyone else in the country for that matter, a party cadre. Through his letters[19] they stayed on top of developments in the new stage of the German movement as well as being able to exercise direct influence on its course. They learned, for example, about opposition within the new GGWA to Lassalle's dictatorial modus operandi and advised him on how to respond. In a letter to Engels in June 1864, Marx said, "I explained that, while we consider it politic to give Lassalle a completely free rein for the time being, we cannot identify ourselves with him in any way. . . ."[20] Engels agreed with Marx that Liebknecht had been comporting himself well. "Clearly it's of the utmost importance to us that Liebknecht should be in Berlin—to spring surprises on Izzy [Lassalle] and also, at an appropriate moment, quietly to enlighten the workers at large about our attitude towards him. At all events, we must keep him there and support him to some extent."[21] In spite of his own dire financial situation Marx sent him money occasionally.

One of the "surprises" that the party sprung on Lassalle was to have Liebknecht help distribute in Germany through the GGWA the "Proclamation on Poland" that Marx wrote for the GWEA. As Jenny Marx explained in her letter to Liebknecht, the leaflet was being sent to him in order "to put a stop to the 'pro-police movement' on the part of certain persons"[22]—a clear reference to Lassalle who was backing the counterrevolutionary policies of Bismarck in regard to the Polish insurrection.

The support that Marx and Engels enjoyed among workers in the Rhine Province was also another potential source of strength that could be called upon to wage the struggle against Lassalleanism. This was clearly evidenced by the visit to London in June 1864 of two workers, political refugees, from Solingen, who declared to Marx that "all the *working men* who were *leaders* of [Lassalle's] movement in the *Rhine Province* [are] . . . now as ever . . . our resolute supporters." Rather, however, than "enlighten the chaps as to our relations, or rather non-relations, with [Lassalle]," Marx and Engels bided their time.[23] With the formation of the IWMA in September, which happened to follow by a month Lassalle's death, the Marx party was now in the most favorable position to take on the politics of their erstwhile comrade and influence the future of the German movement.

With Lassalle's break with scientific communism, the small core of cadre who constituted the Marx party was reduced to a handful. In May 1864 the party experienced its greatest lost in this period with the death, due to illness, of Wolff. For Marx, Wolff was his closest comrade and friend after Engels. Some years later Engels wrote that "For several years Wolff was the only comrade I had in Manchester with the same views as myself; no wonder that we met almost daily. . . ."[24] In his letter to Jenny informing her of his death, Marx wrote: "In him we have lost one of our few friends and fellow fighters. He was a man in the best sense of the word." Marx was clearly devastated by Wolff's death, as another letter to his wife two days later about the funeral reveals. "I naturally made a short funeral oration. It was an office by which I was much affected so that once or twice my voice failed me."[25] A party member to the end, Wolff left the bulk of his modest estate to Marx, which gave his comrade enough economic security for a year to complete the first volume of *Capital*; Marx's tome was, in turn, "Dedicated To My Unforgettable Friend, WILHELM WOLFF, Intrepid, Faithful, Noble Protagonist of the Proletariat." In words less formal than the "Dedication" but with the same meaning, Wolff's death, as Engels wrote to Weydemeyer, "was a loss for the party of an altogether different order from Lassalle's. We shall never again find such a steadfast fellow, who knew how to talk to the people and was always there when things were at their most difficult."[26] With the ranks of the party thinning—due also to other untimely deaths—the birth of the IWMA five months after Wolff's death could not have come sooner.

Beyond "this little corner of the earth":
The Criteria for a New Revolutionary Era

One of the major lessons Marx and Engels had drawn about the 1848–49 upsurge was that it flowed and ebbed with very sharp ups and downs in the capitalist business cycle. Thus, throughout the long lull they watched closely for any signs of an impending capitalist economic crisis. It became, in fact, a standing joke in the party that this search was at times exaggerated, as Liebknecht recounted years later: "Only on the subject of 'industrial crises' [Marx] fell a victim to the prophesying imp, and in consequence was subjected to our hearty derision which made him grimly mad. However, in the main point he was right none the less. The prophesised industrial crises did come—only not at the fixed time."[27] Indeed, a real crisis occurred in 1857, which impelled Marx to work feverishly to complete his scientific work. Jenny Marx described her husband's reaction to the situation in a letter to a party member: "[Y]ou can . . . imagine how HIGH UP [i.e., high in spirit] the Moor is. He has recovered all his wonted facility and capacity for work, as well as the liveliness and buoyancy of a spirit long since blighted by great sorrow, the loss of our beloved child . . ."[28]

While the economic character of the crisis confirmed what Marx had predicted, its political impact was not realized—at least not immediately. At the end of December, almost a year after the crisis began, Engels lamented to Marx in a letter: "Distress has . . . begun to set in among the proletariat. There are as yet few signs of revolution, for the long period of prosperity has been fearfully demoralising."[29] Marx continued to expect a revolutionary upsurge and even took solace in the brief break in the economic crisis at the beginning of 1858. "The momentary LULL in the crisis is, or so it seems to me, most advantageous to our interests—PARTY INTERESTS, I mean. Even in 1848, after the first LULL, England suffered some very severe blows at 2 or 3 INTERVALS, and at that time the crater had already shifted from where it had been in April 1847. . . ."[30] The 1848 events had shown, then, that lulls are to be expected in a crisis and can even be useful for the revolutionary party to use, presumably, to prepare for the next round.

This was the context in which Marx made a most self-revealing comment in a letter to Lassalle six weeks later.

> There are turbulent times in the offing. If I were merely to consult my own private inclinations, I would wish for another few years of superficial calm. There could, at any rate, be no better time for scholarly undertakings and, after all, what has happened over the last ten years must have increased any RATIONAL BEING'S contempt for the masses as for individuals to such a degree that 'odi profanum vulgus et arceo' [I detest and repudiate the common people] had almost become an inescapable maxim. However all these are themselves philistine ruminations which will be swept away by the first storm.[31]

Such candor revealed not only the disciplined revolutionary, who prioritized political over private needs, but also the committed revolutionary whose basic beliefs could be shaken—in this case, the most fundamental of all, confidence in the masses—by an extended drought in the class struggle. Yet it was precisely because the core of his persona was so thoroughly political and not merely "rational" that whatever doubts, if any, he may have harbored had to be qualified with "however." The subsequent first storms in America and Poland confirmed that these were indeed "philistine ruminations."

In an overview of Europe's political terrain in 1858 Engels pointed to what he called "a peculiar revival of political activity." Common to that activity were the increasing demands of Europe's bourgeoisie and middle classes, who had enriched themselves during the decade-long expansion of capitalist production, to eliminate "the political fetters imposed upon them" by "military and bureaucratic despotism"—rule they acquiesced in "to secure the suppression of the proletarian revolution" in 1848–49. The combination of their new wealth and a dormant working class gave them confidence to begin agitating for more democratic space for themselves—demands that were getting a hearing with "a number of reforming princes" such as Czar Alexander II in Russia, the country that "was the first to awake from [the] political lethargy" of the lull. This situation was not unlike that on the eve of the last upheaval. "The year 1858 bears a close resemblance to the year 1846, which also initiated a political revival in most parts of Europe. . . ."[32] Thus, Engels, at least, was still employing 1848 as his model in trying to make sense out of the developments in Europe, at a time when no real revolutionary process was underway.

In England, where Marx and Engels had pinned their hopes on a modern industrial proletarian movement the situation appeared no brighter, especially as it became clear by the end of 1858 that the economic crisis had come to an end. The break with Jones of the Chartist movement had been due to his maneuvering with middle-class forces for electoral reform, leading to concessions that diluted unnecessarily, in their opinion, the original Chartist program. In the end, as Marx had predicted, what remained of the Chartist movement became history, and Jones "IS NOW A RUINED MAN, but the harm he has done to the English proletariat is incalculable. The fault will, of course, be rectified, but a most favourable moment for action has been missed."[33] The crisis, therefore, did not produce an immediate political response as expected, although—a foresighted qualification—"the fault . . . will be rectified." Indeed, this was the case when about a year later the building trades in London began to mobilize, initiating the movement for modern British trade unionism and, thereby, putting in place a key plank for the construction of the IWMA four years later.

If, by the end of 1858, the economic crisis hadn't produced the long-awaited political upsurge, Marx was convinced, nevertheless, that a new revolutionary wave was on the agenda. He had already anticipated that the new revolutionary process might take a different course from that of 1848—at least in its origins. A couple of months prior to the scenario that Engels painted, which viewed 1858 as 1846, he raised this possibility with his comrade in surveying the political map of Europe in October 1858. "Considering the optimistic turn taken by world trade AT THIS MOMENT . . . it is some consolation at least that the *revolution has begun* in Russia. . . ."[34] He was referring to Czar Alexander II's proposal to convene an assembly of the landlord nobility to discuss the end of serfdom, an example of what Engels later meant by "reforming princes" responding, or giving the appearance of responding, to the demands of its bourgeoisie, or in the case of Russia, the nobility, to have more input for itself in the governance process. Such an opening in feudal Russia, as Marx correctly foresaw, had the potential for unforeseen revolutionary consequences.

He then raised, in a comment that has been almost totally ignored, an issue of profound importance. Although convinced that the capitalist mode of production had outworn its welcome, was it really in 1858 fated for extinction given that it had certainly by now created a "world market, at least in outline, and production . . . based on that market"?

> For us the difficult QUESTION is this: on the Continent revolution is imminent and will, moreover, instantly assume a socialist character. Will it not necessarily be CRUSHED in this little corner of the earth, since the MOVEMENT of bourgeois society is still in the ASCENDANT over a far greater area?[35]

Only in hindsight, four decades later, would Engels be able to provide the answer to this dilemma. The problem, of course, as he later wrote, was that the premise was faulty; capitalism had not expended its potential by any means in 1858 and neither was socialist revolution anywhere on the agenda then.[36]

Still, Marx, in referring to the "imminent revolution" as one in "this little corner of the earth," recognized that a socialist revolution in Europe might not be successful since capitalism was still on the ascent. In such a reality the success of Europe's revolution was linked to that of the revolutionary process elsewhere in the capitalist world. Thus, Marx and Engels's agreement at the beginning of 1860 that the "slave movement in America and Russia" was "the most momentous thing happening in the world today." In his preface to *Capital*, written seven years later, three years into the life of the IWMA, Marx could be even more explicit: "As in the 18th century, the American War of independence sounded the tocsin for the European middle-class, so in the 19th century, the American Civil War sounded it for the European working-class."[37] Political reality had revealed by 1867 that of the two "slave movements" in 1860, the one on the other side of the Atlantic was more decisive. Six decades later, however, "the lava [would] flow from East to West."

Marx and Engels's world revolutionary perspective in 1858, which looked beyond "this little corner of the earth," had been foreshadowed by the former's New Year's Day article written for *NRZ* readers a decade earlier. As the German revolution hung in the balance, Marx argued that its outcome was linked to the successful outcome of a global revolutionary process that embraced struggles as diverse as those "waged in Canada as in Italy, in East Indies as in Prussia, in Africa as on the Danube."[38] The years of "swotting" and revolutionary journalism during the lull had allowed both of them to broaden and concretize that perspective, along with the other lessons of 1848, and, thus, be open to the real movement wherever it might erupt. Contrary to the oft-repeated charge that theirs was a Western-Eurocentric perspective, they, unlike any other revolutionaries of their day, were truly internationalists in their outlook. Hence their determination, from that perspective, of a new revolutionary era.

As part of their global view, and of equal significance, the criteria Marx and Engels actually employed to determine the beginning of the new era were not, as had been true for their postanalysis of 1848, the presence or absence of an economic crisis—the 1857 slump, in fact, had not produced a political upheaval—but rather political events, the real movement. Economics was relevant to the extent that capitalism was indeed now a worldwide phenomenon, which, therefore, resulted in a corresponding global political process. This is not to imply that their emphasis on politics in the early 1860s represented a break with their analysis of 1848–49. The fact is that they threw themselves into that revolution on the basis of the real movement and not economic analysis. The latter was utilized only when they sought to determine when the movement had ebbed and to predict when it would begin again. Just as in 1848, however, they began to move in the early 1860s when real forces were in motion. Although capitalism was still ascendant, that did not lead them to adopt a quietist posture. The conclusions they had reached fifteen years earlier about the inadequacies of Feuerbach's materialism required that they not stand on the sidelines while the real movement was in progress. What was different from 1848 was only the scope of that movement—this time of world proportions.[39]

THE FIRST INTERNATIONAL: "A MIGHTY ENGINE AT OUR DISPOSAL"

On September 28, 1864, a meeting organized by English and French trade unionists was held in London to explore the possibility of collaborative work between the workers' movements of these and other nations, in particular, to support the Polish and Italian struggles for self-determination. Another motive had to do with one of the lessons of the 1857–59 economic crisis, that is, through international solidarity trade unionists on both sides of the English Channel could lessen the ability of capital to pit workers of different countries against one another. That the meeting was held in the same hall, St. Martin's, where the historic mass meeting seventeen months earlier in solidarity with the Northern cause in the American Civil War had taken place, and that many of the organizers of the second meeting had a hand in the first was not coincidental. This, indeed, was what Marx meant when he wrote three years later that the U.S. Civil War "sounded the tocsin for the . . . European working-class." His understanding, better, probably, than anyone else in attendance at the meeting, of its historic significance and possession of a party nucleus enabled Marx to quickly emerge as the guiding force in the new body. The convergence between the internationalism of Europe's working class and that of the Marx party is what made this development possible.[40]

The decade-long activity of Marx and Engels in the IWMA, for which there is, unlike the Communist League, ample documentation, cannot be treated here and in the following chapters in all its rich detail and complexity. The focus, rather, is on the continuity with the lessons of 1848 and the most important programmatic additions to that tradition.[41]

The IWMA: From Its Birth

As was the case with his and Engels's involvement with the League of the Just in 1847, Marx was invited by working-class leaders to participate in the founding of what came to be called the International Working Men's Association, the First International. In spite of his relative isolation in London during the previous decade Marx was well known through his writings to working-class leaders on both sides of the English Channel. Since Marx had turned down apparently similar invitations during the lull years, he had to explain in a series of letters to party members, including Engels of course, why he accepted this time. In all the letters he emphasized that the initiators of the new organization were "real workers' leaders in London, with one or two exceptions all workers themselves."[42] Also, they were the same people who had organized the mass meeting in March 1863 in solidarity with the North, the meeting that *"prevented war with the United States."* They had as well organized a gigantic reception for the Italian revolutionary leader Giuseppe Garibaldi, who visited Britain five months earlier. To Weydemeyer, Marx wrote: "I accepted *this time* because it concerns a matter by means of which it is possible to have a significant influence. . . ."[43] To Engels, he wrote: "I knew that on this occasion 'people who really count' were appearing, both from London and from Paris."[44]

What was different, then, about the September 1864 meeting was that leaders who represented real working-class forces that had been in motion not only in London but also in France and Italy initiated it. It may be recalled that virtually the only other political events during the lull in which Marx partook were sponsored by the Chartists, the Labour Parliament in 1854, and the mass protests against Sunday closing laws a year later.[45] Of even greater significance, given the conclusions the Marx party had reached about world politics, was that the meeting was called to further proletarian internationalism, again, by forces who had already been mobilized. Thus, the opportunity to have an impact on the real movement—the same criterion he and Engels employed in accepting the invitation from the League of Just leaders in 1847—and to "recruit our party entirely anew" was an offer that Marx could not refuse. However minuscule the Marx party had become by 1864, it, unlike any other revolutionary current, was able to do the most with this opportunity.

Marx's letter to Engels also detailed how he got involved and how in less than a month after the September meeting he had assumed political leadership of the new association. A provisional organizing committee composed of representatives for various countries was formed at the initial gathering; Marx and Eccarius were chosen to represent Germany. Marx was also selected to serve on the subcommittee to draft the rules and guiding principles of the new body. It was in this capacity that he was instrumental, through conscious intervention on his and Eccarius's part—the legacy of a decade-long functioning as an informal but disciplined party—in writing the founding documents of the IWMA. In view of the diverse political tendencies on the provisional committee—Owenites, old and new Chartists, Proudhonists, Mazzini's partisans—it took, as he explained to Engels, astute political footwork and skillful writing to produce documents that were consistent with or noncompromising of their own principles while acceptable to all these disparate forces. Although all of Marx's proposals were adopted, he was "obliged to insert two sentences about 'DUTY' and 'RIGHT,' and ditto about 'TRUTH, MORALITY AND JUSTICE' in the preamble to the rules. . . ." Since these were the kind of abstract and classless formulations that Marx and Engels had no patience with he added happily that they "are so placed that they can do no harm."[46]

The most important of Marx's drafts, what became known as the "Inaugural Address of the Working Men's Association," was, as he reported to Engels, "adopted with great enthusiasm (UNANIMOUSLY)" by the then General Council (originally called the Central Council), that is, the former provisional committee, of the Association. Again, Marx had to be very adroit in his writing.

> It was very difficult to frame the thing so that our view should appear in a form that would make it ACCEPTABLE to the present outlook of the workers' movement. . . . It will take time before the revival of the movement allows the old boldness of language to be used. We must be *fortiter in re, suaviter in modo* [strong in deed, mild in manner].[47]

This comment captures in many ways Marx's vision and expectations about the new organization. It was a sober recognition that the political consciousness of Europe's proletariat in 1864 was not what it had been in 1848–49.

Marx and Engels were certainly under no illusions about England's working class. To a comment that Engels made in April 1863—"that the English proletariat's revolutionary energy has all but completely evaporated and the English proletarian has declared himself in full agreement with the dominancy of the bourgeoisie"— Marx replied: "How soon the English workers will throw off what seems to be a bourgeois contagion remains to be seen."[48] That Marx was less pessimistic than Engels may have to do with the fact that he had just attended the mass meeting in March in solidarity with the Northern cause. Nevertheless, he was realistic about the prospects in England. At the same time there was the expectation that through patient but principled political work the revolutionary consciousness of the previous upheaval would resurface, if not in England then certainly elsewhere. And *"fortiter in re, suaviter in modo"* indeed became the modus operandi of the Marx party in the IWMA to facilitate this resurgence.

Given the varied political forces that Marx had to maneuver with, Engels replied: "I cannot wait to see the Address . . . it must be a real masterpiece. . . . But it is good that we are again making contact with people who do at least represent their class, which is what really matters ultimately." While welcoming the opportunity for the Marx party to be back in touch with the workers movement, Engels was doubtful that such disparate political forces could coexist for long within the same organization: "I suspect that there will very soon be a split in this new association between those who are bourgeois in their thinking and those who are proletarian, the moment the issues become a little more specific."[49] Although Engels's forecast was eventually correct, Marx's strategy, as we'll see, was to delay the "split"—as it turned out, splits—as long as possible through the tactic of *suaviter in modo* in order to win as many forces as possible to their party's program.

The "Inaugural Address," one of the four most important Marx party documents—the others being the *Manifesto*, the March Address of 1850, and the *Civil War in France*—"was not," Marx replied to Engels, "so difficult [to write] as you think, because we are dealing with 'workers' all the time."[50] Had the General Council (hereafter the GC) been composed, he suggested, of middle-class elements, the task would have been more formidable. Precisely because the Inaugural Address spoke to the reality of Europe's proletariat in the third quarter of the nineteenth century, the "golden age of capital," it could incorporate the political essence, if not the language, of scientific communism. In many ways the *Manifesto*, unlike the Inaugural Address, was more anticipatory than descriptive of the reality of the time in which it was written.

The first five pages of the nine-page document challenged with documentation—almost all of which had been already collected for *Capital*—the claim of the bourgeoisie and its governmental mouthpieces, particularly in Britain, that the enrichment of the former after 1848 represented a gain for the proletariat. Written originally in English with the British working class very much in mind, the document's refutation of this claim rang true for the trade union members on the GC; so did its conclusion about the larger picture.

> In all countries of Europe it has now become a truth . . . that no improvement of machinery, no appliance of science to production, no contrivances of communication, no new colonies, no emigration, no opening of markets, no free trade, nor all these things put together, will do away with the miseries of the industrious masses; but that, on the present false base, every fresh development of the productive powers of labour must tend to deepen social contrasts and point [*sic*] social antagonisms.[51]

Contrary to the oft-made charge that Marx posited that capitalism leads to the absolute impoverishment of the proletariat, the actual claim, as stated in the Inaugural Address, was that of the tendency toward relative impoverishment. While historians continue to debate the merits of Marx's claim as it relates to the third quarter of the nineteenth century, the fact is that leaders of the most class-conscious workers in the then most advanced capitalist country voted with trade union leaders from other countries to adopt unanimously Marx's argument.[52]

The Address then noted that in spite of British capital's "vampire like" exploitation of labor, the latter could claim two significant victories against the former. The first, the passage by Parliament of the Ten Hours Bill in 1847, "told indeed upon the great contest between the blind rule of the supply and demand laws which form the political economy of the middle class, and social production controlled by social foresight, which forms the political economy of the working class." By its pressure on Parliament, therefore, the proletariat had been able for the first time to place social restraints on the capitalist market.

The second victory was that of the "cooperative movement" that was pioneered by Robert Owen. The record of its "social experiments," particularly the "cooperative factories," had amply demonstrated the superiority of production based on "associated labour" over slave or wage labor. Yet the experience since 1848 had shown that for cooperative labor to really "free the masses" it had "to be developed to national dimensions, and, consequently, to be fostered by national means." It's clear that Marx's praise for the second victory was a concession to at least two political tendencies represented on the GC—the Owenites and Proudhonists. Thirteen years earlier he had been less diplomatic about the limitations of the cooperative movement, namely, its parochialism.[53] But in praising cooperative labor Marx was able to make a declaration in favor of socialism—for a society based on "associated labor"—without explicitly saying so, in language that would be acceptable to the varied tendencies represented on the GC.

The qualification about the need for the cooperative movement to assume national dimensions allowed Marx to then immediately make his most important point in the Address (which he would reiterate again in a more detailed programmatic statement on cooperative labor for the IWMA two years later). Because of the obstacles that the bourgeois state would raise against national cooperation, "To conquer political power has therefore become the great duty of the working classes." And the road to political power was through the combination or unification of workers across national boundaries. It was for this purpose that the IWMA came into existence. The success the English working class had achieved in restraining Palmerston from intervening on behalf of the Confederacy was the best example of what proletarian internationalism could achieve. The foreign policy of Europe's heads of state, "in pursuit of criminal designs, playing upon national prejudices, and squandering in piratical wars the people's blood and treasure," required that workers put forward an alternative policy. "The fight for such a foreign policy forms part of the general struggle for the emancipation of the working classes." Thus, lastly, just as the *Manifesto* ended, "Proletarians of all countries, Unite!"[54]

Marx as Political Organizer

The Provisional Rules of the Association, which Marx also wrote, reveal the organizational tactics that he would employ. Parting from the initial draft of a Mazzini partisan on the GC that listed forty separate rules—which Marx characterized to Engels as an attempt to create "a sort of central government of the *European* working classes (with Mazzini in the background, of course)"[55]—he proposed ten rules introduced by a preamble. The ten rules provided for an open and flexible modus operandi. A yearly congress was called for from which the GC, to sit in London, would be selected. The GC, to "consist of working men belonging to the different countries represented in" the IWMA, had the power to coopt new members onto it. The stipulation of "working men," as we'll see shortly, had significant repercussions.

While affiliated "working men's societies" in their respective countries could "preserve their existent organisations intact," IWMA members "shall use their utmost efforts to combine the disconnected . . . societies [in each country] into national bodies, represented by central national organs." At the same time this norm would not be applied rigidly given the political realities of each country and neither would any "independent local society be precluded . . . from directly corresponding with the [GC]." This kind of organizational flexibility—as opposed to "a sort of central government"—is exactly what Marx wanted, certainly at this stage. This would allow the International to make links with the largest number of workers. As well, it gave the Marx party an opportunity to advance its perspective among qualitatively more layers of Europe's modern proletariat than ever before. Indeed, as Engels foresaw, differences and resulting splits would occur as the party argued for its views, but in the process it would "recruit anew." A flexible IWMA structure—*suaviter in modo*—in other words, would give the party enough breathing space for it to grow.

In the very beginning of the preamble to the Provisional Rules, Marx stated, again tactfully, a basic plank of scientific communism.

> [T]he emancipation of the working classes must be conquered by the working classes themselves; that the struggle for emancipation of the working classes means not a struggle for class privileges and monopolies, but for equal rights and duties, and the abolition of all class rule . . .

And then, shortly afterwards, he came back to his central message in the Address but in a less direct manner.

> [T]he economical emancipation of the working classes is therefore the great end to which every political movement ought to be subordinate as a means . . .[56]

For those tendencies in the IWMA who saw the economical struggle as the end and means and, thus, were not persuaded that "To conquer political power has therefore become the great duty of the working classes," the formulation in the Rules allowed a possible escape route, especially if, as was true with the French version of the Rules, "as a means" was conveniently—unbeknownst to Marx initially—left out.[57] This issue, whether it was necessary for the proletariat to conquer political power, more than any other, would be at the heart of the debates and eventual splits in the International.

No "Piedestal" for the Petit Bourgeoisie. Marx was deadly serious about his injunction in the preamble to the Rules that "the emancipation of the working classes must be conquered by the working classes themselves." If there was one lesson from 1848, surely it had been that the proletariat should entertain no illusions about the petit bourgeoisie, let alone the bourgeoisie. After more than a month of working with some of the petit-bourgeois forces on the GC, Marx wrote to Engels that "one has to be all the more careful the moment men of letters, members of the bourgeoisie or semi-literary people become involved in the movement."[58] To address that concern Marx initiated organizational and rule changes that placed severe limits on middle-class participation in the leadership of the IWMA. To head off requests such as that of Louis Blanc, the former head of the Provisional Government of the February Revolution, to become an "honorary member," Marx motivated, as he explained to Engels, the GC to adopt a resolution "that no one (except workers' SOCIETIES) could be *invited* to join and that nobody at all could be an *honorary member.*"[59] Another innovation allowed the GC to "accept or reject . . . delegates" that affiliated bodies elected to it as its representatives.

When a prominent lawyer who had collaborated with the IWMA sought in early 1865 a seat on the GC, Marx convinced other members that his request should be rejected on the basis of the class interests that he represented. "I believe him an honest and sincere man; at the same time, he is nothing and can be nothing save a Bourgeois politician." Precisely because the lawyer aspired to a seat in Parliament, "he ought to be excluded from entering our committee. We cannot become *le piedestal* for small parliamentary ambitions. . . . [Otherwise] others of his class will follow, and our efforts, till now successful at freeing the English working class movement from all middle class or aristocratic patronage, will have been in vain."[60] Hence, very early in the IWMA's existence Marx opposed any efforts to make the International into an electoral conduit for, certainly, the petit bourgeoisie and bourgeoisie itself. Marx's vigilance on this matter was conveyed in a letter to Engels at the end of 1865 in which he complained that in spite of the tremendous workload on him owing to his involvement in the IWMA—he was trying to complete *Capital* at the same time—it was incumbent on him to continue his activism. "If I resigned tomorrow, the bourgeois element, which looks at us with displeasure in the wings (FOREIGN INFIDELS), would have the upper hand . . . [and] I should be doing very serious damage to the cause."[61] Once again, the priority of politics even at the expense of the scientific work.

Other steps that Marx initiated to limit the influence of petit-bourgeois and bourgeois forces in the IWMA included an unsuccessful campaign in 1865 to have London workers buy the majority of the shares of the *Bee-Hive* newspaper, the official trade union paper, which also served as the International's semi-official organ. "Naturally it is impossible to have a movement here without its own press-organ."[62] The failure to do so led to an official break with the paper in 1870 as it increasingly reflected the interests of its bourgeois share owners rather than those of workers—a move that Marx motivated.

Marx also demanded that GC members be active in building the organization by forming branches and signing up new members; they could themselves be barred from the GC if they didn't pay their dues to get their membership cards. This was, clearly, another way of preventing "honorary" membership and to discourage opportunists with parliamentary ambitions, who were not prepared to be activists in the body, from participating. Such norms, were, of course, consistent with Marx's long-held position that only through active involvement in the real movement could the leader or "educator"—to recall the third thesis on Feuerbach—be "educated." He himself was intimately involved in every organizational detail including the signing and issuance of membership cards, the close monitoring of Association documents and finances—at times advancing his own limited funds to keep it afloat—and, not unexpectedly, drawing up the agendas and draft policy statements for congresses. Marx's insistence on this mode of functioning cast him in the role of the GC's disciplinarian. Upon his return to the GC in the first part of 1866 after a short absence for health reasons, he wrote to Engels: "[S]ince my return discipline has by and large been reestablished."[63]

Though it can't be known with certainty, there is nothing to suggest that Marx would have blocked the participation of a petit-bourgeois figure who was willing to put in the necessary time and energy to build the IWMA. His bottom line was whether an individual, regardless of class origins, was prepared to subordinate his or herself to the interests (as, of course, he and Engels understood) of the workers' movement—the criteria to which they held themselves.

A "Literary Man" in the Workers' Movement. A major debate broke out in the first year of the IWMA's existence about the place of "literary men," or intellectuals, in its leadership, that is, individuals who were clearly not workers but who contributed to the organization's advancement. Obviously, this had implications for Marx and Engels, who on occasion described their role in the workers movement as that of "literary representatives of the proletariat." The issue arose within the French section because, as Marx explained to Engels, "the workers seem to want to take things to the point of *excluding* any LITERARY MAN, etc., which is absurd, as they need them in the press, but it is pardonable in view of the repeated treachery of the LITERARY MEN."[64] While the details of this dispute cannot be explored here, suffice it to say that it was resolved through a vote at the IWMA's first congress, at Geneva in 1866. Henri Tolain, the Proudhonist leader of the French section of the International, moved that sections be required to select only "hand-workers" for delegates to a congress. The main opposition to the motion came from the British trade union leaders, one of whom argued that were it not for some of the nonmanual worker members of the GC, the IWMA "would not have struck so deep a root in Britain. Among those members I will mention one only, Citizen Marx [who was not in attendance], who has devoted all his life to the triumph of the working classes."

Another British delegate spoke against the motion and in so doing gave one of the reasons for Marx's absence at the congress as well as offering a glimpse—too often ignored in standard Marxological accounts—of how Marx was viewed by the trade union leaders with whom he worked.

> That distinguished man perfectly understood the importance of having only hand-workers as delegates to this first [congress]. . . . Accordingly, he refused the appointment which was offered him by the [GC]. But that sentiment of delicacy is no reason for passing a rule to exclude him, or any one else, from being sent to our Congresses. On the contrary, men who devote themselves to the cause of the *proletaires* are too rare to make it expedient that they should be "snubbed." The middle class only triumphed when it allied itself with men of Science and it is the pretended science of middle class political economy which gives it prestige and through that prestige, ministers to its power. Let those who have studied political economy from a working class standpoint come, by all means, to our Congresses, there to shiver the fallacies of middle class political economy.[65]

This most remarkable statement, the various dimensions of which cannot, unfortunately, be explored here, helps to explain why Marx was able to exercise such influence in the IWMA. At the same time, he understood, clearly, that "delicacy," or *suaviter in modo*, was a necessary tactic. Geneva was only one of a number of congresses that Marx would miss and while his need to work on *Capital* was certainly a factor it was also the case, as the delegate revealed, that he was concerned about the issue of class baiting. Tolain tried to defend his motion by also drawing on the example of Marx's absence. "By so acting, Citizen Marx intended to inculcate that delegates to working men's Congresses should be hand-workers, and hand-workers only." The majority of the delegates were not persuaded by Tolain's self-serving spin on Marx's absence and voted twenty-five to twenty against his motion.

Given his earlier experiences with class baiting, Marx had already taken steps to guard against a possible challenge to his leadership in the IWMA. When the German workers' movement sought in the fall of 1864 his return to Germany to be president of the newly-formed GGWA in place of the recently deceased Lassalle, he proposed instead that they elect him to be their representative on the GC, with which they readily complied.[66] Marx and Engels's very crucial involvement in the German movement throughout their activism in the IWMA enhanced the legitimacy of first his, and then, later, Engels's leadership in the International. It was certainly one of the factors in the high regard with which Marx was held by the British trade union leaders and why they and the other GC members gladly accepted the decision of the German workers.

The ringing endorsement that Marx was given at Geneva testified to the enormous influence he exercised in the IWMA by the time of its first congress. Even six months after the organization's founding Marx could accurately tell Engels that "I am IN FACT the HEAD of it."[67] He was not far off the mark when he wrote to a party member in Germany, Ludwig Kugelman, shortly after the Geneva congress eighteen months later, "I am in fact having to run the whole Association myself."[68] With such influence, Marx had to be careful how he wielded it. *Fortiter in re, suaviter in modo* was indeed his modus operandi. While, for example, he did not attend the Geneva congress he was instrumental in directing it by writing the main document for its discussions, "Instructions for the Delegates of the Provisional General Council— The Different Questions," and having his closest party members lead the gathering in his absence.[69]

Sensitive, also, to the potential of class baiting, he declined the post of GC president which was offered to him in the aftermath of Geneva, an offer that was in part a "demonstration" to the Proudhonists' exclusionary efforts at the congress. The GC minutes record that Marx "thought himself incapacitated because he was a head worker and not a hand worker."[70] When he opposed, as another example, the efforts of the above-mentioned bourgeois lawyer to be seated on the GC in early 1865, Marx was most careful, as he explained to Engels: "I could, of course, have prevented the matter *by force*, as all the CONTINENTALS [especially the GC members from France] would have voted with me. But I DID NOT LIKE ANY SUCH DIVISION."[71] Rather than provoking a premature split, he achieved his goal by working behind the scenes—the posture he best enjoyed—through letters to other GC members with arguments that indirectly addressed the principal issues at stake.

One last example is particularly instructive. Eccarius, the long-time party member who with Marx's urging and assistance developed as a true worker intellectual became the editor of the *Worker's Advocate*, the official organ of the IWMA between 1865 and 1867(this was during a period when relations with the *Bee-Hive* were severely strained). He got the job, in place of three influential British trade unionists on the GC, mainly because of Marx's endorsement. Marx later had reservations about his intercession on his behalf, especially after it created resentment amongst the trade union contingent on the GC, who eventually managed to relegate Eccarius to a minor role at the paper. He had tried, as he explained in a letter to Engels in April 1866, unsuccessfully to discourage Eccarius from seeking the post. "It was a 'political' error on my part to have given way to his entreaties. . . ." In view of the problems it had created, there was an important political lesson in all of this.

> Avoidance of any appearance of pursuing personal interests or abusing personal influence for clandestine purposes, and good understanding with the English must, of course, be more important to us than satisfying Eccarius' more or less justified ambition. . . . If I even went so far as to muddy myself for his sake, despite his lack of discipline and his wilful behaviour, I was always moved to do so particularly by the consideration that he has always worked with us and never reaped the fruits of it. But one always makes BLUNDERS if one allows oneself to be influenced by such like considerations.

Marx also opined how Eccarius should have functioned: "If he had followed me, operated slowly, maintained a modest posture, everything would be in the best of order."[72] Eccarius, in other words, should have been, like Marx, *suaviter in modo*. Marx, on the other hand, criticized himself for giving in to personal over political concerns about a long-time and loyal party member.[73]

Given the kinds of slanders that he had to confront a few years earlier, the basis for the *Herr Vogt* polemic, it was even more incumbent on party members, and Marx in particular, that they not give opponents a handle to make similar charges but behave only as principled politicians. This was especially the case when it came to dealing with the British trade unionists, whose participation in the IWMA was crucial—at this stage for sure—to its survival. As he had advised budding revolutionaries almost two decades earlier, "Personal considerations must be utterly disregarded, they ruin everything."[74] Marx, nevertheless, maintained his credibility and influence in the IWMA because he recognized his "political error" with regard to Eccarius and, thus, was able to avoid a repeat performance.

A few months before the Geneva congress the Mazzini partisans had all abandoned or been ousted from the GC. From its very beginning the GC had been the site of a low-level guerrilla warfare between Marx and Mazzini's supporters; the evidence is strong that Mazzini orchestrated this from afar. At the root of the conflict were profound differences over political and organizational issues. In explaining to his cousin Antoinette Phillips, a member of the Dutch section of the IWMA, the particulars of the struggle, Marx made an introspective comment about himself and leadership. During his absence from the GC earlier that year owing to health reasons, Mazzini, he said, "had been busy stirring a sort of revolt against my leadership. 'Leadership' is never a pleasant thing, nor a thing I ambition. . . . But having once fairly embarked in an enterprise which I consider of import, I certainly, 'anxious' man as I am, do not like to give way."[75] It was with such determination that Marx was able to frustrate Mazzini's efforts and have the GC declare in his favor against the latter at a meeting in March 1866.

What the preceding suggests is that Marx, had he chosen, could have operated—and, perhaps, gotten away with it—non-democratically. That he didn't is telling and can be taken to mean that he took seriously his injunction that only the working class could emancipate itself. Yet, as he no doubt believed, democratic functioning should be viewed contextually rather than absolutely and, on balance, he comported himself well.

Support from Manchester. With Engels in Manchester, Marx, unlike 1848–49, was pretty much on his own in London in directing the IWMA, especially in its initial period. The problem was not simply one of geography. It's clear from his letters that Engels was lukewarm about the organization's potential, suggesting that Marx could use his time more wisely to complete *Capital.* Marx did his best to get Engels involved by urging him to establish a section in Manchester as well as encouraging his companion, the working-class Irish nationalist Lizzie Burns, to become a member. For almost a half year his urging was to little or no avail. As his above-mentioned reaction to Marx's first detailed letter about the IWMA indicated, Engels was not confident that the disparate forces of whom it was composed could stay together. "I had always half expected that the naive *fraternité* in the INTERNATIONAL ASSOCIATION would not last long," he told Marx in April 1865.[76] However, his letter to Weydemeyer a month earlier, in which he wrote that the IWMA "is going from strength to strength" suggested that he began to have a more positive attitude toward the organization.[77] By the middle of 1865 Engels was clearly on board, as he increasingly collaborated with Marx on tactics and strategy in its direction.

The Marx-Engels correspondence in this period provides more insights into the character of their partnership. Politically, the partnership was even stronger—in spite of Engels's initial coolness toward the IWMA—because of their intense collaboration vis-a-vis the German movement—about which more will be said later. As for the scientific work, Engels provided invaluable insights, especially as an officer in a capitalist industrial firm, for Marx in writing *Capital.* Engels was virtually the sole person on whom Marx tested his arguments and from whom he sought advice for the completion of his magnum opus. Marx also bounced other ideas off Engels and acknowledged that it was Engels who often took the intellectual lead in the partnership. Referring to his reading on human physiology in mid-1864, literature that Engels was apparently familiar with, Marx commented to Engels, "As you know, 1. I'm always late off the mark with everything, and 2. I invariably follow in your footsteps."[78] Indeed, it had been Engels who first declared himself a communist and through his writings in 1844–1845, as already seen, opened Marx's eyes to the importance of political economy as well as the Chartist movement; without the latter, Marx's thesis about the proletariat as the revolutionary class would have remained just that, a theoretical construct. In the current period Engels led the way in Marx's decision to study such diverse subjects as Irish history, differential calculus, and Russian—all of which were related to the party's political and scientific work.

Finally, the material substance that Engels provided to the Marx household was still indispensable, as Marx acknowledged in August 1865, a time when he was, once again, most desperate financially: "The only thought that sustains me in all this is that the two of us form a partnership together, in which I spend my time on the theoretical and party side of the BUSINESS."[79] During this period, in other words, the partnership involved a conscious division of labor in which Engels labored in his family's factory in Manchester to make it possible for Marx to work on *Capital* as well as be the de facto head of the IWMA.

The Scientific Work as Political Ammunition

When Marx told Weydemeyer in 1859 that, in publishing *A Contribution to a Critique of Political Economy* "I hope to win a scientific victory for our party," he was speaking as well about the entire political economy project that had engaged his attention for the last fifteen years. The opening of a new revolutionary era and the founding of the IWMA shortly afterward inspired Marx to expedite the work. With the basic drafts for all three volumes of *Capital* completed by the end of 1865, to which *A Contribution* was the introduction, the party had at last acquired the theoretical arms it needed to take on opponents and recruit the party anew—to influence the real movement. It remained of course for Marx to prepare for publication in 1867 the first of the three volumes. That Marx was able to do so when he was more active than ever in the IWMA—from about February 1866 to April 1867—is evidence that politics indeed inspired his scientific work.[80]

Trade Unions and "Guerilla Warfare." The first opportunity that Marx had to make use of his theoretical work in the IWMA came when John Weston, an old Owenite on the GC put forward to the Council in May 1865 a series of resolutions for adoption: "1. that A GENERAL RATE IN THE RISE OF WAGES would be of no benefit to the workers; 2. that the TRADES-UNIONS for that reason, etc., are *harmful*." As Marx explained to Engels, "If these two propositions, in which *he* alone in our SOCIETY believes, were to be accepted, we should be in a terrible mess, both in respect of the TRADES-UNIONS here and the INFECTION OF STRIKES now prevailing on the Continent."[81] He then added, "I am, of course, expected to produce a refutation." However difficult it would be to "COMPRESS A COURSE OF POLITICAL ECONOMY INTO 1 HOUR . . . WE SHALL DO OUR BEST." The result was a paper that Marx presented that lasted over the course of two GC meetings in June. Although it was the intention of the GC to publish it along with Weston's arguments—the *Bee Hive* newspaper, in which Weston had already presented his views, ran a small notice about Marx's paper—it was never published in Marx's lifetime. Only afterward was his presentation published, known now as *Value, Price and Profits.*[82]

As Marx noted in his letter to Engels the stakes in this debate were high not only for the IWMA but for the entire labor movement. If Weston was correct and convincing, then the very premises upon which the modern class struggle rested could be placed in doubt. Weston's argument, which resembled that of many utopian socialists, was based on assumptions borrowed from Malthus and Ricardo that once informed, particularly those of the latter, Marx and Engels in their earlier analysis of wages and trade unions. Lassalle's "iron law of wages"—namely, that wages under capitalism are always reduced to the minimal means of subsistence—also drew upon such assumptions. If wages were determined exclusively by the minimal needs of workers for their reproduction, then, as Weston reasoned in his first resolution, the capitalists, in order to maintain their profits, would simply raise the price of consumer goods—thus the conclusion that wage rises would simply harm workers. Hence, also, the claim in the second resolution that trade unions were "harmful."

The discoveries of Marx and Engels during their years of "swotting"—especially Marx's theory of surplus value—allowed them to present a much more sophisticated theory of wages and trade unions. The counterresolutions that Marx offered at the conclusion of his paper—agreed to by the majority of the GC—reflected their current thinking and anticipated the more detailed treatment that was given to them in *Capital*.

> Firstly. A general rise in the rate of wages would result in a fall of the general rate of profit, but, broadly speaking, not affect the prices of commodities.
>
> Secondly. The general tendency of capitalist production is not to raise, but to sink the average standard of wages.
>
> Thirdly. Trades Unions work well as centres of resistance against the encroachments of capital. They fail partially from an injudicious use of their power. They fail generally from limiting themselves to a guerilla war against the effects of the existing system, instead of simultaneously trying to change it, instead of using their organised forces as a lever for the final emancipation of the working class, that is to say, the ultimate abolition of the wages system.[83]

Leading up to his conclusions Marx argued that the productivity of labor was decisive in determining the price of consumer goods. As for wages, their level was determined not just by the minimal needs of workers but also by "the satisfaction of certain wants springing from the social conditions in which people are placed and reared up."[84] And as for the relation between profits and wages, this was in turn related to the maximum limits on the former, which were determined by the minimal needs of workers and the length of the work day. Within these limits there was room for lots of variation on profit rates. "The fixation of its actual degree is only settled by the continuous struggle between capital and labor, the capitalist constantly tending to reduce wages to their physical minimum, and to extend the working day to its physical maximum, while the working man constantly presses in the opposite direction. The matter resolves itself into a question of the respective powers of the combatants."[85] The history of the fight over the length of the working day in England had truly revealed that "legislative interference" on the part of workers organized as a class is what made a difference for them. "This very necessity of *general political action* affords proof that in its [i.e., the proletariat's] merely economic action capital is the stronger side."

Yet it was important that workers engage in "economic action," the "everyday struggles," to achieve a "temporary improvement" in spite of the fact that capital does tend to push wages to the minimum. If workers renounced "resistance against the encroachments of capital . . . they would be degraded to one level mass of broken wretches past salvation. . . . By cowardly giving way in their everyday conflict with capital, they would certainly disqualify themselves for the initiating of any larger movement." At the same time no illusions should be had about these "guerilla fights." They are at best defensive struggles inspired by the "*conservative* motto, '*A fair day's wage for a fair day's work!*'" Only through "general political action" would it be possible to end the increasing impoverishment of the working class (it's clear in this period that Marx meant relative and not absolute impoverishment), action that would allow the proletariat "to inscribe on their banner the *revolutionary* watchword, '*Abolition of the wages system!*'"[86]

What Marx proposed, therefore, was a much more revolutionary conclusion than his and Engels's earlier analyses about wages and trade unions permitted. Like Lassalle's views their earlier positions implied that the proletariat could do little to raise their wages owing to the very nature of the capitalist mode of production.[87] The revised perspective gave, as it might be said today, more agency to the proletariat. Like the Inaugural Address, it recognized the relative, not absolute impoverishment of workers, relative because through their struggles, particularly through shortening the work day, workers could actually increase their standard of living; as a whole, however, average wages fall in relation to capital. Although the GC minutes do not indicate if a vote was taken on the two counterposed sets of resolutions, the discussion leaves no doubt that the majority clearly sided with Marx against Weston.

This was Marx's first explicit treatment of the trade union issue. His third resolution in the Weston debate foreshadowed the proposal he made to the delegates at the Geneva congress in 1866, as part of his "Instructions for the Delegates," the first serious discussion in the IWMA on trade unions. Given that the Proudhonists and partisans of Mazzini opposed unions, for reasons not dissimilar to Weston's position, Marx had to be *suaviter in modo* in broaching the question, and only after two years did he feel confident to put forward a position that would win at least majority support.[88]

Marx's proposal, one of nine that he submitted, was entitled "Trade Unions, Their Past, Present and Future."[89] The statement is most significant, as Draper points out, because "it is the first international statement that effectively linked trade-unionism with socialism as part of a revolutionary program."[90] "Their Past," generally, was one as described in the *Manifesto* and the third resolution in the Weston debate. Going farther and more boldly, however, he wrote: "If the Trades' Unions are required for the guerilla fights between capital and labour, they are still more important as *organised agencies for superseding the very system of wages labour and capital rule.*" As for their "Present," again, the third resolution was a harbinger, specifically, with regard to the criticism that they limited themselves to the "guerilla fights." They "kept too much aloof from general social and political movements"— the problem that would be called in Russian revolutionary circles four decades later, "economism." That, however, they had recently become active in England for the fight to extend the suffrage—to be discussed in the next chapter—was a positive sign. This anticipated, in fact, what they would have to do in the "Future."

> Apart from their original purposes, they must now learn to act deliberately as organising centres of the working class in the broad interest of its *complete emancipation.* They must aid every social and political movement tending in that direction. Considering themselves and acting as the champions and representatives of

the whole working class, they cannot fail to enlist the non-society men [i.e., non-organized] into their ranks. They must look carefully after the interests of the worst paid trades, such as the agricultural labourers, rendered powerless by exceptional circumstances. They must convince the world at large that their efforts, far from being narrow and selfish, aim at the emancipation of the downtrodden millions.[91]

This charge to the trade union movement was the most concrete elaboration Marx had ever made on his oft-quoted passage from the *Manifesto*, "The proletarian movement is the self-conscious, independent movement of the immense majority in the interest of the immense majority." Of utmost importance for this book's thesis is the fact that it is a conclusion that Marx drew based on his knowledge and experiences with, firstly, the Chartist and then, later, the trade union movement in England. It may be recalled that in his message to the meeting of the Labour Parliament movement in Manchester in 1854 he specifically advised that its success depended on its going beyond trade unions to the representation of "the labouring classes" as a whole.[92] The essential concern was how to get the proletariat and its class organizations to think and act socially. In the context of the Russian Revolution, this would be one of the central themes in Lenin's famous polemic, *What is to be Done?*

Proudhon Redux. In its totality the Geneva congress proved to be the first major confrontation between the Marxist and Proudhonist programs. On balance there were no clear-cut winners with regard to the "Instructions" that Marx submitted. His proposal on "Trade Unions," which was vigorously defended by the British trade union delegates, was adopted but only after it was diluted a bit owing to the objections of the Proudhonists from Paris. Opposed not only to unions, they viewed strikes with even greater antipathy. Their view, just as Proudhon had claimed, was that workers could best improve their situation by forming mutual credit associations and forming cooperatives.[93] A compromise amendment was added, which grudgingly conceded that while "strikes were sometimes necessary under existing conditions, commended to the workers the 'more elevated aim' of replacing the wage system by an economy 'based on justice and reciprocity.'"[94] Though taking the sting out of Marx's endorsement of the "guerilla fights" of the proletariat, the amendment did not fundamentally undermine his proposal. In anticipation of the next two chapters, Geneva was also "the first tentative encounter in the conflict between centralism and anti-authoritarianism which deepened in intensity throughout the history of the International and dominated its closing years."[95]

Two years later at the Brussels congress in 1868, the Marx party achieved a decisive victory over Proudhonism. With Eccarius and Friedrich Lessner leading the intervention on his behalf—Marx, again, was absent—the congress, in near unanimity, "supported strikes 'as a means of transition from our present state of affairs to one of association'"[96] Even the Proudhonist delegates from Belgium and France had now become, as Marx told Engels, "most emphatically in favour" of trade unions and strikes.[97] One of these delegates, Paul Lafargue, soon became a party member and a son-in-law. On other key issues the Marx party won a majority of the delegates to their views. In some of the debates Eccarius and Lessner quoted extensively from the just-published *Capital* to make their points. As a specific counter to Proudhon's ideas the delegates from Germany introduced a resolution recommending that workers read and translate Marx's tome. A resolution was passed that paid "particular tribute to *Capital*, saying that 'Karl Marx has the inestimable merit of being the first economist to have subjected capital to a scientific analysis.'"[98]

The effective demise of Proudhonism in the International, as well as the registration of it as a spent political force, was accomplished as part of Marx's larger agenda to promote proletarian internationalism. At the same time that he was leading the fight—"*acting* behind the scenes whilst retiring in public," as he described his modus operandi[99]—to have resolutions passed at IWMA congresses in support of trade unions, the right to strike and the eight-hour work day he also wrote the Addresses that the organization sent to Abraham Lincoln and his successor Andrew Johnson. To the former, "the single-minded son of the working class," it was noted that as long as slavery prevailed, "working men . . . were unable to attain the true freedom of labour or to support their European brethren in their struggle for emancipation."[100] For the latter there was advice: "Yours . . . has become the task . . . to preside over the arduous task of political reconstruction and social regeneration. A profound sense of your great mission will save you from any compromise with stern duties . . . to initiate the new era of the emancipation of labour . . ."[101]

All of these initiatives were interrelated, since on the eve of the Geneva congress the recently formed National Labor Union in the United States had just declared in favor of the eight-hour work day movement, which emerged in the wake of the Civil War, confirmation for Marx that labor in America could not advance until slavery had been overthrown. It was, also, an illustration of his point in the preface to *Capital* that "the American Civil War sounded [the tocsin] for the European working-class" (a variation on this theme first appeared in print, incidentally, in the 1864 Address to Lincoln) since it was the Geneva congress that first launched the eight-hour day movement in Europe. Not surprisingly, then, Marx and Engels reacted with alarm when Andrew Johnson did not heed the former's advice and began to compromise with the old slavocracy. When his congressional allies were defeated at the polls in 1866, Marx was "delighted. . . . The workers in the North have at last fully understood that white labour will never be emancipated so long as black labour is still stigmatised"—almost the same words that appeared less than a year later in *Capital*.[102] Any setback to the struggle in the United States, therefore, could be a setback for labor in Europe.

Shortly after the Lausanne congress in 1867, where the Proudhonists had scored some important victories, Marx told Engels that "I shall personally deliver the coup de grâce to those Proudhonist jackasses at the next congress in Brussels." He added that the pressures of getting *Capital* published and his desire to make sure that "our Association is firmly rooted" obliged him to bide time for the Lausanne congress. In spite of the gains the Proudhonists made at the gathering, "our Association has made great progress." He was referring to the enormous growth in members and affiliated trade unions in England and on the continent and the increasing attention given to it by the bourgeois press. A major reason for the IWMA's growth was its assistance to the successful strike of tailors in Edinburgh and London in 1866, which prevented their masters from bringing in scabs from Europe and Germany in particular. This success, in which Marx and his party comrades played a crucial role via their ties to the German movement, which in turn had strong links with the needle trades in their country, was the decisive breakthrough for the International. Marx then put this progress in perspective for both the future and the past.

> [W]hen the next revolution comes, and that will perhaps be sooner than might appear, *we* (i.e., you and I) will have this mighty ENGINE *at our disposal.* COMPARE WITH THIS THE RESULTS OF MAZZINI'S, ETC., OPERATIONS SINCE 30 YEARS! And with no money to boot! And with the intrigues of the Proudhonists in Paris, Mazzini in Italy [and others] in London . . . and the Lassalleans in Germany [again, to be discussed later]! We can be well satisfied![103]

A year later at the end of the Brussels congress, Marx could with justification be even bolder in saying that he and Engels indeed did have a "mighty engine at [their] disposal." In the aftermath of Brussels the "engine" would be severely tested as it was about to meet its greatest challenge.

CONCLUSIONS

On the eve of the IWMA's birth the Marx party consisted of a handful of members and was relatively isolated. Revolutionary figures such as Mazzini and Garibaldi were far better known to Europe's working classes. Within two years, however, it was at the center of the largest international workers organization ever seen, disseminating its perspective and beginning to win new forces—the process of "recruiting our party anew." Precisely because of the "swotting" and political work that the Marx party had done in the decade before the organization's founding it correctly anticipated that new political opportunities were in the offering, as well as being prepared to assume theoretical and organizational leadership. Virtually all of the major programmatic positions of the International originated in the GC, beginning with the Inaugural Address, and were composed by Marx. Applying the major lesson of 1848, Marx effectively, *fortiter in re, suaviter in modo*, minimized the influence of middle-class reformists in the new proletarian body. With the same tactic he displaced the Mazzinists and Proudhonists. Within four years—the high point of the IWMA in terms of membership numbers—a truly international working-class organization existed with the Marx party at the helm.

An essential trait of Marx's modus operandi was to combine daily organizational activism in the most detailed way—what today would be called "licking the stamps" or doing the "s—t work"—with theoretical leadership. The effectiveness of the latter, in fact, was enhanced by that of the former; it made Marx a more credible leader. Marx epitomized the middle-class thinker who subordinated his life to the revolutionary cause of the proletariat. Being a doer as well as a thinker had the added advantage of rendering class baiting ineffective. Thus, the ardent defense of Marx by the British trade union leaders on the GC against the exclusionary attempts of the Proudhonists at the Geneva congress. This model of revolutionary leadership, the theoretician-activist, was unique in the annals of the revolutionary process—the realization of Marx's third thesis on Feuerbach. It was the essence of communist leadership, as Marx and Engels had argued with Heinzen and other opponents on the eve of 1848. Of course, Marx's modus operandi in the IWMA was not something new for him. Though much briefer in existence than the IWMA, the German revolution had well prepared him for such a role. What was new this time was that Marx was a theoretician-activist amongst forces with far more political weight than had existed in the Rhineland in 1848–49.

The vindication Marx and Engels felt about the priority they had given to "swotting" with the publication in 1859 of what proved to be the introduction to *Capital*, namely, *A Contribution to a Critique of Political Economy*, and the steps they took to create a party in waiting was well justified. Without the revolutionary confidence that the working class would be in motion once again and that, therefore, their party would be presented with new opportunities, and the preparatory work it carried out during the dog days of the preceding decade, the Marx party could never have moved so swiftly back to the center stage of revolutionary activity.

CHAPTER EIGHT

The First International:
From Brussels to the Paris Commune

The English working class will never accomplish anything before it has got rid of Ireland.

—Marx to Engels

[T]rue internationalism must necessarily be based upon a distinct national organisation . . .

—Engels to GC

One thing especially was proved by the Commune . . . that "the working class cannot simply lay hold of the ready-made State machinery, and wield it for its own purpose."

—Marx and Engels

[W]hile the Commune was the grave of early specifically French socialism, it was, for France, also and at the same time the cradle of a new international communism.

—Engels

Almost five years after the founding of the IWMA Engels agreed with long-time Marx party stalwart Friedrich Lessner, who also served on the General Council, that indeed "the cause goes better than ever before; years ago at a time when the stupid democratic mob [i.e., the reformists from the 1848 events] complained about reaction and the people's indifference to them, we, Moor and I, were right in foreseeing in the period of this reaction the enormous industrial development of the last 18 years and declared this would result in a sharpening of the contradictions between labour and capital, and more acute class struggle."[1] Engels was certainly justified in his assessment of the times. In that year, 1869, the IWMA was at its zenith in terms of the number of organizational affiliates and individual members. As the recognized international body that assisted and coordinated labor's struggle against capital it was well represented in virtually every western European country—including the

French colonies of Algeria and Guadaloupe—and the United States. That the London *Times*, as well as the other bourgeois press, gave tendentious but extensive coverage to the Brussels congress of the International the year before indicates how far the organization had come from its fledgling existence five years earlier in 1864. With Engels's move to London in 1870 the Marx-Engels team played an even greater role in the International's direction. On no issue was this more apparent than the insurrection in Paris in 1871 that gave rise to the Commune.

THE BREADTH OF THE MARX PARTY ACTIVITIES

With the publication in 1867 of the first volume of *Capital*, Marx, while preparing at the same time the manuscripts for the subsequent two volumes, thought that he would soon have a revision for a second edition. Although he continued his research, political reality, however, namely the challenges and opportunities for the IWMA as it attracted new forces, sidetracked his plans. Some years later Engels wrote that to "describe Marx's activity in the International is to write the history of the Association itself."[2] Since our focus cannot be a history of the organization, the goal here is to provide an overview of Marx's leadership by discussing only some of the key issues—support to striking workers, women and the International, the Irish question—in which he played a major role after the Brussels congress and before the Franco-Prussian War.

The Marx-Engels team also launched a most unique campaign, mainly through correspondence, to publicize *Capital*, which was related in part to its intense involvement in the German movement, both of which were relevant to their work in the International. The tremendous demands on Marx's time were further aggravated by long bouts of illness of one kind or another throughout this period. Engels's move to London in 1870 came none too soon, since the IWMA was about to be sorely tested.

Strike Solidarity

The main reason for the IWMA's growth by the time of its next congress in Basle, Switzerland, in 1869 was the strike wave that had rocked the European continent the two proceeding years; the latter was in turn spurred on by the recession of 1866–1867 that affected most of Europe. Of these fights, the ones in which the IWMA through the GC played a crucial role were the Paris bronze workers' lockout in 1867, the Geneva building trades strike in 1868, and the bloody Charleroi, Belgium, coal miners' confrontation also in 1868. All three struggles were victorious to varying degrees due in part to the kind of national and international solidarity that the GC, working with IWMA affiliates in various countries, was able to generate on their behalf. The IWMA was thus seen by increasing layers of workers, not only in Europe but elsewhere, as an effective fighting force to which it was advantageous to be affiliated and was continuously called upon to provide strike assistance.

As the effective head of the GC Marx was intimately involved in coordinating strike support work. Marx was usually called upon to write position statements and issue appeals on behalf of the IWMA for various work actions. Even in the midst of the Paris Commune in 1871, when tremendous demands were placed on him and the GC to render assistance, Marx found time to support strikes taking place elsewhere, such as the Antwerp cigar workers' strike. He was particularly effective in getting the German workers' movement, owing to his close ties with it through Liebknecht and other party people, involved in international solidarity efforts as needed. A unique contribution the Marx party made, again via the GC and IWMA affiliates, was the codification and dissemination of the lessons of these struggles for workers. In what was probably a first in the history of the workers' movement, a pamphlet on the struggle of the Geneva building trade workers was written and published by long-time Marx party activist Johann Philippe Becker. By putting together an inexpensive brochure—the proceeds from its sales were used for strike support work—Becker could be assured that the story of the strike would get into the hands of workers.

Becker's brochure was publicized in what became in 1868 the first history of the IWMA, Wilhelm Eichoff's *The International Working Men's Association: Its Establishment, Organisation, Political and Social Activity, and Growth.* Eichoff, a Marx party sympathizer and IWMA activist in Berlin, wrote this short work (originally in German) with the assistance of Marx and largely under his direction; Marx, who apparently wrote part of it, also did the final editing.[3] Details on the three above-mentioned strikes, along with all of the official documents of the International until then, made the sixty-page pamphlet an effective recruitment tool for the organization.[4] Only by documenting for workers the experiences of their movement would it be possible to generalize the lessons of the class struggle; to do, in other words, what Marx and Engels had concluded more than two decades earlier was both essential for scientific communism and the necessary step in the proletariat's quest for political power. It is appropriate to note here that about six months before his death in 1895 Engels, who had just completed the third volume of *Capital,* placed high on his list of next writings a history of the International and Marx's involvement in it.[5]

The IWMA's reputation as an effective source of solidarity for workers' struggles, owing largely to Marx's leadership, brought requests from as far away as New Zealand, India, and Argentina for establishing affiliation. Not surprisingly, the activities of the IWMA earned for it the animosity of governments in Europe, who self-servingly viewed the insurgent labor movements in their countries as under the direction of "decrees sent from London"; the result was the first international campaign in red baiting and persecution of trade union activists.[6]

Women and the Worker's Movement

From the very beginning, when he suggested to Engels that his working-class Irish nationalist companion, Lizzie Burns, become a member of the IWMA—"LADIES ARE ADMITTED," as he informed his comrade—Marx was the most conscious of all the GC members in putting the issue of women on the agenda. To do so meant having to oppose the Proudhonist current in the International, especially its French section, who were "resolutely hostile to women working" and the "participation of women in industry."[7]

At the first annual meeting of the association, the London Conference in September 1865, which had the responsibility of drawing up the agenda for the IWMA's first congress in Geneva a year later, it was Marx who proposed that one of the questions for discussion be that of "Female and Child Labour."[8] Along with the proposal to the Geneva meeting on "Trade Unions," referred to earlier, Marx submitted various proposals, two of which, as it turned out, referred explicitly to girls and women. One, on the "Limitation of the Working Day," called for an eight-hour work day and the serious restrictions on "nightwork." This proposal, it said, "refers only to adult persons, male or female, the latter, however, to be rigorously excluded from all *nightwork whatever*, and all sort of work harmful to the delicacy of the sex, or exposing their bodies to poisonous and otherwise deleterious agencies."

The other proposal, "Juvenile and Children's Labour (Both Sexes)," began with an unmistakably clear materialist premise: "We consider the tendency of modern industry to make children and juvenile persons of both sexes co-operate in the great work of social production, as a progressive, sound and legitimate tendency, although under capital it was distorted into an abomination."[9] It then went on to outline a series of concrete proposals to counter the "abomination" through public education for all young people between nine and seventeen years of age. However, unlike the previous proposal this one made no distinction between the sexes. While it is not the place to discuss here the merits of these proposals, suffice it to say that in the context of 1866 these were indeed progressive ideas for the advancement of women.

In June 1867 the GC voted to bring in the only woman to ever serve on it, the well-known secular activist, Harriet Law (1831–1897). Although Marx was absent for the decision—he was busy with the final preparations for *Capital*'s publication in September of that year—it is noteworthy that Lessner, his most loyal party member on the GC, seconded the motion. Whether coincidental or not, Marx, in preparing for the approval of the GC, which now included Law, the agenda for the upcoming congress in Lausanne, proposed two resolutions for debate. The first was "On the practical means by which to enable the [IWMA] to fulfil its function of a common centre of action for the working classes, female and male, in the struggle tending to their complete emancipation from the domination of capital."[10] This appears to be the first instance of Marx explicitly signalling in an IWMA document that the organization, in spite of its name, was not exclusively male. From then on, almost every subsequent address or declaration issued in the name of the organization or an affiliate that Marx either wrote or edited no longer addressed only "working men" but as well "working women."

For the upcoming congress in Brussels, Marx unsuccessfully sought to have Law be elected by the GC as one of its three delegates; she was defeated by one vote.[11] Nevertheless, he was proud of the fact that the International had "appointed a lady, Madame Law, as a member of the [GC]," as he boasted in a letter to Ludwig Kugelmann, a party man and friend in Germany. While the comment was made somewhat jocularly, to be shared with his wife Gertrud who was also close to the Marx family, Marx was nonetheless serious about the issue of women in the workers' movement:

Joking aside, very great progress was demonstrated at the last congress of the American *'LABOR UNION'*. . . by the fact that it treated women workers with full parity; by contrast, the English, and to an even greater extent the gallant French, are displaying a marked narrowness of spirit in this respect. Everyone who knows anything of history also knows that great social revolutions are impossible without the feminine ferment. Social progress may be measured precisely by the social position of the fair sex (plain ones included).[12]

What this comment reveals is not only Marx the advocate of women's "full parity" in the workers' movement but as well a sober and honest assessment of reality at that time; only in the United States, where the IWMA affiliate, the National Labor Union, formed in 1866, advocated equal pay for equal work for women and men, was real progress being made.

On the eve of and after the Basle congress in 1869—which Marx, again, did not attend—he also took the lead in putting women workers on the GC's agenda. Thus his proposal, seconded by party supporter Hermann Jung and agreed upon by the GC, that the "female president Philomène Rozan" of the Lyons silk workers union be given "special credentials" to attend the upcoming congress.[13] At his first GC meeting after the congress Marx, in an optimistic report about developments in the German movement, drew his colleagues' attention to the fact that the bookbinders union in Leipzig had just agreed for the first time to admit women members.[14] Finally, about a year and a half before the IWMA's effective end and in the aftermath of the Paris Commune, where women communards had played a vanguard role, which was duly noted by Marx in his *Civil War in France*, a proposal was put by him to the GC, and later adopted by the London Conference in September 1871: "The Conference recommends the formation of female branches among the working class. It is, however, understood that this resolution does not at all interfere with the existence or formation of branches composed of both sexes."[15] The basis for this proposal was, as Marx noted, the increasing number of women in industrial jobs in some countries. His main concern was that these women workers become union members, and if single-sex unions facilitated that process then so be it. Such a tactic, however, was not meant to rule out what the bookbinders were doing in Leipzig.

With the IWMA closing down shop the Marx party no longer had an organization to concretize its views on women as workers. Yet the perspective that Marx put forward within it during its eight-year existence was far more advanced than anything that had been done on this matter until then and for a long time afterwards.[16] For this reason, as suggested above, it is of utmost importance to put Marx's advocacy of women's rights, or more correctly, working women's rights—from his class perspective the distinction was crucial—in context. Marx was not the first voice in the nineteenth century to recognize the above-quoted relation between social revolution and the advancement of women. Others, such as the utopian socialist Fourier and his feminist co-thinker Flora Tristan (1803–1844), had said as much decades earlier. Moreover, there were contemporary petit-bourgeois forces and opponents like J. S. Mill who were also active in advancing women's rights, particularly the acquisition of the vote. But only Marx led the fight for a working-class perspective on the advancement of women.[17] While Tristan may have been the first to see the need to make the connections between the workers' and women's movements Marx, was unique in his revolutionary approach to the question.[18] With hindsight it is clear that his was a most prescient view whose implementation, had it occurred, would not only have put the proletarian movement on firmer footing but the growing women's movement as well.

The Irish Question

Certainly no programmatic issue between the Brussels congress and the outbreak of the Franco-Prussian War engaged the Marx party more than that of Irish self-determination. The Irish struggle first attracted the GC's attention in 1867 when a group of Irish nationalists, belonging to the conspiratorial Fenian society, were arrested after carrying out an armed attack to free their incarcerated comrades. A broad-based movement emerged to protest the scheduled execution of those who had been charged with the murder of a policeman in the attack. Within the GC and the milieus in which it functioned, Marx, as he told Engels, "sought by every means at my disposal to incite the English workers to demonstrate in favour of FENIANISM."[19] Most GC members, at a special meeting that was attended by the press, voiced strong support for the right of the Irish nationalists to employ armed struggle and vehemently condemned the judgment against them. Marx wrote the GC's appeal to the British Home Secretary to halt the executions but to no avail.

For the most part, however, Marx was not active in the initial round of GC discussions, mainly because he had not worked out in his own mind the broader political perspective on the Irish question.[20] Furthermore, as he explained to Engels, the "delicacy of the situation" required him to be "diplomatic" since he, like Engels, disagreed with the tactics employed by the Fenians. Following a bombing shortly afterward that left scores of innocent working-class Londoners dead and wounded, Marx, in an insight about ultraleft terror that was as accurate then as a century later, characterized the action as "a great folly. The London masses, who have shown much sympathy for Ireland, will be enraged by it and driven into the arms of the government party. One cannot expect the London proletarians to let themselves be blown up for the benefit of FENIAN EMISSARIES. Secret, melodramatic conspiracies of this kind are, in general, more or less doomed to failure."[21] As had been true before and during the 1848 events the Marx-Engels team continued to have no truck with conspiratorial adventures.

In the immediate aftermath of the executions Marx began to revise his position on the Irish question, which was reflected in a presentation he made to a meeting organized by the German Workers' Educational Association on December 16, 1867, which was attended by about a hundred persons, including a number of GC members. First, the Fenian movement, in spite of its tactical limitations, was, unlike previous Irish resistance, "rooted . . . in the mass of the people, the LOWER ORDERS."[22] Second, on the basis of extensive research on the history of English subjugation of Ireland, especially developments in the two preceding decades, Marx concluded—as he outlined to Engels—that from the perspective of the English proletariat and its own revolutionary interests the Irish needed "Self-government and independence from England." They needed as well an "Agrarian revolution" and "*Protective tariffs against England*" in order to successfully industrialize.[23] Hitherto, Marx and Engels had held that the English proletarian revolution was the precondition for Ireland's independence. Their new view was that Irish self-determination was requisite for England's proletarian revolution. Marx's revised view not only laid the basis for, as Henry Collins and Chimen Abramsky perceptively note,[24] the revolutionary socialist answer to the later phenomenon known as underdevelopment but constituted as well the party's first concrete programmatic statement on the relation between the anticolonial struggle and the proletarian revolution—a position that had been anticipated by some of his earlier journalistic writings on China and India.

Toward the end of 1869 the GC was forced to deal with the Irish question again as a mass protest movement emerged that called for amnesty for the remaining Fenian prisoners. The largest of the demonstrations in England, at Hyde Park in London on October 24, found the entire Marx family, owing to the entreaties of the youngest daughter Eleanor, in attendance. At the following GC meeting Marx is reported to have said that the "main feature of the demonstration . . . was that at least a part of the English working class had lost their prejudice against the Irish."[25] Inspired and with a clearer political position, Marx, this time, took the lead in the discussion within the GC. For him there were actually two issues at stake: "(1) The attitude of the British government on the Irish question; (2) The attitude of the English working class towards the Irish."[26] Cognizant of the tendency of the British trade union contingent on the GC of "cringing to" or "flirting with"—as Marx and Engels respectively characterized it—the recently installed liberal Prime Minister Gladstone, Marx, as part of his overall goal of independent working-class political action, consciously sought to drive a wedge between the former and the latter. Hence, in the debate that ranged over three consecutive meetings Marx took every opportunity to expose and denounce the hypocrisy of Gladstone's liberalism on Ireland and proposed a resolution to that effect.

The last paragraph of the unanimously approved resolution required that it be distributed to all IWMA sections in order to be publicized as widely as possible. Toward this end Marx assisted his daughter Jenny in writing her first political tract, a series of eight articles for a French republican newspaper that dealt mainly with the Gladstone government's mistreatment of the Fenian prisoners. For Marx, the denunciation of the British government's policies was intended to be an expression of the IWMA's solidarity with the Irish movement, which would hopefully gain a hearing for it amongst the Irish proletariat. Within a month of the publication of the GC's resolution this policy bore fruit as inquiries were made from Ireland that led to the establishment of the first Irish section of the IWMA.

The second issue at stake, "the attitude of the English working class towards the Irish," was for Marx the more important of the two. In giving Engels a preview of what he would say in the GC debate, Marx made clear that he indeed had revised his views on the Irish question:

[I]t is in *the direct and absolute interests of the* ENGLISH WORKING CLASS TO GET RID OF THEIR PRESENT CONNEXION WITH IRELAND. . . . . For a long time I believed it would be possible to overthrow the Irish regime by ENGLISH WORKING CLASS ASCENDANCY. I always took this view in the *New-York Tribune.* Deeper study has now convinced me of the opposite. The English WORKING CLASS will *never accomplish anything* BEFORE IT HAS GOT RID OF IRELAND. The lever must be applied in Ireland. This is why the Irish QUESTION is so important for the social movement in general.[27]

Marx's revision of his strategy for Ireland was most significant since it makes clear that the revolutionary "lever" for him, contrary to the usual Marxological claim, did not reside exclusively in the advanced industrialized capitalist world. In other words, not only could the revolutionary initiative begin in the colonial or underdeveloped world but under certain conditions it had to. The implications for the largest underdeveloped country in Europe—from where Marx and Engels expected the "lava to flow"—namely, Russia, are, of course, all too obvious.

Although the GC never got around to formally taking up this part of his proposal—owing mainly to Marx's illness in early 1870—he did address it in an internal GC memo to IWMA sections. The growing Bakuninist operation within the International—to be discussed later—objected to the GC's concern with the Irish question. Marx's reply, on behalf of the GC, is one of the most important statements in the Marx party arsenal. It followed on the heels of his argument that while the "revolutionary *initiative*" might come from France, "England ['the *metropolis of capital*'] alone can serve as the *lever* for a serious *economic* Revolution."

> If England is the BULWARK of English landlordism and European capitalism, the only point where official England can be struck a great blow *is Ireland.*
> [T]he English bourgeoisie has not only exploited Irish poverty to keep down the working class in England by *force immigration* of poor Irishmen, but it has also divided the proletariat into two hostile camps. The revolutionary fire of the Celtic worker does not go well with the solid but slow nature of the Anglo-Saxon worker. On the contrary, in all *the big industrial centres in England* there is profound antagonism between the Irish proletarian and the English proletarian. The average English worker hates the Irish worker as a competitor who lowers wages and the STANDARD OF LIFE. He feels national and religious antipathies for him. He regards him somewhat like the *POOR WHITES* of the Southern States of North America regarded black slaves. This antagonism among the proletarians of England is artificially nourished and kept up by the bourgeoisie. It knows that this scission is the true secret of maintaining its power.
> [I]t is a *precondition to the emancipation of the English working class* to transform the present *forced union* (i.e., the enslavement of Ireland) into *equal and free confederation* if possible, into *complete separation* if need be.[28]

Aside from other issues raised in this statement—the last point, for example, would become the core idea in Lenin's position on the right of nations to self-determination—Marx was never as concrete as he was here on the national-race-class issue, which he is often accused gratuitously of ignoring by latter-day critics. What's revealed here—and not for the first time—is a clear recognition of racial and national divisions within the working class. And, as was true in earlier instances, the recognition of this reality was the precondition for the more important task, the waging of a fight to confront the divisions. Working-class unity across national and racial lines could only come about on the basis of equality among nationalities and races. Marx and Engels, in other words, recognized that such divisions were, as might be said today, socially constructed and, therefore, could be deconstructed or challenged. To do so required a conscious political effort, which in this case meant an unambiguous denunciation of England's subjugation of Ireland. Only by taking such a stance would it be possible to bring the English and Irish proletariat into common political work—laying the basis, hopefully, for unity—as happened when Irish sections of the IWMA were subsequently established in Ireland, England, and the United States.

Marx and Engels were also well aware that common political collaboration was a process that could not be declared. Thus, when the British trade union leader and GC member, John Hales, sought to subordinate the Irish branches of the IWMA to the umbrella British section in 1872, on the ground that the branches undermined the "fundamental principle of the Association [which] was to destroy all semblance of the nationalist doctrine," Engels, who was now on the GC, voiced vehement opposition. His reply reflected the essence of the Marx-Engels team's position on the national question vis-à-vis proletarian internationalism.

> The Irish formed a distinct nationality of their own, and the fact that [they] used the English language could not deprive them of their rights [to have their own branches]. . . . There was the fact of seven centuries of English conquest and oppression of Ireland, and so long as that oppression existed, it would be an insult to Irish working men to ask them to submit to a British Federal Council. . . . [Hales's motion] was asking the conquered people to forget their nationality and submit to their conquerors. It was not Internationalism, but simply prating submission. . . . [T]rue Internationalism must necessarily be based upon a distinct national organisation, and they [the Irish branches] were under the necessity to state in the preamble of their rules that their first and most pressing duty as Irishmen was to establish their own national independence.[29]

It is simply disingenuous, then, to suggest, as has been done ad nauseam, that Marx and Engels were principled opponents of nationalism.[30] Precisely because nationalism was a social construct it always had to be contextualized, as in the Irish case. Also, for the Marx party real proletarian internationalism, once again, could only proceed on the basis of the equality of nations; this was especially true for oppressed nations. Engels's stance, which resulted in a resounding defeat for Hales's proposal—the vote was twenty-two to one—was, in fact, a concrete application of Marx's above-quoted point about Ireland's confederation with England to the International itself.

That Marx's revised position was important for the party is testified to by the fact that he previewed it not only for Engels but as well for Kugelmann, another party member.[31] When he sent the internal GC memo to party members in the

United States he asked them "to pay particular attention" to "the main points" quoted above, referring specifically to the parallel he drew about "poor whites" in the United States and English workers.[32] While neither Marx nor Engels ever returned to the Irish question in the detailed way they did between 1867 and 1872, due mainly to the downturn in the Irish struggle in the subsequent decades, the positions they adopted have as much currency today as then.[33]

The Marx-Engels Team in Action

From the time when Engels urged Marx to write a "fat book," they both understood that it was not enough to just get their ideas into print. It was also necessary to make sure that their writings got into the hands of the readers they deemed most important—workers. This in fact had been one of the lessons of the publication of *A Contribution to a Critique of Political Economy* in 1859, whose impact was initially limited since it was greeted by what Marx and Engels called a "conspiracy of silence" by the bourgeois world. To avoid that happening again they took steps even before *Capital's* appearance in September 1867 to ensure that it would get the hearing they desired. The success of this kind of campaign, which was probably unique in their time (and from which many a hard-pressed untenured faculty member in the modern academy might learn a thing or two), would depend, as Marx explained to Kugelmann in Hanover, "on how skillful and active my party friends in Germany are." While "considered criticism . . . from friend or foe" would be valuable in the long run, "its immediate success" would be determined, "to put it bluntly, by making a noise and beating the drum, which compels even adversaries to speak. To begin with, it is less important *what* is said than that *something* should be said. *Above all, no time must be lost!*"[34] Marx, no doubt, was reacting to the fact that his publisher, Otto Meissner, had been slow in getting the book out. He thought a fine opportunity had been missed by its not being available for the just-completed Lausanne congress, where Meissner "could have disposed of many COPIES. . . . And the book would have been discussed there as a real event."[35]

The attention that *Capital* garnered at the IWMA congress a year later in Brussels was due in large part to the campaign that Marx and Engels initiated in the fall of 1867 in collaboration with "party friends" in Germany. As part of their prepublication publicity efforts they were able to get excerpts of the book, mainly the preface, into a few newspapers in Britain, France, Belgium, and Germany. Engels proposed, in view of the absence of notices in the German press about its forthcoming appearance, that he pose as an anonymous academic reviewer and "attack the thing from the bourgeois point of view, to get things under way." Marx agreed, saying that would be "*the best tactic.*" Engels wrote to Kugelmann to get his assistance along the lines of Marx's above-quoted letter, saying further that his reviews should be published in "as many papers as possible, political and other, wherever it can be done. Long and short notices, provided they come thick and fast." [36] About a month later Engels made an even stronger appeal to Kugelmann and declared that he was ready to assist him in any way possible: "[I]n the service of the party I am always on call."[37] Other party members such as Liebknecht and Becker were also recruited in the effort.

As Marx and Engels soon discovered, it was not easy to conduct their campaign from afar. "If we were in Germany," Engels wrote Marx, "we should already have created a stir in all the papers, and have managed to get the book *denounced*, which is always the best thing."[38] In all, Engels was able to get his reviews—one written along lines that Marx outlined—published in seven German newspapers. Kugelmann was also able to get a few short notices printed. The campaign began to pay off as bourgeois scholars took notice. The major breakthrough in Germany came at the end of 1867 with the somewhat favorable review of the Berlin University economist Eugen Dühring—the future target of Engels's famous polemic—which broke the "silence" within the academic community. Another academic in Berlin was so moved by the book, declaring it "'the most significant phenomenon of this century,'" that he "offered Marx a professorship in political economy."[39] Reviews written by others began to appear in both Germany and England. Three months after its publication Marx could report that his "publisher is satisfied with sales in Germany."[40]

Of course, Marx and Engels's main concern in breaking the silence was to get *Capital* into the hands of workers.[41] They recognized that attention from the "tribe of great men" was the means for so doing. Regarding his effort to get an unsigned article published in one prominent reformist paper, Marx told Engels that if it was accepted "then not merely will the attention of the Berlin workers have been drawn to the book through the quotation of passages which are of direct interest to them, but an extremely useful polemic will have been initiated. . . ."[42] In an effort to get the book circulated in the United States, Engels wrote to a party member there:

> I hope you will be able to bring Marx's book to the attention of the German-American press and of the workers. With the 8–hour [day]-agitation that is in progress in America now, this book with its chapter on the *working day* will come at just the right time for you over there, and, in other respects too, it is likely to clarify people's minds on a variety of issues. The future of the party in America will be beholden to you for any step you can take in that direction.[43]

Still, by the end of the year, three months after *Capital's* appearance, the party's efforts had yet to bear fruit, which was reflected in Jenny Marx's comment to Kugelmann about her husband's magnum opus.

> [Y]ou can believe me when I tell you there can be few books that have been written in more difficult circumstances. . . . If the workers had an inkling of the sacrifices that were necessary for this work, which was written only for them and for their sakes to be completed they would perhaps show a little more interest.[44]

By the time of the Brussels congress nine months later Jenny's hopes would begin to be fulfilled. Also, as a harbinger of the future, Marx was notified, a year after *Capital's* publication, that an effort was under way in Moscow to have it translated into Russian, which became, with the completion of the project in 1872, its first translation into another language.

The Marx-Engels team, in addition to their campaign to get *Capital* into the hands of workers, carried out other collaborative work in this period, particularly in regard to the International. From his first visit to Engels after the IWMA's founding, in early January 1865, Marx maintained regular contact with his comrade about how to proceed. By 1866 he was regularly submitting proposals to Engels for his thoughts and approval before putting them before the GC. For example, when he had qualms about whether the Geneva congress that year should be held, it was Engels who counselled that the political costs would be higher if it were postponed.[45]

An especially important programmatic contribution that Engels made were his series of letters that were published in the IWMA's journal in 1866 as "What have the Working Classes to do with Poland?"[46] Written at Marx's behest, their purpose, largely successful, was to strengthen the fight against the Proudhonist objection to the International's support for Polish self-determination. Contrary to the Proudhonist view that political action in general and support to national liberation movements in particular should not concern the International, Engels argued that the proletariat did indeed have an interest in what happened in Poland. The 1848 upheavals had demonstrated that as long as Poland remained dismembered, a reality in which Russia played the pivotal role, then the German working classes could not liberate themselves.

The distinction that Engels sought to make between, on the one hand, "the right of the great European *nations* to separate and independent existence" such as Poland and, on the other, small nations whose "vitality" or viability as independent nation states he doubted was clearly a provisional conclusion, as revealed by the shift that he and Marx made a couple of years later in support of independence for Ireland—presumably, a "small nation." More than anything the distinction was politically motivated—to repudiate Louis Bonaparte's policy, for his own imperial designs, of encouraging the national aspirations of peoples who hitherto, apparently, had not aspired to their own separate nation states. In hindsight, it is apparent that Engels had yet to get a handle on a process that was still in motion—nineteenth-century nation-state formation. Still, his argument in defense of Poland's right to self-determination facilitated the policy shift that he and Marx made in relation to Ireland as well as paving the way to the revolutionary conclusions that Lenin would later reach on the national question.

Toward the end of 1868 Engels informed Marx of his decision to sell his equity in the family-owned business to the other owners in order that he be able to move to London. This would allow him, as he informed Lessner, to put an end to having to "devote all my time to bourgeois activities" so that he could work "*directly* for our cause."[47] He asked Marx to calculate how much he and his family would need annually in order to get a sum that would allow both of them to live for "a number of years without money troubles." After protracted negotiations with his partners, Engels wrote to Marx on July 1, 1869, "Hurrah! Today *doux commerce* is at an end, and I am a free man." By the end of the following September Engels was now living in London, a ten-minute walk from the Marx household. At the first meeting of the GC in October, Engels, upon Marx's motion, was unanimously voted onto the body. For the first time in two decades and until Marx's death in 1883 the Marx-Engels partnership operated from the same location and, thus, in even closer collaboration.[48]

After almost two decades in power Louis Bonaparte's rule was beginning to fray. Demagogue to the end, he tried to prop up his regime by playing his nationalist card once again, this time vis-à-vis another Bonapartist, Otto von Bismarck. The latter, whose rule, unlike the former's, was in the ascent, and with his own nationalist agenda, was only too willing to accommodate this last gasp of a dying dictator by inducing him into a trap that offered no escape—the Franco-Prussian War. One of the key themes in the *Inaugural Address* of the IWMA in 1864 had been the need for a proletarian foreign policy. The war, which effectively lasted from July to September 1870, presented the International with its first real opportunity—aside from making it impossible to hold its annual congress that year—to realize that goal. On the other hand, the Paris Commune in the following year, certainly the most memorable outcome of the war, presented the International with challenges it did not anticipate.

War and Proletarian Internationalism

A few months prior to its declaration of war against Prussia, Bonaparte's government carried out massive arrests of members of the International throughout France. In spite of the crackdown IWMA members in France as well as Germany issued statements and organized demonstrations in opposition to the war drives of their two governments on the eve of and after hostilities began. Such antiwar activities, in the name of proletarian internationalism, had been one of the acquisitions of the IWMA since its inception. Marx's *Inaugural Address*, until then the organization's most widely distributed document, contributed much to this effort. Still, Marx was under no illusion that the workers' movement, certainly at that stage, could stop a war between France and Germany.

Once the war began in July, the GC asked Marx to write a statement on its behalf known later as the *First Address of the General Council of the International Working Men's Association on the Franco-Prussian War*. Along with a *Second Address* that was issued in September they constitute Marx's most important foreign policy statements for the International. The first address called attention to the IWMA's record in opposition to war, the antiwar stances and activities of its affiliates in France and Germany and the exchange of fraternal messages between French and German workers. The latter was "unparalleled in history of the past." The statement, also, predicted with "devastating accuracy," as Collins and Abramsky note, that "[w]hatever may be the incidents of Louis Bonaparte's war with Prussia, the death knell of the Second Empire has already sounded at Paris." Another most prescient observation made the connection between the absence of democracy and the ability of dictators like Bonaparte to wage aggressive wars.

What truly distinguished the IWMA from other antiwar forces was the international campaign that Marx led to publicize its stance and to win others to it.[49] In addition to having two thousand copies printed and distributed in English and another thirty thousand in French and German, the GC was successful in having it reprinted in part or full in newspapers in London and the British provinces, Geneva,

Zurich, Vienna, Augsburg, and New York. A conscious effort was made to get it into the hands of not only opinion makers such as Thomas Huxley and John Stuart Mill—the latter was reported to be "highly pleased with the address"—but as well to organizations and trade unions that the IWMA may or may not have had ties with. The *Address* even found its way, favorably, into a speech by an American statesman, the very influential reconstruction senator Charles Sumner.[50]

The war also witnessed, perhaps a first in the history of warfare, coordinated antiwar actions on the part of the working populations of the belligerent countries. Again, the International, largely under Marx's direction, was responsible for this. The anti-interventionist movement in Britain during the U. S. Civil War, which helped to bring the IWMA into existence, had served, certainly, as an important precedent for such activities.[51]

The *Second Address* made the case against Bismarck's annexation of Alsace-Lorraine following Bonaparte's defeat in September 1870. Amongst his arguments was one of his most prophetic judgments. The "dismemberment of France" would provoke Russian intervention leading to "a *war of races*," that is, a German-Russian war. This in turn, as he explained in a letter to a close party member, would "act as the midwife of the inevitable social revolution in Russia."[52] If the arithmetic was faulty, the algebra was not. It would take another five decades for his forecast to be fulfilled.

Whereas the *First Address* had hoped that the German working class would limit Berlin to only a "defensive" war, the *Second* was more sober about its prospects for staying Bismarck's hand. "If the French workmen amidst peace failed to stop the aggressor, are the German workmen more likely to stop the victor amidst the clangour of arms?" This reality had to be absorbed by the French affiliates of the IWMA in France as well as something even more important. While it was true that the bourgeois republic that was proclaimed in Paris on September 4 left much to be desired given its "dread of the working class . . . [a]ny attempt at upsetting the new Government in the present crisis, when the enemy is almost knocking at the doors of Paris, would be desperate folly. The French workmen must perform their duties as citizens. . . . Let them calmly and resolutely improve the opportunities of Republican liberty, for the work of their own class organisation."[53]

Marx's counsel of revolutionary restraint to the French workers after Bonaparte's surrender was central in his approach to the fast-breaking events in France. For the first time since the 1848 upheavals, revolution was a real possibility in Europe. While France's defeat would, as Marx and Engels had foreseen, create the conditions for a new revolutionary upheaval, the crucial element in its consummation, however, was missing—leadership. In an attempt to overcome this void, Auguste Serraillier, a GC member, went, in consultation with Marx, to Paris at the beginning of September "to arrange matters with the *International* there," that is, to discourage any attempts at premature revolution-making.[54] Engels noted approvingly that Eugène Dupont, another French GC member, understood what needed to be done: "make use of the freedoms inevitably granted by the republic to organize the party in France; act when occasion presents itself, once organisation has been completed; the International to be held on a leash in France until after peace has been concluded."[55] Patience on the part of the French workers, in order to consolidate bourgeois democracy, was what was now needed.[56]

Coupled with his efforts to convince the French affiliates of the IWMA to exercise revolutionary restraint, Marx worked feverishly to put pressure on the Gladstone government to recognize the new French republic and not give in to pressures from the British oligarchy to intervene in the conflict on behalf of Bismarck and his king, William I, a relative of Queen Victoria. As for the first of these two goals, "I have set everything in motion here for the workers to force their government to recognise the French Republic."[57] He was referring to the mass meetings that the GC helped organize throughout England to this end in mid-September. And for the second, "I do everything in my power, through the means of the *International*, to stimulate . . . [the] 'neutrality' spirit and to baffle the *'paid'* (paid by the 'respectables') leaders of the English working class who strain every nerve to mislead them."[58] Although the International was never successful in getting the Gladstone government to recognize the republic, it's nonintervention campaign played no small part in Britain's official neutrality toward the Franco-Prussian events.

The Paris Commune

The Marx-Engels team's counsel of revolutionary restraint notwithstanding, on March 18, 1871, the working masses of Paris took the initiative. More specifically, the National Guard in Paris, a civic militia composed mainly of workers, revolted against the conservative bourgeois republican government at Versailles—headed by the well-known and long-time antirevolutionary, Adolphe Thiers—after it tried to disarm the Guard. Ten days later, following elections that the Central Committee of the National Guard had called for, a new government, or Commune was proclaimed for Paris.

In spite of their warnings against premature revolution making, Marx and Engels quickly threw themselves into the defense of the Commune. One of the immediate tasks was to counter the slanders in the bourgeois press such as the *Times* that the war and uprising had provoked a split between the German and French sections of the International. To this end, Marx, on behalf of the GC, wrote numerous letters to the editors of newspapers in Germany, France, and England, of which a number were actually published. Having beaten back one attack, Marx was then forced to respond to press insinuations that he and the GC had engineered the insurrection. Marx sent off another round of letters, which the *Times* and at least one other London paper published, ridiculing the allegations. As well as a counter campaign, the GC, with Marx's encouragement, took initiatives to win support for the Commune in England. Marx himself began an extensive effort to solicit aid for the insurgents from IWMA sections. To Léo Frankel and Louis Varlin, two of the Commune's leaders and IWMA members, he wrote in the sixth week of its existence: "I have written hundreds of letters on behalf of your cause to all the corners of the earth where we have branches."[59]

Marx's defense of the Parisian insurgents in his letters to party members and close party contacts, specifically Liebknecht and Ludwig Kugelmann, is most instructive, especially since it was done in the heat of the revolt and before the Commune's fate was sealed. Three weeks after the revolt, he told Liebknecht, the

"Parisians are succumbing. It is their own fault but a fault which really was due to their too great *honnêteté* [decency]. The Central Committee [of the National Guard] and later the Commune gave that MISCHIEVOUS *avorton* [degenerate] Thiers, time to consolidate hostile forces, in the first place by their folly of not wanting to start a *civil war*. . . . Secondly . . . they lost precious moments (they should immediately have advanced on Versailles . . .) by the election of the Commune, the organisation of which, etc., cost yet more time."[60]

To Kugelmann, who failed to see the revolt's significance and was, thus, skeptical of it, Marx referred him back to his *Eighteenth Brumaire* where "you will find that I say that the next attempt of the French revolution will be no longer, as before, to transfer the bureaucratic military machine from one hand to another, but to *break* it, and that is essential for every real people's revolution on the Continent. And this is what our heroic Party comrades in Paris are attempting. What resilience, what historic initiative, what a capacity for sacrifice in these Parisians!"[61]

Regarding the "Party," it is clear that Marx was using the term here in the "broad historical sense" that was discussed earlier.[62] As for the *Eighteenth Brumaire*, he was referring to the point in the last section of the book that Bonaparte's rule, before and after his 1851 coup, should be seen in the context of the historical revolutionary process vis-à-vis the abolishment of the state. "First it perfected the parliamentary power, in order to be able to overthrow it. Now that it has attained this, it perfects the *executive power*, reduces it to its purest expression, isolates it, sets it up against itself as the sole target, in order to concentrate all its forces of destruction against it. And when it has done this second half of its preliminary work, Europe will leap from its seat and exultantly exclaim: Well burrowed, old mole!" Bonaparte's rule, in other words, was preparing the ground for doing what until then had never been done. "All revolutions perfected this machine instead of breaking it."[63] Two decades later, the Commune, in its attempts to do exactly the latter, gave Marx cause to leap from his seat in exultation.

About a week later Marx tried again to convey the Commune's significance to Kugelmann. To his revolutionary armchair critique of the Commune, Marx countered with one of his most insightful observations about the reality of the revolutionary process, which in turn helps to explain why after months of counsel of revolutionary restraint he could wholeheartedly embrace the insurrection.

> World history would indeed be very easy to make if the struggle were taken up only on condition of infallibly favourable chances. It would, on the other hand, be of a very mystical nature, if "accidents" played no part. These accidents themselves fall naturally into the general course of development and are compensated again by other accidents. But acceleration and delay are very dependent upon such "accidents," which include the "accident" of the character of those who first stand at the head of the movement.

Marx then applied this very general statement to the March 18 insurrection. Specifically, he argued, a set of fortuitous circumstances—mainly, the presence of Prussians troops outside Paris—

presented the Parisians with the alternative of taking up the fight or succumbing without a struggle. In the latter case, the demoralisation of the working class would have been a far greater misfortune than the fall of any number of "leaders." The struggle of the working class against the capitalist class and its state has entered upon a new phase with the struggle in Paris. Whatever the immediate results may be, a new point of departure of world-historic importance has been gained.[64]

Thus, while ideally a revolution should be initiated under the most propitious conditions, in the real world it doesn't necessarily work that way. "Accidents," in this case the presence of the Prussian forces, may force revolutionaries to act before the situation is ideal.[65] And recalling again one of the lessons that Engels drew in his *Revolution and Counter-revolution* about the 1848 events, "A well-contested defeat is a fact of as much revolutionary importance as an easily-won victory. . . . It is a matter of course that, in every struggle, he who takes up the gauntlet risks being beaten; but is that a reason why he should confess himself beaten, and submit to the yoke without drawing the sword?"[66] For Marx, who once answered the query, "Your idea of misery," in the popular parlor game Confessions with, "To submit," the response of the Communards to Thiers's Prussian supported provocation was one that he viscerally understood; it was as well in the best revolutionary traditions.[67]

In England, Marx worked through the GC to organize solidarity amongst workers there. Early on in the Commune's existence he proposed that the GC send a delegation to meetings of the recently formed British republican movement to win support for the Parisians. The GC and its affiliates in other countries also organized solidarity meetings. The International was able to swing into action because, as Marx told Frankel a month after the Commune was instituted, the "true character of this grand Paris revolution has been explained to workers everywhere in letters from various [GC] secretaries to sections on the Continent and in the United States."[68] In Germany, Marx party activists played an especially important role in the defense of the Commune, for which they were persecuted by the Bismarck government.

While it is true, as Engels wrote three years later, that the "International did not lift a finger to produce" the Commune—although it "was beyond doubt the child of the International intellectually"—he and Marx had very close ties to some of the insurgent leaders, through whom they sought to influence its course.[69] Varlin and Frankel, in particular, even prior to the Commune's establishment, worked actively to implement Marx's counsel of revolutionary restraint.[70] Once the new government was in place Marx took the initiative to send Serraillier back to Paris to intervene in the situation and send reports back to the GC on developments. Shortly afterward Serraillier was elected to the Commune. Marx's need for accurate information was also one of the reasons that the young Russian revolutionary, Elisaveta Dmitriyeva Tomanovskaya, whom the Marx family had befriended the previous summer, went to Paris and organized the Women's Union for the Defense of Paris as a branch of the IWMA and eventually emerged as one of the Commune's leading socialists.[71]

Through a travelling intermediary Marx facilitated the GC's contacts with the Communards. Frankel, who headed the Commune's Commission on Labor and

Exchange, which was at the forefront of its most far-reaching social measures, wrote Marx two days after the body's formation that " 'your advice on what social reforms to carry out will be extremely valuable for our Commission.'"[72] Since for security reasons Marx communicated with Frankel and the other Communard leaders "verbally," via the interlocutor, the only written record of Marx's input concerned advice on how the Commune could sell securities on the London stock exchange and intelligence on the secret agreements between the Versailles government and Bismarck to suppress the Parisian insurgents.[73] A letter from Tomanovskaya suggests that Marx advised the Communards to do what he and Engels had long ago concluded, based on the lessons of 1848, would be necessary for a victory in any new upsurge in Paris. In the words of the young Russian revolutionary, "We must at all costs stir up the provinces to come to our aid."[74]

Marx's correspondence also makes clear that he and Engels supplied the Communards with advice on military defense. About ten days after the Commune's proclamation, Lafargue, who was living in Bordeaux and cognizant of the leadership deficiencies in Paris wrote, "'couldn't Engels come here to put his talents at the disposal of the revolution?'"[75] Two weeks before the Commune's demise on May 28, Jenny Marx foresaw the outcome and the reasons for it in a letter to Kugelmann.

> The lack of military leadership, the entirely natural distrust of everything "military" . . . the quarrels, irresolution and contradictory actions which necessarily result—all these evils, inevitable in a movement so audacious and so youthful, would certainly have been overcome by the core of the sound, self-sacrificing and self-confident workers; but now I think all hope is lost. . . . Another June [1848] massacre lies before us . . .[76]

A day later, Marx, in a letter to Frankel and Varlin, offered advice, which went unheeded, to the Communards to overcome the deficiencies that Jenny noted.[77] "If only the Commune had listened to my warnings! I advised its members to fortify the northern side of the heights of Montmartre, the Prussian side, and they still had time to do this: I told them beforehand that they would otherwise be caught in a trap." In an effort to ensure against the kind of reprisals that were inflicted on the insurgents in June 1848, Marx "demanded that they should at once send to London all the documents compromising the members of the National Defence [i.e., Versailles government officials who had been conniving with Bismarck], so that by this means the savagery of the enemies of the Commune could to some extent be held in check. . . ."[78] Whether Marx and Engels's advice would have prevented or perhaps lessened the dimensions of the notorious slaughter that Versailles carried out against the Communards—beyond anything that Paris had seen then or since—will of course never be known.[79]

Precisely because of the Marx household's personal and political involvement in the Commune and all of the anxiety that entailed, especially with the impending bloodbath, the events took their toll on everyone. To the Kugelmanns, one month after the insurrection, Marx's daughter Jenny wrote: "Mohr and he [Engels] go out for long walks together, whenever Mohr's health permits it. . . . The present state of things causes our dear Mohr intense suffering, & no doubt is one of the chief causes of his illness. A great number of our friends are in the Commune." Almost a month later her mother told the Kugelmanns, "You can't have an idea of how much my husband, the girls and all of us have suffered because of the French events."[80] Evidence, indeed, that whatever reservations Marx had about the Parisians prior to their insurrection he put them aside and totally identified with them as a fellow fighter.

The Civil War in France

Marx's most important and enduring contribution to the Communards came in the immediate aftermath of their demise with the publication in mid-June of *The Civil War in France*. As early as March 28, ten days after the insurrection, he proposed that the GC issue a statement about the events in Paris which was agreed to along with the motion that it be written by him. Marx, however, was only able to read to the GC, for its unanimous approval, what was the third of his drafts on May 30, two days after the last barricades fell. The delay, contrary to much Marxological speculation, was due largely to uncertainly about the revolution's course—particularly in the first three weeks—Marx's illnesses, and most importantly, inadequate information. About the latter, Marx told Frankel in his letter of April 26, "One of these days, the [GC] is to issue an Address. . . . It has put off this manifesto up to now, because it was expecting the Paris Section [of the IWMA] from day to day to supply it with precise information. In vain! Not a word!"[81]

The address that Marx wrote for the GC, written in the heat of the Commune's final days, was as much a defense of the Communards as a political analysis. The earlier drafts indicate that the address was also to have been prescriptive, that is, advice on how to defend and advance the revolution. As a GC document, it also, like the three other most important Marx party political statements—the *Manifesto*, the Address of March 1850, and the *Inaugural Address*—as well as other GC statements that Marx composed, had to take into account the political tendencies within the organization in whose name it was issued.

The political heart of the forty-page document is the third section, which analyzes the Commune itself "where the proletariat for the first time held political power."[82] Because this was also a first in their lives, Marx and Engels milked its every detail available to them to add to the arsenal of lessons they had drawn about the 1848 upheavals.

At the heart of Marx's assessment was the point he had already made to Kugelmann about the Commune fulfilling his prediction in the *Eighteenth Brumaire*. After quoting from the manifesto that the National Guard's Central Committee issued to justify its actions on March 18—"The Proletarians of Paris . . . have understood that it is their imperious duty and their absolute right to render themselves masters of their own destinies, by seizing upon the governmental powers"[83]—Marx declared: "But the working class cannot simply lay hold of the ready-made State machinery, and wield it for its own purpose." This was proven by the fact that the largely working-class National Guard replaced the standing army with itself. Ten days later the Commune was proclaimed. "The first decree of the Commune, therefore, was the suppression of the standing army, and the substitution for it of the armed people." The manner in which the Commune functioned and was organized—"self-government of the producers," or, the "tendency of a government of the people and for the people"[84]—set it apart from anything that had existed until then. "Thus, this new Commune . . . breaks the modern State power."

This conclusion was of such importance to Marx and Engels that they reproduced Marx's above-quoted declaration in the Preface to the 1872 German edition of the *Manifesto*. They noted that the revolutionary program in the second part of the 1848 document "has in some details become antiquated. One thing especially was proved by the Commune, *viz.*, that the working class cannot simply lay hold of the ready-made State machinery, and wield it for its own purpose."[85]

Marx then distilled the Commune's essence.

> The multiplicity of interpretations to which the Commune has been subjected, and the multiplicity of interests which construed it in their favour, show that it was a thoroughly expansive political form, while all previous forms of government had been emphatically repressive. Its true secret was this. It was essentially a working-class government, the produce of the struggle of the producing against the appropriating class, the political form at last discovered under which to work out the economical emancipation of Labour.
>
> Except on this last condition, the Communal Constitution would have been an impossibility and a delusion. The political rule of the producer cannot coexist with the perpetuation of his social slavery. The Commune was therefore to serve as a lever for uprooting the economical foundations upon which rests the existence of classes, and therefore of class rule. With labour emancipated, every man becomes a working man, and productive labour ceases to be a class attribute.[86]

The Commune was not only the fulfillment of the demand that arose in the 1848 upheavals to have a republican government that addressed the social interests of the producers, the "Social Republic," but of more fundamental significance a government whose modus operandi—because it was in the hands of the producing class— set into motion the process to end class oppression and, thus, to undermine the state itself and institute "true democracy."

The actual social policies that the Commune undertook in its short existence "could but betoken the tendency of a government of the people by the people." Thus, Marx recognized, as he explained a decade later, that "the majority of the Commune was in no sense socialist nor could it have been."[87] The Commune, rather, was the beginning of a process that its working-class supporters knew could not be fulfilled overnight. "They know that in order to work out their own emancipation, and along with it that higher form to which present society is irresistibly tending by its own economical agencies, they will have to pass through long struggles, through a series of historic processes, transforming circumstances and men."[88] The Communards, hence, were the very embodiment of Marx's third thesis on Feuerbach: "The coincidence of the changing of circumstances and of human activity or self-change can be conceived and rationally understood only as *revolutionary practice*." Also, as progressive as its social measures were, the "great social measure of the Commune was its own existence." What Marx meant, as he elaborated in the first draft, was that aside from the fact that the Commune "clearly, consciously proclaimed the Emancipation of Labour, and the transformation of Society, as their goal . . . the actual 'social' character of their Republic consists only in this, that workmen govern the Paris Commune!"[89] More important, therefore, than its proclamations and measures as a "Social Republic" was the fact that political power in Paris was in the hands of working people. That and only that reality could be the basis for the realization of the more distant socialist goal.

In both the final version and the first draft Marx provided an analysis for the Communards from a communist perspective on how to realize the worker-peasant alliance.[90] The elaboration in the first draft is worth quoting since it anticipated by more than two decades the definitive Marx-Engels programmatic statement on the peasantry, Engels's *The Peasant Question in France and Germany.*

Given the character of the peasantry's mistreatment at the hands of the French state from 1848 onwards, the Commune, Marx argued, objectively represented its interests. Hence, the reason why Versailles did its utmost to prevent the realization of its worst nightmare—a worker-peasant alliance between Paris and the countryside. Yet it had to be recognized that "[t]here exists of course in France as in most continental Countries a deep antagonism between the townish and rural producers, between the industrial Proletariat and the peasantry." The antagonism was based on "economical differences" between the two groups of producers and upon which "rests superconstructed a whole world of different social and political views." However, the changed economic circumstances of the peasantry, increasingly hard pressed to maintain its way of life in the face of the advance of capitalist relations of production, had put the peasantry in an objectively less antagonistic relation with the proletariat.

> What separates the peasant from the proletarian is, therefore, no longer his real interest, but his delusive prejudice. If the Commune, as we have shown, is the only power that can give him immediate great boons [i.e., benefits] even in its present economical conditions, it is the only form of government that can secure to him the transformation of his present economical conditions, rescue him from expropriation by the landlord on the one hand, from grinding, trudging and misery on the pretext of proprietorship on the other, that can convert his nominal proprietorship of the land in the real proprietorship of the fruits of his labor, that can combine for him the profits of modern agronomy, dictated by social wants, and every day now encroaching upon him as a hostile agency, without annihilating his position as a really independent producer. Being immediately benefited by the communal Republic, he would soon confide in it.[91]

Thus, what Marx proposed here to the Communards was a framework in which to formulate concrete measures to win the peasantry to its side. To the extent that the Commune could assure the peasant that he would not be expropriated but rather would be aided by the new government to become "a really independent producer" then could such a worker-peasant alliance be consummated—a prerequisite for the Commune's survival.

While the *Civil War* remained for Marx and Engels their definitive statement on the Commune, occasional comments they made in subsequent years supplemented its analysis. Away from the heat of the Commune's defense they could afford, for example, to be less reticent, or, perhaps better said, more explicit about the shortcomings of its leadership, especially its "lack of centralisation" and failure to employ more "authoritarian means" to defend itself—claims that can only be noted here.[92]

Three years after the Commune's overthrow Engels, in a critique of the "revolutionary" postmortem blustering of Blanquist refugees in London, made a most sober comment about the revolutionary process.

> A lot of follies [or better, "stupidities" in a rendering by Draper] are unavoidably committed in every revolution, as they are indeed at all other times, and when at last people calm down sufficiently to be able to review events critically, they inevitably draw the following conclusion: we have done many things that it would have been better to leave undone, and have failed to do many things that it would have been better to do, and that is why things took a bad turn. But what a lack of critical attitude is needed to declare the Commune impeccable and infallible and to assert that, every time a house was burned down or a hostage was shot, this was a case of retributive justice, right down to the dot on the "I."[93]

An honest assessment of the Commune, in other words, had to take into account its weaknesses as well as its strengths. That Marx and Engels could say more about the former when things were more "calm" did not in the least detract from the defense and analysis offered in *The Civil War*.

A final issue concerns the debate over whether Marx, like Engels, apparently, considered the revolutionary government to be the dictatorship of the proletariat and the related issue of whether it was in fact. In the above-quoted introduction to the 1891 edition of *The Civil War*, Engels in the very last paragraph wrote: "Of late, the German ["Social-Democratic" in the original] philistine has once more been filled with wholesome terror at the words: Dictatorship of the Proletariat. Well and good, gentlemen, do you want to know what this dictatorship looks like? Look at the Paris Commune. That was the Dictatorship of the Proletariat."[94] The context for this interjection was the recent uproar in the German party on the part of its right wing to distance itself from Marx's phrase (a reflection of the growing influence of the opportunist wing of the party, which will be detailed in the next chapter).[95] In an effort to expose this reformist tendency, which paid lip service to the revolutionary legacy of the Commune, Engels may well have overstated the case of the Commune to score points.

Marx, on the other hand, in no known instance ever wrote that the Commune was the dictatorship of the proletariat. However, an account of a speech he gave at a banquet four months after the Commune's demise reports him saying the following:

> [T]he Commune was the conquest of the political power of the working classes. . . . The Commune could not found a new form of class government . . . [since through its social measures] the only base for class rule and oppression would be

removed. But before such a change could be effected a proletarian dictature would become necessary, and the first condition of that was a proletarian army. The working classes would have to conquer the right to emancipate themselves on the battlefield. The task of the International was to organize and combine the forces of labor for the coming struggle.[96]

How much credence should be given to an account by the bourgeois press, which had on more than one occasion misquoted or tangled Marx's views—in this case a New York paper that Marx would have had probably little opportunity to respond to if he had been misquoted—is problematic. The statement itself, let alone the issue of what Marx really meant, can be read as declaring that the dictatorship of the proletariat either actually existed, or, that it needed to exist for the Commune to go forward.

What is less uncertain is that nothing Marx wrote before, during or after the Commune about the dictatorship of the proletariat and the transition to such a dictatorship suggests that he would have applied the term to the Parisian government. Earlier forecasts referred to a multiclass government—"since power cannot be attained by a single class"—just as had been true with the "Provisional Government in Paris" in the 1848 revolution.[97] Two years later in 1850 he argued, in opposition to the Willich-Schapper faction in the Communist League, that in "France . . . it isn't the proletariat alone that gains power but the peasants and the petty bourgeois as well, and it will have to carry out not its, but *their* measures."[98] The content of *The Civil War* and his comments during the Commune make clear that his expectation about a multiclass alliance was, in his opinion, realized; the "working" or "producing" classes governed Paris, that is, not just the proletariat.

Lastly, while his above-mentioned comment in 1881 that the "majority of the Commune was in no sense socialist" doesn't directly address this issue, it is worth quoting this in context:

> Of one thing you may be sure—a socialist government will not come to the helm in a country unless things have reached a stage at which it can, before all else, take such measures as will so intimidate the mass of the bourgeoisie as to achieve the first desideratum—time for effective action.
>
> You may, perhaps, refer me to the Paris Commune but, aside from the fact that this was merely an uprising of one city in exceptional circumstances, the majority of the Commune was in no sense socialist, nor could it have been. With a modicum of COMMON SENSE, it could, however, have obtained the utmost that was then obtainable—a compromise with Versailles beneficial to the people as a whole.[99]

For Marx, the dictatorship of the proletariat presupposed the existence of a well-developed proletariat that would be in a position to "intimidate the mass of the bourgeoisie." Everything he wrote about Paris and France prior to and after the Commune makes clear that he knew this precondition was nonexistent in 1871. Hence, his counsel of revolutionary restraint to the French movement on the eve of the Commune. Engels himself said as much in 1895 in his "Introduction" to Marx's *The Class Struggles in France*. While both the 1848 and 1871 uprisings had "shown . . . that in Paris none but a proletarian revolution is any longer possible," the Commune and its outcome "proved how impossible even then, twenty years after [the 1848–1851 events] . . . this rule of the working class still was."[100] The 1848 upheavals revealed that the era of the bourgeois as a revolutionary class was over and that of the proletarian revolution had commenced. But the Commune had also revealed that the proletariat was still not in a position to institute its rule.

Thus, it seems reasonable to conclude that if Marx characterized the Commune as a dictatorship it would have been for him a dictatorship of the people's alliance, that is, an alliance of the proletariat and its allies, or, the working classes in its broadest sense.[101]

CONCLUSION

Writing to Kugelmann about *The Civil War* shortly after its publication, Marx said, "It is making the devil of a noise and I have the honour to be THIS MOMENT THE BEST CALUMNIATED AND THE MOST MENACED MAN OF LONDON. That really does one good after a tedious twenty years' idyll in the backwoods."[102] The spate of calumnies that London's bourgeois press launched against the address and its author accused the International of having fomented the Parisian insurrection: "[A]mid the reaction that swept over Europe following the defeat of the Commune, the very success of the *Civil War* . . . helped to brand the International as the greatest threat to society and civilisation."[103] Marx and the organization came under the scrutiny of the British ministry for home affairs.[104] Previous anti-slander campaigns, however, especially the one in 1860 in response to the accusations of the German pedant Karl Vogt, had well prepared Marx and Engels to lead a countercharge. To virtually every false charge they fired off letters to editors on behalf of the GC for almost three months, of which they were successful in having a number actually published. By the end of the summer of 1871 the calumnies had somewhat abated.

The slander campaign, as indicated, testified to the GC's success in widely circulating the document. As well as key figures in the House of Commons, trade unions bodies in London, Manchester, and Birmingham were sent copies. As Marx told the GC, "it was necessary now to circulate the address as widely as possible among the working class."[105] Near the top of the handbill for the second edition was written, "(THIS OUGHT TO BE READ BY EVERY BRITISH WORK-MAN)." The original run of a thousand copies was soon followed by another two thousand as well as a German edition that Engels prepared. "It ran through three editions in two months, sold 8000 copies in the second edition and was translated into most European languages."[106] No other work written by Marx was as widely read so quickly. Nothing he published in the remaining twelve years of his life surpassed its importance. Along with Marx and Engels's supplementary views on the Commune, the *Civil War* would exercise a profound influence on Lenin's "revolutionary practice."

While fending off the slanders from the bourgeoisie the GC organized relief work for the thousands of refugees from the Commune who were fleeing to London. Marx, who two decades earlier had played a leading role in assisting German refugees who arrived in London following the defeat of the 1848–1849 revolution, took the initiative this time. Both he and Engels led the Council's effort to collect and distribute funds to the refugees. The extent of Marx's personal involvement in this effort was disclosed in the remarks of his daughter Jenny in late December 1871 to the Kugelmanns about the difficulty the GC was having in raising sufficient funds for the refugees: "You can imagine . . . how much all these difficulties and troubles worry poor Mohr. Not only that he has to fight with all the Governments of the ruling classes—into the bargain, he has hand to hand combats with the 'fat, fair and forty' landladies, who attack him, because this or that *Communeux* hasn't paid his rent."[107] That Marx, who had his own landlord problems on more than one occasion, had to provide such assistance to the Communards testifies to the desperateness of their situation as well as his unfailing willingness to aid fellow fighters in a time of need.

Ruling class attacks—including even one from the Pope[108]—on the International in the aftermath of the Commune had an unintended consequence. They did more to publicize the organization and its de facto leader than anything until then. For working-class fighters and progressives in whatever corner of the globe who had been inspired by the Parisian insurgents, the calumnious campaign simply raised the International's prestige in their eyes. Requests for affiliation with the International began to pour in from the most far-flung cities in the world. Whether it was workers in Calcutta,[109] New Orleans, San Francisco, Buenos Aires, or Copenhagen, or a group of journalists in Washington D. C., who "were determined that the International should exert an active influence upon American politics,"[110] or the great American abolitionist Wendell Phillips, the requests reflected the undeniable fact that at that historical moment the International was viewed by friend and foe alike as the foremost transnational defender of the producing classes.

Once it was revealed that Marx was the author of the *Civil War* he too was propelled into the public spotlight in a way he had never been before. The reporters who flocked to his home for interviews were in part responsible for making his name, if not a world-wide household name, recognizable, certainly, amongst the most politically conscious everywhere. The result of all of this free publicity was that for the first time in the history of the Marx party the first seeds of its program were being scattered globally. While only a few of these seeds actually germinated—for reasons that will be taken up in the next chapter—the few that did can trace their roots to the gains the party made in the wake of the Paris uprising.

Thirteen years after the Commune's defeat, Engels put it in perspective in terms of building the party, as understood in its broad historical sense. The occasion was the victories that the German party had just scored in the 1884 Reichstag elections, doubling its votes over the 1881 elections.

> I have hopes that in France it will provide fresh impetus for our party. Over there people are still suffering from the aftermath of the Commune. Great though its influence on Europe may have been, it has also seriously set back the French proletariat. To have been in power for three months—and in Paris at that—and not to

have radically altered the world but rather have come to grief through their own incompetence (such being the biased fashion in which the matter is understood today)—is proof that the party is not viable. That is the specious argument usually advanced by people who fail to realise that, while the Commune was the grave of *early* specifically French socialism, it was, for France, also and at the same time the cradle of a new international communism. And this last will be duly set on its feet by the German victories.[111]

Engels's assessment that in spite of the outcome in Paris the seeds of "international communism" had been successfully sown was indeed accurate. Marx, in fact, had alluded to this in his above-quoted remark to Kugelmann during the Commune that "whatever the immediate results may be, a new point of departure of world-historic importance has been gained." That the international communist party was "viable" in 1884, as Engels asserted in opposition to the opinions of demoralized French revolutionaries, was due in no small part to the life and death fight that he and Marx waged in the Commune's aftermath to maintain the International's programmatic integrity—the subject of the next chapter.

CHAPTER NINE

The First International:
The Final Years and Legacy

[T]he workers' party must be constituted not as the tail of some bourgeois party, but as an independent party with its own objective, its own politics.
—Engels, London Conference

[T]here are circumstances where you are in duty bound to occupy yourselves with things much less attractive than theoretical study and research.
—Marx to Nikolai Danielson

I think the next International—after Marx's writings have been at work for some years—will be directly Communist and will openly proclaim our principles.
—Engels to Frederick Sorge

Mohr's life without the International would be a diamond ring with the diamond missing.
—Engels to Laura Lafargue

Russia forms the vanguard of revolutionary action in Europe.
—Marx and Engels

[N]ot until the times get somewhat more turbulent shall we really be aware of what we have lost in Marx. . . . [A]t a revolutionary juncture his judgement was virtually infallible.
—Engels to J. P. Becker

The year and a half that followed the Commune's overthrow found the Marx-Engels team more active than ever in the International. The need for organizational regroupment in the wake of the Paris events resulted in a special leadership meeting in London in September 1871. This gathering made the preparations for what would be the last congress of the International a year later at The Hague. In the meantime, challenges to the International's basic program as well as its very existence emerged full-blown from within. The most serious of these came from the forces associated with the anarchist Mikhail Bakunin. While eventually victorious, the founders of modern communism recognized that this "episode in the history of the party" was over. Following the organization's demise they turned their attention to the realization of the International's program through national parties, especially in Germany and Russia. History would later reveal—specifically with regard to the latter—that while the world's first truly international proletarian organization effectively came to an end at the Hague Congress, its program remained intact, owing to the Promethean struggle that Marx and Engels waged within it in the final years.

THE FIGHT FOR PROGRAMMATIC INTEGRITY

The reactionary response of the bourgeois press in England to Marx's revolutionary defense of the Communards in his *Civil War in France* forced two of the leading British trade union leaders on the GC, George Odger and Benjamin Lucraft, to sever their ties with the International. In their quest to be elected to parliament, once the suffrage laws were liberalized in 1867 and 1869, they increasingly saw the organization as a liability for their hopes of winning the approval of England's liberal bourgeoisie. By collaborating with the latter to fund their electoral aspirations these "labour leaders," as Engels later and derisively described their behavior, intended to "form the foundation of a mighty movement to chain the workers politically still more firmly to the bourgeoisie."[1] Just such a class collaborationist perspective, which challenged the very essence of the program that Marx had fought for from the IWMA's birth, as well as the growing Bakunin operation from within, necessitated the convening of the London Conference.

The Call for Independent Working Class Political Action

The political reality of continental Europe since the last IWMA congress in Basle in 1869—the Franco-Prussian War and the crackdown on IWMA activists by various governments after the Commune—had made it logistically impossible to hold a congress not only in 1870 but also, as it became clear in the weeks after the Commune, in 1871. Hence Engels's motivation for his proposal that the solution to this dilemma be a "private Conference" of the IWMA in London in September.[2] Further GC discussion specified that the meeting would be composed of its members, of whom six were elected to have voting rights—Marx and Engels consciously did not run—and representatives from as many sections as could attend. On the basis of Marx's proposal it was also agreed that the conference would be "confined exclusively to questions of organisation and policy. He thought under the present circumstances the question of organisation was most important."[3]

As it turned out the most important issue that the twenty-three delegates grappled with at the conference was profoundly political albeit with major organizational implications. While neither Marx nor Engels was responsible for raising the matter—that was the work of a Blanquist Communard refugee—their intervention in the discussion was decisive in its outcome (in spite of the fact that neither had voting rights). The issue was political action of the working class. In the IWMA's 1864 Inaugural Address and Preamble to the Rules, both of which Marx had written, the issue was addressed respectively in the following ways: "To conquer political power has therefore become the great duty of the working classes"—which was for Marx the Address' central message—and, "[T]he economical emancipation of the working classes is therefore the great end to which every political movement ought to be subordinate as a means." The French contingent, then under the influence of the anarchist views of Proudhon, had conveniently left out, it may be remembered, "as a means" in its translation of the Preamble in order to rationalize its abstentionist political orientation. This was exactly the bowdlerization that Marx wanted the conference to rectify.

In 1871, the basic question about working-class political action was whether the abstentionist anarchist perspective—advocated now by Bakunin's followers—or the class collaborationist views of the English trade unionists such as Odger and Lucraft were the only alternatives for workers. In his intervention, Engels distilled the essence of the Marx party's politics.

> [F]or us abstention is impossible. The workers' party already exist as a political party in most countries. . . . The experience of real life and the political oppression imposed on them by existing governments . . . force the workers to concern themselves with politics, whether they wish or not. To preach abstention would be to push them into the arms of bourgeois politics. Especially in the aftermath of the Paris Commune which placed the political action of the proletariat on the agenda, abstention is quite impossible.
>
> We seek the abolition of Classes. What is the means of achieving it? The political domination of the proletariat . . . revolution is the supreme act of politics; whoever wants it must also want the means, political action, which prepares for it, which gives the workers the education for revolution and without which the workers will always be duped. . . . But the politics which are needed are working class politics; the workers' party must be constituted not as the tail of some bourgeois party, but as an independent party with its own objective, its own politics.
>
> The political freedoms, the right of assembly and association and the freedom of the press, these are our weapons—should we fold our arms and abstain if they seek to take them away from us? It is said that every political act implies recognition of the status quo. But when this status quo gives us the means of protesting against it, then to make use of these means is not to recognise the status quo.[4]

Marx underscored Engels's point about the educational benefit of political action two months later in a most didactic letter to a party activist in New York, Friedrich Bolte. For the working class to take power it needed to have "a PREVIOUS ORGANISATION" in place or, as Engels explained, "an independent party with its own objective, its own politics." The realization of this would occur, as experience had begun to show, when, through their "separate economic movements," workers united to press for their common class or political interests such as in the fight for the shorter work day. While such struggles presuppose a certain degree of PREVIOUS organisation, they are in turn equally a means of developing this organisation.

Where the working class is not yet far enough advanced in its organisation to undertake a decisive campaign against the collective power, i.e. the political power, of the ruling classes, it must at any rate be trained for this by continual agitation against, and a hostile attitude towards, the policies of the ruling classes. Otherwise it remains a plaything in their hands, as the September revolution in France showed [the bourgeois democratic Third Republic that followed in the wake of Bonaparte's surrender to Bismarck in 1870], and as is also proved to a certain degree by the game that Messrs Gladstone et Co. still succeed in playing in England up to the present time [through the class collaborationist trade union misleadership].[5]

Therefore, through "continual agitation" and a "hostile attitude" toward the ruling classes the working class both learns *and* organizes itself for the "decisive campaign." Hence, as discussed in chapter seven, the importance of the daily fights, the guerrilla wars of workers with capital—the training ground for the fight of fights. The real movement had, thus, allowed Marx to concretize the relatively abstract formulations he had made almost three decades earlier in his *Theses on Feuerbach* about the self-education of the oppressed. Along with Engels's speech, Marx's letter to Bolte constitute the very core of communist "revolutionary practice" or politics.

Engels's speech was clearly directed at the anarchists. Their abstentionist line, however revolutionary it might sound, "would . . . push [the workers] into the arms of bourgeois politics," or make them, as Marx put it to Bolte, a "plaything in their hands"—and, thus, be party, unwittingly perhaps, to Odger and Lucraft's line. Only if the workers had their own "independent party with its own politics" could they avoid the deadly trap of "bourgeois politics." Hence, workers not only had an inherent interest in defending basic democratic rights but were obligated to do so since their existence gave them the space to further their own class interests. The alternative, therefore, to both the Bakuninist and class collaborationist lines was independent working-class political action, the bottom line of both the Inaugural Address and the Preamble—and the heart and soul of the Marx party's politics for at least a quarter of a century. The task now, seven years after both documents had been adopted and after the experience of the Commune, was to make this line a living reality.

Five weeks prior to the Commune, Engels made the same point in a letter to the Spanish section of the IWMA. Regarding its concerns about how to combat the influence of nonworking class parties on workers, he drew on Europe's recent political history.

> Everywhere experience has shown that the best means of freeing workers from this domination . . . is to found in each country a proletarian party with a political programme of its own, a political programme that is very clearly distinguished from those of the other parties since it must express the conditions for the emancipation of the working class. . . . [Given that] the fundamental relations between labour and capital being everywhere the same, and the fact of political domination by the propertied classes over the exploited classes existing everywhere, the principles and the goal of the proletarian political programme will be identical, at least in all the western countries.[6]

Just as he was to do seven months later, he criticized the abstentionist line of the Bakuninists that was then influential in Spain and elsewhere in southern Europe. "To refrain from fighting our enemies in the political arena would be to abandon one of the most powerful means of action, and particularly of organisation and propaganda. Universal suffrage gives us an excellent means of action." Germany, he added, was the best example of what a workers' party could do with the suffrage.

In one of his speeches at the London conference under this point, Marx specifically addressed the matter of workers in parliaments, which "must not be thought that it is of minor importance." When governments prevented duly elected workers' representatives from exercising their parliamentary rights, "the effect of this severity and intolerance on the people is profound." He too, as Engels had done in his letter to the Spaniards, offered the German example for what was possible when more political space existed.

> Whereas if, like [August] Bebel and Liebknecht, they are able to speak from this platform, the entire world can hear them—in one way or the other it means considerable publicity for our principles. . . . When during the [Franco-Prussian War] Bebel and Liebknecht embarked on the struggle against it, and to disclaim responsibility on behalf of the working class with regard to what was happening—the whole of Germany was shaken, and even Munich . . . was the scene of great demonstrations demanding an end to the war.

> The governments are hostile to us. We must answer them by using every possible means at our disposal, getting workers into parliament is so much gaining over them, but we must choose the right men and watch out for the Tolains.[7]

Worker participation in parliaments, therefore, was a means to an end—"a platform . . . for our principles." In a set of minutes that were taken by another conference secretary, the second paragraph begins with Marx saying the following: "Since the July Revolution [1830] the bourgeoisie has always made every effort to unnoticeably create obstacles, in the workers' way. Our newspapers are not reaching the masses—the speakers' platform is the best means of publicity."[8] The promotion of proletarian internationalism, as Bebel and Liebknecht had done, was exactly what the parliamentary platform should be used for.[9]

On the following day of the debate Marx repeated Engels's point about the logic of the abstentionists' "revolutionary" line: "[B]y adjourning politics until after the violent struggle they are hurling the people into the formalist, bourgeois opposition—which it is our duty to combat, as well as the powers-that-be." In concluding both his remarks and the debate on the question of workers' political action he addressed what other speakers had raised, governmental repression of the IWMA in the aftermath of the Commune. "We must tell [these governments] . . . we know that you are the armed force opposing the proletariat—we shall act against you peacefully wherever possible—and take up arms when that is necessary."[10] Thus, if the peaceful road through the employment of basic democratic rights and the parliamentary option was closed to the workers' movement then the International was prepared to pursue armed struggle.

Independent working-class political action—this was the essence of Marx and Engels's intervention. The central theme of their 1850 Address—including the need for workers to have their own candidates in elections—it was the main lesson they drew from the 1848–1849 upheavals. Against the strong opposition of the Bakuninists, they won the majority to this perspective.[11] Engels and Marx, who were authorized to later draw up the resolutions as well as a new set of Rules agreed to at the conference, presented the GC a month later the now famous resolution "IX. Political Action of the Working Class," which incorporated the majority sentiment on this debate. The heart of the resolution is its last five paragraphs, which rectified the bowdlerization of the Preamble six years earlier.

> Considering, that against this collective power of the propertied classes the working class cannot act, as a class, except by constituting itself into a political party, distinct from, and opposed to, all old parties formed by the propertied classes;
> That this constitution of the working class into a political party is indispensable in order to insure the triumph of the social Revolution and its ultimate end—the abolition of classes;
> That the combination of forces which the working class has already effected by its economical struggles ought at the same time to serve as a lever for its struggles against the political power of landlords and capitalists
> The Conference recalls to the members of the *International*: That in the militant state of the working class, its economical movement and its political action are indissolubly united.[12]

The resolution's historic significance is that it constitutes, as a result of their intervention in the Conference—and aside from what they had already been doing in regard to Germany (again, to be discussed later)—the first seeds that Marx and Engels planted for what would eventually be Europe's mass working-class political parties. The resolution is the first explicit international call for such formations. While much would need to be done before its realization, it nevertheless gave those forces who were predisposed to move in this direction the authority, that is, the prestige of the International, to go forth boldly.

Among the other points of agreement at London, two resolutions are noteworthy: the previously discussed one called "Formation of Working Women's Branches"[13] and another entitled "Agricultural Producers." As was the case with the former, the latter, initiated also by Marx, was a product of the lessons he had drawn about the Commune. Specifically, he urged the conference to recognize the importance of the worker-peasant alliance and thus the need for the IWMA to do propaganda work in the countryside. Thus, the wording of the resolution that he and Engels wrote:

1. —The Conference invites the [GC] and the [affiliate sections] . . . to prepare, for the next Congress, reports on the means of securing the adhesion of the agricultural producers to the movement of the industrial proletariate.

2. —Meanwhile, the [affiliate sections] are invited to send agitators to the rural districts, there to organise public meetings, to propagate the principles of the International and to found rural branches.[14]

While the resolution reflects the actual practice of the Marx party in the upheavals of 1848–1849 in Germany and vis-à-vis the Commune as discussed, respectively, in chapters four and eight, it constitutes its first written programmatic statement to that effect. For future revolutionaries in overwhelmingly peasant countries like Russia, such statements would be of invaluable strategic assistance.

Summing up the conference in a letter to Jenny, Marx wrote: "It was HARD WORK. Morning and evening sessions, commission sessions in between, HEARING OF WITNESSES, REPORTS TO BE DRAWN UP AND SO FORTH. But more was done than at all the previous Congresses put together, because there was no audience in front of which to stage rhetorical comedies."[15] The conference's success was due in no small part to Engels's contribution, his most intimate collaboration yet with Marx for such a meeting. His role was crucial especially on the eve of the conference, when Marx was forced by his doctor to leave town for two weeks to recuperate from overwork. In the two months afterwards, he and Marx worked tirelessly with other GC members in writing up and distributing the conference documents and the new set of IWMA rules. There would be an even greater need for Engels's presence, since the victories that the Marx party won at London would surely not go unanswered by its opponents.

Against the Bakunin Operation

The struggle with the Bakunin current in the International concerned a matter of enormous significance, one that would bedevil many a twentieth-century revolutionary—how to deal with political differences within a revolutionary party. It was the first such struggle in the socialist movement for which, due to the conscious effort of Marx and Engels, at the direction of the GC, there is a detailed record from which future revolutionaries could learn. Unfortunately, limitations of space prevent any detailed analysis of what proved to be a very bitter fight. However, a few observations are appropriate.

Bakunin, essentially, began in 1868 to create a secret organization within the International in order to take over and impose his politics. In the process he resorted to very despicable actions including a virulent antisemitic campaign.[16] The main problem, as Marx and Engels argued, was not his ideas—the pluralist character of the IWMA guaranteed his right to participate—but rather secret organizing from within. Such a modus operandi, behind the backs of the working class, was what they found most objectionable in Bakunin's actions. Bakunin's operation, hence, undermined the very essence of working-class independent political action as well as the International's first rule: "The emancipation of the working classes must be conquered by the working classes themselves." Therein lay the fundamental political difference between the Bakuninists and the Marx party.

Marx and Engels were able to amass sufficient evidence to convince firstly the majority of the GC in 1872 and then, later that year, the delegates to the Hague congress that Bakunin's disruption campaign was real. The delegates to the latter voted to oust him and a key leader of his clique from the IWMA. More recently discovered documents, that the International did not have access to, make for an even more damaging case against Bakunin's split operation. As Hal Draper, who provides the most thorough and current investigation of the issue, pointedly notes, Bakunin's has the dubious distinction of being "the first leftist movement to apply its conspiratorial pattern of subversion not to assail society at large or to defend itself against the police, but to destroy other socialists' organization."[17]

There is one charge the Bakunin group made that is worth highlighting because it addressed a major organizational-cum-political difference between the GC majority, led by the Marx-Engels team, and the Bakuninists—the only time in the fight that a substantive issue was openly debated. Claiming that the GC was "authoritarian" in its operations, it argued that the International, "embryo of the future human society, must be, from now on, the faithful image of our principles of liberty and federation." On behalf of the GC, Marx and Engels countered that the IWMA or any revolutionary organization could not serve as a model for a socialist society—in which "the power of the State disappears . . . and the functions of government become simple administrative functions"—since it was absurd to think that the working class could organize itself to take and defend state power without the centralization of authority. Drawing on the lessons of the Commune, they added sarcastically, the "Communards [according to Bakunin's logic] would not have failed if they had understood that the Commune was 'the embryo of the future human society' and had cast away all discipline and all arms, that is, the things which must disappear when there are no more wars!"[18] Of course, as noted earlier, Marx and Engels did criticize the Communards for not centralizing authority sufficiently for its defense.

The Hague Congress and the End of the IWMA

At least five months prior to the Hague congress Marx and Engels had made clear to their closest contacts that they planned to relinquish leadership responsibilities in the IWMA in order to return to the scientific work.[19] Only the necessity of leading the fight against the Bakuninists for the programmatic integrity of the Association, as the epigram that opens this chapter indicates, prevented them from doing this sooner. To Kugelmann at the end of July 1872, Marx wrote, "Before I resign, I want at least to protect it from disintegrating elements."[20] So much then for the charge of Bakunin apologists that the effort to expel the anarchist leader and his closest followers was done in order for Marx and Engels to assume undisputed leadership of the International.

The majority of the GC and the sixty-four delegates at The Hague agreed that in order to "protect it [the IWMA] from disintegrating elements" as well as increasing governmental repression the organization would have to be more centralized and disciplined. This is what Marx saw as the central task of the congress in his opening report to it on behalf of the GC: "You, the delegates of the working class, meet to strengthen the militant organisation of a society aiming at the emancipation of labour and the extinction of national feuds." In a summary speech at the end of the congress, Marx defended the move, one of, he said, the meeting's three major achievements, with the clear understanding that this would not come at the expense of the International's democratic functioning.

> [A]t a time when persecution is being organised, the . . . Congress rightly believed that it was wise and necessary to increase the powers of the [GC] and to centralise,

in view of the impending struggle, activity which isolation would render impotent. . . . [W]ho but our enemies could take alarm at the authority of the [GC]? Has it a bureaucracy and an armed police to ensure that it is obeyed? Is not its authority solely moral, and does it not submit its decisions to the [various national] Federations which have to carry them out?[21]

The "impending struggle" did not suggest that revolution was imminent. Rather, and consistent with Marx and Engels's long-held view that the IWMA was a "mighty engine" for revolution and not "a debating club,"[22] the point was to begin the construction of the kind of organization that could successfully wage a revolution when necessary. As Engels put it afterward, in response to the anarchist-oriented sections who believed their "autonomy" had been compromised by the shift to a more centralized body, "wherever there is an organisation, some autonomy is sacrificed for the sake of unity in action. . . . [T]hey do not realise that the *International* is a society organised for struggle, and not for fine theories. . . ."[23] The Commune revealed in no uncertain terms what would happen if such an organization was not in place: it "fell because there did not appear in all the centres, in Berlin, Madrid, etc., a great revolutionary movement corresponding to this supreme uprising of the Paris proletariat."[24] Hence, their constant refrain, which they made sure was embodied in the Rules, that the IWMA was the "militant organisation" of the working class—an organization for worldwide revolutionary action.

The organizational shifts the delegates voted for were basically those measures adopted by the GC in the aftermath of the London Conference, which required the GC to make sure that sections abided by congress decisions and to empower it with the right to suspend those in noncompliance. The move to a more centralized and disciplined organization was related to what Marx saw as one of the other major achievements of the congress—the decision to make Resolution IX from the London Conference on political action of the working class one of the Association's basic rules. This decision, in his view, recognized that "[o]ne day the worker will have to seize political supremacy to establish the new organisation of labour." How to achieve this would depend on the realities of each country.

[W]e do not deny the existence of countries like America, England, and . . . [perhaps] Holland, where the workers may achieve their aims by peaceful means. That being true we must also admit that in most countries on the Continent it is force which must be the lever of our revolution; it is force which will have to be resorted to for a time in order to establish the rule of the workers.[25]

In other words, what in other contexts Marx and Engels—and at least one of the delegates[26]—called the dictatorship of the proletariat would be necessary in this revolutionary transformation.

Certainly the most controversial decision the congress made, its third achievement in Marx's view, was, upon a proposal from a majority of the GC, the transference of the seat of the GC from London to New York. Engels's justification for this decision, in a series of articles and letters to IWMA supporters after the congress, was consistent, if more explicit, with the motivation he gave to the delegates when it was debated. Basically, he argued, with himself and Marx, as well as a number of other key GC leaders, stepping down after the congress the leadership of the Council would have inevitably come under the influence of either the exile French Blanquists or English trade union reformists had it stayed in London. The reality of the former, whose own brand of "barricadology," distinct but not fundamentally unlike that of the Bakuninists, and the latter, whose reformist politics would have delivered the International to "bourgeois radicals" or even to "the control of the [British] government," made the move necessary.[27] Given the security and other drawbacks to a European site, New York was the best alternative. Reluctantly—as Engels explained to his readers, "it took some pains to carry this transfer through"[28]—the delegates voted by the narrowest of margins for the proposal.

With the International's demise in less than two years after this decision it has been suggested that in making the proposal—with, it should be noted, nine other GC members—Marx and Engels consciously wrote the Association's death warrant.[29] Firstly, that the proposal explicitly stated that the move was "for the "1872/73 year" suggests that the change in venue was not necessarily seen as permanent. For Marx and Engels, certainly, New York provided safe refuge for the organization until more favorable circumstances warranted its return to Europe. "The only country where something could still be accomplished in the name of the International was America," Engels wrote two years later.[30] Their subsequent actions regarding the International lend credence to such an interpretation.[31] From London they continued to be actively involved in its course including many hours spent on preparing documents from The Hague. Only with the very narrow and poorly attended Geneva congress a year later, the last official IWMA congress, did they become convinced that the International was a spent force.[32] And only in hindsight did they see that The Hague "was actually the end."[33]

What about the charge that in leading the successful fight for a more centralized and disciplined IWMA Marx and Engels effectively killed the organization because it forced the Bakuninists into a complete break?[34] Indeed, five months after The Hague Marx told Friedrich Sorge that "the great achievement of the . . . Congress was to induce the rotten elements to *exclude themselves*, i.e. to leave."[35] That the departure of the Bakuninists may have reduced the ranks of the IWMA was for Marx and Engels not a fact to bemoan but rather to be applauded. In a most didactic letter to Bebel in June 1873, Engels began his explanation with a general observation about political success and revolutionary patience.

> Naturally every party leadership wants to see successes. . . . But there are circumstances in which one must have the courage to sacrifice *momentary* success for more important things. Especially for a party like ours, whose ultimate success is so absolutely certain and which has developed so enormously in our own lifetimes and before our own eyes, momentary success is by no means always and absolutely necessary.

Engels, who had been referring to the German situation (again, to be discussed later), then offered the example of his and Marx's actions vis-à-vis the sectarians in the IWMA.

After the Commune it [the IWMA] had a colossal success. . . . We knew very well that the bubble *must* burst. All the riff-raff attached themselves to it. The sectarians within it became arrogant and misused the International in the hope that the most stupid and meanest actions would be permitted them. We did not allow that. Knowing well that the bubble must burst some time, our concern was not to delay the catastrophe but to take care that the International emerged from it pure and unadulterated. The bubble burst at The Hague. . . . [I]f we had come out in a conciliatory way at The Hague, if we had hushed up the breaking out of the split, what would have been the result? The sectarians, especially the Bakuninists, would have got another year in which to perpetuate stupidities and infamies . . . because *principles* would already have been sacrificed at The Hague. Then the International would indeed have gone to pieces . . . through "unity"! . . . And if we had to do it again we would not, taking it all together, act any differently—tactical mistakes are always made, of course.

Of the "more important things," for Marx and Engels the preservation of the political program took precedence over the maintenance of unity for unity's sake. The fight for programmatic integrity was crucial for long-term party building. Engels's assertion, by the way, that "we knew" that "the bubble" had to "burst" was not a self-serving hindsight. He, it may be remembered, was doubtful from the beginning of the IWMA that so many disparate political tendencies could coexist in the same organization.

Finally, an especially perceptive coda on internecine party struggles.

Incidentally, old man Hegel said long ago: A party proves itself victorious by *splitting* and being able to stand the split. The movement of the proletariat necessarily passes through different stages of development; at every stage part of the people get stuck and do not participate in the further advance; and this in itself is sufficient to explain why the "solidarity of the proletariat," in fact, everywhere takes the form of different party groupings, which carry on life-and-death feuds with one another, as the Christian sects in the Roman Empire did amidst the worst persecutions.[36]

Without getting into the details it may be briefly noted, as vindication for Marx and Engels's position, that in the next decade the Bakuninist split operation disappeared ignominiously from the political scene. The Marx party, on the other hand, was indeed more "able to stand the split."

For Marx and Engels the IWMA's end was due mainly to the fact that the International "in its old form has outlived itself." As Engels explained to Sorge two years after The Hague, a particular set of historical circumstances, specifically, the continent-wide repression following the defeat of 1848–1851 had brought it into existence. "In order to produce a new International like the old one—an alliance of all the proletarian parties of all countries—a general suppression of 1864 would be necessary. For this the proletarian world had now become too big, too extensive." The IWMA, in other words, was, to recall Marx's characterization of the Communist League in 1860, "an episode in the history of a party." As for the future, Engels was prescient in his algebra if not his mathematics. "I think the next International—after

Marx's writings have been at work for some years—will be directly Communist and will openly proclaim our principles."[37] Only with the coming of the Russian Revolution would his prediction be fulfilled.

The Marx-Engels team spent more time in the International than any other political organization. It was also the last political formation in which they actively participated as members. As is apparent by now, that experience offers extremely rich insights into their approach to political organizing, which, again, cannot be detailed here. Suffice it to say that, firstly, Marx and Engels always approached organizational questions politically and, thus, had no organizational model suitable for all places and times. Second, many of the positions that Marx and Engels held about how the GC—but not necessarily the organization as a whole—should function and much of their modus operandi on that body, particularly their efforts to make the GC a disciplined, centralized but democratic body as well as one composed of activists, clearly anticipated what would later be called Leninist organizational norms. Lastly, it is noteworthy that during the entire course of the IWMA's existence Marx and Engels almost never referred to "our party" or the "Marx party" in relation to the International. What this suggests is that *the IWMA* was their party or, more correctly, their party in the making. Engels's aforementioned point that the next International "will openly proclaim our principles" is instructive. It recognized that the IWMA's official programmatic statements contained, if not "openly" and everything, much of the substance of the communist program. Marx and Engels, therefore, had every reason to give their loyalty first and foremost to the IWMA and not to the tiny party nucleus they headed at the time of the International's birth. Viewed from the long-term perspective of Engels's statement the IWMA was a very auspicious step in the process of being able to "recruit our party anew."

THE INTERNATIONAL'S LEGACY

More than a year before the Paris Commune, Marx commented to Engels on the prospects for revolution. "I am firmly convinced that although the first blow will come from France, Germany is far riper for a social movement, and will grow far over the heads of the French."[38] Six months later, after the Franco-Prussian War began, Marx and Engels sent a memo to the leadership of the Social Democratic Workers' Party in Germany about the war's significance for the workers' movement in that country. *"This war has shifted the centre of gravity of the continental labour movement from France to Germany.* This means that greater responsibility now rests with the German working class. . . ."[39] While the "first blow" did indeed come from France in the form of the Commune—the last gasp, as Engels would later say, of a revolutionary tradition—Marx and Engels were still convinced that the axis of world revolution had moved east of Paris. It was within this framework that Marx advised Sorge, now the Secretary of the GC in New York, about what to do with the IWMA a year after The Hague congress.

> As I view European conditions, it is quite useful to let the formal organisation of the [IWMA] recede into the background for the time being. . . . Events and the

inevitable development and intertwining of things will of themselves see to it that the International rises again in an improved form. For the present it suffices not to let the connection with the most capable in the various countries slip altogether out of our hands . . .[40]

Party building work would now focus on the construction of workers' parties within "various countries," of which the most important was Germany.

A Reevaluation of the English Movement

Implicit in Marx and Engels's view that the "centre of gravity" of the workers' movement had shifted eastward was a downgrading of the importance of the English movement. It may be recalled that they had once looked to the latter as the vanguard of the workers' movement owing to the advanced character of capitalism in England and the existence of a genuine workers' party, the Chartists. What explains, therefore, their reevaluation—contrary to the standard Marxological myth—of the English movement?

As previously noted, Engels, for certain, began in 1858 to have second thoughts about the revolutionary potential of England. When the Chartist leader Ernest Jones sought then to maneuver with the liberal bourgeoisie by watering down the historical demands of the Chartist program, Engels said it was symptomatic of "the fact that the English proletariat is actually becoming more and more bourgeois." He then offered an explanation: "In the case of a nation which exploits the entire world this is, of course, justified to some extent."[41] The booty of British imperialism, in other words, had begun to compromise England's workers. It was exactly this point that Marx responded to in his comment that the revolutionary movement might be "CRUSHED in this little corner of the earth" because capitalism, with Britain in the lead, was still "ascendant" globally.[42]

Seventeen months prior to the formation of the IWMA Engels was even less optimistic about the prospects in England. To Marx he wrote that "the English proletariat's revolutionary energy has all but completely evaporated and the English proletarian has declared himself in full agreement with the dominancy of the bourgeoisie."[43] Marx, however, was not yet willing to write them off. "How soon the English workers will throw off what seems to be a bourgeois contagion remains to be seen."[44] As had always been true in the history of the class struggle, only the real movement would provide an answer.

The English trade union leaders who were instrumental in the International's foundation came almost exclusively from the building trades and skilled crafts. The latter, in particular, were mainly concerned about their survival in the face of industrial capitalism. They looked to the IWMA somehow not unlike the way the straubinger elements in Germany had once looked to the Communist League. Both the building trades and skilled crafts' officialdom, as would become increasingly clear, were motivated to participate in the IWMA on the basis of narrow economic and political interests and not proletarian internationalism. Unionized industrial workers were in the main conspicuously absent in their affiliation with the IWMA. They were, for the most part, clearly better off than other workers and thus felt more secure.[45] In his *Inaugural Address* Marx had alluded to the stratification in the English working class by noting that "a minority [had gotten] their real wages somewhat advanced" during the unprecedented expansion of British capitalism in the third quarter of the nineteenth century.[46] The political repercussions of these differences within the working class would only become clear in the course of the IWMA's experience in England.

It was the suffrage question and electoral politics that first revealed for Marx the reality of the trade unionists' participation on the GC. Marx and Engels, of course, had long supported worker involvement in the electoral process as long as it was really independent working-class political action (one of the key themes in the *Address of March 1850*). At the same time, the French experience from 1848 through the Bonapartist period had shown that the electoral process was not necessarily a panacea for workers. Universal manhood suffrage would offer little to workers, as Engels explained to German workers, "if one has only a large and ignorant rural population, a well-organised bureaucracy, a well-regimented press, associations sufficiently kept down by the police and no political meetings at all."[47]

Within six months of the IWMA's formation, the GC, with Marx's enthusiastic support, helped to bring into existence the Reform League, the working-class organization that played a key role in pressuring parliament to enact the 1867 Reform Act, which extended the suffrage to the middle class and parts of the better-off workers. At Marx's urging the GC had agreed that it would only support the demand of universal manhood suffrage. A year later, however, Marx reported to J. P. Becker that two of the GC's trade unionists "[W. R.] Cremer and Odger have both *betrayed* us in the Reform League, where they came to a *compromise with the bourgeoisie* against our wishes."[48] The two gave in to the liberal bourgeois elements in the League who would only support household suffrage. Not only was the GC's perspective compromised by Cremer and Odger but the fledgling organization's own agenda suffered as a result of the time and energy that its members devoted to League activities (one of the main reasons why the IWMA did not hold a congress in its first year). At the beginning of 1871, Marx wrote the following to Julian Harney, the former Chartist leader, who was now living in Boston:

> I regret saying, most of the workmen's representatives use their position in our council only as a means of furthering their own petty personal aims. To get into the House of Commons by hook or crook, is their *ultima Thule* ["most cherished goal"], and they like nothing better than rubbing elbows with the lords and M.P.'s by whom they are petted and demoralised.[49]

What Marx witnessed was perhaps the first manifestation of a phenomenon that would be all too common in the subsequent history of the labor movement and its involvement in electoral politics.

If in Marx's opinion the trade unionists Odger and Cremer had sold out the English working class on the suffrage question, he would make sure that they would not be able to do the same on the Irish question. As noted earlier, Marx and Engels's strategy was to craft a GC policy position that made clear that the IWMA's support of the Fenian prisoners and Irish self-determination was unequivocal while attempting, at the same time, to drive a wedge between the trade unionists and the liberal Gladstone government with whom they were flirting. In accord with Marx's strategy, Engels wrote, "it would be fine to get Odger into a pickle."[50] Having witnessed its origins, Marx now sought to undermine this first instance of what later came to be called the labor-liberal electoral coalition. While successful in getting the trade unionists to vote for the resolution, it soon became clear that their true loyalties were with the coalition and not independent working-class politics and proletarian internationalism.

In spite of the vacillation of the trade unionists on the Irish question Marx still felt there was hope for England. Thus his retort to Bakunin who—for his own factional reasons—criticized the GC for trying to provide leadership to the movement in Britain instead of creating a separate leadership body, as was the case in other countries. "The English have all the *material* necessity for the social revolution. What they lack is the *spirit of generalisation and revolutionary ardour*. It is only the [GC] that can provide them with this, that can thus accelerate the truly revolutionary movement in this country, and consequently *everywhere*."[51] The "spirit of generalisation" is what Marx and Engels had long held to be the unique contribution of the communist party to the revolutionary process.[52] Thus, at the beginning of 1870, when he replied to Bakunin on behalf of the GC, Marx apparently thought that there was a "truly revolutionary movement" in England in need of such a leadership. It was in this framework that Engels recommended in May 1871 that the Secretary to the GC be someone who could "spread the [IWMA] amongst the masses of London and . . . render it independent of the aristocracy of the working classes and its acknowledged leaders."[53] The real movement would soon make clear that this was not to be the case.

If Marx's resolution on the Irish question was difficult for the trade unionists to swallow, his *Civil War in France* proved to be indigestible. As noted at the outset of this chapter their disagreement with its line forced those who were still formally members of the GC to completely sever their ties with the IWMA. Under pressure from their liberal allies they chose to distance themselves from the fallen Communards and Marx's uncompromising defense of them. Whatever hopes, therefore, Marx and Engels had once pinned on the English movement had clearly been dispelled by the reaction of their leaders to the demise of the Commune. A new leadership, in their view, would have to emerge to replace them.

The real movement of the Commune and the response of the trade unionists had been instructive. Marx's intervention in the discussion on trade unions at the London Conference in 1871 no doubt reflected the lessons he and Engels had recently drawn based on their English experience. In response to a proposal for an international federation of trade unions, the minutes report Marx saying the following:

> The TRADE UNIONS . . . are an aristocratic minority—the poor workers cannot belong to them. . . . [T]he same goes for workers born in the East End of London; one in 10 belongs to [them]—peasants, day labourers never belong to these societies.

The TRADE UNIONS can do nothing by themselves—they will remain a minority—they have no power over the mass of proletarians—whereas the International works directly on these men—it does not need their organisation in order to carry along the workers. . . . It is the only society to inspire complete confidence in the workers.[54]

While there is nothing in these comments that contradicts Marx's earlier pronouncements on trade unions—in particular, his *Instructions for the Delegates* to the 1866 Geneva congress (see chapter seven)—they were far more critical of them than anything he had ever said.

That Marx, also, proposed at the London Conference the creation of a separate leadership body for Britain in place of the GC suggests that he indeed had reevaluated his position about England's revolutionary role. The English working-class movement would have to create its own leadership, work at its own pace, and hopefully be inspired by revolutionary movements elsewhere such as Germany.

At The Hague Marx left little doubt about what he thought of the trade union misleaders. When one of them questioned the credentials of Maltman Barry with the claim that he didn't represent English workers, Marx retorted: "[I]t does credit to Barry that he is not one of the so-called leaders of the English workers, since these men are more or less bribed by the bourgeoisie and the government."[55] Although his widely publicized remarks led to a complete rupture with the reformists, Marx was unapologetic two years later: "I knew that I was letting myself in for unpopularity, slander, etc., but such consequences have always been a matter of indifference to me. Here and there people are beginning to see that in making that denunciation I was only doing my duty."[56] The time had clearly arrived for Marx, in his dealings with the trade unionists, when *suaviter in modo* had to give way to *fortiter in re*.

In an analysis of the parliamentary elections in 1874, Engels returned to the point that he and Marx had raised in 1858 to explain the political backwardness of the English workers. "This is understandable in a country in which the working class has shared more than anywhere else in the advantages of the immense expansion of its large-scale industry. Nor could it have been otherwise in an England that rules the world market."[57] While politics was also determinant—the willingness of the ruling class to grant the historical demands of the Chartists was particularly important—the impact of the booty of British imperialism on the consciousness of English workers was still for Engels, as late as 1883, decisive. "Participation in the domination of the world market was and is the economic basis of the English workers' political nullity."[58] Only when the world monopoly of Britain's rulers would be challenged by competitors, with the resulting diminution of the booty, would English workers begin to move. Not until the labor upsurge in the late 1880s amongst the lower ranks of the industrial working class, especially in London, would Engels be proven right.

The Struggle for a German Party

Exactly at the same time that Marx, to be joined later by Engels, began to build the IWMA he *and* Engels were actively involved in influencing the construction of what would be the first mass workers' party—in Germany. At the core of their efforts, just as was true for the International, was the fight for independent working-class political action. Success would require an incessant struggle against the legacy that Lassalle had bequeathed to Germany's workers' movement.[59]

In the concrete setting of Germany, independent working-class political action meant independence from the feudal monarchial class led by Bismarck as well as the liberal bourgeoisie grouped in what was called the Party of Progress. Germany's revived labor movement, it may be remembered, came into existence in 1863 with the baggage of Lassalleanism, the essence of which was reliance on Bismarck—what Marx and Engels sarcastically called "royal Prussian governmental socialism"—and a dictatorial leadership. The former trait was in many ways a reaction to the pusillanimity of Germany's liberals. Unlike its counterpart in England, Germany's liberal bourgeoisie, for reasons that Marx and Engels had already explained—the lessons of 1848–1849—was unwilling to support the workers' movement's political aspirations and was, therefore, unable to prevent their independent political action, as had been true in England. Under Lassalle's influence, however, the illusion that workers should in turn look to Bismarck's junkerdom-monarchial class proved to be the bigger obstacle to their political clarity. Such an illusion was aggravated, in their opinion, by two other shortcomings in Lassalle's legacy, the tendencies to view universal manhood suffrage as a panacea for the working class and to deprecate the value of trade union organizing.

Grounded on such theoretical terrain, Germany's first workers' party, the one that Lassalle helped to found in 1863, the General German Workers's Union, or ADAV, was, in Marx's view, deformed at birth. To Engels in early 1865 he wrote: "The sooner it is disbanded, the better. . . . [T]he air must be cleared and the party purged of the stench left behind by Lassalle."[60] Under Lassalle's successors, especially J. B. Schweitzer, the politics and dictatorial mode of functioning of the organization actually worsened.[61] A few years later Engels observed that "unfortunately it appears to be a law of the proletarian movement that everywhere a part of the workers' leaders necessarily become corrupted, though it has happened nowhere else in the general fashion to which Lassalle developed it in Germany."[62] At the same time Marx and Engels took advantage of every opportunity to expurgate Lassalle's "stench," including a brief stint of writing for Schweitzer's paper, Social-Demokrat, until it became clear that his Lassallean course was not to be altered. As part of this effort Marx was successful in getting the paper to reprint the Inaugural Address. After an initial overture, he gave up, however, any hope of the ADAV becoming an affiliate of the International.[63]

Marx and Engels's tactic was to attack Lassalleanism in whatever forum was open to them. In an article on Proudhon written at Schweitzer's request, Marx told Engels that "several very savage blows, ostensibly aimed at Proudhon, strike home at" Lassalle "and was intended to do so."[64] Engels then followed up with a translation of an old Danish folk ballad, "in order . . . to impress on the readers of Social-Demokrat the necessity of struggle against the rural squirearchy."[65] Precisely because Lassalleanism advocated a bloc between the working class and Bismarck's feudal-monarchial coalition it either ignored or played down the exploitation of the peasantry.[66]

When they later broke with Schweitzer's paper they told readers of other German newspapers that they "repeatedly demanded that the language [of the paper] directed at the ministry and the feudal-absolutist party should be at least as bold as that aimed at the men of Progress," in other words, the liberal bourgeoisie.[67] Leading up to the break Marx had tried without success to persuade Schweitzer to abandon his Lassallean perspective.

> It is beyond all question that Lassalle's ill-starred illusion that a Prussian government might intervene with socialist measures will be crowned with disappointment. The logic of circumstances will tell. But the *honour* of the workers' party requires that it reject such illusions, even before their hollowness is punctured by experience. The working class is revolutionary or it is nothing.[68]

Engels's point about the importance of the fight against feudal relations in the countryside makes clear that he and Marx were reaffirming the political strategy they adopted for the German revolution beginning in 1847, most importantly, the strategy of the people's alliance. They said as much when they announced their break with Schweitzer and his paper.[69] This was crucial because that strategy supplied the answer to the perplexing question posed by Germany's reality. If Germany's still-small working class could not count on the cowardly liberal bourgeoisie, then how could it expect to advance without an alliance with Bismarck's junkerdom? The solution was the worker-peasant alliance. To the very end of their lives Marx and Engels would continually try to impress upon the German party the necessity of this strategic alliance.

Their most important literary intervention in this period in the German movement, as well as being one of their major political writings, was Engels's pamphlet *The Prussian Military Question and the German Workers' Party*. Written in close collaboration with Marx, who had in fact proposed its structure and central message—to kill two birds with one stone, that is, the feudal class as well as the liberal bourgeoisie—it constitutes their key statement, albeit implicitly, against Lassalleanism. The issue that prompted the piece was the constitutional conflict between the Prussian Assembly, composed in its majority by the Party of Progress, or the liberal bourgeoisie, and Bismarck's government. More specifically, who of the two had the right to reorganize Prussia's armed forces and what position should the workers' movement take in this conflict?

In the notices that he sent out to publicize the pamphlet, Marx quoted from its programmatic conclusions.

> "The only aspect of army reorganisation in Prussia which is of interest to the German working class is the increasingly thorough implementation of universal conscription."
> The policy which the working class must pursue in the constitutional conflict is: "above all to preserve the organisation of the workers' party as far as present conditions permit; to drive the Party of Progress on to make *real* progress, as far as possible; . . . but to reply to the hypocritical enticements of reaction [Bismarck's government] with the words:
> 'With the spear one should accept gifts, point against point.'"[70]

Marx and Engels had long held that universal conscription was preferable to the traditional caste-like recruitment policies of Prussia's army because it provided the working class with the necessary military skills for taking political power.

But the real intent of the pamphlet was to argue for the independent organization of the working class from both the party of "reaction" as well as the liberal bourgeoisie. Of the two, however, the latter represented an advance for workers because its traditional program, civil liberties and basic democratic rights, were weapons that the working class "needs for its ultimate victory."[71] Thus, and recalling the last section of the *Manifesto*, the workers' party should support the bourgeoisie in its struggle against reaction *"as long as it remains true to itself."* On the other hand, the lessons of 1848–1849 had taught that the German bourgeoisie was fainthearted and that even if the workers' party sought to "drive the Party of Progress, as far as possible" it might not succeed:

> [E]ven then the workers' party would have no choice but . . . to continue its campaign for bourgeois freedom, freedom of the press and rights of assembly and association which the bourgeoisie had betrayed. Without these freedoms it will be unable to move freely itself; in this struggle it is fighting to establish the environment necessary for its existence, for the air it needs to breathe.[72]

Thus, in no uncertain terms Marx and Engels made clear that the fight for bourgeois democracy was to be fought for by the workers' party even when the bourgeoisie was not willing to do so. This conclusion is, therefore, the elaboration and extension, based on the lessons of 1848–1849, of the strategic perspective on the German revolution that they sketched in the final section of the *Manifesto* on the eve of those upsurges.[73] Furthermore, recalling the essence of the *1850 March Address*, the assumption underlying this strategy was that "the workers' party will not play the part of a mere appendage to the bourgeoisie but of an independent party" in order "to educate the individual workers about their class interests [which are "directly opposed to those of the capitalists"] and when the next revolutionary storm comes . . . it will be ready to act."[74]

For the workers' party to successfully carry out a fight for bourgeois democracy it would have to do so in alliance with the rural producers: "[U]ntil such time as the rural proletariat is also swept along into the movement, the urban proletariat cannot and will not achieve anything at all in Germany."[75] With this last advice Engels's pamphlet can truly be said to be the necessary, and as it turned out, their final addendum, again, based on the lessons of the real movement, to the *Manifesto's* program for the German revolution. It was for this reason that Marx and Engels agreed five years later to reissue Engels's *Peasant War in Germany* in order, as stated in the new preface, to stress that it "is the immediate and most urgent task of the German labour movement to breathe life into this class [farm laborers] and draw it into the movement."[76]

Finally, any "gifts" from Bismarck's "Bonapartist" regime, a particular type of "reaction," were to be viewed without any illusions. Thus, as already cited in another context, his advice about the limitations of universal suffrage under a Bonapartist regime. Only as long as Bismarck thought he could, in good Bonapartist fashion, use the workers' movement against the bourgeoisie would he tolerate its existence. "From the moment that this movement turns the workers into an independent force, and thereby becomes a danger to the government, there will be an abrupt end to it all." Thirteen years later, after the German party had become a mass workers' party with its own agenda, Engels's prediction was fulfilled when Bismarck had the party outlawed under his antisocialist law.

Owing largely to the efforts of the Marx-Engels team the pamphlet was widely read and discussed.[77] In campaigning against Lassalleanism they sought at the same time to rebuild their tendency in Germany. In spite of their historical links with the movement there this meant, as they had recognized as early as 1853, having to "recruit our party entirely anew." The campaign they waged to promote *Capital* in 1867–1868 (see chapter eight) was also part of this effort. Above all, as Engels told Marx in 1867, "We must try to establish a direct link with the workers in Germany again, that is what we most lack. . . ."[78] Initially, their only real cadre on the scene was Liebknecht, who, in their opinion, and as already mentioned, had many limitations.[79] In their collaboration with him they were careful, just as had been true with the building of the IWMA, not to subordinate the interests of constructing a mass workers' movement in Germany to the interests of their tendency. It is testimony to the power of their line *and* actions that they were eventually successful after beginning with so few forces.

In retrospect, Liebknecht's greatest contribution to the movement was his recruitment in 1865 of the then twenty-four year old August Bebel to the Marxist tendency.[80] Working together they were largely responsible for constructing an alternative and rival to the ADAV which eventually lead to the formation in 1869 in the city of Eisenach of the Social Democratic Workers Party, or SDAP. It would take the Eisenachers, as they came to be known, some time, however, before they fully adopted a Marxist perspective. Partly for this reason and the fact that he represented the German workers' movement as a whole on the GC Marx was very circumspect in his dealings with both the ADAV—much to the distress of Liebknecht—and SDAP in relation to the International. When, for example, Schweitzer in 1868 opportunistically made overtures to Marx, the latter responded in a cordial but very principled manner. In a very didactic letter he offered a concise as well as insightful definition of a sect, which he accused Lassalle of founding. "The sect ["every sect is religious"] seeks its *raison d'être* and its *point d'honneur* not in what it has *in common* with the class movement, but in the *particular shibboleth distinguishing* it from that movement."[81] Lassalle's particular "shibboleth" or panacea was "state aid" for workers' cooperatives.

Criticizing, then, Schweitzer's recently published proposals for trade union organizing, Marx made one of his most compelling statements about the process of proletarian self-liberation.

> [A] *centralist* organisation, suitable as it is for secret societies and sect movements, contradicts the nature of the TRADE UNIONS. Were it possible—I declare it *tout bonnement* to be impossible—it would not be desirable, least of all in Germany. Here where the worker is regulated bureaucratically from childhood onwards, where he believes in authority, in those set over him, the main thing is *to teach him to walk by himself.*[82]

Very tactfully, Marx had followed Engels's suggestion that "you . . . find occasion to give Schweitzer a piece of your mind concerning his dictatorial ambitions. . . ."[83] Consistent with their long-held view that only the working class could liberate itself Marx sought—unsuccessfully, as he correctly anticipated—to impress upon Schweitzer the importance of workers having enough space to be trained for that process. Trade unions, while clearly not the instrument for proletarian revolution, could play, however, an important role in preparing workers for self-rule—that is, "trade unions as a school for socialism."[84]

In this context there was an important piece of advice that Marx offered to four Lassallean activists with whom he met during his visit to Germany in 1869. The meeting ended, as one of them reported, "with Marx stressing once more the need never to try to cling to individuals but bear in mind the cause, and draw conclusions to only promote it. 'Be it Liebknecht, be it Dr Schweitzer, or be it myself, always think about the cause,'"[85] Also, while in Germany Marx was visited by an emissary from Bismarck who tried, unsuccessfully of course, to bring him on board the latter's train.[86] Bismarck's earlier success in getting Lassalle's support—the rationale, in fact, for Marx's advice to the four Lassalleans—no doubt encouraged him to think he could do the same with Marx. When he realized later that with Marx it was indeed "the cause" that really mattered, Bismarck decided to use in place of the ineffective carrot the stick to attempt to limit his influence.

The increase in the International's prestige was decisive in inducing both the ADAV and SDAP to openly declare their allegiance to its program and, thus, a socialist perspective. This was vindication for Marx and Engels of their strategy of prioritizing in this period the building of the IWMA instead of the German section. It soon became clear, however, that the ADAV, especially because of Schweitzer's leadership, was not sincere in its declaration. It was no accident that Schweitzer found more in common with Bakunin's split operation than the IWMA's program. In their fight against Bakunin's connivance Marx and Engels openly, within the International at least, came out against Schweitzer and in support of Liebknecht and Bebel's SDAP. Their support for the latter, including its later evolution, became a public fact and continued for the rest of their lives, although, as will be seen, not uncritically.

With the outbreak of the Franco-Prussian War, Liebknecht and Bebel, as already noted, in one of the most noble chapters of the socialist workers' movement in Germany or anywhere, openly opposed, as Reichstag members and in the face of overwhelming public support for the war, Bismarck's imperialist ambitions. Their opposition became a pretext for Bismarck to crack down on socialists of all stripes as well as liberals. The persecution of both the ADAV and SDAP created the conditions for the unification of Germany's socialist movement, which took place at the now-famous congress in Gotha in 1875. Because the proposed program of unity was largely based on Lassallean nostrums both Marx and Engels subjected it beforehand to stinging criticisms, the most well-known of them being Marx's *Critique of the Gotha Program.*

In his critique, a letter to Bebel, Engels offered a useful insight on his and Marx's relationship with the SDAP that helps to frame their intervention.

People imagine that we run the whole show from here, whereas you know as well as I do that we have hardly ever interfered in the least with internal party affairs, and then only in an attempt to make good, as far as possible, what we considered to have been blunders—and *only theoretical* blunders at that.[87]

There were enormous "theoretical blunders" in the unity program, in their opinion, that violated the Eisenachers' own program. Two years earlier, as noted above, Engels, in specific reference to the International, had already made clear to Bebel why he and Marx held that programmatic integrity was a greater priority than unity when it came to politics. If there was insufficient support to advance the Eisenach program, then in place of the unity congress the leadership "should simply have come to an agreement about action [with the Lassalleans] against the common foe . . . a longish spell of common activity . . . [would have] prepared the ground" for meaningful and principled unity.[88] "Every step of real movement is more important than a dozen programmes."[89]

There was for the most part nothing in their critiques that was new or hadn't been stated before.[90] As Marx argued, "[T]he whole programme . . . is tainted through and through by the Lassallean sect's servile belief in the state . . ."[91]—the main reason for his earlier criticisms of Lassalle's views. Some of the formulations, it's true, were more concise and pointed. What was different this time is that the *Critique* was an explicit indictment of Lassalleanism in a statement to be circulated to the leadership of the Eisenachers. Previous critiques had been implicit, such as *The Prussian Military Question*, or confined to private correspondence.

While both had threatened beforehand to publicly "disassociate" themselves from the new party and its program, the German Socialist Workers' Party or SAPD, they in fact did not. As Engels explained to Bebel, contrary to their expectations the program did not prove to be an embarrassment to the Marx party.

> [T]he jackasses on the bourgeois papers have taken this programme perfectly seriously, reading into it what isn't there and interpreting it communistically. The workers are apparently doing the same. It is *this circumstance alone* which has made it possible for Marx and myself not to dissociate ourselves publicly from a programme such as this. So long as our opponents as well as the workers continue to read our views into that programme, we are justified in saying nothing about it.[92]

Under these circumstances, party programs, as they had already pointed out, were indeed not as important as the real movement. Engels later agreed with Bebel that the fusion should be seen as "an educational experiment,"[93] perhaps a necessary step in the real movement of forging a communist party. Such an outcome would depend on how the Eisenacher leadership conducted itself vis-à-vis the Lassalleans within the new organization. From this moment onward the Marx-Engels team looked to Bebel rather than Liebknecht to ensure that the "experiment" worked.

Because of their reservations about the fusion, Marx and Engels maintained a vigilant watch over the SAPD's development. Within a couple of years they detected the beginnings of what would later be called "reformism." To Sorge, Marx wrote:

In Germany a corrupt spirit is asserting itself in our party, not so much among the masses as among the leaders (upper class and "workers"). The compromise with the Lassalleans has led to further compromise with other waverers . . . not to mention a whole swarm of immature undergraduates and over-wise graduates who want to give socialism a "higher, idealistic" orientation, i.e. substitute for the materialist basis . . . a modern mythology with its goddesses of Justice, Liberty, Equality and *Fraternité*.[94]

It was precisely this tendency that Engels, with Marx's collaboration, would lead the charge against—one of the subjects of the next chapter.

The Russian Movement

When Marx and Engels determined in 1860 that a new revolutionary era had begun they pointed to the peasant movement then under way in Polish Russia—evidence that in the new era "the lava will flow from East to West." It took them, however (Marx specifically), about seven years to make direct contact with Russia's nascent revolutionary movement. In the meantime, and symptomatic of developments there, revolutionaries in Moscow took the initiative to have *Capital* published in Russian, its first translation into another language.

While conducting his political economy research Marx gained a better appreciation of Russia's importance, which spurred him in early 1870 to learn Russian. As Jenny described it, "he has begun studying Russian as if it were a matter of life and death."[95] After reading *The Condition of the Working Class in Russia* by N. Flerovsky, the Russian Narodnik socialist—a work that Marx described to Engels as "the most important book published since your work on the *Condition of the Working Class*,"[96]—"one feels deeply convinced that a most terrible social revolution . . . is irrepressible in Russia and near at hand. This is good news. Russia and England are the two great pillars of the present European system. All the rest is of secondary importance, even *la belle France et la savante Allemagne*."[97] Five years later Engels accurately foresaw that the social revolution in Russia—whose arrival clearly took longer than he expected—would "have inevitable repercussions on Germany."[98] From this point to the very end of their lives both Marx and Engels gave priority to developments in Russia, a fact that virtually every Marxological account ignores.

Owing in part to the enormous impact that *Capital* had in Russia—the Russian edition sold better than any other one—as well as his renown in connection with the IWMA, Marx was asked in March 1870 by a group of Russian émigrés in Geneva to represent them on the GC in the IWMA, thus beginning his formal links with the generation of Russian revolutionaries from whom would later emerge the leadership of the Russian revolution. In view of his and Engels's long-standing and well-known opposition to the Russian state, Marx found it ironic that he would "be functioning as the representative of *jeune Russie*! A man never knows what he may achieve, or what STRANGE FELLOWSHIP he may have to suffer."[99] As already noted, one of these young émigrés, Elisaveta Tomanovskaya, worked closely with Marx and Engels during the Commune. That these Russian youth adamantly opposed Bakunin no doubt helped to deconstruct the essentialist views—largely negative—

that Marx and Engels had long harbored about the "Russian race." Very soon Engels would say of these youth, "As far as talent and character are concerned, some of these are absolutely among the very best in our party." And in anticipation of a Lenin, "They have a stoicism, a strength of character and at the same time a grasp of theory which are truly admirable."[106]

The Geneva exiles wanted Marx to be their representative because "the practical character of the movement was so similar in Germany and Russia, [and] the writings of Marx were so generally known and appreciated by the Russian youth. . . ."[101] Although the standard charge is that Marx and Engels's perspective did not address the reality of underdeveloped settings such as Russia, radicalizing Russian youth in the 1870s didn't view it that way. It was for this reason that they sought out his views on the prospects and course of socialist revolution in their homeland. Specifically, would Russia have to undergo a prolonged stage of capitalist development or could it proceed directly to socialist transformation on the basis of communal property relations that prevailed in much of the countryside at that time?

Because of the socioeconomic changes that Russia was then undergoing, Marx was reluctant to make any categorical judgements. In a letter in 1877 that he never mailed to the editorial board of the publication of a group of Russian revolutionary democrats, he warned against turning in *Capital* his "historical sketch of the genesis of capitalism in Western Europe into a historical-philosophical theory of general development, imposed by fate on all peoples, whatever the historical circumstances in which they are placed. . . ."[102] What he was willing at that time to say about Russia, based on his intense study, was that if it "continues along the path it has followed since 1861, it will miss the finest chance that history has ever offered to a nation, only to undergo all the fatal vicissitudes of the capitalist system."[103]

When a related question was posed to him in 1881 by one of the founders of the Marx party in Russia, Vera Zasulich, specifically whether the Russian peasant commune could survive in the face of the ever-expanding capitalist mode of production, Marx was again cautious. In order for it to be saved and be the basis for socialist property relations "it would first be necessary to eliminate the deleterious influences which are assailing it from all sides . . . ,"[104] in other words, as one of the drafts of his letter put it, "To save the Russian commune, a Russian revolution is needed."[105] The drafts upon which this reply was based went into far greater detail on the peasant question and revealed how extensively he had been following developments in Russia.

While Marx was cautious about the question, Engels seemed to be more certain—at least in the context of a polemic with a Russian Blanquist who, in Engels's opinion, romanticized the peasant—that the commune would not survive capital's penetration into the countryside. As it turned out, it fell on Engels's shoulders to bring more clarity to this question, since in outliving Marx by twelve years he witnessed developments in Russia's countryside that Marx could only anticipate.

As for the politics and strategy of socialist revolution in Russia, it was Engels in the aforementioned polemic who first predicted what would be involved. Rejecting the Blanquist view that the Russian peasant was "instinctively revolutionary," he warned against "a premature attempt at insurrection" since "Russia undoubtedly is on the eve of a revolution." He provided a most accurate sketch of what would occur, not when he expected but three decades later.

[A] growing recognition among the enlightened strata of the nation concentrated in the capital that . . . a revolution is impending, and the illusion that it will be possible to guide this revolution among a smooth constitutional channel. Here all the conditions of a revolution are combined, of a revolution that, started by the upper classes of the capital, perhaps even by the government itself, must be rapidly carried further, beyond the first constitutional phase, by the peasants, of a revolution that will be of the greatest importance for the whole of Europe.[106]

Marx saw a similar scenario and when the Russo-Turkish War broke out in 1877 they both thought it would precipitate Russia's social revolution. Though this was not the case, they got, once again, the algebra if not the mathematics right since it was indeed a war, the Russo-Japanese War in 1905 that opened up the process that culminated in 1917.

In his polemic with the Blanquist, Engels made clear that in Russia's reality a revolution that began with a conspiracy was certainly justifiable. Never at anytime "in my political career [have I] declared that conspiracies were to be universally condemned in all circumstances."[107] Later, both he and Marx praised Russian revolutionaries such as Vera Zasulich who either carried out or attempted individual acts of terror against Russian rulers. "Against such wild animals one must defend oneself as one can, with powder and lead. Political assassination in Russia is the only means which men of intelligence, dignity and character possess to defend themselves against the agents of an unprecedented despotism."[108]

Both also held that the opening of the social revolution in Russia would spread westward, leading to "*radical change throughout Europe.*"[109] In fact, the "overthrow of Tsarist Russia . . . is . . . one of the first conditions of the German proletariat's ultimate triumph."[110] To J. P. Becker in 1882, Engels counselled that the formation of the next international should only be done when the moment was right.

[S]uch events are already taking shape in Russia where the avant-garde of the revolution will be going into battle. You should—or so we think—wait for this and its inevitable repercussions on Germany, and then the moment will also have come for a big manifesto and the establishment of an *official*, formal International, which can, however, no longer be a propaganda association but simply an association for action.[111]

This was most prophetic since it was indeed the Russian Revolution in 1917 that led to the formation in 1919 of the Third or Communist International which proudly proclaimed its adherence to the Marx program.

Finally, in the "Preface" to the second Russian edition of the *Manifesto* in 1882 they wrote that "Russia forms the vanguard of revolutionary action in Europe." As for the future of the peasant commune in Russia they provided their clearest answer yet: "If the Russian Revolution becomes the signal for a proletarian revolution in the West, so that the two complement each other, the present Russian common ownership of land may serve as the starting point for communist development."[112] To the end of his life, which was only fifteen months away, Marx continued to devote his attention to the peasant question in Russia—the question with which Lenin would begin his revolutionary studies.

A Fighter to the End

Prior to The Hague Congress, as already noted, Marx made clear that he wanted to pull back from active political work in order to return to the scientific work. And indeed to his death in 1883 Marx's public activities diminished considerably. There has been much Marxological speculation about his political inactivity in the last decade of his life. Hobsbawm, in particular, claims that " a mood of withdrawal and disappointment pervades the final years of Marx."[113] Certainly, the personal tragedies took their toll. His reaction to the death of a grandson in 1874, for example, is revealing about Marx the person.

> I am in this respect less stoical than in others and family afflictions always hit me hard. The more one lives, as I do, almost cut off from the outside world, the more one is entangled in the emotional life of one's own circle.[114]

No deaths hit him harder than those of his wife Jenny in December 1881, to be followed thirteen months later by his eldest daughter Jenny Longuet. Almost exactly two months later, March 14, 1883, Engels found Marx at home, as he wrote to Liebknecht, "sound asleep, but it was forever. . . . [A]ll I can say is that, in my opinion, the death, first of his wife, and then, in a most critical period, of Jenny, helped to bring on the final crisis."[115]

In addition to personal tragedies Marx was also burdened by deteriorating health in his last decade, which severely limited his literary output. In spite of both factors, however, it is simply not the case that this was a period of despondency for him. The fact is that to the extent his health allowed he maintained until the very end a rigorous regimen of study related to the completion of *Capital* and intervened on occasion, if not publicly, in the political arena.[116] While his own publications between 1874 and 1883 amounted to less than a tenth of what he had published in just the preceding three or four years, his notebooks indicate that he was doing extensive reading and research on mathematics, political economy, anthropology, colonial policies—with particular focus on India—U. S. developments, and, of course, the Russian rural question.

His occasional forays into politics included efforts to limit Lassalleanism—the *Critique of the Gotha Program* being the most memorable example—and reformism (to be discussed in the next chapter) in the German party. His continuing links with the French movement found him in 1876 and 1877 devoting a tremendous amount of time and energy in translating, with important emendations at his suggestion, Hippolyte Lissagaray's *History of the Commune*, the "best history" in his view of the Paris uprising. As part of his efforts to have it widely circulated, he suggested to leaders of the newly unified German party "that you undertake to bring out this work, which is of importance to our party . . . "[117]

In 1880 he and Engels helped to draft the electoral program of what in his opinion was the *first real workers' movement* in France."[118] In the preamble, which he wrote, Marx made perhaps his most succinct and popular rationale, from a communist perspective, for the participation of the workers' party in elections. He began with the premise "That the emancipation of the producing class ["or proletariat"] is that of all human beings without distinction of sex or race." Also, only on the basis of "collective ownership" of the means of production would liberation be assured. Such an "appropriation" required the "revolutionary action of the producing class . . . organized into an independent political party." To this end, "all of the means at the disposal of the proletariat, including universal suffrage" should be utilized. Taking part in the elections, he emphasized, was a *"means of organisation and struggle."*[119] As further assistance to the French party, Marx drew up a detailed questionnaire on the working conditions of urban and rural workers—the first such inquiry—that was widely distributed throughout France. These workers, the introduction of the questionnaire said, "understand that they alone can describe the hardships they endure with the full knowledge of the matter."[120]

Thirteen months before his death, in very poor health and on his way to Algeria to try to recuperate, Marx rendered his last assistance to the French party by reluctantly granting a meeting in Marseilles to Jules Guesde, a leader of the party and close contact of Marx and Engels. Under attack from opponents within the party, "it was important for him to have an 'official' meeting on my side. After all, one was bound to concede that much to the party."[121]

Finally, Marx intervened, largely through his old IWMA contact, Maltman Barry, in British politics on the occasion of the Russo-Turkish War in 1877. To ensure that Britain would not come to the Czar's assistance, whose overthrow Marx and Engels expected in the event of Russia's defeat, he worked actively "behind the scenes" to promote pro-Turkish sentiment amongst British workers.[122]

Compared to his political activism in the preceding period it is not incorrect to say that "withdrawal" from politics characterized the last decade of his life. To conclude as Hobsbawm does, however, that this reflected a "mood of withdrawal and disappointment" flies in the face of the known facts. His letter to daughter Jenny on the birth of his new grandson is telling about his mood in April 1881. While grandmother Jenny had hoped for a granddaughter, "I prefer the 'manly' sex for children born at this turning point of history. They have before them the most revolutionary period men had ever to pass through. The bad thing now is to be 'old' so as to be only able to foresee instead of seeing."[123] In this very confident view of the future—and indeed accurate one, as history would show—there is no hint of despondency but at most regret in not being able to be a participant. Even after the death of his wife Jenny, his old combative spirit, the inveterate fighter, came alive when his enemies had assumed that her death was occasion for his end.

> The vehemence with which the bourgeois papers in Germany have announced either my demise, or at any rate the inevitable imminence thereof, has tickled me hugely, and the "man at odds with the world" will have to get fit for action again, if only to oblige them.[124]

In his last extant letter to Engels, two months before he died and with his health failing, Marx, the optimist to the end, thought he could "get fit for action again": "I believe that, given patience and rigorous self-discipline, I shall soon get back onto the rails again."[125] The death of daughter Jenny a couple of days later proved to be too much to overcome.

What Hobsbawm and others who subscribe to the view that Marx was demoralized in his last years also ignore is the partnership with Engels. Because of their division of labor, Engels took on tasks that freed Marx up to spend most of his time on the political economy research. Marx could, in other words, withdraw from active politics in good conscience knowing full well that his partner would take up the slack.

Clearly, it was the Russian movement that he and Engels found most heartening. In an overview of the gains of their tendency in various countries, Marx told Sorge at the end of 1880 that "In Russia—where *Capital* is more widely read and acclaimed than anywhere else—our success is even greater."[126] His and Engels's optimism about the Russian movement never wavered. Three months before his death, he expressed his joy to his daughter Laura about the popularity of his ideas in Russia: "Nowhere my success is to me more delightful; it gives me the satisfaction that I damage a power, which besides England, is the true bulwark of the old society."[127] Upon hearing of Marx's death, students in St. Petersburg took up a collection which they sent to Engels to have a wreath placed on his grave—a small but not insignificant sign that his joy about Russia was not unwarranted.

CONCLUSION

At his funeral Engels had every right to declare that "Marx was before all else a revolutionist"—the note on which the first chapter of this volume began. The evidence presented since then leaves no doubt, as Engels continued, that "fighting was his element. And he fought with a passion, a tenacity and a success such as few could rival."

Engels went on to say that "[t]he crowning effort of this part of his work was the creation of the International Working Men's Association of which he was the acknowledged leader from 1864–72."[128] The evidence presented in this and the two preceding chapters substantiates this assessment. Subsequent developments, taken up in part in the next chapter, confirm even more the veracity of Engels's pronouncement on the place of the IWMA in Marx's legacy. Without the IWMA it is highly unlikely—to paraphrase one of his well-known quips—that the revolutionary seeds that Marx sowed would have germinated. His and Engels's constant insistence on independent working-class political action, the main lesson they drew from the 1848–1851 upheavals, was crucial in the later development of Europe's mass working-class parties. Regarding the first of these parties—which became a model for many others—Liebknecht, while speaking "as the representative of the *German Social-Democrats*" at the funeral, didn't exaggerate when he said, Marx was "*the* man who *created* our party, as much as one can speak of creating in this connection."[129]

In this sense, it is equally true that Marx was the founder of Russia's first workers' party, the body from which the leadership of the Revolution of 1917 emerged.

More than a year and a half after his death, with the benefit of more perspective, especially since for the first time in four decades he was without a revolutionary partner, Engels, in a letter to J. P. Becker, the oldest surviving member of their tendency, could be even more insightful about Marx, himself and the partnership.

> [M]y misfortune is that since we lost Marx I have been supposed to represent him. I have spent a lifetime doing what I was fitted for, namely playing second fiddle, and indeed I believe I acquitted myself reasonably well. And I was happy to have so splendid a first fiddle as Marx. But now that I am suddenly expected to take Marx's place in matters of theory and play first fiddle, there will inevitably be blunders and no one is more aware of that than I. And not until times get somewhat more turbulent shall we really be aware of what we have lost in Marx. Not one of us possesses the breath of vision that enabled him, at the very moment when rapid action was called for, invariably to hit upon the right solution and at once get to the heart of the matter. In more peaceful times it could happen that events proved me right and him wrong, but at a revolutionary juncture his judgement was virtually infallible.[130]

Thus, Engels paid Marx the supreme compliment to a revolutionary—one who knows "what is to be done." As for himself and whether his trepidations were warranted, only his play at "first fiddle" would provide the answer—the subject of the next chapter.

CHAPTER TEN

Engels and Revolutionary Continuity

In the service of the party I am always on call.

—Engels to Kugelmann

[R]equests for my assistance are still more frequent than I would wish in view of
my theoretical work. But if a man has been active in the movement for more than
fifty years, as I have been, he regards the work connected with it as a bounden duty
that brooks no delay.

—Engels, *Capital*, III

[T]he [German] party is going bourgeois. That is the misfortune of all extreme parties when the time approaches for them to become "possible."

—Engels to Paul Lafargue

[Without] the victory of the modern industrial proletariat [in the West] . . . Russia can never achieve a socialist transformation.

—Engels

With Marx's death it fell to Engels to carry out the perspective that he and Marx
adopted in the aftermath of the International, that is, priority for the scientific work.
To this end Engels devoted most of the last years of his life to the preparation for
publication of Marx's unfinished manuscripts of *Capital*. Because Marx suggested in
Volume I of *Capital* that the validity of his thesis would be fully realized with the
publication of the subsequent volumes, Engels understood that the integrity as well
as the prestige of the Marx party was at stake. Only in 1894, fifteen months before
his own death, did he complete the project. Owing to his tireless efforts the Marx-
Engels arsenal expanded beyond all that had been published while Marx was alive.
Of major importance for purposes here were the publications dealing with the
lessons of 1848–1849. Consistent, also, with the communist obligation to document the class struggle, Engels in the last months of his life made the initial steps to

prepare an edition of his and Marx's collected works, the necessary effort without which this book itself would have been impossible to write.

At the same time, political reality dictated that he provide leadership to pressing issues. Not the least of these were the varying fortunes of the German party, from its outlawing by Bismarck to its unbanning. The party's successes in the electoral arena, along with the reformist tendencies that these bred, occupied much of Engels's time. As had been the case with his now-deceased partner, Engels waged a life and death struggle for the programmatic integrity of scientific communism. Other national parties, those in France and the United States also required his attention. The Russian party, however, was especially important. Special attention was paid to it, which subsequent history would reveal was fully justified. Lastly, when it appeared that the time was ripe for a new international Engels took an active role in ensuring that it would build upon what he and Marx had been able to accomplish in the first International. In all of this Engels acquitted himself well at "first fiddle."

THE STRATEGY AND TACTICS OF PARTY BUILDING

At his death Marx was the acknowledged leader of the international socialist movement. His was the address to which socialists from every corner of the world wrote to for advice, although much of this correspondence was actually handled by Engels in the last year of Marx's life owing to his poor health. Along with the theoretical work, the other key task Engels set for himself was the maintenance of a center for the movement, which Marx's house had once served as. Explaining to Bebel why he needed to stay in London, "we wish to maintain intact, in so far as it is in my power, the many threads from all over the world which spontaneously converged upon Marx's study."[1]

The German Party and the Fight against Reformism

The skepticism with which Marx and Engels greeted the fusion between the Eisenachers and the Lassalleans at the Gotha congress in 1875 persisted. Two years later Marx told Engels that it had "degraded the party, both in theory and in practice."[2] With regard to theory he, as well as Engels, felt that the concessions that were made to Lassalleanism had undermined the progress that was registered by the formation of the Eisenach or SDAP in 1869. Marx, as already noted, attributed the watering down of their materialist perspective in part to the influx of young intellectuals into the ranks of the new SAPD. For this reason they seized on the opportunity, after requests from Liebknecht and other party leaders,[3] to take on Eugen Dühring, the Berlin academic whose ideas were attractive to a wing within the party. As Engels explained some years later, "it thus became necessary to take up the gauntlet thrown down to us, and to fight out the struggle whether we liked it or not."[4]

Against Herr Dühring. In claiming that he had created a comprehensive system to explain physical and social reality in its entirety Dühring also attacked Marx's views.

But as Engels alluded in a letter to Marx, the two did not have a system to explain all reality in all places at all times and certainly no blueprints for a socialist future.[5] This was exactly the aspect of Dühring's outlook that he attacked in what eventually came to be called *Anti-Dühring*. If it was true, as he argued in that work, that "eternal truths" were unlikely in the natural sciences, in the "historical group of sciences" this was even more the case.

> Anyone . . . who here sets out to hunt down final and ultimate truths, genuine, absolutely immutable truths, will bring home but little, apart from platitudes and commonplaces of the sorriest kind . . .[6]

For the intellectuals who were joining the party, and who in Marx's opinion were not willing to do the hard study that a materialist view required, Dühring offered the kind of ready-made answers that Marx and Engels refused to provide, hence his attractiveness.

Marx and Engels worked out together their plan of attack, which in the end was carried out by Engels. Marx opined that in order for Engels to undermine Dühring's supporters within the party he had to criticize him "without any compunction."[7] Half-jokingly, Engels replied: "It's all very well for you to talk. You can lie in a warm bed—study Russian agrarian relations in particular and rent in general without anything to interrupt you—but I have to sit on a hard bench, drink cold wine, and all of a sudden drop everything else and break a lance with the tedious Dühring. However, it can't be helped."[8]

Within two years, by 1878, Engels had produced not only a response to Dühring but as well the most comprehensive statement on their own outlook. While Engels wrote virtually all of *Anti-Dühring*, Marx wrote one chapter in the political economy section as well as being the sounding board for Engels's argument. A part of the work was published as a separate pamphlet, *Socialism: Utopian and Scientific*, and widely distributed. In the introduction to the French edition of the pamphlet Marx wrote, after "consultation . . . with Engels,"[9] that it "constitutes what might be termed an *introduction to scientific socialism.*" To the leadership of the SAPD Marx advised that "there's much to be learned from Engels's positive exposés, not only by ordinary workers" but even the intellectual element itself within the party.[10] To a British writer who was doing a survey of the socialist movement Marx sent a copy of the work because it was "very important for a true appreciation of German socialism."[11] Though firstly a serialized presentation in the party newspaper *Vorwärts*, then the pamphlet, and later the book itself, *Anti-Dühring* became perhaps the single most influential weapon in the Marx party arsenal for eventually winning the German party to a Marxist perspective. And, in the process "it finished, totally, the appeal of Dühring to German social democrats."[12]

The Circular Letter of 1879. Marx and Engels also fought for programmatic integrity in the new party. The first major test arose in the aftermath of Bismarck's Anti-Socialist Law, which banned the SADP and its press in 1878; an important exemption allowed the party to run candidates in elections and hold seats in the provincial and national Reichstags. An immediate issue that was posed by the law was how the editorial committee that would publish the new party organ, the *Sozialdemodrat*, in exile in Zurich, should function in relation to the rest of the party and its elected leadership. The broader political question was whether the party should accommodate itself to Bismarck's crackdown by adopting a more moderate posture or should maintain a revolutionary perspective.

When the proposed editorial committee in Zurich, which consisted of what Marx derisively called a "social-philanthropist" ("the first man to buy his way into the party")[13] and two adherents of Dühring, one of whom was the then-twenty-nine year old Eduard Bernstein, published an article that confirmed their worst fears, Marx and Engels reacted with a stinging denunciation. Their letter to Bebel and the rest of the party leadership, which has come to be known as the *Circular Letter*, ranks, as Draper correctly argues, in importance with the *Manifesto*, the *Address of March 1850*, the *Inaugural Address*, and the *Civil War in France*.[14]

There are two key themes in the document, which was written by Engels with Marx's collaboration. One, in opposition to Bernstein and the other authors of the article that Engels sardonically called the "Manifesto of the Zurich Trio," unequivocally reaffirmed the historic program of the communist party. In their "Manifesto" Bernstein and his cohorts had proposed that the SAPD abandon its proletarian orientation, make an appeal to both the petit bourgeoisie and the bourgeoisie, and adopt a posture that would be less threatening to the Bismarck regime. "If, Engels replied, they [the "trio"] think as they write, they ought to leave the party or at least resign from office [i.e., the editorial committee]. If they don't, it is tantamount to admitting that they intend to use their official position to combat the party's proletarian character. Hence the party is betraying itself if it allows them to remain in office."[15] Engels threw down the gauntlet because the clear implication of their position, as he bitingly and sarcastically put it, was:

> Therefore elect bourgeois!
> In short, the working class is incapable of emancipating itself by its own efforts. In order to do so it must place itself under the direction of "educated and propertied" bourgeois who alone have "the time and the opportunity" to become conversant with what is good for the workers. And, secondly, the bourgeois are not to be combatted—not on your life—but *won over* by vigorous propaganda.[16]

The goal of the "trio," as he adroitly and succinctly dissected their watered-down version of revolutionary politics, was "to relieve the bourgeois of the last trace of anxiety" by showing it "clearly and convincingly that the red spectre really is just a spectre and doesn't exist." But to shore up its left flank the "Manifesto" made clear that the party's "programme is not to be *relinquished*, but merely *postponed*—for some unspecified period." As he elaborated on what the "trio" wrote:

> They accept it [the "programme"]—not for themselves in their own lifetime but posthumously, as an heirloom for their children and their children's children. Meanwhile they devote their "whole strength and energies" to all sorts of trifles, tinkering away at the capitalist social order so that at least something should appear to be done without at the same time alarming the bourgeoisie.[17]

Engels's sarcasm resonates so well only because it derides an all too familiar political disposition. Precisely because "we are still only too familiar with all these catch-phrases of 1848," could Engels and Marx be so insightful about the "trio."

> These are the same people . . . whose fear of any kind of action in 1848 and '49 held back the movement at every step and finally brought about its downfall; the same people who never see reaction and then are dumbfounded to find themselves at last in a blind alley in which neither resistance nor flight is possible.[18]

Engels then showed how the *Manifesto* had foreseen this kind of development in the German movement and suggested what to do about it. Those who truly believe what the "Manifesto" put forward should form their own party, a "Social-Democratic petty-bourgeois party" separate and apart from a "Social-Democratic Workers' Party" with whom the latter "could negotiate . . . and, according to circumstances, form an alliance with. . . ."[19] Under no circumstances should they be permitted to be in the leadership of the SAPD and should "remain aware that a break with them is only a matter of time."

The other major issue that Engels addressed in the *Circular* concerned the behavior of the Reichstag Fraktion. Here Engels took up a problem that would bedevil many a twentieth-century workers' party wherever it had a parliamentary fraction, that is, how to make it accountable to the party as a whole. Engels, in opposition again to the Zurich "trio," came to the defense of a SAPD member who had publicly and sharply criticized the vote of a Fraktion member for one of Bismarck's capitalism-from-above ventures—a whiff of the "stench" left behind by Lassalle's support to Bismarckian "state socialism." Engels agreed that the vote had "infringed party discipline" and that the deputy deserved to be handled "roughly" since the SAPD's program had specifically opposed both indirect taxation (the means by which the venture would be financed) and the "first and fundamental rule of our party tactics: not a farthing for this government" (from the slogan that Liebknecht made famous in 1871, *"diesem system keinen Mann und keinen Groschen!"*—"for this system, not one man and not one penny!").[20] In a didactic letter to Bebel two months later, Engels made the point—consistent with his and Marx's fundamental views—that was often forgotten by many a "social-democrat" in the subsequent century, which warrants highlighting:

> Social-Democratic deputies must always uphold the vital principle of consenting to nothing that increases the power of the government vis-à-vis the people.[21]

However despicable the behavior of the deputy or the Fraktion as a whole the larger problem was the uproar amongst some of the party leadership, as reflected by the "trio," to the criticism.

> [H]as German Social-Democracy indeed been infected with the parliamentary disease, believing that, with the popular vote, the Holy Ghost is poured upon those elected, that meetings of the faction [Fraktion] are transformed into infallible councils and factional resolutions into sacrosanct dogma?[22]

To combat this "disease," which Marx and Engels first termed in 1849–1850 "parliamentary cretinism," the party norm that the parliamentary representatives were subordinate to the will of the party as a whole had to be upheld.

At the same time Engels recognized that the uproar over the criticism came primarily from those elements, such as the Zurichers, who wanted to make the SAPD less threatening to Bismarck. Their goal was to cast the party organ in a similar fashion. For a party that had been outlawed and had its press forced into exile it was inexcusable in Engels's view to be concerned about sounding too revolutionary. If anything, it had even more of a duty to hold the banner higher. Echoing the theme on which the *Manifesto* began and ended, the party was obligated to "openly proclaim for Europe's benefit the methods and aims of the German party."

Clearly, it was the issue of the composition of the editorial committee that most concerned Marx and Engels. In concluding the *Circular*, Engels warned that if the "trio" constituted the new committee, "then all we could do—much though we regret it—would be publicly to declare ourselves opposed to it and abandon the solidarity with which we have hitherto represented the German party abroad. But we hope it won't come to *that*."[23] In terms less diplomatic, Marx explained to Sorge a day later what was at stake.

> Engels has written a circular (letter) to Bebel, etc. (just for *private circulation* among the German leaders, of course), in which our point of view is plainly set forth. So the gentlemen are forewarned and, moreover, are well enough acquainted with us to know that this means bend or break! If they wish to compromise themselves, *tant pis!* In no circumstances shall we allow them to compromise *us*. . . . [T]hey are already so far infected with parliamentary cretinism as to believe themselves *above criticism* and to denounce criticism as a *crime de lèse majesté!*[24]

In effect, the *Circular* constitutes Marx and Engels's major programmatic statement against opportunism or what would later be called reformism or revisionism.[25] Perhaps it's no accident that one of the targets of their polemic, Bernstein, would some two decades later come to be called the father of revisionism.[26] No other joint document of Marx and Engels so clearly anticipated and critiqued the course of social democracy in the twentieth century.[27] Politically, it stands in direct descent from the *Manifesto* and the *1850 March Address*, further evidence for Lenin's thesis about the centrality of 1848–1849 in Marx and Engels's politics. That this letter only became public in its entirety for the first time in 1931, in a Stalinist publication, when it was then in Moscow's interest to expose the reformist character of social democracy, is also not fortuitous.

Marx and Engels's threat of "bend or break" to the leadership of the SAPD forced Bebel, accompanied by Bernstein, to travel to London to resolve their differences with the "old ones"—testimony to their influence and what was at stake. Although the matter was settled to the satisfaction of both parties, which eventually allowed Bernstein to become editor of the *Sozialdemokrat*, the subsequent history of the party and Bernstein himself revealed that the issue of reformism in the German party would continue to be a problem.[28]

Less it be construed that the "old ones" were unduly harsh with the German leadership, Marx's comment to Sorge a few months later about their intervention is instructive.

> [W]e have eschewed any kind of *public* intervention. It does not befit those who are peacefully—*comparativement parlant*—ensconced abroad to contribute to the gratification of government and bourgeoisie by doing anything to aggravate the position of those who are operating in the homeland under the most difficult circumstances and at considerable personal sacrifice.[29]

Neither did they view their efforts as an imposition of their views. Two years later Engels described to Bernstein their modus operandi vis-à-vis national sections: "[A]ny attempt to influence people against their will would only do us harm, destroy the old trust that dates from the International."[30]

This is perhaps the appropriate place to address the matter of Marx and Engels's relationship to the German party, specifically, their "membership." As discussed in chapter six, they had often spoken of their "party" in two senses, the broad historical communist tendency on the one hand, and the more narrow "Marx party" nucleus on the other. With the emergence of the IWMA in 1864 and, then later, the SAPD in 1875 and other national parties they had to be more precise and circumspect about their party affiliations. Engels made the clearest statement on this a few weeks before Marx's death. He objected to Bernstein's reference to him as "Comrade Engels" in the *Sozialdemokrat* because "comrade," he wrote, should only be employed "to *inform* the reader that the person concerned belongs to the party."

> [W]e here are not in fact "comrades" in the narrower sense of the term. We can hardly be said to belong to the German party any more than to the French, American or Russian. . . . We set no little store by this, our special position as representatives of *international* socialism.

Engels then made another crucial point. "But it also precludes us from belonging to one particular national party—so long, that is, as we are unable to return to Germany and participate immediately in the struggle there."[31] Active participation in the struggle, in other words, was a requirement of party membership—another concretization of the third thesis on Feuerbach. Engels's main point was that his and Marx's relations with the SAPD and the German movement in general were as "representatives of *international* socialism" and not as members of the German party. This was indeed the axis of his intervention into German affairs after Marx's death.

Parliamentary Cretinism and the Electoral Process. The belief that the legislative arena was the be all and end all of politics, "parliamentary cretinism," was a "disease" that Marx and Engels first diagnosed in the context of the 1848 events. Just as had been the case then, its reappearance three decades later in the SAPD could also be traced to illusions about the electoral process. When the German party made its first electoral gains in 1874 Engels warned that "it can hardly be doubted that measures to restrict the franchise will follow, though not for a year or two."[32] He was off by two years, since it was in 1878 that Bismarck, fearful of the SAPD's successes, had it banned. Exactly because he anticipated Bismarck's reaction he also warned that "we all know that, when it comes down to it, nothing can be achieved without force."[33]

Commenting on the Reichstag debate leading up to Bismarck's crackdown, Marx made a more general observation about force and the parliamentary road to social transformation.

> An historical development can remain "peaceful" only for so long as its progress is not forcibly obstructed by those wielding social power at the time. If in England, for instance, or the United States, the working class were to gain a majority in PAR-LIAMENT or CONGRESS, they could, by lawful means, rid themselves of such laws and institutions as impeded their development. . . . However, the "peaceful" move-ment might be transformed into a "forcible" one by resistance on the part of those interested in restoring the former state of affairs; if (as in the American Civil War and the French Revolution) they are put down by *force*, it is as rebels against "law-ful" force.[34]

If, even in the United States and England, there was some likelihood that the peace-ful road was ruled out—in his speech six years earlier after The Hague congress he appeared to be more certain about such an option in both countries[35]—then clearly it was unlikely in Bismarck's Germany. Its impending crackdown against the SAPD "is the necessary prelude to forcible revolutions."[36] Until the end of his life Engels waged an uphill battle within the German party against the "disease" to drive home this point.

Bismarck's ban of the SAPD gave—perhaps intentionally—its parliamentary Fraktion, which tended to be to the right of the membership, far more influence in the SAPD than before. While Engels had no objection to the Fraktion's taking the lead given the constraints of the ban on open party activities—it functioned, he told Karl Kautsky six months after the ban was lifted in 1890, as "a dictatorship which was necessary and excellently carried out"[37]—he held that "they can neither demand nor impose the implicit obedience [of the membership] that could be demanded by the former party leadership, *specifically* elected for the purpose. Least of all under present circumstances, without a press, without mass meetings."[38] In this, Engels was stating an essential principle later associated with democratic cen-tralist organizing, that centralism in action required full democracy in decision making. Because he had more faith in the party's ranks than its leadership he was especially concerned that they have sufficient freedom of action—an issue to be returned to shortly.

Engels also made it clear that elections were important but were not, under cap-italism at least, an end in themselves. One of the key political conclusions of his newly published *Origin of the Family, Private Property and State* book, which was reprinted as an excerpt in *Sozialdemokrat* in connection with the upcoming Reich-stag elections, was that "universal suffrage is the gauge of the maturity of the work-ing class. It cannot and never will be anything more in the present-day state; but that," he continued, "is sufficient. On the day the thermometer of universal suffrage registers boiling point among the workers, both they and the capitalists will know where they stand."[39]

Cognizant of Bismarck's censors, Engels could not be as forthright with his metaphor as he was eight years later when he made this very same point to Paul Lafargue, following electoral gains for the party in France, about the value of elections for the revolutionary process.

> Do you realize now what a splendid weapon you in France have had in your hands for forty years in universal suffrage; if only people knew how to use it! It's slower and more boring than the call to revolution, but it's ten times more sure, and what is even better, it indicates with the most perfect accuracy the day when a call to armed revolution has to be made; it's even ten to one that universal suffrage, intelligently used by the workers, will drive the rulers to overthrow legality, that is, to put us in the most favorable position to make the revolution.[40]

Engels, therefore, leaves no doubt, contrary to all of the social democratic efforts to make him a reformist, that elections under capitalism were only a means, a "gauge," the best in his opinion, to determine when to resort to armed struggle.[41] And this was a gauge to be employed not just in Bismarck's Germany.

This is the framework in which Engels's, as well as Marx's, pronouncements on elections and the use of force for socialist transformation must be understood. Regarding the successes of the SAPD in the 1884 elections, Engels told Bebel: "I am less concerned just now with the number of seats that will eventually be won . . . the main thing is the proof that the movement is marching ahead . . . [and] the way our workers have run the affair, the tenacity, determination and above all, humour with which they have captured position after position and set at naught all the dodges, threats and bullying on the part of the government and bourgeoisie."[42] In other words, the self-organization of the working class was the decisive gain. Or, to Sorge about the successes in the 1887 elections: "It is not at all a question of the number of seats, but solely of the statistical record of the irresistible growth of the party."[43]

And finally, the 1893 elections: "[T]he number of seats is a very secondary consideration. The principal one is the increase of votes . . . [especially in the] rural districts . . . without which we cannot expect to be victorious."[44] Although the Sozialdemokratische Partei Deutschlands or SPD, the new name the party adopted after the ban was lifted in 1890, didn't do as well in the runoff elections in terms of seats, Engels said, "I am prouder of the defeats than of the successes . . . [because] What we won we owe—for the first time—entirely to our own strength . . . [and not to] the help of the liberals and democrats."[45] All of these assessments only make sense when seen from the perspective of elections as a gauge for the best moment when to employ revolutionary force.

Engels, like Marx, was unequivocal on the necessity of force. To Bebel in 1884, when the prospects for lifting the ban against the SAPD seemed likely in return for its renunciation of violence, he counselled steadfastness on principles. "No party, unless it was lying, has ever denied the right to armed resistance *in certain circumstances*. None has ever been able to renounce that ultimate right."[46] To a co-thinker in Denmark in 1889, he wrote: "We are agreed on this: that the proletariat cannot conquer political power, the only door open to a new society, without violent revolution."[47] In his commentary on the party's new program in 1891, the so-called Erfurt Program, Engels argued that the reality of Germany "proves how totally mistaken is the belief that a . . . communist society, can be established in a cosy, peaceful way."[48] To an Italian critic in 1892 Engels replied publicly: "I have never said the socialist party [the SPD] will become the majority and then proceed to take power. On the contrary, I have expressly said," echoing his aforementioned comments to LaFargue, "that the odds are ten to one that our rulers, well before that point arrives, will use violence against us, and this would shift us from the terrain of majority to the terrain of revolution."[49]

Finally, there was Engels's angry reaction to the most famous bowdlerization in the history of the socialist movement, Liebknecht's cut and paste job in the party newspaper *Vorwärts* on his 1895 "Introduction" to Marx's *Class Struggles in France*. What Engels objected the most to about the fabrication, as he explained to Kautsky and Lafargue, was that it was done "in such a fashion that I appear as a peaceful worshiper of legality at any price" in order "to support the tactics of *peace at any price and of opposition to force and violence. . . .*"[50] Even the version that he approved for publication in the SPD's theoretical journal, *Neue Zeit*, after watering it down because of the leadership's fears about government reprisals, had a key paragraph removed. The unexpurgated text made clear that "street fighting" was still on the revolutionary agenda in most places, if not everywhere, but that it would "have to be undertaken with greater forces."[51] This was his last word on the matter, since he died five months later. Had Engels known beforehand that it would be on the expurgated version, which made him appear as an opponent of "street fighting," that subsequent generations of social democrats would be reared, he no doubt would have resisted their entreaties to tone it down.

Underlying Engels's position was a very fundamental principle that informed him and Marx even before they became conscious communists, that is, the importance of adequate preparatory time in order to take power under the best circumstances. Elections were the best measure of that moment because they revealed what the party's strengths were, its level of support and organization. This was the point he was getting at in an article in *Sozialdemokrat* shortly after the government's ban on the party had expired in September 1890, though in language more couched and less provocative. "The attempt must be made to get along with legal methods of struggle for the time being"—the qualifier at the end being crucial. Should the party, he asked, "build barricades" if the regime banned it again? "It will certainly not do its opponents this favour. It will be saved from this by the knowledge of its own position of strength, given it by every general election to the Reichstag. Twenty per cent of the votes cast is a very respectable figure, but this also means that the opponents together still have eighty per cent of the vote." But given the rate of the gains that the party was making in each election "it would be mad to attempt a putsch."[52]

While reformists have tried to use this statement to justify their politics, it's at best a very tortured reading of Engels, which flies in the face of his overall strategy as argued here. His other public and private pronouncements at the time make clear that his call for revolutionary restraint in the *Sozialdemokrat* was exactly that. Precisely because of the gains the party had just made, doubling its vote to 1.5 million from the 1887 election, he expected that Bismarck would take preemptive action. "No doubt they will be the first ones to fire. One fine day the German bourgeois and their government, tired of standing with their arms folded, witnessing the ever increasing advances of socialism, will resort to illegality and violence."[53] However, the regime should remember, he warned in the party press, that "at least one-half of the German socialists have passed through the army" and "amongst them too many who have learned to stand at order arms in a hail of bullets till the moment is ripe for attack."[54]

In letters to Paul and Laura Lafargue Engels revealed the strategy behind his warning—playing for time. In spite of Bismarck's expected actions,

> we must not let ourselves be smashed up before our time. So far we have but one soldier in 4 or 5 and, on a war footing, possibly 1 in 3. We are penetrating the countryside; the elections . . . have proved it. In 3–4 years we shall have the agricultural labourers and day-labourers, i.e. the most solid upholders of the status quo. . . . That is why we must come out for the time being for legal action and not react to the provocations which will be lavished upon us.[55]

Elections, therefore, were the means by which the party could garner the effective forces to successfully wage the violent struggle. And until the most propitious moment, revolutionary restraint. Of course, Engels recognized, consistent with his and Marx's earlier views, that while it would be a "great misfortune" if, because of, for example, a war with Russia, the party was "brought to power prematurely, still one must be armed for this eventuality. . . ."[56] Being "armed" meant above all having a leadership in place that understood what had to be done in such a scenario.

It might be noted that nowhere in this does Engels say anything about winning a majority of the electorate through the elections. The reason, as already suggested, is that he didn't expect the ruling class to allow the electoral process to go that far. Thus, what was crucial for success was winning not just a simple majority in elections but rather, effective supporters, those forces who were willing to vote with their feet to resist the regime and especially those who knew how to use arms. Participating in the electoral process made it possible to determine when the requisite number of such forces had been accumulated. Hence the reason why the conduct of the party's proletarian ranks in the process was more important for him than just the number of votes obtained or seats won. Engels was also aware that the electoral process itself was flawed. Given the constraints on universal suffrage, in that neither women nor anyone under twenty-five could vote, or the gross inequities in the apportionment of electoral districts, the elections were far from an accurate measure of majority sentiment. Lastly, by taking preemptive action, that is, overthrowing the electoral process, the regime would forfeit its claims to legality and thus strengthen the party politically in its use of force. The government then, to employ the above-cited point that Marx made, would be acting as "rebels against 'lawful' force," meaning the majority.

In conclusion, Engels's approach to the electoral process, as a gauge to determine the most propitious moment to use revolutionary force, challenges the claim of twentieth-century Social Democracy that its current is more faithful than any other to Marx and Engels's political legacy. This is especially true when their electoral strategy is coupled with the main lesson that he and Marx drew from the experience of the Paris Commune—that "the working class cannot simply lay hold of the ready-made State machinery, and wield it for its own purposes."

The Lessons of 1848. Since the disease of parliamentary cretinism had first been diagnosed in the context of the 1848 upheavals, Engels thought it important to resurrect the lessons of that momentous period. In the aftermath of Marx's death, when requests came to him to either reprint or write new pieces about his deceased comrade, he seized on the opportunity, not surprisingly, to make political points about the contemporary reality on the basis of those lessons. Among the most important of these writings were his articles "Marx and the *Neue Rheinische Zeitung*" and his "Preface" and introduction, "On the History of the Communist League," to a new edition of Marx's 1853 pamphlet *Revelations Concerning the Communist Trial in Cologne.*

To be fully appreciated Engels's articles must be read in the context of the political situation in Germany that we've been discussing. In *Marx and the NRZ* he affirmed the continuing relevancy of the *Manifesto.*

> Never has a tactical programme proved its worth as well as this one . . . whenever, since [1848] . . . a workers' party has deviated from it, the deviation has met its punishment; and today, after almost forty years, it serves as the guiding line of all resolute and self-confident workers' parties in Europe, from Madrid to St. Petersburg.[57]

Then a discussion of one of the key lessons of 1848.

> [W]e everywhere opposed the democratic petty bourgeoisie as well when it tried to gloss over its class antagonism to the proletariat with the favourite phrase: after all, we all want the same thing; all the differences rest on mere misunderstandings. But the less we allowed the petty bourgeoisie to misunderstand our proletarian democracy, the tamer and more amenable it became towards us. The more sharply and resolutely one opposes it, the more readily it ducks and the more concessions it makes to the workers' party. We have seen this for ourselves.[58]

It's no surprise that Engels wanted the *March 1850 Address* reprinted the next year, since this was exactly one of its central messages. In "On the History of the Communist League" he was explicit in his endorsement of the *Address* which

> . . . is still of interest today, because petty-bourgeois democracy is even now the party which must certainly be the first to take the helm in Germany as the saviour of society from the communist workers on the occasion of the next European upheaval now soon due. . . . Much of what is said there is, therefore, still applicable today.[59]

Lastly, the "Preface" to the reprint of Marx's pamphlet about the Cologne trial was even more insistent on the links between 1848 and 1885. The reasons he thought that its reappearance would be useful were that it would "once again show the old Lassalleans that something was already afoot in Germany before the great Ferdinand's time and, for another, the proceedings of the Prussians did, in fact, even then set the pattern for what the Anti-Socialist Law [the law banning the SAPD that was then in effect] has now made the norm."[60] Regarding the latter point, he explained the significance of Marx's 1849 speech before the Cologne jury.

> [Made] in the face of the government's hypocritical legality it preserves a revolutionary standpoint from which many could take an example even today.—Did we call on the people to take up arms against the government? Indeed we did, and it was our duty to do so. Did we break the law and depart from the foundations of law? Very well, but the laws we broke had already been torn up by the government and trampled upon before the eyes of the people.[61]

Although this was written in 1885 when the ban against the SAPD was still in effect, Engels did not for a minute think that by unbanning the party the regime would achieve any modicum of legality.

The lessons of 1848 were also critical in countering one of the legacies of Lassalleanism, the slogan that was embedded in one of the planks of the party program adopted at the 1875 Gotha unity congress. Specifically, the plank stated: "The emancipation of labor must be the work of the working class, in contrast to which all other classes are but one reactionary class." It was the second clause that Marx objected to in his *Critique* because it simply flew in the face of the real movement of history. That is, under varying situations other classes beside the proletariat could indeed play a progressive role and thus did not in fact constitute "one reactionary class."

When Kautsky kept the phrase in the draft of the Erfurt program in 1891 Engels reacted quickly and successfully to convince him otherwise.[62] It was in fact because of his campaign to eliminate the "stench of Lassalleanism" in the party that he went public for the first time, prior to the congress where the new program would be discussed and much to the consternation of the party leadership, with Marx's *Critique*. In a most didactic letter to Kautsky in 1891 Engels explained that the main problem with the phrase, in addition to what Marx had stated, was that it telescoped the revolutionary process instead of seeing it as a prolonged endeavor. His as well as Marx's constant refrain, based on the lessons of 1848 and other revolutions, particularly the French Revolution, and codified in the *1850 March Address*, had been that the process essentially involved the succession of extreme parties over a period of time.

Engels's letter to Bernstein in 1883 was most explicit on this point.

> [There is] an idea, related to that of one reactionary mass, namely that, with the subversion of the present state of affairs, we shall come to the helm. That is nonsense. A revolution is a lengthy process, cf. 1642–46 and 1789–93, and in order that circumstances should be ready for us and we all for them, all the intermediate parties must come to power in turn and destroy themselves. And then we shall come—and may, perhaps, once more be momentarily routed.[63]

Related to this reality and most important was the fact that the communist workers, who were a minority, would have to ally with other classes, especially the peasantry—the people's alliance—in order to take power. To view everyone other than the proletariat as "one reactionary class" was an obstacle to this alliance. To Kautsky in 1891, he wrote: "So long as we are not strong enough to seize the helm of state ourselves and realise our principles there can be no talk, strictly speaking, of *one* reactionary mass *vis-à-vis us*. Otherwise the whole nation would be divided into a reactionary majority and an impotent minority."[64]

In his above-cited letter to the Danish co-thinker in 1889, Engels reiterated the criteria that he and Marx had long employed in deciding to enter into alliances with other parties:

> [O]nly if the advantage to us [the communist party] is direct or if the historical development of the country in the direction of the economic and political revolution is indisputable and worth while; and provided that the proletarian class character of the Party is not jeopardised thereby. For me this is the absolute limit. You can find this policy set forth as early as 1847 [sic] in the *Communist Manifesto*; we pursued it in 1848, in the International, everywhere . . .[65]

The revolutionary process of 1848 had also taught that alliances with the petit bourgeoisie and reformists should not be confused with membership with them in the same party. The lesson of their vacillating behavior throughout those events was that they should be treated warily. This is why he and Marx proposed in the *Circular Letter of 1879* that that wing of the party, its right wing, leave and form its own organization with which the then SAPD could enter into alliances as the need arose. However, in the aftermath of Bismarck's Anti-Socialist law, constituting the ban, when the Fraktion, which was where this current had its headquarters, gained disproportionate influence in the party, Engels felt it would be tactically unwise to force such a split. His reasons testify to his political acumen.

> These people *live* off the Anti-Socialist Law. Were there to be free discussion tomorrow, I should be all for letting fly at once, in which case they would soon come to grief. But so long as there is no free discussion, so long as they control all the papers printed in Germany and their numbers (as the majority of the "leaders") enable them to make the very most of gossip, intrigue, whispering campaigns, *we*, I believe, must steer clear of anything that might lead to a breach, or rather might lay the *blame* for that breach at our door. That is the universal rule when there is a struggle within one's own party, and now it applies more than ever. The breach must be so contrived that we continue to lead the old party while they either resign or are chucked out.[66]

To fully understand Engels's tactics, it can't be emphasized enough that in his struggle against the reformists Engels kept his eyes on the SAPD's proletarian ranks, the audience he felt that, if given the opportunity to participate in real and open debate, would be won to communist politics. Thus the importance of internal party democracy, which under the ban was not fully possible.

Once, however, the ban was lifted in 1890 Engels was insistent on greater democratic functioning within the party. Hence his letter to Kautsky six months

later demanding that the ranks had " 'to finally stop eternally treating the party officials, their own servants, with kid gloves, and stop standing before them, as before
infallible bureaucrats, so very obediently instead of critically.'"[67] This may have been
the first usage of language that called attention to a phenomenon that would
increasingly afflict not only the German party but other workers' parties—bureaucratization. More than a year later he criticized a related trend in the party, what he
termed the "statification" of the party press. He was referring to the recent congress
decision to subject all party newspapers to the control of the national leadership,
which he felt would undermine the press' ability to be critical. "The party is too
large for rigid discipline; the first need is for a 'formally independent party press.'"[68]
What the sociologist Robert Michels, a one-time SPD member, later termed the
"iron law of oligarchy" (a play on Lassalle's famous formulation) within the German
party, Engels as early as 1890 sought to combat.

Engels offered a sociological explanation for the reformist current within the
German party. As noted before both he and Marx looked askance upon the increasing number of petit-bourgeois and "eddicated" (intellectuals) elements within the
party in the aftermath of the Gotha unity congress. Nine years later Engels, in an
educational comment meant for Paul Lafargue, could be more specific about the
petit bourgeoisie's impact and why they should be kept at arm's length.

> [T]hey bring their narrow class prejudices along with them. In Germany we have
> too many of them, and it is they who form the dead weight which trammels the
> march of the party. It will ever be the lot of the petty bourgeoisie—as a mass—to
> float undecidedly between the two great classes, one part to be crushed by the cen-
> tralisation of capital, the other by the victory of the proletariat. On the decisive day,
> they will as usual be tottering, wavering and helpless . . . and that is all we want.
> Even if they come round to our views they will say: of course communism is the
> ultimate solution, but it is far off, maybe 100 years before it can be realised—in
> other words: we do not mean to work for its realisation neither in our, nor in our
> children's lifetime. Such is our experience in Germany.[69]

Few portraits of the petit bourgeoisie in the Marx-Engels arsenal can rival this one
in both its brevity and insight. The implicit political conclusion, which Engels
alluded to in his *Marx and the NRZ* article, was that the direction in which this class
wavered depended on the resoluteness of the proletarian party. The latter, therefore,
should never bend to these inveterate totterers.

The "eddicated" elements in the party, which he feared would increase with the
lifting of the ban in 1890, presented a somewhat different problem. This was especially true with a current that emerged in the party in the late eighties, known as the
Jungen, or "Youth" tendency, which opposed what it called "the success-hungry parliamentary tendency among the present-day Social Democrats." While at first glance
Engels should have welcomed this development he in fact rejected their overtures to
bloc with them. He did so because he saw in them the same elitist attitude toward
the proletarian ranks of the party that he and Marx had long ago condemned in the
Young Hegelians.

Whatever opinions Engels may have shared with the tendency about the parliamentarians—their critique, in his view, ignored the broader political context, especially, no doubt, the ban, and amounted to no more than "simple trifles"—was overshadowed by their elitist assumptions. In rebuking them he gave the *Jungen* a lesson on how intellectuals should conduct themselves in the workers' party:

> May they come to realise that their "academic education" . . . does not provide them with an officer's commission and a claim to a corresponding post in the party; that in our party everybody must work his way up; that positions of trust in the party are not won simply through literary talent and theoretical knowledge even if both are undoubtedly present, but that this also demands familiarity with the conditions of party struggle and adjustment to its forms, proven personal reliability and constancy of character and, finally, a willingness to join the ranks of the fighters—in short, that they, the "academically educated" all in all have much more to learn from the workers than the workers from them.[70]

Engels's retort was basically and profoundly a concretization of Marx's third thesis on Feuerbach, about the education of the educator, drawing on the four subsequent decades of political and party experience that he and Marx had been through.

While the *Jungen* represented a leftist, or perhaps more correctly, an ultraleft current in the SAPD, Engels understood all too well that they shared a fundamental trait with the petit-bourgeois Reichstag Fraktion that they were so critical of—the belief that not only did they know what was best for the proletariat but that only they should be entrusted with its implementation.[71] This did not exhaust Engels's explanation of the emergence of the reformist tendency within the German party. A few years later he offered, to be discussed shortly, an additional reason. It was, by the way, in his rejection of the *Jungen*, that Engels repeated, at least twice, Marx's oft-quoted—almost always decontextualized and misinterpreted—quip about "Marxism." "Marx foresaw such disciples when he had this to say at the end of the seventies about the 'Marxism' raging among certain Frenchmen . . . 'I know only this, that *I* am not a 'Marxist.'"[72]

Finally, that Marx and Engels were adamant opponents of the parliamentary disease did not in the least mean that they ignored forms of democratic governance. To the contrary, and hence Engels's rebuttal in 1892 to an Italian critic who made such an allegation: "Marx and I, for forty years, repeated ad nauseam that for us the democratic republic is the only political form in which the struggle between the working class and the capitalist class can first be universalised and then culminate in the decisive victory of the proletariat."[73] He said as much six months earlier in his critique of the draft program for the Erfurt congress: "If one thing is certain it is that our party and the working class can only come to power under the form of a democratic republic."[74] In fact, his main criticism of the draft document was that it failed to make an explicit call for a democratic republic. If the party leadership was afraid that such a call would provoke the government—which, as he pointedly noted, spoke volumes about the existing political reality in Germany and confirmed his argument about the unlikelihood of peaceful change—then, "What . . . in my opinion should and could be included is the demand for *the concentration of all political power in the hands of the people's representatives.*" In proposing this formulation as a substitute Engels suggests what for him was the content of the democratic republic. It should be kept in mind that Marx and Engels understood that parliamentary government was only one species of representative government. Engels's proposal is helpful because it points to the critical distinction he and Marx made between the form and content of governance. So too is his most instructive criticism in 1884 of Bernstein's invocation in an article of the "concept of democracy."

> That concept changes according to the *demos* and hence does not get us one step further. What in my view should have been said is this: For the seizure of political power, democratic *forms* are also necessary to the proletariat for whom, however, like all political forms, they are only a means. But if, today, you want democracy as an *end*, you have to look for support to the peasants and petty bourgeoisie, i.e. to classes which are in decline and which, from the moment they try to preserve their existence by factitious means, are *reactionary* in their relations with the proletariat. Another thing that should not be forgotten is that the *logical* form of bourgeois rule is, precisely, a democratic republic which, however, has become too much of a risk only because of the progress already made by the proletariat, but which, as France and America go to show, is still feasible simply as bourgeois rule.[75]

Not only does Engels clarify the difference between the substance and form of democracy—the all too important question of who constitutes the "people" is the heart of the matter—but as well outlines his and Marx's long-held political strategy for converting form into substance.

Of even greater value, because it anticipated an issue that would trip up many a would-be revolutionary in the following century, is his letter in 1894 to Paul Lafargue sixteen months before his death. Specifically, he criticized the view of a current within the French party that confused the substance of republican government with its form. They were under the illusion, in his opinion, that because "we have a republic in France . . . we can use the government to introduce socialist measures!" He then began his educational.

> A republic, in relation to the proletariat, differs from a monarchy only in that it is the *ready-made* political form for the future rule of the proletariat. You [in France] have the advantage of us in that it is already in being; we, for our part, shall have to waste 24 hours creating it. But a republic, like any other form of government, is determined by what composes it; so long as it is the form of *bourgeois* rule, it is quite as hostile to us as any monarchy whatsoever (save in the *forms* of that hostility). Hence it is a gratuitous illusion to treat it as an essentially socialist form; to entrust it, whilst it is dominated by the bourgeoisie, with socialist tasks. We can wring concessions from it, but never look to it to carry out our job. Even if we were able to control it by a minority so strong that it could become a majority from one day to the next.[76]

In no uncertain terms Engels took to task the illusion that the bourgeois-dominated state could be expected to carry out "socialist tasks," an assumption, however, that many a Social Democratic and Stalinist party in the twentieth century came to hold. Little wonder that this most prescient letter is almost never cited.

There is also the intriguing suggestion in his letter that new forms of rule could be expected to emerge with socialist revolutions. Whether the soviets that emerged in the Russian revolution constituted such an innovation is of course a subject that must be reserved for another volume. The main point, however, is that the Marx-Engels team took seriously forms of governance, particularly, in order not to confuse substance with forms.

The Peasant Question. A widely-held myth, which this book has also challenged, is that Marx and Engels either ignored or dismissed the peasantry. Not surprisingly then, Engels continued to underscore the importance of the peasant question until the very end. This was reflected in his republication and writing priorities. Although he was unable, as intended, to do a major revision of his *Peasant Wars in Germany*, he did write an important piece at the end of 1882 entitled *The Mark*, on the history of rural property relations in Germany. *"Very good!"* was Marx's reaction to Engels's manuscript, the last one he would ever read. Appended to subsequent editions of his very popular pamphlet, *Socialism: Scientific and Utopian*, its purpose was made clear in the first paragraph.

> [I]t is necessary that socialist working-men, and through them the peasants, should learn how the present system of landed property, large as well as small, has arisen. It is necessary to contrast the misery of the agricultural labourers of the present time and the mortgage-servitude of the small peasants, with the old common property of all free men in what was then in truth their "fatherland," the free common possession of all by inheritance.

In the context of Bismarck's escalating national chauvinist campaign, it was crucial that the workers' movement not concede the rural areas to him. Engels concluded his article with an appeal to the peasantry to consider the socialist alternative. Since German peasants, like all of Europe's peasantry, were faced with further decline—as a result mainly of "American competition"—"the restoration of a free peasant class, starved and stunted as it is, has this value,—that it has put the peasant in a position, with the aid of his natural comrade, the worker, to help himself, as soon as he once understands *how.* . . . Think well on it, German peasants. Only the *Social-Democrats* can help you."[77] Engels provided a sketch of the "how" that he would eventually elaborate on—to be discussed shortly. Four years later Engels followed up *The Mark* by republishing, with an introduction he wrote, Wilhelm Wolff's very influential 1849 *NRZ* articles, *The Silesian Billion*, which explained how the Junker class enriched itself at the expense of the peasantry through the redemption of feudal dues (see chapter four); again, the continuing relevancy of the lessons of 1848.

One of the features of the parliamentary disease, as Engels analyzed it in his critique of the Erfurt draft program, was the tendency of "striving for the success of the moment" at the expense of the "future of the movement," that is, "opportunism." In the electoral arena this translated into the disease of "vote-catching." It was exactly this secondary affliction, specifically, the "striving" by reformist forces in both the German and French parties to win the peasant vote at the expense of principles that convinced Engels to write in 1894, seven months before his death, what came to constitute the Marx party's most comprehensive programmatic statement on the peasant question.

For the most part there is nothing in *The Peasant Question in France and Germany* that either Marx or Engels hadn't said before. Marx's first draft of the *Civil War in France* (see chapter eight) and marginal notes to Bakunin's book *Statehood and Anarchy*[78] in 1874 clearly anticipate much of what Engels wrote. Its value of course, just as Engels intended, was that it made their views public for the first time in a comprehensive document. Specifically, it put forward a perspective on how socialist workers could win over the peasantry, in order to realize the worker-peasant alliance. Of the various rural social layers, it was the small peasants who constituted the swing vote on the socialist revolution, the segment to which he devoted most of his attention. Firstly, the party shouldn't offer any false hopes and had to candidly state and explain to them that under capitalism

> we foresee the inevitable doom of the small peasant but that it is not our mission to hasten it by any interference on our part.
>
> Secondly, it is just as evident that when we are in possession of state power we shall not even think of forcibly expropriating the small peasants (whether with or without compensation) as we shall have to do in the case of the big landowners. Our task relative to the small peasant consists, in the first place, in effecting a transition of his private undertaking, private property to a co-operative one, not forcibly but by dint of example and the proffer of social assistance for this purpose.[79]

Contrary then to all of the forcible expropriations of small peasants carried out in the name of Marxism in the twentieth century, none had any affinity with what Marx and Engels advocated. This would also apply, as Engels makes clear, to what he calls middle peasants. The justification for the expropriation of the large estates was the exploitation of the rural proletariat employed on them. Yet, "we by no means consider compensation as impermissible in any event; Marx told me (and how many times!) that in his opinion we would get off cheapest if we could buy out the whole lot of them."[80] It should be kept in mind that Engels wrote this with France and Germany in mind; he and Marx always contextualized their programmatic discussions based on the reality of the particular setting.[81]

Commenting on that wing of the SPD, led by Georg Vollmar, that wanted to catch the peasant vote at the expense of programmatic integrity Engels told Paul Lafargue:

> You will have seen in *Vorwärts* [the official organ of the SPD] Bebel's speech in the 2nd electoral constituency of Berlin. He complains with reason that the party is going bourgeois. That is the misfortune of all extreme parties when the time approaches for them to become "possible."[82]

Not surprisingly, it was Bebel who complained about the reformist direction of the party, an assessment with which Engels agreed. Of all the SPD leaders, including

Kautsky, as well as party leaders anywhere in the world, it was Bebel for whom Engels had the highest regard. To his old comrade J. P. Becker he wrote in 1884: "There is no more lucid mind in the whole of the German party, besides which he is utterly dependable and firm of purpose."[83] Or, to Sorge a few months later: "Luckily we have Bebel [in Germany] who invariably gets hold of the right end of the stick. . . . Ever since I have conducted the 'official' correspondence with Bebel instead of with Liebknecht, not only does all go smoothly, but something actually comes of it, and my views are presented to the chaps in their entirety."[84] His confidence in him explains why the Engels-Bebel correspondence, in terms of party strategy and tactics, is perhaps the richest in the Marx party arsenal after that of Marx and Engels themselves. As his comment to Sorge indicates, Liebknecht's stock with Engels plummeted as Bebel's rose. This remained the case until the end.

The reformist trend that Bebel called attention to was one that both Marx and Engels had earlier diagnosed, what Engels later called "opportunism." Engels's hope was that principled political differences would provoke the right wing into a split after the ban was lifted in 1890. Hence the necessity of programmatic integrity. As for Bebel's prognosis about the SPD, Engels responded that "our Party cannot go beyond a certain limit in this respect without betraying itself. . . ."[85] Only hindsight would reveal that, contrary to what Engels thought, the "bourgeois" trend had indeed gone "beyond a certain limit." The parliamentary disease had metastasized into a cancer within the SPD. The campaign for catching the peasant vote signalled the beginning of revisionism in the German party. Vollmar was its political leader and Bernstein, not long afterwards, became its theoretician. The consequences were devastating. Revisionism enabled the imperialist yearnings of Germany's bourgeoisie, leading to the bloodbath of World War I—which Engels, as will be seen shortly, foresaw. The SPD was the only organized political force that could have halted this development. As Engels understood all too well, and as demonstrated by his actions, there was nothing inevitable about this outcome.

Party Building in Other Countries

At the end of 1894, Engels described his busy schedule to Laura Lafargue, Marx's second daughter and wife of Paul Lafargue, which included his reading regimen:

> I have to follow the movement in five large and a lot of small European countries and the U.S. America. For that purpose I receive 3 German, 2 English, 1 Italian *dailies* and from Jan. 1, the Vienna daily, 7 in all. Of *weeklies* I receive 2 from Germany, 7 Austria, 1 France, 3 America (2 English, 1 German, 2 Italian, and 1 each in Polish, Bulgarian, Spanish and Bohemian, three of which in languages I am still gradually acquiring.[86]

Engels's need to stay on top of developments in the real movement, especially in locations where the Marx party had a base, was very much due to the many requests for advice from around the world that poured into his study. Since it's impossible here to do justice to the myriad aspects of Engels's party-building efforts, the focus here in only on what he saw as the key issues in some of these countries. This allows us to see also how he adjusted strategy and tactics for the particular setting.

The fight against opportunism and reformism in the German party had its counterpart in France and much of his advice for the former was also meant for the latter (in particular *The Peasant Question in France and Germany*). The program that Marx and Engels drafted for the Workers Party in France in 1880 (see previous chapter), and adopted by it that same year, became increasingly distasteful to its right wing. Within a couple of years it split and formed an organization based on what it called *"politiques des possibilités,"* that is, feasible politics. The Possibilists, he insisted, were certainly not a workers' party and at best the "embryo" for the future *"tail of the radical bourgeoisie."* His doubts about its long-term success were confirmed within a decade.

As had been true on two previous crisis-ridden moments in France's history, a "Man on Horseback" appeared at the end of the 1880s. This time he would, for the price of the republic, recover the nation's dignity by putting an end to corruption and parliamentary gridlock, and return Alsace-Lorraine, which had been acquired by Germany in the Franco-Prussian War, to its rightful owner. This most recent reincarnation of Bonapartism, whose siren call had an eerily modern ring, General Boulanger, a former Minister of War, posed a real challenge to the Workers' Party, as Engels clearly recognized.

Engels had to first convince the party, particularly Lafargue, that the threat of a Boulanger dictatorship via either elections or a coup d'état was serious and, if successful, would be a major set back for the cause. He would "do away with parliamentarism, purge the judges under the pretext of corruption, establish a strong-fisted government and a mock parliament, and crush Marxists, Blanquists and Possibilists all together. And then, ma belle France—you'll have got what you asked for."[87] Communists, then, could not be indifferent to threats to bourgeois democracy.

While, as discussed earlier in this chapter, Engels stressed that communists should entertain no illusions about the bourgeois republic, the defense of bourgeois democracy was very much in the interests of the workers' movement. If Boulanger were to be defeated, "the liberties conquered by the Socialists would not only be maintained but gradually extended, so that our Party would be in a better position for fighting its way than anywhere else on the Continent.[88] What Engels sought most was to get Lafargue to see that the alternatives before France's workers were not, as Boulanger and the Radicals (France's liberal party) framed the debate, between "Bonapartism" and "parliamentarism." He understood all too well the ineffectiveness of the liberal alternative, namely more parliamentarism—the phenomenon that was driving the lower classes into the arms of Boulanger. The "third" alternative was the basic plank in the communist program—independent working-class political action. The Workers' Party, he advised, should use its election campaigns to this end. Elections could also be used to demand the arming of the people, the "only guarantee against Caesaristic velleities on the part of popular generals." Again, a few months later: "The Republic will always be in danger so long as the soldier has a rifle and the worker has none."[89] In effect, Engels provided the first Marxist lesson, all but ignored by the Marxological fraternity, on how to combat what in hindsight was the prototypical expression of a phenomenon that would rear its ugly head in the twentieth century in a much more advanced and virulent form—fascism.[90]

It was largely through his correspondence with Laura and Paul Lafargue that Engels conducted his campaign. In the process he became even better acquainted with Laura's political acumen, which he soon recognized was superior to that of her husband. "I really think you are about the only person who can keep his or her head above water and clear in Paris" he told her at the beginning of 1890.[91] Partly for that reason, in a letter meant for both their eyes, he urged Laura to become a member of the editorial board of the party's newly founded paper in 1892.

> Now my dear Löhr [Laura's nickname] a few words with you. In that new daily paper you are an absolutely necessary factor. . . . [W]hat I want to drive into you, poking your ribs with both my forefingers, is that you must be a regular member of the rédaction and paid accordingly. Paul is too much an hidalgo [gentleman] to think of, or to press, such matters, but "it mun be done" as they say in Lancashire, and I think it is my duty to call your and Paul's attention to it. The subject is too important to be neglected . . .[92]

For the sake of the party they *both* had to put aside any late-nineteenth-century sensibilities they might have held about her, as Paul's wife, being on the editorial board. A small but not insignificant example of Engels's intervention in a national party to advance the interests of the movement as a whole.

Commenting on the so-called "Marxist" party in England at the end of 1894, Engels wrote to Sorge, the Marx party's most faithful cadre in the United States: "The Social-Democratic Federation, just like your German Socialist Labor Party, has managed to transform our theory into the rigid dogma of an orthodox sect." In this sentence Engels aptly summarized what remained even till his death the fundamental shortcoming of those who paraded as "Marxists" in both the United States and England. Much of the advice he proffered to overcome this problem for one country was as relevant to the other.

Sectarianism, Marx and Engels had long held, was symptomatic of the backwardness of the working-class movement—"the stage of infantile diseases." Sects could rule the day as long as no real workers' party existed. Once one came into being the sects would be confined to the dustbin of history. Thus, their eyes were on the prospects and signs for just such parties in the two countries. Whereas in Germany and France, countries with a much longer tradition of independent working-class political action, the key task was programmatic integrity in order to sharply differentiate the revolutionary workers' party from pseudo currents, in the United States and England it was to just get a workers' party off the ground. For the moment, program could take a back seat; not every "i" had to be dotted or "t" crossed, as Engels had said in another context. It would be through the experiences of the real movement, including its mistakes, that the programmatic issues would be resolved. The role of a communist vanguard was to go through the experiences with workers to help draw the lessons rather than carping from the sidelines about the theoretical inadequacies of the newly emerging workers' movements. All of this, of course, was consistent with their long-held views about the education of the educator as well as the masses.

In the English case it may be remembered that Marx and Engels had predicted that once the crumbs from the booty of British imperialism (the Irish question was also relevant) to its working class had begun to diminish, English workers would begin to move. He tried in 1881, in fact, to stimulate the process—specifically, campaign for the creation of a workers' party—in a series of articles he wrote for Britain's leading labor paper. His efforts came to naught. Thus, Engels was most heartened when London's East End proletariat, largely unskilled workers and not the labor aristocracy, began its strike wave in the early 1890s, an upsurge in which Eleanor Marx, the youngest daughter, played a major role, in consultation with Engels. Regarding "the leading men and women" of the strikes, "In them I see the *real* beginning of the movement here."[93]

The formation of the Independent Labour Party shortly afterwards (and two and a half years before his death), which eventually became Britain's first mass workers' party, was for Engels confirmation of his projection. Under no illusions, however, about the new party's leadership, "I am counting on the masses to keep the leaders in order."[94] The main thing was that the process was off the ground.

While Engels did what he could to rectify the subjective or agential obstacles to the formation of a workers' party in the United States, he recognized that the structural ones, "peculiar" to that country, required revolutionary patience, as he frequently reminded his American comrades. (It might be mentioned here that Engels visited the United States for the first time in 1888 in order to get a firsthand view.) In a remarkably insightful letter to Sorge at the end of 1893, he outlined what he saw those obstacles to be. First, an electoral system inherited from England that employed the winner-take-all procedure that was a disincentive to the protest vote. Second, divisions within the working class between the "native-born and the foreigners," between the European immigrants, "And then the Negroes." Lastly, "the workers . . . have been exposed to a prosperity no trace of which has been seen here in Europe for years."[95]

Regarding the "Negroes," Engels was no doubt referring to the consequence of Reconstruction's defeat. On more than one occasion, as already noted, Marx had stated that "labor cannot emancipate itself in the white skin where in the black it is branded." Reconstruction's overthrow allowed the "branding" process to go forth with a vengeance. Yet Engels was not pessimistic and expected that conditions would one day be "ripe for a socialist workers' party" in the United States.[96]

There were many other national movements, such as the one in Italy, for example, to which Engels rendered invaluable assistance.[97] But none held his attention, in terms of the immediacy of revolution, as the Russian movement did. He continued to believe, as Marx had, that it was in Russia that the ingredients existed for a revolution that, as they wrote in the "Preface" to the Second Russian Edition of the *Manifesto*, would be "the vanguard of revolutionary action in Europe."

The spate of political assassinations that began in 1877 impressed Marx and Engels with Russia's volatility. Just as in the case of Vera Zasulich's assassination attempt (noted in the previous chapter), they praised the assassins—members of Narodnaya Volya (People's Will)—of Czar Alexander II in 1881. To daughter Jenny, Marx wrote that they were "sterling chaps through and through, without melodramatic posturing, simple, matter-of-fact, heroic. . . . [T]hey . . . are at pains to teach Europe that their *modus operandi* is a specifically Russian and historically inevitable mode of action which no more lends itself to moralising—for or against—than does the [recent] earthquake in Chios [Greece]."[98] For Engels, they were "our people" whose actions had helped to create a "revolutionary situation" in Russia.[99]

As Marx's comment to Jenny indicates, neither he nor Engels praised terrorism as a tactic suitable for all places at all times. Thus, in the same article in which he condemned a terrorist bombing in London in January 1885—"Irish hands may have laid the dynamite, but it is more than probable that a Russian brain and Russian money were behind it"—he publicly defended Narodnaya Volya.

> The means of struggle employed by the Russian revolutionaries are dictated to them by necessity, by the actions of their opponents themselves. They must answer to their people and to history for the means they employ. But the gentlemen who are needlessly parodying this struggle in Western Europe in schoolboy fashion . . . who do not even direct their weapons against real enemies but against the public in general, these gentlemen are in no way successors or allies of the Russian revolutionaries, but rather their worst enemies.[100]

In the specific conditions of Russia, terror was justifiable, but not in western Europe, at least at that moment.

Since Engels followed closely the debate within the Russian movement on the use of terror—"these Russian quarrels are not uninteresting," he told Laura Lafargue[101]—he could respond to Zasulich's request to comment on Georgi Plekhanov's polemic, *Our Differences*, against Narodnaya Volya's overall perspective and tactics. The Russian situation was so unstable, he pointed out, that it "is one of those special cases where it is possible for a handful of men to *effect* a revolution. . . . Well, if ever Blanquism, the fantasy of subverting the whole of a society through action by a small group of conspirators, had any rational foundation, it would assuredly be in St. Petersburg." However—a most important qualifier—"Once the match has been applied to the powder, the men who have sprung the mine will be swept off their feet by an explosion a thousand times more powerful than they themselves . . ."[102]

For Engels, then, the important thing was "that revolution should break out" and it was "of little concern to me" whether it be Blanquist conspirators or not since the pent-up energy in Russia was such that "1789, once launched, will before long be followed by 1793," meaning the "revolution in permanence." "Men who have boasted of having *effected* a revolution have always found on the morrow that they didn't know what they were doing; that once *effected*, the revolution bears not resemblance at all to what they had intended."[103]

At this time Engels began a regular correspondence and contact with Zasulich, Plekhanov, and other leaders of the recently formed Emancipation of Labor group, the first explicitly Russian Marxist organization.[104] As he and Marx had earlier noted, the seriousness with which they took the study of their writings was singular amongst all their party contacts. They sought his views on the key theoretical issue that Marx had earlier been asked to address—whether Russia could bypass capitalist development and proceed directly to socialism based on the common ownership of property of the traditional peasant commune. There were of course enormous political implications in the answer to this most vital question.

After almost a decade and a half had lapsed since their last thorough discussion of this topic, Engels made his final and definitive judgment in 1894. Russia's recent development, as he and Marx had suspected, was decidedly capitalist, and the "proletarianisation of a large proportion of the peasantry and the decay of the old communistic commune proceeds at an ever quickening pace." Whether enough of the traditional communes remained for a "point of departure for communistic development," Engels could not say.

> But this much is certain: if a remnant of this commune is to be preserved, the first condition is the fall of tsarist despotism—revolution in Russia. This will not only tear the great mass of the nation, the peasants away from the isolation of their villages . . . and lead them out onto the great stage . . . it will also give the labour movement of the West fresh impetus and create new, better conditions in which to carry on the struggle, thus hastening the victory of the modern industrial proletariat, without which present-day Russia can never achieve a socialist transformation, whether proceeding from the commune or from capitalism.[105]

Thus, in no uncertain terms, and contrary to all of the future Stalinist distortions of Marx and Engels's views, Russia could "never achieve a socialist transformation" *without* the overthrow of the bourgeoisie in western Europe by its own proletariat. Russia would not only be the "impetus" for the socialist revolution in the West, as Marx and Engels had been saying for two decades, but its own revolution was inextricably linked to that outcome. This forecast would be profoundly and tragically confirmed by subsequent history.

Engels also noted in his assessment that the Russian bourgeoisie, like its German counterpart, was content to allow a despotic autocrat—the Czar—to rule in its place because it "offers it more guarantees than would changes even of a bourgeois-liberal nature." This was advantageous to the socialist revolution because the bourgeoisie's cowardly behavior meant that Russia's small but growing proletariat, just as was true for Germany—but unlike England—would be forced to combine the fight for economic and social advancement with the struggle for political democracy; to ensure, in other words, that the revolution would go beyond the boundaries of its bourgeois democratic tasks to become permanent. The German proletariat was thus the west European working class that was expected to be the immediate recipient of Russia's "impetus." It was exactly this point, the vanguard role of the proletariat in Russia's as well as Germany's coming revolution, that Engels made to Zasulich at his last New Year's Eve celebration, an insight she quickly conveyed to her comrades in the Emancipation of Labour Group.[106] History would again confirm Engels's prescience.

TOWARD A NEW INTERNATIONAL

Following Marx's death in 1883, Engels made it clear that given the priority of the scientific work, he would only "take to the saddle if need arose"—that is, if politically necessary.[107] Such a situation appeared in 1889, which led Engels to put on hold for a half-year his literary endeavors to take the initial steps in what would eventually become the Socialist or Second International—the body that directly nurtured Europe's mass working-class parties.

As important as proletarian internationalism was for the revolutionary process, between not only German and Russian workers but workers in every country, Marx and Engels were cautious about the need to form a new international in the aftermath of the IWMA.[108] The priority then, as they saw it, was the construction of national workers' parties. However, with the growth of socialist workers' parties in many European countries in the 1880s—due in no small part to the assistance Engels provided—there was increasing clamor for international collaboration. This was the climate that produced independent calls to hold an international socialist congress in Paris on the centennial of the 1789 French Revolution.

If such a congress was going to be held, about which Engels had his doubts, he wanted to make sure that it conclude at least on the same programmatic level that the IWMA had ended. The possibility was quite real that without his strong intervention the very forces that he and Marx had once battled together, and he alone since his partner's death, might dilute what the IWMA had accomplished and claim the mantle as the representatives of international socialism. To this end, to prevent this from happening, he subordinated his other priorities. Basically, he used his political influence, mainly through correspondence with the Lafargues, and Bebel and meetings in London, to ensure that a congress take place in Paris that was consistent with the fundamental precepts of the Marx party. And once it became clear that the Possibilists from France and reformists from England would lead a rival congress at the same time in the French capital, it was crucial that the Marxist congress, as it came to be known, would be far more successful and not appear to be the culprit for competing meetings. Largely because of his tireless and timely efforts, Engels's hopes were fulfilled.

He explained to Sorge and Lafargue why he "put [his] shoulders to the wheel" to make the congress a success: "[I]t is again the old split in the International that comes to light here, the old battle of the Hague. The adversaries are the same, but the banner of the Anarchists has been replaced by the banner of the Possibilists." Hence, "it was this, and this alone what made me take the matter up in such good earnest. . . . [T]he position we conquered upon the anarchists after 1873 was now attacked by their successors, and so I had no choice."[109] It was only at a similar congress two years later in Brussels that Engels felt that the anarchist ghost had finally been laid to rest.

Having done his utmost to ensure its success, Engels, however, didn't attend the Paris meeting. His experiences in the IWMA had taught him well, as he explained to Laura Lafargue a month in advance: "I must keep away . . . [otherwise] I should come back here with a load of tasks. . . . Those things one cannot decline at a congress, and yet I must, if the 3rd volume [of *Capital*] is to see the light of day."[110]

Engels had also advised against the reconstitution of a new international at the congress, which did not occur. Given both the German and Austrian parties' persecution at the hands of their respective states, "they cannot afford to play at international organisations which are at present as impossible as they are useless."[111] In his opinion, the meeting's most significant accomplishment, aside from "the fact that the unanimity of the socialist parties of Europe is demonstrated to all the world," was the decision to have coordinated international workers' rallies on May 1. "That is the best thing our congress did."[112] The May Day demonstration in London the following year, in which he both participated as well as assisted in organizing with Eleanor Marx, was attended by more than two hundred thousand.

The "Marxist congress," as it was called by friend and foe alike, also passed a number of significant resolutions. One of the first testifies to, as asserted in chapter eight, the advanced character of the Marx party on the gender question: "Congress declares it is the duty of male workers to admit female workers as equal in their ranks on the basis of the principle of 'equal work, equal pay' for workers of both sexes without discrimination of nationality."[113]

Even more pertinent to the central argument of this book, the "Congress noted that, as the possession of political power was what enabled capitalists to rule, workers in countries where they had the vote should join the socialist parties and elect them to office. Elsewhere, workers should use all possible means to obtain the suffrage."[114] The roots of these positions could be traced, of course, to the independent working-class political action perspective that Marx fought so hard for in the IWMA. They constitute the necessary link in the continuity of the Marxist project from the latter to the Socialist International, again, the body that nurtured Europe's mass workers' parties.

Although not planned for at the Paris meeting, similar congresses were convened in its aftermath, the next in 1891 in Brussels and in Zurich in 1893, which Engels attended, his first public visit to the continent in almost two decades. While Engels helped to build the congresses he did so as long as it was in his view a continuation of the fight against the anarchists and reformists. He was still doubtful that the time was ripe for the formation of a new international.

Though Engels was opposed to the launching of a new body, it did not in the least imply that he minimized the coordination and linkages between the workers' movements of various countries. All of his activities, especially his intervention into national parties, was done exactly from such a perspective. In almost every letter to party leaders he raised the international repercussions, both negative and positive, of particular policies in order to foster proletarian international solidarity.

Since the formal organization that emerged in 1900 from the parties that convened the occasional congresses came to be known as the Socialist International it might be noted here what Engels thought about the adjectives, "socialist" and "communist." A year and a half before his death he wrote that he and Marx had never called themselves social democrats because for most of their lives the "elasticity" of that label was unsuitable "to describe our special standpoint." In 1894, however,

the situation is different, and the word can be allowed to pass, unfitting as it remains for a party whose economic programme is not just generally socialist, but directly communist, and whose ultimate political aim is to surpass the entire State, and thus democracy too. The names of *real* political parties never fit exactly; the party develops, but the name stays.[115]

That the Socialist International did not emerge as Engels thought it should, on the basis of a revolutionary upsurge, is not insignificant. It's "unfitting" name may have been a harbinger of its destiny. Nineteen years later, on the heels of the Russian Revolution, a new international was formed, as Engels had predicted in 1882, and called itself the Communist International. In the immediate wake of the IWMA in 1874, Engels, it may be recalled, thought that "the next International—after Marx's writings have been at work for some years—will be directly Communist and will openly proclaim our principles."[116] Whether or not the new body deserved to be called communist, as Marx and Engels understood the appellation, is the stuff of another volume.

In his reply to the French party's greetings to him on his seventieth birthday in 1890, Engels wrote: "The moment I am no longer of any use to the struggle, may it be granted to me to die."[117] Five years later that moment arrived when he was incapacitated by, unbeknownst to him, throat cancer. Within a few months, on August 5, 1895, he died. As testimony to what he and Marx had achieved the funeral, though small—about eighty people—at his request, was a truly international affair. Representing the German party, Liebknecht, in his remarks cited at the beginning of chapter one, was as accurate about his contribution to the movement as Engels had been about Marx in his graveside speech twelve years earlier.[118] But it was Eleanor Marx who perhaps best captured him, in a short biographical sketch written five years before his death. Engels, she wrote, "has a stronger sense of duty and above all of Party discipline than anybody," a characteristic that rested on what she noted to be his "most essential quality . . . his absolute selflessness."[119]

ENGELS'S CONTRIBUTION: AN ASSESSMENT

One of the favorite pastimes of the Marxological fraternity is to engage in Engels bashing. If this coterie of critics were to be believed, it was Engels who either began or prepared the way for the Stalinist and/or reformist corruption of Marx's ideas. While there have been two recent and thoughtful rejoinders to this charge[120] (essentially from within the circle and suggestive that this diversion is no longer in vogue), they too suffer from what the bashers succumb to—a failure to treat Marx and Engels as they saw themselves and what they in fact were, first and foremost, political activists.

Terrell Carver's *The Intellectual Relationship*, perhaps the most well known of this genre of Engels-as-the-problem literature, best illustrates its major shortcoming.[121] Carver argues that the "intellectual relationship between the two living men . . . was very much a story of what they accomplished independently, though their accomplishments were by no means theoretically coincident."[122] He also accuses Engels of converting Marx's ideas, after his death, into an overarching "system of knowledge"—something with which Marx would have rightly disagreed—with physical science as his model, to be applied to the study of "history, 'thought' and, somewhat implausibly, current politics." This is not the place to critique, a not too difficult exercise, Carver's argument within the arena in which he prefers to operate—the realm of ideas (which is essentially what the aforementioned rejoinders do).

The problem with Carver and his critics, as already suggested, is that they operate within the realm of ideas while Marx and Engels long ago abandoned the ethereal for terra firma—politics. Thus, his problem with Engels's supposed application of a "system of knowledge . . . to current politics" is entirely of his making and not that of Engels. Had he taken the time to examine Engels's politics he might have recognized the straw man he erected for himself. And herein lies the crux of the matter. Given, as substantiated throughout this book, that Marx and Engels prioritized politics and that their "intellectual" and scientific endeavors were motivated primarily by political considerations, then to what extent is the alleged dichotomy that Carver claims to find in their "texts" reflected in their politics? In other words, in the arena that was most important to them, politics, is there any evidence of the supposed dichotomy? Carver's thesis falls flat precisely because there is no such evidence.

While Carver doesn't even bother to make a case for such a political dichotomy there are those who claim that Engels paved the way for the reformism of twentieth-century social democracy. The evidence presented in this chapter, especially in the section on "Parliamentary Cretinism," has, hopefully, made clear that any attempt to link Engels to this current flies in the face of everything he did to head off such a development.[123] Again, there is nothing to suggest that his practice deviated in the least from that of his partner.

As for the claim, which is only implicit in Carver, that he provided if not the political then the intellectual foundations for Stalinism—Carver and those who imply this are all too aware, as substantiated on more than one occasion in this chapter, that nothing in his practice laid the basis for Stalinist politics—this too is beside the point. Neither Marx nor Engels would have looked for the answer to the emergence of Stalinism in the realm of ideas—Engels's alleged positivism—but rather in a material understanding of politics. Carver and his co-thinkers would find, if they took Marx and Engels as they saw themselves, that avenue of inquiry to explaining Stalinism much more rewarding than their idealist approach; but that too is the subject of another book.

That those who subscribe to the dichotomy thesis, such as Carver, ignore Marx and Engels's politics is not surprising since it is especially clear in this arena that they operated as a team, as demonstrated throughout this book. When Carver claims that it was in 1859 that Engels publicly distanced himself from Marx's epistemology for the first time, he conveniently overlooks Marx's comment a year later in *Herr Vogt* that "we ["*Engels* and myself"] work to a common plan and after prior agreement."[124] Engels's instruction to Bernstein in 1882—while Marx was alive—to print in the *Sozialdemokrat* that "Marx and I always agree beforehand on any public move we make,"[125] is completely supported by the record, Carver's protestations to the contrary notwithstanding. This was exactly their modus operandi until the end and nowhere was this clearer than in their politics.

Certainly one of the most outstanding qualities of Engels that we unfortunately have not been able to discuss, simply for lack of space, was his perspicacity about the past and the future. Though he perhaps overstates, the historian Perry Anderson is not off the mark when he writes: "Engels's *historical* judgements are nearly always superior to those of Marx."[126] If true—Anderson makes a convincing case—then critics of Engels such as Carver are obligated to explain why such a defective methodology as he is claimed to have employed could be so rewarding.

The same can be said about his forecasts. While, as we've noted on occasion, his and Marx's arithmetic about the future may have been faulty, the algebra was nonetheless elegant. Among his many insights none were as uncannily accurate as his predictions about a future European conflagration and its outcome. Marx, as noted in chapter eight, had also, as early as 1870—and no doubt in collaboration with Engels—begun to make such predictions. While a general European war was not inevitable—"A revolution in Russia . . . would save Europe from the misfortune of a general war"[127]—if it broke out, "one thing is certain":

> This war, in which fifteen to twenty million armed men would slaughter one another and devastate Europe as it has never been devastated before . . . would either lead to the immediate triumph of socialism, or it would lead to such an upheaval in the old order of things, it would leave behind it everywhere such a heap of ruins, that . . . the socialist revolution, set back by ten or fifteen years, would only be all the more radical and more rapidly implemented.[128]

Nine years earlier, in 1882, he foresaw—in anticipation of Sarajevo in 1914—that the Czar's agents, owing to their "pan-Slav and rabble-rousing in Herzegovina" and elsewhere in the Balkans, "may well find themselves with a war on their hands, a war neither they, nor Austria nor Bismarck will be able to control."[129]

If Engels didn't quite get all of the particulars right about how World War I came about, its toll and outcome, it's only because he operated with a theoretical perspective and not a crystal ball. While others may have foreseen the war, Engels was no doubt unique, together with Marx, in anticipating its revolutionary outcome first for Russia and then for the rest of Europe. His foresight was due largely to the theoretical framework both he and Marx employed. For both of them the test of their method was not prediction for prediction's sake but its ability to grasp political reality in order to assist the proletariat and its allies in its fight to take power— to ensure that conflagrations such as World War I would not be inevitable. As long as Engels's critics ignore the terrain on which he and Marx operated, their sideline carping will remain simply that.[130]

Two years before his death Engels was feted in Zurich and other European capitals as the veritable head of the international socialist movement. With not a hint of false modesty he accepted the accolades in the name of his deceased partner. To the International Socialist Workers' Congress in Zurich—attended by more than

400 delegates of socialist organizations and workers' parties from eighteen countries—he said: "Marx is dead, but were he still alive there would be not one man in Europe or America who could look back with such justified pride over his life's work."[131] Engels himself had every reason to be just as proud. What he had been able to accomplish in the decade after Marx's death, in effect doing the work of two in the context of an even larger movement, and with more to come in the next two years—let alone his invaluable contribution to their revolutionary partnership during Marx's lifetime—erased any doubts he might have had harbored about his ability to play at first fiddle.

Conclusions

The timeworn ad nauseam treatment of Marx—as well Engels, though less so—as only a thinker, or even worse, a quixotic thinker, flies in the face of everything they both were about, what they did, *and* what they accomplished. The evidence is unambiguous that they were indeed first and foremost political beings and to treat them otherwise is not only inadequate but disingenuous. From their youth until their deaths, politics—revolutionary politics—was the axis around which their lives revolved. And it was exactly the combination of their communist politics and activism as a team that allowed them to make the most decisive contribution to the nineteenth century's democratic movement—the central argument of this book.

An Overview of the Evidence

The reality of Prussian authoritarianism, and not, as suggested far too often by the Marxological industry, philosophical musings or parent-child angst, was decisive in the political trajectory of the young Marx and Engels. The issues that drove them and their cohorts are still some of the same ones mutatis mutandis that bring conscious human beings into politics today. How would the German nation acquire political democracy? Which social layer would play the decisive role in its realization? Could the unwashed masses really be entrusted with self-rule? It was, above all, the search for answers to these questions—the same ones that activists in South Africa, for example, grappled with for decades—that led the two young radical democrats to what they called scientific communism. For the young Marx, in particular, a radical journalist, Prussian state censorship ensured that the quest for such answers would be no mere academic exercise. Indeed, Marx's road to communism originated in his uncompromising fight for freedom of the press and other basic democratic rights—a trait that remained at the very core of both their political beings until the very end.

The first task in Marx and Engels's quest for answers was to "settle accounts" with their own intellectual traditions, in particular, German philosophy. The "ruthless criticism" of received wisdom was their method. Philosophy proved inadequate in answering the questions they sought to answer. At best it might furnish methodological insights but at worst it smacked of apriorism and intellectual elitism. Even the best that philosophy had to offer, that is, the materialist Ludwig Feuerbach, suffered from a fatal flaw—his failure to study and partake in politics. Only a study of the "real movement," that is, the actual course of history and its motor forces, rather than preconceived schemes or blueprints, and only through "practical activity," that is, politics, could answers be obtained.

The real movement of history taught a lesson to Marx and Engels that remained at the core of their political beings—a profound faith in the ability of the oppressed to liberate themselves. Marx's break with Ruge was due fundamentally to their differences on this vital point. Ruge's lack of faith typified a core characteristic of social reformers of all stripes, whom Marx and Engels would encounter in various incarnations and do battle with for the rest of their lives. At the core of the petit bourgeoisie and its reformist politics was a lack of faith in the ability of the oppressed to do it for themselves and, thus, the need for some other social class or individuals, be it an enlightened dictator, the liberal bourgeoisie, or a "handful of chosen men," to do it on their behalf. Exactly because Marx and Engels held otherwise they could reach their unique insight that distinguished them from the reformists. Through struggle, that is, the unwashed masses prepare themselves for self-rule—obviating the need for well-meaning social reformers or other "saviors" of the oppressed.

Thus, from a study of the real movement of history, Marx formulated his third thesis on Feuerbach about the education of the educator and the education of the oppressed through struggle to prepare themselves to take power and construct a new society. To the end, they forever came back to this thesis, variably expressed, in numerous assessments and pronouncements. Their own lifelong tendency to prioritize political over scientific work, whenever there was real motion, was the realization of this thesis, specifically, the point about the education of the educator.

The real movement of history also taught that as long as social inequality persisted, that is, class society, "true democracy"—the "sovereignty of the people"—was impossible. Thus, the need for a social or socialist revolution that would eliminate private ownership of the means of production and hence class rule, which would in turn obviate the need for the state, including the democratic state. But the prerequisite for the socialist revolution was the democratic revolution—the best terrain on which the oppressed could prepare itself for taking power and self-rule. While Marx and Engels clearly saw the limitations of bourgeois democracy, their strategy was to push it as far left as possible by advocating forms and practices, such as the republican form of government, that allowed the largest number of the populace to exercise control over the state.

They concluded, on the basis of the study of history and the real movement in progress, the Silesian weavers strike and the reality of France—what Marx saw with his own eyes during his stay in Paris—and England—Engels's contribution about the latter had an enormous impact on Marx—that the proletariat constituted the really revolutionary class. The real movement had demonstrated that the proletariat could both act *and* think; philosophers, whom Marx had previously called "thinking humanity," were thus expendable. From this reading of history and the current reality they arrived at their new world outlook.

Engels's definition of communism, in his 1847 polemic with Heinzen, the essence of which would be reiterated a year later in the *Manifesto*, encapsulates what they had arrived at. "Communism is not a doctrine but a *movement*, it proceeds not from principles but from *facts* . . . insofar as it is a theory . . . [it] is the theoretical summation of conditions for the liberation of the proletariat." To paraphrase the *Manifesto*, scientific communism, their new outlook, is the generalized lessons of the class struggle in the interests of the proletariat. In this sense, Marxism is the quintessential work in progress—dependent on the unfolding of the class struggle, the real movement of history. Armed with these conclusions, Marx and Engels never looked back to the intellectual milieu from which they emerged.

The conclusions they drew from the settling of accounts required them, therefore, to link up with other fighters, particularly the proletariat, the only class that had the interest and capability to end class rule. Their strategy was to differentiate themselves from other currents that competed for the ear of the proletariat by critiquing their views and besting them in debate. While brief, the Communist Correspondence Committees experience allowed them to first formulate some of their most basic strategic and organizational views. Most importantly it facilitated their linkage with the proletarian fighters they now sought. However, as much as they strove to link up with these forces, in the final analysis it was thinking proletarian fighters who, after being won to their perspective, chose them to be their leaders. The convergence of the Marx-Engels team and the advanced guard of Germany's still nascent proletariat resulted in the formation of the Communist League, the first communist workers' party. With common agreement to end its conspiratorial style of organizing, the CL commissioned Marx, with Engels's assistance, to draw up a programmatic statement, the *Manifesto*.

In many ways a grand and anticipatory statement, the *Manifesto* could only serve as a guide to action in the most general sense. Most fundamentally, "in the movement of the present [of the working class] . . . they [communists] . . . represent and take care of the future of that movement." Little was offered, however, beyond this general perspective and, hence, the very brief programmatic section at the end on Germany. The document hedged on that most crucial question—would the German bourgeoisie act "in a revolutionary way." As communists and not inevitablists, they understood that only the real movement, in which they had to participate, would provide an answer as well as point the way to a more specific guide. This is exactly what happened when the 1848 revolution broke out in Germany. They immediately supplemented the *Manifesto* with the *Demands*, which constituted a programmatic strategy for forging the people's alliance of the peasantry, urban petit bourgeoisie and proletariat in the lead. Hence, in spite of what the *Manifesto* did or did not say, their practice at the beginning of, during, and after the 1848 events gives lie to the oft-repeated ad nauseam charge that they neglected the peasantry. The worker-peasant alliance was vital to their strategy.

In the framework of both the *Manifesto* and *Demands* Marx and Engels threw themselves wholeheartedly into the democratic movement in first Brussels and then Germany and quickly emerged as the leaders who constituted its most extreme wing. Though modified in the course of the upheavals, their overall strategy was, again, to push the democratic revolution as far left as possible—to provide the most favorable terrain upon which to launch the socialist revolution. The indisputable fact is that the Marxist current, as it began to be known, was, particularly through the *NRZ*, "Organ of Democracy," the most consistent voice for democracy in all of Germany during the revolution. At a certain stage, certainly the late fall of 1848, Marx was the effective leader of the most militant defenders of the increasingly threatened democratic space.

In so doing they had to also battle against the workerist current within the CL and Germany's nascent labor movement, which dismissed the importance of the democratic revolution and the people's alliance. Their error, in Marx and Engels's view, was to put the economic cart before the political cart. While they were forced to modify their strategy owing to the cowardly and fainthearted behavior of respectively the bourgeoisie and the petit-bourgeois democrats, Marx and Engels never forsook the basic goal of promoting the democratic revolution. Hence, the significance of the people's alliance, especially their tireless effort to construct the worker-peasant alliance—the first such effort in the history of socialism. Even before it became certain that the bourgeoisie could not be depended on, their practice had been to actively involve the proletariat in the fight for democracy in order that they be in the most favorable position to move to the next stage of the struggle. To draw on the South African example again, it was and continues to be (though today to a lesser extent) exactly this question—should revolutionary workers be in the forefront of the democratic revolution or waiting on the sidelines for the socialist revolution?—that is debated within the workers' movement.

Marx and Engels's democratic stripes were most visible on another crucial question—the right of national self-determination. Throughout the momentous two years, they established and fought for a policy through the pages of the *NRZ* that they maintained to the end—support for the right of oppressed nations to become independent. Workers of an oppressor nation, they constantly underscored, could not achieve their own liberation without the liberation of the oppressed nation.

As communists Marx and Engels sought immediately to draw a balance sheet of the 1848 events in order to distill its lessons, to generalize the lessons of the class struggle in the interests of the proletariat. For Germany they produced one of their most important party documents, the *Address of March 1850*, as well as Engels's *revolution and Counter-Revolution*. The French events were analyzed, firstly, in a series of Marx's articles plus one they co-authored, which Engels later published as *The Class Struggles in France* and, secondly, in Marx's book *The Eighteenth Brumaire*. Their basic conclusion was that the defeat of the revolutions signalled the end of one era and the beginning of another, the era of socialist revolution.

Related to this conclusion was another fundamental lesson: the bourgeoisie had proven through its behavior that it no longer had an interest in leading the charge for democracy. More alarmed by the militancy of the growing proletariat than the authoritarian antidemocratic character of a feudal oligarchy—in the case of Germany—or a dictator, in the form of Louis Bonaparte—it was willing to forfeit its right to rule in its own name and acquiesce in Bonapartist rule. Neither were the petit-bourgeois democrats to be looked to, as events had also shown. Their record had been at best one of vacillation. Only through independent working-class political action with the proletariat leading the people's alliance of the peasantry and urban petit bourgeoisie would democratic rule be instituted. Marx and Engels's very intimate involvement in the 1848–49 events along with the democratic credentials that they had earned gave them not just the right but the political expertise to draw such conclusions.

In no instance was the behavior of the reformist, the moderate republican, or perhaps the reluctant democrat more instructive than in the case of Tocqueville—one of twentieth-century liberalism's favorite alternatives to Marx. Tocqueville epitomized the response of that milieu to the revolution. Because of his deep-seated fear of the masses, his horror of their coming to power via a revolution, he helped to pave the way for the Bonapartist dictatorship. While some might claim or would like to think that he did so unwittingly—as was truthfully the case with many reformists—the fact is that he consciously rejected the only road he knew could prevent the republic's overthrow—revolutionary mobilization of the masses. While in Germany Marx and Engels were doing everything they could to do just that, in order to advance the democratic revolution, in France Tocqueville did everything he could to crush it. While Tocqueville may have written that he really wanted to maintain the republic—perhaps with an eye on his epitaph—he wasn't willing to do what would have been necessary in the reality of France in 1848–1851 to ensure its success. Tocqueville, in other words, in sharp contrast to Marx and Engels, failed to vote with his feet for democracy. He feared more what those such as Marx and Engels were fighting for, namely, that the political revolution become, as the *1850 Address* put it, the "revolution in permanence."

With the counterrevolution on the offensive and the prospects for a new revolutionary upsurge unlikely, which they concluded on the basis of their economic analysis, Marx and Engels made the requisite political and, therefore, organizational adjustments and focused on what they called their scientific work. It allowed them to reflect back on the 1848 events and draw more lessons, not the least of which was an even greater appreciation of the necessity of the worker-peasant alliance. Contrary, however, to the usual Marxological portrait of them in this period, the long lull in the class struggle from 1851 to 1864, their decision to disband the CL did not mean that their foray into party politics had come to an end. For them the long lull was an opportunity to prepare through "swotting" (study and research), for the next upsurge and to have in place a party nucleus to be able to take advantage of that moment when it arrived. This is what distinguished the Marx party from any other radical current during that period and explains largely why it, as opposed to any other, could move so quickly to the leadership of that political upsurge. It had, through its writings and research *and* political practice—however limited compared to the previous period—its political weapons in place. How a party conducts itself in the absence of class battles is, hence, as vital as how it does so in the midst of an upsurge.

In determining when the next upsurge would occur Marx and Engels employed not just economic criteria but political ones as well. Also, contrary to another myth, their terrain was not just, as they called it, their "little corner of the earth," namely, western Europe, but the entire world. Thus the reason they judged a new revolutionary era in the offering when the slaves and serfs in, respectively, the United States and Russia began to show signs of resistance at the beginning of 1860. Like other German revolutionaries they saw the U.S. Civil War as an opportunity to continue Germany's democratic revolution by supporting the one taking place on the other side of the Atlantic. Their global perspective allowed them to see the war's significance in a way that even the most perceptive historians miss. The U.S. Civil War, Marx often wrote, was the signal for Europe's working class just as the American War of Independence had been the signal for its bourgeoisie.

In the context of what he saw as a new revolutionary era, whose vanguard was the Civil War, Marx immediately seized the opportunity to step into the leadership of the real movement—in part the response of the English proletariat to the Civil War's signal—that led to the birth of the International Workingmen's Association. Armed with the central lesson of 1848, he made sure that this first truly international working-class organization was founded on two basic principles, enshrined in its founding documents, which he wrote: "[T]he emancipation of the working classes must be conquered by the working classes themselves" and "[T]o conquer political power has therefore become the great duty of the working class." From the IWMA's beginning to the end, Marx, largely on his own at the outset and then later with Engels, fought—"*fortiter in re, suáviter in modo*" (strong in deed, mild in manner)—to make these goals—independent working-class political action—a reality. "*Suaviter in modo*" also meant a nonsectarian and flexible organizational modus operandi in order to attract the largest number of workers to the International. Because of his success, it was not for naught that Engels considered the IWMA to be Marx's "crowning achievement."

A fight for independent working-class political action in the IWMA was necessary because many of the various currents who initially comprised the IWMA did not agree with this perspective. Much of English trade union officialdom, especially amongst the skill trades and artisans, looked instead to the liberal bourgeoisie and its politicians for leadership—the origins of the twentieth century's labor-liberal electoral coalition—while the Proudhonists and Bakuninists simply rejected working-class involvement in the political arena. There was nothing inevitable about Marx's perspective being accepted; it had, in other words, to be fought for. To ensure that the working class did it for themselves Marx also took steps to limit the influence of the liberal bourgeoisie, petit-bourgeois reformers such as John Stuart Mill and others from his milieu, and aspiring parliamentary careerists in the International. Again, his efforts were completely consistent with his long-held position, encapsulated in the third thesis on Feuerbach, about the education of the oppressed. His own involvement in the IWMA was the quintessential embodiment of the theoretician-activist—another concretization of the third thesis about the education of the educator. In all of this Marx and Engels were informed by the lessons of 1848—complete distrust of the bourgeoisie and wariness of the petit bourgeoisie.

A crucial aspect of independent working-class political action was not only Marx's promotion of proletarian internationalism, through, for example, strike support and antiwar work, but as well efforts to broaden the social consciousness of workers around questions as diverse as Irish self-determination and the advancement of working-class women. Both he and Engels recognized, especially as a result of the English reality, that trade union consciousness did not inevitably lead to social consciousness, that is, solidarity with the oppressed in its majority; again, it had to be fought for. Their pronouncements *and* activities around both the Irish—as part of the issue of nationalism and proletarian internationalism—and women's questions give lie, once again, to the ad nauseam repeated charge that they neglected national/ethnic and gender issues.

The Paris Commune and the ensuing fight against Bakunin's split operation severely tested the IWMA and were largely responsible for its demise. Through their intimate involvement with the Commune, the closest that they ever came to seeing a proletarian revolution, Marx, in particular, on behalf of the IWMA, was able to employ the lessons of 1848 as well as add to them—conclusions that were forever enshrined in his *Civil War in France*. While Marx and Engels had counselled revolutionary restraint prior to the uprising, consistent with their long-held view about the necessity of adequate preparatory time, they threw themselves into its defense once it was underway. Their unsuccessful effort, for example, to get the communards to make links with France's peasantry was a clear application of a key lesson from 1848—the necessity of the worker-peasant alliance.

However ill-prepared the insurgents were, any revolutionary worth his or her salt was obligated to come to their defense and not critique them from the sidelines. Consistent again with the third thesis on Feuerbach, revolutionary practice was necessary for the education of both the masses and the educator. This was exactly one of the major points that Marx made in the *Civil War* about the communards: "They know that in order to work out their own emancipation, and along with it that higher form to which present society is irresistibly tending by its own economical agencies, they will have to pass through long struggles, through a series of historic processes, transforming circumstances and men." While, as Marx pointed out some years later, the Commune "was in no sense socialist, nor could it have been," its most important accomplishment was the fact that it was a beginning, because political power was for the first time in the hands of Paris' working masses—the necessary prerequisite to socialist transformation. And it was on the basis of this reality that another lesson was drawn—so important that Marx and Engels thought it required an addendum to the *Manifesto*—namely, that "the working class cannot simply lay hold of the ready-made State machinery, and wield it for its own purpose." This, in Marx's opinion, was confirmation of one of his conclusions in the *Eighteenth Brumaire* about the opening up of the new era of proletarian revolution in the aftermath of 1848.

The Bakunin fight was a severe test of Marx and Engels's democratic stripes, which in the end they wore well. It reveals that they clearly recognized the potential for "dictators"—as they called them—in the workers' movement, just as they had in the case of Proudhon and Lassalle, and were vigilant in combating them. What they objected to the most in Bakunin's operation was its covert character, behind the backs of workers—a "handful of chosen men" if ever there was one. In successfully challenging the operation Marx and Engels provided many lessons, which they consciously documented, about democratic functioning and the handling of political differences in the workers' movement—issues that would trip up many a twentieth-century would-be revolutionary.

The reason that Engels regarded the IWMA to be Marx's "crowning achievement" was that it laid the seeds for the first truly independent working-class political parties. It was in fact the London Conference in 1871, a year before the IWMA's effective demise, that made the first explicit call, in Resolution IX, for such formations. The subsequent growth of Europe's mass working-class political parties has its roots in that historical decision, one in which Marx and Engels, again, played a decisive role. The arguments they made on its behalf could be traced back to the lessons of 1848 and the third thesis on Feuerbach. The Hague Congress a year later, a much more representative gathering and the last congress of the International, ratified that decision.

The programmatic gains of the IWMA, particularly the call for independent working-class political action, became the axis around which first Marx and Engels, and then Engels on his own, did political work in relation to the various national movements in its aftermath. They waged a constant and often uphill battle to make this call a reality. While Britain soberly illustrated that indeed there was nothing inevitable about independent working-class political action, Germany, on the other hand, revealed what could be done through conscious intervention in the context of a favorable set of political circumstances. It was there, after many fits and starts, that the Marx party had its greatest success. That Europe's working class had the first example in 1869 in Germany of a workers' party that Marx and Engels could point to for emulation was due in no small part to their efforts. Their success in Germany required a fight once again against those in the workers' movement who deprecated the democratic revolution. Engels's pamphlet *The Prussian Military Question*, a key weapon in their intervention, was the first document in the post-1848 period—drawing on its lessons—to call on the workers' party to take the lead, independently of the liberal bourgeoisie, in the democratic revolution. And as part of this call was the necessity, once again, of the worker-peasant alliance.

In spite of the gains in Germany, Marx and Engels were under no illusions about the party's future. They were thus quite critical of the first appearances of a reformist tendency amongst its leadership, the reason for their *Circular of 1879*. Written in order to nip this development in the bud, it uncannily anticipated the course of twentieth-century social democracy, which they clearly would have had no truck with. The main target of their critique was the reformist belief that workers couldn't do it for themselves and therefore needed to align with petit-bourgeois reformists and the enlightened bourgeoisie—a violation of their own core beliefs as well as the lessons of 1848. They both, especially Engels after Marx's death, consciously resurrected the 1848 events in order to educate a new generation of worker-activists on the necessity of independent working-class political action. His decision to have the *1850 March Address* reprinted—in spite of latter-day social-democratic efforts to have Marx and Engels disown it—was part of this campaign.

The "disease" of parliamentary cretinism was symptomatic of reformism and thus the target of Marx and Engels's critique. Again, they drew on their experiences from 1848 to combat it. Having outlived Marx by twelve years, Engels witnessed the electoral gains of the German party, gains that contributed in part to the "disease." He, thus, tried in vain to inculcate in the party a revolutionary perspective on the electoral process. That is, electoral gains were not to be seen as an end in themselves but rather a gauge to determine the most propitious time, on the basis of the degree of self-organization of the working class and its allies, to resort to armed struggle to take power. Contrary then to later social-democratic efforts to recast him in their own image and in spite of all the bowdlerization that he was subjected to by the German party leadership, Engels can in no way be held responsible for the eventual metastasization of the disease. Engels's efforts notwithstanding, the reformist tendency, unbeknownst to him at the time of his death in 1895, had succeeded in becoming its dominant trend.

As important as the German movement was for Marx and Engels, they had long held that its advancement was intimately connected with revolutionary developments elsewhere. Thus their detailed attention to other national movements. As always, their bottom line was independent working-class political action, be it in France, England, or the United States. At the same time they tailored their strategy and tactics depending on the stage of development of such action. The French case provided as well a most instructive example of the Marx party's defense of bourgeois democracy as a result of the Bonapartist threat of General Boulanger in 1889, giving lie to the oft-repeated suggestion that Marx and Engels were indifferent to democratic governance (an issue to be discussed later). Engels's advice to his U.S. and English contacts testifies to the importance they gave to workers doing it for themselves. Their collective action as a class was more important than theoretical clarity, since it was through the former that the latter emerged. For these two countries the main task was the creation of a workers' party. Coupled with this advice was Engels's incessant fight against sectarianism and the treatment of his and Marx's ideas as dogma—a phenomenon that would become all too common in their aftermath.

But it was in Russia, contrary to the usual Marxological charge about their exclusive preoccupation with the proletariat of western Europe, that they placed their greatest hopes for a revolutionary breakthrough. Not only were conditions ripe there, which they had been saying since about 1870, but Russia was the country in whose revolutionaries they had the most confidence. As a group, the Russians, they felt, were better acquainted with their writings—those of both Marx and Engels—than any other national party. Engels's opinion of them in 1872—"They have a stoicism, a strength of character and at the same time a grasp of theory which are truly admirable"—was one he maintained to the end. After many years of detailed study, which Marx initiated, Engels concluded that a bourgeois democratic revolution was on Russia's agenda, one that would be based on the worker-peasant alliance.

Whether the revolution would become permanent, that is, would effect socialist transformation, depended, contrary to later Stalinist misrepresentations, on whether Europe's proletariat would carry out its own revolution. Germany, they felt, would be the immediate recipient of Russia's spark. As they wrote in the preface to the 1882 Russian edition of the *Manifesto*, "Russia forms the vanguard of revolutionary action in Europe." With the Russian revolution, they felt, a new international would come into existence that "will be directly Communist and will openly proclaim our principles." History would confirm the prescience of their judgments.

The Three Arguments

To what extent do the facts presented in this book allow for the making of a more than credible case for the claims that (1) no two people contributed more to the struggle for democracy in the last century than Marx and Engels, and (2) their effectiveness was due to their being first and foremost political activists who constituted a revolutionary partnership, and (3) the lessons they drew as communists from the 1848 revolutions?

Beginning with the second claim, the easiest of the three to substantiate, the record leaves little doubt—contrary to the insinuations of Engels bashers—that Marx and Engels were indeed a political team and one that was maintained even after Marx's death. From their fateful ten-day meeting in Paris in 1844 to Engels's death in 1895, they were a revolutionary partnership in both word and deed. There is nothing to suggest that Marx was exaggerating when he publicly stated in 1860 that "we [*Engels and myself*"] work to a common plan and after prior agreement" or that he later changed his view. Most importantly, it is what they did, in its totality, that justifies this conclusion.

If it is indisputable that they constituted a team, what about the second part of this claim that they owed their effectiveness as democrats and communists to the partnership? One way to approach this is to pose the question whether either one would have been as effective without the other. Since there is virtually unanimous agreement that Engels's effectiveness derived from his alliance with Marx—his reference to himself as "second fiddle" in the partnership was in part a recognition of this reality—the question really is about the advantages Marx derived from his partnership with Engels. Obviously, as seen throughout their collaboration, Marx's accomplishments in both the literary and political arena would have been severely limited without the material assistance that Engels provided beginning in 1850. His comment to Engels, about a year after he had become active in the IWMA, "that the two of us form a partnership together, in which I spend my time on the theoretical and party side the business" while Engels labored in his family's factory in Manchester, acknowledged this fact. Their division of labor was, therefore, crucial for Marx's effectiveness.

Beyond, however, the level of material assistance, Engels, throughout the course of their partnership, provided other and even more valuable assistance. Through Engels's eyes, it may be remembered, even before the alliance commenced, Marx first learned about the revolutionary potential of the proletariat, specifically the Chartist movement and its fight to extend democracy to the masses. During their trip to England in 1845 Engels introduced Marx to the Chartists as well as the leaders of the German proletariat in London, on the basis of which they helped initiate their first political formation, the Society of Fraternal Democrats.

From the earliest days of the partnership it was Engels who appeared, according to the extant correspondence, to be the team's taskmaster. Certainly, the pressure he exerted at the outset on Marx to publish became a refrain that the latter would hear until the end. Because they constituted a political team their combined efforts facilitated the creation of both the Communist Correspondence Committees and the Communist League, the two organizations that launched their revolutionary careers and earned them recognition that they would not otherwise have enjoyed. Engels's programmatic contributions were crucial to the CL's basic perspective. Most relevant is the fact that it was Engels, apparently, who first outlined the strategy for the democratic revolution, which was not reflected in the *Manifesto*, that he and Marx actually employed in the 1848–1849 upheavals. Specifically, in both his *Principles of Communism*, the draft that Marx employed for the *Manifesto*, and his polemic with Heinzen, he spelled out the "people's alliance," that is, the proletariat in coalition with the peasantry and urban petit bourgeoisie. The *Demands* that he and Marx wrote to supplement the *Manifesto* were the concretization of this strategy in the German setting.

At virtually every step in the course of the 1848 events Marx and Engels's success in implementing the people's alliance rested on their partnership as the core of a larger political team. In no instance was this clearer than the September events in Cologne, the high-water mark of the worker-peasant alliance. When Engels was forced to leave Prussia his dispatches on the national revolutions, especially the Hungarian struggle, made it possible for the *NRZ* to continue to be the most consistent defender of national self-determination in the democratic movement. Finally, Engels's assistance in drawing a balance sheet on the 1848 revolutions was no more apparent than his writing in Marx's name *Revolution and Counter-revolution in Germany*.

During the long lull in the class struggle between the 1848 upheavals and the formation of the IWMA in 1864, Engels's material assistance to Marx and his family took the form not only of direct monetary contributions but also writing in his name for various publications, for which Marx received compensation; again, this allowed Marx to spend more time on the political economy project. Because this period was also very trying for Marx personally, Engels's moral support was equally important. This is what Marx alluded to when, following the death in 1855 of his third child in the space of five years, he told him: "Amid all the fearful torments I have recently had to endure, the thought of you and your friendship has always sustained me, as has the hope that there is still something sensible for us to do together in the world." Along with the material and moral support, Engels was there when Marx needed his political acumen. His pamphlet *Po and Rhine*, the only programmatic document they issued during this period, reaffirmed the Marx party's claim to be the most consistent defenders of the right of national self-determination.

It was Marx who, as noted, took the lead on the IWMA; Engels had to be won over to its significance. Once convinced he provided invaluable political as well as material assistance to Marx. From Manchester he helped Marx strategize on the General Council debates on the trade union, Irish and Polish self-determination questions and the growing fight with Bakunin's operation. All of these issues had enormous implications for independent working-class political action. With Marx increasingly burdened with IWMA obligations, Engels's intervention in the German movement, as strikingly illustrated by his pamphlet *The Prussian Military Question*, made it possible for Marx to point to the German party as a model of such action. His relocation to London in 1870 came none too soon, as the IWMA was to face its greatest challenges with the Paris Commune and the Bakunin fight. Though it cannot be proven, it seems unlikely that Marx would have been as effective on both fronts without Engels's presence. That the Marx party was able to maintain the banner of independent working-class political action at the end of the IWMA in 1872 was again due in no small part to Engels's assistance.

In the IWMA's aftermath and Marx's return to the political economy project, Engels increasingly took up the political slack. This was also necessitated by Marx's deteriorating health. Thus, by the time of his death in 1883, Engels had largely assumed most of the party responsibilities that Marx had once shouldered. In no instance was this clearer than in their fight for programmatic integrity in the German party. Done in close collaboration with his partner, it was Engels who largely conducted this effort. Both his *Anti-Dühring* and *Circular Letter of 1879* should be seen in this context. And until the end, as chapter ten makes clear, he waged a ceaseless if at times uphill battle to make real his and Marx's political bottom line, independent working-class political action. His decision to "take to the saddle" once again, to organize the International Socialist Congress in 1889, was very much related to this campaign. All of this, it must be remembered, was done while he devoted most of his remaining years to completing Marx's political economy project and republishing his earlier writings, all of which further enhanced his partner's stature within the working-class movement.

In sum, then, the Marx-Engels partnership was highly effective because it drew on the strengths and assets of two individuals who were not only enormously talented but as well thoroughly convinced of the primacy of political action—the need for the educator to participate in the real movement of history even at the expense of the scientific work—and that ideas and perspectives had to be fought for. "Ideas," Marx had written in 1844, "cannot carry out anything at all. In order to carry out ideas men are needed who can exert practical force." No political team in history so epitomized this truth.

Very early, also, in their political careers Marx and Engels concluded that to be effective fighters they needed a perspective, a program. This is exactly what the second argument of this book speaks to. On the basis of both a reading of political history and their participation in the 1848 upheavals they reached one of their major programmatic conclusions—that only an alliance of the peasantry and urban petit bourgeoisie led by the proletariat could ensure the extension of democracy. Thus, the necessity of independent working-class political action—their bottom-line program. The question, then, is to what extent did this conclusion enable Marx and Engels to be effective? Their effectiveness can be assessed on at least two levels—the extent to which, in the aftermath of the 1848 upheavals, they successfully implemented their bottom-line program and second, the impact of this success on politics, that is, the real movement. Since, as Engels claimed, the IWMA was Marx's "crowning achievement," another way of posing the question is whether Marx's success in building the IWMA in the way he did was due to his being armed with their basic programmatic conclusion and, secondly, whether the IWMA was effective because it was based on this program. The second level of effectiveness begins to address the first argument of this book, about which more will be said shortly. The IWMA experience, of course, does not exhaust Marx and Engels's practice in the aftermath of the 1848 events but it was certainly the most important since it had decisive repercussions for their other practice. Thus, it would be useful to comment on other areas of their practice beyond the IWMA, especially their intervention in the German movement. Clearly it is not possible to "prove"—at least in the space of this book—the second argument. One problem is that their long-term effectiveness—the second level—can only be examined in their aftermath, the subject of another book. With that said, however, a more than credible case can be made that their basic program was critical in their achievements.

There is no gainsaying that the IWMA and the German party, beginning, in the case of the latter, with the Eisenachers' SDAP, were indeed independent working-class political organizations, a fact in which Marx and Engels played no small role. Their conscious intervention into both was crucial, especially since neither body was initiated by them. In other words, there was nothing inevitable about the direction of the two formations. Because independent working-class political action was so basic to what Marx and Engels were about they were supersensitive to any efforts to undermine it. At each step their vigilance stymied would-be saviors of the proletariat in whatever incarnation they took.

In the case of the IWMA in London, defensive shields had to be raised against the entreaties of the liberal bourgeoisie, aspiring parliamentarian careerists, and petit-bourgeois do-gooders—all of whom Marx successfully frustrated. Marx and Engels's actions were informed by the bottom-line programmatic position they had distilled from the real movement. As such it was a necessary condition in explaining their behavior; they had to at least be convinced politically in order to act politically. This does not in the least ignore other explanatory factors such as the many talents they employed in their successes; the tactic of *fortier in re, suaviter in modo* in the case of the IWMA was no doubt of importance. But in the final analysis a profound conviction in their program was the necessary underpinning for their success.

In Germany, to a somewhat similar array of nonproletarian suitors was added a much greater threat—Bismarck, to whom on a platter the Lassallean misleadership tried to offer the fledgling labor movement. Again, Marx and Engels were a, if not the, key roadblock to these designs, a fact that Bismarck acknowledged in his unsuccessful effort to woo Marx to his side. A strategic plank in their fight against the Lassallean "stench," such as the "one reactionary mass" slogan and workerist opposition to the democratic revolution, was, it should be remembered, their promotion of the people's alliance, the backbone of which was the worker-peasant alliance. That Marx and Engels were in the main successful in implementing their perspective of independent working-class political action in the German movement does not ignore the subsequent course of the SPD. As noted in chapter ten, Engels recognized a year before his death the possibility "that the party is going bourgeois," which he discounted. History would, however, prove him wrong. But as long as he and Marx were alive the indisputable fact is that the revisionist tendency, which they attacked as early as 1879 in their *Circular*, was not able to lead, at least not openly, the party in this direction, owing largely to their opposition. Whether this trend was inevitable or not is a question that later Marxists would have to grapple with—again, a subject for another volume.

That they were less successful in implementing this perspective in the English case testifies to the weight of other factors. In their view, the crumbs to the English working class from the imperialist ventures of its rulers, along with the concessions the latter made to the historic Chartist program, was the main obstacle to independent working-class political action there. Yet they remained optimistic that the objective obstacles would eventually be removed, a prediction Engels felt was fulfilled with the creation of England's first truly workers' party in 1893.

The English case, especially vis-à-vis the German one, alludes to the other dimension of Marx and Engels's effectiveness—the extent to which the implementation of their basic program increased the political efficacy of the adopting organizations. The first and most sweeping argument of this book, that no two people did more to advance the fight for democracy in the nineteenth century, is very much related to this dimension. Of the three arguments, as noted in the Preface, this is the most difficult to actually prove. An adequate proof, again, would require a volume that focused on the agential factor in the nineteenth-century democratic movement in its entirety and comparatively. Yet, if Rueschemeyer, Stephens, and Stephens are correct, which indeed seems to be the case, that the self-organization of the working class was responsible for the democratic breakthrough in the last century, then a prima facie case can easily be made that Marx and Engels were more than just effective. No other nineteenth-century figures played so decisive a role in the implementation of independent working class political action, the sine qua non for the self-organization of the working-class and, hence, the democratic breakthrough. Their effectiveness, therefore, surpassed that of any other political actors in modern history.

In considering this conclusion the reader should keep in mind the history of their lifelong commitment to the democratic struggle as detailed in this book. Draper's point about Marx's democratic credentials are instructive: "Marx was the first socialist figure to come to an acceptance of the socialist idea *through* the battle for the consistent extension of democratic control from below. He was the first figure in the socialist movement who, in a personal sense, came through the bourgeois-democratic movement: *through* it to its farthest bounds, and then out by its farthest end. In this sense, he was the first to fuse the struggle for consistent political democracy with the struggle for a socialist transformation."[1] Their contribution to the democratic breakthrough, therefore, was not inadvertent but purposive.

As for the particulars of Marx and Engels's practice and the self-organization of the working class it was primarily through the IWMA that they made their contribution. Though the bourgeoisie ascribed more influence to the organization than it actually had, the perception of influence—due largely to its independent character—became a source of influence. For politicizing workers throughout the world the IWMA and its memory was a model and source of inspiration. While the particulars of this process are beyond the province of this book, the mass working-class political parties that emerged in the last two decades of the nineteenth century, the concrete expressions for Rueschemeyer, Stephens, and Stephens's self-organization of the working classes, had their roots in one way or another in the IWMA, owing to the stature it had achieved. The German party and its achievements, in which Marx and Engels again played no small role, was also influential in serving as a model—which they often pointed to—for other national parties. But its embrace of independent working-class political action was due in part, as noted in chapter nine, to what they achieved with the IWMA.

Though the end of the IWMA meant that Marx and Engels lacked their own organization to promote their bottom line political position, they nonetheless exercised enormous influence in national parties in its aftermath precisely because of the influence they had won via the IWMA. The French and Russian cases illustrate the breadth of their interventions. The French case is noteworthy for Engels's campaign to convince the leadership of the Workers' Party, mainly the Lafargues, to defend bourgeois democracy against an aspiring Bonapartist dictator, giving lie to the oft-repeated charge that Marx and Engels gave insufficient attention to democratic forms and substance. As for Russia, they were convinced that a democratic revolution was a necessity and a possibility. They helped to educate the first generation of Russian socialists that only with such a revolution, based on the worker-peasant alliance, would it be possible to get to the socialist revolution—with the important proviso that the latter would have to be linked to the struggle of workers in western Europe, beginning with Germany, to take power, that is, to carry out their own socialist revolutions. A definitive case for Marx and Engels's decisive role in the establishment of mass workers' parties elsewhere in Europe would require from leaders of those parties the kind of testimony that German party leader Wilhelm Liebknecht supplied at Marx's funeral—Marx "was *the* man who *created* our party."

If Germany was a model of independent working-class political action, England exemplified until 1893 the model that Marx and Engels adamantly opposed, the class collaborationist labor-liberal coalition. The formation in 1893 in England of the first real independent workers' party was for Engels confirmation of their basic perspective, that is, workers would have to do it for themselves if they wanted to advance their interests. A detailed comparison—beyond the scope of this book—of German and English workers prior to 1893 might determine the comparative advantages, for these two cases at least, of independent working-class political action. While material and political gains for workers were important, they were not, it should be remembered in such a comparison, the sole criteria for Marx and Engels. Rather, and of higher priority for them, was the value of workers' self-education and self-organization through their own struggles for material and political gains, the necessary preparation for taking power and running a society in the interests of the majority. Subsequent history would show that German workers had a much higher level of revolutionary consciousness, in spite of their leadership—a fact that Marx and Engels recognized quite early—than their English counterparts, the result, perhaps, of their longer history of independent political action.

Was Marx and Engels's contribution to the democratic struggle, as I claim in my first argument, unequalled? Weren't there other figures who made at least as significant a contribution? Again, only a separate volume could provide a definitive answer. Yet the comparison in chapter five of the practice of Marx and Engels with that of Tocqueville is most telling and suggests where not to look for an answer. When confronted with the choice of popular control from below or a dictator from above, Tocqueville voted with his feet for the latter. The fact is that Tocqueville was not unique for those who are usually identified, at least today, with the democratic movement in the last century. The problem, of course, is today's construction of that movement, more specifically, the confusion of nineteenth-century liberalism with democracy. As Alan Kahan rightly points out about liberalism between 1830 and 1870, "All liberals reject universal suffrage and democracy in the here and now. All theoretically support it under certain conditions to be met at some point in the (generally distant) future."[2] As well as Tocqueville, the other key liberal figure that Kahan's generalization applies to is J. S. Mill. Marx and Engels understood this side of Mill quite well and, thus, made sure that his influence in the International would be limited.[3] Therefore, if there were individuals who rivalled Marx and Engels's contribution to the democratic struggle, they're not likely to be found in the ranks of nineteenth-century liberalism.

A couple of final comments about the arguments of this book. By now it should be clear that Marx and Engels would not have been surprised at the chief finding of Rueschemeyer, Stephens, and Stephens about the critical role of the working class in the institutionalization of democracy, the point of departure for this book. As not only participants but architects of the self-organization of the working class they witnessed its origins and development and understood as communists its significance for the democratic revolution. Because they were so intimately involved with the process they had a much more nuanced understanding of what was involved, in terms of tactics and strategy, than the more global analysis of Rueschemeyer, Stephens, and Stephens (as well, to be discussed shortly, they had no illusions about what was involved). The centrality of the worker-peasant alliance to their strategy can't be emphasized enough. Göran Therborn's earlier work, which Rueschemeyer, Stephens, and Stephens draw on, does recognize the role of that alliance in some settings, though he too seems to be unaware of Marx and Engels's historic contribution to its implementation.[4] And nowhere was their influence more visible on this score than in the Russian Revolution—again, a subject for another book. Thus, recent scholarship seems at last to have grasped what the founders of modern socialism understood all too well about the process of democratization.

The unique contribution of this book is a close reading of Marx and Engels's practice and their undertanding of that practice—a necessary correction to Rueschemeyer, Stephens and Stephens's overly deterministic explanation of the democratic breakthrough. Again, no claim is being made here for a conclusive treatment of the crucially important agential factor in the breakthrough. I claim only to lay the basis for the centrality of Marx and Engels's role. This more politically robust explanation of the breakthrough provides an additional benefit. If the IWMA was the incubator for the self-organization of the working class, then the U.S. Civil War was the impetus for the first democratic wave—thus, pushing the date for its onset a number of decades earlier than what Rueschemeyer, Stephens and Stephens propose. As Marx said on more than one occasion, the War was the "tocsin" or signal for independent working class political action. What he and his partner grasped better than any of their contemporaries—and many thereafter—was the global character of the democratic struggle, a fact that rings even truer today.

To conclude, then, a more than credible case can be made that (1) Marx and Engels were the leading protagonists in the democratic movement in the nineteenth century because they (2) constituted a revolutionary partnership and (3) were largely effective in instituting independent working-class political action, the basis for the self-organization of the working class. In substantiating the second and third arguments, demonstrated clearly by the evidence presented in this book, a prima facie, if not conclusive, case can be made for the first and most sweeping argument.

The Depoliticization of Marx and Engels: Toward an Explanation

Since the standard apolitical portrait of Marx—Engels, again, less so—is so at odds with what this book presents, an explanation or, at least, a step toward one is required to account for the emergence and persistence of this myth. At least two reasons, it seems to me, can be advanced to this end. They both have to do in varying degrees with a glaring fact about Marxology, the source of the myth—very much an academic enterprise.

The first reason, as suggested by the history of Marxology, is that with the rise of Stalinism in the thirties the academy became a refuge for those who resisted the orthodoxy of Moscow and its sycophants in the West. In the academy one could study what Marx and Engels wrote without reprobation and recriminations and be creative with their ideas while critiquing at the same time what was being done in their names. From the Frankfurt School to its descendants in the post–World War II period, especially the fifties and "turbulent" sixties and seventies, the academy was the most likely place where their readings could be read free of Moscow's templates.[5]

However well intentioned the effort was to create a refuge in the academy, it had two unintended and negative consequences. One was that it created the false impression that a real refuge had been created. It mistook the academy for the real movement where, outside the academy, Stalinism was enormously influential—in both the advanced capitalist world as well as the so-called Third World. Marx and Engels would have argued that the fight against Stalinism had to be waged in the real movement, in politics and not in the academy. As long as Stalinism was triumphant outside the hallowed halls there was no real refuge.

Second, like the refuge that medieval monastic life provided for the ancient classics, the academy's sanctuary for Marx and Engels's writings tended to scholasticize its refugees, divorcing them increasingly from the terrain on which they were meant by their authors to operate—the real movement. Just as was true for ancient knowledge in the monastic world, the academy's protection came with a price—increasing obscurantism. To better grasp what happened it is important to understand the practice of the scholar-intellectual in whose hands Marx and Engels's project became a ward.

By and large the political theorists and humanities scholars who were most attracted to their ideas were not activists (except perhaps when inspired by the real movement). Their mode of production is, like many academic intellectuals (but not all), profoundly individual.[6] Collective action, the subordination of themselves when necessary to the real movement is simply not their thing. At times the real movement may force them to descend from the heavens to Earth to become participants (but even then more likely as observers, advisors, or teachers as opposed to students of the real movement). Marxologists and political theorists, in general, find uninteresting that which Marx and Engels spent most of their time on—politics. Thus the focus on their "texts" and the creation of a canon, focusing especially on Marx's precommunist days, in the tradition of more conventional theory. The meetings, factional struggles, policy statements, party publications are unworthy of serious consideration. George Lichtheim's comment about the IWMA is classic: "a wearisome tale of complicated maneuvering in the pursuit of which much toil and virtue were consumed."[7] With that he feels justified in devoting less than three percent of his highly acclaimed *Marxism: An Historical and Critical Study* to the IWMA.

Some academics who might be inclined to be sympathetic may not be equipped experientially to understand and grasp Marx and Engels's political practice. Put simply, it is far easier for a revolutionary activist, someone who has to grapple with many of the same political and organizational problems, to understand and appreciate their practice than someone who is not. For a Lenin—the quintessential revolutionary—their writings in their entirety were invaluable; he couldn't get enough. The unavoidable fact is that there is in general an inverse relationship between the years spent in the academy and the time spent in revolutionary politics. Finally, political scientists who study the "real world" should in theory find what Marx and Engels did most of the time attractive. Their problem, by and large, is both political and intellectual. As for the former, their political leanings do not dispose them to be open to that side of Marx and Engels; thus the failure until now of looking at their contribution to the transition to democracy.[8] Regarding the latter, the actual study of politics, due in part to methodological traditions as varied as positivism, textual analysis, and postmodernism, is of little interest for much of the discipline.

A second reason for the depoliticization is political, specifically, the fallout from the split in the international socialist movement during World War I into Social Democracy and Communism. The adherents and/or fellow-travellers of the former, many of whom would exercise a conscious and unconscious influence on the portrayal and interpretation of Marx and Engels in subsequent decades—especially in the academy, where many did their "practice"—viewed the latter as Leninists-cum-Stalinists. To the extent that Leninism was equated with voluntarism and/or activism, then anything smacking or suggestive of such in Marx and Engels was either ignored or falsified. Their "party" activities were denied along with anything suggestive of political strategy and tactics such as their usage of the "dictatorship of the proletariat." In other words, every effort had to be made to erect the proverbial Chinese wall between the practice of Marx and Engels on the one side and Lenin on the other. Some of these Marxologists were actually former "party people" like Lichtheim. "Former" is the operative word. In departing from Stalinist formations they oftentimes left as demoralized and disillusioned used-to-be's. Hence, their tendency to go even further in depoliticizing Marx and Engels or misreading them through their own disillusionment with party activities. For those few within the academy who approach them as first and foremost political people, they are less likely, it appears, to be Marxologists but rather self-conscious Marxists or sympathizers whose experiences in the laboratory of politics and the class struggle have been on balance positive—a category in which I include myself.

The two reasons offered here for the depoliticization of Marx and Engels do not in the least deny that other factors are at play. They represent at best a preliminary inquiry into this most salient and disingenuous feature of the Marxological industry.

Marxism after Marx and Engels

To treat Marx and Engels as political people without at least acknowledging all that was done in their names in their aftermath would be inconsistent with what they were about. If, to pose the issue more concretely, they had every reason to be proud of their accomplishments at the end of their lives, would they feel the same today? It should be said immediately, and as alluded to on many occasions throughout the book, this question can only be answered in a subsequent volume. Consistent with their methodology, any effort to explain the reality of Social Democracy and Stalinism in the twentieth century would have to be materially and politically situated. However, it is possible to address the more specific issue whether the rise of Stalinism can be traced to them if not through sins of commission then by omission or default. Is it true, as is often charged, that Stalinism has its roots in their failure to take seriously, or as the more milder version of this critique goes, to be explicit about democratic governance? As one recent critic argued, it is the "silences" in their "classic texts" on democratic forms and civil liberties that explain in part why subsequent revolutionaries erred on the question of democracy.[9]

The reader of this book should certainly know by now that this charge is utterly groundless (I leave aside the question of the origins of Stalinism, which, again, can only be explored in another volume). It reflects amongst circles that should know better the depths of the ignorance about the very core of Marx and Engels's practice—the legacy of treating them solely through their "classic texts." To recall Engels's response in 1892 to a similar charge: "Marx and I, for forty years, repeated ad nauseam that for us the democratic republic is the only political form in which the struggle between the working class and the capitalist class can first be universalised and then culminate in the decisive victory of the proletariat."[10] Or, his educational to Bernstein in 1884: "For the seizure of political power, democratic *forms* are also necessary to the proletariat for whom . . . like all political forms, they are only a means. But if . . . you want democracy as an *end*, you have to look for support to the peasants and the petty bourgeoisie. . . ." Democratic forms, hence, were extremely important in order to realize the substance of democracy.

Encapsulated in Engels's comments was his and Marx's fundamental strategy. To briefly recapitulate, their politics begins with the quest for democracy. Their unique and decisive contribution was the claim that only if political power were in the hands of the proletariat, what they sometimes called the dictatorship of the proletariat, would democracy be realized. Like other socialists they understood, of course, that its realization was dependent on the elimination of social inequality. But the latter could only proceed with the dictatorship of the proletariat. (The people's alliance, the backbone of which was the worker-peasant alliance, was the means to that dictatorship.) Previous efforts at democracy, they argued, had been limited, as Engels tried to educate Bernstein years later, because of the narrow view of who constituted the "demos" in the democracy. What was unique about the proletariat was that its liberation could only be realized through the liberation of all other oppressed layers that had historically been excluded from the "demos." (They included, by the way, women as part of the historically oppressed who too would benefit from the proletariat's fight, contrary to the claims of some, such as the aforementioned critic.)

The charge that they paid insufficient attention to forms of democratic governance is simply not true but, more importantly, it reveals a lack of understanding of Marx and Engels's politics. There had been historically no want of insights on democratic governance, which they duly acknowledged. What was of greater import and missing in everything that had been done till then was the problem of the "demos," that is, how to extend democracy to the most oppressed, the majority that had always been excluded. Their priority, which is what they devoted their lives to, was to get political power into the hands of the proletariat. It was from that vantage point that they addressed matters of governance and administration, which, for them, always had to be contextualized. They indeed had no patience with abstract principles of governance and viewed with suspicion constitutional engineering. "The machinery of government cannot be too simple. It is always the craft of knaves to make it complicated and mysterious."[11] Thus their criticism of what they labelled "the Montesquieu-[Jean Louis] Delolme worm-eaten theory of division of powers" principle. In the context of the German Revolution of 1848, this principle, as they argued in the pages of the *NRZ*, was an obstacle to democracy.

It should also be remembered that from the beginning of their political activities they fought against potential and real dictators in the workers' movement, be it Proudhon, Bakunin, or Lassalle. They motivated and implemented organizational norms that were designed to limit such developments, although they were under no illusions that such norms in and of themselves would prevent this from happening. The detailed attention they gave, especially Marx in the CL and IWMA, to organizational matters was also part of this effort. Marx's warning to Schweitzer about centralist norms in German trade unions underscores his approach to governance: "Here [Germany] where the worker is regulated bureaucratically from childhood onwards, where he believes in authority, in those set over him, the main thing is *to teach him to walk by himself.*"[12] While it is true that the German party would in their aftermath be subjected to what came to be called the "iron law of oligarchy," they nonetheless recognized its early symptoms and did everything they could to head it off.

Thus, to fully understand Marx and Engels's views on democracy is to know what they did as well as what they wrote, in other words, their practice. Critics and sympathizers who depend on the "classic texts" run the risk of getting at best only half the picture. Their "theory of democracy" combines both their pronouncements and their practice. Their most basic premise was that democracy had to be fought for. The best texts, constitutions or intentions could never ensure the institution of democracy—witness the fate of Germany's well-crafted liberal constitution of 1849, or the ill-fated maneuvers of Tocqueville the politician about the same time—only a fight would do that. Their unique contribution was an understanding of the class forces that had it in their interest and capability to effectively carry out such a fight. History revealed, as substantiated by Rueschemeyer, Stephens, and Stephens, that Marx and Engels were indeed correct in their analysis and their decision, therefore, to prioritize the empowerment of the proletariat in the fight for democracy's realization.

At the same time, Marx and Engels had no illusions about workers' parties as they began to be formed in the 1870s and 1880s. Their *Circular of 1879* comments on more than one occasion about the German party becoming "bourgeois," and anticipation of the problem of its bureaucratization testify to their sobriety. Of particular importance, given the subsequent course of Social Democracy, they entertained no illusions about the electoral process as a means for taking state power. Elections were not an end in themselves but only a "thermometer"—the best, in Engels's opinion—to determine the most propitious time to resort to armed struggle. Also, as Engels emphasized in his warnings about the Bonapartist threat in France in 1889, workers' parties that were devoid of proletarian internationalism were susceptible to national chauvinism, which would in turn undermine democracy and, thus, the socialist struggle. Democratic gains would be tenuous as long as state power remained in the hands of the bourgeoisie—an insight that resonates even better at the end of the twentieth century than it did then.

If the critics' charge is that Marx and Engels failed to specify models of governance for a postrevolutionary society, they would gladly plead guilty for reasons that have already been discussed—their life-long disdain for socialist blueprints. If implicit in the criticism is the assumption that democratic governance can be assured by the availability of such prescriptions, they are surely mistaken. They would do well to take to heart Marx and Engels's oft-repeated observation, again based on a reading of history, about the unforeseen aspects of the revolutionary process.[13] As the Paris Commune had demonstrated, only the real movement could settle questions about the modes of governance in a postcapitalist world. The duty of communists was to distill the lessons of such experiences (the point made earlier about Marxism being the quintessential work in progress).

There is another vital point about Marx and Engels's practice that's been noted on a number of occasions in this book but is virtually ignored by the critics—the importance of adequate preparatory time for revolutions. In other words, the circumstances under which a revolution is made is determinant in whether the masses can rid "itself of all the muck of ages and become fitted to found society anew," that is, to, amongst other things, successfully institute democratic functioning. Thus, the reason for their constant counsel of revolutionary restraint in order that the masses take power under the best possible circumstances. At the same time, they correctly understood that in some circumstances revolutionary forces might be forced to take power prematurely, as in the case of the Commune. And not the least of the circumstances that might force such action was the international setting. But it was exactly such incalculables as these that explain their "silences," not out of disregard for democratic governance but rather a profound understanding of the reality of revolutionary transformation.

Without getting into the track record of socialist revolutions in the twentieth century, I would only remind the reader of Marx's pregnant observation in the *Eighteenth Brumaire* about the difficulty, relative to bourgeois revolutions, in carrying out such transformations:

> [P]roletarian revolutions . . . criticise themselves constantly, interrupt themselves continually in their own course, come back to the apparently accomplished in order to begin it afresh, deride with unmerciful thoroughness the inadequacies, weaknesses and paltrinesses of their first attempts, seem to throw down their adversary only in order that he may draw new strength from the earth and rise again, more gigantic, before them, and recoil again and again from the indefinite prodigiousness of their own aims, until a situation has been created which makes all turning back impossible, and the conditions themselves cry out:
>
> Hic Rhodus, hic salta!
> Here is the rose, here dance!

No two political leaders in all of history provided their followers with as much foresight as did Marx and Engels. They did as much as any mortals could do to prepare their cadre for the "situation . . . which makes all turning back impossible," namely, the future battles. History, in turn, would judge whether those who spoke and acted in their names took full advantage of what was bequeathed to them. But, again, that's another story.

Notes

PREFACE

1. Dietrich Rueschemeyer, Evelyne Stephens, John Stephens, *Capitalist Development and Democracy* (Chicago: University of Chicago Press, 1992), p. 141. By "working class" they mean "employed manual labor outside of agriculture" (p. 59). What Marx and Engels understood by "working class"—not inconsistent with this definition—will become clear as part of the explication of their political strategy and tactics.

2. Eric Hobsbawm, *The Age of Empire: 1875–1914* (New York: Pantheon Books, 1987), p. 127.

3. As many forests as have been felled for the Marxological industry, it is telling that the number of books that prioritize Marx and Engels's political activities can literally be counted on one hand and a couple of fingers. There is, in chronological order of publication: David Riazanov's 1927 classic, *Karl Marx and Friedrich Engels: An Introduction to Their Lives and Work* (New York: Monthly Review Press, 1973), which remains the best introduction; Boris Nicolaievsky and Otto Maenchen-Helfen, *Karl Marx: Man and Fighter* (New York: Penguin, 1983); Oscar Hammen's *The Red '48ers: Karl Marx and Frederick Engels* (New York: Charles Scribner's Sons, 1969); Richard N. Hunt's, in spite of its title, *The Political Ideas of Marx and Engels, Vols. I and II* (Pittsburgh: University of Pittsburgh Press, 1974, 1984); Hal Draper's four-volume work, *Karl Marx's Theory of Revolution* (New York: Monthly Review Press, 1977–1990)—hereafter, *KMTR*; Alan Gilbert's *Marx's Politics: Communists and Citizens* (New Brunswick, N.J.: Rutgers University Press, 1981); and lastly, David Felix's thoroughly tendentious work, *Marx as Politician* (Carbondale, Ill.: Southern Illinois University Press, 1983). None of these books, however, provides a detailed analysis of the party activities of the Marx-Engels team from beginning to the end as is done here. Draper informed me before his death in 1990 that he had intended to do such a work but apparently was unable to complete a manuscript.

4. Taylor, *From Napoleon to the Second International* (London: Hamish Hamilton, 1994), p. 312.

5. Terrell Carver, ed., *The Cambridge Companion to Marx* (Cambridge: Cambridge University Press, 1991), p. 12. Carver's recent and admittedly "defensive" response to his critics reveals that he still can't get beyond his self-centered and, thus, apolitical reading of the Marx-Engels partnership. They "must be treated," according to him, "much as we treat ourselves as

intellectuals and as persons" or "the way that most of us live out the relationships from which we construct our intellectual and personal lives"; "The Engels-Marx Question: Interpretation, Identity/ies, Partnership, Politics," *Engels After Marx*, eds. Manfred B. Steger and Terrell Carver (University Park: The Pennsylvania State University Press, 1999), pp. 34–35.

6. The reasons for the depoliticization of Marx, and to a lesser extent Engels, are discussed in the "Conclusions."

7. The one exception to this is my discussion in chapter eight of Engels's characterization of the Paris Commune as the dictatorship of the proletariat.

8. For more details see his *KMTR, I,* pp. 3–4.

9. Draper's two companion volumes to his *Chronicle, The Marx-Engels Register: A Complete Bibliography of Marx and Engels's Individual Writings,* and *The Marx-Engels Glossary: Glossary to the Chronicle and Register and Index to the Glossary,* are also invaluable reference works. All three are published by Schocken Books, New York, 1985–1986.

CHAPTER ONE.

THE DEMOCRATIC URGE AND COMMENCEMENT
OF A REVOLUTIONARY PARTNERSHIP

1. Karl Marx and Frederick Engels, *Collected Works,* Vol. 24, p. 585. Hereafter, citations from the *Collected Works* will be designated by the volume as 4, for example, and then the page(s).

2. 42, pp. 567–68.

3. *Marx and Engels through the Eyes of their Contemporaries* (Moscow: Progress Publishers, 1978), pp. 8–9.

4. 2, pp. 408–9.

5. V. E. Kunina, ed., *Frederick Engels: His Life and Works—Documents and Photographs* (Moscow, Progress Publishers, 1987), p. 433.

6. For the relevant biographical details see Boris Nicolaievsky and Otto Maenchen-Helfen, *Karl Marx: Man and Fighter* (New York: Penguin Books, 1983), Franz Mehring, *Karl Marx: The Story of His Life* (London: George Allen & Unwin, 1951); Riazanov's *Karl Marx and Frederick Engels,* and Draper's *The Marx-Engels Chronicle: A Day-by-Day Chronology of Marx and Engels' Life and Activity* [hereafter, *Chronicle*] (New York: Schocken Books, 1985). Although clearly anti-Marxist, Hammen's *The Red '48ers* provides useful contextual information. The same can be said for Felix's *Marx as Politician*

7. Marx's rebellious tendencies were clearly evident in citing approvingly in the foreword to what was to have been his published dissertation the work of a friend that yearned for an alternative to the current regime.

Other than of course his own writings, perhaps the best detailed treatment of the evolution of Marx's political ideas before the *Communist Manifesto* is Draper's *Karl Marx's Theory of Revolution: Vol. I. State and Bureaucracy* [hereafter, *KMTR, I*] (New York: Monthly Review Press, 1977). Gary Teeple's *Marx's Critique of Politics: 1842–1847* (Toronto: University of Toronto Press, 1984) is useful at the level of ideas but limited because it ignores Marx's practice during this period including, most importantly, the partnership he formed with Engels.

8. 1, p. 130.

9. 1, p. 382.

10. 1, pp. 137–38.

11. 1, p. 133.

12. 1, 392

13. Ibid.

14. 1, p. 395.

15. 1, p. 400.

16. 3, p.133

17. Ibid., p. 134. Regarding the importance of the exchange of letters as well as their limitations, see Marx and Engels's comments in *The German Ideology* (5, p.236), on the problem of imprecise formulations. Also, see Engels's letter in Dec. 1890 (Draper, *Chronicle,* p. 261) regarding a request to reprint the exchange and why he objected unless done as part of a collected works publication.

18. Ibid., p. 141

19. Ibid., p. 142.

20. Ibid., p. 144.

21. 3, p. 186–87.

22. 3, p. 201. It is interesting to note that in his discussion of the song, Marx does not refer to the line, "the constables serve their Graces [i.e., the manufacturers]" (see Draper, *KMTR,* I, p. 177, for a translation of the entire song). This was clearly a recognition by the strikers that the state served the interests of the manufacturers. The reason that Marx may not have commented on this very important expression of class consciousness of the strikers is that he himself had yet to formulate such a position—i.e., a class theory of the state. By the following year, however, he, along with Engels, would do exactly that.

23. Draper, *Chronicle,* p. 16.

24. 3, pp. 202–6.

25. Draper, *KMTR, I,* p. 181. For the entire letter, see 3, p. 580.

26. One of the few Young Hegelians who agreed with Marx was Georg Jung. He wrote to Marx in June 1844 that the "Silesian weaver's strike is a brilliant confirmation of M's thesis in *DFJ* on the role of the proletariat" (Draper, *Chronicle,* p. 17).

27. 2, p. 267.

28. Hammen, p. 40.

29. 2, pp. 373–74.

30. 3, p. 393.

31. Ibid., p. 397.

32. 3, 416.

33. The standard biographies on Marx and Engels say that in the first meeting between the two, November 16, 1842 (Draper, *Chronicle,* p. 13), Marx was standoffish, thinking that Engels was associated with the "Free" group. While this may be true, it is clear from his references to Marx in the English press that the meeting did not prejudice Marx in Engels's eyes.

34. Felix, p. 35.

35. This appears to be the case because the extant correspondence between them at this early period is almost exclusively Engels's letters to Marx; the latter's letters have never been

located. It appears that Engels destroyed them in 1848 in anticipation of a police crackdown (Draper, *Chronicle*, pp. 36–37).

36. Draper, *KMTR, I*, p. 223.

37. 4, p.86

38. Ibid., p. 84.

39. Ibid., p. 119.

40. 38, pp. 3–6. This comes from the earliest surviving letter in the correspondence between Marx and Engels.

41. 38, p. 18.

42. 38, p. 17.

43. Shortly after Marx's death in 1883, Engels discovered the uncompleted manuscripts for the remaining volumes of *Capital*. He noted that Marx kept secret the progress he was making knowing that had Engels been aware he would have "pestered [him] until he consented to its publication" (47, p. 3).

44. 38, p. 3.

45. 38, p. 27.

46. 38, p. 9.

47. See above, fn. 35.

48. Felix, pp. 36–37.

49. 38, p. 10.

50. 38, p. 23.

51. 38, p. 5. For a more detailed treatment by Engels on this point see his "Speeches in Elberfeld" in 1845, 4, pp. 248–49.

52. 4, pp. 262–63.

53. He said as much almost fifty years later in the "Preface" to a reprint of *The Condition of the Working-Class in England* (27, p. 261). At the same time this conclusion should be qualified by noting a comment Engels made in a letter to Marx, a couple of months before the Elberfeld speeches. Referring to his stinging attack on the English bourgeoisie in *The Condition*, which he was then writing, he says, "[M]y blows . . . are meant for . . . the German bourgeoisie, to whom I make it plain enough that they are as bad as their English counterparts . . ." (38, p. 11). But then, about a month later, he reported that at that time, support for communism came mainly from "the middle class." The reason, as he explained to probably surprised English readers, was that "this class in Germany is far more disinterested, impartial, and intelligent than in England . . . because it is poorer. . . . We, however, hope to be in a short time supported by the working classes who always and everywhere must form the strength and body of the Socialist party . . ." (4, p. 230).

Also, there is some evidence that already within two months of the Elberfeld speech, Engels was reconsidering his views about large and small capital. Referring specifically to communist intervention in the Associations for the Benefit of the Working Classes, he reported on their success in critiquing "middle-class . . . measures . . . to benefit working people. . . . Thus the intention of the middle classes, to dupe the working classes, by hypocrisy and sham philanthropy, has been totally frustrated" (4, p. 237). What might explain the apparent discrepancy between the Elberfeld speech and this comment is that Engels may have looked more favorably on capitalists who attended communist-organized public events where he and other communists spoke than on those who participated in the Associations.

54. 4, p. 721.

55. 38, p. 22.

56. For the complete draft of the plan, see 4, p. 666.

57. Teeple argues convincingly (chap. 5) that much of the content of the planned book was realized in other writings during this period.

58. See above, p. 5.

59. 38, p. 22.

60. 5, p. 6. These quotes are from the version of the *Theses* edited by Engels in 1888 in order to make them more readable.

61. 6, p. 662.

62. See above, p. 12.

63. See Engels's article, 6, pp. 3–14, on the proceedings of the conference for which he utilized coverage in the English press.

64. 4, pp. 613–44. Although the *Marx-Engels Werke* dates this piece to Spring 1845, that is, before the England trip, the *MECW*, more accurately points out that while the translation of Fourier's writings were no doubt done earlier, the introduction, interpolations, and ending "were most probably written not before August . . ." (p. 713). They returned to Brussels about August 24. See, also, Draper, *Register*, p. 111.

65. Ibid., p. 614.

66. Engels's rejection of an "absolute method" very early in his political life is noteworthy given the oft-repeated charge—to be addressed in chapter ten—that that was exactly what he did to Marx's views.

67. 26, 314.

68. 4, p. 646.

69. Ibid., pp. 647–48.

70. 5, p. 236.

71. 29, p. 264.

72. 26, p. 520.

73. In support of this see Draper, *Chronicle*, pp. 229 and 263.

74. 5, pp. 52–53.

CHAPTER TWO.
FROM THEORY TO PRACTICE:
TOWARD A COMMUNIST PARTY

1. 26, pp. 318–19.

2. Draper, *Chronicle*, p. 22.

3. 38, pp. 38–39.

4. Hammen, p. 142.

5. For anti-Marxists such as Felix or Hammen, Marx's besting of Weitling was the onset of Marxist "liquidations" or "purges ." Draper convincingly refutes such a reading in his *KMTR, II,* pp. 654–59.

6. <u>38</u>, p. 537.

7. <u>6</u>, p. 45.

8. <u>6</u>, p. 47.

9. Again, see Draper, *KMTR, II,* pp. 654–59.

10. <u>6</u>, pp. 54–56.

11. About a month before writing to Köttgen, Marx complained of his personal financial straits and his limited options for getting money. "No doubt there are sundry bourgeois in Cologne who would probably advance me the money for a definite period. But some time ago these people adopted a line that in principle is diametrically opposed to my own, and hence I should not care to be beholden to them in any way" (<u>38</u>, p.43). Thus, at the personal level Marx, quite early, avoided financial arrangements that might be politically compromising. A self-financed communist movement was the way to avoid such a problem at the organizational level.

12. The theoretical roots of this line can be found in various statements by Engels— Marx, to a lesser degree—written prior to this letter. For a useful overview, see Draper, *KMTR, II,* pp. 169–79.

13. <u>38</u>, p. 71.

14. <u>38</u>, p. 82.

15. Draper, *KMTR, II,* p. 547. Draper also provides more details on the various usages of the term.

16. Alvin Gouldner, *Against Fragmentation* (New York: Oxford University Press, 1985), p. 102, and Peter Jones, *The 1848 Revolutions* (New York: Longman, 1991), p. 8. Although Gouldner is mistaken in his claim that Marx mistook artisans for the industrial proletariat, he does provide some useful background material on their changing situation. For a firsthand account of an artisan's reality and radicalization, see the autobiography of the long-time Marx party activist Frederick Lessner, *Sixty Years in the Social-Democratic Movement* (London: The Twentieth Century Press, 1907), particularly chapters I and II.

17. <u>20</u>, p. 28. He also wrote that during his Paris stay he got to know Proudhon and "In the course of lengthy debates often lasting all night, I infected him with very much to his detriment with Hegelianism . . ."

18. Engels encouraged Marx to prioritize *The Poverty of Philosophy* over *The German Ideology*: "[S]hould the placing [with publishers] of our manuscripts [*The German Ideology*] clash with the placing of your book, then, for heaven's sake, chuck the manuscripts into a corner, for it's far more important that your book should appear. We're neither of us likely to make much more out of our work in that quarter" (<u>38</u>, p. 114). (Hammen's rendering of the last sentence, p. 128, is more readable: "Neither of us bit off very much in our work on it.")

19. Draper, *KMTR, II,* p. 81.

20. <u>6</u>, p. 211.

21. Ibid., p. 212.

22. Nicolaievsky and Maenchen-Helfen, p. 115.

23. Felix, p. 69.

24. Hobsbawm, pp. 143–44.

25. It is instructive to look at Blanqui's organizational norms in order to put in perspective what Marx and Engels advocated. See Paul Corcoran, ed., *Before Marx: Socialism and Communism in France, 1830–48* (New York: St. Martin's Press, 1983), pp. 34–35.

26. See above, p. 13.

27. This might explain why there is virtually nothing in the Marx-Engels writings of this period in criticism of Blanqui who more than anyone was identified with conspiratorial organizing. That is, their significant opponent was Weitling and not Blanqui, who never identified himself as a communist. To the extent that Weitling, the self-styled communist, advocated the Babouvian model then it was he whom Marx and Engels had to debate on this question.

28. Felix, p. 69, and Gouldner, p. 94.

29. Hunt, p. 264.

30. Nicolaievsky and Maenchen-Helfen, pp. 115–16.

31. Draper, *Chronicle*, p. 24.

32. See for example, Gouldner, pp. 104–5.

33. 6, pp. 83–84.

34. 38, p. 91.

35. That Marx was unaware, as late as December, of the changes underway in the League, is indicated by a comment he made in a letter of the 28th of the month: "[T]here is a large faction in the German communist party which bears me a grudge because I am opposed to its utopias and its declaiming" (38, p. 105).

36. Draper, *Chronicle*, p. 25.

37. 26, p. 320.

38. Hammen, p. 160.

39. Hammen, p. 160.

40. 17, pp. 79–80.

41. His letter of March 7, to Roland Daniels (38, pp. 110–11), while intentionally not specific—owing to security concerns—indicates the urgency and seriousness that he lent to this effort.

42. 6, p. 594.

43. 6, p. 303.

44. There has been much speculation about Marx's absence. While it is probably true that he was strapped for money he was able to scrape up enough to finance the publication of his anti-Proudhon tract, *The Poverty of Philosophy*, which appeared a month after the congress. Clearly, then, he prioritized the usage of the limited monies at his disposal. Also, as Nicolaievsky and Maenchen-Helfen persuasively argue, the money that the Brussels commune raised to send Wolff to the congress could have been used to send Marx. Their claim is "that before associating himself definitely with the League Marx wanted to await the results of the congress" (p. 132). Another possibility is that Marx saw Engels's participation as sufficient for their team, given the history of class baiting within the League. This might explain why Marx asked Wolff, whose peasant origins would have made him less vulnerable to such sniping, to attend.

45. 6, p. 595.

46. 45, p. 288.

47. 6, p. 603.

48. 38, p. 134.

49. Although Belgium was nominally a constitutional monarchy, sarcastically called by Marx and Engels "the model constitutional state," it was not in their opinion another Britain. In spite of its bourgeois revolution in 1830, political democracy was still curtailed and its monarch, King Leopold, was a near autocrat. Leopold's presence represented in their view, "thermidorian rule," i.e., a counterrevolution in power (7, p. 165).

50. 6, p. 294.

51. This alliance of the "people" has generally been ignored in most accounts of Marx and Engels's political strategy. It is crucial in any discussion on Lenin's understanding of the politics of Marx and Engels. For two exceptions to this major oversight, see Mary-Alice Waters, "The Workers' and Farmers' Government: A Popular Revolutionary Dictatorship," *New International* 1, 3 (1984), and John Ehrenberg, *The Dictatorship of the Proletariat: Marxism's Theory of Socialist Democracy* (New York: Routledge, 1992). Draper, *KMTR, II*, particularly chapters 7–10, recognizes the alliance in their writings but less explicitly than the aforementioned writings.

52. 6., p. 321.

53. Engels may have been drawing on Marx's brief treatment of this matter in *The Poverty of Philosophy*, where he quotes the British economist and utopian John Bray in order to refute Proudhon: "Mr Bray [unlike Proudhon and his panaceas] . . . proposes merely measures which he thinks good for a period of transition between existing society and a community regime" (6, p. 142).

54. Riazanov, p. 75.

55. Riazanov, *The Communist Manifesto of Karl Marx and Friedrich Engels* (New York: Russell and Russell, 1963), p. 291. See Appendix E for the entire issue.

56. 6, pp. 349–50.

57. Felix, p. 72.

58. 17, p.80.

59. There had been a precedent for the League's charge to Marx and Engels. In 1838, Wilhelm Weitling "was commissioned by the League [of the Just] to prepare its first major publication," *Die Menschleit, wie sie ist und wie sein sollte* (Carl Wittke, *The Utopian Communist: A Biography of Wilhelm Weitling Nineteenth-Century Reformer* [Baton Rouge: Louisiana State University Press, 1950]), p. 23.

60. Riazanov, *Karl Marx and Friedrich Engels*, p. 75.

61. 6, p. 388.

62. Hammen, p. 169.

63. The entire letter is in Riazanov, *Karl Marx*, p. 78. It is odd that the *MECW* failed to include this most important document in what is otherwise a fairly complete collection of materials relevant to the *Manifesto's* origins. Could it be that the editors were perpetuating Moscow's long tradition of mythologizing the founders of the world communist movement?

64. Hunt, p. 189.

CHAPTER THREE.

THE REVOLUTIONS OF 1848–1849:
PARTICIPATING IN THE "REAL MOVEMENT"

1. Lenin, *Collected Works*, Vol. 13 (Moscow: Progress, 1978), p. 37.

2. 41, p. 87.

3. 41, p. 82.

4. This translation is Draper's in his *The Annotated Communist Manifesto* (Berkeley: Center for Socialist History, 1984), p. 32, which in many ways is superior to the Authorized English Translation (AET) of 1888. Hereafter, however, I will utilize the AET version unless stated otherwise.

5. The relevant section in Engels's *Principles of Communism*, "Question 25," spells out the *raison d'être* of this strategy.

6. The significance of the change that Engels made in 1888 is quite important and is related to what will be discussed later in this chapter, the actual course of the German bourgeoisie in the 1848–1849 revolution.

7. Interestingly, when Engels quoted from this section of the *Manifesto* for an article he wrote in 1884 he transcribed it as follows: "In Germany the Communist Party fights with the bourgeoisie whenever it acts in a revolutionary way, against the absolute monarchy, the feudal landowners and *philistinism*" [italics added] (26, p. 121). By substituting "philistinism" for "petty bourgeoisie" Engels may have been making an effort to correct the original language of the *Manifesto* to reflect what actually happened in the course of 1848–49. Of course, in his Authorized English Translation of 1888 Engels retained the original language.

8. Draper, *The Annotated*, pp. 110–11, argues persuasively that the oft-quoted phrase in the *Manifesto*, the "idiocy of rural life" is in fact a mistranslation. The more accurate translation would be "privatized isolation of rural life." The most significant exception to this silence concerns Poland, where it says that communists support the Polish party "that insists on an agrarian revolution as the prime condition for national emancipation. . . ." In speeches that Marx and Engels were making at the time the *Manifesto* was about to be published they argued that Poland's national liberation depended on a radical land reform in order to mobilize the peasantry.

9. Just as Marx was completing the *Manifesto* Engels was writing about politics in Switzerland where he noted that its peasantry had so far followed the lead of the bourgeoisie: "[T]hey are owners, like the bourgeoisie, and for the moment their interests are almost identical with those of the bourgeoisie." As for this momentary alliance, "it is true that a time will come when the fleeced and impoverished section of the peasantry will unite with the proletariat, which by then will be further developed, and will declare war on the bourgeoisie . . ." (6, p. 525). Armed, therefore, with its historical materialist view, the Marx party was theoretically equipped to attempt to win over the peasantry in the impending German revolution.

10. 6, 468.

11. 6, p. 472.

12. The best evidence for this comes from Jenny Marx's memoirs (Felix, pp. 249–50).

13. 6, p. 649.

14. 6, p. 651.

15. Nicholaievsky and Maenchen-Helfen, pp. 159–60. The source for this is an account written about a year later by Sebastian Seiler, a CL member who worked closely with the

Marx party. This appears to be the only extant source on Marx's strategy during his brief sojourn in Paris. It suggests that the eventual return to Germany was a tactical move in the face of the increasing clamor within the exile community to take part in the upheavals within Germany. If, as Marx and Engels may have reasoned, the exiles were going to return by hook or crook, then at least their party should provide the leadership to avoid what they correctly foresaw would be a fiasco with the expedition.

16. Hammen, pp. 200–1, provides useful details on these events. As a member of the Marx party, Jenny Marx worked in opposition to the expedition through contacts within Germany to make sure that the expedition not be confused with the efforts of the CL and its public face, the German Worker's Club (38, pp. 539–40).

17. Nicolaievshy and Maenchen-Helfen, pp. 167–68.

18. See Engels's brief discussion on the admission requirements he subjected a new recruit to about the middle of March 1848 (38, pp. 163–64).

19. 38, p. 162.

20. 38, p. 594. Engels was critical of the way the protest had been organized—"with appalling stupidity" (p. 159)—foreshadowing a sharp dispute that would soon take place between the organizers and the Marx party.

21. David McLellan, *Karl Marx: His Life and Thought* (New York: Harper and Row, 1973), p. 194.

22. See 7, pp. 3–4, for the *Demands*, and pp. 601–2 for details on their publication and reprinting.

23. 7, p. 4.

24. Gilbert, pp. 161–65, provides a useful discussion and critique of other characterizations of the *Demands*.

25. Draper, *Chronicle*, p. 31. See also, McLellan, 193. This was also the same government that was only too happy to finance the ill-fated armed expedition of German exiles which the Marx party was adamantly against. The regime's motives, as Marx and Engels probably became aware, had nothing to do with revolutionary internationalism but rather a desire to rid itself of potential allies for its own proletariat, whom, as most astute observers recognized, it would soon have to confront (see Nicolaievsky and Maenchen-Helfen, pp. 156–62). Bernard Moss's apologia for the reformists in his "Marx and Engels on French Social Democracy: Historians or Revolutionaries?" *Journal of the History of Ideas* (1985) ignores this most important fact in explaining Marx and Engels's distrust of them.

26. 7, 535.

27. 38, p. 172.

28. Draper, *Chronicle*, p. 32, and Hammen, p. 255. For a useful discussion on the political and historical context of the business community of Cologne from which Camphausen came and which might have some bearing on his politics, see J. M. Diefendorf, *Businessmen and Politics in the Rhineland, 1789–1834* (1980) .

29.Nicolaievsky and Maenchen-Helfen, pp. 168–69.

30. Riazanov, *Karl Marx and Frederick Engels,*p. 88.

31. On Gottschalk's usage of this term, see Draper, *KMTR* II, pp. 207–8. A major thesis of P. H. Noyes, *Organization and Revolution: Working-Class Associations in the German Revolutions of 1848–1849* (Princeton: Princeton University Press, 1966), is that Marx and Engels failed to provide leadership to the workers' movement. What Noyes misses is that they did

indeed have a strategy for the working class but in alliance with the petit bourgeoisie and small peasantry. They, as opposed to Gottschalk, saw that it was through such an alliance that workers would be in a better position to further their interests, i.e., through the fight for the bourgeois democratic revolution. For a more recent rendering of Noyes's argument, see Jonathan Sperber, *Rhineland Radicals: The Democratic Movement and the Revolution of 1848–1849* (Princeton: Princeton University Press, 1991).

32. Hammen, p. 377.

33. Noyes, pp. 293, 305–6.

34. 26, p. 325.

35. Hammen, p. 217, and Draper, *Chronicle*, p. 32.

36. 26, p. 122.

37. 10, p. 5.

38. Hammen, p. 220.

39. 17, p. 80.

40. Hammen, p. 221.

41. 26, pp. 324–25.

42. Hunt, pp. 173–74. As Hunt correctly notes, the Marx-Engels biographers in Moscow—which is reflected also in the *MECW*—never recognized that Marx shelved the CL. They in fact excluded this portion of Röser's testimony in 38 (pp. 550–54) and *MEGA*₂ III/3 (pp. 738–40) and said editorially that on this point he was in error (38, p. 640). Hunt's explanation for Moscow's myopia, that Marx's shelving of the CL was un-"Leninist," may be true as "Leninism" was understood in the former USSR.

43. 7, p. 15.

44. 7, p. 51.

45. 10, p. 346.

46. Quoted in Draper, *KMTR,*III, p. 153.

47. George Duveau, *1848: The Making of a Revolution* (Cambridge: Harvard University Press, 1967), pp. 155–56.

48. 7, p. 144.

49. 7, pp. 351.

50. 7, p. 92.

51. 7, pp. 166–67.

52. Two months later Engels reiterated this approach in reference to the Prussian regime's practice of deploying young men from one province to police in other provinces, i.e., to pit Germans against one another—its divide and rule strategy(7, p. 400). In another article the *NRZ* reprinted a report from Prague about efforts within Germany to generate opposition to Berlin's denial of Czech self-determination (7, p. 215). Again, Marx and Engels didn't ignore or deny the reality of national chauvinism. Their concern was how to wage a fight against it.

53. Sperber, pp. 170–72.

54. 7, pp. 248–49.

55. 7, p. 251.

56. See above, p. 3.

57. Z, pp. 258–59.

58. Felix, p. 84. According to Sperber, "Its circulation was not limited to the provincial metropolis; the paper was found in the most obscure corners of the Prussian Rhine Province. It was read out loud at meetings of the democratic club in Münstermaifeld and posted for the public to read by radicals in the Eifel town of Adenau. Articles from it were reprinted in the *County Intelligencers* of Wittlich and Bitburg, and were discussed, a correspondent claimed in the taverns of the metalworking town of Velbertin, a 'democratic oasis' in the . . . [Prussian loyalist] ocean of the Bergishes Land" (p. 212).

59. For some details on these discussions, see Hammen, pp. 259–60.

60. Ibid. p. 260.

61. Z, pp. 294–95.

62. Hammen, p. 260. The following comment by Eric Hobsbawm, certainly no fly-by-night Marxologist, indicates the depth of ignorance about Marx and Engels's activities vis-à-vis the peasantry: "We may note in passing that during 1848–49 Marx and Engels, like most of the left underestimated the revolutionary or even the radical potential of the countryside, in which they took little interest" (*The History of Marxism*, Vol. I, ed. Hobsbawm [Bloomington: Indiana University Press, 1982], p. 241).

63. Hammen, p. 268.

64. Z, pp. 556–57. Hammen, who interprets the facts to fit his thesis that Marx and Engels were antidemocrats, introduces Marx's remarks with the qualifier, "in contrast to the forthright Weitling . . ." Hammen's legerdemain shows that even when a researcher has the facts—as he generally does, which makes his book far more useful than the usual Marxological tract—the politics of the investigator is in general determinant in how the facts are to be interpreted. This seems to be especially true when it comes to writing about Marx and Engels.

CHAPTER FOUR.
THE END OF THE REVOLUTIONARY UPSURGE
AND THE LESSONS OF STRUGGLE

1. On the particulars of both events see Z, pp. 411–66 and the relevant notes; also, Hammen, pp. 272–311.

2. Z, p. 430.

3. Z, p. 431.

4. What Marx and Engels meant by "dictatorship of the proletariat" will be discussed later in this chapter. The most detailed treatment of their usage of "dictatorship" can be found in Draper's *KMTR, III: The "Dictatorship of the Proletariat"* (1986), "Part I: Dictatorship: Its Meaning in 1850."

5. Three years later Marx disputed the provision in the French constitution of November 1848 that "the division of powers is the primary condition of a free government." "Here we have the old constitutional folly. The condition of a 'free government' is not the *division*, but the *unity* of power. The machinery of government cannot be too simple. It is always the craft of knaves to make it complicated and mysterious" (10, p. 570).

6. Hammen, p. 295.

7. Z, pp. 585.

8. Z, p. 444.

9. Hammen, p. 284.

10. Hammen, p. 303.

11. *7*, p. 464.

12. Hammen, p. 310.

13. *38*, p. 179. The translation here is actually from Hammen, p. 312.

14. *7*, p. 595.

15. *7*, p. 571. Other newspapers reported on the meeting at which the debate took place, including the *NRZ*. See especially the latter's coverage since it no doubt reflected what Marx thought was most important about the debate (p. 570).

16. *7*, p. 573.

17. *7*, p. 504.

18. *7*, p. 496.

19. *7*, p. 506. Again, as in the case of Marx's usage of "dictatorship," no more should be read into this other than what he intended—the employment of any means necessary to defend and advance the interests of the majority against a counterrevolutionary minority. For a more thorough discussion of this usage see the special note, "The Meaning of 'Terror' and 'Terrorism'" in Draper, *KMTR, III*, pp. 360–74.

20. Draper argues, *KMTR,II*, pp. 219–38, that the question about the behavior of the bourgeoisie had not been an open one. Rather, Marx and Engels actually expected the German bourgeoisie to act in a revolutionary way. While Draper offers persuasive evidence for this interpretation, the total body of evidence leads me to believe that they went back and forth on this question; whatever the case, they recognized that only reality would provide an answer.

21. *7*, p. 492.

22. *8*, p. 3.

23. *8*, p. 21. Three weeks earlier Marx had himself raised the taxation issue in regard to Frederick IV's directive of October 15 to the civic guard to "not forget *that you obtained the weapons from me . . .*" Marx pointed out to his readers that this was a bogus claim since it was taxes, "the *work of the nation*," that made the purchase of weapons by the government possible. Monarchs, he continued, can only deliver to the people what the people have given to them through taxes, what he called the "*economic secret*" behind the power of monarchs. "Therefore the initial causes for the overthrow of the kings . . . have always been *questions of taxation*" (*7*, p. 477).

24. Hammen, p. 340.

25. *8*, pp. 39–40. In his capacity as a Rhineland Democratic Association official Marx wrote to Ferdinand Lassalle—the first extant correspondence between them—in Düsseldorf to request that the democratic body in the town support the campaign, "to be advocated specially in rural areas" (*38*, p. 180).

26. Hammen, p. 345.

27. *8*, p. 41.

28. *38*, p. 181.

29. *8*, pp. 106–7.

30. *7*, p. 74.

31. Marx said as much as early as 1845; *4*, p. 265.

32. 6, p. 529. Whether Marx and Engels actually thought the bourgeoisie would "fight bravely" to institute bourgeois democracy is open to debate. What is certain is that they knew only the real movement would provide an answer.

33. 8, p. 178. For a discussion on the history and usage of "social republic" see Draper, *KMTR, II*, pp. 204–5, 232–34.

34. 8, p. 215.

35. Ibid. Marx's notebooks indicate that a year earlier he had been doing intense reading on British imperialism in Africa and elsewhere throughout what is referred to currently as the Third World. See Marx and Engels, *Gesamtausgabe (MEGA₂) IV. Bd. 6, Text* (Berlin, 1983).

36. 8, pp. 227–28.

37. 8, p. 390. On the discussions within the Worker's Society, see Hammen, pp. 360–61. Contrary to Hammen, the context of this quote makes clear that "the party" is indeed the "people's alliance" of the *Demands* and not the communist party of the *Manifesto*.

38. 8, p. 514.

39. 8, pp. 288–89.

40. 8, p. 390.

41. Ibid., p. 391.

42. 9, p. 282.

43. McLellan, *Karl Marx: His Life and Thoughts* (New York: Harper and Row, 1973), p. 220, gives a liberal interpretation of the break by suggesting that Marx was under pressure from left critics of "his temporising attitude" toward the petit-bourgeois democratic milieu. Apparently, it doesn't occur to McLellan that it was the "temporising attitude" of the democrats that led the *NRZ* to reevaluate its relationship with the Democratic Association.

44. 24, pp. 141, 146.

45. Ibid., p. 146. As Sperber notes, Silesia, "a center of antifeudal peasant uprisings," was well disposed to give a favorable hearing to the *NRZ* articles(p. 485).

46. Hunt, pp. 270–71 and 240.

47. 8, p. 341.

48. 8, pp. 527–28.

49. 9, p. 487.

50. 9, p. 378.

51. 9, pp.448–49. This was in spite of the fact that Engels had made clear to the Committee that his intentions were otherwise. Although Engels was certainly circumspect in his behavior, the fact that "he demanded that the . . . Committee should disarm Elberfeld militiamen who were hostile to the revolution and distribute their arms among workers . . . [and] proposed that the bourgeoisie should pay a firm tax, to be used for the maintenance of the armed detachments" perhaps explains why the bourgeoisie was uncomfortable with his presence (L. F. Ilyichov et al., *Frederick Engels: A Biography* [Moscow: Progress Publishers, 1974], p. 145).

52. Hammen, p. 400.

53. 38, p. 203.

54. 38, p. 207. Engels's, "The Campaign for the German Imperial Constitution" (10, pp. 147–239) provides the details of his participation in the military campaigns of the revo-

lution, beginning with Elberfeld. See also "From the Indictment of the Participants in the Uprising in Elberfeld in May 1849" (10, pp. 602–4). The accounts make clear that he played a major role in the Elberfeld events.

55. 38, p. 213.

56. For a glimpse of Marx's educational activities see the reminiscences of Wilhelm Liebknecht, the future German social democratic leader, who came into the orbit of the Marx party about this time (*Marx and Engels Through the Eyes of Their Contemporaries* [Moscow: Progress, 1978], pp. 66–72).

57. 10, p. 600.

58. Draper, *KMTR, II*, p. 599. See his special note on the many Marxological efforts to prove that Marx supposedly never agreed with the document and Draper's very persuasive refutation. An additional comment is in order about those Marxologists who dismiss the document on the grounds that it was a party statement, or the "work of a committee" (Hunt, p. 243). Such an attitude often reveals the Marxologist's own class situation and hence failure to take Marx and Engels as they wanted to be regarded—as political people who took party work seriously and were willing to support party policies that may not have been worded exactly as they might have wanted or inclusive of all they advocated, i.e., the reality of working within a group and not as individuals. The milieu that breeds the Marxological enterprise makes it difficult for its practitioners to understand individuals who voluntarily subordinate their lives to political party activity.

For this particular group of Marxologists the basic problem is their profound disagreement with the political content of the "Address." Thus, Hunt's social democratic and anti-Leninist bias must be kept in mind in reading his conclusion that "It would be best to disregard the document altogether as a source for the political doctrines of Classical Marxism" (p. 248).

59. Riazanov, *Karl Marx and Frederick Engels*, p. 100.

60. 38, p. 550.

61. Engels said as much in a letter the following year in defense of the "Address" against the howls of petit-bourgeois democrats: "Why . . . the present outcry about a programme that merely sums up in a very calm and, above all, quite impersonal manner, what has already long been in print? . . . Any democrat with a modicum of intelligence must have known from the start what was to be expected of our party—the document cannot have taught him much that was new . . . no one . . . could have ever believed that the communists had, after 1850, turned away from the principles and the policy of the *Neue Rheinische Zeitung*" (38, p. 393). Further evidence, therefore, that the "Address," contrary to the claims of Hunt and other Marxologists, was not some Blanquist or ultraleft aberration on Marx's part.

62. See fn. 58.

63. 10, p. 375.

64. Marx elaborated on the crisis of the French peasant in *The Class Struggles in France, 1848 to 1850*, written almost at the same time as the "Address." As for the resolution of this crisis, "Only the fall of capital can raise the peasant; only an anti-capitalist, a proletarian government can break his economic misery, his social degradation. The *constitutional republic* is the dictatorship of his united exploiters; *the social-democratic, the Red republic*, is the dictatorship of his allies" (10, p. 122).

Noteworthy also is that "the revolutionary faction of the Chartists opposes this demand for parceling out [land] with the demand for the confiscation of all landed property, and insists that it should not be distributed but remain national property" (10, p. 515).

65. 10, p. 318.

66. Ibid., pp. 319–20.

67. 10, p. 56.

68. Ibid., pp. 69–70.

69. See 10, 387–88, for the full text of Marx's reply. Draper's, *KMTR, III—The "Dictatorship of the Proletariat"* is very useful for a repudiation of the claim that Marx's usage of the term represented a Blanquist deviation on his part. However, Draper's thesis that "*For Marx and Engels . . . 'dictatorship of the proletariat' meant nothing more and nothing less than 'rule of the proletariat,' the 'conquest of political power' by the working class, the establishment of a workers' state in the first postrevolutionary period"* (p. 213), is also problematic. I would argue that the use of force—"sweeps away by force the old conditions of production"—which elsewhere in the *Manifesto* is referred to as "despotic" means, was a key component of Marx's meaning. Also, Draper is in error if he is suggesting that Marx expected the dictatorship of the proletariat to be the first form of governance after the overthrow of the bourgeoisie. In his debate with Weitling (see chapter three, pp. 80–81), for example, Marx indicated that the first government would be composed of "heterogeneous elements," i.e., a multiclass government. Also, in *Class Struggles* (see above fn. 64) he foresaw a "dictatorship of his [the peasantry's] allies" as the replacement for the bourgeois dictatorship. See also, chapter six, p. 145, for a later instance of Marx's reference to a multiclass government on the day after the revolution.

70. Europe's peasants, they noted, did not benefit from the economic revival. Their situation had even deteriorated. In spite of that, "The history of the last three years has, however, provided sufficient proof that this class of the population is absolutely incapable of any revolutionary initiative" (10, p. 509). A very similar statement was made by Engels a year later in his *Revolution and Counter-Revolution in Germany* (11, p. 12). The validity of this claim notwithstanding, it would be an error, on the basis of Marx and Engels's actual practice in the 1848–49 events, to interpret it, as is often done, to mean that they dismissed the peasantry. From their perspective and experience the operative word is "initiative."
Most importantly, these words were written before the December 1851 coup of Bonaparte, which evoked a massive uprising of the peasantry in opposition. Marx and Engels took note of these events, which was reflected in their later accounts. Thus, the *Eighteenth Brumaire* and Engels's important follow-up article, "Real Causes why the French Proletariat remained comparatively inactive in December last" (11, pp. 216–17), both discuss those peasants that did take revolutionary initiatives vis-à-vis those, the majority, that did not.

71. 10, pp. 509–10. There is some evidence that Marx had anticipated such a shift as early as December 1849. In a letter that month to Joseph Weydemeyer, a close *NRZ* collaborator, he wrote that "with trade still *en ascendant*, the mass of the workers in France and Germany, etc., as well as the entire strata of tradesmen, etc., though perhaps revolutionary in words, are certainly not so *en réalité*" (38, p. 220).

72. 27, pp. 512, 520.

73. 40, p. 41. This translation, more readable, is from Draper, *KMTR, II*, p. 383.

74. In this context Marx's views on the situation in Italy should be mentioned, especially since he expressed them about this time. Mazzini, in his opinion, was misleading the movement because "by failing to turn to the part of Italy that has been repressed for centuries, to the peasants, he is laying up fresh resources for the counter-revolution" (38, p. 454).

75. 11, pp. 6–7.

76. 27, p. 508. Engels's observation only makes sense if it is realized that the last article in *The Class Struggles* was taken from the "Review" article discussed above, i.e., the article in which Marx and Engels had concluded that the revolutionary upsurge had come to an end.

77. 11, pp. 106–7.

78. 4, p. 119.

79. 8, p. 51.

CHAPTER FIVE.
INTERPRETING THE 1848–1851 EVENTS IN FRANCE: MARX AND ENGELS VERSUS TOCQUEVILLE

1. I am most thankful to Ron Aminzade, Roger Boesche, Mary Dietz, Lisa Disch, and Lansiné Kaba for their comments on earlier drafts of this chapter.

2. Priscilla Robertson, *Revolutions of 1848: A Social History* (Princeton: Princeton University Press, 1971), p. 422.

3. Hammen, p. 382.

4. Carl Schurz, *The Reminiscences of Carl Schurz*, Vol. I, 1829–1852 (New York: The McClure Co., 1907). Marx and Schurz were political opponents with each making disparaging comments about the political activities of each other (*Reminiscences*, pp. 139–40, and 10, pp. 347–47, and pp. 372–73.) Nevertheless, Schurz's account substantiates in general the picture that Marx and Engels drew about the German events.

5. P. J. Proudhon, *The General Idea of the Revolution in the Nineteenth Century* (1851) and *The Social Revolution Demonstrated by the Coup d'Etat* (1852). In his "Classical Social Theory and the French Revolution of 1848" (*Sociological Theory* 7, 2 [Fall, 1989]), Craig Calhoun offers Proudhon as an alternative to Marx for an interpretation of 1848. In claiming, however, that Proudhon represented "the now submerged tradition which took the French revolutionary ideals of equality and justice to a radical extreme, which combined them with communitarian notions of solidarity . . . which counted on the direct action of 'the people'" (219), he fails to mention Proudhon's second volume as well as his later support of Bonaparte—let alone the profoundly antidemocratic side of Proudhon.

6. V. Hugo, *Napoléon le petit* (London, 1852). Marx had the following opinion of the work: "Victor Hugo confines himself to bitter and witty invective against the responsible publisher of the coup d'état. The event itself appears in his work like a bolt from the blue. He sees in it only the violent act of a single individual. He does not notice that he makes this individual great instead of little by ascribing to him a personal power of initiative such as would be without parallel in world history" (21, pp. 56–57). As for Blanc's book, he wrote: "If read carefully . . . it makes the fellow look like an ass for it shows that on every crucial occasion the worker acted without his knowledge or consent . . ." (40, p. 310).

7. For this to be a fair comparison the emphasis is on those sections of *Class Struggles* written before the Fall of 1850.

8. Roger Price, *The Revolutions of 1848* (Atlantic Highlands, N.J.: Humanities Press, 1988), p. 64. For other comparisons of Marx and Tocqueville regarding the 1848 revolutions, see Edward T. Gargan, *Alexis de Tocqueville: The Critical Years, 1848–1851* (Washington, D.C.: Catholic University Press, 1955) and Irving M. Zeitlin, *Liberty, Equality, and Revolutions in Alexis de Tocqueville* (Boston: Little Brown, 1971), particularly chapter six. And more recently, Craig Calhoun, op. cit. The emphasis here, however, is on their politics.

9. J. P. Mayer, "Introduction," to *Recollections: The French Revolution of 1848*, ed. J. P. Mayer and a. P. Kerr (New Brunswick, N. J.: Transaction Books, 1987), pp. xxxii–iii. This is the edition of the *Recollections* employed here.

10. See George Kelly's *The Human Comedy: Constant, Tocqueville, and French Liberalism* (Cambridge: Cambridge University Press, 1992), p. 235, in which he argues that Tocqueville's writing of history as a private memoir represented a liberal retreat from politics. In his authoritative biography, *Tocqueville* (New York: Farrar, Straus, Giroux, 1988), André Jardin states that "we should not necessarily believe him when he declares that they are not destined for the public. . . . No doubt he did not intend to release them to the public during his lifetime. But his reflections on his age led Tocqueville to a concern for what posterity would think of him." (p. 453)

11. Tocqueville, *Recollections*, pp. 12–13.

12. Alan S. Kahan, *Aristocratic Liberalism: The Social and Political Thought of Jacob Burkhardt, John Stuart Mill, and Alexis de Tocqueville* (New York: Oxford University Press, 1992), p. 72.

13. 6, p. 381.

14. Another writing that Tocqueville may also have had in mind was Proudhon's highly popular *Qu'est-ce que la propriété?*, published in 1840, which popularized the aphorism, "property is theft."

15. Although Tocqueville, according to Roger Boesche (in a private communication), once referred to himself as a "liberal of a new kind," and Engels referred on occasion to the faction that Tocqueville belonged to as "Liberal," I will employ, given the present-day debates that surround the usage of this appellation, for the most part the self-descriptions that Tocqueville employed to describe his political tendency in *Recollections*.

16. Marx's critique at the end of 1847 of Alphonse de Lamartine's praise of private property for not distinguishing between bourgeois and other forms of private property could just as well have applied to Tocqueville (6, p. 405). Lamartine became the effective head of the government that emerged from the February revolution.

17. 10, 54–55.

18. Tocqueville, *Recollections*, p. 73.

19. Ibid., pp. 74–75. That socialists did accede to positions of authority in some locales such as Rouen in the aftermath of February might explain Tocqueville's assessment. See Aminzade, *Ballots and Barricades: Class Formation and Republican Politics in France, 1830–1871* (Princeton: Princeton University Press, 1993), p. 182, for particulars.

20. Ibid., p. 62. As to which "absolute systems" he is referring to, it is unclear. It's possible he may have had Marx and Engels in mind but it is doubtful since their *Manifesto* had yet to appear in French. A more likely candidate for Tocqueville's criticism was Lorenz von Stein, whose *Der Socialismus und Communismus des heutigen frankreichs*—a second edition came out in 1848—was certainly much better known among the circles that he frequented than the *Manifesto*.

21. Tocqueville, pp. 75–76.

22. Quoted in Irving Zeitlin, *Liberty, Equality, and Revolution in Alexis de Tocqueville* (Boston: Little Brown, 1971), pp. 106–7.

23. Ibid., p. 105.

24. *Democracy in America*, ed. Phillips Bradley, trans. Henry Reeve, Francis Bowen, and Phillips Bradley, 2 Vols. (New York: Vintage Books, 1945), p. 6.

25. See Peter McPhee, "The Crisis of Radical Republicanism in the French Revolution of 1848," *Historical Studies* 16, 162 (1974), who suggests that another explanation for the revolutionary republican view of February was the institution of universal manhood suffrage which, for them, meant that the provisional government was to be defended at all costs.

26. Tocqueville, p. 76.

27. For the anti-Marxist Daniel Mahoney, Tocqueville's conclusion is "one of the most intriguing and unsettling remarks in his *Recollections.*" That his hero could envision the possibility of socialism is "unsettling" for Mahoney, who reveals a profound ignorance of what Marx and Engels actually advocated. Nevertheless, he is correct to criticize any interpretation of his remarks to mean that Tocqueville was "somehow open to Marx and his view of the social question." Another problem that Mahoney has is reconciling Tocqueville's remarks with his "Speech on the Right to Work" made to the Constituent Assembly on September 12, 1848. The latter, in Mahoney's opinion, makes it clear that Tocqueville was unequivocal in his opposition to socialism. Be that as it may, the fact is that two years later in his *Recollections* he certainly seems to equivocate. Mahoney should at least address this apparent discrepancy, which could reasonably be interpreted to mean that in his private memoirs Tocqueville was less certain about his opposition to socialism than in his public remarks two years earlier. See his "Tocqueville and Socialism," *Tocqueville's Defense of Human Liberty: Current Essays* (New York: Garland Publishing, 1993), p. 179.

28. Tocqueville, *Recollections*, p. 96.

29. Tocqueville, *Recollections*, p. 97.

30. 10, p. 61.

31. According to Ron Aminzade (private communication) Ledru-Rollin later admitted that the policies of his provisional government with regard to the peasantry were an error.

32. 10, pp. 67–69.

33. Tocqueville, *Recollections*, p. 144.

34. 7, p. 164.

35. Tocqueville, *Recollections*, p. 136. See Calhoun, op. cit., p. 221, for a discussion on whether Tocqueville and Marx were correct in their characterization.

36. 10, p. 56.

37. Mark Traugott, *Armies of the Poor: Determinants of Working-Class Participation in the Parisian Insurrection of June 1848* (Princeton: Princeton University Press, 1985), disputes Marx and Tocqueville's characterization of the Gardes Mobiles.

38. Tocqueville, *Recollections,* p. 165.

39. 10, pp. 66–67.

40. Tocqueville, *Recollections*, p. 147.

41. Ibid., pp. 147–48.

42. Ibid., p. 148.

43. Ibid., pp. 148–49.

44. While Marx gives a figure of "over 3,000 prisoners" having been massacred, Charles Tilly, *The Contentious French* (Cambridge, Mass.: Harvard University Press, 1986), p. 384, says that 1,400 "died in the June days."

45. Marx's sarcasm about the angst of the likes of a Tocqueville was biting: "It is well known how the bourgeoisie compensated itself for the moral anguish it suffered by unheard of brutality, massacring over 3,000 prisoners" (10, 68).

46. Tocqueville acknowledges in a marginal note to the chapter in *Recollections* that covers this period that "There is a great gap in this chapter" (p. 167).

47. Jardin, p. 416.

48. Jardin, p. 419. About a month before the debate on the right to work issue Proudhon, a member of the Assembly, caused quite an uproar—reported by the *NRZ*—by making a prolonged attack on private property. Along the way he exclaimed, " 'By recognising in the Constitution the right to work, you have proclaimed the recognition of the abolition of property'" (*7*, p. 323). It may have been Proudhon's heresy that Tocqueville had in mind in his lambasting the constitutional proposal.

49. Mahoney, p. 186.

50. Tocqueville comes very close to admitting this having been the case. When the draft committee was set up in May 1848, he said that the "thing that most effectively deprived [it] of its freedom of mind was, one must admit, fear of outside events and the excitement of the moment. It is difficult to appreciate how much this pressure of revolutionary ideas affected even those minds least subject to such influence, and how it almost unconsciously drove them farther than they meant to go, and sometimes even in a different direction. There is no doubt that, had the Committee met on the 27th June [i.e., after the defeat of the revolt] instead of the 16th May, its work would have turned out to be entirely different" (*Recollections*, p. 169). In other words, the concession to the workers regarding work and assistance would not have been included in the draft from the beginning.

51. Jardin, p. 419.

52. Tocqueville, *Recollections*, p. 178.

53. Jardin, p. 420.

54. See chapter four, p. 92.

55. *10*, p. 79.

56. Tocqueville, *Recollections*, p. 166.

57. Jardin, pp. 438–39.

58. Kelly's argument, above, fn. 10, that *Recollections* was not the private memoir that its author claimed it to be has merit. By failing to discuss the Roman betrayal Tocqueville was in all likelihood attempting to influence his image for subsequent generations.

59. *9*, p. 477.

60. *Recollections*, p. 211.

61. *10*, pp. 92–93.

62. Tocqueville, *Recollections*, p. 220.

63. Ibid., pp. 219–20.

64. Ibid., p. 223.

65. Ibid., pp. 225–26.

66. This followed discussions that Tocqueville had with Bonaparte on May 15, 1851. It is not clear from his memoirs if this was the same or a different meeting referred to above in which Tocqueville raised various options for the president on how to stay in office.

67. *10*, p. 142.

68. *10*, p. 580. This comes from Marx's article, "The Constitution of the French Republic Adopted November 8, 1848," the only thing he wrote on the French situation between his and Engels's last article in *Class Struggles* and the *Eighteenth Brumaire*. It is also noteworthy

because of its detailed analysis of the democratic limitations of the constitution, giving lie once again to the oft-repeated charge that he short-shrifted such matters.

69. Tocqueville, *Recollections*, p. 292.

70. *Correspondence and Conversations of Alexis de Tocqueville with Nassau William Senior*, quoted in Zeitlin, p. 118.

71. Jardin, p. 461. Sixteen years earlier, in his *Democracy in America*, Tocqueville asked if was possible to have an alternative to the American path to republican democracy "in which the majority, repressing its natural instinct of equality, should consent, with a view to the order and the stability of the state, to invest a family or an individual with all the attributes of executive power? Might not a democratic society be imagined in which the forces of the nation would be more centralized than they are in the United States; where the people would exercise a less direct and less irresistible influence upon public affaires, and yet every citizen, invested with certain rights, would participate, within his sphere, in the conduct of the government?" Tocqueville answered affirmatively. Thus, his willingness to acquiesce in Bonaparte's coup may have reflected his earlier vision about an alternative path to democracy via the investiture of "an individual with all the attributes of executive power."

72. It is true that in the "Foreword" to his *Old Regime*, Tocqueville suggested that his analysis of 1789 would serve to explain subsequent events such as 1830 and 1848. Since he died before doing a planned follow-up volume, it is not known how specific he intended to be in an analysis of 1848. At best, *Old Regime* is an implicit critique of the bourgeoisie in 1848 as well as Bonaparte's Second Empire.

73. 11, p. 118.

74. 11, p. 135.

75. 11, p. 155.

76. 11, p. 168.

77. Jardin, pp. 458–59.

78. While Tocqueville enthusiastically voted against the impeachment motion on June 13, he in fact helped lead the charge against it as the Assembly member who headed the Ministry of Foreign Affairs; he did not, apparently, vote to abolish universal manhood suffrage. He was clearly opposed to the decision, as he explained to Bonaparte in their meeting on May 15, 1851. " 'I regard that law . . . as a great misfortune, almost as a crime. It has deprived us of the only moral force society possesses today, that is to say, the moral power of universal suffrage, without ridding us of the dangers of that voting system. We are left to face a multitude, but an unauthorized multitude' "(*Recollections*, pp. 291–92). As noted earlier, Tocqueville was no partisan of universal suffrage before 1848. His apparent change of heart in 1851 should be weighed in that light as well as his well-known fears about the "unauthorized multitude."

79. 11, p. 176.

80. See especially chapter six, "a Premature Totalitarian: Louis Bonaparte," in James H. Meisel's *Counter-Revolution: How Revolutions Die* (New York: Atherton Press, 1966). Trotsky drew upon Marx's analysis of Bonapartism to dissect both fascism and Stalinism.

81. Alasdair MacIntyre, "The Indispensability of Political Theory," *The Nature of Political Theory*, eds. David Miller and Larry Siedentop (Oxford: The Clarendon Press, 1983), p. 27.

82. Whether Marx and Engels's line would have been more effective if given an opportunity for implementation in France is of course purely academic. What can be said is that

they strove mightily to realize their line in the German setting. While unsuccessful, they had no hesitation in faulting the Tocquevillian counterparts in Germany who too feared its masses and did what they could to hold their "revolutionary passions" in check. Tocqueville, who visited Germany in May 1849, held views about the upheavals there that would have certainly placed him and Marx on the opposite sides of the barricades had he been able to carry out his line there.

83. <u>21</u>, p. 57

84. *Democracy in America*, Vol. 1, pp. ix–x.

85. This might explain why the treatment in *Democracy in America* on the origins of the U.S. political system virtually ignores the Revolutionary War and its role in bringing the republic into existence. The Revolution simply "broke out . . . battles were fought and victories obtained for it; it became the law of laws" (*Democracy in America*, Vol. I, p. 58). The role of class struggle in all of this is either denied or ignored. Marx, by the way, had apparently read *Democracy*, as suggested by his comment in his 1843 article, "On the Jewish Question," <u>3</u>, p. 151.

86. Tocqueville, *Mon Instinct, mes opinions,*" quoted in Antoine Rédier, *Comme disait M. de Toqueville* (Paris, 1925), p. 48; quoted in Jack Hayward, *After the French Revolution* (New York: New York University Press, 1991), p. 149. See also, Jardin, p. 305, for a more abbreviated version of this statement.

87. <u>6</u>, p. 382.

88. Gargan, p. 225.

CHAPTER SIX.
POLITICAL ADJUSTMENTS TO THE
LONG LULL IN THE CLASS STRUGGLE

1. According to McLellan, pp. 234–35, the Address' "bombastic style, lack of realism and excessive optimism concerning contact with workers' organisations and the army make it doubtful that Marx and Engels played a large part in drawing it up, though they must have acquiesced in its final form as they never disavowed it—and it was even reprinted by Engels." McLellan, who provides no hard evidence to support his claim about the document's authorship, may be guilty of the same exegetical exercise that other Marxologists perform on the March 1850 Address. See chapter four, fn. 58.

2. <u>10</u>, pp. 373–74.

3. Ibid., pp. 375, 377.

4. Draper, *KMTR*, III, pp. 206–11. See the entire chapter 12 for his most detailed analysis of the episode, and Part III, which demolishes Marx's alleged "Blanquist aberration."

5. In a letter dated June 27, 1850, Marx wrote in reference to a governmental crisis in England that "a truly revolutionary movement will get under way here" (<u>38</u>, pp. 238–39)—indicating that as late as then he still held hopes for a new upsurge.

It is interesting to note that at about the time of his reassessment, probably near the beginning of August, Marx and Engels seriously considered emigrating to the United States Toward the end of August, Marx "asks Rothacker [a one-time League member] who is going to America, to make contacts for this purpose and to survey the prospects for founding a paper" (Draper, *Chronicle*, p. 51). This suggests that they indeed did conclude that revolution was not on Europe's agenda for some time to come.

6. 38, p. 551. This comes from Peter Röser's testimony(see chapter three, p. 78).

7. Ibid., p. 551.

8. Marx's rationale was that the revision of the 1847 Rules by the Authority in London in 1848—see chapter four, p. 98—meant that there were gross inconsistencies in the then-current Rules that needed to be reconciled.

9. The editors of the *MECW* write that the "circular" refers to the March "Address," although the "last circular" before the meeting was the June "Address." In his translation, Draper, *KMTR, II*, p. 604, renders the phrase as the "next-to-last circular" which would clearly then be the March "Address." Because the minutes of the September 1 meeting are not available it is not clear what exactly were the issues in the debate, which could help in clarifying which of the two "Addresses" is being referred to. More important, is the fact that Marx is defending here the "Addresses"—I include both since Marx and Engels saw them as a package—in spite of one of the premises upon which they were based, namely, an imminent renewal of the revolutionary wave. This is important in view of various Marxological attempts to have Marx and Engels disown them on the utterly spurious claim that they represented their momentary lapse into Blanquism and that only with their reassessment of the period did they return to their social-democratic senses.

10. 10, pp. 626–27.

11. 10, pp. 286–87.

12. 10, p. 628.

13. See chapter five, pp. 117, 122–23, respectively, on his influence in the workers' movement prior to the February Revolution and the ineptness of his government.

14. 10, pp. 628–29.

15. See chapter three, pp. 80–81.

16. 10, pp. 483–84.

17. Draper, *KMTR, II*, p. 606.

18. 10, p. 633.

19. For the details of Cologne's actions see 10, p. 708–9 n.446.

20. See chapter two, p. 54.

21. See chapter four, p. 98.

22. 10, p. 529.

23. Ibid., p. 530.

24. 10, p. 627.

25. 6, pp. 355–56.

26. 43, p. 495. In 1875 Marx publicly praised both Willich and Schapper, the former for his outstanding job as a colonel in the Union Army in the U.S. Civil War (24, p. 52).

27. P. N. Fedoseyev et al., *Karl Marx: A Biography* (Moscow: Progress Publishers, 1989), p. 249.

28. 39, pp. 137–38.

29. 39, pp. 576–78.

30. 39, p. 259. The reference to "my livelihood" is the journalistic work, about which more will be said later, that brought in some income beginning in 1851. The "Economy" refers, of course, to his long-awaited opus on political economy. German booksellers were presumably

"alienated" because their prospective author was certainly persona non grata in Germany—as far as the Prussian state was concerned. For an honest overview of the personal trials and tribulations of the Marx family during this period—the most difficult of their lives—see McLellan, op. cit., pp. 262–80 and 325–33.

31. 39, p. 580.

32. 39, p. 247.

33. 17, p. 81.

34. 41, p. 82.

35. Engels's sister Marie recognized that his move to Manchester was a temporary measure and one having to do with the pace of the class struggle: "[A]s soon as you believe that favourable chances have reappeared for your party you will at once give up business and will again work for your party" (L. F. Ilyichov et al., *Frederick Engels: A Biography* [Moscow: Progress Publishers, 1974], p. 167).

36. 38, p. 286.

37. 38, p. 287.

38. 38, p. 290.

39. 38, p. 382.

40. The preceding quotes from Engels's letter to Weydemeyer of 12 April 1853 are from 39, pp. 308–9. Note Engels's usage of "Marx party," i.e., without quotation marks, signifying its acceptance as normal discourse. This comes five months after the Cologne trial in which its derisive usage achieved its greatest currency, mainly at the hands of the Prussian authorities. In the *Revelations* pamphlet the term was always used with quotation marks.

41. 38, p. 230.

42. *Marx and Engels Through the Eyes of Their Contemporaries*, op. cit., p. 71. One of the best examples of how Marx encouraged party members in scientific work was his relationship with Johann Eccarius, a tailor, who with Marx's assistance, became a working-class intellectual. For the details on their relationship, which is also a powerful refutation of Shlomo Avineri's claim that Eccarius came in for "unearned contempt" from Marx, see Draper's "Two Adventures in Sophisticated Marxology," *KMTR, II*, pp. 644–53.

43. 39, p. 367.

44. Karl Marx, *A Contribution to the Critique of Political Economy* (1859), 16, pp. 470–71. The " 'great men' of the exile" comes from the title of the manuscript by the same name that Marx and Engels wrote in 1852 that exposes in satirical form the reformist *émigré* would-be leaders including the Willich-Schapper party.

Engels's assertion that the Marx party avoided the demoralization that afflicted much of the rest of the political exile community after the 1848–49 revolutions challenges the picture painted by Isaiah Berlin, *Karl Marx: His Life and Environment* (London: Oxford University Press, 1963), chapter 8, "Exile in London: The First Phase." According to Berlin, "[T]he complete absence of any symptom of revolution, at times tended to induce a sense of hopeless stagnation which demoralized and embittered all but very few of the men engaged in it. In the case of Marx desperate poverty and squalor were added factors in desiccating his never unduly romantic or pliant character. While these years benefited him as a thinker and revolutionary, they caused him to retire into the narrow circle composed of his family, Engels, and a few intimate friends . . ." (p. 181). Typical of Marxological accounts, the truths in this assessment are overshadowed by an unsupported insinuation, in this case that Marx, too, was one of the "embittered" and "demoralized," that flies in the face of the actual record.

45. 40, p. 354.

46. 40, p. 377.

47. 41, p. 193.

48. 41, p. 82.

49. 41, p. 194. The book also sparked a lot of interest in the German-American press. The pre-publication orders from the United States, which party members like Weydemeyer helped to generate, were influential in convincing the Berlin publishers to undertake the project; see Karl Obermann, *Joseph Weydemeyer: Pioneer of American Socialism* (New York: International Publishers, 1947), pp. 100–1. Even Willich promoted the book in the United States; more about later.

50. Typical of the descriptions of Marx and Engels's political activities in this period is that of Nicolaievsky and Maenchen-Helfen, op. cit.: "After the dissolution of the Communist League . . . no other organization existed" (p. 243). Or McLellan, op. cit., referring to the post-League period: "For the next ten years Marx was a member of no political party" (p. 252). Or Avineri, op. cit.: "Since the early 'fifties Marx had consistently divorced himself from any connection with such ["conspiratorial"] political organizations. . . . Even during 1857–58, when he envisaged a possible radicalization that might lead to revolution, Marx did not try to prepare for it by forming or joining a revolutionary group" (p. 257). Mehring, op. cit., at least acknowledges the existence of political relations: "[T]hey were both too passionately political not to feel in the long run the lack of a party, for their supporters, as Marx himself admitted, did not represent a party" (p. 249). Again, as is often true with Marxological accounts, none of these statements are false; they are simply partially true.

The only exceptions to this myopia are the brief treatments in Monty Johnstone, "Marx and Engels and the Concept of the Party," *The Socialist Register, 1967*, eds. Ralph Miliband and John Saville (London: Merlin Press, 1967), pp. 128–31, and John Molyneux, *Marxism and the Party* (London: Pluto Press, 1978), pp. 23–25.

51. 41, p. 87.

52. 39, p. 290. See similar remarks that Marx made about eight months later, Ibid., p. 386.

53. 39, 293.

54. 2 Samuel 15:18. This verse refers to the struggle between King David and Absalom and the assumption of the former that he had the allegiance of these two parties.

55. 38, p. 290.

56. 38, p. 394. Engels's usage of "general staff" is noteworthy since Hunt, *II*, op. cit., claims that Marx and Engels never spoke in these terms: ".[T]he image of the vanguard as the 'general staff' of the revolution, made famous by Lenin, was expressed clearly . . . by Bakunin several decades earlier, and was just as repudiated by Marx and Engels" (p. 323).

57. Johnstone, op. cit., p. 129.

58. 39, pp. 195–96.

59. 39, p. 68.

60. 40, p. 38.

61. 13, pp. 50–51, and p. 58. See the former for details on the initial meeting and how Marx viewed its importance.

62. Along with dire financial circumstances and near poverty conditions, the Marx's eight-year-old son Edgar died from gastric illness, the third child to die in five years. To Engels he wrote: "I've already had my share of bad luck but only now do I know what real unhappiness is. I feel BROKEN DOWN." But then he added: "Amid all the fearful torments I have recently had to endure, the thought of you and your friendship has always sustained me, as has the hope that there is still something sensible for us to do together in the world" (39, p. 533).

63. 40, p. 344.

64. 40, p. 210.

65. 43, p. 211.

66. 38, pp. 290–91.

67. 38, pp. 402–3.

68. 38, pp. 481, 489.

69. 39, p. 41.

70. 41, p. 117.

71. 39, p. 554.

72. 39, p. 507.

73. 40, p. 25. Marx's reply to the Rhineland workers is nonextant.

74. 40, pp. 435–36. Three years earlier, when it became clear to Marx and Engels that Lassalle's actions were problematic, Engels wrote to Marx, "If he can be induced to commit a direct and OVERT ACT against the party, then we shall have him. But as yet there would seem to be none of that and in any case a row would be quite out of place" (40, p. 27). Disciplinary actions in the party, therefore, had to be based on behavior—cf. p. 146, above, regarding the expulsion of Willich-Schapper faction.

75. 40, p. 538.

76. 40, pp. 437, 447. The "manifesto" was never published, however, due in all likelihood to the fact that the war ended sooner than expected, July 1859.

77. 40, pp. 319–21.

78. 40, p. 323.

79. For the most insightful and thorough analysis of the break between the Marx party and Lassalle, which disputes the Marxological claim that Marx had a personal dislike for Lassalle, see Draper, *KMTR, IV,* specifically, chapter 3 and Special Note A.

80. 40, pp. 437–38.

81. 40, p. 446.

82. 41, p. 54. Of particular importance for the party, of course, was its reputation vis-à-vis the workers' movement and the German wing specifically. Thus, Marx proudly reported in *Herr Vogt,* that the GWEA, which included opponents of the party, on February 6, 1860, "passed a unanimous resolution 'to brand as slander' Vogt's allegation that I had 'exploited' the German workers in general and the London workers in particular" (17, p. 264).

83. 41, p. 87. The best overview of the issues involved is provided by Riazanov, pp. 117–21, who writes of *Herr Vogt*'s importance: "Even in Marx's lifetime, students of the decade between 1849–1859 acknowledge that there was no other work that had such an insight into the parties of this epoch as did this work of Marx."

84. 40, p. 439.

85. <u>40</u>, p. 472.

86. <u>40</u>, p. 451.

87. Draper, *Chronicle*, p. 101.

88. <u>41</u>, p. 84.

89. <u>40</u>, p. 393.

90. <u>16</u>, pp. 216–17, 240.

91. For details on the pamphlet's impact, see <u>16</u>, p. 663 n182.

92. <u>40</u>, p. 586 n52.

93. <u>40</u>, p. 44.

94. Draper, *Chronicle*, p. 83.

95. <u>40</u>, p. 41.

96. <u>38</u>, pp. 454–56.

97. <u>40</u>, pp. 419–20.

98. For details on Lassalle's maneuvers, see Draper, *KMTR, IV*, pp. 54–58.

99. <u>40</u>, p. 445.

100. <u>13</u>, p. 657.

101. <u>40</u>, p. 552.

CHAPTER SEVEN.
A NEW REVOLUTIONARY ERA AND THE
BIRTH OF THE FIRST INTERNATIONAL

1. <u>41</u>, pp. 4 and 7.

2. On Weydemeyer's role in generating such sentiments in the German-American community, see Karl Obermann, *Joseph Weydemeyer: Pioneer of American Socialism* (New York: International Publishers, 1947), especially chapter IV.

3. For details on their participation as well as others in the war, see A. E. Zucker, ed., *The Forty-Eighters: Political Refugees of the German Revolution of 1848* (New York: Columbia University Press, 1950), particularly chapter seven.

4. Royden Harrison, in his very useful essay, "British Labour and American Slavery," argues persuasively that it was rank and file proletarian support for the Northern cause that was decisive since a significant element of the trade union leadership and its newspapers were either sympathetic to the Confederacy or nonsupportive of the North; *Before the Socialists: Studies in Labour and Politics, 1861–1881* (London: Routledge and Keagan Paul, 1965).

5. Draper, *Chronicle*, p. 116, says Marx was able to do this through Eccarius who had close contact with the English trade union movement and its leaders. Harrison, op.cit., p. 72, on the other hand, disputes the claim that Marx "organised the meeting," saying rather that it was really the work of the positivist academic Edward Beesly; this isn't, however, inconsistent with Draper's claim.

6. <u>19</u>, p. 154. Modern scholarship has by and large confirmed Marx's insights about the role of England's working class in restraining the efforts of official England in intervening on behalf of the Confederacy. The most recent assessment can be found in Howard Jones, *Union in Peril: The Crisis over British Intervention in the Civil War* (Chapel Hill: The University of North Carolina Press, 1992), pp. 155–56, 260. In addition to Harrison's article,

op. cit., Philip Foner's *British Labor and the American Civil War* (New York: Holmes and Meier, 1981) is still the most authoritative historiographical treatment of the issue.

7. Six weeks earlier Marx, in a letter to Ludwig Kugelman, wrote: "We are obviously heading for revolution—something I have never once doubted since 1850. The first act will include a by no means gratifying rehash of the stupidities of '48–'49. However, that's how world history runs its course, and one had to take it as one finds it" (41, p. 437).

8. See chapter three, pp. 75–76.

9. 41, p. 477.

10. 41, pp. 477–78.

11. 19, pp. 296–97.

12. Fedoseyev et al., op. cit., p. 361.

13. Ibid. "The Moor" of course was Marx.

14. See Marx's letter to Engels of September 12, 1863 (41, p. 493) for a few details on his efforts.

15. 41, p. 400.

16. 41, p. 467.

17. Ibid. It might be appropriate here to address Marx's usage of quite derogatory language (certainly by today's standards)in another letter to Engels about Lassalle–particularly, his "nigger" origins (41, p. 390). Marx employed the term in other contexts in letters but never in published writings. According to the editors of the *MECW*, it did not have the "more profance and unacceptable status" of later history (42, p. xl). Whether the editors' note is an apologia is neither here nor there. Marx and Engels, like all mortals, were products, obviously, of the world in which they lived. Their comments in personal correspondence that were unambiguously racist, sexist, or antisemitic must be seen in context and in relation to their entire corpus of writings and actions. For what it's worth, Marx was fondly known, as noted earlier (p. 172), by close friends and family as "Moor" owing to his dark features and had a son-in-law, Paul Lafargue, a mulatto, who was also fondly called in family circles, "African" and "Negrillo."

18. It was for this reason that Lassalle, as mentioned above in chapter six, p. 185, offered upon a platter to Bismarck the newly born German labor movement in return for state-supported workers' enterprises. Unbeknownst to Marx at the time, in the Summer of 1863, Lassalle, the head of the new GGWA, met secretly with Bismarck to effect such a quid pro quo. In his letter to the Chancellor, which included the statutes of the GGWA, Lassalle gloated over "the constitution of *my* empire, which perhaps you'd have to envy me! But this miniature picture will plainly convince you how true it is that the working class feels instinctively inclined to dictatorship if it can first be rightfully convinced that such will be exercised in its interests. . . ." He then proposed to Bismarck that the Crown become, in partnership with him lording over the German working class, a "social dictatorship" (Draper, *KMTR, IV*, p. 55). How perceptive Marx had been a few months earlier in suspecting Lassalle of aspiring to be "a future working men's dictator"! Regarding Marx's views on the "iron law of wages," see below, p. 189.

19. By this time Engels, apparently for security reasons, was responsible for keeping correspondence from party members such as Liebknecht in what Marx referred to as "the archives" (41, p. 537).

20. 41, p. 537.

21. 41, p. 539.

22. 41, p. 586.

23. 41, p. 533.

24. 24, p. 170.

25. 41, pp. 523 and 525, for both letters.

26. 42, p. 38.

27. Karl Liebknecht, *Karl Marx* (London: Journeyman Press, 1975) p. 59. For a discussion on the source of the error with Marx and Engels's analysis of capitalist business cycles in this period and how they later corrected it, see Ernest Mandel, *The Formation of the Economic Thought of Karl Marx* (New York: Monthly Review Press, 1971), chapter 5.

28. 40, p. 566. The Marx's eight-year-old son Edgar had died about a year and a half earlier; see chapter six, fn. 62.

29. 40, p. 223.

30. 40, p. 243.

31. 40, p. 271. The Latin verse is from Horace, *Odes*, III, I, 1, according to the editors. Compare Marx's comment with that of Jenny in October 1863 to a close friend about the deplorable state of politics in Germany: "One often feels tempted to turn away in disgust from all politics, and indeed I wish we could observe the scene purely as 'amateurs'; but for us, unfortunately, it always remains a vital question" (41, p. 582). Like her husband, Jenny too was political to the core in spite of herself.

32. 16, pp. 123–24.

33. 40, p. 375.

34. 40, p. 346.

35. Ibid., p. 347.

36. See chapter four, p. 109.

37. *Capital, Vol. I* (New York: International Publishers, 1972), p. 9.

38. See chapter four, p. 95.

39. The argument made here is more in line with Alan Gilbert's critique of Sheldon Wolin and others who suggest or contend that the mature Marx became an economic determinist. While Gilbert comes closer to the truth in arguing that if anything Marx gave greater priority to politics in the aftermath of 1848–49, a close reading of his and Engels's involvement in those revolutions, as described in chapters three and four, makes clear that they were just as political then as later. It is true, as they themselves mentioned on occasion—see above, p. 152—they matured politically as a result of the earlier experiences. See Gilbert's "The Storming of Heaven: Politics and Marx's *Capital*," *Marxism*, eds. J. Roland Pennock and John Chapman, [*Nomos*, XXVI] (New York: New York University Press, 1983).

40. Henry Collins and Abramsky's chapter, "Origins of the First International," in their *Karl Marx and the British Labour Movement* (London: Macmillan and Co., 1965), pp. 14–29, remains the best explanation for the IWMA's emergence.

41. One of the most striking characteristics of the Marxological literature is the grossly inadequate—let alone tendentious—treatment of this most vital period in the lives of Marx and Engels. For Shlomo Avineri, *Karl Marx* (Cambridge: Cambridge U.P.,1968), for example, the IWMA gets about six or seven paragraphs, while Berlin, op. cit., manages to eke out about twenty-five pages in his almost three hundred-page tome. Things improve a bit with

McLellan, op. cit., in which a little more than a tenth of the entire volume summarizes their involvement in the body. George Lichtheim, *Marxism* (New York: Praeger, 1962), who devotes less than three percent of his book to the IWMA, excuses his short shrift of any serious discussion of the rich programmatic debates in the organization on the grounds of it being "a wearisome tale of complicated maneuvering in the pursuit of which much toil and virtue were consumed" (p. 109).

42. 42, p. 47.

43. 42, p. 44.

44. 42, p. 16.

45. See chapter six, pp. 157–58.

46. 42, p. 18. The section of the Provisional Rules in which these formulations appear are as follows: "[T]his International Association and all societies and individuals adhering to it, will acknowledge truth, justice, and morality, as the basis of their conduct towards each other, and towards all men, without regard to colour, creed, or nationality;

They hold it the duty of a man to claim the rights of a man and a citizen, not only for himself, but for every man who does his duty. No rights without duties, no duties without rights;" (20, p. 15).

47. 42, p. 18. The one modification that Marx had to make in his draft, after some debate in the Council, was that the word "profitmongers," in reference to opponents of the Ten Hours' Bill that was passed by parliament in 1847, was eliminated. The vote was eleven to ten for its removal. It should be noted that in addition to Marx and Eccarius two other party members, Pfänder and Friedrich Lessner, were on the GC, having just been coopted onto it—a practice that was agreed on at the initial meeting of the GC—upon a motion and second by Marx and Eccarius respectively. For details see *MEGA*₂, Bd. 20, Abt. 1, p. 276, and Collins and Abramsky, op. cit., p. 43.

48. 41, pp. 465 and 468 respectively.

49. 42, p. 20.

50. 42, p. 22.

51. 20, p. 9.

52. For some discussion on the issue of relative impoverishment in modern scholarship see Eric Hobsbawm, *The Age of Capital: 1848–1875* (London: Weidenfeld and Nicolson, 1975), pp. 219–23, and Harrison, op. cit., pp. 22–25. The latter argues that while real wages did rise for the proletariat during this period, "the share of wages in the national income declined after 1850" (p. 23). This would support, therefore, Marx's argument about the tendency to "deepen social contrasts." Of particular significance, in Harrison's opinion, was the differentiation within the working class—the emergence of what Marx called "a minority of the working classes [that] got their real wages somewhat advanced" (20, p. 9).

53. See the two articles by Ernest Jones that were published in 1851 on cooperation, "under," according to Marx, "my direction" (42, p. 15).

54. In his letter to Engels that describes the tact he employed in writing the Address, Marx notes pointedly: "Insofar as INTERNATIONAL POLITICS is mentioned in the 'Address,' I refer to COUNTRIES and not to NATIONALITIES, and denounce Russia, not the *minores gentium* [smaller nations]" (42, p. 18). What this suggests is that Marx was concerned that the call for proletarian internationalism not be undermined by any appearance of appeals to nationalism or national prejudices.

Collins and Abramsky, op.cit., still the best single volume on Marx's involvement in the IWMA, point out that, in contrast to the other GC members who understood internationalism in a more limited sense, "Only Marx proposed that the workers should organise internationally to win political power and use it to change the social system. His tactics throughout the history of the International can only be understood in the light of his overriding aim, an aim which few of his English associates shared or even understood" (p. 50). This is indeed an accurate insight as the evidence presented in the rest of this and the next chapter will make clear.

55. 42, p. 17.

56. 20, p. 14.

57. In a "Confidential Communication" in 1870 Marx notes that the omission was made by the "Paris Committee," i.e., Proudhonists, of the IWMA. "When questioned by the [GC], the Paris Committee excused itself by the difficulties of its political situation" (21, p. 121).

58. 42, pp. 54–55

59. The actual resolutions were as follows: "That persons residing in any part of England can join the Association, but that no member can be elected upon the General Committee who is unable to attend its meetings, and assist in its deliberations." And secondly: "That organised bodies of working men be invited to join this Association in their cooperative capacity, the amount of their contributions to be left to their means and discretion" (20, pp. 17–18). By requiring that GC members had to be active participants the first resolution effectively barred honorary or paper membership.

60. 42, pp. 92–93. Marx, in a letter to Engels in May 1865, voiced similar suspicions about Ernest Jones: "[B]etween ourselves, *he* is *only* trying to use our Association for electoral agitation" (42, p. 155). When Jones asked Marx in November 1868 to assist in his parliamentary bid, the latter politely declined. One of the reasons Marx gave was that the GC "does not get mixed up in ELECTIONEERING" (43, p. 166).

61. 42, p. 207.

62. 42, p. 50.

63. 42, p. 268.

64. 42, p. 109.

65. This and the other quotes from the session at the Geneva congress which addressed this issue are from *MEGA*₂, Bd. 20, I, pp. 706–7.

66. See Marx's letter to a former CL member, along with the accompanying notes, for the details on this (42, pp. 3–4).

67. 42, p. 130.

68. 42, p. 328.

69. See, in particular, his letter to Johann Philipp Becker, a former CL member who was in exile in Geneva, on the eve of the meeting, with very concrete instructions about how the congress should be led (42, pp. 314–15).

70. 20, p. 412. For the record, it might be noted that in 1862 Marx, who, in an effort to "prevent myself and my family from actually being relegated to the streets," tried to get a job as a clerk for the railroad—which might have qualified him for a "manual worker"—but was denied owing to his unintelligible handwriting (41, pp. 435–36).

71. 42, p. 109.

72. This and the preceding quotes are from 42, p. 253.

73. For a detailed treatment of Marx's long-time relationship with Eccarius and a convincing refutation of charges that Marx mistreated him, see, again, Draper, "Poor Eccarius and the Marx-Monster," *KMTR, II*, pp. 644–53.

74. See chapter two, p. 35.

75. 42, p. 243.

76. 42, p. 141.

77. 42, p. 125.

78. 41, p. 546.

79. 42, p. 172.

80. For a similar reading of Marx the activist, see Gilbert, "The Storming of Heaven: Politics and Marx's *Capital*," op. cit., p. 162.

81. 42, p. 159. The minutes for the GC meeting at which Weston made his proposals are not extant.

82. Marx's daughter, Eleanor, was responsible for its publication in 1898 under this title. As it became clear to Marx that its publication by the GC might attract the attention of leading intellectuals who had ties to the labor movement such as John Stuart Mill, he consulted Engels about the desirability of so doing since it might preempt the soon to appear *Capital*. See their exchange, 42, pp. 162–63, and 168.

83. 20, p. 149.

84. Ibid., p. 145.

85. Ibid., p. 146.

86. Ibid., pp. 146 and 148–49.

87. In Part I of the *Manifesto* it says, for example, that wages are "restricted almost entirely to the means of subsistence. . . . In proportion, therefore, as the repulsiveness of the work increases, the wage decreases." Or, later, the "modern laborer . . . instead of rising with the progress of industry sinks deeper and deeper below the conditions of existence of his own class."

88. Draper, *KMTR, II*, p. 99, who provides the best overview of the evolution of Marx and Engels's views on trade unions, is correct in saying that the "document is . . . not a statement that fully reflects where Marx's thinking was by 1866; it included only as much as Marx thought could be adopted at this juncture by the international congress."

89. Unfortunately it is not possible here to look at the other proposals that Marx submitted, which included such topics as "Limitation of the Working Day," "Juvenile and Children's Labour (Both Sexes)," "Co-operative Labour," "Direct and Indirect Taxation," "Polish Question," "Armies," and matters related to the organization and activities of the IWMA. As a whole they reveal how Marx concretized in policy terms many of the theoretical issues raised in *Capital*—published a year later—and give lie to the frequent charge that the more mature Marx abandoned his earlier humanistic concerns. For example, it was crucial to limit the working day—the specific proposal was for eight hours—in order "to restore the health and physical energies of the working class, that is, the great body of every nation, as well as to secure them the possibility of intellectual development, sociable intercourse, social and political action" (20, p. 187).

90. Draper, *KMTR, II*, p. 99.

91. <u>20</u>, p. 192.

92. See chapter six, p. 158.

93. For the best summary of Marx's critique of Proudhon and his ideas see his lengthy letter to J. B. Schweitzer of Jan. 24, 1865, written shortly after Proudhon's death (<u>20</u>, pp. 26–33).

94. Collins and Abramsky, op. cit., p. 117.

95. Ibid., p. 124.

96. Ibid., p. 141.

97. <u>43</u>, p. 95.

98. McLellan, op. cit., p. 381.

99. <u>42</u>, p. 290.

100. <u>20</u>, p. 20.

101. <u>20</u>, p. 100.

102. <u>42</u>, p. 334 These were the congressional elections in November 1866—"the most important off-presidential election in our history," according to Samuel Eliot Morrison (*The Oxford History of the American People*, New York, 1965, p. 715).

103. <u>42</u>, pp. 423–24.

CHAPTER EIGHT.
THE FIRST INTERNATIONAL:
FROM BRUSSELS TO THE PARIS COMMUNE

1. <u>43</u>, p. 252.

2. <u>24</u>, p. 190.

3. <u>21</u>, pp. 517–18.

4. Institute of Marxism-Leninism, *The General Council of the First International, 1868–1870* (Moscow: Progress Publishers, 1974), p. 46 [hereafter, <u>GC</u>]. Eichoff's pamphlet was the "only systematic exposition of . . . [the IWMA's] principles published in Germany during its life-time . . ." (Roger Morgan, *The German Social Democrats and the First International, 1864–1872* [Cambridge, 1965], p. 238).

5. Engels, Paul and Laura Lafargue, *Correspondence, Vol. 3, 1891–1895* (Moscow: Foreign Languages Publishing House, 1963), p. 347. Concerned about the accuracy of the historical record of the IWMA, Marx, in 1878, wrote a short piece to correct the misinformation that a former GC member and later opponent of Marx, George Howell, provided that year in an article claiming to be a history of the International; see <u>24</u>, pp. 234–39. Owing largely to the priority he placed on finishing *Capital* after the organization's effective demise in 1873, Marx, however, never got around to writing anything more detailed than this on the IWMA.

6. On the details of governmental harassment and persecution of IWMA activists and affiliates see Eichoff's aforementioned report, and Marx's reports to the Basle and Hague congresses in 1869 and 1872 respectively (<u>21</u>, pp. 68–82, and <u>23</u>, pp. 219–27). If subsequent Marxological accounts have failed to appreciate the political importance of the IWMA in Marx's practice, Europeans governments—France, Belgium, Austria, and Switzerland in particular—certainly did not dismiss what one French government-sponsored newspaper referred to as the "foreign Machiavelli" (<u>21</u>, p. 75) who was apparently orchestrating the strike wave sweeping Europe in 1869.

7. Edith Thomas, "The Women of the Commune," *The Massachusetts Review* 12, 3 (1971), p. 411. Proudhon's own views on women were notorious, as exemplified by his "famous dictum that woman is either housewife or courtesan" (Persis Hunt, "Feminism and Anti-Clericalism under the Commune," ibid., p. 431). Marx's initiative also meant having to oppose the Lassallean-influenced "anti-feminist" stance of the German workers' movement. See Werner Thönnessen, *The Emancipation of Women: The Rise and Decline of the Women's Movement in German Social Democracy 1863–1933* (London: Pluto Press, 1976), pp. 15–27.

8. *MEGA₂*, Bd. 20, p. 466.

9. For these and the other proposals see 20, pp. 187–89, and chapter seven, fn. 89.

10. 20, p. 203.

11. GC, 1866–1868, p. 247.

12. 43, pp. 184–85. Marx's relations with Kugelmann, interestingly, cooled after a visit to his family in 1874. The reason was Marx's objections, as he explained to Engels, to the way that he treated his wife Gertrud: "[T]his arch-pedant, this pettifogging, bourgeois philistine has got the idea that his wife is unable to understand him, to comprehend his Faustian nature with its aspirations to a higher world outlook, and he torments the woman, who is his superior in every respect, in the most repulsive manner. So it led to a quarrel between us . . ." (45, p. 46).

Perhaps this is the appropriate place to take up the oft-repeated charge that Marx fathered a child by his housekeeper Helene Demuth—the suggestion, then, that his private practice vis-à-vis women was less than exemplary. According to Allen Wood, however, "it is now widely held that [Marx] was not" the father (Ted Honderich, ed., *The Oxford Companion to Philosophy* [New York: Oxford University Press, 1995], p. 524).

13. GC, 1868–1870, p. 139.

14. Ibid., pp. 170 and 453.

15. 22, p. 424.

16. Another example of what happens when Marx and Engels are not treated as political people is the enormous mountain of misrepresentations that claim to be explications of their views on women. The most representative collection of this can be found in *Women, Class, and the Feminist Imagination: A Socialist-Feminist Reader*, eds. Karen V. Hansen and Ilene Philipson (Philadelphia: Temple University Press, 1990), particularly Part I, "The Past." Almost invariably, the exegesis involves the selection of statements from their well-known writings upon which an entire edifice is erected. Never is there any effort to look at their practice, let alone contextualize what they wrote *and* did.

17. Most interestingly, in the United States, where Marx thought the best progress was being made on women in the worker's movement, it had been Marx party members and associates who, more than a decade earlier, played a vanguard role in this development. "No one worked harder or more effectively to bolster support for women's rights in the immigrant labor movement than Mathilde Giesler Anneke" who had once been part of the *NRZ* milieu in Cologne. In 1853 she joined forces with Joseph Weydemeyer to continue her work. For details see Bruce Levine, *The Spirit of 1848: German Immigrants, Labor Conflict, and the Coming of the Civil War* (Urbana: U. of Illinois Press, 1992), pp. 124–25.

18. In an otherwise intelligent discussion of the similarities and differences between Tristan and Marx, Máire Cross and Tim Gray, *The Feminism of Flora Tristan* (Oxford: Berg, 1992), fall prey to gratuitous Marx bashing with the completely unsubstantiated charge that "Marx dismissed women workers as deferential and lacking in political nous, thereby difficult

to organise and mobilize" (pp. 135–36)—a claim that flies in the face of the evidence presented here. It's easy to get away with such fables when, as with Cross and Gray, Marx's political activities are ignored. Nancy Folbre makes similar misrepresentations in her "Socialism, Feminist and Scientific," *Beyond Economic Man: Feminist Theory and Economics,* eds. Marianne A. Ferber and Julie A. Nelson (Chicago: University of Chicago Press, 1993), pp. 94–110.

19. 42, p. 460.

20. His letter of November 30 to Engels makes clear that this was the case(42, pp. 485–87).

21. 42, p. 501.

22. 21, p. 194. When Marx's daughter Jenny wrote in 1869 to Kugelmann that "We are all of us downright Fenians" (43, p. 548), she was referring to the Marx household's identification with that side of Fenianism and not with what Marx and Engels characterized as its weakness, the tendency toward ultraleft adventurism.

23. 42, pp. 486–87.

24. Collins and Abramsky, p. 134.

25. GC, 1868–1870, p. 172.

26. GC, 1868–1870, pp. 176–77.

27. 43, p. 398.

28. 21, pp. 88–89.

29. GC, 1871–1872, pp. 197–98. Engels's comment was recorded in the GC minutes which were read and approved at the following meeting with him in attendance. During the Austro-Prussian War in 1866 the GC had a debate on the "QUESTION OF NATIONALITY in general and the attitude we should adopt to it," as Marx told Engels afterwards(42, p. 287). The GC minutes, unfortunately, provide little or no detail about what Marx said. His aforementioned letter indicates that he sought to avoid the GC taking "a one-sided course," that is, knee-jerk reaction in support or opposition to nationalism. As to the latter, he clearly rejected the view put forward that "any nationality and even nations are " *des préjugés surannés* [outdated prejudices]."

30. While Walker Connor is sufficiently informed to know that for Marx and Engels "national movements were not to be treated in isolation but viewed against this broader backdrop" i.e., the global revolutionary process, he faults them for "inconsistency" with what he calls "classical Marxism." The latter, according to Connor, is "philosophically incompatible" with nationalism. The "incompatibility" is, rather, in Connor's mind. What he fails to grasp, and what Marx and Engels clearly understood, is that nationalism is indeed a social construction and always in transition. Their dialectical approach allowed for the kind of flexibility to understand their moving target that his more rigid methodology, which he would impose on them, cannot. See the first chapter, "Three Strands of Nationalism in Marx and Engels," in his *The National Question in Marxist-Leninist Theory and Strategy* (Princeton: Princeton University Press, 1984).

31. See his letter to Kugelmann of November 29, 1869, which was written ten days prior to the one to Engels and with a more elaborate presentation of the argument—43, pp. 390–91.

32. 43, pp. 474–75. Marx, by the way, was not alone in drawing the parallel between English anti-Irish sentiment and southern U.S. white working-class racism. Another GC

member, the British trade union reformist Mottershead, said as much at one of their meetings in 1872. The Irish in England "were looked down upon by the English workers much the same as the mean Whites of the South looked down upon Negroes" (GC, 1871–1872, p. 196).

33. Engels had intended to write a major work on Irish history and to that end collected numerous materials during his visit there in 1869—which he made available to Marx for his researches on the Irish question—and mastered the Gaelic language; he only got as far as the first chapter of the project owing to the intervention of political reality in 1870. For details on what he intended, see 21, 488.

34. 42, p. 442. The correspondence makes clear that Marx's urgings had little to do with bringing attention to himself but rather to the book.

35. 42, p. 427.

36. 42, p. 444.

37. 42, p. 468.

38. 42, p. 462.

39. 43, p. 597.

40. 42, p. 488.

41. That Marx and Engels saw the text as a weapon to be employed by the movement was indicated when Liebknecht suggested in 1871 that Engels's 1844 article that inspired Marx's political economy research be republished. Engels objected because it is now "*quite obsolete* and full of inaccuracies that could only confuse people." It would be better, he told Liebknecht, to "print more extensive excerpts from *Capital*" (44, pp. 135–36).

42. 42, p. 495.

43. 42, pp. 451–52.

44. 42, pp. 578–79.

45. 42, p. 265.

46. 20, pp. 152–61.

47. 43, p. 252.

48. Unfortunately for those interested in how the partnership operated, the historical record would never be as clear as it had been in those two decades when there had been a paper trail in the form of correspondence almost every other day.

49. For an assessment of the address vis-à-vis the positions of other currents, see Collins and Abramsky, pp. 179–80. As to how Marx and Engels dealt with other antiwar forces, see also, 44, pp. 31–35.

50. GC, 1870–1871, p. 87.

51. Possibly another precedent were the antiwar activities of students in France, Germany, and Italy on the eve of the Austro-Prussian War in 1866. For details, see Frederick Lessner, *Sixty Years in the Social-Democratic Movement* (London: Twentieth Century Press, 1907), pp. 36–38, and *MEGA*$_2$, Bd. 20, pp. 421–25.

52. 44, p. 57.

53. 22, p. 269.

54. 44, p. 64.

55. 44, p. 67.

56. The revolutionary uprising that occurred in Lyons following news of Bonaparte's surrender was stark confirmation of what happened when impatience ruled the day. The process, as Marx described, was proceeding well—spreading also to Marseilles and Toulouse—until "the asses, Bakunine and Cluseret [a military adventurist who went through numerous incarnations—see Draper, *Glossary*, p.43], arrived at Lyons and spoiled everything. The Hotel de Ville was seized—for a short time—and most foolish decrees on the *abolition de l'état* and similar nonsense were issued. . . . [T]he very fact of a Russian . . . pretending to impose himself as the leader of a *Comité du Salut de la France* was quite sufficient to turn the balance of public opinion" (44, pp. 88–89). Anarchist leadership for a revolution was a contradiction in terms. The outcome was a fiasco that deprived Paris of the kind of regional support it sorely needed six months later.

57. 44, p. 70.

58. 44, p. 14. As part of their effort to maintain British "neutrality" in the final months of the war and shortly before the Commune, Marx and Engels led a very heated debate in opposition to the British trade unionists on the GC who advocated that Britain declare war on Germany. For details, see GC, 1870–1871, pp. 106–57 passim.

59. 44, p. 149. Typical of the Marxological enterprise is Ronald Payne's misrepresentation that Marx "in fact . . . wrote very few letters and contented himself with ineffectual gestures, while claiming always that 'our party' was responsible for the revolution" (*Marx: A Biography* [New York: Simon & Schuster, 1968], p. 420). While it is likely that Marx was using "hundreds" figuratively, based on the letters that the editors of the *MECW* project have included—which, however, does not take into account letters that were indeed written by other GC members—the subsequent discussion makes clear that Marx and Engels did not engage in empty gestures on behalf of the Communards.

60. 44, p. 128.

61. 44, p. 131.

62. See above, chapter six, p. 155.

63. 11, pp. 185–86.

64. 44, p. 136–37.

65. See chapter six, p. 152, for earlier comments by Marx and Engels on the revolutionary party taking power prematurely.

66. 11, p. 68.

67. On the particulars about the situation that faced the Parisians see Stewart Edwards, *The Paris Commune, 1871* (New York: Quadrangle Books, 1973), especially chapters 3 and 4, which is still the best modern account of the Commune and largely confirms Marx's assessment. Prosper-Olivier Lissagaray's *History of the Paris Commune* (London: New Park Publications, 1976), first published in 1876, and which Marx had a hand in its writing, is the best contemporary account by a participant. A later classic, Frank Jellinek's *The Paris Commune of 1871*, first published in 1937 concluded that "Marx's analysis does fit a larger proportion of the facts than any other, and does so more convincingly" (pp. 389–90). The point made here about Marx's embracement of the Commune is at sharp variance with interpretations that suggest otherwise such as McLellan's, pp. 393–94 and that of Royden Harrison, "Marx, Engels, and the British Response to the Commune," *The Massachusetts Review* 12, 3 (1971), p. 473.

68. 44, p. 141.

69. 45, p. 41.

70. For details on this see Edwards, pp. 125–26.

71. For details of her activities and valor as a fighter, see her letter to Jung (which he reported on—GC, 1870–1871, p. 184). Also, her report to the Commune's Labor Commission that was headed by Frankel proposed that women's work be reorganized through "free producers' co-operatives" along with other very advanced measures that suggest the influence of Marx; see both in the collection of Commune documents edited by Stewart Edwards, *The Communards of Paris, 1871* (Ithaca, N.Y.: Cornell University Press, 1973), pp. 133–36.

72. Edwards, *The Paris Commune*, p. 257.

73. 44, pp. 142, 148–51.

74. Edwards, *The Communards*, p. 134.

75. Maximilian Rubel and Margaret Manale, *Marx Without Myth* (New York: Harper & Row, 1975), p. 263. According to Collins and Abramsky, "Lafargue no doubt had in mind the plan of military operations worked out by Engels for the defense of Paris against the Germans. After Engels's death, his literary executors, August Bebel and Eduard Bernstein, destroyed the plan because they wanted to remove evidence of Engels's 'treason' to the 'fatherland'" (Collins and Abramsky, p. 193n).

76. Marx and Engels, *Writing on the Paris Commune*, ed. Hal Draper (New York: Monthly Review Press, 1971), pp. 222–23.

77. 44, pp. 148–49.

78. 44, p. 151 for this and the preceding quote. The advice that Marx was referring to here was offered in the letter cited above in fn. 73.

79. According to Edwards, "There is no exact figure, but something in the order of 25,000 Parisians were killed, compared to the Versailles losses in battle of 877 dead and 6,454 wounded. . . . The exact number of arrested is not certain . . . maybe 50,000" (*The Paris Commune*, pp. 346–47).

80. Marx and Engels, *Writings on the Paris Commune*, p. 222.

81. 44, p. 141.

82. Their assessment in the "Preface" to the 1872 German edition of the *Manifesto*, about which more will be said shortly (23, p. 175).

83. See Edwards, *The Paris Commune*, pp. 155–56, for a longer excerpt from the statement. That the Central Committee statement employed "proletarians" is noteworthy given subsequent debates about Marx's characterization of the Commune as the proletariat in power for the first time. This is not the place to take up this question—again, see Edwards for the most current scholarship on the Commune's social composition—but simply useful to point out that within the National Guard at least such a denomination would not have seemed odd.

84. 22, pp. 328, 332, 339. The latter quote was inspired of course by Lincoln's famous phrase. The U.S. Civil War continued to weigh heavily on the minds of everyone—hence, the title of the document—including Thiers, who tried to liken his war against the Communards to that of Lincoln's against the Confederacy. To counter this claim Marx, throughout the address, refers disparagingly to Versailles' actions as that of the "slaveholders' rebellion."

85. 23, p. 175.

86. 22, pp. 334–35.

87. 46, p. 66.

88. <u>22</u>, p. 335.

89. <u>22</u>, p. 499. The documents of the Commune that Edwards has assembled, *The Communards of Paris*, reveals that the most class-conscious component of the Commune's leadership, other than that of the IWMA members, was the National Guard's Central Committee. In addition to the manifesto following the March 18 events, which Marx quoted, their declaration in early April is also instructive. Amongst its exhortations is, "Workers, make no mistake—this is all-out war, a war between parasites and workers, exploiters and producers" (p. 80).

90. <u>22</u>, p. 337. Apparently, the only concrete step the Communards took to win the peasantry to their cause was the issuance at the end of April or beginning of May of a manifesto, "To the Working People of the Village"; Marx referred to its contents in *Civil War*. According to Draper, the document "had to be distributed to the rural areas by scatter-drops from balloons: such was the effect of the blockade. The Parisians were unable to send organizers and agitators into the country districts to carry their message, which was summarized in the manifesto as 'The land to the peasant, the tool to the worker, work for all'" (Draper, *KMTR, II*, p. 394). In her letter of April 24 to Jung, Tomanovskaya wrote: "We did not get the Manifesto to the farm-workers out soon enough. I do not think it was written at all and this in spite of all our warnings" (Edwards, *The Communards*, p. 134; see also, above, p. 214). Draper offers evidence that Marx did not think highly of the manifesto because it failed to provide a concrete program to win over the peasantry.

91. <u>22</u>, pp. 494–95.

92. For details see <u>23</u>, p. 425; <u>44</u>, p. 293; <u>27</u>, pp. 187, 514.

93. <u>24</u>, p. 18.

94. <u>27</u>, p. 191.

95. For details on the context see Draper, *KMTR, III*, pp. 312–17.

96. <u>22</u>, p. 634.

97. See chapter three, pp. 80–81.

98. See above, chapter six, p. 145. Note the similarity of this remark with the one Engels made three years later about the revolutionary party coming to power prematurely—see chapter six, p. 152—and the parallels with Marx's analysis of the Commune and its outcome.

99. <u>46</u>, p. 66.

100. <u>27</u>, p. 514.

101. This interpretation, hence, challenges that of Draper, (*KMTR,III*, pp. 269–78, 292–94), who argues that "Marx had no compunction about applying the term to the Paris Commune." Draper rests his case on the above-quoted 1871 newspaper account of Marx's banquet speech, which is odd. As he notes elsewhere, Marx was so frequently misquoted that he "made a practice of *not* writing in corrections to editors who printed mistatements about him . . ." (*KMTR, II*, p. 589n). As for the argument presented here about Marx's views before, during, and after the Commune, Draper certainly recognizes, in his first volume at least (particularly chapters 7, 8, and 9), the people's alliance as a vital component of Marx and Engels's reading of the class character of the revolutionary transition, he has virtually nothing to say about it in his third volume. No doubt this omission is due to the purpose of the latter, an encyclopedic treatment of the term "dictatorship of the proletariat." However, a thorough effort to determine if Marx really applied the phrase to the Commune would have to take into account the actual content of his views on the politics of the revolutionary transition before, during, and after the 1871 upheaval.

102. 44, p. 158.

103. McLellan, p. 401.

104. This is indicated by a request to Marx from an official in the ministry to submit to him all of the official documents issued by the GC (see 44, pp. 169–70).

105. GC, 1870–1871, p. 225.

106. McLellan, p. 400.

107. 44, p. 566.

108. For details of the Pope's opinion of the International, see GC, 1870–1871, p. 242.

109. Regarding the request from Calcutta, the GC secretary, according to the minutes of August 15, 1871, "was instructed . . . also to urge the necessity of enrolling natives in the Association" (GC, 1870–1871, p. 258), thus, making clear that the new affiliate was not to be an exclusively expatriate body.

110. Ibid., p. 241.

111. 47, p. 211.

Chapter Nine.
The First International:
The Final Years and Legacy

1. 23, pp. 614–15.

2. There had been a precedent for such a conference when in 1865 the GC, at Marx's urging, decided that it would be premature to hold a congress that year for the fledgling organization and convened instead a conference, also in London.

3. GC, 1870–1871, respectively pp. 244–45, and 259.

4. 22, pp. 417–18.

5. 44, pp. 258–59.

6. 22, p. 278.

7. All of Marx's quotes are from 22, p. 617. Henri Tolain, an IWMA leader of the French section, was elected to the National Assembly prior to the Commune but sided with Versailles against the Parisian insurgents; the section with the GC's endorsement expelled him.

8. 22, p. 617n.

9. Two days later under another point Marx reiterated his praise for Bebel and Liebknecht by adding that as part of their protest against the war "they refused to vote any subsidy" for the government's actions (22, p. 619). Their refusal stands in sharp contrast to those deputies from the same party who did vote some four decades later for such subsidies on the eve of World War I—the issue that finally split the Socialist or Second International.

10. See 22, p. 618 for all of these quotes.

11. For details on the discussion and votes see $MEGA_2$, I, Bd. 22, pp. 695–712.

12. 22, p. 427.

13. See chapter eight, p. 201 for details.

14. 22, pp. 426 and 686.

15. 44, p. 220.

16. Draper, *KMTR, IV*, pp. 291–94, argues convincingly that Bakunin may have been one of the first proponents of "racist anti-semitism," i.e., what Hitler perfected, as opposed to historical anti-Jewish sentiment.

17. Draper, *KMTR, IV*, p. 271. Engels, in fact, said as much in a report to the GC on Bakunin's operation on the eve of the Hague congress(GC, 1871–1872, p. 511). Boris Nicolaevsky, "Secret Societies and the First International," *The Revolutionary Internationals*, ed. Milorad Drachkovitch (Stanford University Press, 1966), argues that Mazzini through his supporters on the GC, against whom Marx waged a successful fight in the early years of the IWMA, carried out the first such conspiratorial campaign in the IWMA. Aside from the fact that the evidence he offers is sketchy, that neither Marx nor Engels ever said such about Mazzini's efforts or compared it to Bakunin's suggests that Nicolaevsky may be reading more into those events than is warranted.

18. 23, pp. 115 and 121, for these quotes.

19. See in particular, 44, pp. 386–87, 582, and 23, p. 265.

20. 44, p. 413.

21. 23, p. 255.

22. GC, 1866–1868, p. 157.

23. 23, p. 283.

24. 23, p. 256.

25. 23, p. 255.

26. The speaker was the Blanquist Edouard Vaillant who, speaking for the resolution's inclusion said, "Economic struggle must be inseparable from political struggle and the abolition of class rule must be carried through in the revolutionary process by means of the dictatorship of the proletariat" (*The Hague Congress of the First International, Minutes and Documents*, [Moscow: Progress Publishers, 1976], p. 160). See Draper, *KMTR, III*, pp. 284–86, for a useful discussion on Marx's influence on the Blanquist usage of "dictatorship of the proletariat" at this moment.

27. As already stated, the British trade unionists' issue will be addressed later in this chapter. Regarding the Blanquists, while Marx and Engels were willing to bloc with them against the Bakuninists, they had no illusions about their politics. As with the Bakuninsts, their conspiratorial approach to politics inevitably breeds "a dictatorship of one or several individuals" as opposed to "a dictatorship . . . of the entire revolutionary class, the proletariat (24, p. 13).

28. 23, p. 266. In a completely gratuitous remark, Collins and Abramsky suggests that "it is doubtful without a good deal of mandate [i.e., credential]-fixing before the Congress [by Marx and Engels presumably] it could have been carried at all" (op. cit., p. 264). They provide not a shred of evidence for this insinuation nor is there anything in the record to make such a case. It was precisely because of the possibility of such a charge—i.e., "an artificial majority"—that Marx and Engels opposed having the congress in London (see 44, p. 408).

29. On one end of the spectrum is the more circumspect McLellan, p. 410, while at the other end is the judgment of Paul Thomas,*Karl Marx and the Anarchists* (London: Routledge &Kegan Paul, 1980) p. 328, that in proposing the move "Marx had destroyed the International in order to save it."

30. 45, p. 42.

31. Nicolaievsky and Maenchen-Helfen, p. 391, have a similar interpretation.

32. See their letters to Sorge right after the Geneva congress, 44, pp. 535–37. The IWMA was officially dissolved at a meeting in Philadelphia in 1876.

33. 45, p. 42.

34. See Jacques Freymond and Miklos Molnár, "The Rise and Fall of the First International, " *The Revolutionary Internationals*, ed. Milorad Drachkovitch (Stanford University Press, 1966) pp. 29–31.

35. 44, pp. 475–76.

36. All quotes here from 44, pp. 512–14.

37. All the quotes here are from Engels's letter to Sorge, 45, p. 42.

38. 43, p. 429.

39. 22, pp. 261–62.

40. 44, p. 535.

41. 40, p. 344.

42. See chapter seven, p. 177.

43. 41, p. 465.

44. 41, p. 468.

45. See Collins and Abramsky for details on the composition and limitations of the British trade union participation in the IWMA, pp. 59–81.

46. See also chapter seven, fn. 52.

47. This is from Engels's pamphlet, *The Prussian Military Question and the German Workers' Party*, 20, p. 74, about which more will be said later.

48. 42, p. 314.

49. 44, pp. 100–1.

50. 43, p. 388. The vacillation of Odger and the other trade unionists on Irish self-determination anticipated the behavior of the reformists within the Second International on the colonial issue, i.e., their failure to condemn outright the imperialism of their respective ruling classes.

51. 21, p. 87.

52. See chapter three, p. 60.

53. 44, p. 147.

54. 22, p. 614.

55. *The Hague Congress: Minutes and Documents*, p. 124.

56. 45, p. 18. For evidence that substantiates Marx's charges see Collins and Abramsky, p. 260, and Royden Harrison, *Before the Socialists*, chapter IV.

57. 23, p. 613. In their otherwise useful discussion of the difficulties of the IWMA in England, chapter XIV and Conclusions, Collins and Abramsky, unfortunately, do not address this factor.

58. 47, p. 55.

59. An aspect of the Lassalle legacy that continued into modernity is the awe in which Franz Mehring's well-known biography, *Karl Marx*, is held, oftentimes cited as the "standard" or "classical" account. What is seldom recognized, as Draper persuasively argues (*KMTR, IV*, pp. 305–18), is that Mehring was and remained a Lassallean and it was thus from that perspective that his biography was written, with all the repercussions of such a bias.

60. 42, pp. 75–77.

61. On some details of this deterioration and the extent to which Schweitzer compromised himself to Bismarck's government, see Raymond H. Dominick III, *Wilhelm Liebknecht and the Founding of the German Social Democratic Party* (Chapel Hill: University of North Carolina Press, 1982), pp. 104–5. Dominick cites a memo of Bismarck in 1871 in which the Chancellor wrote that with the ADAV " 'not only is a material understanding still possible, but a timely intervention by the state will also succeed in reconciling the majority of the workers with the existing order. . . .'" There is nothing to suggest that Bismarck's expectations were ill founded.

62. 43, p. 336.

63. For a useful account of the relationship between the German movement and the IWMA, see Roger P. Morgan, op. cit.

64. 42, p. 67.

65. 20, p. 89. The piece, apparently, was responsible for a provision being introduced in the Prussian Assembly that would allow rural workers to form unions (see, 42, pp. 94 and 608).

66. It may be recalled, see chapter seven, that Marx and Engels six years earlier criticized Lassalle's drama *Franz von Sickingen* for its lauding of the landed nobility and failure to take the side of the peasantry.

67. 20, p. 80.

68. 42, p. 96.

69. 20, p. 80.

70. 20, p. 86.

71. 20, p. 77.

72. 20, p. 78.

73. In a pre-publication notice Engels wrote that the "pamphlet bases itself once more on the standpoint adopted by the literary representatives of the proletariat of 1846–1851 [i.e., Marx and Engels] and develops this standpoint as against both reaction and the progressist bourgeoisie . . ." (20, p. 81).

74. 20, p. 78.

75. 20, p. 75.

76. 21, p. 100.

77. For some details on their campaign to publicize the pamphlet, see 20, pp. 456–57.

78. 42, p. 430.

79. See chapter six, p. 162, for their earlier opinion of Liebknecht. Dominick, op. cit., in his generally sympathetic portrayal of Liebknecht substantiates many of Marx and Engels's charges. In his above-quoted statement about the significance of the Franco-Prussian War for the German movement, Marx told Engels, "I have once and for all abolished the fulsome 'identity' of interests between him and myself which our Wilhelm [Liebknecht] invents to others whenever it suits his purposes" (44, p. 59).

80. On the commencement of his relationship with Bebel, see Dominick, op. cit., pp. 120–22. Liebknecht's recruitment of Bebel to the Marxist tendency did not mean that he had become a communist, at least not initially. In a comment to Engels in 1869 about Bebel, which also spoke volumes about his opinion of Liebknecht, Marx said "I believe Bebel to be

useful and able. He only had the particular misfortune to find his 'theoretician' in Mr Wilhelm" (43, p. 249). To Kugelmann a few months later Engels wrote: "If Bebel only had some theoretical knowledge . . . he seems to me to be quite a capable fellow, who simply has this one shortcoming" (ibid., p. 313). Within a few years, however, they would hold him in the highest regard.

81. 43, p. 133.

82. 43, p. 134.

83. 43, p. 118.

84. 43, 629.

85. 43, p. 630. For another rendering of this quote and details on the context, see Draper, *KMTR, II*, p. 587.

86. 42, p. 361. See also, Marx's revelations in 1878 about an earlier effort to recruit him to Bismarck's cause; 24, pp. 230–33.

87. 45, p. 65.

88. Dominick, pp. 243–45, provides a useful discussion and evidence on the lack of communist understanding within the Eisenach camp itself in order to argue that Marx and Engels's criticisms were unrealistic. He ignores, however, their awareness of the fact that "circumstances at the time precluded this" (45, p. 70), that is, advancing beyond the Eisenach program, and recommendation for joint political work between the ADAV and SDAP as a prelude to unity.

89. 45, p. 70. It was Liebknecht more than any other Eisenacher who engineered the fusion and therein, in Marx and Engels's opinion, lay the problem. As even a sympathetic biographer admits, "Typically, Liebknecht shunted theory into a corner when its consequences became uncomfortable" (Dominck, op. cit., p. 164). To forge ahead with the fusion Liebknecht held from Bebel Marx's critique (a fact that Dominick seems not to be aware of)—a harbinger of things to come in his modus operandi in the German party; see Draper's note on this in *KMTR, IV*, pp. 70–71.

90. The obvious exception is Marx's brief but most significant discussion on the norms of distribution and equality in a postcapitalist society. Also, both he and Engels treat the dictatorship of the proletariat in a manner that supports my argument in chapter four about force being a necessary component of their understanding of such a state; see respectively, 24, p. 95, and 45, p. 64. Further evidence comes in the form of Marx's marginal notes on Bakunin's book *Statehood and Anarchy*, particularly, 24, p. 517, which was also written about this time.

91. 24, p. 97.

92. 45, p. 98.

93. 45, p. 98.

94. 45, p. 283.

95. Rubel, p. 252. This is a better rendering than that provided by the *MECW* editors in 43, p. 551. Almost two decades earlier Engels taught himself Russian though not, apparently, for the political reasons that motivated Marx.

96. 43, p. 424.

97. 43, p. 450. As noted in chapter eight, p. 210, Marx foresaw that a war with Germany would be "the midwife of the inevitable social revolution in Russia."

98. 45, p. 103. I'm referring, of course, to the revolutionary upheavals in Germany that followed in the wake of the Russian Revolution in 1917.

99. 43, p. 462.

100. 44, p. 396.

101. GC, 1868–1870, p. 220.

102. 24, p. 200.

103. Ibid., p. 199.

104. 24, p. 371.

105. 24, p. 359.

106. 24, p. 50.

107. 24, p. 37.

108. 24, p. 252. For Marx's praise of Russian terrorists such as Zasulich, see 46, pp. 45 and 83.

109. 45, p. 296.

110. 24, p. 103.

111. 46, p. 198.

112. 24, p. 426.

113. Hobsbawm, *Age of Capital*, p. 115.

114. 45, p. 31.

115. 46, p. 458.

116. Alan Gilbert, "The Storming of Heaven," (p. 162) suggests that Marx's literary output after the 1848–1851 period was positively related to upsurges in the class struggle. "A relatively calm, scholarly atmosphere [after 1872] did not inspire the completion of *Capital*." It's true that under the pressure of events in the 1860s Marx was perhaps more inspired to get his ideas into print. The evidence presented here, however, makes clear that he worked hard, by doing the research, to complete the project.

117. 45, p. 150. His daughter Eleanor translated the work into English, which was eventually published in 1886.

118. 46, p. 44. For the program, which was slightly amended by leaders of the French party, the Parti Ouvrier Français, see 24, pp. 637–38.

119. 24, p. 340.

120. 24, p. 636.

121. 46, p. 199.

122. 45, pp. 292 and 447.

123. This comment makes clear, as already discussed—see chapter seven, fn. 17—that Marx and Engels were very much products of the world in which they lived when it came, in this case, to views about women. And yet, as discussed in chapter eight and elsewhere, they were very much advanced for their time.

124. 46, p. 170.

125. 46, p. 425.

126. 46, p. 45.

127. 46, p. 399.

128. 24, p. 464.

129. 24, p. 470.

130. 47, p. 202.

CHAPTER TEN.
ENGELS AND REVOLUTIONARY CONTINUITY

1. 47, p. 17.

2. 45, p. 246.

3. 45, p. 120. Regarding Dühring's influence, Liebknecht wrote to Engels: "He has gained a strong grip on many of our people (notably in Berlin) and must be dealt with *firmly*" (*Frederick Engels: A Biography* [Moscow: Progress Publishers, 1974], p. 295).

4. 27, p. 278.

5. 45, p. 123.

6. Engels, *Anti-Dühring: Herr Eugen Dühring's Revolution in Science* (Moscow: Progress Publishers, 1969), p. 109.

7. 45, p. 119.

8. 45, p. 122.

9. 46, p. 15.

10. 45, p. 218.

11. 45, p. 334. These endorsements by Marx are supplied in order to later dispute Carver's suggestion (p. 124) that Marx showed no enthusiasm for the book.

12. Steenson, op. cit., p. 194.

13. 45, p. 259.

14. Draper, *KMTR, II*, pp. 516 and 600.

15. 45, p. 403.

16. Ibid.

17. Ibid., p. 405.

18. Ibid., pp. 406–7.

19. Ibid., p. 408.

20. Ibid., p. 399.

21. 45, pp. 423–24.

22. 45, p. 400.

23. Ibid., p. 408.

24. 45, p. 413–14.

25. Engels characterized this development in the German party as "opportunism." While indeed opportunism and reformism are distinct, subsequent history would reveal that the former paved the way to the latter.

26. It is also understandable why so few Marxologists, many of whom are social democrats or lean in that direction, either ignore the document or downplay its significance, such as Berlin who can with a straight face say, "The attack on the Gotha Program was Marx's last violent [whatever that means] intervention in the affairs of the [German] party. No similar

crisis occurred again in his lifetime, and he was left free to devote his remaining years to theoretical studies . . ." (Berlin, op.cit., p. 268).

27. McLellan, pp. 437–38, is one of the few Marxologists to even quote from the *Circular*. Yet, he, for whatever reasons, focuses on those sections that underscore Marx and Engels's historical positions rather than those cited here that anticipate social democracy's future.

28. Contrary to what McLellan suggests (p. 438), Marx did have an opinion of Bernstein and company, at least in September 1879, which was not very flattering: "They are poor *counter-revolutionary* windbags" (45, p. 413). While Engels began to look favorably on Bernstein afterward it is not clear if Marx changed his view. Three months before his death Engels wrote to him: "You are right when you say that Bernstein doesn't always allow himself adequate time for reflection" (46, p. 413).

29. 46, p. 42.

30. 46, p. 150.

31. 46, p. 447. Engels began his objection with, "I detest anything that smacks of title-mongering." This had been a long-held position of his.

32. 45, pp. 6–7.

33. 45, p. 9.

34. 24, p. 248.

35. See chapter nine, p. 231.

36. 24, p. 249.

37. *Selected Correspondence*, p. 407.

38. 46, p. 8.

39. 26, p. 272.

40. *Engels-Lafargue Correspondence*, Vol. III, p. 211.

41. This is exactly the point that Manfred Steger fails to grasp in his attempt to justify the subsequent revisionism of Bernstein; see his "Friedrich Engels and the Origins of German Revisionism: Another Look," in Steger and Carver, op. cit. Adam Przeworski, in the first chapter of his *Capitalism and Social Democracy* (Cambridge: Cambridge University Press, 1985), gives a reformist spin to Engels but less direct. J. D. Hunley, *The Life and Thought of Friedrich Engels: A Reinterpretation* (New Haven: Yale University Press, 1991), in his chapter, "Engels's Alleged Reformism," pp. 96–111, provides a useful introduction to and refutation of such claims.

42. 47, p. 210. Within his own framework Engels was very sober about electoral results in Germany. "In Germany it is easy to vote for a Social Democrat because we are the only real opposition party and because the Reichstag has no say in things, so that ultimately it doesn't matter whether one votes at all, or for which of the 'dogs that we are' one does vote." (47, p. 342). Thus, he recognized quite early the issue of the protest vote in relation to the "wasted" vote.

43. Marx and Engels, *Letter to Americans, 1848–1895* (New York: International Pubishers, 1969), p. 176.

44. *Engels-Lafargue Correspondence*, III, pp. 262–63.

45. *Engels-Lafargue Correspondence*, III, pp. 273–74.

46. 47, p. 223.

47. *Selected Correspondence*, p. 386.

48. 27, p. 227.

49. 27, p. 271.

50. *Selected Correspondence*, p. 461.

51. 27, p. 519.

52. 27, pp. 78–79.

53. 27, p. 241.

54. 27, pp. 6 and 10.

55. *Engels-Lafargue Correspondence*, II, pp. 365–67. Note here, to be addressed shortly, the importance that he lent to the electoral victories in the rural areas.

56. *Letters to Americans*, p. 238. This was a remarkably prescient insight since it *was* war with Russia that brought the German party to power in 1918. But the revolutionary wing of the party led by Rosa Luxemburg and Karl Liebknecht lacked the ingredient that Engels said would be crucial in such a scenario—a revolutionary leadership that knew what had to be done. The outcome tragically revealed that this was indeed a premature accession to power.

57. 26, p. 121.

58. Ibid., p. 125.

59. 26, pp. 326–27.

60. 47, p. 305.

61. 26, pp. 306–7.

62. Apparently it was Bebel who wanted the slogan reinserted into the final draft; see Gary Steenson, *Karl Kautsky, 1854–1938: Marxism in the Classical Years* (Pittsburgh: University of Pittsburgh Press, 1991), p. 99.

63. 47, pp. 35–36.

64. *Selected Correspondence*, p. 409.

65. *Selected Correspondence*, p. 387.

66. 47, p. 145.

67. Draper, *Chronicle*, p. 263.

68. Ibid., p. 273.

69. 47, p. 497.

70. 27, pp. 70–71.

71. For a discussion of the *Jungen* and Engels's response, see Stanley Pierson, *Marxist Intellectuals and the Working-Class Mentality in Germany, 1887–1912* (Cambridge, Mass.: Harvard University Press, 1993), chapter one.

72. 27, p. 70. See also, *Engels-Lafargue Correspondence*, II, p. 386. Draper's discussion of the misrepresentations of Marx's meaning is insightful (*KMTR, II*, pp. 5–11). As this quote suggests, it should be clear by now that Marx and Engels were comfortable with people calling themselves their "followers" or "disciples" or even "Marxists" as long as they were faithful to their perspective. Thus, Marx's reference in 1881 to Paul Lafargue as "one of my direct disciples" (46, p. 61).

73. 27, p. 271.

74. 27, p. 227.

75. <u>47</u>, pp. 119–20.

76. *Engels-Lafargue Correspondence*, III, pp. 325–26.

77. <u>24</u>, pp. 441, 456.

78. <u>24</u>, pp. 517–18.

79. <u>27</u>, p. 496.

80. Ibid., p. 500.

81. Draper's three chapters in his *KMTR, II,* pp. 317–452, is still by far the most thorough treatment of Marx and Engels's views on the peasant question in various countries including France and Germany.

82. *Engels-Lafargue Correspondence*, III, p. 344. In November 1887 he said almost exactly the same thing about the German party in a letter to Paul Lafargue (Volume II, p. 72).

83. <u>47</u>, pp. 201–2.

84. <u>47</u>, pp. 245–46.

85. *Engels-Lafargue Correspondence*, III, p. 344.

86. *Engels-Lafargue Correspondence*, III, p. 347.

87. Draper, *KMTR, IV*, p. 236.

88. *Engels-Lafargue Correspondence*, II, pp. 302–3.

89. *Engels-Lafargue Correspondence*, II,, pp. 50 and 66 respectively.

90. Unlike the Marxologists, Trotsky, who did more than anyone else to advance a Marxist analysis of fascism and should, therefore, have been interested in Engels's perspective, seemed also not to be aware of this episode in Engels life. There is no reference at all to Boulanger in the collection of his writings on fascism, *The Struggle Against Fascism in Germany* (New York: Pathfinder Press, 1971). The simple reason may have been that most of the relevant correspondence was not published until 1956, sixteen years after Trotsky's assassination—enough time, however, for the Marxologists to have discovered this treasure.

91. *Engels-Lafargue Correspondence*, II, p. 356.

92. *Engels-Lafargue Correspondence*, III, p. 177.

93. *Engels-Lafargue Correspondence*, II, p. 330.

94. *Letters to Americans*, p. 248.

95. *Letters to Americans*, p. 258.

96. Ibid.

97. Engels's three-page letter in January 1894 to Filippo Turati, the Italian Socialist Party leader, which was published in its theoretical organ, is perhaps the most concise summary of their strategy and tactics for party building to be found in the Marx-Engels arsenal. It was particularly relevant for overwhelmingly peasant countries whose working class was just developing. An issue that neither he nor Marx had explicitly addressed was that of the workers' party taking seats in a government dominated by the bourgeois parties. Drawing on the lessons of France in 1848, he warned against such a move saying, *"That is the greatest danger"* (*Selected Correspondence*, p. 446).

98. <u>46</u>, p. 83.

99. <u>46</u>, p. 208.

100. <u>26</u>, p. 294. Note the similarities between this and their private critique of the Fenian terrorists in 1867, chapter eight, p. 202.

101. <u>47</u>, p. 264.

102. <u>47</u>, p. 280.

103. Ibid., p. 281.

104. On some details of Zasulich's close relationship with Engels, especially after she moved from Geneva to London in 1894, see Jay Bergman, *Vera Zasulich: A Biography* (Stanford: Stanford University Press, 1983), chapter four, and Draper, *Chronicle*, pp. 286, 288.

105. <u>27</u>, p. 433.

106. Draper, *II*, pp. 271–72.

107. <u>47</u>, p. 17.

108. Marx's letter in 1881 to D. Nieuwenhuis was unequivocal in his opposition to forming a new international, saying that the "critical conjuncture . . . has not yet arrived" (<u>46</u>, p. 67).

109. *Selected Correspondence*, p. 382, and *Engels-Lafargue Correspondence*, II, p. 277.

110. *Engels-Lafargue Correspondence*, II, p. 275.

111. *Engels-Lafargue Correspondence*, II, p. 282.

112. *Engels-Lafargue Correspondence,* II, p. 303.

113. Donald Sassoon, *One Hundred Years of Socialism: The West European Left in the Twentieth Century* (New York: The New Press, 1996), p. xx.

114. Ibid., p. xxi.

115. <u>27</u>, pp. 417–18. See chapter six, p. 148, regarding their earlier view of "social democracy" and this chapter, p. 257, on the "elasticity" with which he used the label.

116. See chapter nine, p. 234.

117. <u>27</u>, p. 87.

118. See chapter one, p. 2.

119. *Marx and Engels Through the Eyes of Their Contemporaries*, p. 211.

120. Hunley, and S. H. Rigby, *Engels and the Formation of Marxism: History, Dialectics, and Revolution* (Manchester: Manchester University Press, 1992).

121. While Carver, op. cit., is, relatively speaking, the most vocal member of this current, there are others who have played a supporting role. See in particular Terrence Ball's "Marxian Science and Positivist Politics" in the collection which he co-edited with James Farr, *After Marx* (Cambridge: Cambridge University Press, 1984). For an overview of the historiography of the issues see Rigby's "Introduction."

122. Carver, p. 151.

123. Hunley, as already mentioned, also disputes this charge with adequate evidence, although in a manner that fails to fully see Engels as a political person.

124. <u>17</u>, p. 114.

125. <u>46</u>, p. 292. This is exactly why Carver has to perform so many contortions in his attempt to erect a Chinese wall between Marx and Engels with regard to *Anti-Dühring*. See the relevant section in this chapter as well as Rigby, pp. 150–60, for evidence to refute such a claim. Furthermore, if there's any shred of truth in Carver's argument about Engels's different methodology, then it too should have been reflected in his editing and writing of Volumes II and III of *Capital*—evidence he can't produce.

126. Perry Anderson, *Lineages of the Absolutist State* (New York: New Left Books, 1974), p. 23n.

127. Draper, *Chronicle*, p. 250.

128. 27, p. 245.

129. 46, p. 192.

130. To his credit Rigby at least acknowledges Marx and Engels's politics, which he attempts to refute. In so doing he reveals his grossly inadequate knowledge about their political activities and political reality and, as other theorists are prone to do, falls into the trap of treating their writings as texts. Though his approach to Engels is political to the core, Lawrence Wilde's critique of his politics is narrow and lacks the kind of broader international perspective as provided here, especially the place of Russia in Engels's calculations; see his, "Engels and the Contradictions of Revolutionary Strategy," in Steger and Carver, op. cit.

131. 27, p. 404.

CONCLUSIONS

1. Draper, *KMTR, I,* p. 59.

2. Alan Kahan, *Aristocratic Liberalism: The Social and Political Thought of Jacob Burck-hardt, John Stuart Mill, and Alexis de Tocqueville* (New York: Oxford University Press, 1992), p. 140.

3. As well as Kahan's, C. B. Macpherson's third chapter in his *The Life and Times of Liberal Democracy* (Oxford: Oxford University Press, 1977), provides details on Mill's democratic limitations.

4. Göran Therborn, "The Rule of Capital and the Rise of Democracy," *New Left Review* No. 103 (May–June 1977), pp. 23–28.

5. Paul Thomas's "Critical Reception: Marx then and now," Carver, *The Cambridge Companion to Marx*, is suggestive in this regard as well as Jacques Derrida's *Spectres of Marx: The State of the Debt, the Work of Mourning, and the New International* (New York: Routledge, 1994).

6. Drawing on "Kautsky's well-known articles on the intelligentsia," which no doubt reflected the SPD leader's visceral understanding of the academic enterprise, Lenin, in his *One Step Forward, Two Steps Back*, wrote: "No one will venture to deny that *the intelligentsia* . . . is characterised, by and large, *precisely by individualism* and incapacity for discipline and organisation" (Lenin, *Collected Works*, Vol. 7, p. 267).

7. See chapter seven, fn. 41.

8. There are a few notable exceptions to this record: Arthur Rosenberg, *Democracy and Socialism: A Contribution to the Political History of the Past 150 Years*, trans. George Rosen (New York: A. A. Knopf, 1939), which, by the way, was favorably reviewed in the American Political Science Review upon its appearance; and more recently, Michael Levin, *Marx, Engels and Liberal Democracy* (New York: St. Martin's Press, 1989), and Stephen Eric Bronner, "The Democratic Legacy of Karl Marx and Frederick Engels," in his *Socialism Unbound* (New York: Routledge, 1990). None of these, however, presents the kind of details, especially their party activities, as is done here.

9. Carollee Bengelsdorf, *The Problem of Democracy in Cuba: Between Vision and Reality* (New York: Oxford University Press, 1994), especially her "Introduction." Robert Heilbroner, in his more popular, *Marxism: For and Against* (New York: W. W. Norton, 1981), chapter five, makes a similar criticism.

10. See chapter ten, p. 268.

11. 10, p. 570. For some context see chapter four, pp. 85–86.

12. See chapter nine, p. 243.

13. See chapter ten, p. 276, in relation to Russian developments. In regard to the U. S. movement, Engels made a similar comment in 1887: "The real movement always looks different to what it ought to have done in the eyes of those who were tools in preparing it" (*Letters to Americans*, p. 192).

Bibliography of Works Cited

PRIMARY SOURCES

Marx, Karl, and Frederick Engels. *Collected Works.* New York: International Publishers, 1975+ [in progress]. This is the primary source for all of Marx and Engels's extant writings and utterances. Of the projected fifty volumes for this series forty-seven have been published to date. Citations from the *Collected Works,* hereafter *MECW,* will be designated by the volume, as 47, for example, and then page(s).

Marx, Karl, and Friedrich Engels. *Gesamtausgabe (MEGA).* Berlin: Dietz Verlag, 1975+ [in progress]. The major difference between this new *MEGA* series—hereafter, *MEGA*₂— and the *MECW* is that it includes correspondence to Marx and Engels and their excerpt notebooks. Of the projected 114 volumes, forty-six have been published to date.

———. *Selected Correspondence.* Moscow: Progress Publishers, 1975

———. *Letters to Americans, 1848–1895: A Selection.* New York: International Publishers, 1969.

———. *Writings on the Paris Commune,* ed. Hal Draper. New York: Monthly Review Press, 1971.

Marx, Karl. *Capital, Volumes I–III.* New York: International Publishers, 1972.

Engels, Frederick. *Anti-Dühring: Herr Eugen Dühring's Revolution in Science.* Moscow: Progress Publishers, 1969.

Engels, Frederick, and Paul and Laura Lafargue. *Correspondence, Volumes I–III.* Moscow: Foreign Languages Publishing House, 1960.

Institute of Marxism-Leninism. *The General Council of the First International. Minutes, 1866–1872.* Moscow: Progress Publishers, 1974.

———. *The Hague Congress of the First International, September 2–7, 1872. Minutes and Documents.* Moscow: Progress Publishers, 1976.

SECONDARY SOURCES

Aminzade, Ron. *Ballots and Barricades: Class Formation and Republican Politics in France, 1830–1871.* Princeton: Princeton University Press, 1993.

Anderson, Perry. *Lineages of the Absolutist State.* New York: New Left Books, 1974.

Ball, Terence, and James Farr, eds. *After Marx*. Cambridge: Cambridge University Press, 1984.

Bengelsdorf, Carollee. *The Problem of Democracy in Cuba: Between Vision and Reality*. New York: Oxford University Press, 1994.

Bergman, Jay. *Vera Zasulich: A Biography*. Stanford: Stanford University Press, 1983.

Berlin, Isaiah. *Karl Marx: His Life and Environment*. London: Oxford University Press, 1963.

Bronner, Stephen Eric. *Socialism Unbound*. New York: Routledge, 1990.

Calhoun, Craig. "Classical Social Theory and the French Revolution of 1848." *Sociological Theory* 7(Fall, 1989).

Carver, Terrell. *Marx & Engels: The Intellectual Relationship*. Bloomington: Indiana University Press, 1983.

———, ed. *The Cambridge Companion to Marx*. Cambridge: Cambridge University Press, 1991.

Collins, Henry, and Chimen Abramsky. *Karl Marx and the British Labour Movement*. London: Macmillan, 1965.

Connor, Walker. *The National Question in Marxist-Leninist Theory and Strategy*. Princeton: Princeton University Press, 1984.

Corcoran, Paul, ed. *Before Marx: Socialism and Communism in France, 1830–48*. New York: St. Martin's Press, 1983.

Cross, Máire, and Tim Gray. *The Feminism of Flora Tristan*. Oxford: Berg, 1992.

Derrida, Jacques. *Spectres of Marx: The State of the Debt, the Work of Mourning, and the New International*. New York: Routledge, 1994.

Dominick III, Raymond H. *Wilhelm Liebknecht and the Founding of the German Social Democratic Party*. Chapel Hill: University of North Carolina Press, 1982.

Draper, Hal. *Karl Marx's Theory of Revolution, Vols. I-IV*. New York: Monthly Review Press, 1977–1990.

———. *The Annotated Communist Manifesto*. Berkeley: Center for Socialist History, 1984.

———. *The Marx-Engels Chronicle: A Day-by-Day Chronology of Marx and Engels's Life and Activity*. New York: Schocken, 1985.

———. *The Marx-Engels Register: A Complete Bibliography of Marx and Engels's Individual Writings*. New York: Schocken, 1985.

———. *The Marx-Engels Glossary: Glossary to the Chronicle and Register, and Index to the Glossary*. New York: Schocken, 1986.

Duveau, George. *1848: The Making of a Revolution*. Cambridge, Mass.: Harvard University Press, 1967.

Edwards, Stewart. *The Paris Commune, 1871*. New York: Quadrangle Books, 1973.

———. *The Communards of Paris, 1871*. Ithaca: Cornell University Press, 1973.

Ehrenberg, John. *The Dictatorship of the Proletariat: Marxism's Theory of Socialist Democracy*. New York: Routledge, 1992.

Fedoseyev, P. N. et al. *Karl Marx: A Biography*. Moscow: Progress Publishers, 1989.

Felix, David. *Marx as Politician*. Carbondale: Southern Illinois University Press, 1983.

Folbre, Nancy. "Socialism, Feminist and Scientific," *Beyond Economic Man: Feminist Theory and Economics*, eds. Marianne A. Ferber and Julie A. Nelson. Chicago: University of Chicago Press, 1993.

Foner, Philip. *British Labor and the American Civil War.* New York: Holmes and Meier, 1981.

Freymond, Jacques, and Miklos Molnár. "The Rise and Fall of the First International, " *The Revolutionary Internationals,* ed. Milorad Drachkovitch. Stanford: Stanford University Press, 1966.

Gargan, Edward T. *Alexis de Tocqueville: The Critical Years, 1848–1851.* Washington, D.C.: Catholic University Press, 1955.

Gilbert, Alan. *Marx's Politics: Communists and Citizens.* New Brunswick: Rutgers University Press, 1981.

Gilbert, Alan. "The Storming of Heaven: Politics and Marx's *Capital,*" *Marxism,* eds. J. Roland Pennock and John Chapman. *Nomos* XXVI. New York: New York University Press, 1983.

Gouldner, Alvin. *Against Fragmentation.* New York: Oxford University Press, 1985.

Hammen, Oscar. *The Red '48ers: Karl Marx and Frederick Engels.* New York: Charles Scribner's Sons, 1969.

Hansen, Karen, and Ilene Philipson, eds. *Women, Class, and the Feminist Imagination: A Socialist-Feminist Reader.* Philadelphia: Temple University Press, 1990.

Harrison, Royden. *Before the Socialists: Studies in Labour and Politics, 1861–1881.* London: Routledge and Keagan Paul, 1965.

———. "Marx, Engels, and the British Response to the Commune," *The Massachusetts Review* 12 (1971).

Hayward, Jack. *After the French Revolution: Six Critics of Democracy and Nationalism.* New York: New York University Press, 1991.

Heilbroner, Robert. *Marxism: For and Against.* New York: W. W. Norton, 1981.

Hobsbawm, Eric. *The Age of Capital: 1848–1875.* London: Weidenfeld and Nicolson, 1975.

———, ed. *The History of Marxism,* Vol. I. Bloomington: Indiana University Press, 1982.

———. *The Age of Empire: 1875–1914.* New York: Pantheon Books, 1987.

Hugo, Victor. *Napoléon le petit.* London, 1852.

Hunley, J. D. *The Life and Thought of Friedrich Engels: A Reinterpretation.* New Haven: Yale University Press, 1991.

Hunt, Richard N. *The Political Ideas of Marx and Engels, Vols. I and II.* Pittsburgh: University of Pittsburgh Press, 1974, 1984.

Ilyichov, L. F. et al. *Frederick Engels: A Biography.* Moscow: Progress Publishers, 1974.

Jardin, André. *Tocqueville.* New York: Farrar, Straus, Giroux, 1988.

Johnstone, Monty. "Marx and Engels and the Concept of the Party." *The Socialist Register, 1967,* ed. Ralph Milliband and John Saville. London: Merlin Press, 1967.

Jones, Howard. *Union in Peril: The Crisis over British Intervention in the Civil War.* Chapel Hill: The University of North Carolina Press, 1992.

Jones, Peter. *The 1848 Revolutions.* New York: Longman, 1991.

Kahan, Alan S. *Aristocratic Liberalism: The Social and Political Thought of Jacob Burkhardt, John Stuart Mill, and Alexis de Tocqueville.* New York: Oxford University Press, 1992.

Kelly, George. *The Human Comedy: Constant, Tocqueville, and French Liberalism.* Cambridge: Cambridge University Press, 1992.

Kunina, V. E., ed., *Frederick Engels: His Life and Works—Documents and Photographs.* Moscow: Progress Publishers, 1987.

Lenin, V. I. *Collected Works.* Moscow: Progress Publishers, 1977.

Lessner, Frederick. *Sixty Years in the Social-Democratic Movement.* London: The Twentieth Century Press, 1907.

Levin, Michael. *Marx, Engels and Liberal Democracy.* New York: St. Martin's Press, 1989.

Levine, Bruce. *The Spirit of 1848: German Immigrants, Labor Conflict, and the Coming of the Civil War.* Urbana: University of Illinois Press, 1992.

Lichtheim, George. *Marxism: An Historical and Critical Study.* New York: Praeger, 1962.

Liebknecht, William. *Karl Marx: Biographical Memoirs.* London: The Journeyman Press, 1975.

Lissagaray, Prosper-Olivier. *History of the Paris Commune.* London: New Park Publications, 1976.

MacIntyre, Alasdair. "The Indispensability of Political Theory." In *The Nature of Political Theory,* ed. David Miller and Larry Siedentop. Oxford: The Clarendon Press, 1983.

McLellan, David. *Karl Marx: His Life and Thought.* New York: Harper and Row, 1973.

McPhee, Peter. "The Crisis of Radical Republicanism in the French Revolution of 1848." *Historical Studies* 16 (1974).

Macpherson, C. B. *The Life and Times of Liberal Democracy.* Oxford: Oxford University Press, 1977.

Mahoney, Daniel. "Tocqueville and Socialism." In *Tocqueville's Defense of Human Liberty: Current Essays,* ed. Peter Lawler and Joseph Alulis. New York: Garland Publishing, 1993.

Mandel, Ernest. *The Formation of the Economic Thought of Karl Marx.* New York: Monthly Review Press, 1971.

Marx and Engels Through the Eyes of Their Contemporaries. Moscow: Progress Publishers, 1978.

Mehring, Franz. *Karl Marx: The Story of His Life.* London: George Allen & Unwin, 1951.

Meisel, James H. *Counter-Revolution: How Revolutions Die.* New York: Atherton Press, 1966.

Molyneux, John. *Marxism and the Party.* London: Pluto Press, 1978.

Morgan, Roger. *The German Social Democrats and the First International, 1864–1872.* Cambridge: Cambridge University Press, 1965.

Morrison, Samuel Eliot. *The Oxford History of the American People.* New York: Oxford University Press, 1965.

Moss, Bernard. "Marx and Engels on French Social Democracy: Historians or Revolutionaries?" *Journal of the History of Ideas* (1985).

Nicolaievsky, Boris, and Otto Maenchen-Helfen. *Karl Marx: Man and Fighter.* New York: Penguin, 1983.

Noyes, P. H. *Organization and Revolution: Working-Class Associations in the German Revolutions of 1848–1849.* Princeton: Princeton University Press, 1966.

Obermann, Karl. *Joseph Weydemeyer: Pioneer of American Socialism.* New York: International Publishers, 1947.

Payne, Ronald. *Marx: A Biography.* New York: Simon & Schuster, 1968.

Pierson, Stanley. *Marxist Intellectuals and the Working-Class Mentality in Germany, 1887–1912.* Cambridge, Mass.: Harvard University Press, 1993.

Price, Roger. *The Revolutions of 1848.* Atlantic Highlands, N.J.: Humanities Press, 1988.

Proudhon, P. J. *The General Idea of the Revolution in the Nineteenth Century.* Paris, 1851.

———. *The Social Revolution Demonstrated by the Coup d'Etat of December 2.* Paris, 1852.

Przeworski, Adam. *Capitalism and Social Democracy.* Cambridge: Cambridge University Press, 1985.

Riazanov, David. *Karl Marx and Friedrich Engels: An Introduction to Their Lives and Work.* New York: Monthly Review Press, 1973.

Rigby, S. H. *Engels and the Formation of Marxism: History, Dialectics, and Revolution.* Manchester: Manchester University Press, 1992.

Robertson, Priscilla. *Revolutions of 1848: A Social History.* Princeton: Princeton University Press, 1971.

Rosenberg, Arthur. *Democracy and Socialism: A Contribution to the Political History of the Past 150 Years,* trans. George Rosen. New York: A. A. Knopf, 1939.

Rubel, Maximilien, and Margaret Manale. *Marx Without Myth: A Chronological Study of His Life and Work.* New York: Harper and Row, 1975.

Rueschemeyer, Dietrich, Evelyn Stephens, and John Stephens. *Capitalist Development and Democracy.* Chicago: University of Chicago Press, 1992.

Schurz, Carl. *The Reminiscences of Carl Schurz,* Vol. I, 1829–1852. New York: The McClure Co., 1907.

Sperber, Jonathan. *Rhineland Radicals: The Democratic Movement and the Revolution of 1848–1849.* Princeton: Princeton University Press, 1991.

Steenson, Gary. *"Not One Man! Not One Penny!": German Social Democracy, 1863–1914.* Pittsburgh: University of Pittsburgh Press, 1981.

———. *Karl Kautsky, 1854–1938: Marxism in the Classical Years.* Pittsburgh: University of Pittsburgh Press, 1991.

Steger, Manfred B., and Terrell Carver, eds. *Engels After Marx.* University Park: The Pennsylvania State University Press, 1999.

Taylor, A. J. P. *From Napoleon to the Second International.* London: Hamish Hamilton, 1994.

Teeple, Gary. *Marx's Critique of Politics: 1842–1847.* Toronto: University of Toronto Press, 1984.

Therborn, Göran. "The Rule of Capital and the Rise of Democracy." *New Left Review* No. 103 (May-June 1977).

Thomas, Edith. "The Women of the Commune." *The Massachusetts Review,* 12(1971).

Thomas, Paul. *Karl Marx and the Anarchists.* London: Routledge & Kegan Paul, 1980.

———. "Critical Reception: Marx then and now." In *The Cambridge Companion to Marx,* ed. T. Carver. Cambridge: Cambridge University Press, 1991.

Thönnessen, Werner. *The Emancipation of Women: The Rise and Decline of the Women's Movement in German Social Democracy 1863–1933.* London: Pluto Press, 1976.

Tilly, Charles. *The Contentious French.* Cambridge, Mass.: Harvard University Press, 1986.

Tocqueville, Alexis de. *Democracy in America,* ed. Phillips Bradley, trans. Henry Reeve, Francis Bowen, and Phillips Bradley, 2 Vols. New York: Vintage Books, 1945.

———. *Recollections: The French Revolution of 1848*, eds. J. P. Mayer and P. Kerr . New Brunswick, N.J.: Transaction Books, 1987.

Traugott, Mark. *Armies of the Poor: Determinants of Working-Class Participation in the Parisian Insurrection of June 1848*. Princeton: Princeton University Press, 1985.

Trotsky, Leon. *The Struggle Against Fascism in Germany*. New York: Pathfinder Press, 1971.

Waters, Mary-Alice. "The Workers' and Farmers' Government: A Popular Revolutionary Dictatorship." *New International* 1(1984).

Wittke, Carl. *The Utopian Communist: A Biography of Wilhelm Weitling, Nineteenth-Century Reformer*. Baton Rouge: Louisiana University Press, 1950.

Wood, Allen. "Karl Marx." In *Oxford Companion to Philosophy*, ed. Ted Honderich. New York: Oxford University Press, 1995.

Zeitlin, Irving. *Liberty, Equality, and Revolution in Alexis de Tocqueville*. Boston: Little, Brown, 1971.

Zucker, A. E., ed. *The Forty-Eighters:Political Refugees of the German Revolution of 1848*. New York: Columbia University Press, 1950.

Index

When only the italicized title is given, the work is by Marx and/or Engels. Works by other authors will have the author's name in parentheses following the italicized title. Periodicals are italicized followed by their place of publication in brackets.

Bebel, August, 227, 232, 242, 243–44, 254, 256, 258, 271–72, 278, 344n. 75, 346n. 9, 349n. 80, 354n. 62

Becker, Johann Philippe, 199, 206, 236, 247, 251, 272, 337n. 69

Bee-Hive [London], 184, 186, 189

Belgium, Brussels, 20, 50, 53–54, 58, 314n. 49. *See also* Democratic Association (Belgium)

Bengelsdorf, Carollee, 357n. 9

Bentham, Jeremy, 17

Bergman, Jay, 356n. 104

Berlin. *See* Revolutions of 1848–1849

Berlin, Isaiah, 330n. 44, 335n. 41, 352n. 26

Bernstein, Eduard, 256, 258–59, 265, 269, 272, 304, 344n. 75, 353nn. 28, 41

Beust, Friedrich von, 92

Bismarck, Otto von, 166, 172, 174, 209–10, 214, 239, 241–43, 256, 258, 260, 263, 297, 334n. 18, 349n. 61, 350n. 86

Blacks, 193, 204, 275, 334n. 17, 341n. 32

Blanc, Louis, 50, 115, 117, 183, 323n. 6, 329n. 13

Blanqui, Auguste, Blanquists, 39, 142, 145, 151, 218, 246, 273, 276, 313nn. 25, 27, 329n. 9, 347n. 27

Boesche, Roger, 324n. 15

Bolsheviks, 146, 152

Bolte, Friedrich, 225–26

Bonaparte, Louis, 101, 108, 110, 115, 118, 128–29, 130–38, 208, 209–12, 288

bonapartism, 110, 273, 288, 305

Born, Stephen, 46, 68–70, 71, 97, 114

Boulanger, General, 273

bourgeois democracy. *See* democracy and bourgeois democratic revolution

bourgeoisie, 42, 79, 84, 90, 93–96, 107, 129, 176, 272. *See also* liberal bourgeoisie

Bourgeoisie and the Counter-Revolution, 93–95, 103, 159

Bray, John, 314n. 53

British imperialism, 235, 238, 275, 298

Bronner, Stephen, 357n. 8

Brown, John, 170

Buonarroti, Filippo, 17, 39

bureaucracy, 3, 78, 96

Burns, Lizzie, 188, 199

Burns, Mary, 12

business cycles, 120, 144, 153, 175, 198, 322n. 71, 335n. 27. *See also* economic crises

Calhoun, Craig, 323n. 5

California, 108

Camphausen, Ludolf, 67, 73, 77, 84–85, 316n. 28

Canada, 95

Capital, ix, 11, 16, 19, 20, 33, 151, 153–54, 155–56, 160, 167, 169, 177, 181, 184, 185, 188–90, 193, 195, 198–200, 246, 248, 253, 278; Engels's input, 188, 310n. 43; promotional campaign, 206–7, 242, 342n. 41; in Russia, 154, 207, 245, 246, 250

capital and the capitalist mode of production, 118, 123, 126, 177. *See also* bourgeoisie

Carr, E. H., 74

Carver, Terrell, ix, 280–82, 307n. 5, 356nn. 121, 125

Cavaignac, Louis Eugène, 126

Central Authority. *See* Communist League

Central Committee of European Democracy, 147

Charleroi, 198

Chartists, 11, 12, 21–22, 31, 41, 42, 54, 69, 108, 142, 156–58, 176, 179, 188, 192, 235, 238, 294–95, 298, 321n. 64

children, 200

China, 203

Circular Against Kriege, 32–33, 39. *See also* Kriege

Circular Letter of 1879, 255–59, 266, 292–93, 296, 298, 305, 352n. 26

civil liberties, vii, 3, 4, 24, 35, 77–78, 94, 225–26, 241, 303–4; freedom of the press, 3, 4, 10, 68, 72, 98–99, 285

Civil War in France, 103, 179, 201, 215–21, 237, 256, 271, 291

class baiting, 32, 34, 43, 144, 185–86, 194, 313n. 44, 337n. 70

Class Struggles in France, 107–9, 110, 115–36, 219–20, 262, 321n. 64, 323n. 76

Cluss, Adolf, 149–50, 158, 159
Collins, Henry and Abramsky, Chimen, 203, 209, 336n. 54, 347n. 28
Cologne, 66, 84. *See also* 1848–1849 Revolutions
Cologne Democratic Society (Association), 70, 72, 80, 86, 88, 92, 97, 98, 320n. 43
Cologne Society of Workers and Employers, 80
Cologne Workers' Society, 67, 70, 72, 77, 78–80, 86–88, 92, 95–97
committee of public safety, 86, 88, 91, 100, 131
communism, 4, 5, 7, 13, 23, 26, 32–33, 36, 52, 84, 114, 116, 118, 143, 148, 172, 195, 221–22, 237, 249, 279–80, 287, 305; transition to, 47, 51, 143–45
Communist Correspondence Committees (CCC), 30–38, 41–44, 155, 295. *See also* party
Communist (Third) International, 233–34, 247, 280
Communist League(CL), 45, 98, 233, 287, 295; Central Authority, 43–47, 50–55, 58, 62, 65, 70, 98, 102–3, 105, 143–46, 178; Cologne trial, 149, 167; end of, 148, 150–51; expulsion of Willich-Schapper faction, 146; founding congress, 46–50, 313n. 44; principles and rules, 46–47, 49–50, 53–54, 63–64, 69, 98, 143, 146–47, 149, 316n. 18; revival, 102; role in 1848–1849 revolutions, 57–72; second congress, 53–54; split, 143–47; suspension, 71–72, 98, 103, 106. *See also* party
Communist Manifesto, vii, 26, 38, 51, 53, 59–61, 64–65, 66, 72, 74, 84, 102–4, 106, 108, 111, 117–18, 143–45, 149, 152, 156, 158, 164, 169, 171, 180–82, 191–92, 215, 241, 256–58, 264, 266, 287, 291, 295; Preface to German edition of 1872, 216; Preface to Russian edition of 1882, 247, 275; propaganda work, 64, 75, 80, 86, 93, 159; translations, 95, 315nn. 7, 8; writing of, 54–55
Condition of the Working-Class in England, 11, 16, 19, 21

Condition of the Working Class in Russia (Flerovsky), 245
Connor, Walker, 341n. 30
consciousness, 6–7; trade union, 68–69, 191, 235–38, 291, 348n. 45
conscription, 240–42
conspiratorial organizations, 12, 39, 40, 46, 52–53, 59, 71, 107, 287, 347n. 27
The Constitution of the French Republic, 326n. 68
constitutions and constitutional monarchy, 4, 19, 51, 67, 68, 93, 95, 114, 127–29, 135–37, 305, 314n. 49, 318n. 5
A Contribution to the Critique of Political Economy, 154–55, 164, 189, 195, 206, 331n. 49
cooperatives, 181–82, 242
Corcoran, Paul, 313n. 25
Cremer, W. R., 236
Crimean War (1854–1856), 167
Critique of the Gotha Program, 243–44, 248, 265, 350n. 90, 352n. 26
Cross, Máire and Gray, Tim, 340n. 18

Dalai Lama, 153
Dana, Charles, 159–60
Daniels, Roland, 313n. 41
defense work, legal and political, 98–99, 148–51, 211–14, 220, 265
Demands of the Communist Party in Germany, 64–65, 67, 70, 72, 79, 86, 88, 90, 93, 123, 287, 295
democracy and bourgeois democratic revolution, vii, 20, 27, 61, 67–68, 84, 103–4, 119, 120, 125, 137, 170, 269, 286, 304; Belgium, 62, communism and, 1, 24, 35, 51, 104, 241, 273; governance, 268–69, 299, 303–5; liberal, 10, 50, 54, 58, 74, 103; nationalism and, 42; socialism and, vii, 35, 47, 94–95, 110–11, 241. *See also* liberal democracy
Democracy in America (Tocqueville), 120, 138, 327n. 71, 328n. 85
Democratic Association (Belgium), 50, 54, 62
"democratic breakthrough," vii–viii; Marx and Engels's role in, vii–viii

Independent Labour Party (Britain), 275, 299
India, 199, 203, 248, 346n. 109
Instructions for the Delegates of the Provisional General Council, 186, 191
intellectuals, 114, 254–55, 267–68, 357n. 6. *See also* academics
International Socialist Workers' Congress, 282–83, 296
International Working Men's Association (IWMA), xi, 155, 158, 163, 169, 174, 176, 178–238 (Ch. 7–9), 250, 278, 290, 296–97, 299, 301, 302, 339n. 6, 348n. 32; Basle Congress, 198, 201, 224; British section, 205, 348nn. 45, 57; Brussels Congress, 192, 194, 200; founding, 178–79, 188; French section, 199, 211, 215, 225; General Council (GC), 181, 182, 184, 186–87, 208, 213, 215, 336n. 47; Geneva Congress, 185, 191–93, 200, 208, 238, 338n. 89; Geneva Congress (1873), 232; German section, 211; The Hague Congress, 223–24, 229–34, 238, 248, 260, 347nn. 28, 29; intellectuals, 185; Lausanne Congress, 193, 200; London Conference, 199, 201, 224–29, 292, 346n. 2; membership, 183–84, 193–94, 197–98, 199, 221, 337n. 59; move to New York, 231–32, 234; organization, 182, 230–31; peasantry, 228; principles and rules, 179–83, 225–29, 336n. 46; Russian movement, 245; Spanish section, 226; struggle against Bakuninists, 229–30; United States, 198, 210, 221, 232. *See also* anti-war work, Bakunin and Bakuninists; Ireland, Paris Commune, strike solidarity, women, Socialist (Second) International
The International Working Men's Association: Its Establishment, Organization, Political and Social Activity, and Growth (Eichoff), 199
internationalism and proletarian internationalism, 12, 42, 53, 69, 75, 95, 177–79, 182, 193, 205, 209–11, 227, 278, 291, 305, 336n. 54
Ireland, Irish: struggle for independence, 12, 202–6, 208, 236–37, 291, 342n. 33
"iron law of oligarchy," 267, 305

"iron law of wages," 173, 189
The Italian War and Prussia's Tasks (Lassalle), 161
Italian War of 1859, 161, 163, 167
Italy, 76, 95, 164–66, 178, 322n. 74, 355n. 97

Jardin, André, 126, 324n. 10
Jellinek, Frank, 343n. 67
Johnson, Andrew, 193
Johnstone, Monty, 331n. 50
Jones, Ernest, 157–58, 176, 235, 336n. 53, 337n. 60
Jones, Howard, 333n. 6
Jones, Peter, 312n. 16
June Revolution (1848), 74–75, 107–8, 123
Jung, Georg, 309n. 26
Jung, Hermann, 201, 344n. 71
Jungen, 267–68, 354n. 71

Kahan, Alan, 300, 324n. 12
Karl Kautsky, 260, 262, 265, 266, 272, 357n. 6
Kelly, George, 324n. 10
Kersausie, Joachim René, 124
Kommunistische Zeitung [London] 52
Kossuth, Lajos, 95
Köttgen, Gustav, 33, 51, 68
Kriege, Hermann, 32–33, 39, 159
Kugelman, Gertrud, 200
Kugelman, Ludwig, 186, 200, 206–7, 211–12, 214–15, 220, 221, 230
Kunina, V. E., 308n. 5

labor aristocracy, 236–37, 275
Labour Parliament movement, 157–58, 179
Lafargue, Laura, 263, 272, 274, 276, 278, 299
Lafargue, Paul, 192, 261, 262, 267, 269, 271, 274, 278, 299, 334n. 17
Lamartine, Alphonse de, 324n. 16
land reform, 105–6, 123. *See also* peasantry
Lassalle, Ferdinand, Lassalleans, 99, 154, 155, 161–62, 164, 166–67, 173–74, 186, 189, 191, 194, 239–45, 248, 254, 257, 265, 297–98, 319n. 25, 332nn. 74, 79, 334n. 18, 348n. 59
Law, Harriet, 200

press, 51, 57–58, 91, 156, 158–60, 267, 274; primacy of principles, 50, 187, 233, 244; programs, 244; propaganda, 64, 80, 86, 98, 151, 155–57, 172, 206–7, 209–11, 220; publications, 154–56, 158, 206–7, 242; relations with opponents, 142; rules, 46–49; splits, 180, 183, 233, 266; strategy and tactics for constructing, 38, 155–56, 195, 221, 232–33, 242, 244, 355n. 97. *See also* alliance of the people, Communist Correspondence Committees, Communist League, conspiratorial organizations, League of the Just

passive resistance, 91–92

Payne, Ronald, 343n. 59

Peasant Question in France and Germany, 217, 271, 273

Peasant War in Germany, 109, 241, 270

peasantry, x, 51, 61, 64–65, 68, 105, 126, 165–66, 217, 228, 239, 287, 315n. 8 (61), 322n. 70, 355n. 81; in France, 109, 122–23, 214, 217, 271, 321n. 64, 325n. 31; in German Revolution (1848–1849), 78–80, 86, 88, 91, 94, 97, 101, 106, 142, 166–67, 318n. 62; in Germany (post-1850), 239, 241, 270–71, 349n. 65; in Switzerland, 315n. 9. *See also* Russia

The People's Paper [London], 158

permanent revolution, 95, 100, 104, 105–6, 130, 276, 289

personal, the, and politics, 35, 175, 187

petit bourgeoisie, 25, 51, 60–61, 64, 78, 80, 103–4, 106, 148, 165, 183, 264, 267, 315n. 7

petitions, 34–35, 68, 92

Pfänder, Karl, 43, 145, 336n. 47

Philippe, Louis, 19, 39, 62, 74, 116

Phillips, Antoinette, 187

Phillips, Wendell, 221

philosophy, 5–8, 13, 17, 20–21, 22–23, 25, 147, 285–86

Pierson, Stanley, 354n. 71

Plekhanov, Georgi, 276

Po and Rhine, 161, 163–65, 167, 295

Poland: self-determination, 54, 75, 78, 170–72, 176, 178, 208, 315n. 8

Political Action of the Working Class, 228–29

political economy, 150, 185, 188–92, 207, 245, 250, 255. *See also* Capital

pope, 129–31, 221

Possibilists (France), 273, 278

Poverty of Philosophy, 26, 31, 37, 49–50, 312n. 18. *See also* Proudhon

Price, Roger, 115, 323n. 8

Principles of Communism, 52–53, 54, 74, 75, 148, 295, 315n. 5

Proclamation on Poland, 172, 174

profits, 190

proletariat, 8, 18–19, 24, 27, 41, 59, 107, 125–26, 286; political rule and dictatorship of, 51, 80, 85, 107–8, 144–45, 182, 215–16, 218–19, 225, 231, 303, 304, 318n. 4, 322n. 69, 345n. 101, 347n. 26, 350n. 90. *See also* working class

Proletarierbund [New York], 159

property and property relations, 116, 118, 121, 122–23, 127

Proudhon, Pierre-Joseph, Proudhonists, 31, 36, 37–38, 49–50, 114, 137–36, 179, 185, 186, 191, 192–94, 199, 208, 225, 239, 290, 323n. 5, 326n. 48, 337n. 57, 339n. 93, 340n. 7

provisional governments, 80–81, 85–86, 89, 105, 122–23, 144–45, 219

Prussia, 2–3, 66; Constitutional Assembly, 68, 75, 84–86, 90, 93, 95, 100, 105–6, 128

Prussian Military Question and the German Workers' Party, 240–41, 244, 292, 296, 349nn. 73, 77

Przeworski, Adam, 353n. 41

publishing, Marx and Engels's approach to, 16–17, 25–26, 34, 155–56

Qu'est-ce que la propriété? (Proudhon), 324n. 14

race and race relations, 193, 204–6, 249, 334n. 17, 336n. 46, 341n. 32, 347n. 16

radicals, 117

Recollections (Tocqueville), 115–35

red baiting, 199

"Red or Social Republic," 86–87, 100, 108, 211–17, 320n. 33, 321n. 64

Die Reform [New York], 159
Reform Act of 1832, 118
Reform Act of 1867, 236
Réforme [Paris], 117
"reformism," 244, 352n. 25. *See also* revisionism
Reform League, 236
reforms and reformists, 35, 117, 148, 218, 232, 238, 266–67, 270–72, 273, 279, 280, 286, 289, 293; revolution and, 52, 73, 95, 105–6, 314n. 53
refugee support work, 102, 143, 145, 220–21
relative deprivation, 119–20
religion, 5, 32–33, 146
republic, 65, 67, 73, 87, 117, 119, 125–26, 268–69, 286
republicans, 117–18
Revelations Concerning the Communist Trial in Cologne, 149–50, 264
revisionism, 258, 298, 352n. 25, 353n. 41. *See also* reforms and reformists
revolution: causes and conditions for, 117–18, 177, 212–13; democratic and political, 9, 42, 47, 60, 65, 69, 80; force as a means to, 261–62; internationalism and, 53; leadership, 124, 210, 237, 331n. 56; parliamentary means to, 260; peaceful road, 231, 260, 268; preparatory steps to, 7, 26–27, 52, 124, 156, 195, 212–13, 262, 306; process of, 26, 35, 51, 60, 80–81, 104–5, 144–45, 152, 177, 195, 212–13, 218, 237, 246–47, 265; role of petit bourgeoisie, 264; taking power prematurely, 152, 354n. 56. *See also* arms and armed struggle, communism, socialism and socialist revolution
Die Revolution [New York], 159
Revolution and Counter-Revolution in Germany, 110, 160, 165, 213, 295
revolutionary practice, 21, 22, 26, 184, 194–95, 226, 286, 291, 296, 305
revolutionary restraint, 74, 87, 118, 123, 161, 210–13, 219, 247, 262, 306
"revolutionary terror," 90
Revolutions of 1848–1849, vii, viii, 57–139 (Ch. 3–5); reassessment of chances for a new upsurge, 143–44. *See also* alliance

of the "people"; Communist League; Germany; lessons of revolution; liberal bourgeoisie; nationalism and nationality; *Neue Rheinische Zeitung (NRZ)*; peasantry; revolution; Tocqueville, Alexis de
Rheinische Zeitung (RZ) [Cologne]: Marx as editor of, 3–5, 66–67
Rhineland, 2–3, 16–19, 73–74, 160, 165, 174
Rhineland Democratic Association, 91
Riazanov, David, 53–54, 55, 103, 307n. 3
Ricardo, David, 189
Rigby, S. H., 356n. 120, 357n. 130
Robertson, Priscilla, 323n. 2
Roman Revolution, 130–31, 135
Rosenberg, Arthur, 357n. 8
Röser, Peter, 71–72, 103, 151, 317n. 42, 329n. 8
Rozan, Philomène, 201
Rubel, Maximilian and Manale, Margaret, 344n. 75
Rueschemeyer, Dietrich, Stephens, Evelyne and Stephens, John, vii–viii, 298–99, 300–1, 305, 307n. 1
Ruge, Arnold, 5–10, 13, 23, 26, 60, 73, 90, 147, 286
Russia, x, 75, 101, 154, 167, 170, 171–72, 176–77, 204, 207, 208, 229, 293–94; peasantry, 246–48, 276–77; Revolution, 57, 68–69, 191–92, 210, 234, 245, 246–47, 251, 270, 280, 282, 294, 300; revolutionary movement, 245–48, 250–51, 275–77, 299, 350n. 95
Russian Social Democratic Labor Party, 146
Russo-Japanese War, 247
Russo-Turkish War, 247, 249

Sassoon, Donald, 356n. 113
Schapper, Karl, 32, 39–41, 47–49, 52, 55, 62, 70, 78–80, 86, 88, 92, 97, 98, 102, 143–48, 163, 167, 329n. 26
Schleswig-Holstein, 42
Schramm, Konrad, 145
Schurz, Carl, 115, 323n. 4
Schweitzer, J. B., 239–40, 242–43, 304–5, 349n. 61
"scientific work," 141, 143, 148, 151, 152–55, 163, 188–93, 248, 253, 289

working class, viii, 307n. 1; independent
political action of, vii–viii, 66, 96,
103–6, 173, 183, 224–29, 239, 249–50,
273, 279, 288, 290, 292, 296–97,
299–301; self-education of, 59–60, 226,
300; self-liberation, 59, 90, 147–48,
242–43, 256, 261, 286, 299. *See also*
elections, England, France, Germany,
United States

World War I, 272, 282, 346n. 9, 354n. 56
Worringen, 79–80, 86–88, 92

Young Hegelians, 4–5, 10–11, 14–15, 45,
267

Zasulich, Vera, 246–47, 275–77, 356n. 104
Zeitlin, Irving, 120, 323n. 8
Zucker, A. E., 333n. 3